Advanced Visual Basic

Kip R. Irvine
Miami-Dade Community College-Kendall

Scott/Jones Inc., Publishers
P.O. Box 696, El Granada, CA 94018
scotjones2@aol.com
(415)726-2436 or Fax: (415) 726-4693
http://www.scottjones.pub.com

Advanced Visual Basic
Kip R. Irvine

Copyright © 1998 by Scott/Jones, Inc.

All rights reserved. No part of this book may be reproduced or transmitted in any form without the written permission of the publisher.

ISBN: 1-57676-002-2

Composition: Kip R. Irvine
Book Manufacturing: Malloy Lithographing, Inc.
Text Design: Kip R. Irvine
Cover Design: Cyber Island Graphics

9 8 7 Z Y X

All product names identified in this book are trademarks or registered trademarks of their respective companies, and are appropriately capitalized. Visual Basic, Word 97, Excel 97, and Access 97 are trademarks of Microsoft Corporation. VB/HelpWriter is a trademark of Teletech Systems, Delphi is a trademark of Borland International, Crystal Reports is a trademark of Crystal Computer Services.

Additional Titles Of Interest From Scott/Jones

The Windows 95 TextBook: Extended Edition
The Windows 95 TextBook: Standard Edition
Short Course in Windows 95
Stewart Venit

The Access 7 Gudebook: Full Course
The Access 7 Gudebook: Short Course
Maggie Trigg
Phyllis Dobson

Additional Books in Visual Basic

Visual Basic 5 CourseBook
Forest Lin

Introduction to Programming Using Visual Basic
Gary Bronson

Visual Basic with Applications, 2nd Edition
Mark Simkin

Introduction to Programming Using Visual Basic
Forest Lin

Other Programming Language Texts by Scott/Jones

Assembly Language for the IBM-PC Family, 2nd Edition
William Jones

C by Discovery, 2nd edition
L.S. Foster

Problem Solving with C
Jones and Harrow

C Through Objects
John Connely

*This book is dedicated to
the many excellent students
at Miami-Dade Community College
who have helped me learn to teach
Visual Basic*

Table of Contents

1 Designing and Coding Programs — 1

1.1 Application Development Cycle — 2
- 1.1.1 Interviewing Management and Users 2
- 1.1.2 Creating Program Specifications 2
- 1.1.3 Performing a Feasibility Review 2
- 1.1.4 Designing the Application 3
- 1.1.5 Design Goals 4
- 1.1.6 Implementing the Application 5
- 1.1.7 Testing the Application 5

1.2 Sample Design: Mozart Music Sales — 6
- 1.2.1 Program Specifications 6
- 1.2.2 Program Design 7

1.3 User Interface Design — 10
- 1.3.1 Avoiding Crowding Forms 10
- 1.3.2 Setting the Tab Order 11
- 1.3.3 Keyboard Input 12
- 1.3.4 Using Standard Menus 13

1.4 Coding Guidelines — 13
- 1.4.1 Declaring Variables and Constants 13
- 1.4.2 Naming Variables and Constants 14
- 1.4.3 Naming Controls 15
- 1.4.4 Naming Procedures and Methods 16
- 1.4.5 Indenting Code 17
- 1.4.6 Predefined VB Constants 17
- 1.4.7 Line Continuation 18
- 1.4.8 App Object Properties 18

1.5 Error Handling — 20
- 1.5.1 Causes of Errors 20
- 1.5.2 On Error GoTo Statement 20
- 1.5.3 Resume Statement 21
- 1.5.4 Using the Err Object 23

1.6	Reducing Code Size	24
1.7	Improving Execution Speed	25

    1.7.1   Code Optimization 25
    1.7.2   Display Optimization 26
    1.7.3   Perceived Speed Optimization 26

1.8	Review Questions	27
1.9	Chapter Exercises	29

2 Building an Invoice Application — 33

2.1	Mozart Music Sales - 1	33

    2.1.1   Objectives 34
    2.1.2   Program Specifications 34
    2.1.3   Program Design 34
    2.1.4   Program Implementation 36

2.2	Mozart Music Sales - 2	39

    2.2.1   Program Specifications 40
    2.2.2   Program Design 40
    2.2.3   Program Implementation 42

2.3	Mozart Music Sales - 3	45

    2.3.1   Program Specifications 46
    2.3.2   Program Design 46
    2.3.3   Program Implementation 47

2.4	Common Dialog Control	52

    2.4.1   ShowOpen, ShowSave Methods 52
    2.4.2   Example: Selecting and Opening a File 53
    2.4.3   ShowColor Method 55
    2.4.4   ShowFont Method 56

2.5	Saving and Retrieving Program Settings	57

    2.5.1   Viewing the System Registry 57
    2.5.2   Visual Basic Procedures 60
    2.5.3   SaveSetting Procedure 60
    2.5.4   GetSetting Function 60
    2.5.5   Example Program: Save/Retrieve Data Path 61
    2.5.6   GetAllSettings Function 62

2.6	Review Questions	63
2.7	Chapter Exercises	65

3 Chapter 3: Arrays and Collections — 71

3.1 Object Variables — 71

- 3.1.1 Declaring and Assigning Objects 71
- 3.1.2 Declaring and Assigning Object Arrays 73
- 3.1.3 Creating a Control Array in Design Mode 74
- 3.1.4 Creating a Control Array at Runtime 75

3.2 The MixUp Game — 76

- 3.2.1 Program Specifications 76
- 3.2.2 Program Design 77
- 3.2.3 Program Implementation 77

3.3 Using Visual Basic Collections — 82

- 3.3.1 Built-In Collections 82
- 3.3.2 Programmer-Defined Collections 83
- 3.3.3 Collection Methods and Properties 84
- 3.3.4 Example: Resizing Controls on a Form 86

3.4 The Glossary Program — 88

- 3.4.1 Program Design 88
- 3.4.2 Program Implementation 89

3.5 Random-Access Files — 92

- 3.5.1 Opening a File 92
- 3.5.2 Writing Records 93
- 3.5.3 Reading Records 93
- 3.5.4 Example: Customer Accounts Program 94
- 3.5.5 Program Design 94
- 3.5.6 Program Implementation 96

3.6 Creating MDI Applications — 98

- 3.6.1 MDI Bitmap Viewer Program 99
- 3.6.2 Program Design 100
- 3.6.3 Program Implementation 101

3.7 Review Questions — 104

3.8 Chapter Exercises — 106

4 Object-Oriented Programming — 117

4.1 Classes and Objects — 117

- 4.1.1 Object-Oriented Design 118
- 4.1.2 Class Modules 120
- 4.1.3 Creating Instances of a Class 122
- 4.1.4 Properties 123
- 4.1.5 Event Handlers 125
- 4.1.6 Methods 126

4.1.7 New and Set Statements 126

4.2 Student Class Example 127

    4.2.1 Program Design 127
    4.2.2 Program Implementation 128

4.3 Student Collection Class 130

    4.3.1 Program Design 130
    4.3.2 The Main Form 131
    4.3.3 The clsStudent Class 133
    4.3.4 The clsStudentCollection Class 134

4.4 Doctors Office Scheduling Program 136

    4.4.1 Program Specifications 136
    4.4.2 Program Design 137
    4.4.3 Program Implementation 141
    4.4.4 The clsPatient Class 142
    4.4.5 The clsApptCalendar Class 144
    4.4.6 The clsAppointment Class 146
    4.4.7 The frmInput Form 149

4.5 Review Questions 152

4.6 Chapter Exercises 155

5 Introducing Databases 165

5.1 Tables and Databases 166

    5.1.1 Introduction 166
    5.1.2 Defining Tables 166
    5.1.3 Recordset Objects 167
    5.1.4 Field Types in Databases 168
    5.1.5 Using Data Controls 169
    5.1.6 Using Data-Bound Controls 170

5.2 Using Microsoft Access 172

    5.2.1 Creating a Database 172
    5.2.2 Creating the SalesStaff Table 173
    5.2.3 Creating Indexes 174
    5.2.4 Entering Table Data 175

5.3 Viewing the SalesStaff Table 175

    5.3.1 The Database Table 176
    5.3.2 Display the Table 176
    5.3.3 Adding New Records 177
    5.3.4 Changing the Record Order 179

5.4 Moving the Recordset Pointer 181

    5.4.1 Example: SalesStaff Table 182

5.5 Data-Bound List, Combo, and Grid 183

        5.5.1   Data-Bound List Control 183
        5.5.2   Data-Bound Combo Control 186
        5.5.3   Data-Bound Grid Control 188

5.6   Mozart Music Sales - 4   190

        5.6.1   Program Specifications 190
        5.6.2   Program Design 190
        5.6.3   Program Implementation 191

5.7   Mail-Order Computer Sales   193

        5.7.1   Program Specifications 193
        5.7.2   Program Design 194
        5.7.3   The Computer Database 195
        5.7.4   Program Implementation 196

5.8   Searching for Records (SalesStaff 3)   199

        5.8.1   Table Seek Method 200
        5.8.2   Using an SQL Search 202
        5.8.3   Example: A Simple Query Program 203
        5.8.4   FindFirst, FindNext, and Other Search Methods 205

5.9   Review Questions   206

5.10 Chapter Exercises   208

6   Data Access Objects   221

6.1   Using the Data Access Object Library   221

        6.1.1   Workspaces 222
        6.1.2   OpenRecordset Method 222
        6.1.3   TableDefs Property 223

6.2   Project: Personal Contact Manager - 1   225

        6.2.1   Program Specifications 225
        6.2.2   Program Design 226
        6.2.3   Implementation: module1 230
        6.2.4   Implementation: frmMain 233
        6.2.5   Implementation: frmSplash 234
        6.2.6   Implementation: frmEdit 235
        6.2.7   Conclusion 235

6.3   Project: Personal Contact Manager - 2   236

        6.3.1   Program Specifications 236
        6.3.2   Program Design 236
        6.3.3   Program Implementation 237

6.4   Project: Doctors Office Appointments - 2   241

        6.4.1   Program Specifications 241
        6.4.2   Program Design 242
        6.4.3   Implementing the Appointment Program 244

- 6.4.4 The Main Form: frmMain 244
- 6.4.5 Implementing the clsAppointment Class 245
- 6.4.6 The clsApptCalendar Class 247
- 6.4.7 Implementing the clsPatient Class 250
- 6.4.8 The frmDisplay and frmInput Windows 252
- 6.4.9 Conclusion 253

6.5 Multiuser Database Processing — 253

- 6.5.1 Example: Record-Locking Program 254
- 6.5.2 Program Implementation 256
- 6.5.3 BeginTrans, CommitTrans, and Rollback 258

6.6 Review Questions — 259

6.7 Chapter Exercises — 263

7 Relational Databases — 271

7.1 Database Design — 272

- 7.1.1 Terminology 272
- 7.1.2 Designing a Database 273

7.2 Using the SQL Language — 274

- 7.2.1 Structure of an SQL Statement 274
- 7.2.2 A Sample Database 275
- 7.2.3 SELECT Statement 276
- 7.2.4 WHERE Clause 277
- 7.2.5 Selecting from Multiple Tables 280
- 7.2.6 JOIN Clause 281
- 7.2.7 Creating Queries in Microsoft Access 284

7.3 SQL Action Queries — 285

- 7.3.1 UPDATE Statement 285
- 7.3.2 DELETE Statement 286
- 7.3.3 INSERT INTO Statement (Append Queries) 287

7.4 Creating Tables and Indexes — 288

- 7.4.1 Creating Indexes 288
- 7.4.2 Creating Tables 288
- 7.4.3 Removing Tables and Indexes 289

7.5 Application: Stellar Car Rental — 290

- 7.5.1 Overview 290

7.6 Table Descriptions — 291

- 7.6.1 Vehicle Inventory 292
- 7.6.2 Vehicle Descriptions, Types, and Status 293
- 7.6.3 Rental Prices 293
- 7.6.4 Customers, Reservations, and Invoices 294

7.7 Validation Rules — 295

Table of Contents   xi

       7.7.1   Creating Validation Rules in Access 296
7.8   Table Relationships   297
       7.8.1   Creating Table Relationships 298
7.9   Designing the Interface   302
       7.9.1   Vehicle Reservations 303
7.10   Reservation Implementation   307

       7.10.1   Module1 307
       7.10.2   The clsVehicleType Class 309
       7.10.3   The clsReservation Class 310
       7.10.4   The frmReserv Form 317
       7.10.5   The frmCustomer Form 319
       7.10.6   The frmFindFile Form 320
       7.10.7   The frmPrices Form 321

7.11   Review Questions   322

7.12   Chapter Exercises   324

8   Reports and Online Help   329

8.1   Crystal Reports   329

       8.1.1   Creating a Columnar Report 330
       8.1.2   Dividing a Report Into Groups 335
       8.1.3   Adding Selection Criteria 337
       8.1.4   Creating a Cross-Tab Summary Report 340
       8.1.5   Using the Crystal Reports Custom Control 343
       8.1.6   Sample Application: Concert Ticket Reports 345
       8.1.7   Program Implementation 347

8.2   Creating Online Help   350

       8.2.1   The User Assistance Model 350
       8.2.2   StatusBar Control 351
       8.2.3   Creating Online Help Files 354
       8.2.4   VB/HelpWriter Lite 355
       8.2.5   Example: Stellar Car Rental Reservations 355
       8.2.6   Adding Help Commands to the Menu 358
       8.2.7   Expanding the Help File 359
       8.2.8   Adding Jumps 362

8.3   Review Questions   364

8.4   Chapter Exercises   367

9   Object Linking and Embedding (OLE)   369

9.1   OLE Fundamentals 369

        9.1.1   Embedding and Linking 371
        9.1.2   Insertable Objects 371
        9.1.3   Example: Creating a WordPad Document 373

9.2 OLE Container Control   373

        9.2.1   Example: Creating an Embedded Word Object 373
        9.2.2   Example: Creating an Embedded Excel Worksheet 377
        9.2.3   CreateLink Method 382

9.3 OLE Container Program   383

        9.3.1   Program Specifications 383
        9.3.2   Creating a New Excel Worksheet 383
        9.3.3   Creating a New Word Document 384
        9.3.4   Inserting an Excel Worksheet 385
        9.3.5   Inserting a Word Document 385
        9.3.6   Program Implementation 386

9.4 OLE Automation   388

        9.4.1   Visual Basic for Applications 388
        9.4.2   Example: Creating a Word Document 389
        9.4.3   Word Classes, Properties, and Methods 390
        9.4.4   OLE Automation with Excel 394
        9.4.5   Excel: Statistical Score Analysis 395

9.5 College Admissions Program   398

        9.5.1   Program Specifications 398
        9.5.2   Program Design 398
        9.5.3   Program Implementation 402
        9.5.4   Conclusion 407

9.6 Review Questions   407

9.7 Chapter Exercises   409

10 Tapping Into the Windows API   415

10.1 The Need for External Procedures   415

        10.1.1   Static and Dynamic Linking 416

10.2 Declaring and Calling DLL Procedures   417

        10.2.1   The Declare Statement 417
        10.2.2   The API Viewer Utility Program 418
        10.2.3   First Example: Flashing a Window Caption 419

10.3 Parameters in DLL Procedures   421

        10.3.1   String Parameters 422
        10.3.2   Numeric Parameters 423
        10.3.3   User-Defined Types 424
        10.3.4   Example: GetWindowsDirectory 424

10.4	Reading and Writing Application INI Files	426
	10.4.1 Maintaining a Program's INI File 427	
10.5	Example: The clsIniFile Class	429
	10.5.1 Class Description 430 10.5.2 A Short Test Program 430	
10.6	Review Questions	433
10.7	Chapter Exercises	434

11 Creating ActiveX Controls   439

11.1	ActiveX Components	439
	11.1.1 Types of Objects Provided by Components 440 11.1.2 ActiveX Controls 441	
11.2	Creating a Student ID Number Text Box	442
	11.2.1 Creating a Test Program 443 11.2.2 Adding an Event to the Control 445 11.2.3 Comments 447	
11.3	AddAppointment ActiveX Control	447
	11.3.1 Program Specifications 447 11.3.2 User Interface 448 11.3.3 Saving and Restoring Properties 450 11.3.4 Raising Events in ActiveX Controls 451 11.3.5 Implementing Property Procedures 453 11.3.6 AddAppointment Control Source Listing 454 11.3.7 Client Program Listing 457	
11.4	Creating an ActiveX DLL	458
	11.4.1 The DoctorSchedule ActiveX DLL 458 11.4.2 Client Program Implementation 460 11.4.3 Instancing Property 461 11.4.4 DoctorSchedule Implementation 462 11.4.5 The clsSchedule Class 463 11.4.6 The clsAppointment Class 465 11.4.7 The clsPatient Class 466 11.4.8 Testing the Compiled Component 466	
11.5	Creating an Out-Of-Process Component	467
	11.5.1 Converting DoctorSchedule to ActiveX EXE 467	
11.6	Where To Go From Here	468
11.7	Review Questions	469
11.8	Chapter Exercises	471

A	**Visual Basic Review**		**475**
A.1	Competency Review Test		476
A.2	Data Types, Variables, and Constants		478
	A.2.1	Data Types 478	
	A.2.2	Boolean 478	
	A.2.3	Byte, Integer, Long 478	
	A.2.4	Single, Double, Currency 479	
	A.2.5	String 480	
	A.2.6	Date 480	
	A.2.7	Object 481	
	A.2.8	Variant 481	
	A.2.9	Declared Constants 481	
	A.2.10	Static Arrays 482	
	A.2.11	Dynamic Arrays 482	
	A.2.12	Collections 483	
	A.2.13	User-Defined Types 483	
A.3	If Statements		484
	A.3.1	Compound Expressions (And, Or, Not) 484	
	A.3.2	Block IF Statement 484	
	A.3.3	Using ELSE 484	
	A.3.4	Select Case 485	
A.4	Loops		486
	A.4.1	For-Next Statement 487	
	A.4.2	Do-While Statement 487	
	A.4.3	Do-Until Statement 488	
	A.4.4	While-Wend Statement 488	
A.5	Procedures		489
	A.5.1	Declaring a Subroutine Procedure 489	
	A.5.2	Procedure Parameters 490	
	A.5.3	Declaring a Function Procedure 491	
	A.5.4	Passing Arguments by Reference 492	
	A.5.5	Passing Arguments by Value 493	
	A.5.6	Private and Public 494	
	A.5.7	Optional Parameters 494	
	A.5.8	Parameter Arrays 495	
A.6	String Handling		495
A.7	Forms		497
	A.7.1	Properties 497	
	A.7.2	Methods 499	
	A.7.3	Sample Form-Loading Program 500	
	A.7.4	Events 502	
A.8	Standard Visual Basic Controls		503

	A.8.1	Label 503	
	A.8.2	Text 503	
	A.8.3	Command Button 504	
	A.8.4	Option Button 504	
	A.8.5	Frame 505	
	A.8.6	Check Box 505	
	A.8.7	Image 506	
	A.8.8	Line 506	
	A.8.9	Timer 506	
	A.8.10	Scroll Bars 506	
	A.8.11	List Boxes and Combo Boxes 507	
	A.8.12	Default Properties 509	
A.9	Coding Guidelines		509
	A.9.1	Naming Controls 509	
	A.9.2	Using General Procedures 510	
A.10	Tools for Input-Output		511
	A.10.1	Print Method 511	
	A.10.2	Format$ Function 511	
	A.10.3	MsgBox Procedure 512	
	A.10.4	MsgBox Function 513	
	A.10.5	InputBox Function 515	
	A.10.6	Printer Object 516	
	A.10.7	Screen Object 516	
	A.10.8	Application Object 517	
A.11	Creating Menus and Toolbars		517
	A.11.1	Common Menu Types 517	
	A.11.2	Creating a Simple Menu 518	
	A.11.3	Menu Properties 519	
A.12	Sequential Files		521
	A.12.1	Basic Syntax 521	
	A.12.2	Reading From an Input File 521	
	A.12.3	Writing to an Output File 524	
A.13	Answers to the Competency Test Questions		525

B Standard VB4 Add-Ins   529

B.1	Using VisData		529
	B.1.1	Creating the Database 529	
	B.1.2	Creating the SalesStaff Table 529	
	B.1.3	Creating Indexes 532	
	B.1.4	Entering Table Data 534	
	B.1.5	Creating Validation Rules 535	
	B.1.6	Setting Table Relationships 536	
B.2	Using Data Manager		536
	B.2.1	Creating the Database 537	

	B.2.2	Creating the SalesStaff Table 538	
	B.2.3	Editing a Table Design 539	
	B.2.4	Creating Indexes 540	
	B.2.5	Entering Table Data 542	
B.3	Using the Data Form Designer		543
	B.3.1	Code Modifications in the Author Form 545	
	B.3.2	Create the Main Window 545	
	B.3.3	Add Another Table 546	

C   Answers to Odd-Numbered Review Questions

Chapter 1	549
Chapter 2	550
Chapter 3	551
Chapter 4	552
Chapter 5	553
Chapter 6	554
Chapter 7	556
Chapter 8	557
Chapter 9	558
Chapter 10	559
Chapter 11	560

Preface

At any time, I enjoy bringing out a new programming book. But it's especially pleasant to write about Microsoft Visual Basic®. Visual Basic 3 and Visual Basic 4 made a huge impact on the programming world and set the standard for visual interface programming. Now, with the transition to Visual Basic 5, programmers are more excited than ever to be creating ActiveX controls and programming on the Internet. Microsoft-certified Visual Basic consultants can almost name their own price if they have experience with the latest tools and techniques.

Why This Book Was Written

During the last few years, colleges everywhere have found Visual Basic to be a popular and useful vehicle for teaching Windows Programming applications and concepts. At Miami-Dade, we began teaching the course in late 1995. Soon afterward, we realized that Visual Basic should be taught at the intermediate and advanced levels, to people who take programming *very* seriously. We immediately found professional programmers and would-be programmers filling the second-semester Visual Basic classes. For two years I have been creating and refining stacks of course handouts and sample programs for this course, and getting great help from students. To say that students have *taught me to program* in Visual Basic is an understatement, because so many of them have shared their considerable knowledge and skills.

Features of This Book

Every experienced instructor knows that students have a variety of learning styles. Some learn from manuals; others from sample programs; some prefer the "human" touch, being able to spend one-on-one time with an instructor; some learn from step-by-step exercises. To help address different learning styles, this book contains a number of pedagogical features that serve to reinforce each other during the learning process:

- *Object-oriented programming.* During the survey and reviewing process for this book, we found that many instructors wanted object-oriented programming to be emphasized much more strongly than in existing Visual Basic textbooks. I completely agree! Therefore, objects are used throughout the book, with special emphasis on class design in Chapter 4, integration with databases in Chapter 6, OLE objects in Chapter 9, and designing ActiveX components in Chapter 11.

- *Discussions about program design, coding style, object-oriented concepts.* These concepts are at the core of a solid computer science education.

- A *short table of contents* is displayed at the beginning of each chapter. People like to see what the chapter is about, at a glance.

- *Pop-up programming tips* that show up in gray-shaded boxes. The reader can ignore these without disturbing the flow of the main text body, and come back to them later. It's surprising how often these little tips become useful when programs won't work!

- *Reference information* on Visual Basic, the Jet Database Engine, Crystal Reports, the Windows API, ActiveX components, and online help. The Microsoft manuals and online help are wonderful, but it's not easy to limit the scope of information. In this book, you find lots of tables and lists, just when you need to use them in a program.

- *Hands-on programming examples* that guide the reader while working at the computer. These are short and simple, designed to demonstrate concepts, and it's always nice to have something to do at the computer.

- *One or two moderately complex applications* that are specified, designed, and implemented in each chapter. The source code for these programs is on the student disk. Anyone who has written real-world applications can appreciate the importance of careful design and planning. Students, lacking that experience, should not be misled into thinking that all Visual Basic programs are trivial in size and complexity.

- *Review questions* at the end of each chapter. Some are no-brainers, some require thought. But you can trace the origin of every question back to a specific spot in the reading, in case you didn't read the chapter carefully enough the first time (who does?). Answers to the odd-numbered questions are in Appendix C. Answers to the even-numbered questions are printed in the Instructor Manual.

- *End-of-Chapter programming exercises* that offer a variety of programming challenges, from easy to difficult. The solutions to these programs are printed in the instructor's manual and are placed on the disk that accompanies the instructor's manual. In the writing of these programs, we gain valuable experience in problem solving. The programs can be fun, frustrating, exhilarating, aggravating, inspiring, and many other things. But they *do* teach you to program.

- *A Visual Basic review tutorial* for programmers who are experienced in other languages is available in Appendix A. This doesn't replace a beginning course in programming by any means, but it can be great for people who already know what they want to do, and just need the tools to do it.

- A *competency exam* located in Appendix A to help professors and students move more rapidly into Visual Basic. Students can judge their own mastery of fundamental topics, on their own time. Each question in the test is keyed to a particular topic in the Visual Basic review tutorial (Appendix A).

- *Tutorials for VB add-ins*, Data Manager and VisData. These are handy utilities for students who do not have Microsoft *Access* available. The tutorials are in Appendix B.

- *Programs supplied on disk* are indicated by a small computer disk icon in the margin. A disk with the letter S inside refers to a program on the student diskette that accompanies this book. A diskette with the letter I inside refers to a program on the instructor disk that accompanies the instructor manual. The name of the directory holding the program is always shown below the disk. For example, the following icons indicate a program in the \College directory on the student disk, and a program in the \Karate1 directory on the instructor disk.

A Quick Survey of Chapter Topics...

Chapters 1-10 are compatible with Visual Basic 4.0. All chapters are compatible with Visual Basic 5.0:

- Chapter 1, **Designing and Coding Programs**, explains the application development cycle, user interface design, coding guidelines, error handling, and performance optimization.

- Chapter 2, **Building an Invoice Application,** develops a point-of-sale application in several stages, introduces the common dialog control, and shows how to save and restore system registry settings.

- Chapter 3, **Arrays and Collections,** introduces objects, collections, random files, MDI applications, and an event-driven computer game that is always popular with students.

- Chapter 4, **Object-Oriented Programming,** goes head-on into object-oriented programming, with classes, objects, methods, properties, collection classes, and a complete application for scheduling doctors office appointments.

- Chapter 5, **Introducing Databases,** shows how to create a database, use the data, data-bound grid, list, and combo controls, and shows how to use Seek and FindFirst to search for records.

- Chapter 6, **Data Access Objects,** concentrates on data access objects and multi-user databases, and develops two database applications in stages.

- Chapter 7, **Relational Databases,** shows how to design multi-table databases, create SQL queries and data definition statements, create validation rules, and goes through the steps of coding a multi-table database application.

- Chapter 8, **Reports and Online Help,** shows how to use Crystal Reports to create professional-looking reports, and how to create online help files for users of an application.

- Chapter 9, **Object Linking and Embedding,** introduces object linking and embedding (OLE), showing how to integrate Visual Basic with Microsoft Word and Excel, using OLE containers and objects.

- Chapter 10, **Tapping into the Windows API,** focuses on calling DLL procedures and taking advantage of the Windows *application programmer's interface* (API).

- Chapter 11, **Creating ActiveX Components,** shows how to create ActiveX components using Visual Basic 5, with examples of ActiveX controls, a DLL, and an out-of-process component server.

- Appendix A: **Visual Basic Review,** is a quick-start tutorial on the essentials of Visual Basic for readers who are already experienced programmers.

- Appendix B: **Standard VB4 Add-Ins,** is a tutorial on using the VisData, Data Manager, and Data Form Designer programs that are shipped with Visual Basic 4.

- Appendix C: **Answers to Odd-Numbered Review Questions,** contains answers to the review questions located at the end of each chapter. (The even-numbered answers are supplied in the Instructor's manual.)

Chapter Sequence Flowchart. It is often more useful for professors to cover chapters in a different order from the sequence presented in the book. The following sequences of chapters are possible, given built-in dependencies between topics:

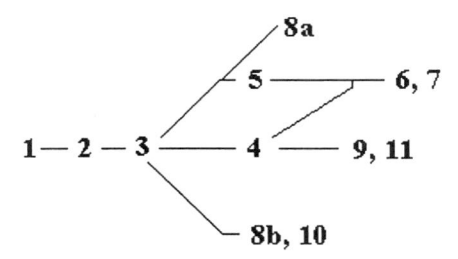

```
                        8a
                       /
                      5 ———— 6, 7
                    /       ↗
   1 — 2 — 3 ——— 4 ———— 9, 11
                    \
                      8b, 10
```

* Chapter 8a indicates Crystal Reports, and Chapter 8b indicates Online Help.

Immediately after Chapter 3, you can cover Chapters 5, 8, and 10 without any difficulties. After Chapter 4, Chapters 9 and 11 may be covered. After Chapters 4 and 5, Chapters 6 and 7 may be covered. One alternate approach, for example, is to begin databases before object-oriented programming, so the sequence would be 1-3, 5, 4, 5-6, 8-11. Another approach would be to emphasize ActiveX controls earlier in the course, so the sequence would be 1-3, 4, 11, 5-7, 8, 9, 10.

Supplemental Materials and Teaching Aids

The following learning aids are furnished with each copy of the book:

- Review Questions at the end of each chapter.
- Answers to the odd-numbered review questions in Appendix C.
- A disk containing all sample programs.

Preface

- Access to the following author and publisher Web sites where additional sample programs are available:

  `http://www.pobox.com/~irvinek/vbook`
  `http://www.scottjonespub.com`

The following teaching aids are furnished to the instructor in the instructor's guide:

- A printed test bank of short-answer, multiple-choice and True/False questions, with two sets of 40 questions per chapter.

- Additional programming exercises designed to enhance the use of this book.

- Answers to all even-numbered review questions in the book.

- A disk containing the test bank questions for each chapter.

- A disk containing solution programs for all programming exercises in the book. Updated solutions and additional programming exercises will be posted on the author and publisher web sites listed earlier. (Files exclusively for instructor use will be encrypted with password-protection.)

Acknowledgements

- First, let me warmly thank Richard Jones, the publisher, who provided a lot of the inspiration and guidance for this book. Through our many conversations, we developed the ideas that eventually brought this book to life. Cathy Baehler, of Baehler Editing, helped eliminate many typos and minor errors that slipped by me.

- **Kathy Blicharz,** Professor, Pima College in Tucson, Arizona, was instrumental in testing and reviewing this book as it was under development during the first half of 1997. She had many fine suggestions that affected the book's design.

- **Merrill Parker,** Professor, Chattanooga State Technical Institute, reviewed several chapters and created an excellent competency test for Visual Basic fundamentals, found in Appendix A.

- **Edward Wittke,** Project Data Manager, University of Arizona, contributed a tremendous amount of time and energy to proofreading the book. He provided many excellent suggestions for corrections, improvements and clarifications.

Many thanks to the following instructors who reviewed the book's outline and/or manuscript:

Mary Amundson-Miller, Greenville Technical College
Kamran Azad, Orangeburg Technical College
Collin Ballance, Nashville State Technical Institute
Allen Brooks, Linfield College
Jesse Cabrera, San Antonio College
Randolph Campbell, Morningside College
Brad Chilton, Tarelton State College
Alejandro Ferro, Miami-Dade Community College
Rob Fitzgerald, University of North Florida

Lee Hunt, Collin County Community College
Mozelle Johnson, Pima Community College
Jeffrey Kent, Los Angeles Valley College
Carol Peterson, South Plains College
Jeff Scott, Blackhawk Technical Institute
Cherie M. Stevens, South Florida Community College
Michael J. Walton, Miami-Dade Community College-North
Melinda White, Santa Fe Community College

The following persons classroom tested this book during 1997:

- Kathy Blicharz, Pima College

- Kai Liang, Miami-Dade Community College-Kendall, who also created some great programming projects involving financial calculations.

- David Victor, Miami-Dade Community College-Kendall

Special thanks to Eduardo Molieri, who wrote most of the solution programs for the chapter exercises. Eduardo is also the co-author of the Instructor's Manual accompanying this book.

TypeSetting

Typesetting of this book was done by Kip Irvine, using Microsoft Word 97. Any suggestions, criticism, and locations of misprints would be warmly appreciated. Please send e-mail to: **kip.irvine@pobox.com** or call Kip Irvine at **305-237-2806** (Miami-Dade Community College). The editor, Richard Jones, can be reached at: **Scotjones1@aol.com**.

About the Author

Kip Irvine holds a M.S. (computer science) and D.M.A. (music composition) from University of Miami; Professor of Computer Information Systems, Miami-Dade Community College-Kendall, 1983+; published textbooks are *COBOL for the IBM Personal Computer* (Prentice Hall, 1987), *Assembly Language for the IBM-PC* (Macmillan, 1990 & 1993), *C++ and Object-Oriented Programming* (Prentice Hall, 1997), and the current book, *Advanced Visual Basic*; other interests are Tae Kwon Do, 'Cello, and sailing.

1 Designing and Coding Programs

Chapter Contents

Application Development Cycle
    Interviewing Mangagement and Users
    Creating Program Specifications
    Performing a Feasability Review
    Designing the Application
    Design Goals
    Implementing the Application
    Testing the Application
Sample Design: Mozart Music Sales
    Program Specifications
    Program Design
User Interface Design
    Avoiding Crowding Forms
    Setting the Tab Order
    Keyboard Input
    Using Standard Menus
Coding Guidelines
    Declaring Variables and Constants
    Naming Variables and Constants
    Naming Controls
    Naming Procedures and Methods
    Indenting Code
    Line Continuation
    App Object Properties
Error Handling
    Causes of Errors
    On Error GoTo Statement
    Resume Statement
    Using the Err Object
Reducing Code Size
Improving Execution Speed
    Code Optimization
    Display Optimization
    Perceived Speed Optimization
Review Questions
Chapter Exercises

1.1 Application Development Cycle

1.1.1 Interviewing Management and Users

Some programs are designed, coded, tested, and installed before their users even get to see the programs. Any suggestions or input are useless at that point, unless the design team is willing to re-engineer the programs. Needless to say, such programs do not generate a lot of support from the very people who will use them!

A good designer talks to the people who will actually use the software. The designer analyzes the application's requirements, and in many cases, involves one or more users in helping to design the program's visual interface. At the same time, a company's management will generally know what types of input and output information are needed for the application. Often, this knowledge will have to be built over a period of interviews, demonstrations, brainstorming sessions, and thoughtful analysis. Open and candid communication is essential between the designer and users at all levels.

1.1.2 Creating Program Specifications

Using the application requirements, the designer, along with management, will generate a list of specifications. The specifications spell out, item by item, what the program will do. For a very simple program, the specifications may be only a single paragraph; for a complex program, the specifications may resemble a legal document. Here, for example, are the specifications for a simple program that we will write in Chapter 2, called Mozart Music Sales:

The Mozart Music Store needs a simple invoice program that can be filled in by a store clerk (the *user*) when a compact disc or cassette tape is purchased. In our store, we use a 5-digit SKU number to uniquely identify all items.

On startup, the program displays the current date so that it may be verified by the store clerk. When the user selects a SKU number from an existing list of numbers, the program displays the album title that matches the number. The clerk looks at the item for a label indicating one of three price codes (A, B, or C) and enters the same code into the computer by clicking with the mouse. The clerk also selects the recording format (CD or tape). The program immediately calculates the sale amount, tax, and net price. The user can also click on a check box if the customer is entitled to a 10% discount. When the user decides to quit the program, the program confirms before terminating.

1.1.3 Performing a Feasibility Review

While the specifications are being developed, an experienced designer will be conducting an ongoing "reality check". This involves not only a knowledge of the application itself, but the strengths and weaknesses of Visual Basic. In addition, most designers do a considerable amount of research learning about the hundreds of third-party products that enhance the capabilities of Visual Basic.

Can the application requirements be met, given the available hardware and software? In general, 32-bit Visual Basic applications require 16 MB of RAM to run adequately, preferably on a Pentium or higher processor. Programs running on a network have more demanding database server requirements than stand-alone programs.

Is there enough time to design, code, and test the program? Deadlines should be set for each phase of the project: specifications, design, coding, and testing. If any of these steps end up being repeated, all subsequent deadlines must be renegotiated.

Are there enough programmers (particularly with experience in developing similar applications in Visual Basic) involved in the project? This is an important consideration, because every project needs a designer or programmer who can avoid the costly mistakes that result from inexperience. It is generally unwise to expect even an experienced programmer to learn Visual Basic and write a professional application at the same time. Invariably, code written at the beginning of the project will have to be rewritten near the end of the project, once the programmer has discovered better ways of doing things.

Extra time must be included for fixing bugs and providing for at least a minimal set of modifications that are outside of the original specifications.

1.1.4 Designing the Application

During the design phase of the project, the project specifications are translated into a detailed description of the program in terms that programmers can understand. Programmers are not expected to know anything about the application domain, for instance, so any special processing requirements must be spelled out. The design includes descriptions and examples of input/output data, illustrations of sample screens and reports, and data validation requirements.

Visual Design. Another aspect of the design is the visual component of the program. This can be achieved by creating the forms and controls even before any code has been written. This technique is called *prototyping*, and helps the client or user of the program visualize the finished product.

Procedural Design. The designer can use a procedural approach, which involves breaking down the program specifications into a hierarchy of high- and low-level *tasks*, or *processes*. This is the traditional method, used with success over the last 30-40 years, but it suffers from one major drawback: the program structure is greatly influenced by restrictions in the programming language, rather than being a reflection of the physical entities that make up the application. Procedural designs are gradually being replaced by object-oriented designs as computer languages evolve.

Object-Oriented Design. This approach to design focuses on the physical entities that make up an application problem. The design emphasizes the interactions between objects, as well as the responsibilities and characteristics of objects. In the design of a doctor's office scheduling program, for instance, the physical entities might be the Patient, Doctor, Schedule, and Appointment. Each of these could be translated into a class, with methods and properties. A Schedule might have the following methods and properties:

Methods:
    AddNewAppointment
    RemoveAppointment
    ShowAllAppointments
    ShowAppointmentsByDoctor

Properties:
    Appointments (a collection of Appointment objects)
    NumberOfAppointments
    LastUpdate   (date when schedule was last updated)

A *method* represents an action that may be performed by the object, or a message that might be sent or received by the object. Methods are implemented as procedures. A *property* is a data value stored inside the object. Properties can have built-in validity checks, to make sure they always have reasonable values.

1.1.5 Design Goals

There are some basic goals to strive for when designing programs:

Simplicity. The design should be as *simple* as possible, while still fulfilling all of the program specifications. Avoid cluttering designs with lots of unnecessary features. A simple design can more easily be communicated between programmers and designers. In a Visual Basic program, simplicity is important in both the visual design and the design of the code inside modules and forms.

Flexibility. A well-executed design is *flexible* enough to accomomdate the inevitable changes that will occur during the lifetime of the application. Changes may appear at the specification level, design level, or implementation level. Each change has a cascading effect on the levels after it, so a change to the program specifications will affect the design, which will in turn affect the implementation. On the other hand, a change to the program's implementation will generally not affect the design.

Extensibility. Well-designed software is *extensible,* meaning that additions of new features at both the large-scale level and at the detailed level are possible without destroying the original program. We extend Visual Basic programs by adding new modules and forms, and by modifying the procedures, methods, and properties of existing modules.

Reusability. When the same software can be moved from one program to other programs, we say that it is *reusable*. This can be achieved in Visual Basic by encapsulating code inside class modules, and by loading these modules into multiple projects. In particular, the use of OLE automation servers and ActiveX controls makes it easier to allow many programs to share the same executable program code. The concept of *plug-in component*s is fundamental to Visual Basic, beginning with the standard controls and custom controls in the toolbox window.

1.1.6 Implementing the Application

The *implementation phase* of a software project is usually what the programmers have been waiting for. The program design has been built from the specifications, the visual interface has been evaluated and approved by the users, and the project has been determined to be feasible. All projected deadlines are reasonable, adequate programming and testing personnel have been brought into the project, and any required software tools have been purchased and mastered.

Programming Teams. If a team of programmers is creating the application, each programmer will be assigned certain sections of the program to work on. Some might develop classes and objects that will be used by other project members. Others will be involved in fully developing the visual interface. Generally, a project leader will coordinate the actions of the programmers. Procedures will be established for the sharing of source code among the team, using library software such as *SourceSafe,* which is distributed with the Visual Basic Enterprise Edition. This software allows one to track all changes made by programmers, revert to previous versions of the software, and check source code modules in and out of a library. Strict coding guidelines are important at this phase, to ensure that all source code in the application has a similar look and feel.

Allow for Changes. In the best of all possible worlds, once a program's specifications and design were approved by a client, no more changes would be made to the program. This would be great, but clients, who are usually not programmers themselves, often expect changes to be made at the last minute. If the consultant/programmer appears to be too rigid in not allowing changes to be made, the client may possibly dislike the final product. Most consultants get used to the idea that last-minute changes will be made, and build this cost into the original consulting fee. Fortunately, Visual Basic programs lend themselves well to visual modifications. Deeper, structural modifications are much more difficult, because they may involve moving large blocks of code between modules, creating new modules, redesigning classes, and so on.

1.1.7 Testing the Application

The testing phase of the application's development is in many ways the most important. This is the last point at which designers can verify that the program accomplishes the tasks outlined by the program specifications. Possible design flaws might be uncovered at this point, requiring a modification to the design and re-coding of certain parts of the program.

Companies with experience in developing high-quality software have strict procedures in place for the design, documentation, coding, and testing of software. Often a separate testing department will thoroughly test daily updates of the software, document each bug they find, and pass this information on to the programmers. After each bug is fixed, the same section of software must be re-tested, to ensure that a new bug was not created in the process of fixing the existing bug.

A *test suite* should be created for the program; this is a sequenced series of inputs designed to fully exercise the program and uncover any flaws. There are independent companies who only test other companies' software. They have considerable experience in developing high-quality test suites.

An ongoing problem in software development is the lack of adequate testing. Programming shops in small companies often have no formal testing procedures. In extreme cases, the programmer is given no assistance in the design, documentation, and testing phases of a project. Most programmers like to write programs, and are not likely to create great documentation and/or user manuals.

In small shops, the testing of the program is often left up to the programmer who wrote the actual code. This is a mistake, because most programmers tend to run their programs the same way, with the same types of inputs. A user who knows nothing about the program makes a much better tester, because he/she will provide unanticipated inputs and actions. Often, the intense pressure of constant deadlines imposed by management tends to make programmers release code into production before it is adequately tested.

1.2 Sample Design: Mozart Music Sales

Now that we have reviewed the overall process of application development, let's look at an example in which a set of specifications are developed into a program design. This is a relatively simple invoice program for a music store that sells music tapes and CDs.

1.2.1 Program Specifications

The Mozart Music Store needs a simple invoice program that can be filled in by a store clerk (the *user*) when a compact disc or cassette tape is purchased. The store uses a 5-digit number called an *SKU number* to uniquely identify all items. On startup, the program will display *a splash screen* that identifies the program's name, revision date, and other identification information.

When the user selects an SKU number from an existing list of available numbers, the program displays the album title that matches the number. The clerk looks at the item for a label indicating one of three price codes (A, B, or C) and enters the same code into the computer by clicking with the mouse. The clerk also selects the recording format (CD or tape). The program immediately calculates the sale amount, tax, and net price. Also provided is a check box which can be clicked if the customer is entitled to a 10% discount.

Chap 1: Designing and Coding Programs

As each item is added to the current invoice, the price of each item is displayed, and the program displays a running invoice total with the sales tax and net amount. The program saves the contents of the current invoice in a text file and gradually accumulates multiple invoice records in the same file.

The user can choose to clear all fields on the form and start a new invoice. When the user wants to quit the program, a confirmation dialog should display before the program ends.

1.2.2 Program Design

This program should have a simple, straightforward user interface, with a minimum of clutter on its main window. We want to focus the user's attention on a few vital pieces of information. We display the name of the store on the Form's title bar, and the date is displayed in a label. Combo boxes can be used for the list of SKU numbers and salesperson names. Each group of option buttons should be surrounded by a frame, so the two groups can operate independently. The program will automatically recalculate and display the numeric amounts whenever the user changes the price code, format, or discount.

The splash screen (Figure 1) appears first, before the main form. There is a timer control on the window, allowing it to automatically disappear after two seconds have passed. In the lblRevisionDate label, insert the current date. The icon, shown in an image control is one of the icons that is supplied with Visual Basic, having the filename misc31.ico.

Figure 1. Sample Splash Screen.

Main Window. The main window (Figure 2) will have a menu, which will allow us to add new commands to the program without cluttering up the form with buttons. The main window contains a list box called lstInvoice that displays the album title, SKU number, and item price. The salesperson name is selected from a combo box. The user selects a SKU number as in the previous program, and the item's title appears. The user selects a price code and format. Optionally, the discount check box is selected. When the user clicks on the Add button, the current album is added to the list box. At the same time, we display the total sales for the invoice in the labels on the right side of the form.

Figure 2. Mozart Music Sales, Main Window.

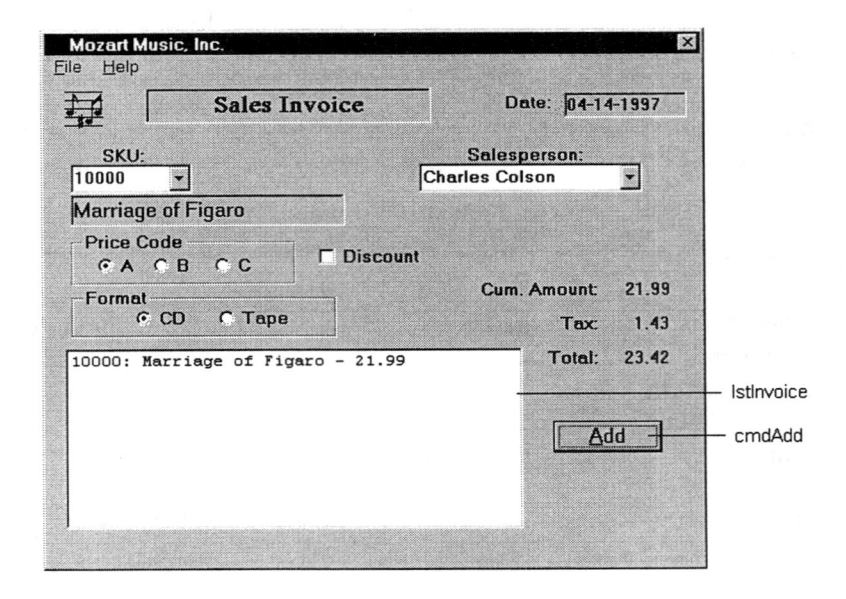

In Figure 3, two items have been added to the invoice, totaling $37.98 before taxes.

Figure 3. Sample Items Added to Invoice.

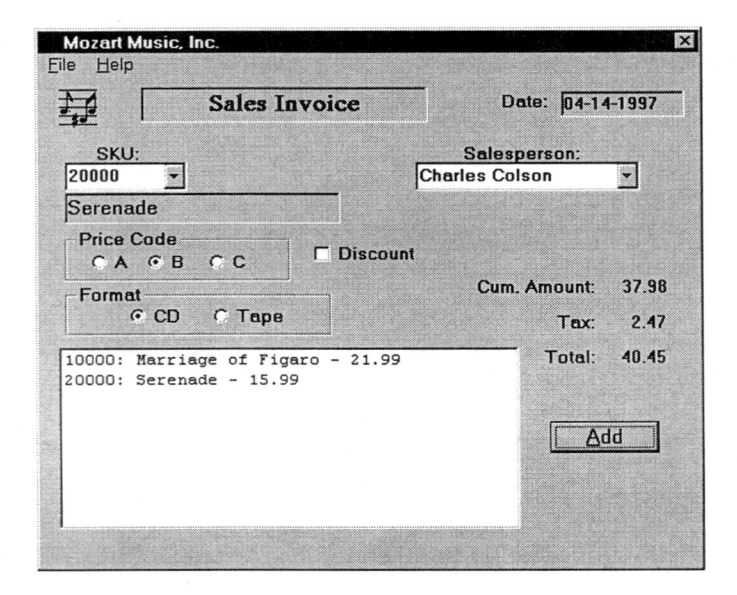

Menu Design. In order to reduce the cluttering of command buttons on the form, we will create a menu for this program and transfer most of the button commands to the menu. The menu has the following layout and selections. The Name property of each menu item appears on the right side:

```
File                                         mnuFile
   New invoice            Ctrl+N             mnuFileNew
   Save                   Ctrl+S             mnuFileSave
   Exit                   Ctrl+X             mnuFileExit
Help                                         mnuHelp
   About Mozart Sales     F1                 mnuHelpAbout
```

Notice that shortcut keys such as *Ctrl+N* and *Ctrl+S* are shown for each menu choice. The user can also activate the File menu by pressing *Alt-F*, and the New invoice item by pressing *N*. Although a splash screen is generally not the same as the form displayed by the Help/About command, we will use the same form for both for now.

Saving the Invoice. When the user has entered all the required data for the current invoice, the invoice is saved to a file by clicking on the File/Save menu command. But if the salesperson is not selected, Figure 4 shows the displayed reminder.

Figure 4. Saving the Invoice.

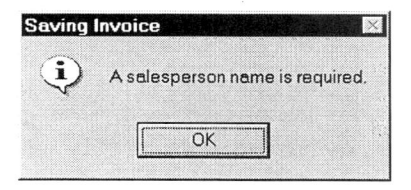

Input Files. From input text files, we fill one combo box with a list of SKU numbers, another combo box containing names of salespeople, and an array of strings containing the names of titles. The file called "sperson.txt", contains the names of salespeople that we intend to load into a combo box. Here are sample names:

```
Adrian Adams
Barbara Baker
Charles Colson
Daniel Del Terzo
Erin Easterbrook
Fay Franklin
George Gomez
Henry Heller
```

The second file, called "titles.txt", contains a list of SKU numbers and album titles:

```
10000,"Marriage of Figaro"
20000,"Serenade"
22222,"Cosi Fan Tutti"
```

```
    30000,"Requiem"
    33333,"Symphony in G Minor"
    40000,"Piano Concerto in C Major"
    44444,"Sinfonia Concertante"
    50000,"Mozart's Greatest Hits"
```

With the design information shown in this section, we should have enough information to begin coding the Mozart Music Sales program. The complete solution to this program will be shown in Chapter 2.

1.3 User Interface Design

The user interface of a program is that part of the program that interacts with users. It usually incorporates various types of input from the keyboard and mouse. Output will usually be to the screen or printer. Over the years, applications written for Windows 3.1, Windows 95 and Windows NT have established a standard look and feel. Microsoft publishes guidelines for the design of windows, menus, dialog boxes, and so on. Good sources of examples can be found in the Microsoft Office applications such as Word, Excel, Access, PowerPoint, and Project. The following topics consist of suggestions that you might want to follow.

1.3.1 Avoiding Crowding Forms

When you place controls too close together on a form, you give the impression of crowding, and the user has to work harder at focusing on information that is most important. If you really have a lot of information to display, or your program requires a great deal of input from the user, consider some alternatives.

Divide the form into several different forms, all accessible from a starting form. Use command buttons or a menu to let the user show the other forms. Provide hints on the starting form as to what the other forms contain, so the user will not have to spend a lot of time searching for the desired form.

Use the custom SSTab control (Figure 5) to overlay groups of controls on the same form. Each group of controls appears on a separate tab, similar to the tabs on a set of file folders. For example we can place a customer's address on one tab, and show his list of payments and credits on separate tabs. Any buttons that affect the entire form, however, should be separate from the SSTab control.

Figure 5. SSTab Control Example.

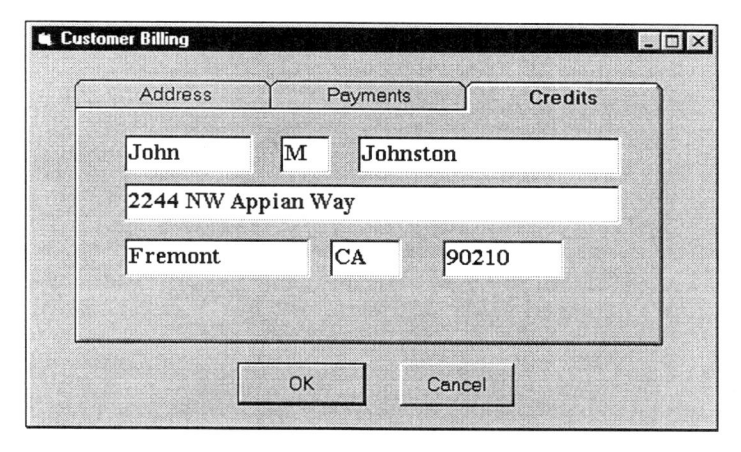

Watch Your Form's Size. A common problem occurs when you create a program on a computer with a high-resolution monitor, and then run the program on a low-resolution monitor. Many programmers work in 1024 x 768 mode (or higher), but their program users use a standard 640 x 480 VGA monitor. The result is that forms appear only partially on the screen, or are too large for the screen. Of course, you should always test your programs in standard VGA mode before delivering them to end-users. You can also calculate the size of any window at runtime, using the Width, Screen.TwipsPerPixelX, Height, and Screen.TwipsPerPixelY properties. For example, the following statements calculate the current form's height and width, in pixels, and display an error message if either is too large:

```
If (Width / Screen.TwipsPerPixelX) > 640 Then
   MsgBox "Form is too wide."
End If
If (Height / Screen.TwipsPerPixelY) > 480 Then
   MsgBox "Form is too tall."
End If
```

This code can be placed in the Form_Load event handler of a form.

1.3.2 Setting the Tab Order

Every control that involves user input has a property called TabStop, which can be either True or False. If this property is True, the user can press the Tab key to move to this control when the program is running. The TabIndex property allows you to set the order in which controls will receive the focus when the user tabs between controls. After all of the controls have been positioned on your form, you should give some attention to the order of tab stops. Start with the control that you want the user to begin with; set its TabIndex to 0. Then move to the next control in the desired tab order, and set its TabIndex to 1, and so on.

A group of option buttons presents a special case when dealing with tab stops. The buttons should have their TabIndex values numbered sequentially. But when you run the program, notice that you can use the Tab key to move only to the first button in the group (the one with the lowest TabStop value). To move to the other buttons, you have to use the keyboard arrow keys. Pressing the Tab key will just take you to the next control following the group of option buttons.

1.3.3 Keyboard Input

When it has the focus, a control has the ability to respond to keyboard keys. The following event procedures trap keyboard events, shown here for a list box named List1:

```
Private Sub List1_KeyPress(KeyAscii As Integer)
Private Sub List1_KeyDown(KeyCode As Integer, Shift As Integer)
Private Sub List1_KeyUp(KeyCode As Integer, Shift As Integer)
```

The **KeyPress** event interprets ANSI characters only, so it is used for standard keyboard keys such as 'A', '7', Enter, Tab, Backspace, and so on. If the user will be pressing an extended key (F1-F12, Ins, Del, arrow keys, Home, End, and so on), the KeyPress event will not be activated.

The **KeyDown** and **KeyUp** event procedures respond to the pressing and releasing of extended keyboard keys, once that are generally non-displayable. When the key is pressed, the KeyCode parameter contains a numeric value that your program can act on. Table 1 shows a list of the more common keyboard constants along with their matching descriptions.

Table 1. Keyboard Constants.

Constant	Description
vbKeyBack	Backspace
vbKeyTab	Tab
vbKeyReturn	Enter
vbKeyEscape	Esc
vbKeyPageUp	PgUp
vbKeyPageDn	PgDn
vbKeyEnd	End
vbKeyHome	Home
vbKeyLeft	Left arrow
vbKeyUp	Up arrow
vbKeyRight	Right arrow
vbKeyDown	Down arrow
vbKeyInsert	Insert
vbKeyDelete	Delete
vbKeyF1	F1 function
vbKeyF2	F2 function
...	...
vbKeyF12	F12 function

You can easily retrieve these values and paste them in your programs, using the View/Object Browser menu command. Look upder "Visual Basic Objects and Procedures", and look in the sub-category "KeyCodeConstants". For example, the following event procedure would be activated if the user pressed a key while the list box had the focus:

```
Private Sub List1_KeyDown(KeyCode As Integer, Shift As Integer)
```

Chap 1: Designing and Coding Programs 13

```
        If KeyCode = vbKeyDelete Then
            mnuMemberRemove_Click
        End If
    End Sub
```

The statments say to call the mnuMemberRemove_Click procedure when the user presses the Delete key. All other keys are ignored.

1.3.4 Using Standard Menus

The menus of applications written for Microsoft Windows have a standard look and feel. This is in a large part due to the fact that many of the submenu names are standardized. Microsoft Word, for example, contains the submenus listed in Table 2. Of course, most Visual Basic applications will not have the same submenus; but whenever program operations can be logically grouped under these categories, standard submenu names should be used.

Table 2. Microsoft Word Menu Sample.

Name	Description/Choices
File	New, Open, Close, Save, Save As, Print, Print Preview, file history list.
Edit	Undo, Cut, Copy, Paste, Clear, Select All, Find, Replace, Go To.
View	Lets the user switch between different formats, or views of the information in the current window.
Insert	Insert application-specific data into the current window.
Format	Change the style or appearance of data in the current window.
Tools	Application-specific tools, set program options.
Window	New, tile, cascade, split, show list of open windows.
Help	Contents, index, context-sensitive help, about the application.

1.4 Coding Guidelines

1.4.1 Declaring Variables and Constants

It's easy to make a mistake when typing the names of variables and constants. If you use the **Option Explicit** command in the declarations section of all modules, Visual Basic will flag the misspelling before the program runs. If you omit this command, a brand-new variable will be created when the program runs, which is probably not what you intended. This type of error is quite difficult to catch, particularly in large programs. Option Explicit can be automatically placed in each new module as it is created: select the Tools/Options menu command, click on the Environment tab, and check the "Require Variable Declaration" option.

1.4.2 Naming Variables and Constants

For identifiers defined at the global or form level, always choose identifier names that are descriptive, because you will have to remember these names as you are writing the program, and later, when you or anyone else returns to the program to perform maintenance.

Table 3 contains both good and bad examples of variable names.

Table 3. Examples of Variable Names.

Good	Poor
lastName	ln
hourlyPayRate	rate
transactionCount	tc
highestScore	high
numQuestionsAsked	qAsk

Variable names inside procedures should also be meaningful if possible, particularly in longer procedures where the variable is used quite a bit. On the other hand, variables used for loop counters and those holding temporary values need not be descriptive. For example, a loop counter called j is perfectly acceptable because its usage is clear from the context:

```
Dim j As Integer
For j = 1 To QuestionCount
    '....
Next j
```

In the VB 5.0 *Programmers Guide*, Microsoft recommends using standard prefixes at the beginnings of variables and constants that indicate their type (Table 4).

Table 4. Standard Prefixes for Variables.

Data Type	Prefix	Example
Boolean	bln	blnFound
Byte	byt	bytRasterData
Collection object	col	colWidgets
Currency	cur	curRevenue
Date (Time)	dtm	dtmStart
Double	dbl	dblTolerance
Error	err	errOrderNum
Integer	int	intQuantity
Long	lng	lngDistance
Object	obj	objCurrent
Single	sng	sngAverage
String	str	strFName
User-defined type	udt	udtEmployee
Variant	vnt	vntCheckSum

Microsoft also recomments using a scope prefix at the beginning of identifiers: g = global, m = module, (no prefix) = local. Table 5 lists examples of variables that use both prefixes. The most important principle is that once you create a system, be consistent.

Table 5. Recommended Scope Prefixes.

Global	Module	Local
gblnFileFound	mblnFileFound	blnFileFound
gcurSalary	mcurSalary	curSalary
gstrLastName	mstrLastName	strLastName

1.4.3 Naming Controls

It's a good idea to use standard prefixes for form, control, and menu names, to help identify them in program code. The default names given to controls such as Form1, Command1, and Option1 are not descriptive enough to be a help in understanding their purpose within the program. You definitely do not want to use names that look like ordinary variables. Table 6 contains a list of standard prefixes for forms, menus, and other controls, suggested by the Visual Basic *Programmers Guide*.

Table 6. Standard Prefixes for Controls.

Control Type	Prefix	Example
3D Panel	pnl	pnlGroup
Animated button	ani	aniMailBox
Check box	chk	chkReadOnly
Combo box, drop-down list box	cbo	cboEnglish
Command button	cmd	cmdExit
Common dialog	dlg	dlgFileOpen
Communications	com	comFax
Control (specific type is unknown)	ctr	ctrCurrent
Data control	dat	datBiblio
Data-bound combo box	dbcbo	dbcboLanguage
Data-bound grid	dbgrd	dbgrdQueryResult
Data-bound list box	dblst	dblstJobType
Directory list box	dir	dirSource
Drive list box	drv	drvTarget
File list box	fil	filSource
Form	frm	frmEntry
Frame	fra	fraLanguage
Gauge	gau	gauStatus
Graph	gra	graRevenue
Grid	grd	grdPrices
Horizontal scroll bar	hsb	hsbVolume
Image	img	imgIcon
Key status	key	keyCaps
Label	lbl	lblHelpMessage
Line	lin	linVertical
List box	lst	lstPolicyCodes
MAPI message	mpm	mpmSentMessage
MAPI session	mps	mpsSession

MCI	mci	mciVideo
MDI child form	mdi	MdiNote
Menu	mnu	mnuFileOpen
MS Flex grid	msg	msgClients
MS Tab	mst	MstFirst
OLE	ole	oleWorksheet
Outline	out	outOrgChart
Pen BEdit	bed	BedFirstName
Pen HEdit	hed	hedSignature
Pen ink	ink	inkMap
Picture	pic	picVGA
Picture clip	clp	clpToolbar
Report	rpt	rptQtr1Earnings
Shape	shp	shpCircle
Spin	spn	spnPages
Text box	txt	txtLastName
Timer	tmr	tmrAlarm
UpDown	upd	updDirection
Vertical scroll bar	vsb	vsbRate
Slider	sld	sldScale
ImageList	ils	ilsAllIcons
TreeView	tre	treOrganization
Toolbar	tlb	tlbActions
TabStrip	tab	tabOptions
StatusBar	sta	staDateTime
ListView	lvw	lvwHeadings
ProgressBar	prg	prgLoadFile
RichTextBox	rtf	rtfReport

1.4.4 Naming Procedures and Methods

Procedures and methods are action statements, so their names should contain verbs. Can you tell which of the following procedure names correctly convey their meaning, and which names are somewhat cryptic?

```
1    CalculateWeeklyPay
2    WeeklyPay
3    AverageAllScores
4    AverageScore
5    LookUpPurchasePrice
6    LUPP
7    RandomizeButtons
8    RndButtons
9    AddNewRecord
10   NewRecord
```

Some of these names appear to be variables or constants, because they don't imply any action. If you guessed that the odd-numbered names were the best, you're right!

1.4.5 Indenting Code

Always indent statements inside loops and If statements. Nothing is more annoying to read than a program containing nested loops and If statements that does not use proper indentation. For example, the following code has no indentation. Does it make any sense?

```
Do While Not EOF(1)
Input #1, payRate, hours
If payRate > 0 Then
If hours > 0 Then
weeklyPay = hours * payRate
lblWeeklyPay = Format$(weeklyPay, "currency")
Else
MsgBox "Hours are invalid", vbInformation, "Error"
End If
Else
MsgBox "Rate is invalid", vbInformation, "Error"
End If
Loop
```

Here is the same code, indented correctly:

```
Do While Not EOF(1)
   Input #1, payRate, hours
   If payRate > 0 Then
     If hours > 0 Then
        weeklyPay = hours * payRate
        lblWeeklyPay = Format$(weeklyPay, "currency")
     Else
        MsgBox "Hours are invalid", vbInformation, "Error"
     End If
   Else
     MsgBox "Rate is invalid", vbInformation, "Error"
   End If
Loop
```

Who would ever imagine that having beautiful code is important? But it's true—most experienced programmers have a distinctive coding style, that could almost be called a "signature".

1.4.6 Predefined VB Constants

Whenever possible, use the Visual Basic predefined symbolic constants that apply to control properties. A few constants that are often modified at run time are listed in Table 7. The complete set may be viewed using the Visual Basic Object Browser.

Table 7. Selected Control Property Constants.

Control.Property	Symbol	Constant
CheckBox.Value	vbUnchecked	0
	vbChecked	1
	vbGrayed	2
Form.Windowstate	vbNormal	0
	vbMinimized	1
	vbMaximized	2
MousePointer	vbDefault	0
	vbHourglass	11

1.4.7 Line Continuation

Avoid letting source code extend beyond the right edge of the screen, because it becomes almost impossible to read. If necessary, use the underscore (_) character to continue a line. The underscore must be preceded by at least one space, and must be the last character on the line. For example, we could break the line after a comma separating the procedure arguments:

```
MsgBox "Hours worked must be greater than zero.", _
       vbExclamation, "Error"
```

It is not possible, however, to break a line in the middle of a string. The following would be an error:

```
MsgBox "Hours worked must be greater _
    than zero.", vbExclamation, "Error"
```

If you really must break a line within a string, create two strings and use the (+) concatenation operator to reconnect them. The following would be correct:

```
MsgBox "Hours worked must be greater " _
    + "than zero.", vbExclamation, "Error"
```

1.4.8 App Object Properties

Visual Basic creates a built-in App (application) object for each running program. These properties can be set in design mode. In Visual Basic 4.0, select Make **EXE File** from the File menu, and click on the Options button (Figure 6). In Visual Basic 5.0, select **Project Properties** from the Project menu, and click on the Make tab (Figure 7).

Fill in the version number boxes, and from the Type listbox, select the element you wish to change; type a description into the Value text box. For example, you might want to assign values to Company Name, Product Name, and Legal Copyright. Notice that the executable program's icon can be selected from the list of icons already assigned to the various forms in the project.

Chap 1: Designing and Coding Programs 19

Figure 6. VB 4.0 Application Object Settings.

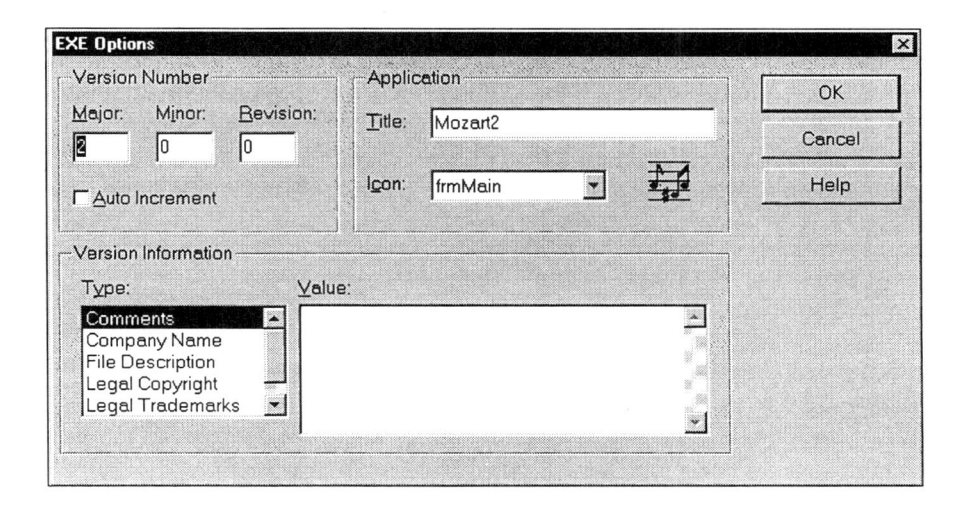

Figure 7. VB 5.0 Application Object Settings.

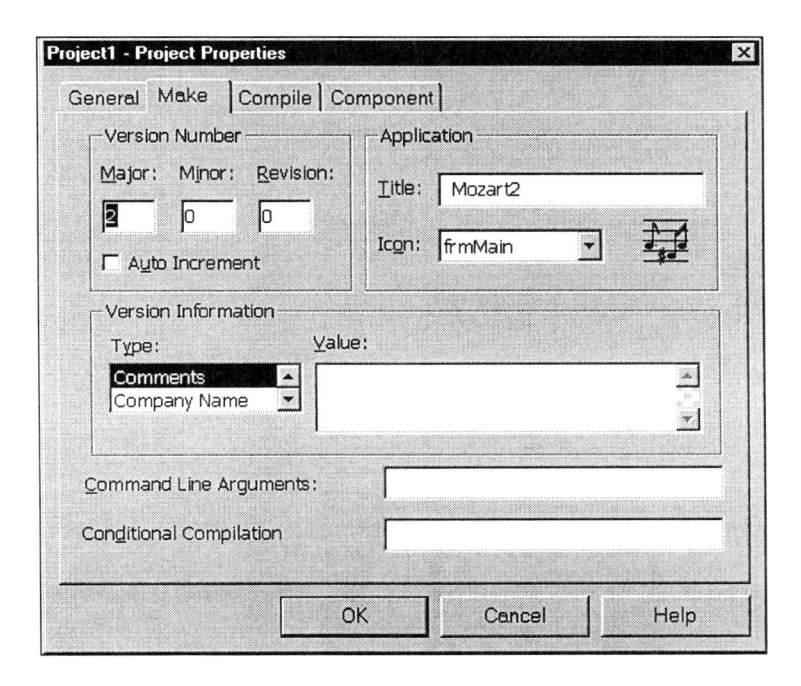

1.5 Error Handling

1.5.1 Causes of Errors

Accidents happen, of course, and computer programs are no exception to the rule. Professional programmers spend a lot of their time planning for the inevitable runtime errors that can stop a program, and writing code that handles the errors in a reasonable way. Some runtime errors are caused by factors outside the programmer's control—incorrect user input, for example. But programs still must recover from these errors and take whatever action is necessary. Here is a partial list of common errors which you are likely to encounter:

- An invalid numeric value is assigned to a numeric variable.
- An input file cannot be found.
- An attempt is made to read past the end of a file.
- An input file contains invalid data.
- An output file cannot be created.
- A string function receives an invalid argument, such as an empty string.
- A non-numeric value is used in a calculation.
- An attempt is made to divide by zero.
- An array subscript is out of bounds.
- A reference is made to a form name for which no instance exists.

Visual Basic provides a way to recover from runtime errors, so a program can take any or all of the following actions when an error has occurred:

- Diagnose the error.
- Notify the user that an error has occurred.
- Ignore the error and continue to the next program statement.
- Attempt to correct the error and continue the program.
- Abort the program.

Error handling is somewhat of an art among professional programmers, and many take pride in writing programs that are nearly "bullet-proof". On the other hand, it is nearly impossible to anticipate everything that can go wrong in a program, and one could spend an excessive amount of time writting error-trapping code. The managers of a project also affect the degree of error checking by pressuring programmers into deadlines that do not allow adequate time for testing and debugging.

1.5.2 On Error GoTo Statement

\OnError

The **On Error Goto** statement enables an error handler and specifies the location of the error handler. An *error handler* is a block of code is identified by a label, containing statements that attempt to report and/or deal with the error. For example, it might be as simple as displaying a message box.

In the following example, if the Open statement fails because the file was not found, the program immediately branches to the label OpenFile1 and an error message displays. On the other hand, if the file is opened successfully, the program continues to execute the statements following the Open, up to the Exit Sub statement:

```
Public Sub OpenFile( filename As String )
  Dim fileNum As Integer
  On Error Goto OpenFile1:
  fileNum = FreeFile
  Open filename For Input As fileNum
  MsgBox "File was opened."
  Close fileNum
  Exit Sub
OpenFile1:
  MsgBox Error$, vbInformation, "OpenFile"
End Sub
```

In this example, we called the **Error$** function to get the error messsage passed by Visual Basic and placing it inside a message box. The **Exit Sub** statement prevents the program from "falling into" the error handler when no error has occurred. Functions use **Exit Function**, and property procedures use **Exit Property.**

1.5.3 Resume Statement

In some situations, you might want to resume processing at the statement immediately following the one that caused the error:

```
OpenFile1:
  MsgBox Error$,vbInformation,"OpenFile"
  Resume Next
```

Another possibility is to resume processing at the same statement that caused the error. In the next example, we call the **InputBox** function to ask the user for a new filename and attempt to open the file again:

```
Public Sub OpenFile( filename As String )
  Dim fileNum As Integer
  On Error GoTo OpenFile1
  fileNum = FreeFile
  Open filename For Input As fileNum
  MsgBox "File opened successfully", vbInformation, ""
  Close fileNum
  Exit Sub
OpenFile1:
  filename = InputBox("The file: " + filename + _
    " was not found. Please enter the " _
    + "correct filename.", "OpenFile Procedure")
  If Len(filename) > 0 Then Resume
End Sub
```

Figure 8 displays the dialog window seen by the user.

Figure 8. Dialog Box: File Not Found.

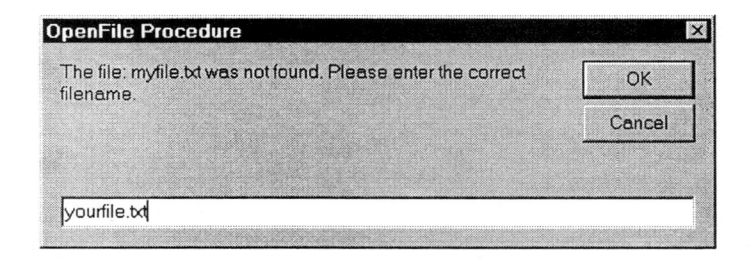

If the Cancel button is clicked, a zero-length filename is returned, and we immediately exit the OpenFile procedure. In the absence of any On Error Goto statement, the program would display the default error window and halt, as in Figure 9.

Figure 9. Unhandled Runtime Error.

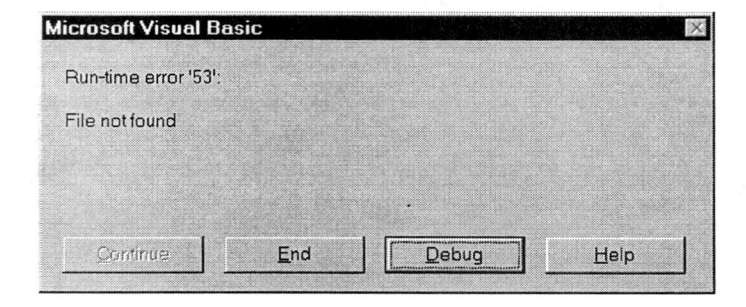

Error handling is automatically disabled when execution leaves the current procedure. Error checking can also be turned off inside the current procedure by using the **On Error Goto 0** statement.

Automatic Backward Chaining. Sometimes you can purposely avoid handling an error, with the expectation that the error will be handled by the previous procedure in the current procedure call stack. Suppose that cmdOpen_Click called OpenFile, and the latter did not have any error handler. The error could still be handled inside cmdOpen_Click:

```
Private Sub CmdOpen_Click()
   On Error GoTo CmdOpen1
   Openfile fileName
   Exit Sub
CmdOpen1:
   MsgBox "The file: " & fileName & " could not be opened."
End Sub

Public Sub OpenFile( filename As String )
   Dim fileNum As Integer
   fileNum = FreeFile
   Open filename For Input As fileNum
   MsgBox "File opened successfully", vbInformation, ""
```

```
        Close fileNum
    Exit Sub
End Sub
```

If an error occurs inside OpenFile, control *immediately* leaves that procedure and branches to the error handler in cmdOpen_Click. In general, a procedure call stack can be unwound as far as necessary in order to locate an error handler, or if there are no more procedure calls left, the default error window is displayed and the program halts.

> ***VB Configuration Tip:*** To prevent the program from halting when an unhandled error occurs inside the GetApps method, you must set one of the VB environment options. In **VB5**, select **Options** from the **Tools** menu, and click on the **General** tab. Select the option button labeled "Break on Unhandled Errors." (In **VB4**, click on the **Advanced** tab to locate the same option button.)

1.5.4 Using the Err Object

Visual Basic creates an object called **Err** whenever a runtime error occurs, and you can access the Err.Number and Err.Description properties separately:

```
OpenFile1:
    MsgBox Err.Description, , "Error " & Err.Number
```

If the program could not open a file, "File Not Found" error message would be displayed, With "Error 53" as the message box caption.

The Err.Raise Method. An error handler can check for specific error codes and provide more specific help to the user. For example, we can revise the earlier example that displayed an input box when a file is not found. If error 53 occurs, we ask for a new filename; for all other errors, we display the error number, matching message, and exit the procedure:

```
OpenFile1:
  Select Case Err.Number
    Case 53: filename = InputBox("The file: " + filename + _
          " was not found. Please enter the " _
        + "correct filename.", "OpenFile Procedure")
        If Len(filename) > 0 Then Resume
    Case Else
      MsgBox Err.Description, , "Error " & Err.Number
  End Select
```

The Err.Raise method is useful when testing error handling code, because you can simulate the occurrence of a runtime error.

```
    Public Sub OpenFile( filename As String )
      Dim fileNum As Integer
      On Error GoTo OpenFile1
      fileNum = FreeFile
      Open filename For Input As fileNum
      Err.Raise 53                    'TEST the FileNotFound error
```

```
MsgBox "File opened successfully", vbInformation, ""
Close fileNum
Exit Sub
(etc...)
```

> ***Programming Tip:*** To make programs more self-documenting, a good technique is to predefine useful runtime error constants. For example:
>
> ```
> Const errFileNotFound = 53
> ```
>
> Then your error handlers can be more descriptive:
>
> ```
> OpenFile1:
>   Select Case Err.Number
>     Case errFileNotFound: filename = InputBox("The file: " +
>     (etc.)
> ```

1.6 Reducing Code Size

There are a number of techniques you can use to reduce the size of a compiled Visual Basic program. This type of optimization can reduce the amount of memory used by the program, and help it to load more quickly. First, however, do not bother to reduce the length or number of identifier names, comments, or blank lines. Doing so will have no effect on the executable program size. The following suggestions appear in the Visual Basic 5 *Programmers Guide*:

- Reduce the number of loaded forms. A form consumes a great deal of memory when loaded, so you can load forms only when they are needed, and unload them when unneeded. The Unload statement does not release all memory used by a form, unless you also set any references to the form to Nothing:

  ```
  Set frmCustomer = Nothing
  ```

- Reduce the number of controls on each form. Rather than using a large number of separately named controls on the same form, use a control array.
- Use labels instead of text boxes when a value is simply being displayed.
- Keep data in disk files or resources and load only when needed. Large bitmaps and strings, for example, can be loaded from files at runtime.
- Organize your modules. Visual Basic loads modules "on demand", meaning that a module is only loaded into memory when one of its procedures or variables is referenced. If related procedures are grouped inside the same modules, fewer modules will be loaded at the same time.
- Consider alternatives to Variant data types. A Variant variable takes up at least 16 bytes of storage, so it should only be used when the type of data assigned to the variable cannot be known at compile time.

- Use dynamic arrays rather than fixed-size arrays. Dynamic arrays can be reduced in size or erased at runtime using the Erase and ReDim statements. When used on a fixed-size array, however, the Erase statement does not reduce memory usage.
- Reclaim space used by strings or object variables. Global strings and object variables, in particular, remain active for the entire life of a program. Setting a string variable to "" reclaims its storage, and setting an object variable to Nothing reclaims most of its storage.
- Eliminate dead code (code that is never executed). Debug.Print statements, incidentally, do not take up space in compiled programs unless the statements call other functions.
- Reduce the number of unused variables.

1.7 Improving Execution Speed

There are three types of speed: *code speed* (the actual time spent performing calculations and executing code), *display speed* (the time spent displaying graphics or painting the screen), and *perceived speed* (how fast your program appears to run).

A major factor in customer satisfaction with a program has to do with the program's *perceived* execution speed. The time spent waiting for such tasks as loading and displaying a form, loading a listbox from a database, for example, can be quite obvious. Of course, many performance factors are beyond the range of the programmer's control, such as CPU speed, memory size, disk access time, and so on.

1.7.1 Code Optimization

The VB 5 *Programmers Guide* lists the following ways to optimize your program's code:

- *Avoid using variant variables.* A variant variable has to be converted to the appropriate data type at run time, whereas typed variables do not require any conversion.
- *Use long integer variables and integer math* if only whole numbers are involved, rather than floating-point or currency variables. Because the native data type of the CPU is 32 bits, the Long data type is also more efficient than Integer or Byte.
- *Store frequently used properties in variables.* It takes less processing time to get and set the value of a variable than it does to access an object's property.
- *Replace procedure calls with inline procedures.* If a loop is executed hundreds or thousands of times, calling a procedure from within the loop slows the program down slightly. Instead, place the procedure body inside the loop.
- *Use constants rather than variables whenever possible.* The value of a constant never changes, so the compiler can substitute the same value into each place where the constant is referenced. A variable, on the other hand, can change value while a program is running, so the variable's value has to be retrieved whenever the variable is referenced.
- *Pass arguments ByVal instead of ByRef*, unless the called procedure has to modify the passed argument.
- *If you use optional arguments*, make them typed rather than Variant (this is possible because of a new feature in VB 5.0).
- *Use collections properly.* Use the For Each...Next statement rather than the For...Next statement. Avoid using Before and After arguments when adding objects to a collection. Use keyed collections rather than arrays for groups of objects of the same type.

1.7.2 Display Optimization

The VB 5 Programmers Guide suggests the following ways to optimize a program's display speed:

- *Set the ClipControls property* of forms, picture boxes, and other containers to False. This will improve the speed at which forms containing a large number of controls are redrawn. ClipControls only needs to be True when using graphics methods such as Line or PSet.
- *Set AutoRedraw to False* if a program draws graphics on a form that must be redrawn frequently. When the form is covered up and then exposed again, place your graphics drawing statements inside the Paint method.
- *Use image controls* instead of picture box controls. Image controls are much simpler, use less memory, and display more quickly. They are ideal for displaying icons, bitmaps, and metafiles.
- *Hide controls when setting control properties* so that all modified controls on the same form can be repainted at the same time. Otherwise, the form repaints after each control is modified.
- *Use Line instead of Pset* when drawing graphics lines. Also, use shape and line controls for simple graphical elements, and use graphics methods for more complex drawings.

1.7.3 Perceived Speed Optimization

A program that seems to do its work quickly when the user is waiting will appear to run more quickly. Here are some techniques that you can use to improve this:

- *Keep forms hidden but loaded.* As we have already pointed out, keeping hidden forms in memory uses up more memory while the program is running. But it takes less time to show a form than it does to load it from disk and then show it.
- *Preload data.* Whenever the user already expects there to be a pause in the program, you can load all data that will be needed in the near future. This will eliminate delays during time-critical moments.
- *Use timers that work in the background.* If a program is waiting for a user input or action, it can perform background operations until the user responds. A timer control allows a program to activate a background processing routine at regular time intervals.
- *Use progress indicators.* The ProgressBar control can show the status of a slow operation, as is generally done by software installation programs. The progress bar will let the user know that the program has not simply frozen up. The hourglass mouse cursor may also be used during short delays. To use it, do the following:

```
Screen.MousePointer = vbHourglass
   (do the slow operations here)
Screen.MousePointer = vbDefault
```

- *Speed the start of your application.* Users hate to click on a program icon and stare at an empty screen for several seconds while all of the program DLLs load. Instead, you can use the Show method in the Form_Load event to show the program's startup form (called a *splash screen*). The startup form should be both simple and attractive. The program's other, larger forms can be loaded in the background while the user is reading the startup form. The VB5 documentation uses the following example, which would be in the startup form:

```
Sub Form_Load()
    Me.Show              ' Display startup form.
    DoEvents             ' Ensure startup form is painted.
    Load MainForm        ' Load main application form.
    Unload Me            ' Unload startup form.
    MainForm.Show        ' Display main form.
End Sub
```

The Professional and Enterprise editions of VB5 let you divide a program into an executable file and multiple DLL files. The executable file can be small, allowing it to load quickly.

1.8 Review Questions

1. During which step in the application development cycle would you develop the user interface?
2. Why is it important for a program designer to speak to those persons who will use the final program?
3. Why is it important to review specifications for feasibility before proceding to the design stage?
4. What is a common mistake made by companies developing programs in Visual Basic for the first time?
5. What is *prototyping*?
6. What is a major drawback of procedural design?
7. In what way is object-oriented design most different from procedural design?
8. Is the Visual Basic toolbox built around a procedural approach, or an object-oriented one?
9. What entities (objects) would be important in a doctor's office scheduling program? (This is an open-ended question, so your choices do not have to agree with those stated earlier in the chapter.)
10. How is a method different from a property?
11. For an Employee object, would PayRate be a method or a property?
12. Why is *flexibility* an important goal in application design?
13. What is meant by *extensibility* in the context of application design?
14. How does the concept of *reusability* apply to the way Visual Basic was designed?
15. When a programming team is working on a project, how can they be sure that two programmers will not inadvertently modify the same source code at the same time?
16. Which type of modification to a program design is usually more difficult to achieve: visual or structural? Why?
17. What is a common mistake made in small programming shops regarding the testing and validation of software?

18. What is *a test suite*, and why is it useful?
19. Why should a program not be placed into production immediately after several bugs have been fixed?
20. Which property is used to set the tab order for each of the controls on a form?
21. Which three events are triggered when the user presses and releases a key?
22. Which keyboard event procedure is best for ANSI characters?
23. What are several standard submenu names found in Windows applications?
24. How does using Option Explicit help to catch programming errors?
25. What basic principles should you follow in naming variables?
26. What basic principles should you follow in naming procedures?
27. What are the recommended prefixes for variables of the following types: Integer, Long, String, Currency, Single, Boolean.
28. What are the recommended prefixes for names of the following controls? text box, list box, combo box, label, form, menu, command button.
29. What are the three types of identifier scope?
30. Explain the meaning of each of the following:

    ```
    On Error GoTo <label>
    On Error Resume Next
    Error$
    ```

31. Name several of the most common types of runtime errors found in Visual Basic programs.
32. If you need to have a large number of controls on a form, what is one way that you can make more efficient use of memory?
33. Which type of control uses more memory: a label, or a text box?
34. Name several ways of helping Visual Basic programs use less memory.
35. How does grouping related procedures in the same module make more efficient use of memory?
36. Why are Variant type variables somewhat wasteful of memory?
37. What are the three main categories (mentioned by this chapter) of measuring execution speed?
38. Name several ways of optimizing the speed of a program's code.
39. Why would we want to store frequently-used object properties in ordinary variables?
40. How does the ClipControls property affect the optimization of a program's display?
41. Why would a progammer want to load several forms into memory before displaying them? How would this affect the program's use of memory?
42. How is a program able to perform background operations while waiting for user input?

43. How can a programmer give the illusion that a large program loads into memory quickly?

1.9 Chapter Exercises

1.9.1 Changing Form Colors

This programming exercise is just for fun: Select a program that you have already written; Add a Timer control to one of the program's forms, set the timer's interval property to 200, and place the following statement inside the timer's event handler:

```
BackColor = RGB(Rnd * 256, Rnd * 256, Rnd * 256)
```

This statement assigns a random background color to the current form. You should see the form's background change color five times per second. If this seems to easy, write statements that randomly select different controls on the current form (from the Controls collection) and change their foreground and background colors. And if you want to try something else, modify the timer event handler so that it gradually fades from one color to another.

1.9.2 Freight Forwarding Service (Design)

Design the visual interface for a program that will help a freight forwarding service keep track of small and medium-sized packages. All freight will be domestic, i.e., within the same country. The user should be able to perform the following tasks:

- Enter the following information about a package that will be sent from the current location to some other address: 5-digit package ID, recipient name, street, city, state, postal code, weight (in pounds), shipping cost, type of shipment (5-day, 2-day, overnight), and insured value.
- After all information for a package is entered, add the package ID and recipient name to a list box. Provide a way for the user to save all package information, along with today's date and time, in a file.
- Design a menu for the program; design a splash screen.

1.9.3 Freight Forwarding Service (Implementation)

Using the design from the previous exercise, implement the Freight Forwarding Service program. Save all package data in a text file or random-access file. (If you know how to use Access databases, you can save the package information in a database table.)

Provide the following validation before allowing a package to be saved:

- The package ID must be five digits long.
- The weight (W) must be in the range $0 < W <= 70$.
- No fields may be blank.
- The insured value (I) must be in the range $0 <= I <= 1000$.

1.9.4 Express Travel Agency (Design)

The Express Travel Agency needs to keep track of the vacation plans of its customers who are travelling by air. Design the visual interface for a program that lets a travel agent view and edit each customer's flight itinerary. The following information is required for each leg of the journey: Departure date and time, flight number, departure airport, airline, number of passengers in group, arrival date and time, arrival airport.

Here is a sample of the complete travel information for a customer named Carol Johnson, showing subsequent legs of the same journey from Miami to Los Angeles for four passengers:

```
Johnson, Carol
10/20/1997, 08:30, 456, MIA, AAL, 4, 10/20/1997, 11:45, DFW
10/20/1997, 12:30, 967, DFW, AAL, 4, 13:45, LAX
//
```

Design a splash screen for the program, and design a menu for the main window.

1.9.5 Express Travel Agency (Implementation)

Implement the Express Travel Agency program that was designed in the previous exercise. Add the following features:

- The flight information must be typed into a text file, random-access file, or database, and saved in such a way that it may be read and displayed by a Visual Basic program.
- Your program must read the flight information file, display the information, and allow the user to modify any of the fields. Provide a way for modified records to be saved in a separate file.
- Use the On Error GoTo statement to display a message if the flight information file cannot be found, and use the InputBox function to let the user enter a new file name. (The InputBox function is explained in Appendix A.)
- *Extra:* If you are using a random-access file or database, save any modified records in their original input file (i.e., update the records).

1.9.6 Multiple-Choice Test (Design)

Design the visual interface for a simple program that administers a multiple-choice test. The test should display a sequence of questions, provide up to five answer choices, and let the user select an answer. When the user clicks a button to go to the next question, the question number and answer choice will be recorded in a file.

At the beginning of the test, let the student select his/her student ID number from a list box. This ID number will be saved in the output file, along with the answer given to each question.

Design the format of the input file, making sure that each question is numbered, contains a question stem (1 to 20 lines of text), and up to five answer choices. Each answer choice may be between 1 and 5 lines long.

1.9.7 Multiple-Choice Test (Implementation)

Implement the multiple-choice test program that was designed in the previous exercise. Be sure that all test questions will fit in the test window, and use scroll bars if necessary. Do not let the student skip a question without giving an answer.

Also, provide a separate program for the instructor who will display the test results. This program must open the test results file, and display each student ID and corresponding list of answers. Provide a way for the instructor to search for a student ID.

2 Building an Invoice Application

Chapter Contents

Mozart Music Sales - 1
    Objectives
    Program Specifications
    Program Design
    Program Implementation
Mozart Music Sales - 2
    Program Specifications
    Program Design
    Program Implementation
Mozart Music Sales - 3
    Program Specifications
    Program Design
    Program Implementation
Common Dialog Control
    ShowOpen, ShowSave Methods
    Example: Selecting and Opening a File
    ShowColor Method
    ShowFont Method
Saving and Retrieving Settings
    Viewing the System Registry
    Visual Basic Procedures
    SaveSetting Procedure
    GetSetting Function
    Example Program: Save/Retrieve Data Path
    GetAllSettings Function
Review Questions
Chapter Exercises

2.1 Mozart Music Sales - 1

This chapter builds a Visual Basic application from the ground up, taking it through several revisions. The design concepts from the previous chapter will be applied here, as the specifications are translated into a visual and functional design for a sales invoice program called *Mozart Music Sales*. The approach introduced here will serve as a model for other applications introduced later in the book.

2.1.1 Objectives

In this project, we hope to accomplish a number of important objectives. Many of the skills may be a review for you, but we want to establish a common base of program design, coding style, and error-handling techiques that will be used throughout the book. The objectives are as follows:

- Translating program specifications into a design.
- Implementing a program design.
- Retrieving and displaying the current date.
- Selecting items from a combo box.
- Using option buttons, grouping within frame controls.
- Creating and indexing into an array of strings.
- Writing a general calculations procedure.
- Displaying a message box with a Yes/No choice.
- Reading from a text file and filling a combo box.
- Using the On Error GoTo statement.

2.1.2 Program Specifications

The Mozart Music Store needs a simple invoice program that can be filled in by a store clerk (the *user*) when a compact disc or cassette tape is purchased. In our store, we use a 5-digit SKU number to uniquely identify all items. This number may also be read by a bar-code reader.

Upon starting, the program immediately displays the current date so that it may be verified by the store clerk. When the user selects a SKU number from an existing list of numbers, the program displays the album title that matches the number. The clerk looks at the item for a label indicating one of three price codes (A, B, or C) and enters the same code into the computer by clicking with the mouse. The clerk also selects the recording format (CD or tape). The program immediately calculates the sale amount, tax, and total price. The user can also click on a check box if the customer is entitled to a 10% discount.

When the user decides to quit the program, the program should confirm before terminating.

2.1.3 Program Design

This program should have a simple, straightforward user interface, with a minimum of clutter on its main window. We want to focus the user's attention on a few vital pieces of information. We display the name of the store on the Form's title bar, and the date is displayed in a label. Combo boxes can be used for the list of SKU numbers and salesperson names. Each group of option buttons should be surrounded by a frame, so the two groups can operate independently. The program will automatically recalculate and display the numeric amounts whenever the user changes the price code, format, or discount.

Figure 1 contains a sample of the main form, after the user has selected the SKU number, salesperson, price code, format, and discount. We show the names of controls which will be referenced by program code. The remaining controls can use default names.

Figure 1. Mozart Music Main Form.

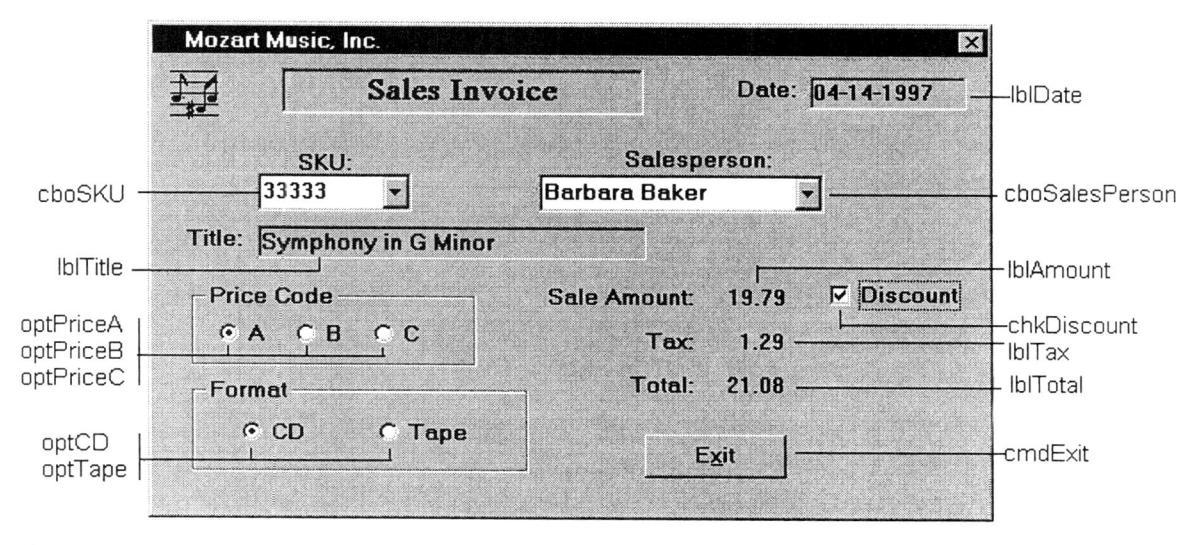

If the user clicks on Exit, we display a message box that confirms before quitting (Figure 2).

Figure 2. Exit Program Dialog.

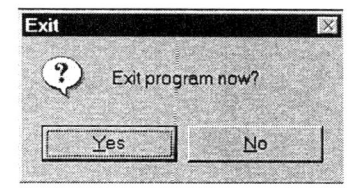

Input Files. From input text files, we fill one combo box with a list of SKU numbers, another combo box containing names of salespeople, and an array of strings containing the names of titles. The file called "sperson.txt", contains the names of salespeople that we intend to load into a combo box. Here are sample names:

```
Adrian Adams
Barbara Baker
Charles Colson
Daniel Del Terzo
Erin Easterbrook
Fay Franklin
George Gomez
Henry Heller
```

The second file, called "titles.txt", contains a list of SKU numbers and album titles:

```
10000,"Marriage of Figaro"
```

```
20000,"Serenade"
22222,"Cosi Fan Tutti"
30000,"Requiem"
33333,"Symphony in G Minor"
40000,"Piano Concerto in C Major"
44444,"Sinfonia Concertante"
50000,"Mozart's Greatest Hits"
```

2.1.4 Program Implementation

The main form, called **frmMain**, should have the following properties set at design time:

```
BorderStyle    =   3   'Fixed Dialog
Caption        =   "Mozart Music, Inc."
```

The following controls have specific properties that should be set at design time:

```
cboSalesPerson.Sorted = True
cmdExit.Caption = "E&xit"
lblAmount.Alignment = 1        'Right Justify
lblTax.Alignment = 1           'Right Justify
lblNetTotal.Alignment = 1      'Right Justify
```

The following declarations are placed at the module level. Always use *Option Explicit*, to force variables to be declared. Otherwise, trivial misspellings of variables result in annoying, hard to catch logic errors:

```
Option Explicit
Const DiscountRate As Single = 0.1       ' standard discount rate
Const TaxRate As Single = 0.065          ' standard sales tax rate
Const MaxTitles As Integer = 100         ' max number of album titles
Const TitleFilename As String = "titles.txt"
Const SalesPersonFilename As String = "sperson.txt"
Dim title(MaxTitles) As String ' array of album titles
```

> *Programming Tip:* To simplify program maintenance, it's a good idea to give names to constants that will be used throughout a program. If you ever need to change the discount rate, for example, it can be changed here. To change the names of the files holding the album titles or the salesperson names, just change the constant definition.

Calculations. In all calculation procedures such as this, there is a standard sequence of steps:

1. Declare any local variables needed by the procedure.
2. Use If statements to query the values of option buttons and check boxes.
3. Copy any numeric data from text boxes into the procedure's local variables.
4. Perform validity checks on all data that will be used in calculations.

5. Perform the calculations.

6. Copy the calculated values into appropriate labels on the form.

Step 2 is unnecessary if there are no option buttons or check boxes. Step 3 may also be omitted in programs such as the current one, where the user has not entered any values into text boxes. But you should be careful to avoid performing calculations directly with text box values. Instead, convert them to numeric values, using the Val function. Step 4 is particularly important in programs that allow for a variety of user input.

The calculations are placed in a general procedure, so that it can be called from each of the click events for the option buttons and check box:

```
Private Sub CalcPrice()
  Dim itemPrice As Single, tax As Single, netAmount As Single
  itemPrice = 0
  If optCD.Value And optPriceA.Value Then itemPrice = 21.99
  If optCD.Value And optPriceB.Value Then itemPrice = 15.99
  If optCD.Value And optPriceC.Value Then itemPrice = 6.99
  If optTape.Value And optPriceA.Value Then itemPrice = 10.99
  If optTape.Value And optPriceB.Value Then itemPrice = 8.99
  If optTape.Value And optPriceC.Value Then itemPrice = 5.99

  If itemPrice <> 0 Then
    If chkDiscount.Value = vbChecked Then
      itemPrice = itemPrice - (itemPrice * DiscountRate)
    End If
    tax = itemPrice * TaxRate
    netAmount = itemPrice + tax
    lblAmount.Caption = Format$(itemPrice, "fixed")
    lblTax.Caption = Format$(tax, "fixed")
    lblNetTotal.Caption = Format$(netAmount, "fixed")
  End If
End Sub
```

We've used actual numbers for the prices here, which makes the program somewhat inflexible. With a little more work, we could read the prices from a file. Also, notice that we bypass the calculations if itemPrice equals zero. This would happen if the user had not yet clicked on the Price code and Format option buttons.

A call to the **CalcPrice** procedure must be placed in the click event of each option button and check box that might affect the price. In optCD_Click, for example, we call CalcPrice:

```
Private Sub optCD_Click()
  CalcPrice
End Sub
```

> *Programming Tip:* When using an option button in an expression, remember that the Value property is either True or False. The following two expressions are equivalent:
>
> ```
> If optCD.Value = True And optPriceA.Value = True Then ...
> If optCD.Value And optPriceA.Value Then ...
> ```
>
> The Value property of a check box, on the other hand, is either vbUnchecked (0), vbChecked (1), or vbGrayed (2). Don't make the mistake of testing for values of True or False:
>
> ```
> If chkDiscount.Value = True Then ...        'Incorrect
> If chkDiscount.Value = 1 Then ...           'Adequate
> If chkDiscount.Value = vbChecked Then ...   'Preferred
> ```

Album Titles. When the user clicks on a SKU number in the cboSKU combo box, we use the ListIndex property to locate the album title in the title array:

```
Private Sub cboSKU_Click()
   lblTitle.Caption = title(cboSKU.ListIndex)
End Sub
```

Reading Information from Text Files. Text files containing the salesperson names and the album titles should be stored in the same directory as the project file. In **Form_Load,** we tell the program to change the current drive and directory to the same location as the project file. Two procedures are used to load the combo boxes:

```
Private Sub Form_Load()
   ChDrive App.Path              'path of Application object
   ChDir App.Path
   lblDate.Caption = Date$       'get today's date
   LoadSalesStaff
   LoadTitles
   optPriceA.Value = True
   optCD.Value = True
End Sub
```

Notice that the optPriceA and optCD option buttons are set as defaults. This is the easy way to make sure the user doesn't forget to enter this information.

The **LoadTitles** procedure loads the album titles from a text file into an array, and it loads all SKU numbers into a combo box. The **On Error GoTo** statement jumps to the label **LoadTitles1** if the input file cannot be opened or read. The Error$ function returns the error message that was generated by Visual Basic:

```
Private Sub LoadTitles()
   Dim j As Integer, sku As String, fileNum As Integer
   On Error GoTo LoadTitles1
   fileNum = FreeFile             'get next available file number
   Open TitleFilename For Input As fileNum
   Do While Not EOF(fileNum)
     Input #fileNum, sku, title(j)
     cboSKU.AddItem sku
```

```
      j = j + 1
    Loop
    Close fileNum
    Exit Sub
LoadTitles1:
    MsgBox Error$ + ": " + TitleFilename, _
        vbInformation, "LoadTitles"
    Exit Sub
End Sub
```

The **LoadSalesStaff** procedure loads the cboSalesPerson combo box with names of the store's sales staff:

```
Public Sub LoadSalesStaff()
    Dim aName As String, fileNum As Integer
    On Error GoTo LoadSalesStaff1
    fileNum = FreeFile
    Open SalesPersonFilename For Input As fileNum
    Do While Not EOF(fileNum)
        Input #fileNum, aName
        cboSalesPerson.AddItem aName
    Loop
    Close fileNum
    Exit Sub

LoadSalesStaff1:
    MsgBox Error$ + ": " + SalesPersonFilename, _
        vbInformation, "LoadSalesStaff"
End Sub
```

Confirming Before Exiting. The call to MsgBox asks the user to confirm before exiting the program. This is considered good style because the user might have clicked on the Exit button by mistake:

```
Private Sub cmdExit_Click()
    Dim choice As Integer
    choice = MsgBox("Exit program now?", vbYesNo _
        + vbQuestion, "Exit")
    If choice = vbYes Then Unload Me
End Sub
```

2.2 Mozart Music Sales - 2

Let's improve the Mozart Music Invoice program and correct some of the first version's limitations. For example, we would like to add a splash screen and a menu system. This new program can accumulate several products on the same invoice and save an invoice in a file. Before you begin, create a new directory called **Mozart2** and copy the Mozart1 files into this new directory. This is very important because you may want to review the first version of the program at a later time. The same approach should be used when you are working on class projects—save complete copies of your project at each stage in its development, just in case you want to undo some of the changes you've made.

2.2.1 Program Specifications

- Primarily, we're interested in being able to list multiple items on the same invoice. For each of these items, we want to display the price. The program should also display a running invoice total along with the sales tax and net amount.
- The program should save the contents of an invoice in a text file, and gradually accumulate all invoice records in the same file.
- The user must be able to clear all fields on the form and start a new invoice.
- The main form will have a menu, which will allow us to ease future expansion to the program without cluttering up the form with buttons.

2.2.2 Program Design

The frmSplash form (Figure 3) appears first, before the main form. There is a Timer control on the window, allowing it to automatically disappear after two seconds have passed. The icon, shown in an image control is one of the icons that is supplied with Visual Basic, having the filename misc31.ico.

Figure 3. The frmSplash Form.

A number of changes will be made to the main window, shown in Figure 4. A list box called lstInvoice will be added to the program, that displays the album title, SKU number, and item price. The salesperson name is selected from a combo box. The user selects a SKU number as in the previous program, and the item's title appears. The user selects a price code and format. When the user clicks on the **Add** button, the current item is added to lstInvoice. The total sales for the invoice is displayed on the right side of the form.

Figure 4. Mozart Music - 2, Main Window.

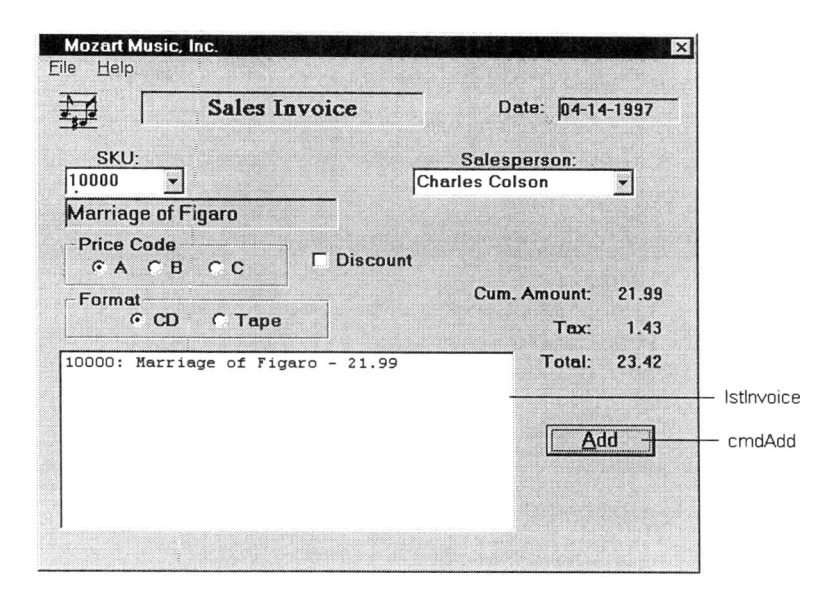

In Figure 5 two items have been added to the invoice, totaling $37.98 before taxes.

Figure 5. Mozart Music - 2, Adding Items.

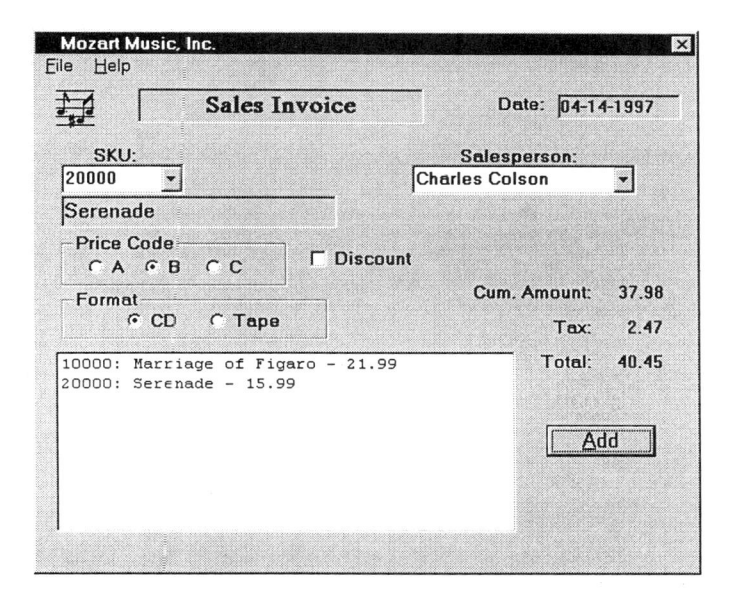

Creating a Menu. In order to reduce the cluttering of command buttons on the form, we will create a menu for this program and transfer most of the button commands to the menu. Table 1 shows the menu's layout and selections. The Name property of each menu item appears on the right side.

Table 1. Menu Design for Mozart Music Sales.

Menu Caption	Shortcut	Item Name
File		mnuFile
New invoice	Ctrl+N	mnuFileNew
Save	Ctrl+S	mnuFileSave
Exit	Ctrl+X	mnuFileExit
Help		mnuHelp
About Mozart Sales	F1	mnuHelpAbout

Notice that shortcut keys such as *Ctrl+N* and *Ctrl+S* are shown for each menu choice. The user can also activate the File menu by pressing *Alt-F*, and the New invoice item by pressing *N*. Although the Help/About command generally does not display the splash screen, we will allow frmSplash to be displayed here.

Saving the Invoice. When the user has entered all the required data for the current invoice, the invoice is saved to a file by clicking on the File/Save menu command. But if the salesperson was not selected, the following reminder appears (Figure 6).

Figure 6. Error Message - Salesperson Name Missing.

2.2.3 Program Implementation

The frmSplash form. The following is a complete listing of frmSplash. Notice that we use the properties of the built-in App object to fill in the company name, program name, as well as the program's major and minor version numbers:

```
Option Explicit

Private Sub Form_Load()
  lblCompanyName.Caption = App.CompanyName
  lblProgramName.Caption = App.ProductName
  lblVersion.Caption = "Version " & App.Major & "." & App.Minor
  lblRevisionDate.Caption = "Revision date: 07-01-1997"
End Sub

Private Sub Timer1_Timer()
  Unload Me
End Sub

Private Sub cmdOk_Click()
  Unload Me
End Sub
```

The frmMain form. The following is a complete listing of frmMain:

```
Option Explicit
Const DiscountRate As Single = 0.1    ' standard 10% discount
Const TaxRate As Single = 0.065       ' sales tax rate
Const MaxTitles As Integer = 100      ' max number of album titles
Const TitleFilename As String = "titles.txt"
Const SalesPersonFilename As String = "sperson.txt"
Const InvoiceFilename As String = "invoices.txt"
Dim title(MaxTitles) As String        ' array of album titles
Dim sku(MaxTitles) As String          ' array of SKU numbers
Dim totalAmount As Single
```

In CalcPrice, after itemPrice is calculated, it must be added to the total amount of the invoice. The total amount is used when calculating the tax and net amount. Notice that CalcPrice is now a function, because itemPrice must be returned to the caller:

```
Private Function CalcPrice() As Single
   Dim itemPrice As Single, tax As Single, netAmount As Single
   If optCD.Value And optPriceA.Value Then itemPrice = 21.99
   If optCD.Value And optPriceB.Value Then itemPrice = 15.99
   If optCD.Value And optPriceC.Value Then itemPrice = 6.99
   If optTape.Value And optPriceA.Value Then itemPrice = 10.99
   If optTape.Value And optPriceB.Value Then itemPrice = 8.99
   If optTape.Value And optPriceC.Value Then itemPrice = 5.99

   If chkDiscount.Value = vbChecked Then itemPrice = itemPrice - _
               (itemPrice * DiscountRate)

   totalAmount = totalAmount + itemPrice
   lblAmount.Caption = Format$(totalAmount, "fixed")
   tax = totalAmount * TaxRate
   netAmount = totalAmount + tax

   lblTax.Caption = Format$(tax, "fixed")
   lblNetTotal.Caption = Format$(netAmount, "fixed")
   CalcPrice = itemPrice
End Function

Private Sub cboSKU_Click()
   lblTitle.Caption = title(cboSKU.ListIndex)
End Sub
```

Adding an Item to the Invoice. The previous version of this program called the CalcPrice procedure from each of the option buttons' Click events. We no longer need to do this. The same is true for the Discount check box. Instead, the user clicks on the "Add" button to add the item to the invoice, and the following code executes:

```
Private Sub cmdAdd_Click()
'Calculate the price of the current item and
'add it to the invoice listbox.
```

```
      Dim n As Integer, itemPrice As Single
      n = cboSKU.ListIndex
      If n = -1 Then Exit Sub
      itemPrice = CalcPrice
      lstInvoice.AddItem cboSKU.Text + ": " + title(n) _
         + " - " + Format$(itemPrice, "fixed")
   End Sub
```

When the user clicks on the Exit button, the program confirms with a message box before unloading the main window:

```
   Private Sub mnuFileExit_Click()
      Dim choice As Integer
      choice = MsgBox("Exit program now?", vbYesNo _
            + vbQuestion, "Exit")
      If choice = vbYes Then Unload Me
   End Sub
```

When the user selects the **File/New invoice** menu command, all controls are reset to the way the form looked when it was loaded. Notice that we set the Text property of the combo boxes—this is only possible if the Style property of the boxes is not equal to "Dropdown List":

```
   Private Sub mnuFileNew_Click()
   'Clear all choices on the form. Note: Modifying the
   'Text property of a combo box is not possible if its
   'style is "Dropdown List".

      cboSalesPerson.Text = ""
      cboSKU.Text = ""
      lstInvoice.Clear
      lblTitle.Caption = ""
      lblAmount.Caption = "0.00"
      lblNetTotal.Caption = "0.00"
      lblTax.Caption = "0.00"
      optPriceA.Value = False
      optPriceB.Value = False
      optPriceC.Value = False
      optTape.Value = False
      optCD.Value = False
      chkDiscount.Value = vbUnchecked
      totalAmount = 0
   End Sub
```

The **File/Save** menu command saves the current invoice to a file after making sure that a salesperson's name has been selected. In error checking statements such as these, it is useful to use the SetFocus method to move to the field causing the error so the user can immediately correct the problem. The current invoice is appended to the existing invoice file:

```
   Private Sub mnuFileSave_Click()
   'Save the invoice in a text file, after making sure
   'that the salesperson name is not blank.
```

Chap 2: Building an Invoice Application   45

```
    If Len(Trim$(cboSalesPerson.Text)) = 0 Then
      MsgBox "A salesperson name is required.", _
             vbInformation, "Saving Invoice"
      cboSalesPerson.SetFocus
      Exit Sub
    End If

    Dim j As Integer, fileNum As Integer
    fileNum = FreeFile
    Open InvoiceFilename For Append As fileNum
    Write #fileNum, Date$, cboSalesPerson.Text
    For j = 0 To lstInvoice.ListCount - 1
      Write #fileNum, lstInvoice.List(j)
    Next j
    Write #fileNum, Val(lblAmount), Val(lblTax), _
             Val(lblNetTotal)
    Write #fileNum, "---------------------------"
    Close #fileNum
    MsgBox "Saved this invoice in file [" + _
      InvoiceFilename + "].", vbInformation, ""
End Sub
```

The only changes to **Form_Load** are that we now show a splash screen and initialize totalAmount:

```
Private Sub Form_Load()
    'Set the current drive letter and path to that
    'of this program. Then load both combo boxes.

    frmSplash.Show vbModal
    ChDrive App.Path
    ChDir App.Path
    lblDate = Date$
    LoadSalesStaff
    LoadTitles
    optPriceA.Value = True
    optCD.Value = True
    totalAmount = 0
End Sub
```

2.3 Mozart Music Sales - 3

In Version 3 of the Mozart Music Sales program we generate a unique number for each invoice and we allow items to be removed from an invoice. These changes appear simple, yet require some planning and careful debugging. As is often true, a small change to the program specifications can turn out to be both challenging and interesting for the programmer. Also, don't forget to create a new directory called **Mozart3** and copy all project files from Mozart2 into Mozart3.

2.3.1 Program Specifications

- The program will allow the user to remove an item from the invoice by selecting it from the invoice list box and clicking on the Remove button.
- The program will sequentially number each invoice by generating an invoice number when a new invoice is created. The invoice number will appear on the form.
- The user will be able to type in the name of a salesperson not currently in the combo box, and by clicking on a button, will be able to add the name to the permanent list of salespeople.

2.3.2 Program Design

The main window now displays the current invoice number in the upper left corner. This number is generated automatically, each time the program runs. It does this by reading the previous invoice number from a file, and adding 1 to the number. Figure 7 shows the main window as it appears after adding a few items to the invoice.

Figure 7. Mozart Music - 3, Main Window.

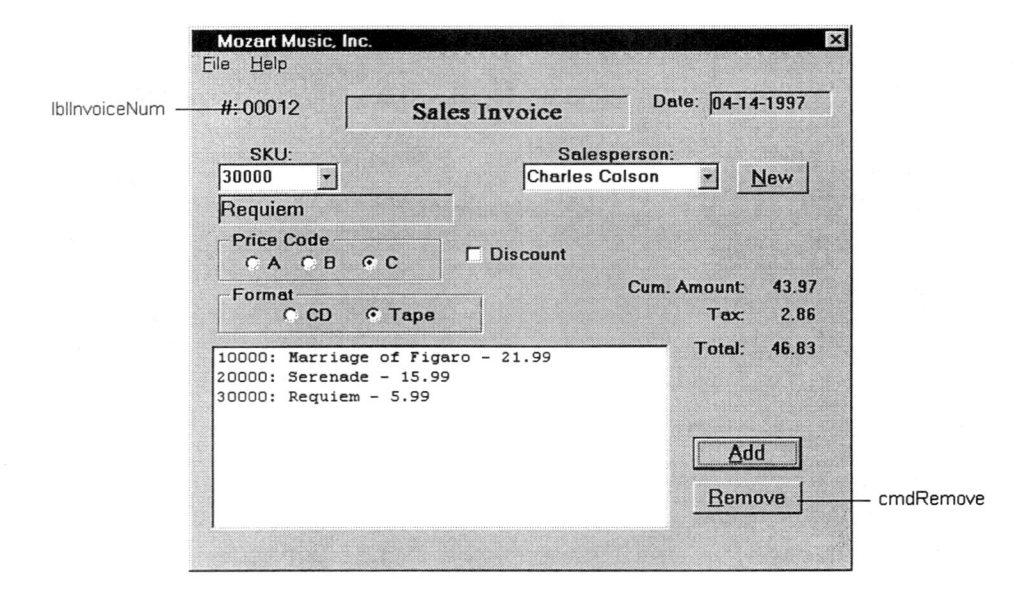

This version of the program allows the user to remove an item from the invoice. When this happens, the total sale, tax, and net amount are recalculated. The user can also add the name of a new salesperson by typing it into the combo box and pressing the New button. Because the Sorted property of the combo box is set to True, the new name will be added in alphabetical order. When exiting the program, the user will get a different message if the invoice has not yet been saved (Figure 8).

Figure 8. Exit Program Confirmation.

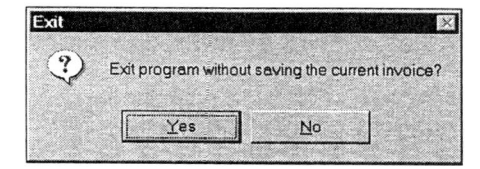

2.3.3 Program Implementation

The itemPrices collection holds the prices of items that have been added to the invoice. We now allow the user to remove items from the invoice; we must recalculate the total invoice amount whenever an item is added or removed.

> ***Programming Tip***: In general, try to declare as few variables the public or module level as possible. Instead, declare local variables inside procedures. Fixing a program bug involving a local variable only requires looking at a single procedure. On the other hand, a bug involving a global or module-level variable is harder to track down because its value may have been modified by many different procedures.

A complete listing of the program code in frmMain is shown here:

```
Option Explicit
Const DiscountRate As Single = 0.1       ' standard discount rate
Const TaxRate As Single = 0.065          ' standard sales tax rate
Const MaxTitles As Integer = 100         ' max number of album titles
Const InvoiceFilename As String = "invoices.txt"
Const InvNumFilename As String = "lastinv.txt"
Const TitleFilename As String = "titles.txt"
Const SalesPersonFilename As String = "sperson.txt"
Dim title(MaxTitles) As String           ' array of album titles
Dim invoiceNum As Integer                ' invoice ID number
Dim itemPrices As Collection             ' prices of invoice items
Dim invoiceSaved As Boolean              ' True if invoice has been saved

Private Function CalcPrice() As Single
' Calculate price of an item, based on the
' media format and price code.
  Dim itemPrice As Single
  If optCD.Value And optPriceA.Value Then itemPrice = 21.99
  If optCD.Value And optPriceB.Value Then itemPrice = 15.99
  If optCD.Value And optPriceC.Value Then itemPrice = 6.99
  If optTape.Value And optPriceA.Value Then itemPrice = 10.99
  If optTape.Value And optPriceB.Value Then itemPrice = 8.99
  If optTape.Value And optPriceC.Value Then itemPrice = 5.99

  If chkDiscount.Value = vbChecked Then
     itemPrice = itemPrice - (itemPrice * DiscountRate)
  End If
```

```
      CalcPrice = itemPrice      'function return value
   End Function
```

This array, called itemPrices, is used by the CalcTotals procedure to calculate the total invoice amount:

```
Public Sub CalcTotals()
'Calculate and display invoice totals.
   Dim j As Integer, tax As Single
   Dim netAmount As Single, totalAmount As Single
   totalAmount = 0
   For j = 1 To itemPrices.Count
     totalAmount = totalAmount + Val(itemPrices(j))
   Next j
   lblAmount.Caption = Format$(totalAmount, "fixed")
   tax = totalAmount * TaxRate
   netAmount = totalAmount + tax
   lblTax.Caption = Format$(tax, "fixed")
   lblNetTotal.Caption = Format$(netAmount, "fixed")
End Sub
```

Invoice Numbering. A new invoice number is generated when the user selects New from the File menu. Unfortunately, if the invoice has not been saved, the old invoice number could disappear. To prevent this from happening, a variable called invoiceSaved indicates when the current invoice has been saved. If this variable is True, a new number will be generated; otherwise, the same number will be retained. The user is not permitted to save the same invoice twice—otherwise the program would create a file containing revised versions of the same invoice. **GetNewInvoiceNumber** opens a file containing the most recently used invoice number, and calls **IncrementInvoiceNumber** to increment and display the number:

```
Public Sub GetNewInvoiceNumber()
   Dim fileNum As Integer
   fileNum = FreeFile
   On Error GoTo GetNewInvoice1
   Open InvNumFilename For Input As fileNum
   Input #fileNum, invoiceNum
   Close fileNum
   IncrementInvoiceNumber
   Exit Sub
GetNewInvoice1:
   MsgBox Error$ + ": " + InvNumFilename, _
      vbInformation, "GetNewInvoiceNumber"
   Exit Sub
End Sub

Public Sub IncrementInvoiceNumber()
   invoiceNum = invoiceNum + 1
   lblInvoiceNum = Format(invoiceNum, "00000")
End Sub

Private Sub LoadTitles()
```

Chap 2: Building an Invoice Application

```vb
'Read product titles and SKU numbers from a text file.
  Dim j As Integer, sku As String
  Dim fileNum As Integer
  fileNum = FreeFile
  On Error GoTo LoadTitles1
  Open TitleFilename For Input As fileNum
  Do While Not EOF(fileNum)
    Input #fileNum, sku, title(j)
    cboSKU.AddItem sku
    j = j + 1
  Loop
  Close fileNum
  Exit Sub

LoadTitles1:
  MsgBox Error$ + ": " + TitleFilename, _
    vbInformation, "LoadTitles"
  Exit Sub
End Sub

Public Sub LoadSalesStaff()
'Read names of sales staff from a text file.
  Dim aName As String
  Dim fileNum As Integer
  fileNum = FreeFile
  On Error GoTo LoadSalesStaff1
  Open SalesPersonFilename For Input As fileNum
  Do While Not EOF(fileNum)
    Input #fileNum, aName
    cboSalesPerson.AddItem aName
  Loop
  Close fileNum
  Exit Sub
LoadSalesStaff1:
  MsgBox Error$ + ": " + SalesPersonFilename, _
    vbInformation, "LoadSalesStaff"
  Exit Sub
End Sub


Private Sub cboSKU_Click()
  lblTitle = title(cboSKU.ListIndex)
End Sub

Private Sub cmdAdd_Click()
'Calculate price of current item and add it to
'the invoice listbox.
  Dim n As Integer, itemPrice As Single
  n = cboSKU.ListIndex
  If n = -1 Then Exit Sub          'no item was chosen
  itemPrice = CalcPrice
```

```
    itemPrices.Add itemPrice
    lstInvoice.AddItem cboSKU.Text + ": " + title(n) + _
      " - " + Format$(itemPrice, "fixed")
    CalcTotals
End Sub
```

Adding a New Salesperson. A new feature in the program lets the user can type in the name of a new salesperson and add that name to the combo box. A blank name cannot be entered:

```
Private Sub cmdNew_Click()
  If Len(Trim$(cboSalesPerson.Text)) = 0 Then
    MsgBox "The salesperson name cannot be blank.", _
           vbInformation, "New Salesperson"
  Else
    cboSalesPerson.AddItem cboSalesPerson.Text
  End If
End Sub
```

Removing Items. The user now can select an item and delete it from the invoice list box. When an item is removed, its price is subtracted from the total invoice amount and its price is removed from itemPrices:

```
Private Sub cmdRemove_Click()
'Remove the selected item from the invoice listbox
'and recalculate the invoice totals.
  Dim n As Integer
  n = lstInvoice.ListIndex
  If n = -1 Then Exit Sub
  lstInvoice.RemoveItem n
  itemPrices.Remove (n + 1)
  CalcTotals
End Sub
```

The itemPrices.Remove method requires an integer index argument. The collection indexes range from 1 to *n*, where n is the number of items.

Form_Load calls a procedure called GetNewInvoiceNumber, which retrieves the most recent invoice number from a file, increments it, and displays it. The last statement in this procedure creates a new Collection object and assigns its reference to itemPrices:

```
Private Sub Form_Load()
'Set the current drive letter and path to that of
'this program. Then load both combo boxes.
  frmSplash.Show vbModal
  ChDrive App.Path
  ChDir App.Path
  lblDate.Caption = Date$
  GetNewInvoiceNumber
  LoadSalesStaff
  LoadTitles
  optPriceA.Value = True
  optCD.Value = True
```

Chap 2: Building an Invoice Application

```
    Set itemPrices = New Collection
End Sub
```

The program prompts the user before unloading the current form. If the invoice has not yet been saved, the message points this out:

```
Private Sub mnuFileExit_Click()
   Dim choice As Integer, msg As String
   If invoiceSaved Then
      msg = "Exit program now?"
   Else
      msg = "Exit program without saving " + _
            "the current invoice?"
   End If
   choice = MsgBox(msg, vbYesNo + vbQuestion, _
            "Exit")
   If choice = vbYes Then Unload Me
End Sub
```

Creating a New Invoice. The event handler for the File/New menu command has two new statements. The invoice number is incremented if the current invoice has been saved, and the File/Save menu item is enabled:

```
Private Sub mnuFileNew_Click()
'Clear all choices on the form. Note: Modifying
'the Text property of a combo box is not possible
'if its style is "Dropdown List".
   cboSalesPerson.Text = ""
   cboSKU.Text = ""
   lstInvoice.Clear
   lblTitle.Caption = ""
   lblAmount.Caption = "0.00"
   lblNetTotal.Caption = "0.00"
   lblTax.Caption = "0.00"
   optPriceA.Value = False
   optPriceB.Value = False
   optPriceC.Value = False
   optTape.Value = False
   optCD.Value = False
   chkDiscount.Value = vbUnchecked
   If invoiceSaved Then IncrementInvoiceNumber
   mnuFileSave.Enabled = True
End Sub
```

Saving an Invoice. Several lines have been added to the mnuFileSave_Click procedure, that save the current invoice number in a file, set a switch indicating that the invoice has been saved, and disable the File/Save menu choice:

```
Private Sub mnuFileSave_Click()
   If Len(Trim$(cboSalesPerson.Text)) = 0 Then
      MsgBox "A salesperson name is required.", _
            vbInformation, "Saving Invoice"
      cboSalesPerson.SetFocus
```

```
        Exit Sub
    End If
    'Save the invoice in a text file.
    Dim j As Integer
    Dim fileNum As Integer
    fileNum = FreeFile
    Open InvoiceFilename For Append As fileNum
    Write #fileNum, Date$, cboSalesPerson.Text
    For j = 0 To lstInvoice.ListCount - 1
       Write #fileNum, lstInvoice.List(j)
    Next j
    Write #fileNum, Val(lblAmount), Val(lblTax), _
          Val(lblNetTotal)
    Write #fileNum, "--------------------------"
    Close fileNum

    'Save the updated invoice number in a text file.
    fileNum = FreeFile
    Open InvNumFilename For Output As fileNum
    Print #fileNum, Format$(invoiceNum, "00000")
    Close fileNum
    invoiceSaved = True
    mnuFileSave.Enabled = False
    MsgBox "Saved this invoice in file [" + _
       InvoiceFilename + "].", vbInformation, ""
End Sub

Private Sub mnuHelpAbout_Click()
    frmSplash.Show vbModal
End Sub
```

2.4 Common Dialog Control

The common dialog control lets you create standard Windows dialog boxes for opening and saving files, selecting colors and fonts, printing documents, and displaying help files. The common dialog control icon appears on a form only in design mode. At runtime, you determine which type of window will be displayed by calling one of the following methods associated with the control:

- ShowColor: Display a color palette.
- ShowFont: Display a font dialog.
- ShowHelp: Display a help topic.
- ShowOpen: Display a File/Open dialog.
- ShowPrinter: Display a printer dialog.
- ShowSave: Display a File/SaveAs dialog.

2.4.1 ShowOpen, ShowSave Methods

The ShowOpen and ShowSave methods display the same dialog seen in all Windows applications when the user is asked to select a file. Before calling either of these methods, you should set certain properties in the common dialog control. Table 2 contains a list of the

Chap 2: Building an Invoice Application

properties used most often. For complete descriptions of all file dialog properties, see the help topic "Common Dialog Control," click on the *Properties* hyperlink and click on "File Dialog Properties."

Table 2. File Open/Save Dialog Properties.

Property	Description
CancelError	When set to True, a trappable error will occur when the user clicks on the Cancel button (default value = False).
DefaultExt	If the user types a filename with no extension, the default extension will be automatically appended to the filename. This is most useful when calling the ShowSave method.
DialogTitle	The title that appears at the top of the dialog window.
FileName	Before the dialog is shown, this can be a default filename; after the dialog closes, this is the complete path and filename selected by the user.
FileTitle	Just the filename selected by the user, with no path.
Filter	A list of file types and default extensions. This makes it easier for the user to know what types of filenames are being displayed.
FilterIndex	The starting position in the list of file types specified by the filter property, starting with 1, which is the default.
Flags	An integer that specifies options that refine the behavior of the window.
InitDir	The initial disk directory to be used when the dialog first appears.
MaxFileSize	The maximum length of a filename that may be entered by the user (the default is 256 characters).

2.4.2 Example: Selecting and Opening a File

In the next example, a File/Open dialog displays a list of Access database files. The name of the sample common dialog control is CommonDialog1. The window appears when ShowOpen is called, and the statements following it are not executed until the window closes:

```
Private Sub cmdOpenFile_Click()
  On Error GoTo OpenFile1
  With CommonDialog1
    .CancelError = True
    .DialogTitle = "Opening Microsoft Access Database"
    .Filter = "Access databases|*.mdb|All files|*.*"
    .FilterIndex = 1
    .Flags = cdlOFNFileMustExist
    .ShowOpen
    Debug.Print "Just the filename: " + .FileTitle
    Debug.Print "Complete path and filename: " + .Filename, , ""
  End With
  Exit Sub
```

```
    OpenFile1:
      'no action: user clicked "Cancel"
    End Sub
```

If the user clicks on "Cancel", a trappable error is generated; the On Error Goto statement tells the program to jump to the OpenFile1 label. Figure 9 shows a sample of the dialog window, showing the file types combo box temporarily pulled down by the user.

Figure 9. Open Database Dialog.

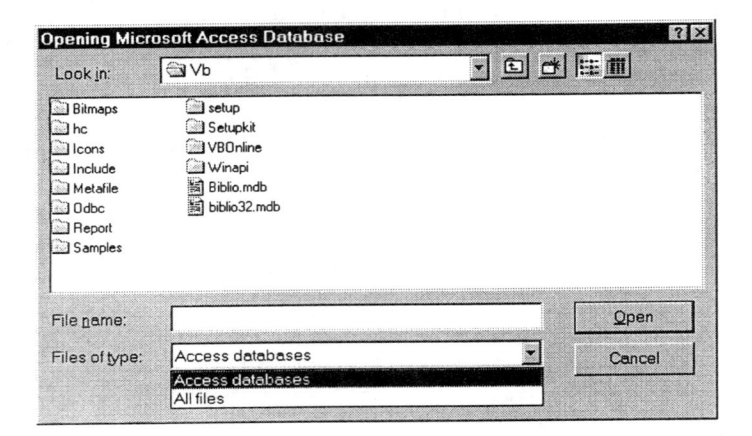

By default, the first filename mask in the Filter property determines the type of files displayed in the window. If the user clicks on "All files", the window will show all files in the directory matching "*.*". This is standard behavior in all Windows applications. The Flags property in this example was set to the predefined constant **cdlOFNFileMustExist**; this causes an error message to be displayed if the user enters a filename that cannot be found (Figure 10).

Figure 10. File Doesn't Exist Error.

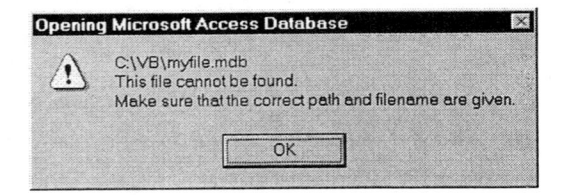

> *Tip:* For a list of predefined constants that may be used in the Flags property, see the help topic "Flags Property (File Dialog)".

2.4.3 ShowColor Method

A common dialog control can make it possible for the user to customize a program's appearance. The ShowColor method implements the common dialog as a color pallete, identical to the one used when we set the ForeColor or BackColor properties of controls in design mode. The following properties are used the most often:

- **CancelError:** When set to True, a trappable error will occur when the user clicks on the Cancel button.
- **Color:** The color chosen by the user, saved as a long integer. Color values are usually displayed as hexadecimal constants.
- **Flags:** An integer that specifies options that refine the behavior of the window.

Setting the DialogTitle property, curiously, has no effect. A useful value to place in the Flags property is the predefined constant **cdlCCRGBInit**, which lets us set the initial color value for the dialog box. The following statements let the user select the background color for the current form:

```
Private Sub cmdBackColor_Click()
  On Error GoTo BackColor1
  With CommonDialog1
    .CancelError = True
    .Flags = cdlCCRGBInit
    .Color = Me.BackColor   'get current color
    .ShowColor
    Me.BackColor = .Color   'use the new color
  End With
  Exit Sub
BackColor1:
  'no action: user clicked "Cancel"
End Sub
```

Figure 11 contains an example of a color dialog (printed here in grayscale).

Figure 11. Windows Color Dialog.

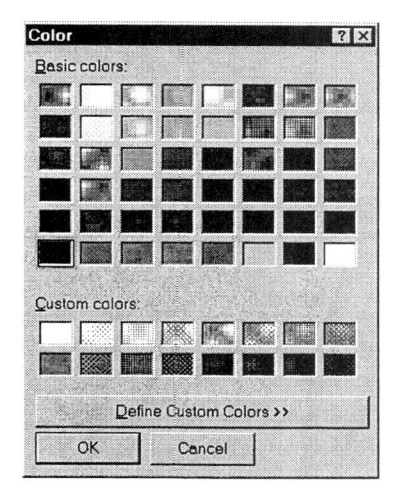

2.4.4 ShowFont Method

The ShowFont method lets the user select a font and its various attributes. The font dialog box can display fonts for the screen, for the printer, or for both. Some of the more commonly used properties of the Font dialog box are listed in Table 3.

Table 3. Font Dialog Properties.

Property	Description
CancelError	When set to True, a trappable error occurs when the user clicks on the Cancel button.
Flags	An integer that specifies options that refine the behavior of the window.
FontBold	Each character appears in bold type.
FontItalic	Each character appears in italic type.
FontName	Sets the name of the font.
FontSize	Sets the size of the font, in points.
FontStrikethru	Each character is overtyped with a horizontal line.
FontUnderline	Each character is underlined.

One of the following constants must be assigned to the Flags property before showing the font dialog: **cdlCFScreenFonts**, **cdlCFPrinterFonts**, or **cdlCFBoth**. The first tells the control to list only the screen fonts; the second lists only printer fonts; and the third lists both screen and printer fonts. The next example displays all available screen fonts and lets the user select one for the text control named **Text1**. The font name and point size are displayed in Text1:

```
Private Sub cmdFonts_Click()
  On Error GoTo ShowFonts1
  With CommonDialog1
    .CancelError = True
    .Flags = cdlCFScreenFonts
    .ShowFont
    Text1.FontName = .FontName
    Text1.Text = .FontName + " " & .FontSize _
        & " point."
    Text1.FontSize = .FontSize
    Text1.FontBold = .FontBold
    Text1.FontItalic = .FontItalic
  End With
  Exit Sub
ShowFonts1:   'No action is taken.
End Sub
```

Figure 12 contains a sample of the dialog window that would be displayed by the preceding code:

Figure 12. Font Dialog Example.

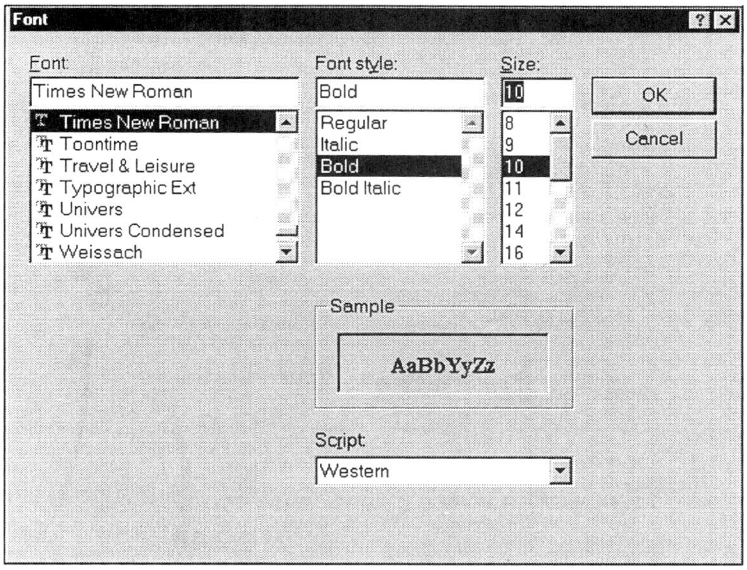

2.5 Saving and Retrieving Settings

Microsoft Windows has been evolving into a object-oriented operating system, where rather than focusing on the various installed programs, the emphasis is on objects created by the user. When you create a document, for example, it may contain graphs, worksheets, sound and video, bitmaps, and other objects created by various applications. Windows needs to have a way of keeping track of which installed programs are associated with each of these objects. When the user selects an object for editing, the appropriate application can be activated.

Most application programs need to save certain configuration information on an ongoing basis. The information might include size, color, and font settings for the program's windows, locations of data used by the program, and other user configuration options.

Application INI Files. Windows 3.x provides a standard way for saving and retrieving configuration information: A file is created called *appname*.**ini**, where *appname* is the program's name. This file is usually saved in the same directory as Windows itself, so it may easily be found by the program that needs it. Unfortunately, an INI file can easily be deleted, or modified by a user with a text editor such as NotePad. Also, over time old INI files tend to be left around when programs are updated or removed from the system.

2.5.1 Viewing the System Registry

The *system registry* is a hierarchical database that Windows uses to keep track of the associations between objects and applications, as well as configuration information for both the operating system and application programs. Under Windows 3.1, most system information was kept in the win.ini, progman.ini, and system.ini files. This has changed under Windows 95 and Windows NT, which both store a great deal of system setup information in the system registry. The system registry also contains classes, properties, and methods that have been *exposed* (made public) by Windows applications. This is part of a process called OLE automation.

You can view the system registry by running the **RegEdit** program that is supplied with Windows. From the **Start** menu in Windows 95, click on **Run** and enter the name **RegEdit**. The program's opening window appears in Figure 13.

Figure 13. Registry Editor Example.

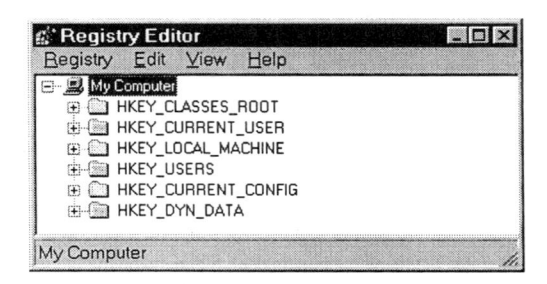

This outline may be expanded by double-clicking first on HKEY_CURRENT_USER, then on Software. Figure 14 shows the topics that appear.

Figure 14. Registry: Software Entry.

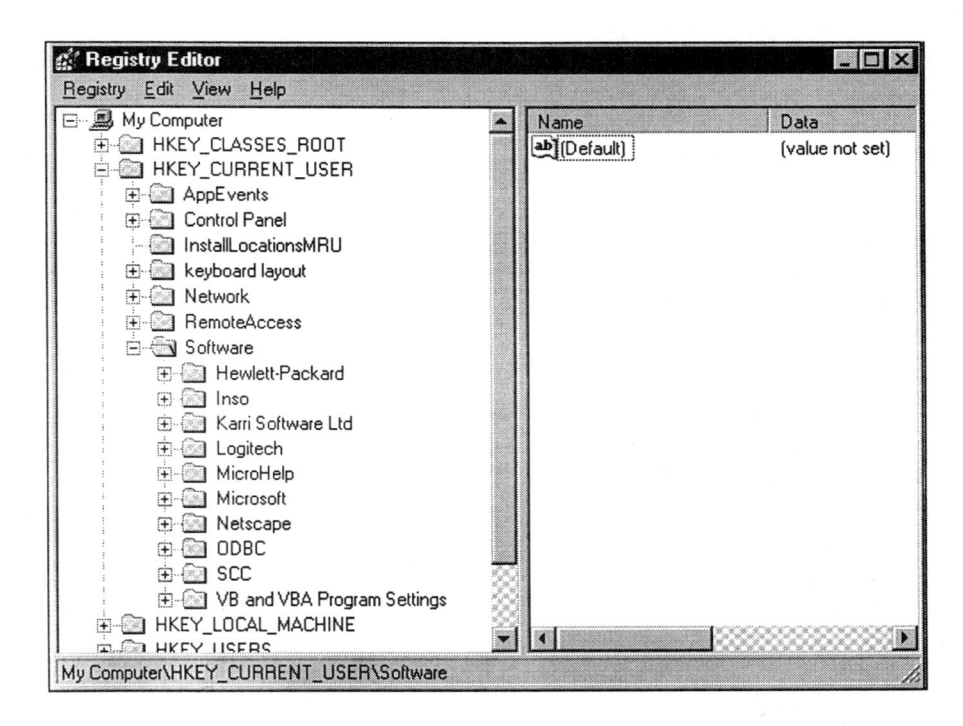

Chap 2: Building an Invoice Application   59

If you expand the *Microsoft* topic, note that Windows saves quite a bit of information about you—the user who installed Microsoft products (Figure 15).

Figure 15. Registry: Software/Microsoft/User Information.

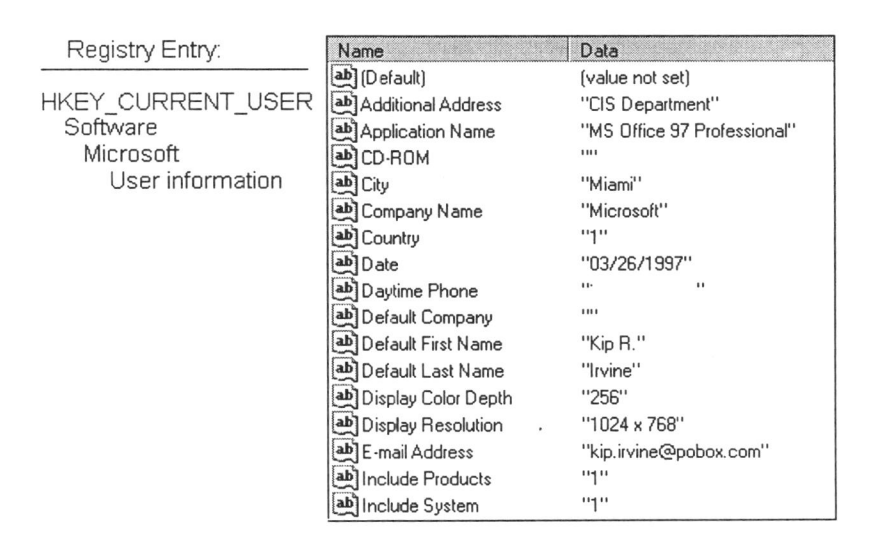

Registry Entry:
HKEY_CURRENT_USER
  Software
    Microsoft
      User information

Name	Data
(Default)	(value not set)
Additional Address	"CIS Department"
Application Name	"MS Office 97 Professional"
CD-ROM	""
City	"Miami"
Company Name	"Microsoft"
Country	"1"
Date	"03/26/1997"
Daytime Phone	" "
Default Company	""
Default First Name	"Kip R."
Default Last Name	"Irvine"
Display Color Depth	"256"
Display Resolution	"1024 x 768"
E-mail Address	"kip.irvine@pobox.com"
Include Products	"1"
Include System	"1"

Similarly, find the VBA (Visual Basic for Applications) topic and select Microsoft Visual Basic (Figure 16).

Figure 16. Registry: Visual Basic for Applications.

Registry Editor
Registry Edit View Help

- VBA
  - Excel
  - **Microsoft Visual Basic**
  - MSAccess
  - Office
- Windows
- Word
- Netscape
- ODBC

Name	Data
(Default)	(value not set)
BackGroundCompile	0x00000001 (1)
CompileOnDemand	0x00000000 (0)
FullModuleView	0x00000001 (1)
RequireDeclaration	0x00000001 (1)
SyntaxChecking	0x00000000 (0)

My Computer\HKEY_CURRENT_USER\Software\Microsoft\VBA\Microsoft Visual Basic

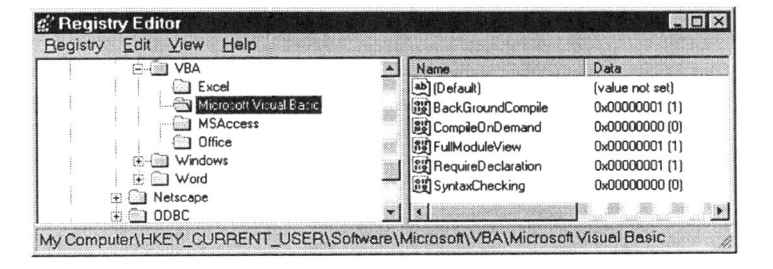

You probably recognize these settings as ones found in the Tools/Options settings in Visual Basic. A value of 1 indicates that the option was checked. Understandably, the system registry should not be directly modified by anyone other than an expert.

The INI files and system registry are not intended to take the place of application databases that would typically hold a much larger amount of data. You would not, for instance, place an employee salary history in the system registry. But, you might place the file path of the employee database in the registry so your program can find it when it starts up.

2.5.2 Visual Basic Procedures

Because Visual Basic programs still run in both 16-bit and 32-bit environments, the procedures that deal with configuration information are able to adapt to both systems. The SaveSetting procedure, for example, saves program information. Under Windows NT or Windows 95, it saves the information in the Windows registry; under Win16, it saves the information in an INI file.

2.5.3 SaveSetting Procedure

The SaveSetting procedure saves a string value associated with a key in a specified section of an application's configuration. The syntax is:

```
SaveSetting appname, section, key, setting
```

Where *appname* is a string containing the name of the program or application; *section* is a string containing the name of the section where the information is located; *key* is the name of the key being saved, and *setting* is the value that will be displayed next to the key. An error occurs if the key setting could not be saved for any reason.

For example, we might want to save the location of data files used by the Mozart Music Sales program before the program exits. The section will be called **Directories**, the Key will be **InvoiceFile**, and the path to the file will be "C:\Mozart\Data\invoices.mdb":

```
SaveSetting "Mozart", "Directories", _
    "InvoiceFile", "C:\Mozart\Data\invoices.mdb"
```

This will create the Directories section if it did not already exist.

2.5.4 GetSetting Function

The GetSetting function returns a string value associated with a key from a program's configuration. The syntax is:

```
GetSetting(appname, section, key [,default]) As String
```

Where *appname* is the program name, *section* is the section name, *key* is the name of the key, and *default* is the value to be returned by the function if a matching key cannot be found or if the value is empty. If *default* is omitted, it is assumed to be an empty string. The return value of GetSetting is a string containing the key's value.

When our program starts up, for example, we could retrieve the location of the invoice database used by the Mozart Music Sales program. The section name is **Directories**, the Key is **InvoiceFile**:

```
Dim InvoiceFile As String
InvoiceFile = GetSetting("Mozart", "Directories", "InvoiceFile")
```

2.5.5 Example Program: Save/Retrieve Data Path

We can write a simple program that demonstrates the GetSetting and SaveSetting procedures. When the program starts, the user enters a path in a text box that identifies the location of the program's data files (Figure 17).

\Settings

Figure 17. Program Settings Window.

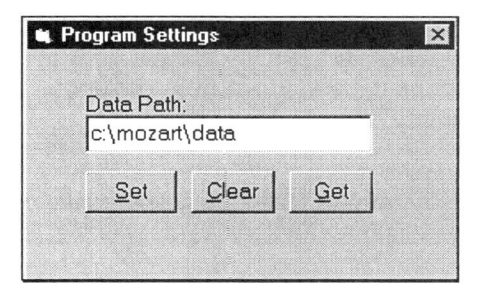

After clicking on the **Set** button, click on the **Clear** button to clear the text box. Click on the **Get** button to retrieve the Data Path setting from the registry. The original data path (c:\mozart\data) should appear in the text box.

Using the **RegEdit** program, we can verify the Mozart—Settings—DataPath entry:

```
HKEY_CURRENT_USER
  Software
    VB and VBA Program Settings
      Mozart
        Settings
          DataPath="c:\mozart\data"
```

Here is the program listing:

```
Private Sub cmdClear_Click()
  txtDataPath.Text = ""
End Sub

Private Sub cmdGet_Click()
'Get the DataPath value.
  txtDataPath.Text = GetSetting("Mozart", "Settings", _
    "DataPath", "(not found)")
End Sub

Private Sub cmdSet_Click()
'Set the DataPath value.
  SaveSetting "Mozart", "Settings", "DataPath", _
    txtDataPath.Text
End Sub
```

2.5.6 GetAllSettings Function

\Showall

The GetAllSettings function returns a list of key settings and their respective values from an application's Windows registry entry. The syntax is:

```
GetAllSettings(appname, section) As Variant
```

Where appname is a string containing the name of the application, section is a string containing the name of the section. The return value is a two-dimensional array of strings containing all the keys and their respective values in the specified section. Or, if either the appname or section does not exist, the function returns an uninitialized Variant. It is a good idea to call the Visual Basic **IsEmpty** function to prevent a runtime error that would be caused by trying to access the function's empty return value.

For example, the following code retrieves all system registry settings for the VisData program, section VISDATA4, and displays them in a list box:

```
Dim MySettings As Variant
Dim j As Integer, st1 As String * 20
MySettings = GetAllSettings("VisData","VISDATA4")
If IsEmpty(MySettings) Then
  MsgBox "No Settings were found.", , ""
Else
  For j = LBound(MySettings, 1) To UBound(MySettings, 1)
    LSet st1 = MySettings(j, 0)
    List1.AddItem st1 + MySettings(j, 1)
  Next j
End If
```

Figure 18 shows a sample of the program's output. Notice that we used a Courier font in the list box to line up the columns.

Figure 18. Settings for VisData.

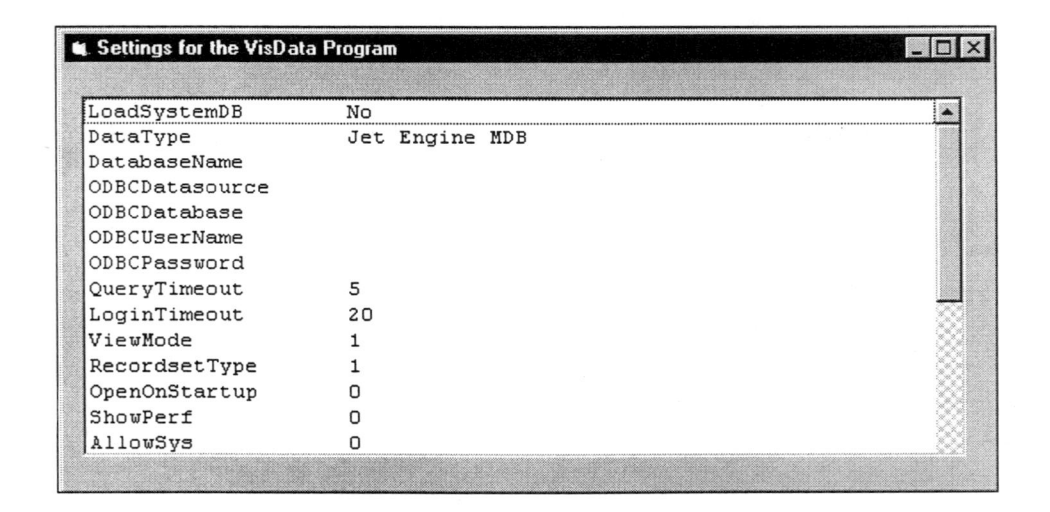

```
Settings for the VisData Program                    _ □ ×
LoadSystemDB         No
DataType             Jet Engine MDB
DatabaseName
ODBCDatasource
ODBCDatabase
ODBCUserName
ODBCPassword
QueryTimeout         5
LoginTimeout         20
ViewMode             1
RecordsetType        1
OpenOnStartup        0
ShowPerf             0
AllowSys             0
```

2.6 Review Questions

The following questions refer to Version 1 of the Mozart Music Sales program:

1. In the Mozart Music Sales program, what determines the price of an album?
2. How many different prices are there?
3. How does the program retrieve the title of an album?
4. How does the program obtain the list of SKU numbers and matching titles?
5. In what way is the program's calculation of an album price very inflexible?
6. Which BorderStyle property prevents the user from re-sizing the main window?
7. What modification would have to be made to this program so that it could be used in different states of the U.S.?
8. Can the chkDiscount.Value property be equal to either True or False?
9. What types of validity checks does the program perform on the input values for the calculation of the album price?
10. Which Visual Basic function (used in this program) causes the numeric values to print with two digits after the decimal point?
11. How many different controls call the CalcPrice procedure?
12. Which property of the cboSKU control is essential in locating the album title?
13. How does the program ensure that the user will not forget to select a price code (A, B, C) and recording format (CD, tape)?
14. What does the FreeFile function do?
15. How is the Error$ function used in this program?
16. Why is it important to use the Exit Sub statement in the LoadSalesStaff procedure?

The following questions refer to Version 2 of the Mozart Music Sales program:

17. How is Version 2 of Mozart Music Sales fundamentally different from Version 1?
18. What arithmetic operation is carried out when a new item is added to the invoice?
19. What output file is created by this program, and what does it contain?
20. What happens if the user does not click the mouse on the splash window?
21. How are *shortcut keys* used in this program?
22. Which input fields cannot be blank when an invoice is saved?
23. Why is it no longer necessary to call CalcPrice from each of the option buttons?
24. In order to modify the Text property of a combo box, what must be the value of its Style property?
25. How do you open a text file so that new records can be added to the file without erasing existing records?
26. What does vbModal mean? What is its opposite?

The following questions refer to Version 3 of the Mozart Music Sales program:

27. How is Version 3 of the Mozart Music Sales program different from Version 2?
28. How does the program deal with new salespeople whose names are not already in the combo box?
29. How does the program "remember" the previous invoice number when it is about to create a new invoice?
30. If the user accidentally enters the wrong information for an item and adds it to the invoice, what remedy does the program offer?
31. How many items can be placed on a single invoice?
32. Suppose the user is currently editing Invoice number 20001. If the user quits without saving the invoice, what will the invoice number be the next time a new invoice is created?
33. Why is it important to have the itemPrices collection when removing an item from the current invoice?
34. When an element is deleted from the middle of an array, what is the algorithm for adjusting the positions of all subsequent members?

The following questions refer to the Common Dialog Control:

35. How is the CancelError property used? Does it signify an error on the programmer's part?
36. Which method is used for opening files?
37. How is the FileTitle property different from the FileName property?
38. How can multiple file types be placed in the Filter property?
39. If the user enters a filename that doesn't exist, how is the FileOpen dialog able to display an error message?
40. Which method is used when displaying a color palette?
41. How can the Font dialog box be made to show both screen and printer fonts?

The following questions refer to saving and retrieving program settings:

42. How are Windows 3.x and Windows 95 different in the way they store program settings?
43. What happens in the SaveSetting procedure if the application name or section name does not exist?
44. Which section of the system registry stores settings of Visual Basic programs?
45. How many key values can be stored in a single section, using SaveSetting?
46. What does GetSetting return if the key name cannot be found in the specified section?
47. What is the structure of the data returned by the GetAllSettings function?

2.7 Chapter Exercises

2.7.1 Mozart Music Prices

Prices for various configurations of CDs and tapes in the Mozart Music program are explicitly coded in the CalcPrice procedure:

```
Private Sub CalcPrice()
    Dim itemPrice As Single, tax As Single, netAmount As Single
    ItemPrice = 0
    If optCD.Value And optPriceA.Value Then itemPrice = 21.99
    If optCD.Value And optPriceB.Value Then itemPrice = 15.99
    If optCD.Value And optPriceC.Value Then itemPrice = 6.99
    If optTape.Value And optPriceA.Value Then itemPrice = 10.99
    If optTape.Value And optPriceB.Value Then itemPrice = 8.99
    If optTape.Value And optPriceC.Value Then itemPrice = 5.99
    (etc...)
```

Revise Version 3 of the Mozart Music program so that it reads the various prices from a text file when the program begins.

2.7.2 Mozart Music Instruments

The Mozart Music store has decided to computerize its sales of musical instruments. Each instrument has both a purchase price and a monthly rental rate (Table 4).

Table 4. Instrument Price Table.

Instrument	Purchase Price	Monthly Rental Rate
Flute	415	40
Alto Saxophone	500	55
Tenor Saxophone	600	75
Bb Clarinet	325	42
Oboe	275	28
Bassoon	654	45
Violin	189	28
Viola	225	38
Cello	575	45
Electric Guitar	425	36

These instrument names and prices should be kept in a file and loaded by the program at runtime.

Add a new form to the program that allows the user to select an instrument from a combo box, select from Purchase and Rental option buttons, and enter the number of rental months. The program should display the cost of the purchase or rental and print an invoice (on the printer or screen) containing the customer name, instrument, address, phone, date, and rental or purchase amount.

2.7.3 Mozart Music Color Settings

In the Mozart Music Sales program, add an Options/Colors menu selection that displays a color common dialog window and allows the user to select the background color of the main window and its controls. As soon as the user selects the new color, the BackColor properties of the form and controls should be updated. Save the colors in the system registry whenever they are changed by the user. Load the color settings from the system registry when the program starts up.

2.7.4 Mozart Music File and Directory Settings

Create program settings for the Mozart Music Sales program that keep track of the following:

- Complete path to the Salesperson file.
- Complete path to the Album Title file.
- Complete path to the Invoice file.

Provide an Options/Files menu selection that will allow the user to customize these settings and save changes. When the program starts up, let it load the settings from the system registry. Use a common dialog control that will let the user browse the disk and select filenames.

2.7.5 Hardbodies Health Club

Write a program that will manage the membership list of a health club. For each member who joins the club, the user will enter the following information: member ID, last name, first name, middle initial, date joined, street, city, state, zip, home phone, membership fee.

The membership fees are determined by the following schedule:

Paid yearly in advance:	$350.00
Paid quarterly in advance:	$450.00
Paid monthly in advance:	$650.00

When all data have been added to the form, print an invoice for the customer and append all information to a text file. Or, if you know how to create random-access files, save the information in a random-access file. (Chapter 3 has a section explaining the use of random-access files, if you wish to read ahead.)

2.7.6 Health Club Class Schedule

Write a program that will keep track of the class schedules for the Hardbodies Health Club. Display a list box containing the instructor names that have been read from a text file. Display another list box containing the days and times of individual classes. Let the user select an instructor, select a class, and click a button called Schedule that matches the instructor to the class. When the program ends, write all information to a text file in such a way that the program can load and display the list of scheduled classes. When you run the program again, it should display the saved schedule.

2.7.7 Depreciation Schedule

Create a program that displays a tax depreciation schedule for items purchased by a business. Load a listbox containing item names from a sequential file. Load an array of matching prices from the same file. When one of these items is clicked, its depreciation schedule appears in the listbox on the right side of the form. The depreciation occurs over a five-year period. There are two forms of depreciation: straight-line and accelerated. The straight-line method lets you deduct up to 20% of the cost of the item per year. The accelerated method allows 40% the first year, 25% the second, 20% the third, 10% the fourth, and 5% the fifth year. Figure 19 contains a sample of the program window.

Figure 19. Depreciation Main Window.

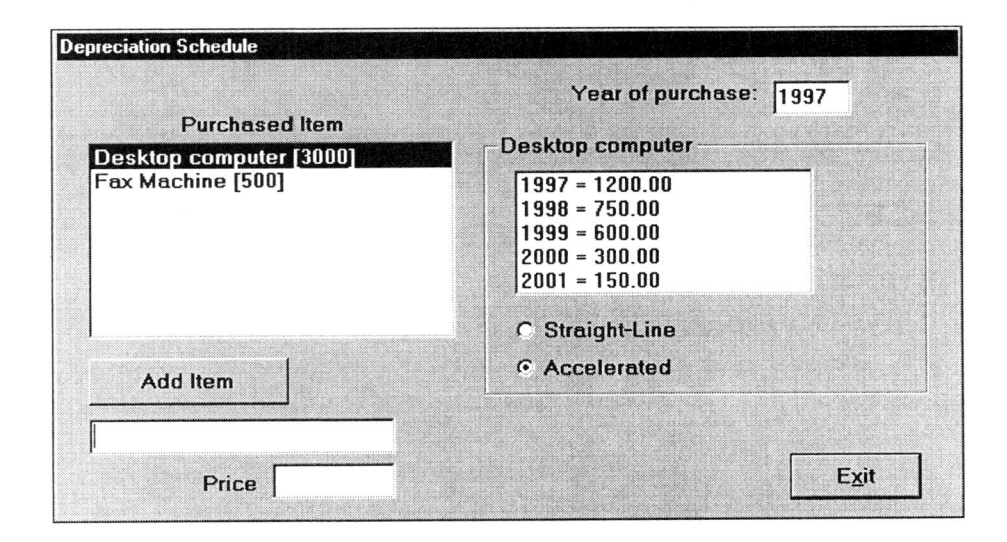

When the user changes an option button, the depreciation schedule recalculates. You can also add new items to the listbox on the left, by typing in the small text controls near the bottom, and by clicking on "Add Item". Notice the frame around the listbox and option buttons on the right side of the window.

2.7.8 Time Clock Program

Write a program that keeps track of the amount of billable time you spend on consulting projects. The program will read the Client file as input, and it will append records to the Billing file:

Client: id (Long), clientName (String)
Billing: date, clientId (Long), startTime, stopTime

All dates and times are stored in Date/Time variables. The Client file should contain at least five names. The Billing file should be empty. When you start working on a project, click on the Start button; when you stop, click on the Stop button. At that moment, the program shows the number of elapsed minutes, and writes a record to the Billing file. Here are two sample records:

```
Date          CustID   Start   Stop    Elapsed
02-01-1998    1101     21:51   22:10   19
02-02-1998    2034     10:20   12:25   125
```

Figure 20 shows a sample of the main window. The name of the selected client should appear in the window caption.

Figure 20. TimeClock Program.

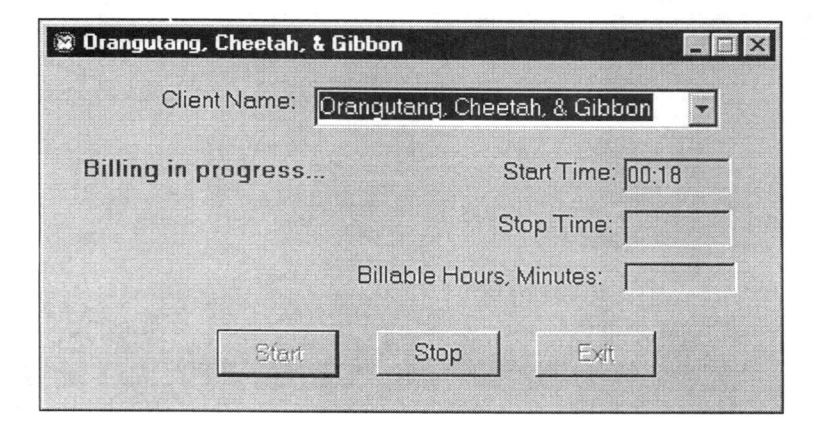

It is important to coordinate the command buttons carefully to make sure the user cannot click out of sequence. The following table shows the two possible program states that affect the buttons. The program is in State 1 when it starts; after clicking on Start, the program enters State 2:

Chap 2: Building an Invoice Application

State	Start	Stop	Exit
1	Enabled	Disabled	Enabled
2	Disabled	Enabled	Enabled

Also, when the user clicks on the Start button, display a status message "Billing in Progress..." to clearly show that the clock is running. It is fun to use a timer control to vary the ForeColor property of this status message once every 1/2 second. Figure 21 shows the same program after the Stop button has been clicked—the stop time and the number of billable hours and minutes are displayed.

Billing File. The program must append a new record to the Billing file when the Stop button is pressed. The client name is chosen from a combo box. All times are displayed as 24-hour clock values. The following expression returns time of day in hh:mm format:

```
Format$(Now, "hh:mm")
```

Figure 21. After Clicking on the Stop Button.

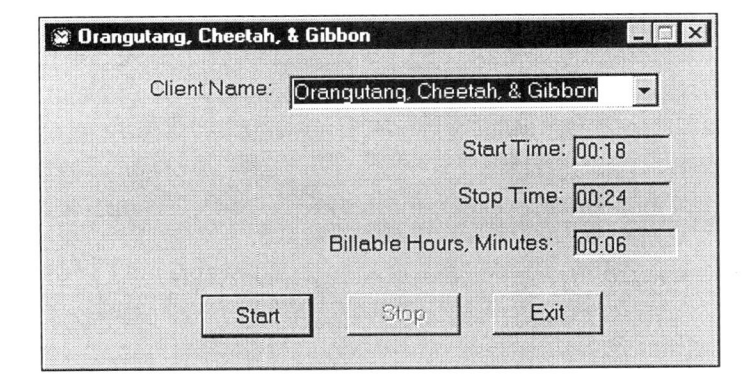

Select an icon for the main window, possibly a clock. Compile the project to an EXE program so it can be run as a stand-alone program. ***Hint:*** The standard Timer function returns the number of seconds that have elapsed since midnight.

3 Objects and Collections

Chapter Contents

Object Variables
    Declaring and Assigning Objects
    Declaring and Assigning Object Arrays
    Creating a Control Array in Design Mode
    Creating a Control Array at Runtime
The MixUp Game
    Program Specifications
    Program Design
    Program Implementation
Using Visual Basic Collections
    Built-In Collections
    Programmer-Defined Collections
    Collection Methods and Properties
    Example: Resizing Controls on a Form
The Glossary Program
    Program Design
    Program Implementation
Random-access Files
    Opening a File
    Writing Records
    Reading Records
    Example: Customer Accounts Program
    Program Design
    Program Implementation
Creating MDI Applications
    MDI Bitmap Viewer Program
    Program Design
    Program Implementation
Review Questions
Chapter Exercises

3.1 Object Variables

3.1.1 Declaring and Assigning Objects

A number of object types are predefined in Visual Basic. All forms in a project, for example are predefined. For example, suppose that the frmEdit form had already been added to the current project; the following code would create a new instance of frmEdit, assign a value to its caption, and display the form:

```
Dim F As New frmEdit
F.Caption = "New form"
F.Show vbModal
```

Visual Basic controls are also predefined object types: CheckBox, CommandButton, Control, ComboBox, Data (data control), DirListBox, DriveListBox, FileListBox, Frame, HScrollBar, Image, Label, Line, ListBox, OptionButton, PictureBox, Shape, TextBox, Timer, and VScrollBar.

Example: Jumping Button Program. You can have a lot of fun showing this program to friends: It displays a command button that says "Click Here". The trouble is, when the user tries to click on the button, it scoots away to a random location. No doubt, there are any number of variations that can be made on this program, involving sound, more buttons, other graphics, and so on. The program creates two instances of the same form, and on each form, manipulates a button as an object. First, here is the code in module1.bas. The ShowAnyForm procedure's first parameter is of type Form, a predefined type in Visual Basic:

```
Public Sub ShowAnyForm(F As Form, mode As Integer)
    F.Show mode    'mode is either vbModal or vbModeless
End Sub
```

In other words, forms and controls can be passed as procedure parameters. We demonstrate this when calling ShowAnyForm from Main:

```
Public Sub Main()
    Dim F1 As New frmJump
    F1.Caption = "Jumping Button 1"
    ShowAnyForm F1, vbModeless

    Dim F2 As New frmJump
    F2.Caption = "Jumping Button 2"
    F2.Top = F1.Top + F1.Height + 100    'place below first window
    ShowAnyForm F2, vbModeless
End Sub
```

This is frmJump shown in design mode:

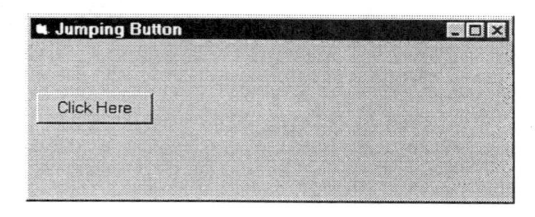

Code in frmJump. The RandomMove procedure moves the button (B) to a random location on the current form. Notice that the procedure parameter is of type CommandButton, a predefined type:

```
Private Sub RandomMove(B As CommandButton)
    B.Left = Rnd * (Me.Width - B.Width)
    B.Top = Rnd * (Me.ScaleHeight - B.Height)
```

Chap 3: Objects and Collections

```
    End Sub
```

The MouseMove event executes when the mouse is moved over the button; therefore, the button always moves away before it can be clicked:

```
    Private Sub cmdTest_MouseMove(Button As Integer, _
        Shift As Integer, X As Single, Y As Single)
      RandomMove cmdTest
    End Sub
```

3.1.2 Declaring and Assigning Object Arrays

Until now, we have used unique names for all controls placed on the same form because the names clearly identify the controls' meanings. For example, a form containing an employee record might contain text boxes named txtID, txtLastName, txtFirstName, txtSalary, and so on. But many programmers prefer to assign a single name to a group of text boxes, option buttons, check boxes, or some other type of control. A subscript is used to select individual members of a control array.

Imagine that an employee record might be represented by an array of text boxes named txtEmployee. One could use a loop to check for missing input, clear the boxes, write them to a file, and so on. A control array uses less memory than the same number of separately named controls. Similarly, an array of option buttons or check boxes can streamline the processing of these controls.

An array of control or form objects can be a great convenience, making it possible to carry out the same operations on each element. A control array, for example, can be created in two ways:

- In *design* mode, assign a value to the Index property of a control.
- In *run* mode, use the Load statement to create new instances of an existing control.

Using program code, you can declare arrays of controls and forms:

```
    Dim formList(0 to 10) as Form
    Dim cmdQuest(0 to 50) as CommandButton
    Dim allOptions(0 to 10) as OptionButton
```

The **Set** statement must be used when assigning an existing object to an array element:

```
    Set formList(0) = frmMain
    Set cmdQuest(j) = cmdChoiceA
```

In other words, frmMain would have to be the name of a form that was already part of the current project, and cmdChoiceA would be a command button on the current form.

Usage. When using an array of objects, you can easily manipulate the properties and methods of all members of the array. For example, to clear ten text controls on the same form, a loop simplifies the task:

```
    Dim j As Integer
```

```
For j = 0 to 9
   txtEmployee(j).Text = ""
Next j
```

The same operation on separately named controls is not as concise:

```
txtID.Text = ""
txtLastName.Text = ""
txtMiddleInit.Text = ""
txtFirstName.Text = ""
txtSalary.Text = ""
txtPhone.Text = ""
txtStreetAddress.Text = ""
txtCity.Text = ""
txtState.Text = ""
txtZip.Text = ""
```

It is also important to write self-documenting code. If a statement contains the identifier **txtEmployee(1),** the program listing may be hard to understand. A possible remedy is to declare constants identifying the fields and use the constants as subscripts into the array when referencing individual fields:

```
Const ID  = 0;
Const LastName = 1
Const MiddleInit = 2
(etc.)

Debug.Print txtEmployee(LastName).Text
```

3.1.3 Creating a Control Array in Design Mode

In design mode, you can create a control array that contains multiple instances of the same type of control. For example, three option buttons named optColor(0), optColor(1), and optColor(2) would be considered a control array. Each has a different value in its Index property (0, 1, 2). In fact, when the index property of a control is given a value, even zero, the control automatically becomes part of a control array.

You can use the Windows clipboard to copy and paste multiple instances of the same control onto a form by following these steps:

1. Create the first instance of the control by dragging it from the toolbox onto a form.

2. Select the control with the mouse and copy it to the Windows clipboard.

3. Paste the clipboard contents onto the form. When you are asked whether you want to create a control array, answer Yes. The control will appear in the upper left corner of the form.

4. Use the mouse to drag the new control to its desired location.

5. Repeat steps 3 and 4 to create more instances of the control.

Once properties such as Font, ForeColor, BackColor, and Alignment have been set for the first instance of a control, each copy of the control pasted onto the form is automatically assigned the same properties. In Figure 1, for example, the form contains an array of text controls named **txtArray**.

Figure 1. Control Array of Text Boxes.

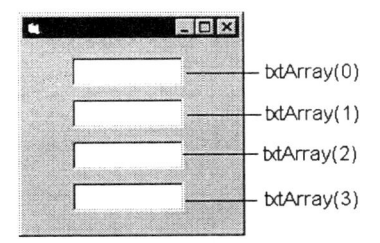

Only a single event handler is required for an entire control array. For example, the Change event for our array called **txtArray** has a parameter called **Index** that identifies which member of the array has had its contents changed:

```
Private Sub txtArray_Change(Index As Integer)
   txtArray.Text(Index) = Ucase$(txtArray.Text(Index))
End Sub
```

3.1.4 Creating a Control Array at Runtime

A control array can be created at runtime, as long as a single instance of the control already exists. By default, the existing control is given an index of zero. For example, we would like to create an array of command buttons called cmdBtn. Each would automatically have the same properties as cmdBtn(0):

```
For j = 1 To 9
   Load cmdBtn(j)         'create a button
Next j
```

The original instance of cmdBtn that was placed on the form does not have to be an array.

Because the new buttons all have the same Left and Top properties, the buttons are placed on top of each other. Each new button is positioned just to the right of the previous one:

```
Private Sub cmdStart_Click()
   Dim leftpos As Integer, j As Integer
   Dim buttonWidth As Integer

   'Get the size and position of the first button.
   leftpos = cmdBtn(0).Left
   buttonWidth = cmdBtn(0).Width

   'Position the other buttons and make them visible.
   For j = 1 To 9
      Load cmdBtn(j)
```

```
        leftpos = leftpos + buttonWidth + 30
        cmdBtn(j).Left = leftpos
        cmdBtn(j).Caption = j
        cmdBtn(j).Visible = True
    Next j
End Sub
```

Let's implement this code in a short program, shown before and after the user clicked on "Start" to create the buttons (Figure 2).

Figure 2. Creating a Button Array.

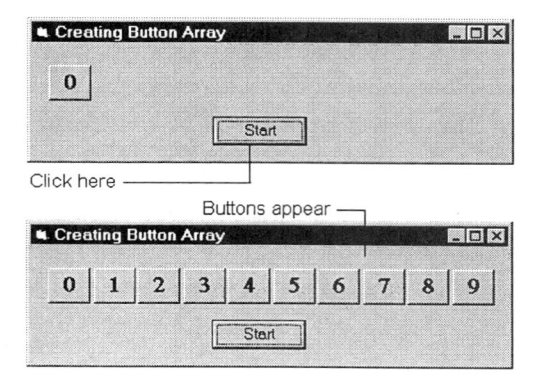

3.2 The MixUp Game

Let's program a simple mind game called "MixUp", where twenty-four buttons cover twelve pairs of images. This is a game that children typically play called *concentration*. The game consists of a collection of cards, in which each card has a picture on one side and is plain on the other. This program provides an excellent way to learn to coordinate user-driven events with timed events. We use control arrays, program switches, and build the solution in individual steps.

3.2.1 Program Specifications

- The user starts a game by selecting the **New Game** command from the **File** menu. This activates a timer that counts the number of elapsed seconds in the game. The images under the buttons are placed in random order.
- During each turn, the user clicks on a pair of buttons; the buttons temporarily disappear, revealing the images underneath.
- If the user finds two matching images, the user is awarded one point and the matching images disappear. If the images do not match, the two buttons reappear, hiding the images.
- The game continues until the user has found all matching images and the program displays a message saying that the game is finished. At any time, the user can start a new game or exit the program.

3.2.2 Program Design

Figure 3 shows a sample of the main window just after a game has started. Each button hides a different image.

Figure 3. Mixup Game, Just Starting.

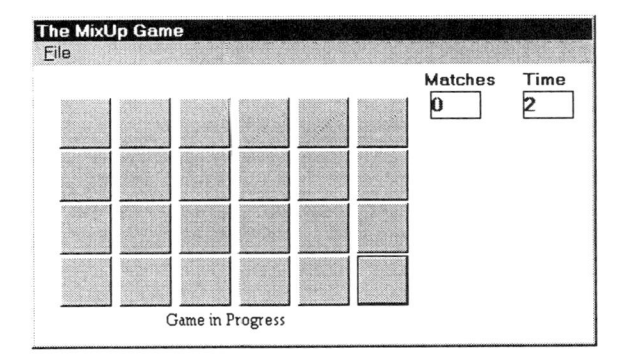

The user clicks on two buttons, making them disappear and exposing the images underneath. Because the images don't match, the buttons reappear after a short delay (Figure 4).

Figure 4. After Two Buttons Have Been Selected.

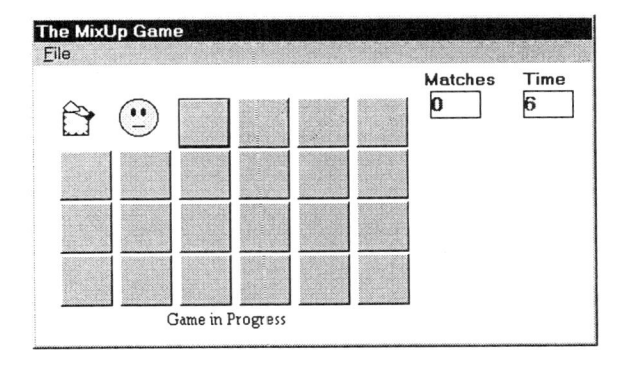

The program uses two timer controls: one to regulate the delay between the moment the second button is clicked and the moment when the buttons reappear. The second timer control counts the total elapsed time for the game. The timer controls are not seen by the user, but they appear on the form in design mode.

3.2.3 Program Implementation

> *Tip:* This project is called an *Assisted Project,* meaning that you will be given background information and hints toward completing the program. But not all of the program's source code is shown—you have to complete it yourself.

Step 1: Select the Icons. Find twelve icons and place them in the same directory as your program. Rename the icon filenames to "0.ico", "1.ico", and so on. This will make it easier to randomly select icons when the game starts to run. You might want to look in the Visual Basic **\icons** directory.

Step 2: Design the Main Form. Name the program's main form **frmMain**. Using the mouse, drag 24 image controls on your program's main form, naming them Img(0), Img(1), and so on. Do not place any pictures in these images. Arrange the images in four rows of six images each: Img(0) through Img(5) appear in the first row; Img(6) through Img(11) appear in the second row, and so on.

> *Design Tip:* When you have to create a lot of controls that have identical properties, a quick way to do it is to create the first one, set its properties, and copy it to the Windows clipboard (press Ctrl-C). Then press Ctrl-V to paste a copy of the control onto the form, and drag the control to its desired position. Each pasted control will be given a new Index value, and the controls will belong to a control array.

Using the mouse, place 24 command buttons on the program's main form so they cover the image controls, naming them cmdBtn(0), cmdBtn(1), and so on. It is very important that the indexes of the buttons match the indexes of the images underneath the buttons. For example, Img(6) must be covered by cmdBtn(6). Also, place two timer controls on the form and name them tmrButton and tmrSeconds. Each timer's Interval property should be set to 1000 (milliseconds):

```
tmrButton.Interval = 1000
tmrSeconds.Interval = 1000
```

Create the following menu. Uncheck the Enabled property of mnuStopGame, so this option will be disabled when the program starts up:

&File	mnuFile
&New game	mnuNewGame
&Stop game	mnuStopGame
E&xit	mnuExit

Add the remaining controls and properties to the form. You may want to set the Icon property of frmMain, and set the form's Caption property to "The MixUp Game". There are two labels on the form, showing the player's score and the number of elapsed seconds, named lblScore and lblTime. There is a label called lblStatus at the bottom of the form showing the current game status as either "Game in Progress" or "Game Stopped".

Step 3: Create the Code Module. Create a code module called **Module1** and declare the following variables and constants:

```
Option Explicit
Const MaxButtons As Integer = 23    'Number of buttons, minus 1
Public PlayingGame As Boolean       'True if game in progress
Public score As Integer             'number of matches
Public timeVal As Integer           'elapsed time, in seconds
Public currImage As Integer         'may be 0, 1, or 2
```

Chap 3: Objects and Collections

```
Public Icons(0 To MaxButtons) As String   'icon names
Public image1Index As Integer      'index of 1st button pushed
Public image2Index As Integer      'index of 2nd button pushed
```

The **Icons** array contains the names of icon files that will be loaded by the program into the image controls. The names will be shuffled in random order to make the game more interesting. We use **image1Index** and **image2Index** to keep track of the most recent two buttons pushed by the user. The need for these variables will be more evident when the rest of the program is finished.

Create a **Main** procedure in Module1 and set the project's startup form to Sub Main. (In VB5, this is done by selecting Project Properties from the Project menu, and select Startup Object.) In the following listing of the Main procedure, the Randomize statement tells Visual Basic to begin the random number sequence with a different value each time the program is run; this ensures that the ordering of icons will be different:

```
Public Sub Main()
  ChDrive App.Path
  ChDir App.Path
  Randomize       'seed the random number generator
  PlayingGame = False
  AssignIconNames
  frmMain.Show vbModal
End Sub
```

Step 4: Starting a Game. The first thing the user will do is to click on the "New game" menu command. This calls InitializeGame:

```
Private Sub mnuNewGame_Click()
  InitializeGame
End Sub
```

Step 5: Initializing a Game. The **InitializeGame** procedure is called whenever the user starts a new game. It calls ShuffleIcons to change the order of the icon names, loads the image controls using LoadPicture, and makes all the buttons visible:

```
Public Sub InitializeGame()
  Dim j As Integer
  currImage = 1
  score = 0
  timeVal = 0
  ShuffleIcons

  For j = 0 To MaxButtons
    frmMain.Img(j) = LoadPicture(Icons(j))
    frmMain.Img(j).Visible = True
    frmMain.cmdBtn(j).Visible = True
  Next j

  With frmMain
    .lblStatus.Caption = "Game in Progress"
    .lblTime.Caption = 0
```

```
      .lblScore.Caption = 0
      .tmrSeconds.Enabled = True
      .mnuNewGame.Enabled = False
      .mnuStopGame.Enabled = True
   End With
   PlayingGame = True
End Sub
```

The **AssignIconNames** procedure builds an array of strings containing icon file names such as "0.ico", "1.ico", and so on. Notice that each icon name is stored in the **Icons** array twice, so that matching icons will exist:

```
Public Sub AssignIconNames()
   Dim j As Integer
   For j = 0 To 11
      Icons(j) = j & ".ico"
      Icons(j + 12) = j & ".ico"
   Next j
```

The **ShuffleIcons** procedure rearranges the icon names much as one might shuffle a deck of cards. Each time the loop repeats, a random integer *n* is selected between 0 and MaxButtons. The icon name at position *n* is exchanged with the icon name at position *j*. The loop repeats, *j* is incremented, and another random exchange takes place:

```
Public Sub ShuffleIcons()
   Dim temp As String, j As Integer, n As Integer
   For j = 0 To MaxButtons
      n = Int((MaxButtons + 1) * Rnd)
      temp = Icons(j)
      Icons(j) = Icons(n)
      Icons(n) = temp
   Next j
End Sub
```

The **Rnd** function generates a pseudo-random real number between 0.0 and 1.0 (but not including 1.0). We multiply this number by 24 (MaxButtons + 1) and truncate the result to an integer, producing a value between 0 and 23.

Step 6: Activate the Buttons. You could run the program at this point, but it wouldn't do very much. The buttons are not yet able to respond to mouse clicks. Let's try a simple experiment, by placing the following code in the Click event of the button array:

```
Private Sub cmdBtn_Click(Index As Integer)
   cmdBtn(Index).Visible = False   'hide this button
End Sub
```

Run the program, click on buttons, and you will find that each button disappears and reveals the picture underneath. This is a good starting point, but we need to use a timer control to make the buttons reappear. This can be done by setting the Enabled property of tmrButton to True, and saving the value of Index in a variable:

```
Private Sub cmdBtn_Click(Index As Integer)
   cmdBtn(Index).Visible = False   'hide this button
```

Chap 3: Objects and Collections

```
      image1Index = Index            'save this index
      tmrButton.Enabled = True
   End Sub
```

In the Timer event procedure, make the button visible again and turn off the timer:

```
   Private Sub tmrButton_Timer()
      tmrButton.Enabled = False
      cmdBtn(image1Index).Visible = True
   End Sub
```

Run the program again. If you click on a button, it should reappear after one second. But if you click on two or more buttons in rapid succession, the program doesn't work properly yet because the buttons are not properly coordinated.

Step 7: Coordinating the Buttons. When playing the MixUp game, the user clicks on the first button, but the program does nothing until the second button is clicked. Only then is the timer enabled. This means we have to keep track of two buttons and their index positions. Notice how currImage becomes useful—it counts the number of buttons clicked by the user:

```
   Private Sub cmdBtn_Click(Index As Integer)
      If currImage = 1 Then           'is this the first selection?
         image1Index = Index          'save this index
         currImage = 2                'get ready for second button
      ElseIf currImage = 2 Then       'is this the second selection?
         image2Index = Index          'save this index
         tmrButton.Enabled = True     'start the timer
      End If
      cmdBtn(Index).Visible = False   'hide this button
   End Sub
```

Only after the second button is clicked do we enable the tmrButton timer. This means, of course, that the timer event procedure must be revised. It makes both buttons visible again and resets currImage to 1:

```
   Private Sub tmrButton_Timer()
      tmrButton.Enabled = False
      currImage = 1
      cmdBtn(image1Index).Visible = True
      cmdBtn(image2Index).Visible = True
   End Sub
```

The variable **currImage** is called a *switch* because it flips back and forth between the values 1 and 2. Run the program again. It should only activate the timer after the second button is clicked. You are given one second to look at the icons before the buttons reappear and cover the icons.

Step 8: Checking for Matching Pictures. There is still more to be done in this program. For example, the program has to know when two pictures selected by the user are matched. It is not possible to compare the Picture properties of two image controls, because the value returned by the Picture property is a unique integer that does not correspond to the icon that was originally placed in the image. However, we can compare the icon names, which were saved in the Icons() array in the AssignIconNames procedure. The procedure that checks for matching pictures can use the following comparison:

```
If Icons(image1Index) = Icons(image2Index) Then
  score = score + 1
    '...(etc.)
```

Recall that **image1Index** and **image2Index** were taken from the Index parameter in the cmdBtn_Click event handler. They tell us which two buttons were clicked, and therefore, which two image controls were under the buttons. This is why it was so important to align the Index properties of the buttons and images when the form was designed. If we had mistakenly put Img(3) under cmdBtn(4), for example, it would be nearly impossible to figure out why the program was not detecting matching pictures.

Where will the program check for matching pictures? It could be inside the tmrButton_Timer event procedure, or even inside the cmdBtn_Click procedure. When matching images are found, their Visible properties can be set to False, making the images disappear.

Step 9: Other Details. There are a few other details to take care of in the program. For example, the second timer counts the number of seconds elapsed from the beginning of the game. This is easily accomplished by incrementing a counter inside the Timer event of **tmrSeconds** and copying the counter to a label on the form called **lblTime**.

The user cannot be allowed to click on more than two buttons at the same time. After the second button is clicked, you might want to disable the entire form until a tmrButton.Timer event has occurred.

The program must determine when the user has finished the game. One way is to set up a loop that iterates through all the buttons, checking their Visible property. If all the buttons are invisible, the user must have matched all of the pictures. Perhaps there are other ways to do this that are yet easier.

3.3 Using Visual Basic Collections

3.3.1 Built-In Collections

Collections are the powerful relatives of arrays in Visual Basic. A collection can contain strings, numbers, forms, buttons, and other types of objects. The objects in a collection are called *members*. Visual Basic programs automatically have several built-in collections. One, called **Forms**, contains all forms that have loaded into memory. Another, called **Controls**, contains all of the controls on a single form.

Suppose that a program loaded three forms called Form1, Form2, and Form3. The following statements would print the names of the forms by using a subscript to refer to each member of the collection:

Chap 3: Objects and Collections

```
Private Sub Command1_Click()
  Dim j As Integer
  For j = 0 To Forms.Count - 1
    Debug.Print Forms(j).Name
  Next j
End Sub
```

Every collection has a **Count** property that returns the number of items in the collection.

Similarly, every form contains a **Controls** collection, a collection of all controls on the form. The following statements iterate through the collection in frmMain and display their names:

```
Dim j As Integer
For j = 0 To frmMain.Controls.Count - 1
  Debug.Print frmMain.Controls(j).Name
Next j
```

The following code does the same thing, using a **For Each** loop. This loop does not require a loop counter, but we do have to declare an object variable that matches the general type of all of the controls:

```
Dim ctrl As Control
For Each ctrl In frmMain.Controls
  Debug.Print ctrl.Name
Next ctrl
```

Fortunately, all controls have a **Name** property, so the reference to **ctrl.Name** is valid.

A Visual Basic program does not terminate until all of its forms have been unloaded. For that reason, it often helps to use a loop at the end of the Main procedure to unload all members of the Forms collection:

```
Dim frm As Form
For Each frm In Forms
  Unload frm
Next frm
```

3.3.2 Programmer-Defined Collections

In addition to using Visual Basic's built-in collections, you can create your own and take advantage of their power and convenience. This is much more effective than trying to simulate the actions of a collection with array variables. To declare and create a collection object, use the **Dim** statement with the **New** operator:

```
Dim MyFriends as New Collection
```

Or, you can just declare a variable that will refer to the collection, and at a later time, use the **New** operator to create the actual collection object. This separation of tasks lets you determine exactly when the collection is created, a feature that programmers generally like:

```
Dim MyFriends as Collection
 .
 .
 .
Set MyFriends = New Collection
```

Using Keys to Identify Members. The members of a collection can be accessed using numeric indexes (subscripts), or each member can be associated with a unique string, called a *key*. For example, we might want to create a collection in which each person's social security number is the *key,* and the person's name is the *member:*

SSN (key)	Name (member)
222-33-4444	Jones, S.
123-65-4321	Gonzalez, J.
987-65-4234	Chong, A.
879-56-3435	Schwartz, E.

No two members can have the same key value, and the key must be a string expression.

To remove a collection, set its identifier to **Nothing** (a Visual Basic keyword):

```
Set MyFriends = Nothing
```

3.3.3 Collection Methods and Properties

Collections have three methods: **Add, Item,** and **Remove.** They have one property, **Count**. The **Count** property indicates the number of members in the collection:

```
MsgBox "There are " & MyFriends.Count & _
 " members currently in the MyFriends collection.", _
 vbInformation,""
```

Add Method. To add a member to a collection, use the **Add** method. The syntax is:

```
object.Add( member, key, before, after )
```

The object must be a collection object. *member* is the object to be added; it is the only required parameter. *key* is a unique string value that is associated with the item. The key can be used to quickly look up a specific member. The following would be valid add statements:

```
Dim MyFriends As new Collection
MyFriends.Add "Jones, S."
MyFriends.Add "Jones, S.", "222-33-4444"
```

The Add method generates a runtime error if an attempt is made to insert a new member whose key is already in the collection, so you should provide an On Error GoTo statement to handle the error.

The *before* parameter specifies a relative position in the collection. The member to be added is placed in the collection before an existing member identified by the *before* argument. If *before* is an integer expression, it must be a number between 1 and Count. If *before* is a string expression, then the position will be determined by the key value of an existing member.

The *after* parameter specifies a relative position in the collection. The member to be added is placed in the collection after the member identified by the after argument. If *after* is an integer expression, it must be a number from 1 to the value of the collection's Count property. If *after* is a string expression, then the position will be determined by the key value of an existing member.

Any type of object can be inserted in a collection, and the members of a collection need not be the same type. Of course, not all collections are useful:

```
MyFriends.Add 26
MyFriends.Add 284.5
MyFriends.Add "Fish"
MyFriends.Add Form1
MyFriends.Add True
```

Item Method. Collections are designed to make searching for members very easy, as long as you know their corresponding key values. The **Item** method returns the object that is associated with the key value. The syntax is:

```
object.Item( index )
```

If *index* is an integer expression, it identifies the index position of the member that is to be retrieved. User-defined collections are indexed from 1 to Count. If *index* is a string expression, it causes a search for a member with a matching key value. The Item method generates a runtime error if no matching member is found in the collection.

In the following example, we search for the key "123-65-4321", and the value "Gonzalez, J." is assigned to nameFound:

```
Dim MyFriends As new Collection
MyFriends.Add "Gonzalez, J.", "123-65-4321"
'(...add other members...)

Dim nameFound As String
nameFound = MyFriends.Item( "123-65-4321" )
```

The Item method only makes a copy of the member, but does not alter or remove it from the collection.

Remove Method. Use the **Remove** method to remove a member from a collection. The syntax is:

```
object.Remove index
```

As with the Item method, *index* may either be an integer expression or a string value that matches one of the keys in the collection. For example,

```
MyFriends.Remove "222-33-4444"
```

The Remove method generates a runtime error if no matching member is found in the collection.

Removing All Collection Members. The following **ClearCollection** procedure is a general-purpose loop that removes all members of a user-defined Collection object:

```
Public Sub ClearCollection(coll As Collection)
  Dim obj As Variant
  For Each obj In coll
    coll.Remove 1
  Next obj
End Sub
```

3.3.4 Example: Resizing Controls on a Form

You may have noticed that some Window applications are able to adjust the height and width of controls on a window when the window is resized by the user. One way to do this is to compare the new dimensions of the window to its previous dimensions, and use this ratio to scale the positions and dimensions of all of the controls in the window.

Let's write a general-purpose procedure in Visual Basic that will adjust the width and horizontal positions of all controls on a form when the form is re-sized. For example, start with the form as it appears in design mode (Figure 5).

Figure 5. Before Resizing the Form.

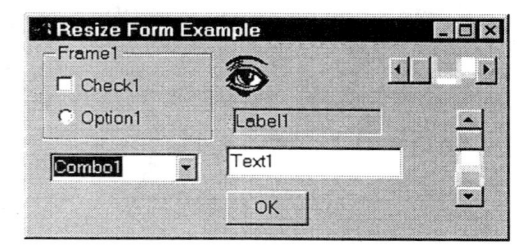

When we run the program, the user drags the right side of the window and all of the controls automatically adjust their Left and Width properties (Figure 6). The Stretch property of the Image control equals True.

Figure 6. After Resizing the Form.

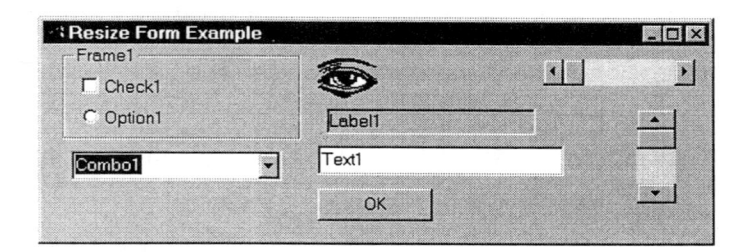

First, it is necessary to create a form-level variable that saves the current width, and initialize the variable in the Form_Activate procedure:

```
Dim saveWidth As Integer

Private Sub Form_Activate()
   saveWidth = Width
End Sub
```

A **Form_Resize** event is generated when a form is first shown, and when the user resizes the form with the mouse. Here is the code for that event handler:

```
Private Sub Form_Resize()
   ResizeControls Me, saveWidth
End Sub
```

All that remains, then, is to create the ResizeControls procedure that takes the current form and its previously saved width, and resizes the form's controls.

Implementation. The **ResizeControls** procedure would be placed in a general code module so it could be called from anywhere in a program. We start out by calculating the ratio (changeFactor) between the old and new widths of the form. Then, we iterate through the form's collection of controls:

```
Public Sub ResizeControls(F As Form, oldWidth As Integer)
   Dim ratio As Single, ctrl As Control
   If oldWidth < 1 Then Exit Sub    'Cannot divide by zero!
   ratio = F.Width / oldWidth
   On Error Resume Next
   For Each ctrl In F.Controls
     ctrl.Width = ctrl.Width * ratio
     ctrl.Left = ctrl.Left * ratio
   Next ctrl
   oldWidth = F.Width
End Sub
```

Some types of controls such as Timer and CommonDialog do not have Height and Width properties, so the On Error Resume Next statement lets the loop continue when an invalid property is referenced.

Of course, we have only resized and moved the controls in the horizontal direction. In the chapter exercises, you will be asked to augment this procedure so it resizes controls both vertically and horizontally. Another improvement might be to adjust the Font.Size property of the controls.

3.4 The Glossary Program

To better demonstrate the use of Collections and searching for values using keys, let's create a program called Glossary. In this collection, programming terms will be the *keys*, and the term definitions will be the *members*. For example:

```
term:        variable
definition:  A named storage area in a program.
```

3.4.1 Program Design

The program will have the ability to load a glossary from a specially prepared text file in which each term is followed by its definition. We will use a common dialog control to let the user select the file to be loaded into the glossary. Figure 7 shows the program's main form.

Figure 7. Glossary Program, Main Window.

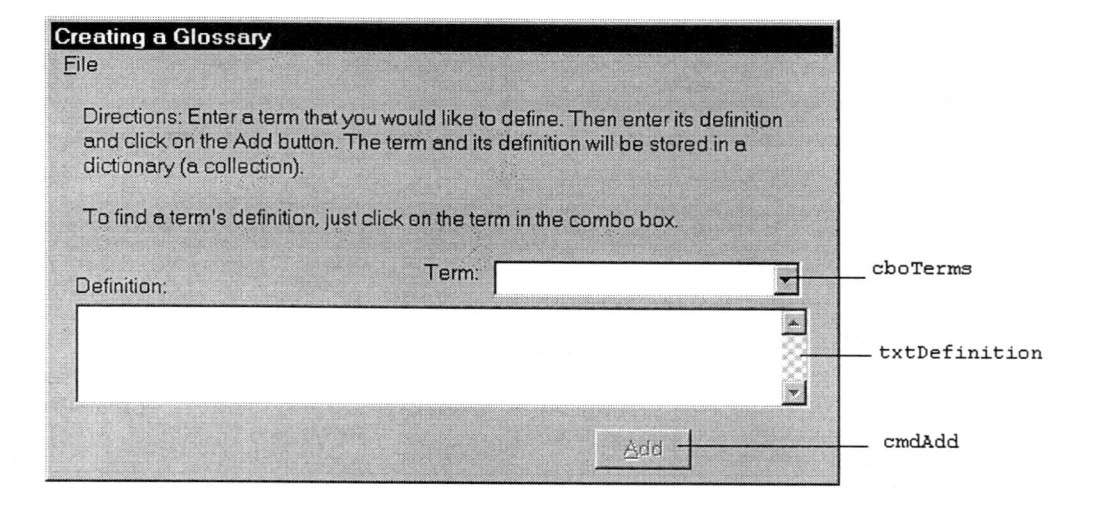

After clicking on the File/New command, a File/Open dialog lets the user select a glossary file. Once a file has been loaded, the user can select a term from the combo box. When a term is chosen, its definition appears in the Definition text box (Figure 8).

The user can also add new terms and definitions to the glossary (Figure 9). The program does not save the revised glossary to disk, but that is a task requested by one of the Chapter Exercises.

Figure 8. Definition Found.

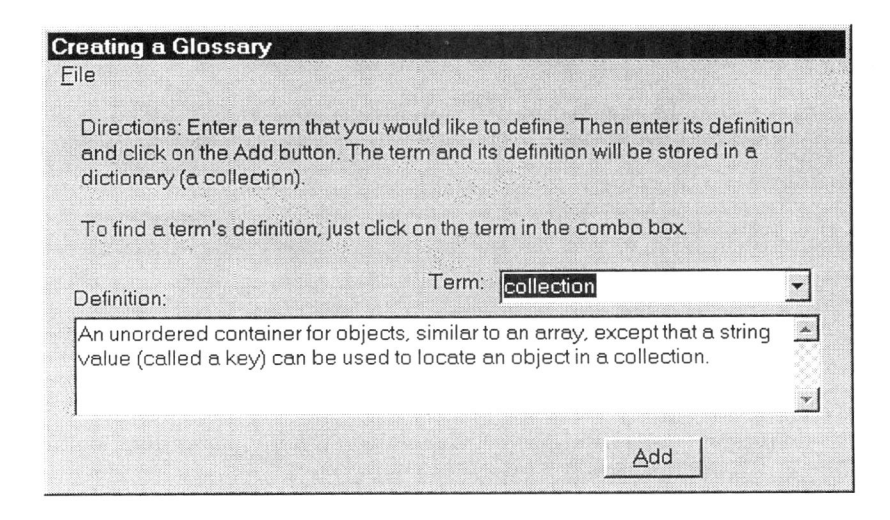

Figure 9. Adding a New Term & Definition.

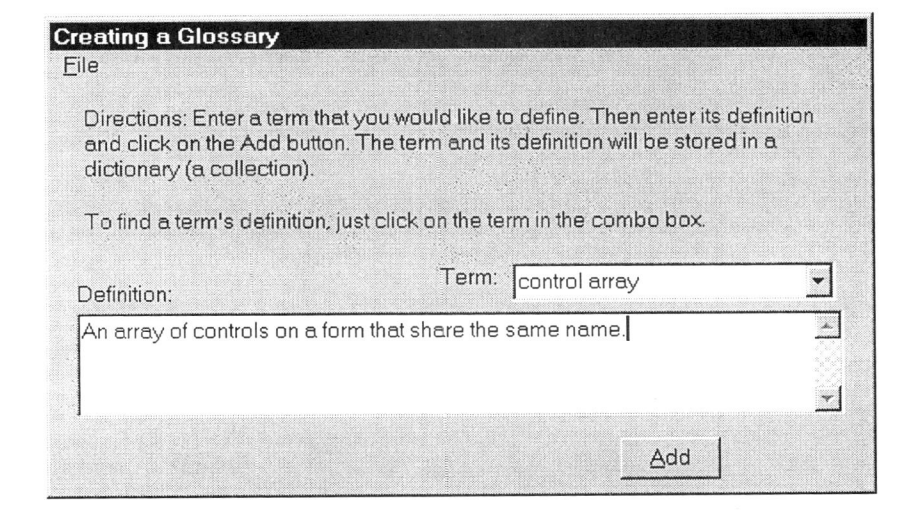

3.4.2 Program Implementation

The glossary is declared at the module level so it can be shared by all functions on the form. The **DuplicateKeyError** constant is used for comparison to runtime error codes returned by Visual Basic when inserting a new term in the glossary. The Form_Load procedure creates the empty collection:

```
Option Explicit
Const DuplicateKeyError = 457
Dim glossary As Collection
```

```
Private Sub Form_Load()
  Set glossary = New Collection
End Sub
```

When the user decides to add a new term to the glossary, the term is added to both the collection and combo box. If the term is already in the glossary, a duplicate key error message is displayed:

```
Private Sub cmdAdd_Click()
  On Error GoTo Add1
  glossary.Add txtDefinition.Text, cboTerms.Text
  cboTerms.AddItem cboTerms.Text
  cboTerms.Text = ""
  txtDefinition.Text = ""
  Exit Sub
Add1:
  If Err.Number = DuplicateKeyError Then
    MsgBox "This term was already added to the " _
      + "glossary.", vbInformation, ""
  Else
    MsgBox Error$, vbInformation, "Error"
  End If
End Sub
```

When the user clicks on a term in the combo box, **FindDefinition** is called:

```
Private Sub cboTerms_Click()
  FindDefinition cboTerms.Text
End Sub
```

FindDefintion calls the collection's Item method, which in turn returns the definition associated with the term. Suitable error handling is included:

```
Private Sub FindDefinition(key As String)
  On Error GoTo Find1:
  txtDefinition.Text = glossary.Item(key)
  Exit Sub
Find1:
  Select Case Err.Number
    Case 5
      MsgBox "'" + key + "' was not found " _
        + "in the glossary.", _
        vbInformation, "Error"
    Case Else
      MsgBox Error$, vbInformation, "Error"
  End Select
End Sub
```

When the user decides to open a glossary file, ShowOpen is called:

```
Private Sub mnuFileOpen_Click()
  On Error GoTo FileOpen1
```

Chap 3: Objects and Collections

```
    With cdFile
      .CancelError = True
      .DialogTitle = "Open Glossary File"
      .Filter = "Glossary file|*.gls|All files|*.*"
      .fileName = "*.gls"
      .ShowOpen
      ReadGlossaryFile .fileName
    End With
    Exit Sub
FileOpen1:
    'no action taken - user clicked on Cancel
End Sub
```

The **ReadGlossaryFile** procedure clears out the current glossary, opens the file for input, reads the keys and definitions, and handles possible duplicate key errors:

```
Public Sub ReadGlossaryFile(fileName As String)
    Dim key As String, definition As String
    Dim elt As Object, fileNum As Integer
    On Error GoTo ReadGlossary1
    ClearAll    'clear the collection, etc.
    fileNum = FreeFile
    Open fileName For Input As fileNum
    Do While Not EOF(1)
      Line Input #fileNum, key
      Line Input #fileNum, definition
      glossary.Add definition, key
      cboTerms.AddItem key
    Loop
    Close fileNum
    Exit Sub
ReadGlossary1:
    If Err.Number = DuplicateKeyError Then
      MsgBox "Glossary file contains a duplicate keyword.", _
        vbInformation, "Error"
    Else
      MsgBox Error$, vbInformation, "Error Reading Glossary File"
    End If
End Sub
```

The **Add** button is only enabled when both a term and definition have been entered:

```
Private Sub txtDefinition_Change()
    cmdAdd.Enabled = (Len(cboTerms.Text) > 0) And _
                    (Len(txtDefinition.Text) > 0)
End Sub
```

The **ClearAll** procedure iterates through the collection and removes each member. The parameter passed to the Remove method is always 1 because we just keep removing the first member until there are none left:

```
Public Sub ClearAll()
    Dim elt As Variant
```

```
        txtDefinition.Text = ""
        cboTerms.Clear
        For Each elt In glossary
            glossary.Remove 1
        Next
End Sub
```

3.5 Random-Access Files

Random-access files provide an efficient way of storing and retrieving data in such a way that records may be modified selectively. Sequential files may only be processed in sequential record order, hence the name *sequential*. Processing begins at the first record, and continues in sequence to the last record, unless the process is halted and the file closed. A random-access file, on the other hand, does not have to be processed in sequence. You can select any record, read it, and modify it in place.

There are some other important differences between sequential and random-access files:

- Each record in a random-access file is identified by a unique integer between 1 and 2,147,483,647, called a *record number*. Sequential files do not explicitly number their records.
- A sequential file may not be open for both input and output at the same time. Random-access files, on the other hand, can be open for both operations at the same time.
- Sequential records can vary in length. Random-access file records must all be the same length, for a very good reason: the physical position of any record can be found by multiplying the record number by the record length.
- Sequential records are translations of internal binary data into a text representation. Random-access records require no such translation.
- When opening a random-access file, a specific description of the record structure must be supplied by the programmer, showing the number of bytes allocated to each field. A sequential file has no such requirement. Different records may contain completely different sequences of fields.

Once a random-access file has been created, changing the lengths of its records is somewhat difficult. A new record description would have to be created, a new file opened, and all records would have to be copied from the old file to the new one. When designing the record layout for a random-access file, programmers will sometimes leave some slack space at the end of each record for additional data, to avoid having to undergo the time-consuming file copy process we just described. *Note:* Random-access files are not database files. Databases are introduced in Chapter 5.

3.5.1 Opening a File

The general syntax for opening a random-access file is:

```
Open pathname For Random [Access access] As filenumber Len=reclength
```

where *pathname* is the directory path plus the filename, and *reclength* is the integer length of each record in the file. The value of *access* indicates the types of operations that will be permitted on the file: **Read**, **Write**, or **Read Write**. If *access* is omitted, Read Write is assumed. For the pathname, it is suggested that you use a distinctive filename extension such as **.rnd** to indicate that the file is a random-access file.

3.5.2 Writing Records

Use the **Put** statement to write a record to a random-access file. The syntax is:

```
Put filenumber, [recnumber], varname
```

where *filenumber* is the number of a file that has already been opened, *recnumber* is an integer that indicates which record is to be written, and *varname* is the name of a variable that contains the data to be written to the file.

If *recnumber* is omitted, then the record read will be either the one following the most recent Put or Get operation, or the record number returned by the most recent Seek operation. In the following statements, for example, records 10, 11, and 12 are written to the file:

```
Put 1, 10, myRec
Put 1, , myRec
Put 1, , myRec
```

If a file is empty and you write to the tenth record, space for nine empty records will automatically be saved in the file before the tenth record is inserted. This must be done, so that when a request to read the tenth record is given later on, Visual Basic can calculate the physical location of the record.

3.5.3 Reading Records

Use the **Get** statement to read a record from a random-access file. The syntax is:

```
Get filenumber, [recnumber], varname
```

where *filenumber*, *recnumber*, and *varname* have the same meanings as in the Put statement. If *recnumber* is omitted, then the record read will be either the one following the most recent Put or Get operation, or the record number returned by the most recent Seek operation.

Moving the Record Pointer. The **Seek** statement can be used to position the record pointer in a random-access file. Its syntax is:

```
Seek filenumber, position
```

If the next Put or Get statement does not specify a record number, the record affected will be the one positioned by calling Seek. If recNum were equal to 20 in the next example, the Get statement would read myRec from record 20:

```
Seek 1, recNum
Get 1, , myRec
```

3.5.4 Example: Customer Accounts Program

Let's create a short program that keeps track of charges and payments by customers. A single random-access file (customers.rnd) will store all records, using the customer ID number as the record number. We will limit ID numbers to the range 1 to 9999, to prevent the file from becoming too large. If each record were 40 bytes long, for example, the file could be as large as (40 * 9999) = 399,960 bytes.

3.5.5 Program Design

The user first enters a customer ID and clicks the Get button. If the ID is found in the file, the rest of the customer record is displayed. The main form, called **frmCustomer**, lets the user enter a customer ID, name, amount of payments, and amount of charges for each customer (Figure 10).

Figure 10. Customer Accounts Program.

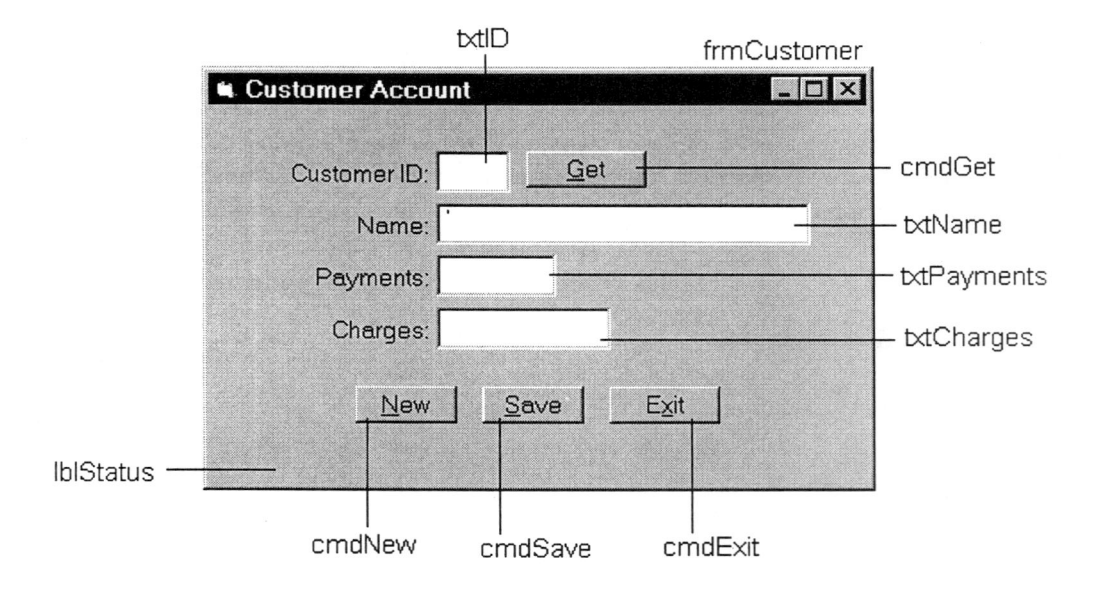

New. To create a new customer record, just blank all of the fields and let the user type in all required data.

Save. To save a customer record, the user types in an ID number (between 1 and 9999), a name, total payments, total charges, and clicks the Save button. An example is shown in Figure 11.

Figure 11. Saving a New Customer.

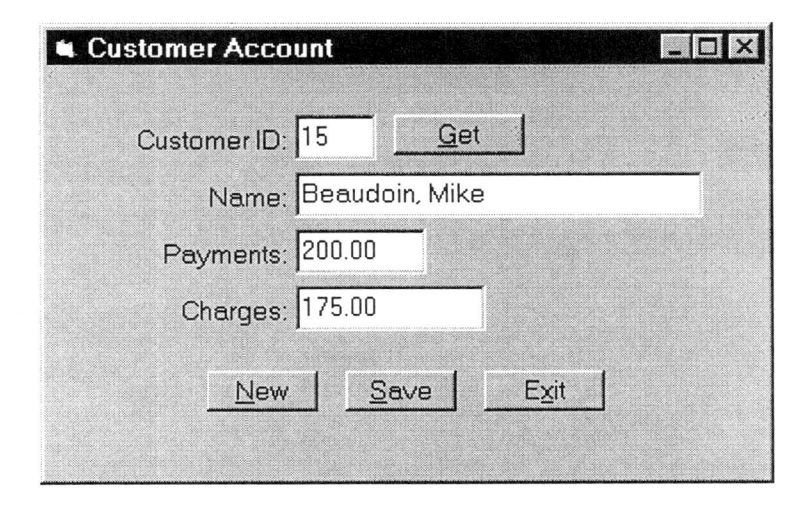

Each record is saved in the same random-access file, using the customer ID as the record number.

Finding Records. To find an existing customer, the user enters a customer ID number and clicks on the Get button (see Figure 12). The status line at the bottom of the form indicates whether or not the record was found.

Figure 12. Searching for a Customer.

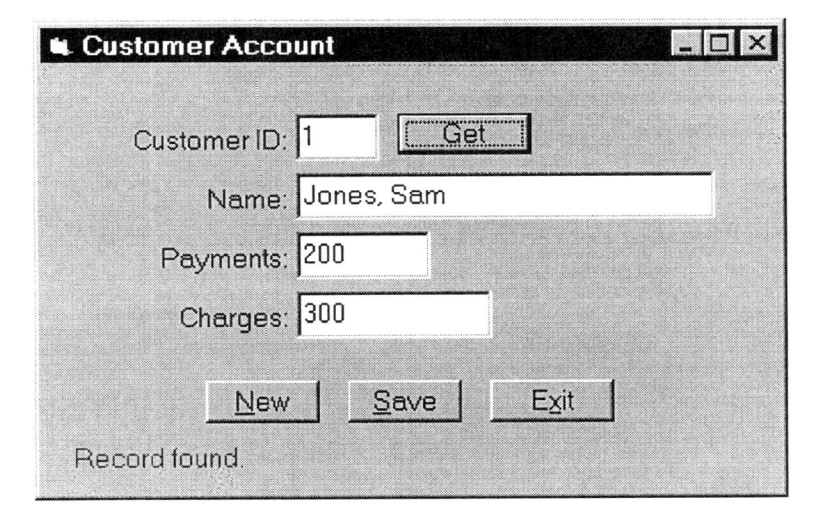

Or, if the record is not found, the status line displays a message to that effect. After finding a record, the user can modify some of its fields and click the Save button to save the record.

3.5.6 Program Implementation

In the declarations section of the main form, declared constants hold the name of the random-access file and the length of each record (CustomerLen). fileNum is the number of the open customer file:

```
Option Explicit
Const CustomerFile As String = "customers.rnd"
Const CustomerLen As Integer = 40
Dim fileNum As Integer
```

Also in the declarations section, **Customer** is declared as a user-defined type, containing all of the fields that belong in each record of the customer file. It is important to know the length of each field so the record length can be calculated:

```
Private Type Customer         ' Lengths
   id As Integer              '    4
   name As String * 20        '   18
   payments As Currency       '    8
   charges As Currency        '    8
   unused As String * 2       '    2
End Type
```

Notice that two unused bytes were left at the end of the Customer type. This allows for a small amount of expansion for additional data when needed.

We set the directory and path, get the next available file number, and open the random-access file in Form_Load. The file stays open for the program's duration:

```
Private Sub Form_Load()
   ChDrive App.Path
   ChDir App.Path
   fileNum = FreeFile
   Open CustomerFile For Random As fileNum _
       Len = CustomerLen
End Sub
```

Creating a new customer record involves clearing all of the text controls on the form:

```
Private Sub cmdNew_Click()
    txtId = ""
    txtName = ""
    txtPayments = ""
    txtCharges = ""
End Sub
```

When the user clicks the **Save** button, the ID number is checked for an acceptable value. We fill in each of the fields in the Customer record variable (called cust), and write the record to the file at the position indicated by the ID number:

```
Private Sub cmdSave_Click()
   Dim cust As Customer, id As Integer
   On Error GoTo SaveRecord1
```

Chap 3: Objects and Collections

```
      id = Val(txtId.Text)
      If id < 1 Or id > 9999 Then
        MsgBox "Customer ID must be between 1 and 9999."
        txtId.SetFocus
        Exit Sub
      End If
      cust.id = id
      cust.name = txtName.Text
      cust.payments = Val(txtPayments.Text)
      cust.charges = Val(txtCharges.Text)
      Put fileNum, cust.id, cust
      Exit Sub
  SaveRecord1:
      MsgBox Error$, vbCritical, "Error"
  End Sub
```

To retrieve an existing record, the user types a record number into txtId. If the ID field in the record does not match its record number, we assume the record was never initialized:

```
  Private Sub cmdGet_Click()
      Dim recNum As Integer, cust As Customer
      Dim id As Integer
      On Error GoTo GetRecord1
      id = Val(txtId.Text)
      Get fileNum, id, cust
      If cust.id <> id Then
        lblStatus = "Record not found."
        txtName.Text = ""
        txtPayments.Text = ""
        txtCharges.Text = ""
      Else
        lblStatus = "Record found."
        txtName.Text = cust.name
        txtPayments.Text = cust.payments
        txtCharges.Text = cust.charges
      End If
      Exit Sub
  GetRecord1:
      MsgBox Error$, vbCritical, "Error"
  End Sub
```

When the user clicks the **Exit** button, the main form unloads, triggering the Form_Unload event. We close the customer file just as the form is about to be unloaded:

```
  Private Sub cmdExit_Click()
      Unload Me
  End Sub

  Private Sub Form_Unload(Cancel As Integer)
      Close fileNum
  End Sub
```

Comments. Because this is a simple program, error checking was kept to a minimum. An improved version of the program would make sure that a record was never saved if any of its fields were blank, and each of the numeric fields would be checked for reasonable ranges of values. A nice improvement would also be to let the user select customer names from a list box when searching for customers.

3.6 Creating MDI Applications

A *multiple-document interface* (MDI) window is a special type of window that acts as a container for other windows, each of which is called an *MDI child*. Each child window must stay within the boundaries of the containing window, which is called the *MDI parent*. For example, Microsoft Word is an MDI application, where each document window is an MDI child. If the MDI parent is minimized or closed, the child windows are generally minimized or closed also.

Visual Basic restricts you to only one MDI form per program, but there can be a virtually unlimited number of child forms. To create an MDI form in VB4, select **MDI Form** from the Insert menu. In VB5, select **Add MDI Form** from the Project menu. Any other form can be an MDI child window, as long as its MDIChild property is set to True.

Most programs using an MDI form allow the user to create multiple instances of a child form inside the MDI parent. For example, if the MDI parent has a menu containing the Window/New command, the following procedure creates and displays a new copy of frmChild:

```
Private Sub mnuWindowNew_Click()
   Dim newdoc As New frmChild
   newdoc.Show vbModeless
End Sub
```

As soon as the first child form appears, its menu replaces the menu on the main MDI form. After the user has created several new forms this way, the MDI form and its child forms might appear as in Figure 13.

Note: MDI child forms cannot be shown with vbModal.

Figure 13. MDI Window Example.

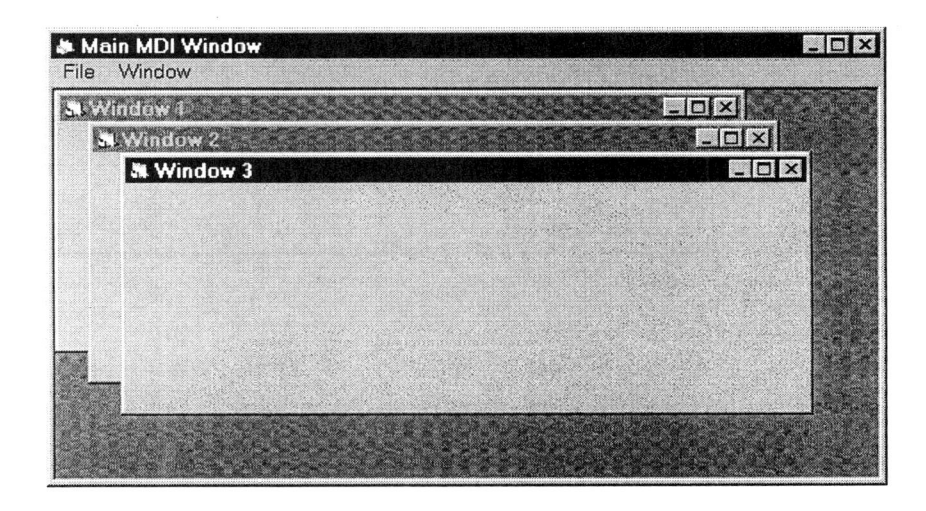

When a child form is minimized, it appears as a button along the bottom of the MDI parent form. The child forms can be tiled, cascaded (overlapped), or the icons arranged by calling the Arrange method and passing it one of the following Visual Basic constants:

```
frmMDI.Arrange vbCascade
frmMDI.Arrange vbTileHorizontal
frmMDI.Arrange vbTileVertical
frmMDI.Arrange vbArrangeIcons
```

3.6.1 MDI Bitmap Viewer Program

It is often useful to create an array of child forms, to allow processing them as a group. In the sample MDI program that we are about to create, each child window will display a different bitmap. Arbitrarily, we will limit the program to twenty child windows. We store each instance of frmChild in an array called ChildWindow. The variable WinCount keeps track of the number of child forms created so far:

```
WinCount = WinCount + 1
Set ChildWindow(WinCount) = New frmChild
ChildWindow(WinCount).Show vbModeless
```

This makes it easy to perform the same operation on all child windows. For example, the following statements close all windows and set WinCount to zero:

```
Dim j As Integer
For j = 1 To WinCount
  Unload ChildWindow(j)
Next j
WinCount = 0
```

The project includes the following modules: frmMDI (parent), frmChild (child), and Module1.

3.6.2 Program Design

The MDI parent, called **frmMDI**, has no controls on it. The child window, **frmChild**, has an image control and a common dialog control. Figure 14 shows the form in design mode.

Figure 14. MDI Parent Window.

When the user clicks on the image control or chooses the File/Open from the menu, the program displays a File/Open dialog box and lets the user select a bitmap or metafile image that will be displayed on the form.

Each child window can hold a different graphic image. The name of each image file appears in the form's caption. In Figure 15, for example, we have loaded two metafiles from the Visual Basic home directory and tiled the windows vertically.

Figure 15. Displaying Two Metafiles.

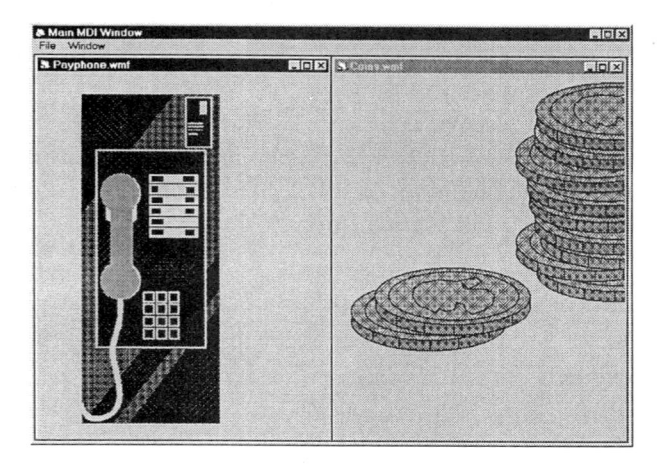

Properties and Menus. The following properties apply to frmChild and frmMDI:

```
frmChild.MDIChild = True
frmMDI.Caption = "Main MDI Window"
```

The **frmMDI** menu is intentionally simple because it only appears when there are no open child windows:

&File	mnuFile
E&xit	mnuFileExit
&Window	mnuWindow
&New	mnuWindowNew

The **frmChild** window has the following menu:

&Window	mnuWindow
&New	mnuWindowNew
&Cascade	mnuCascade
A&rrange Icons	mnuArrange
&Tile	mnuWinTile
&Horizontally	mnuTileHoriz
&Vertically	mnuTileVert
&All Windows	mnuAllWindows
&Minimize	mnuWinMinimize
&Close	mnuWinCloseAll
&Restore	mnuWinRestore

The WindowList option should be checked. At run time, this causes a list of all open child windows to be displayed at the bottom of the menu.

3.6.3 Program Implementation

Here is a complete listing of Module1. The Main subroutine is the project's startup procedure:

```
Const MaxWin As Integer = 20
Public ChildWindow(1 To MaxWin) As frmChild
Public WinCount As Integer
```

The startup procedure, **Main**, shows frmMDI as a modeless window because that is the only way MDI forms can be shown:

```
Public Sub Main()
  WinCount = 0
  frmMDI.Show vbModeless
End Sub
```

OpenNewWindow creates a new frmChild object and assigns it to the ChildWindow array:

```
Public Sub OpenNewWindow()
'Create and open a new child window.
  If WinCount = MaxWin Then
```

```
        MsgBox "Cannot create any more windows", _
            vbInformation, ""
        Exit Sub
    End If
    WinCount = WinCount + 1
    Set ChildWindow(WinCount) = New frmChild
    ChildWindow(WinCount).Caption = "Window " & WinCount
    ChildWindow(WinCount).Show vbModeless
End Sub

Public Sub RemoveAllWindows()
'Loop through the ChildWindow array and unload
'all windows.
    Dim j As Integer
    For j = 1 To WinCount
      Unload ChildWindow(j)
    Next j
    WinCount = 0
End Sub
```

SetAllWindowState sets the WindowState property of all the child windows to the value passed in the parameter **stateVal** as vbMaximized, vbMinimized, or vbNormal:

```
Public Sub SetAllWindowState(stateVal As Integer)
'Loop through the ChildWindow array and set the
'windowstate of each one
    Dim j As Integer
    For j = 1 To WinCount
      ChildWindow(j).WindowState = stateVal
    Next j
End Sub
```

MDI Parent Form. This is a listing of the frmMDI (parent) form:

```
Private Sub mnuFileExit_Click()
    End
End Sub

Private Sub mnuWindowNew_Click()
    OpenNewWindow
End Sub
```

MDI Child Form. This is a listing of the frmChild form:

```
Private Sub Img_Click()
    OpenImageFile
End Sub

Private Sub mnuFileOpen_Click()
    OpenImageFile
End Sub

Private Sub mnuWindowNew_Click()
```

Chap 3: Objects and Collections 103

```
    OpenNewWindow
End Sub

Private Sub mnuArrange_Click()
   frmMDI.Arrange vbArrangeIcons
End Sub

Private Sub mnuCascade_Click()
   frmMDI.Arrange vbCascade
End Sub

Private Sub mnuFileExit_Click()
   RemoveAllWindows
   End
End Sub

Private Sub mnuTileHoriz_Click()
   frmMDI.Arrange vbTileHorizontal
End Sub

Private Sub mnuTileVert_Click()
   frmMDI.Arrange vbTileVertical
End Sub

Private Sub mnuWinMinimize_Click()
   SetAllWindowState vbMinimized
End Sub

Private Sub mnuWinCloseAll_Click()
   RemoveAllWindows
End Sub

Private Sub mnuWinRestore_Click()
   SetAllWindowState vbNormal
End Sub

Private Sub OpenImageFile()
'Let the user open a graphic image (bitmap or
'metafile).
   On Error GoTo OpenImage1
   With cmdialog1
      .DialogTitle = "Open Bitmap or Metafile"
      .CancelError = True
      .filename = "*.bmp;*.wmf"
      .Filter = "Bitmaps(*.bmp;*.wmf)|*.bmp;*.wmf"
      .ShowOpen
      Img = LoadPicture(.filename)
      Me.Caption = .FileTitle
   End With
OpenImage1:
   'user clicked Cancel--no action taken.
End Sub
```

3.7 Review Questions

The following questions refer to control arrays and form arrays:

1. What advantages does a control array have over explicitly named controls? (For example, an array of text boxes.)
2. How may a control array be created in *design* mode?
3. How may a control array be created at runtime?
4. What are Visual Basic's object type names for check boxes, command buttons, and option buttons?
5. Assuming that **frmAuthor** was a form in the current project, write a statement that assigns a reference to the form to an object variable called **aForm**.
6. How can declared constants help to make a control array of text boxes more self-documenting? Assume that the text boxes correspond to fields in a file.
7. Show an example of creating a new instance of a form and assigning it to an object variable.
8. Show an example of a procedure that has a form variable as a parameter.
9. Write a loop that creates a control array of 10 command buttons, assigns values to their captions, and makes all of the buttons visible.

The following questions refer to the MixUp game in Section 3.2:

10. What does the LoadPicture function do?
11. If the Picture properties of two identical bitmaps are compared, will the picture properites be equal?
12. How are the two timer controls used in this program?
13. Why is it important for the Index properties of the Image controls to exactly match the indexes of the command buttons?
14. How does the program determine if two images are identical?
15. What does the program do when the two selected images match?
16. What does the program do when the two selected images do not match?
17. Which statement in the program ensures that a different sequence of images will be generated each time the program is run?
18. What is the purpose of the **currImage** variable?
19. What is the purpose of the **image1Index** and **image2Index** variables?
20. Why shouldn't the **tmrButton** control be enabled in *design* mode?
21. How can you prevent the user from clicking on more than two buttons in rapid succession?
22. How can the program determine when the game is over?

The following questions refer to collections:

23. What is the purpose of the built-in **Forms** collection?

24. What assumption does the following loop make about the controls on the current form? Might this loop cause a runtime error?

    ```
    Dim j As Integer
    For j = 0 To Controls.Count - 1
      Controls(j).Text = ""
    Next j
    ```

25. Write a For-Each statement that iterates through all of the controls on a form.

26. Can the key value in a collection be a String, Long, or Single data type?

27. In a collection containing social security numbers and names of people, which field (ssn or name) is likely to be the key field? Why?

28. What problem might there be with a collection that uses last names of people as keys?

29. Can members of a collection be accessed randomly? How about sequentially?

30. Can a collection contain objects of different types?

31. Describe the meaning of each parameter in the Collection.Add method.

32. In the Collection.Add method, which parameter is required?

33. Describe the Collection.Item method and show an example.

34. What is the lowest index value in a user-defined collection?

35. When resizing the controls on a form, why is it important to calculate the ratio between the old form width and the new form width?

The following questions refer to the Glossary program in Section 3.4:

36. Does Visual Basic generate a runtime error when duplicate key values are inserted into a collection?

37. How does a program know when the Item method in a collection fails to find a matching key?

38. When iterating through a collection, what happens if you try to repeatedly remove the member in position 1?

The following questions refer to random-access files, in Section 3.5:

39. What is the single greatest advantage that random-access files have over sequential files?

40. What restriction applies to random-access files that does not apply to sequential files?

41. What is the lowest record number in a random-access file?

42. Can a random-access file be open for input and output at the same time?

43. How practical is it for a single random-access file to have two different record formats?
44. Why is it useful to leave some empty space at the end of each random-access file record?
45. If record number 100 is saved in an empty random-access file and the record length is 50, how large will the file be?
46. In the Customer Accounts program, what user-defined type was created?

The following questions refer to MDI Applications, in Section 3.6:

47. Why is a MDI parent window called a *container*?
48. In the sample MDI program what type of object was placed in each instance of the MDI child window?
49. What happens to the menu on an MDI parent window when one of the MDI child windows is activated?
50. Why was it useful to create an array of MDI child windows in the program?

3.8 Chapter Exercises

3.8.1 Resizing Controls on a Form

We showed an example in this chapter of a procedure that horizontally resizes the controls on a form. Improve the ResizeControls procedure so that it also resizes controls in the vertical direction. Use a test program to demonstrate your procedure.

3.8.2 Glossary Program

Modify the Glossary Program presented in Section 3.4 so that if new entries have been added to the glossary, the program prompts the user to save the glossary when the program exits. Use a File/Save common dialog control, to allow the user to select the name of the file that will hold the revised glossary.

3.8.3 The Buttons Control Array

Make some improvements to the program in section 3.1.4 that created an array of command buttons:

- Shuffle the order of the button captions.
- Resize the buttons when the user uses the mouse to resize the form.
- Ask the user to enter the number of buttons that will be displayed. Then arrange the buttons in separate rows, ten to a row.
- Let the user unload the buttons from the form before the program ends.

3.8.4 Sorted Collection

Write a program that contains a sorted collection of Employee records. Sort the collection on the idNumber field, which is the key for each item. The data value to be inserted is the employee's last name:

```
Dim idNumber As String * 9
Dim lastName As String * 30
```

Creating a sorted collection is not as difficult as it sounds. The trick is to create an Insert procedure that will place each new item in the proper position in the collection. To get you started in the right direction, the following program creates a sorted collection of names. Of course, there are no key fields in this example, so it will have to be modified before it can be applied to Employee records:

```
Dim coll As Collection

Public Sub Main()
   Set coll = New Collection
   Insert "Jones"
   Insert "Smith"
   Insert "Baker"
   Insert "Adams"

   'Display the collection:
   Dim obj As Variant
   For Each obj In coll
     Debug.Print obj
   Next obj
End Sub

Public Sub Insert(st As String)
'Insert string in alphabetical order.
   Dim j As Integer
   For j = 1 To coll.Count
     If st < coll.item(j) Then
        coll.Add st, , j    'insert before pos j
        Exit Sub
     End If
   Next j
   coll.Add st    'insert at end
End Sub
```

3.8.5 Indexed Random-Access File

Combine your knowledge of random-access files and collections to create an index for the Customer Accounts random-access file in Section 3.5.4. The file should be indexed on the customer ID field.

You no longer have to use a numeric customer ID as the record number. Instead, each customer ID must be a string containing exactly six digits. Add at least ten records such as the following to the file:

```
Record
Num        ID number      Name
1          000111         Beaudoin, Mike
2          000120         Adams, Bill
3          001200         Charles, Anne
4          020302         Davidson, Gonzalo
5          (etc.)         (etc.)
```

Build a collection called **Index** that contains entries in which the ID number is the key and the record number is the member:

Member	Key
1	000111
2	000120
3	001200
4	020302

When the user enters a customer ID and clicks the Get button, your program should look up the ID number in the index and retrieve the person's record number. Using the record number, read the correct record from the random-access file and display the customer's information. When the program exits, save the index in a text file. When the program starts up again, read the index file back into the Index collection.

3.8.6 MixUp Game

Make the following improvements to the MixUp Game that was presented in Section 3.2:

- Let the user choose from several difficulty levels. At higher levels, the timer delay could be decreased; a different set of icons could be loaded that contains pictures that are very similar. For example, Visual Basic is shipped with icons representing different phases of the moon, which might be quite challenging.
- Create a file containing the best scores by players of the game. Perhaps the twenty players with the lowest time values could have their names displayed in a "hall of fame" window.
- Rather than storing the icons in separate files, place them in an ImageList control.
- Let the user select the number of buttons and images to be used. You would have to expand the control arrays at runtime.

3.8.7 Mozart MDI Application

Use Version 3 of the Mozart Music Sales program in Chapter 2 as a basis for this project. Place the invoice in an MDI child window. Allow the user to edit and create two or three invoices at the same time, each in a separate window. If the user does not save an invoice, its corresponding invoice number is dropped.

3.8.8 Mozart Music User-Defined Types

Enhance the previous exercise as follows:

- Create a user-defined type that represents a single item in an invoice. For example:

```
Type InvoiceItem
   skuNumber As Long
   title As String
   price As Currency
End Type
```

- Create a user-defined type for the invoice itself and let it contain an array of InvoiceItem objects:

```
Const MaxItemCount As Integer = 20

Type Invoice
   invoiceID As Long
   invoiceDate As Date
   salesPerson As String
   ItemList(0 To MaxItemCount) As InvoiceItem
   itemCount As Integer
   totalAmount As Currency
   tax As Currency
   netAmount As Currency      'totalAmount + tax
End Type
```

Notice that itemCount keeps track of how many items have been added to the invoice. Enclosing all invoice-related variables in a user-defined data type is a good idea. For example, it makes it easier to track down the variables, and it is easier to pass the variables as a single procedure argument.

> *Design Tip:* User-defined types are an important step in the direction of object-oriented programming. The concept behind object-oriented *classes* is that they are essentially user-defined types with additional capabilities and protections.

3.8.9 Classical Music CD Catalog

Anyone who collects classical music CDs often encounters an annoying problem: it is nearly impossible to remember exactly which recordings of which compositions are in the collection. To help remedy this problem, you can create a cataloging program suited to your needs.

There are a number of shareware programs for cataloging CDs available on the Internet and other online services, but nearly all are oriented towards popular music. For example, they often represent an entire album as a single data entity. Or, they organize data entries according to star performers. The composers of the songs themselves may only be a footnote.

In the proposed CD cataloging system, each composition is assigned a separate entry. Your instructor will determine whether the information is to be stored in (1) a sequential file, (2) a random-access file, or (3) a database.

From the user's point of view, the greatest inconvenience in using a music cataloging program is having to enter a large amount of data. To help reduce typing for the user, you can use combo boxes for the composer, instrumentation, soloist, and conductor fields. Store these values in text files or database tables, and load the combo boxes at runtime. New names can be added to the files whenever necessary.

Figure 16 shows a sample of the program's main window; feel free to design a more interesting one of your own.

Figure 16. Music CD Catalog, Main Window.

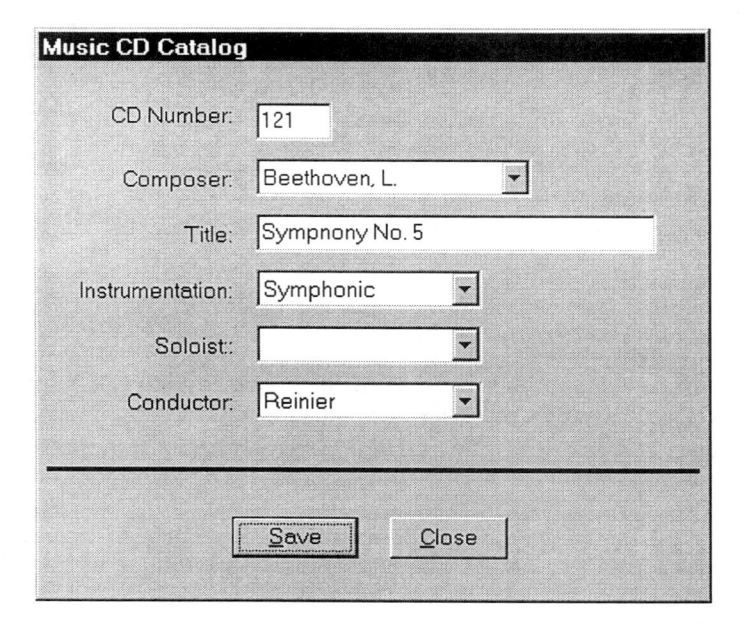

Not all entries will have a soloist, as is the case in this sample containing Symphony No. 5 by Beethoven. The Save button saves the CD information in a file or database, and the Close button closes this window and ends the program.

3.8.10 Searching the Classical Music Catalog

Using the music cataloging program from the previous exercise, allow the user to search for records using any *one* of the following fields: CD number, Composer, Title, Instrumentation, Soloist, Conductor. The user should be able to select the search value from one of the combo boxes shown here. The program will then build a list of composition names and CD numbers and place it in a list box. For example, if the user wants to find all compositions by J.S. Bach, the composer's name is selected before clicking on **Find** (Figure 17).

Figure 17. Searching for a Single Composer's Compositions.

```
Music CD Catalog

        CD Number: [    ]

         Composer: [Bach, J.S.      ▼]

            Title: [                ]

    Instrumentation: [           ▼]

          Soloist: [           ▼]

        Conductor: [           ▼]

                ─────────────────

              [ Find ]  [ Save ]  [ Close ]
```

The program then builds a list of compositions by that composer. Optionally, the list can be sorted alphabetically by title (Figure 18).

Figure 18. Found: Compositions by a Single Composer.

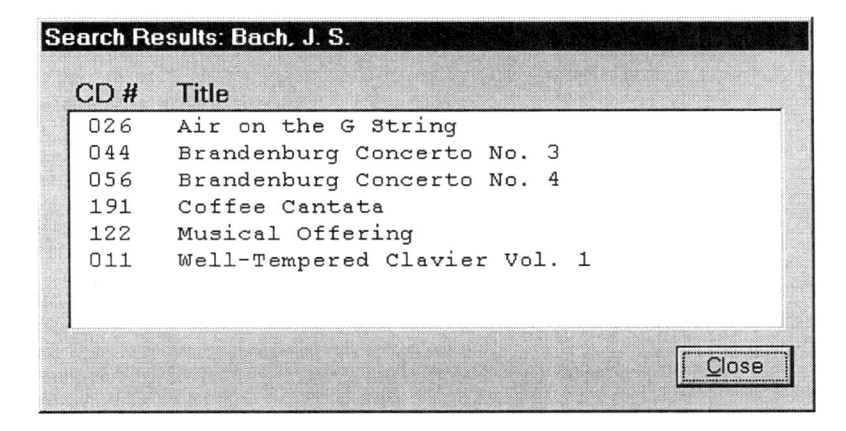

```
Search Results: Bach, J. S.

CD #    Title
026     Air on the G String
044     Brandenburg Concerto No. 3
056     Brandenburg Concerto No. 4
191     Coffee Cantata
122     Musical Offering
011     Well-Tempered Clavier Vol. 1


                                   [ Close ]
```

If the user selects one of the titles by double-clicking in the list box, the program should return to the main window and display all the details of the selected title. Suppose the user selected *Air on the G String*; the details might be displayed as in Figure 19.

Figure 19. Details of a Single Title.

[Music CD Catalog dialog box showing CD Number: 026, Composer: Bach, J.S., Title: Air on the G String, Instrumentation: Chamber, Soloist: (blank), Conductor: Mariner, with Find, Save, and Close buttons.]

3.8.11 Cleaning Equipment Rental Wizard

A *wizard* is a popular type of user interface tool used in computer applications today that guides the user through a short series of logical steps in solving a problem. Wizards are a subset of a larger class of problem-solving and advice-giving software called expert systems. In Microsoft Access, for example, the *Database Wizard* helps a user to design a new database; there are wizards to help you import and export data, build a form, and so on. Along the way, the user makes decisions that affect the wizard's path through the process. A wizard ensures that the following are done:

- A user who is new to the software will be able to build an application component or complete a multi-step task.
- Critical steps will be carried out in the correct order.
- All necessary information will be collected.
- Steps can be retraced and repeated without disturbing the logical sequencing of information.
- The user is being educated along the way; various possibilities and options are presented in a logical manner.

Cleaning Equipment Rental Wizard. For this project, you must create a program that contains an Equipment Rental Wizard. The program will gather all information needed for selecting the items to be rented, the rental duration, price, date, delivery instructions, and customer data. The program's implementation should use some of the techniques presented in this chapter, such as form and control arrays, collections, random-access files, and MDI windows.

Here are the steps to follow in filling out the rental reservation form:

1. Select the device to be rented. The program should help the user narrow down the choices. Present a list of common household tasks, let the user select one, and ask the user pertinent questions about the scope or size of the task.

2. Enter the number of rental days. Various options might be presented, showing how a discounted rate can apply as the rental duration grows.

3. Select home delivery or customer pick-up. Home delivery might carry a surcharge for the larger items.

4. Verify that the customer was trained in the use of the equipment (this might be an insurance requirement for the store).

5. Get the customer's name, address, phone, and credit card data.

6. Compute the total rental charge, including sales tax and delivery.

7. Print a customer invoice.

Equipment. To avoid making the wizard become too complicated, limit the choices to the following equipment:

    300 psi water pressure cleaner
    1000 psi water pressure cleaner
    10-gallon steam industrial-quality carpet cleaner
    5-gallon steam carpet cleaner for medium-sized jobs
    hand-held carpet cleaner for small jobs
    10-gallon shop vacuum
    home carpet vacuum
    floor polisher

3.8.12 Yachting Regatta - 1

The SeaWind Yacht Club keeps track of the results of multiple sailboat races that together make up a single regatta. Write an MDI application that lets the user display and modify information for several races and several sailboats. Create separate MDI child windows for RaceInfo and BoatInfo, both user-defined types. Store the RaceInfo objects in a collection that has a key built from a combination of each boat number and race number. Store the BoatInfo objects in a collection that has a key based on the boat number.

The data for these collections may be read from one of the following types of files, to be determined by your instructor: sequential files, random-access files, database tables.

Create a user-defined type called **RaceInfo** that contains the fields shown in Table 1.

Table 1. The RaceInfo Table.

Field	Data Type	Description
Boat Number	Integer	Identifies the boat. Matches one of the boat numbers in the *BoatInfo* file.
Race Number	Integer	Unique for each race (1..10).
Starting Time	Date/Time	Time when the race started.
Finishing Time	Date/Time	Time when the race ended.
Handicap Minutes	Integer	Number of minutes to be added to the boat's actual completion time.
Adjusted Time	Integer	Length of time taken to complete the race, adjusted by the boat's handicap.
Comments	String	Notes concerning special race conditions or pending protests involving this boat.

Create a user-defined type called **BoatInfo** that contains the following fields, and store the records in a random-access file:

Field	Data Type	Description
Boat Number	Integer	Matches boat numbers in the *RaceInfo* file.
Boat Name	String	The boat's name.
Owner Name	String	Last name, first initial.
Handicap Factor	Single	0.0 to 2.00, used when calculating the Handicap Minutes in the *RaceInfo* table.

3.8.13 Yachting Regatta - 2

Yacht2

Continue the the Yachting Regatta program from the previous exercise. Provide the following additional features:

- When displaying the RaceInfo window, let the user quickly display information about the current boat by selecting *BoatInfo Window* from the menu.
- Add the following fields to the **RaceInfo** user-defined type:

Field	Data Type	Description
Race date	Date	Date of the race.
Scratch Boat Time	Long	Number of minutes estimated for completion of the race by a pre-selected boat, called the "scratch boat".

- Calculate the *handicap minutes* and *adjusted time* for each boat in each race, using the formula described in the next paragraph. Display these values in the *RaceInfo* window (these two fields were originally left empty.)

Handicap. In sailboat races involving boats of different sizes and configurations, boats vary greatly in their speed. Therefore, a handicapping system is used that will give each boat a more or less equal chance of winning the race. In this program, we will calculate the handicap minutes (HCM) for a boat in a particular race by multiplying the scratch boat time (SBT) by the boat's handicap factor (HCF). A fast sailboat would have a large handicap factor, and a slow boat would have a small one. Here are some examples of calculations:

Race #	Boat #	SBT	HCF	HCM
1	1	180	.8	144
1	2	180	.5	90
1	3	180	.1	18
2	1	60	.8	48
2	2	60	.5	30
2	3	60	.1	6

For the same boat, more handicap minutes are applied to a longer race than a shorter one.

3.8.14 Yachting Regatta - 3

Using the Yachting Regatta programs from the previous exercises, calculate and display the ranking of each boat for each race. For each race, the boat in first place will have the lowest adjusted time. The adjusted time (AT) is calculated from the starting time (ST), finishing time (FT) and handicap minutes (HCM) as follows: AT = (FT - ST) + HCM. For each race, produce a table such as the following:

Results for Race # 1:

Boat Name	Rank	Adjusted Time
Blue Star	1	220
Windward Passage	2	270
Ticonderoga	3	275
Kialoa II	4	280
Queen Mab	5	310
Novia del Mar	6	400

3.8.15 Yachting Regatta - 4

Using the Yachting Regatta programs from the previous exercises, calculate the overall ranking of each boat, inclusive of all races. The boat's rank in a particular race determines the number of points counted against the boat. The boat with the highest overall ranking is the one with the lowest overall points. For example, if boat X's rank in four races was 1, 1, 4,

5, it would have 11 overall points. If boat Y's rank in four races was 2, 3, 3, 4, it would have 12 overall points. Therefore, boat X would be awarded a higher overall ranking.

3.8.16 Customer Accounts

Implement an index for the Customer Accounts program. For convenience, each customer's ID number was directly used as a record number. Unfortunately, using customer ID numbers as record numbers results in a great deal of wasted space if the file contains few records. If a file contained 500 customers, for example, 95% of the disk space used by the file would be empty.

A better solution would be to create an index for the file, and use the index to keep track of the positions of the records. The index, which could be implmented as an array, would contain both the customer ID numbers and their corresponding record numbers. Table 2 shows a possible sequence of customer numbers as they are added to the file.

Table 2. Customer Records Added to the File.

Customer ID	Record Number
1000	1
1234	2
1111	3
2021	4
1046	5
1872	6
2649	7
...	...

The result is that very little space is wasted. A customer ID can be modified without moving the record to a new position, and records can be deleted by setting the customer ID to a predefined value such as **0000** (see Table 3). Then, when a new record is inserted, the index can be searched for the first available position. A new customer record could be inserted at record position 5.

Table 3. Making Space for Inserted Records.

Customer ID	Record Number
1000	1
1234	2
1111	3
2021	4
0000	5
1872	6
2649	7
...	...

4 Object-Oriented Programming

Chapter Contents

Classes and Objects
    Object-Oriented Design
    Class Modules
    Creating Instances of a Class
    Properties
    Event Handlers
    Methods
    New and Set Statements
Student Class Example
    Program Design
    Program Implementation
Student Collection Class
    Program Design
    The Main Form
    The clsStudent Class
    The clsStudentCollection Class
Doctors Office Scheduling Program
    Program Specifications
    Program Design
    Program Implementation
    The clsPatient Class
    The clsApptCalendar Class
    The clsAppointment Class
    The frmInput Form
Review Questions
Chapter Exercises

4.1 Classes and Objects

One of the most exciting developments in computer software over the last ten years has been *object-oriented programming* (OOP). It is a way of designing and coding applications that has led to using interchangeable software components to build larger programs. Object-oriented programming languages first appeared in the early 1980s, with Algol, SmallTalk, and C++. The legacy from these somewhat advanced languages is the gradual development of object-like visual tools for building programs. In Visual Basic, for example, forms, buttons, check boxes, list boxes, and other controls are ideal examples of objects. Object-oriented designs help to produce programs that lend themselves well to ongoing development and expansion.

A *class* is a program structure that defines a distinguishing set of characteristics that identifies a new type. To use an analogy from nature, mammals in the cat family (*Felidae*) have similar characteristics: sharp claws, whiskers, paws, and a carnivorus diet. We could speak of the *Felidae* class, and individual instances of cats would be called *objects,* or *instances*. Similarly, in a computer program, all class instances would share common characteristics. Visual Basic controls and forms, for example, are classes. In the Toolbox window, each type of control represents a class. When you select the CommandButton control from the toolbox and place it on a form, you are creating an *instance* of the CommandButton class. An instance is also called an *object* (Figure 1).

Figure 1. CommandButton Class and CommandButton Object.

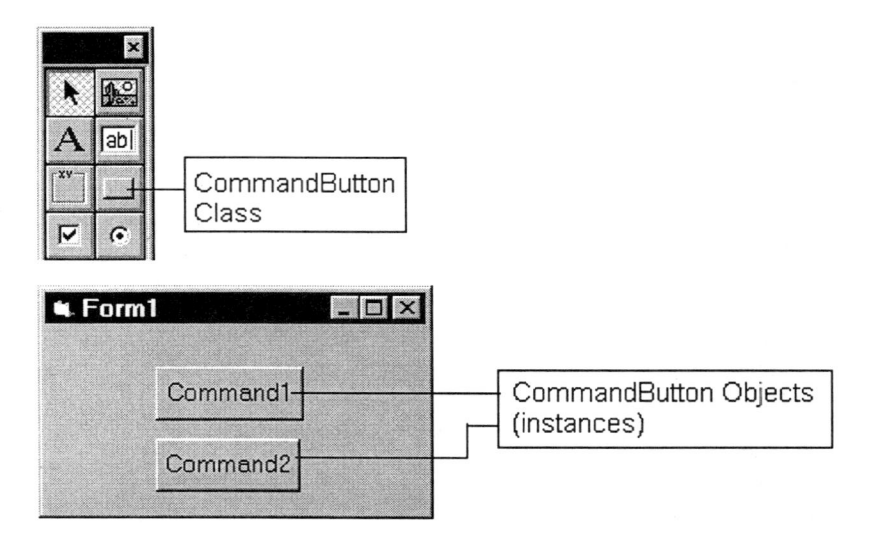

Properties and Methods. The way a program communicates with each object is determined by the properties and methods defined in the object's class. The CommandButton class, for example, has *properties* such as Left, Top, Caption, and Name. Each CommandButton object contains its own unique set of property values. In the example just shown, the two command buttons had different values in their Top, and Caption properties. *Methods,* on the other hand, are shared by all instances of a class; so the Move method in the CommandButton class is the same for all CommandButton objects. What about event handlers? We have seen that the Click event procedures for different buttons usually contain different code. This shows us that each object can have a unique set of event procedures.

4.1.1 Object-Oriented Design

Object-oriented programming is not just a matter of randomly dropping classes and objects into a program. The real challenge is to design classes in such a way that the resulting objects will effectively cooperate and communicate. The primary goal is to address the needs of the application, or problem being solved. A secondary goal is to design classes that can outlive the current application and possibly be useful in future programs.

The first step after creating the program specifications is to analyze the application requirements. Object-oriented analysis, as it is called, can often start with a detailed description of the problem to be solved. A term often applied to this process is called *finding the classes*. In every problem and every application, there are classes waiting to be found. It is the designer's job to discover just what those classes are. A famous sculptor once said that inside every block of marble, there is a work of art waiting to be discovered by the artist.

Finding the Classes. Classes are the fundamental building blocks of object-oriented applications. When designing object-oriented programs, we first select classes that reflect physical entities in the application domain. For example, the user of a record-keeping program for a college might describe the application's requirements as follows:

> We need to keep a **list of students** that lets us track the courses they have completed. Each student has a **transcript** that contains all information about completed courses. At the end of each semester, we will calculate the grade point average of each **student**. At times, users will search for a particular **course** taken by a student.

Notice the highlighted nouns and noun phrases in this description: list of students, transcript, student, and course. These would ordinarily be classes in our program's design.

Looking for Control Structures. Classes can also be discovered in the description of processing done by an application, or in the description of control structures. For example, what if the application involved scheduling of college classes for students? Here is another possible description from the program specifications:

> We also want to schedule classes for students, using the college's master schedule to determine the times and room numbers for each student's class. When the optimal arrangement of classes for each student has been determined, the student's class schedule will be printed and distributed.

In this description, we anticipate a need for a controlling agent that could be implemented as a class. We might call it **Scheduler**, a class that matches up each student's schedule with the college master schedule.

Describing the Classes. The next step, after finding the classes in an application, is to describe the classes in terms of attributes and operations. *Attributes* are characteristics of each object that will be implemented as properties; attributes describe the properties that all objects of the same class have in common. Classes also have *operations*, which are actions that class objects may perform, or messages to which they can respond. Operations are implemented as class methods. Using the record-keeping application that we described earlier, Table 1 describes some of the attributes and operations that will be important.

Table 1. Sample Attributes and Operations.

Class	Attributes (properties)	Operations (methods)
Student	ID, LastName, FirstName, Transcript	Print, Input
StudentList	AllStudents, Count	Add, Remove, FindStudent
Course	Semester, Name, Grade, Credits	Print, Input
Transcript	CourseList, Count	Print, Search, CalcGradeAvg

The sets of attributes and operations are often incomplete during the early stages of design because it is difficult to anticipate all the requirements of the application. As a design develops, the need often arises for additional properties and methods that improve communication between objects. Rather that being seen as a weakness, however, one of the strengths of the object-oriented design process is that it accommodates ongoing modifications.

Interface and Implementation. The class *interface* is the portion that is visible to the outside world, that is, to the users of the class. The interface provides a way for class users to communicate (send messages) to class objects. In Visual Basic, we create the interface by declaring public properties and methods.

The class *implementation* is the portion of the class that is hidden from class users; it is created from private instance variables, private properties, and private methods. The hiding of data and procedures inside a class is achieved through a process called *encapsulation*. In this, it might be helpful to visualize the class as a "capsule" around its data and procedures.

Inheritance. In passing, we will mention that Visual Basic is not completely object-oriented, primarily because it leaves out an essential feature: inheritance. *Inheritance* lets programmers create new classes that inherit, or derive characteristics of existing classes. For example, you might want to start with a Student class that has only general information for all types of students. Then specialized types of students might require the creation of classes such as GraduateStudent, ExchangeStudent, StudentEmployee, and so on. These new classes would share all the characteristics of the Student class, and they would each add new characteristics that made them specialized.

4.1.2 Class Modules

In Visual Basic, you define a class by creating a *class module.* A class module is a module that contains variables, properties, and methods. The properties and methods are implemented as public procedures, and variables are generally private. (The Visual Basic documentation refers to a class module as a *ClassModule object*, but in this case, the use of the word "object" tends to obscure the distinction between a class and an object.)

To add a class module to a project in Visual Basic 5, select **Add Class Module** from the Project menu. In Visual Basic 4, select **Class Module** from the Insert menu. After adding a class module, bring up the Properties window and set the **Name** property of the class to a descriptive name (such as clsStudent). Your class module will be saved as part of the current project.

Once a class module has been created, program statements can be used to create instances of the class. Subject to memory limitations, you can create as many instances of the same class as you wish. The same program may also contain multiple class modules, each defining a different type of object.

> *Programming Tip:* In our sample programs, names of class modules always begin with a "cls" prefix. This is not required by Visual Basic, but the naming convention helps when looking at program source code. So we choose names such as clsStudent, clsSchedule, and clsTranscript.

The following is a suggested layout for class modules. Nothing in Visual Basic dictates this order, but programs are usually easier to read if the source code is arranged in a consistent manner:

    Comments about the class
    Constant declarations
    Instance Variables
    Public Properties and Methods
    Private Properties and Methods

Here is a short class called **clsEmployee**, containing examples of each type of class element:

```
'The clsEmployee class encapsulates data
'relating to a single employee.

Option Explicit
Const MaxSalary As Currency = 100000    'Constant declaration
Private idNumberP As Long               'Private instance variables
Private lastNameP As String
Private modifiedP As Boolean

'********* Public Properties and Methods **********

Public Property Get IdNumber() As Long
End Property

Public Property Let IdNumber( idval As Long )
End Property

Public Sub CalcAvgerageSalary()
End Sub

'********* Private Properties and Methods **********

Private Property Get Modified() As Boolean
End Property
```

```
Private Property Let Modified( newval As Boolean )
End Property

Private Sub Class_Initialize()
End Sub

Private Sub Class_Terminate()
End Sub

Private Function GetRecentPayrate() As Single
End Function
```

4.1.3 Creating Instances of a Class

To create an instance of a class, you first declare a variable of the class type. You then use the **New** statement to create a class instance and the **Set** statement to assign the instance to a variable. For example, we create instances of the clsStudent class called **s1** and **s2**:

```
Dim s1 As clsStudent, s2 As clsStudent
Set s1 = New clsStudent
Set s2 = New clsStudent
```

When an object is no longer needed, it can be removed by setting its variable to **Nothing** (a Visual Basic keyword):

```
Set s1 = Nothing
```

This releases all memory used by the object. In general it's always a good idea to remove objects that are no longer needed so the program can use the memory for new objects.

> ***Programming Tip:*** You can declare an object variable, create a class instance and assign the object reference to the variable all in the same statement:
>
> ```
> Dim aStudent As New clsStudent
> ```

You can use a loop to create an array of objects:

```
Dim st(1 To 10) As clsStudent
Dim j As Integer
For j = 1 To 10
   Set st(j) = New clsStudent
Next j
```

And another loop to release the memory used by the array:

```
Dim j As Integer
For j = 1 To 10
   Set st(j) = Nothing
Next j
```

If an object is created inside a procedure, it is removed automatically when the procedure ends. This is called *going out of scope*. An object declared at the Form level is automatically released when all references to the form are set to Nothing.

At the moment, we only create instances of classes contained in the same project. In a later chapter we will show how to create an instance of a class that is in another program. Such a program is called an *ActiveX Server*.

4.1.4 Properties

To the user of an object, a *property* acts like a data value belonging to the object. Actually, a property consists of one or two procedures that control access to variables that have been encapsulated in the object. The variables are called *instance variables*, and are declared in the class module that defined the object.

Let's assume that the clsStudent class has three properties called IdNumber, LastName, and FirstName. An application program can create a new clsStudent object and assign a value to its IdNumber property:

```
Dim stu As clsStudent
Set stu = New clsStudent
stu.IdNumber = "12345"
```

The same property can also be retrieved and printed:

```
Debug.Print stu.IdNumber
```

In the clsStudent module's declarations section, we declare the instance variables idNumberP, lastNameP, and firstNameP, having nearly the same names as the properties. The letter P appended to each name indicates that it is a private instance variable:

```
Option Explicit
Const IDSize = 6
Private idNumberP As String, lastNameP As String, _
        firstNameP As String
```

> ***Programming Tip:*** To prevent a name clash between instance variables and their corresponding property names, it is a good idea to append a special character to each instance variable name. One advantage to this approach is that it is easy to spot instance variable names in program code. In the examples here, we will append a trailing 'P' to each instance variable name, but other programmers use similar techniques that are just as good.

Let's create two property functions for each variable that set and return its value. To create a property, select the Insert/Procedure menu command. When the Insert Procedure dialog box appears, type in a name for the procedure and click on the Property option. First, create a property called **IdNumber.** The *All Local variables as Statics* check box, if checked, would allow all local variables inside the procedure to retain their values between procedure calls. At the moment we have no need of this option. The following procedures are automatically pasted into the class module. They are incomplete, but they provide a framework that you can fill in:

```
Public Property Get IdNumber()

End Property

Public Property Let IdNumber(vNewValue)

End Property
```

Get is a keyword that indicates that the procedure returns the value of the property. It is a function, so we specify the return type and place an assignment statement in the procedure body that returns the value of the instance variable called idNumberP:

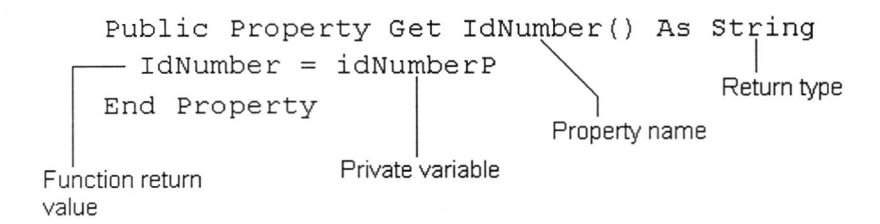

```
Public Property Get IdNumber() As String
    IdNumber = idNumberP
End Property
```

- Function return value
- Private variable
- Property name
- Return type

Let is a keyword that indicates that the procedure assigns a value to the property. This is how we might implement the procedure, which assigns the **id** parameter to the instance variable:

```
Private idNumberP As String
    .
    .
    .
Public Property Let IdNumber(id as String)
    idNumberP = id
End Property
```

You do not have to use the default property names. For example, you could rename the Let property to SetIdNumber. If you want a property to be read-only, just omit the Let procedure for that property.

Public Properties, Private Instance Variables. Properties are part of the class interface and instance variables are not. The last thing we would want is for the user of an object to directly modify an instance variable, because we would have no ability to prevent invalid values from being placed in the object. This is why instance variables are declared *private*, making them hidden inside the object. It is much easier to debug programs in which we enforce this hiding, because we often include error trapping in property/Let procedures. In the IdNumber property, for example, we might include some error trapping to make sure **id** has the correct number of digits:

```
Const IDSize As Integer = 6

Public Property Let IdNumber(id as String)
    id = Trim$(id)
```

```
    If Len(id) = IDSize Then
       idNumberP = id
    Else
       MsgBox "Error: Student ID number must be " _
           & IDSize & " digits long.", _
           vbInformation, ""
    End If
End Property
```

Of course, we could also check each character to make sure it was a digit.

The following statements create a clsStudent object and set its properties:

```
Dim aStudent As clsStudent
Set aStudent = New clsStudent
aStudent.IdNumber = "123456"
aStudent.LastName = "Baker"
aStudent.FirstName = "Samuel"
```

The following statements get the properties of aStudent and copy them to labels on the current form:

```
lblIdNumber.Caption = aStudent.IdNumber
lblLastName.Caption = aStudent.LastName
lblFirstName.Caption = aStudent.FirstName
```

4.1.5 Event Handlers

There are two standard event handlers associated with each class object. **Class_Initialize** is automatically invoked by Visual Basic whenever an object is created, and **Class_Terminate** is automatically invoked when an object is destroyed. Neither procedure may contain any parameters or return type. Here, for example, we set properties to default values when an object is created:

```
Private Sub Class_Initialize()
   IdNumber = "000000"
   LastName = "(unknown)"
   FirstName = "(unknown)"
End Sub
```

In the following **Terminate** event handler, we print a debugging message:

```
Private Sub Class_Terminate()
   Debug.Print "Student object terminated."
End Sub
```

In most cases, the Terminate event provides an opportunity to close files and release memory that was allocated by this class object.

4.1.6 Methods

In addition to properties, class modules can contain methods. A *method* is a procedure that acts upon an object. Methods and properties together form what we call the *class interface.* An interface is a simplified language or protocol that users of an object use when communicating with it. In fact, calling a method is often described as *message passing.* For example, the debug window has a method called Print; when we pass a Print message to the Debug object, it prints a string into the window:

```
Debug.Print "The value of N is ";N
```

You can create other useful methods that enhance the class. For example, the following **AsString** method converts the clsStudent properties to a single string with an end-of-line character after each:

```
Public Function AsString() As String
'Return a string representation of the current
'Student object:
  AsString = "ID Number:  " + IdNumber + vbCrLf + _
     "Last Name:  " & LastName + vbCrLf + _
     "First Name: " & FirstName + vbCrLf
End Function
```

4.1.7 New and Set Statements

The **Set** statement assigns an object to a variable. Rather than copy the entire object, however, a *reference* to the object is assigned. You might think of a reference as a kind of alias—another name for the same object. This means that no new copy of the object has been created. For example, we might assign frmMain to myForm, using the Set statement:

```
Dim myForm As Form
Set myForm = frmMain
```

both myForm and frmMain refer to the same form. When we change the caption of myForm, we also change the caption of frmMain:

```
myForm.Caption = "This Caption has Changed"
```

On the other hand, the **New** statement creates a new instance of an object type. So if you combine New with Set, the receiving variable refers to a separate object. In the next example, the caption of frmMain is unchanged as we show a separate form on top of the original one and change its caption:

```
Dim myForm As Form
Set myForm = New frmMain
myForm.Caption = "This Caption has Changed"
myForm.show vbModal
```

4.2 Student Class Example

4.2.1 Program Design

Let's write a short program that inputs the ID, first name, and last name of a student. There is only one class, called clsStudent. The program will create an object, fill it with data, retrieve the same data, and display the values.

The user interface is in frmMain, where the user can enter the ID, first name, and last name of a student (Figure 2). When the Get button is clicked, the data is transferred to a clsStudent object. The Clear button clears the text boxes, and the Get button retrieves the fields from the object.

Figure 2. Student Class Program, Main Form.

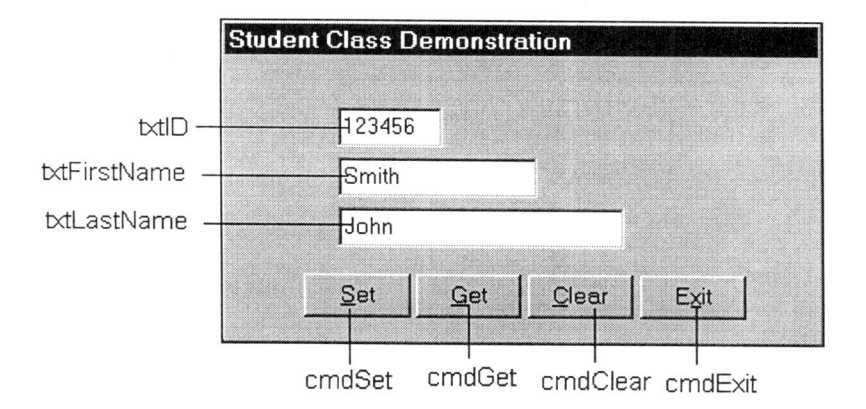

Error Trapping. If the user assigns an ID number that is not six digits long, the following message appears when the Set button is clicked:

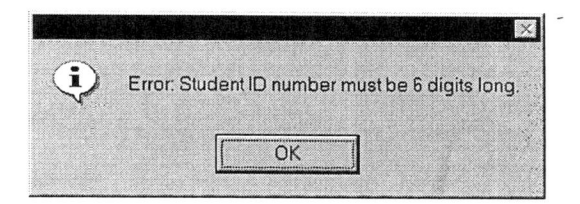

This message was generated by the property procedure inside the clsStudent class. The user can fix the error and try again until a correct value is entered. Similarly, error messages display when a blank last name or first name are entered.

4.2.2 Program Implementation

The frmMain Form. The program's window, called frmMain, is responsible for creating an instance of clsStudent that will be used for both input and output:

```
Option Explicit
Dim aStudent As clsStudent

Private Sub Form_Load()
   Set aStudent = New clsStudent
End Sub

Private Sub cmdClear_Click()
   txtID.Text = ""
   txtLastName.Text = ""
   txtFirstName.Text = ""
End Sub

Private Sub cmdExit_Click()
   Set aStudent = Nothing
   Unload Me
End Sub
```

When the **Get** button is clicked, the program retrieves the ID, FirstName, and LastName properties from aStudent, the clsStudent object:

```
Private Sub cmdGet_Click()
   txtID.Text = aStudent.ID
   txtFirstName.Text = aStudent.FirstName
   txtLastName.Text = aStudent.LastName
End Sub
```

When the **Set** button is clicked, the program copies the contents of the text boxes into the clsStudent object:

```
Private Sub cmdSet_Click()
   aStudent.ID = txtID.Text
   aStudent.FirstName = txtFirstName.Text
   aStudent.LastName = txtLastName.Text
End Sub
```

The clsStudent Class. Here is a listing of the clsStudent class source code. The three instance variables are private.

```
'Description of the clsStudent class.
Option Explicit
Private idP As String
Private lastNameP As String
Private firstNameP As String

Private Sub Class_Initialize()
   ID = "000000"
   LastName = "(unknown)"
```

Chap 4: Object-Oriented Programming

```
    FirstName = "(unknown)"
End Sub

Public Property Get ID() As String
   ID = idP
End Property
```

The **Let ID** property procedure checks the length of the ID that was passed to it:

```
Public Property Let ID(IDnum As String)
   Const IDSize = 6
   IDnum = Trim$(IDnum)
   If Len(IDnum) = IDSize Then
      idP = IDnum
   Else
      MsgBox "Error: Student ID number must be " _
              & IDSize & " digits long.", _
              vbInformation, ""
   End If
End Property

Public Property Get LastName() As String
   LastName = lastNameP
End Property
```

Similarly, we check the **LastName** property to make sure that a blank name is never assigned to the lastNameP instance variable:

```
Public Property Let LastName(aName As String)
   aName = Trim$(aName)
   If Len(aName) > 0 Then
      lastNameP = aName
   Else
      MsgBox "Error: Student's last name cannot " _
         + "be blank.", vbInformation, ""
   End If
End Property

Public Property Get FirstName() As String
   FirstName = firstNameP
End Property
```

And the **FirstName** property cannot be blank:

```
Public Property Let FirstName(aName As String)
   aName = Trim$(aName)
   If Len(aName) > 0 Then
      firstNameP = aName
   Else
      MsgBox "Error: Student's first name cannot " _
         + "be blank.", vbInformation, ""
   End If
   firstNameP = aName
```

```
End Property
```

Summary. As you can see, this program did not do very much; it is surprising, at first, that object-oriented programs seem so long. In general, this holds true, because a lot of the extra code exists to "seal off" and encapsulate the private data in classes. Next, we're going to show how a program might coordinate the use of two classes—a student class and a collection class.

4.3 Student Collection Class

Most object-oriented applications do not have just a single class; instead, they are implemented as the interaction between two or more classes. There is a name for a group of classes that work closely together: a *component*. Component classes belong together and are mutually dependent on each other.

It is often useful to use diagrams to express class relationships. In the following example, the clsStudentCollection class and clsStudent class exhibit a *containing* relationship. That is, a collection of students *contains* one or more student objects:

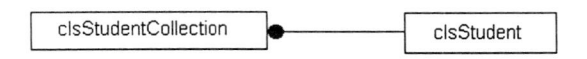

```
| clsStudentCollection |●————————| clsStudent |
```

The class that owns, or contains another object will have the solid circle at its end of the connecting line. There are quite a number of diagramming methods for class relationships, but this one was chosen for its simplicity.

4.3.1 Program Design

In this program, the user can input information for a student and have the student object added to a collection. The collection is represented by the clsStudentCollection class. The program also allows the user to search for a student either by ID number or by last name. The main window is shown in Figure 3.First, the user enters the data for several students and click on the Add button several times. Next, by clicking on Show All Students, the listing appears in Figure 4.

Figure 3. Student Collection Class, Main Window.

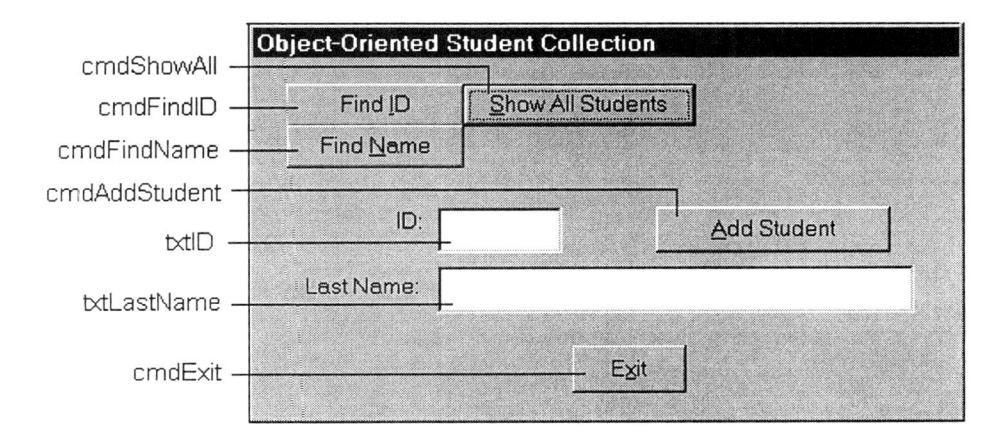

Figure 4. Displaying All Students.

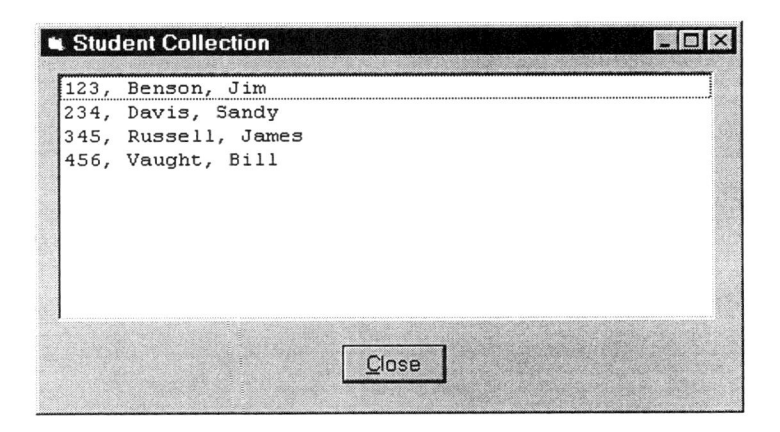

The user can enter an ID number and ask the collection to locate the matching student. The Find ID button activates the search (Figure 5). The user can also enter a last name and click on **Find Name**; this asks the collection to search for a matching student.

4.3.2 The Main Form

The code in frmMain, the startup form for this program is listed here. A new student collection object is created when the form loads:

```
Option Explicit
Dim studentList As clsStudentCollection
Dim aStudent As clsStudent

Private Sub Form_Load()
  Set studentList = New clsStudentCollection
End Sub
```

Figure 5. Searching for a Student ID.

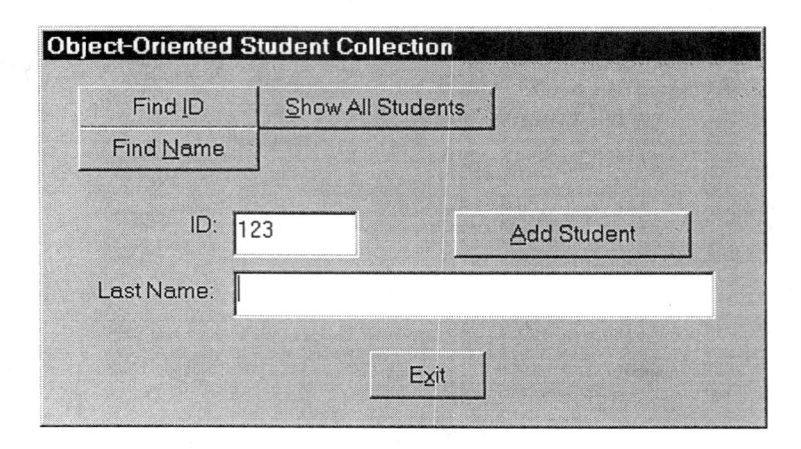

Add. To add a new student to the collection, the program creates an instance of clsStudent, sets its properties with data from text boxes on this form, and calls the Add method in the clsStudentList class:

```
Private Sub cmdAddStudent_Click()
  If Len(Trim$(txtID.Text)) = 0 Or _
     Len(Trim$(txtLastName.Text)) = 0 Then Exit Sub
  Set aStudent = New clsStudent
  aStudent.ID = txtID.Text
  aStudent.LastName = txtLastName.Text
  studentList.Add aStudent
  Set aStudent = Nothing
End Sub
```

Find an ID. To find a student, the program creates a student object, set its ID number, and calls the FindByID method in the clsStudentList class. If a value of True is returned, a text box is filled with the student's last name:

```
Private Sub cmdFindID_Click()
  Dim aStudent As New clsStudent
  aStudent.ID = Val(txtID.Text)
  If studentList.FindByID(aStudent) Then
    txtLastName.Text = aStudent.LastName
  Else
    txtLastName.Text = "(not found)"
  End If
  Set aStudent = Nothing
End Sub
```

Find a Name. To find a person by name, we call the FindByLastName method, and fill a text box with the student's ID number if found:

```
Private Sub cmdFindName_Click()
  Dim aStudent As New clsStudent
  aStudent.LastName = txtLastName.Text
  If studentList.FindByLastName(aStudent) Then
```

```
      txtID.Text = aStudent.ID
    Else
      txtID.Text = "????"
    End If
    Set aStudent = Nothing
End Sub
```

Show All. To display a list of all students, the program gets a copy of the student collection and uses a For-Each statement to fill a list box on another form (frmDisplay) with the student names and ID numbers:

```
Private Sub cmdShowAll_Click()
  Dim coll As Collection
  Set coll = studentList.Students
  For Each aStudent In coll
    frmDisplay.List1.AddItem aStudent.AsString
  Next aStudent
  frmDisplay.Show vbModal
  Set coll = Nothing
  Set aStudent = Nothing
End Sub
```

4.3.3 The clsStudent Class

Here is a listing of the clsStudent class source code. To save space, we have eliminated the student's first name from the class, and the property procedures are not checking the input values:

```
Option Explicit
Private idP As String
Private lastNameP As String

Private Sub Class_Initialize()
  ID = 0
  LastName = "(none)"
End Sub

Public Property Get ID() As String
  ID = idP
End Property

Public Property Let ID(vNewValue As String)
  idP = vNewValue
End Property

Public Property Get LastName() As String
  LastName = lastNameP
End Property

Public Property Let LastName(lname As String)
  lastNameP = lname
End Property
```

The **AsString** method returns a string representation of the object properties:

```
Public Function AsString() As String
   AsString = ID & ", " & LastName
End Function
```

4.3.4 The clsStudentCollection Class

The **clsStudentCollection** class encapsulates a Collection object, and provides methods and properties that make the collection easier to use. The collection only holds clsStudent objects. Here is a listing of the clsStudentCollection source code:

```
'The clsStudentCollection class.
Option Explicit
Private studentsP As Collection

Public Property Get Count() As Integer
'Return the number of students.
   Count = studentsP.Count
End Property
```

The **Students** property returns a reference to the collection of students, which makes it possible for the caller to have full read-write access to the collection.

```
Public Property Get Students() As Collection
'Return a reference to the student collection.
   Set Students = studentsP
End Property
```

This approach carries a certain amount of risk that the user will wipe out the collection without any knowledge on the part of the clsStudentCollection class. But exported objects such as Access, Word, and Excel also allow read/write access to their collection objects.

The **Add** method attempts to add the student to the collection. If the program attempts to add a duplicate key, a runtime error is automatically generated:

```
Public Function Add(aStudent As clsStudent) As Boolean
   On Error GoTo AddError
   studentsP.Add aStudent, aStudent.ID
   Add = True
   Exit Function
AddError:
   MsgBox Error$, vbInformation, "clsStudentCollection.Add"
   Add = False
End Function
```

The Class_Initialize event handler creates a new Collection object and assigns it to studentsP, an instance variable:

```
Private Sub Class_Initialize()
   Set studentsP = New Collection
End Sub
```

The **FindByID** method searches the collection for a matching ID, using the collection's key field. Recall that **Set** must be used when assigning a clsStudent object to **aStudent:**

```
Public Function FindByID(aStudent As clsStudent) As Boolean
  On Error GoTo NotFound
  Set aStudent = studentsP.Item(aStudent.ID)
  FindByID = True
  Exit Function
NotFound:
  FindByID = False
End Function
```

The **FindByLastName** method loops through the collection, looking for any records that match the last name of the student that was passed as an argument to the function:

```
Public Function FindByLastName(aStudent As clsStudent) As Boolean
  Dim stu As clsStudent
  On Error GoTo FindError
  For Each stu In studentsP
    If aStudent.LastName = stu.LastName Then
      aStudent.ID = stu.ID
      FindByLastName = True
      Exit Function
    End If
  Next stu
  FindByLastName = False
  Exit Function
FindError:
  MsgBox Error$, , ""
End Function
```

The **Class_Terminate** event handler is responsible for releasing all of the memory used by the collection of students. It is necessary to iterate through the collection and destroy the student objects one by one; after this, the collection itself is destroyed:

```
Private Sub Class_Terminate()
  Dim stu As Object
  For Each stu In studentsP
    Set stu = Nothing
  Next stu
  Set studentsP = Nothing
End Sub
```

Cascading Terminate Events. It is important to realize that the Terminate event often has a cascading effect on all instance variables within the class. If designed correctly, your classes can properly clean up all object references that depend on each other. For example, suppose that each student object contained a transcript; this transcript would ordinarily be released by the Class_Terminate event inside the clsStudent class:

```
' clsStudent class (hypothetical)
Private transcriptP as clsTranscript
.
.
```

```
Private Sub Class_Terminate()
  Set transcriptP = Nothing
End Sub
```

The clsTranscript class might have contained a collection of clsCourse objects, so its Terminate procedure would iterate through the courses and destroy each one:

```
'   clsTranscript class (hypothetical)
Private coursesP As Collection
    .
    .
    .
Private Sub Class_Terminate()
  Dim crs As Object
  For Each crs In coursesP
    Set crs = Nothing
  Next crs
  Set coursesP = Nothing
End Sub
```

And this process would continue until all references to objects that originally stemmed from the collection of students were destroyed. Before object-oriented programming languages were invented, memory cleanup of this sort was tedious, error-prone, and difficult to maintain.

4.4 Doctors Office Scheduling Program

It is now time to create a more complex program involving multiple classes and forms. The program schedules and displays appointments made by patients at a medical office. We assume that several doctors work at the office, and that all current patient names are on file. The program will display past appointments for record-keeping purposes, and will schedule upcoming appointments. An essential element in this program's design is that we show how different classes can interact, forming useful relationships.

One interesting difference between this program and the Student program is that the classes in this program now have a visual component, as they load and display their own forms.

4.4.1 Program Specifications

- A patient can request an appointment with a specific doctor at a specific date and time.
- When an appointment is scheduled, the program will store the appointment data in a file for easy retrieval. For each appointment, we need to identify the patient, the doctor, the date and time, and the purpose of the appointment.
- The program will let the user view all appointments currently scheduled, or all appointments scheduled for a chosen patient.

Data Files. The program must read two input text files: One contains a list of doctors ID numbers and names, and the other contains a list of patient ID numbers and names. Here are sample records from the doctors.txt file:

```
"ARON","Aronowitz, D."
"CHONG","Chong, A."
"ROBINS","Robinson, M."
"RODRIG","Rodriguez, C."
"SARKAR","Sarkar, S."
```

Here are sample records from the patients.txt file:

```
1001,"Adams, J."
1004,"Bustamante, M."
1010,"Davis, M."
1020,"Erhart, A."
1022,"Feinstein, G."
1023,"Gonzalez, J."
1025,"Harrison, G."
1050,"Iams, B."
(etc.)
```

The program will also create an output file named appts.txt that contains appointments made by the user. The field order is: doctorId, patientId, date/time, purpose. Here are some sample records:

```
"ARON",1001,#1997-10-01 16:20:00#,"Sore shoulder"
"ARON",1050,#1997-10-02 13:30:00#,"Sore throat"
"SARKAR",1025,#1997-10-05 09:30:00#,"Yearly check-up"
"ARON",1010,#1997-10-05 08:30:00#,"Bunion on toe"
```

4.4.2 Program Design

Classes. The clsPatient class represents a single patient. The clsAppointment class represents a single appointment. The clsApptCalendar class represents the appointment calendar that contains clsAppointment objects. Figure 6 shows a useful diagram of the relationships between classes in this program.

Figure 6. Diagram of Class Relationships.

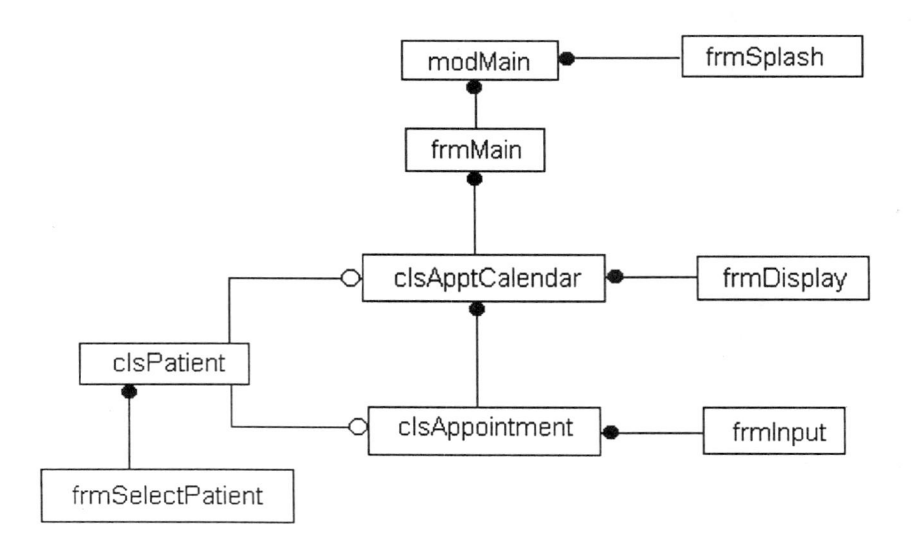

```
                    ┌─────────┐     ┌──────────┐
                    │ modMain │●───│ frmSplash │
                    └─────────┘     └──────────┘
                         ●
                    ┌─────────┐
                    │ frmMain │
                    └─────────┘
                         ●
              ┌──○──┌──────────────┐    ┌───────────┐
              │     │ clsApptCalendar │●──│ frmDisplay │
              │     └──────────────┘    └───────────┘
    ┌──────────┐         ●
    │ clsPatient │        │
    └──────────┘         │
          ●     ┌──○──┌──────────────┐    ┌──────────┐
          │     │     │ clsAppointment │●──│ frmInput │
    ┌──────────────┐   └──────────────┘    └──────────┘
    │ frmSelectPatient │
    └──────────────┘
```

Recall that a line with a solid circle at the beginning indicates a containing relationship (also called a *has-a* relationship). The diagram shows that modMain creates and shows both frmSplash and frmMain. The frmMain form contains an instance of clsApptCalendar, which in turn creates and displays instances of frmDisplay and clsAppointment. The clsAppointment class displays an instance of frmInput.

The clsPatient object exists separately from the other classes; it is not contained within any other class. The open circle placed on the line between the clsApptCalendar and clsPatient classes indicates a *link* relationship (also called a *uses-a* relationship). This relationship is based on the idea that clsApptCalendar sends messages to clsPatient, but the latter is not contained within clsApptCalendar.

User Interface. The program first displays a splash screen with a built-in timer control that removes the window if the user has not clicked on OK after three seconds (Figure 7).

Figure 7. Splash Screen, Doctor's Office Scheduling.

Chap 4: Object-Oriented Programming

The main window (Figure 8) uses a command button for each of the program's functions. The Select Doctor button is disabled because that function has not been implemented yet.

Figure 8. Doctors Office Schedule, Main Window.

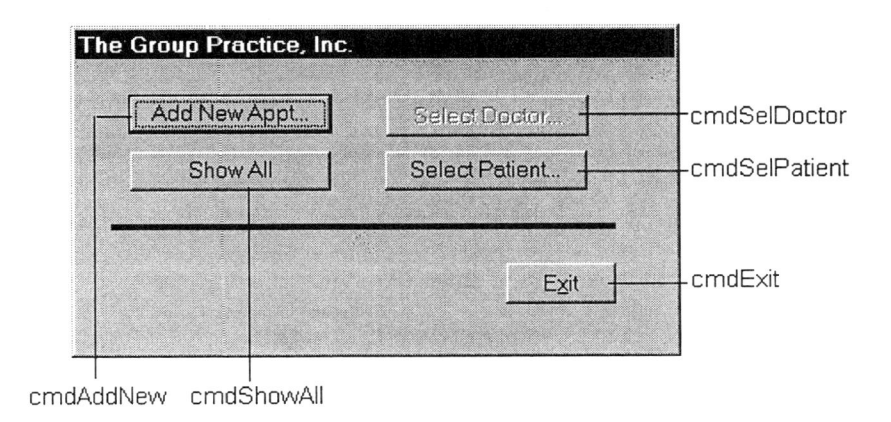

If the user clicks on "Add New Appt...", the Add Appointment window appears. The user selects a doctor ID and patient name from existing lists (Figure 9). The user also enters the date and time of the appointment and a description of the purpose of the visit.

Figure 9. Adding a New Appointment (#2).

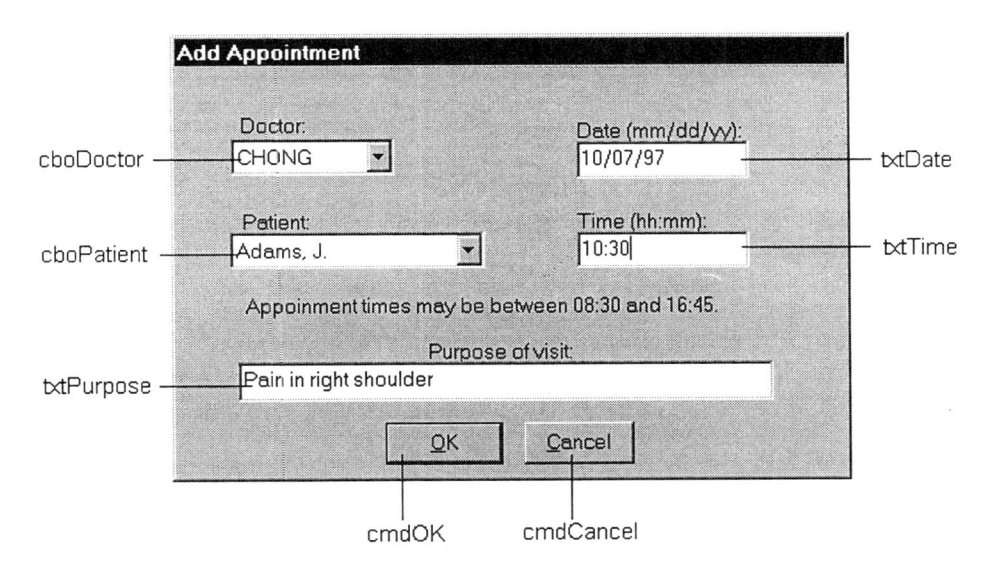

If the user clicks on **OK**, the appointment is saved; if the user clicks on **Cancel**, the appointment is discarded. Error checking is in place for each of the fields; if an invalid date is entered, for example, the following message displays:

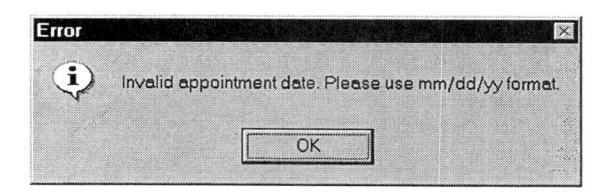

If the appointment time is before 8:30 a.m. or after 4:45 pm, the following message displays:

Back in the main window, the user can also view a list of all appointments in the calendar by clicking the **Show All** button (Figure 10). The list box uses a fixed-width font (Courier New, 8 pt) so the columns can be lined up.

Figure 10. Viewing All Appointments.

The user can also view all appointments made by a single patient. A combo box lists the patient names. Once a name has been selected, a window displays the appointments (Figure 11).

Figure 11. Appointments for a Single Patient.

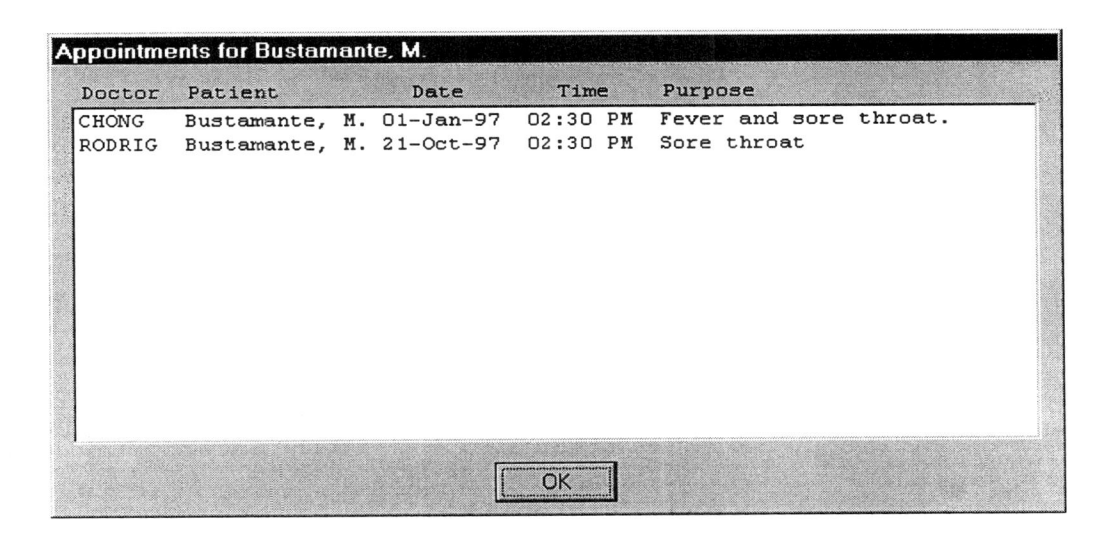

```
Appointments for Bustamante, M.
 Doctor  Patient       Date       Time    Purpose
 CHONG   Bustamante, M. 01-Jan-97  02:30 PM Fever and sore throat.
 RODRIG  Bustamante, M. 21-Oct-97  02:30 PM Sore throat

                            [  OK  ]
```

4.4.3 Program Implementation

The project consists of the modules listed in Table 2.

Table 2. Modules in the Doctors Office Scheduling Program.

Name	Description
modMain	Global identifiers and Main() procedure
frmMain	Main form
frmInput	User inputs a new appointment
frmDisplay	Display list of appointments
frmSelectPatient	Select a patient from a list
frmSplash	Splash screen with program name
clsAppointment	Class module
clsApptCalendar	Class module
clsPatient	Class module

Module1.bas:

```
Public Const DoctorFilename As String = "doctors.txt"
Public Const PatientFilename As String = "patients.txt"
Public Const ApptFilename As String = "appts.txt"

Public Sub Main()
  ChDrive App.Path
  ChDir App.Path
  frmSplash.Show vbModal
  frmMain.Show vbModal
End Sub
```

frmMain:

```
Dim calendar As clsApptCalendar

Private Sub Form_Load()
  Set calendar = New clsApptCalendar
End Sub

Private Sub cmdShowAll_Click()
  calendar.ShowAllAppointments
End Sub

Private Sub cmdAddNew_Click()
  calendar.AddAppointment
End Sub

Private Sub cmdSelPatient_Click()
  calendar.ShowPatientAppointments
End Sub

Private Sub cmdExit_Click()
  Unload Me
End Sub

Private Sub Form_Unload(Cancel As Integer)
  Set calendar = Nothing
End Sub
```

frmSplash:

```
Private Sub cmdOk_Click()
  Unload Me
End Sub

Private Sub Timer1_Timer()
  Unload Me
End Sub
```

4.4.4 The clsPatient Class

The **clsPatient** class represents a single patient. It displays the frmSelectPatient form:

```
Dim patientIDP As Long
Dim patientNameP As String

Public Property Let PatientID(idVal As Long)
  patientIDP = idVal
End Property

Public Property Get PatientID() As Long
  PatientID = patientIDP
End Property
```

```
Public Property Let PatientName(nameVal As String)
   patientNameP = nameVal
End Property

Public Property Get PatientName() As String
   PatientName = patientNameP
End Property
```

SelectByName is called when the user wants to select a name from a list of patients. The frmSelectPatient form is used here, and the resulting patient ID and name are inserted in the current object's properties:

```
Public Sub SelectByName()
'Let the user select a patient name from a list.

   Dim IDtemp As Long, nameTemp As String
   Dim j As Integer, fileNum As Integer
   On Error GoTo SelectByName1
   Load frmSelectPatient
   frmSelectPatient.cboPatient.Clear

   'Load combo box and an array of patient
   'ID numbers.
   fileNum = FreeFile
   Open PatientFilename For Input As fileNum
   j = 0
   Do Until EOF(fileNum)
      Input #fileNum, IDtemp, nameTemp
      frmSelectPatient.cboPatient.AddItem nameTemp
      frmSelectPatient.cboPatient.ItemData(j) = IDtemp
      j = j + 1
   Loop
   Close fileNum
   frmSelectPatient.Show vbModal
   PatientID = frmSelectPatient.PatientID
   PatientName = frmSelectPatient.cboPatient.Text
   Exit Sub
SelectByName1:
   MsgBox Error$, vbInformation, "clsPatient.SelectByName"
End Sub
```

LookupPatientName is really a method relating to the class itself, rather than a specific instance of clsPatient. Given an ID number, this method searches the patient file for a matching record and returns the patient's name:

```
Public Function LookupPatientName(id As Long) As String
'Search the patient file for an ID number; if
'found, return the patient's name.
   Dim fileNum As Integer, IDtemp As Long
   Dim nameTemp As String
   fileNum = FreeFile
```

```
    Open PatientFilename For Input As fileNum
    Do While Not EOF(fileNum)
      Input #fileNum, IDtemp, nameTemp
      If id = IDtemp Then
        LookupPatientName = nameTemp
        Close fileNum
        Exit Function
      End If
    Loop
    LookupPatientName = ""
    Close fileNum
    Exit Function
GetName1:
    MsgBox Error, vbCritical, "clsPatient.LookupPatientName"
End Function
```

The frmSelectPatient Form. The frmSelectPatient form is displayed by **clsPatient**. When the user clicks on the cboPatient combo box, we retrieve the patient's ID number from the ItemData array. This array was initialized when the combo box was filled by the clsPatient.SelectByName procedure:

```
Option Explicit
Dim patientIDP As Long

Private Sub cboPatient_Click()
'User has selected a patient's name from
'the combo box. Set the PatientID property.
  Dim n As Integer
  n = cboPatient.ListIndex
  If n >= 0 Then              'n is >= if a patient was selected
    patientIDP = cboPatient.ItemData(n)
  End If
  Hide
End Sub

Public Property Get PatientID()
  PatientID = patientIDP
End Property

Private Sub cmdCancel_Click()
  patientIDP = 0
  Unload Me
End Sub
```

4.4.5 The clsApptCalendar Class

The **clsApptCalendar** class represents the entire appointment calendar for the office. It creates patient, doctor, and appointment objects. It displays the frmDisplay and frmSelectpatient forms.

Chap 4: Object-Oriented Programming 145

The **AddAppointment** method calls InputFromUser in the clsAppointment class, takes the resulting appointment, and appends it to the appointment file:

```
Public Sub AddAppointment()
  On Error GoTo AddAppt1
  Dim fileNum As Integer
  Dim anAppt As New clsAppointment
  If anAppt.InputFromUser Then
    fileNum = FreeFile
    Open ApptFilename For Append As fileNum
    anAppt.AppendToFile fileNum
    Close fileNum
  End If
  Set anAppt = Nothing
  Exit Sub

AddAppt1:
  MsgBox Error$, vbCritical, "clsApptCalendar.AddAppointment"
  Set anAppt = Nothing
End Sub
```

ShowAllAppointments opens the appointment file, loads a list box with all appointments, and shows the frmDisplay form containing the list box:

```
Public Sub ShowAllAppointments()
    frmDisplay.List1.Clear
    frmDisplay.Caption = "All Appointments"
    On Error GoTo ShowAllAppts1

    Dim anAppt As New clsAppointment
    Dim fileNum As Integer
    fileNum = FreeFile
    Open ApptFilename For Input As fileNum
    Do Until EOF(fileNum)
      anAppt.ReadRecord fileNum
      frmDisplay.List1.AddItem anAppt.AsString
    Loop
    Close fileNum
    frmDisplay.Show vbModal
    Set anAppt = Nothing
    Exit Sub

ShowAllAppts1:
  MsgBox Error$, vbCritical, _
    "clsApptCalendar.ShowAllAppointments"
End Sub
```

The **ShowPatientAppointments** method lets the user select a patient by name, searches the appointment file, and inserts appointments for the patient into a list box:

```
Public Sub ShowPatientAppointments()
'First, let user select a patient.
  Dim aPatient As New clsPatient
```

```
  aPatient.SelectByName
  If aPatient.PatientID = 0 Then Exit Sub   'cancelled
  frmDisplay.List1.Clear
  frmDisplay.Caption = "Appointments for " + aPatient.PatientName
  On Error GoTo ShowPatientAppts1

  'Get list of all appointments that match the patient ID.
   Dim searchID As Long, fileNum As Integer
   Dim anAppt As New clsAppointment
   searchID = aPatient.PatientID
   fileNum = FreeFile
   Open ApptFilename For Input As fileNum
   Do Until EOF(fileNum)
     anAppt.ReadRecord fileNum
     If anAppt.PatientID = searchID Then
       frmDisplay.List1.AddItem anAppt.AsString
     End If
   Loop
   Close fileNum
   frmDisplay.Show vbModal
   Set anAppt = Nothing
   Exit Sub

ShowPatientAppts1:
  MsgBox Error$, vbCritical, _
    "clsApptCalendar.ShowPatientAppointments"
End Sub
```

The frmDisplay Form. The frmDisplay form is displayed by clsApptCalendar:

```
Option Explicit

Private Sub cmdOk_Click()
  Unload Me
End Sub
```

4.4.6 The clsAppointment class

The **clsAppointment** class defines a single appointment made by a patient to see a single doctor at a specific date and time. It displays the frmInput form:

```
Option Explicit
Const EarliestApptTime As Date = #8:30:00 AM#
Const LatestApptTime As Date = #4:45:00 PM#

'Instance variables:
Private doctorIDP As String
Private patientIDP As Long
Private apptDateP As Date
Private apptTimeP As Date
Private purposeP As String
```

Chap 4: Object-Oriented Programming

```
Private Sub Class_Initialize()
  DoctorID = ""
  PatientID = 0
  Purpose = ""
End Sub

Public Property Get DoctorID() As String
  DoctorID = doctorIDP
End Property

Public Property Let DoctorID(newValue As String)
  doctorIDP = newValue
End Property

Public Static Property Get PatientID() As Long
  PatientID = patientIDP
End Property

Public Static Property Let PatientID(newValue As Long)
  patientIDP = newValue
End Property

Public Property Get ApptDate() As Date
  ApptDate = apptDateP
End Property

Public Property Let ApptDate(newValue As Date)
  apptDateP = newValue
End Property

Public Property Get ApptTime() As Date
  ApptTime = apptTimeP
End Property

Public Property Let ApptTime(newValue As Date)
  apptTimeP = newValue
End Property

Public Property Get Purpose() As String
  Purpose = purposeP
End Property

Public Property Let Purpose(newValue As String)
  purposeP = newValue
End Property
```

The **InputFromUser** method initializes the frmInput form with the names of doctors and patients, and uses the form to get all data relating to a single appointment. If the user cancels, the method returns False:

```
Public Function InputFromUser() As Boolean
  With frmInput
```

```
        .FillComboBoxes
        .EarliestApptTime = EarliestApptTime
        .LatestApptTime = LatestApptTime
        .Show vbModal
    End With

    'Update the class properties.
    If frmInput.SaveAppt Then
        DoctorID = frmInput.DoctorID
        PatientID = Val(frmInput.PatientID)
        ApptDate = frmInput.txtDate.Text
        ApptTime = frmInput.txtTime.Text
        Purpose = frmInput.txtPurpose.Text
        InputFromUser = True
    Else
        InputFromUser = False
    End If
    Unload frmInput
End Function
```

The **AsString** method returns a string representation of an appointment with fixed-length display columns, suitable for inclusion in a list box:

```
Public Function AsString() As String
'Create a string representation of this
'appointment.
    Dim D As New clsPatient
    Dim doctor As String * 8
    Dim patient As String * 15
    doctor = DoctorID
    patient = D.LookupPatientName(PatientID)
    AsString = doctor & patient & _
        Format$(ApptDate, "Medium Date") & "  " & _
        Format$(ApptTime, "Medium Time") & "  " & _
        Purpose
    Set D = Nothing
End Function
```

ReadRecord reads appointment data from a text file:

```
Public Sub ReadRecord(fileNum As Integer)
'Transfer data from input file to this object
'(The Input# statement cannot be used directly
' with class properties.)

    Dim F1 As String, F2 As Long
    Dim F3 As Date, F4 As String
    On Error GoTo ReadRecord1
    Input #fileNum, F1, F2, F3, F4
    DoctorID = F1
    PatientID = F2
    ApptDate = DateValue(F3)    'extract just the date
    ApptTime = TimeValue(F3)    'extract just the time
```

```
         Purpose = F4
      Exit Sub
   ReadRecord1:
      MsgBox Error$, vbCritical, "clsAppointment.ReadRecord"
   End Sub
```

AppendToFile writes the current appointment to a text file:

```
   Public Sub AppendToFile(fileNum As Integer)
   'Given a file number (to an open text file),
   'append the current appointment to the file.

      On Error GoTo AppendToFile1
      Write #fileNum, DoctorID, PatientID, ApptDate + _
            ApptTime, Purpose
      Exit Sub
   AppendToFile1:
      MsgBox Error$, vbCritical, "clsAppointment.AppendToFile"
   End Sub
```

4.4.7 The frmInput Form

The **frmInput** form is displayed by the clsAppointment class when the user wants to input an appointment. After being loaded into memory, two properties are set by clsAppointment: EarliestApptTime and LatestApptTime. These limit the range of appointment times:

```
   ' Instance variables:
   Option Explicit
   Private saveAppt_ As Boolean          'read-only
   Private earliestApptTimeP As Date     'write-only
   Private latestApptTimeP As Date       'write-only
   Dim doctorIDP As String               'read-only
   Dim patientIDP As String              'read-only

   Private Sub Form_Activate()
     lblTimeRange = "Appointment times may be between " _
        & Format$(earliestApptTimeP, "hh:mm") & " and " _
        & Format$(latestApptTimeP, "hh:mm") & "."
   End Sub

   Public Property Let EarliestApptTime(early As Date)
      earliestApptTimeP = early
   End Property

   Public Property Let LatestApptTime(late As Date)
      latestApptTimeP = late
   End Property

   Public Property Get DoctorID() As String
      DoctorID = doctorIDP
   End Property
```

```
Public Property Get PatientID() As String
  PatientID = patientIDP
End Property

Public Property Get SaveAppt() As Boolean
' True indicates that the user wants to
' save this appointment.
  SaveAppt = saveAppt_
End Property

Private Sub cboDoctors_Click()
  doctorIDP = cboDoctors.Text
End Sub

Private Sub cboPatients_Click()
'When the user selects a patient name, get the ID number
'from the ItemData property of the combo box.

  Dim n As Integer
  n = cboPatients.ListIndex
  patienvtIDP = Format$(cboPatients.ItemData(n), "0000")
End Sub

Private Sub cmdCancel_Click()
  saveAppt_ = False
  Me.Hide
End Sub

Private Sub cmdOk_Click()
  If ValidateFields Then
    saveAppt_ = True
    Me.Hide
  End If
End Sub
```

The **FillComboBoxes** method fills the input form with the doctor IDs and patient names. We also build an array of patient ID numbers:

```
Public Sub FillComboBoxes()
' Fill the combo boxes containing the doctor
' IDs and patient names.

  Dim fileNum As Integer
  Dim tempID As String, tempName As String
  fileNum = FreeFile
  Open DoctorFilename For Input As fileNum
  Do While Not EOF(fileNum)
    Input #fileNum, tempID, tempName
    cboDoctors.AddItem tempID
  Loop
  Close fileNum
```

Chap 4: Object-Oriented Programming

```
    Dim longID As Long, j As Integer
    j = 0
    Open PatientFilename For Input As fileNum
    Do While Not EOF(fileNum)
       Input #fileNum, longID, tempName
       cboPatients.AddItem tempName
       cboPatients.ItemData(j) = longID
       j = j + 1
    Loop
    Close fileNum
End Sub
```

The privat **ValidateFields** method has the rather tedious job of checking to make sure the user has selected both a doctor and patient, has entered a valid date and time for the appointment, and has entered some explanation of the appointment's purpose. Although error checking takes some effort to code, its reward is evident when a program withstands input from untrained users without breaking down:

```
Private Function ValidateFields() As Boolean
   ValidateFields = False
   'Check for a doctor ID.
   If cboDoctors.ListIndex = -1 Then
     MsgBox "A doctor must be selected", _
       vbInformation, "Error"
     Exit Function
   End If

   'Check for a patient name.
   If cboPatients.ListIndex = -1 Then
     MsgBox "A patient must be selected", _
       vbInformation, "Error"
     Exit Function
   End If

   'Check for an appointment date.
   If Not IsDate(txtDate.Text) Then
     MsgBox "Invalid appointment date. Please use " _
       + "mm/dd/yy format.", vbInformation, "Error"
     Exit Function
   End If
   If Trim$(txtPurpose.Text) = "" Then
     MsgBox "A purpose for the appointment must be given.", _
       vbInformation, "Error"
     Exit Function
   End If

   ' Begin checking the appointment time. Possible runtime
   ' error if invalid format is used.
   On Error GoTo BadTimeFormat
   Dim n As Date
   n = TimeValue(txtTime.Text)
```

```
        'Check for valid time range.
        If n < earliestApptTimeP Or n > latestApptTimeP Then
          MsgBox "Appointment time is either too early or too late. ", _
            vbInformation, "Error"
          Exit Function
        End If
        MsgBox "Appointment confirmed.", vbInformation, ""
        ValidateFields = True
        Exit Function

    BadTimeFormat:
        MsgBox "Invalid appointment time. Please enter in hh:mm format", _
          vbInformation, "Error"
    End Function
```

4.5 Review Questions

1. What are the names of three object-oriented programming languages that appeared in the early 1980s?

2. What is the most obvious influence on Visual Basic produced by more traditional object-oriented programming languages?

3. How would you define the word **class** in object-oriented terms?

4. How is an object different from a class?

5. Do the icons in the Visual Basic toolbox represent classes or objects?

6. How are properties different from methods?

7. Is there a separate copy of the SetFocus method in every command button on the same form?

8. Does each command button on the same form have its own copy of the Visible property?

9. Do all option buttons on the same form share the same event handler?

10. How do classes relate to physical entities in real-world programming applications?

11. In a student record-keeping program, what attributes might be assigned to a Transcript class?

12. What is encapsulation?

13. What essential feature of object-oriented programming was left out of Visual Basic?

14. What type of relationship exists between the classes: ExchangeStudent, GraduateStudent, and Student?

15. Does every instance of a class have to be assigned its own class module?

16. Code a Dim statement that declares a variable of type clsTranscript.

17. Code a statement that creates a clsTranscript object and assigns it to the variable from the previous question.

18. Code a statement that releases the memory used by the object variable used in the previous two questions.
19. Code a single statement that both declares an object variable and creates a new instance of the clsTranscript class.
20. What happens to an object that is created inside a procedure when the procedure finishes?
21. What is an *instance variable*?
22. Can the name of an instance variable be the same as the name of a property within the same class?
23. What two procedures are used to get and set the value of a property?
24. Can two different classes have a property by the same name? If so, can you think of an example?
25. Code an example of a property called LastName that assigns a new value to an instance variable called lastNameP.
26. Why are instance variables usually declared private in classes?
27. How might a class object prevent an out-of-range value from being assigned to one of its properties?
28. How does one create a read-only property?
29. What event procedure is automatically executed when a class object is created?
30. What event procedure is automatically executed when a class object is destroyed?
31. Fill in the missing word: A class interface is composed of properties and _____.
32. What is meant by the term *message passing* in reference to class objects?
33. In the classes shown in this chapter, what does the AsString method accomplish?
34. How might a *private* method be used?
35. At the end of the following example, how many clsStudent objects exist?
    ```
    Dim st1 As New clsStudent
    Dim st2 As clsStudent
    Set st2 = st1
    ```

36. At the end of the following example, how many clsStudent objects exist?
    ```
    Dim st1 As New clsStudent
    Dim st2 As clsStudent
    Set st2 = st1
    Set st1 = Nothing
    ```

The following questions refer to the Student class program shown in Section 4.2:

37. Does the clsStudent class load and display frmMain, or is it the other way around?
38. What error checking is performed by the ID property?

39. What error checking is performed by the LastName property?

The following questions refer to the Student Collection Class program shown in Section 4.3:

40. How does a *containing* relationship exist between the classes in this program?

41. How is the standard Collection class used in this program?

42. In this program, do any of the classes load and display forms?

43. In the clsStudentCollection class, how does the Add method prevent the user from inserting two students with the same ID number?

44. What operation is carried out by the Terminate event in the clsStudentCollection class?

45. What does the FindByID method do in clsStudentCollection?

46. What happens when the Collection.Item method fails to find a matching key value?

47. What disadvantage might there be to letting the Students property return a reference to the collection object inside the student collection (clsStudentCollection)?

The following questions refer to the Doctors Office Scheduling program, presented in Section 4.4:

48. What three classes are used on the Doctors Office Scheduling program?

49. What major difference exists between this program and the Student Collection Class program, in the use of form modules?

50. What information is stored in the two input files?

51. What data items are stored in the output file?

52. What relationship is there between the clsApptCalendar and clsAppointment classes?

53. What relationship exists between the clsApptCalendar and clsPatient classes?

54. What does the SelectByName method in the clsPatient class do?

55. Does the LookupPatientName method relate to a single instance of the clsPatient class?

56. How is the ItemData array important when the user clicks on a name in the cboPatient combo box?

57. The AddAppointment and ShowAllAppointment methods in clsApptCalendar create instances of which other class?

58. Which method in the clsApptCalendar class lets the user select a patient name and view appointments for that one person?

59. How does the clsAppointment class make sure that appointments are not scheduled too early in the morning?

60. What data does a clsAppointment object contain?

61. Which form is controlled and displayed by the clsAppointment class?

62. How does the ReadRecord method in the clsAppointment class extract the appointment time and date values from a single field in the appointment.txt file?

63. What validations are performed on the user's input in frmInput before an appointment is saved?

4.6 Chapter Exercises

4.6.1 Doctors Office: Self-Referencing

It is possible, with a little effort, to call a class method from one of the forms owned by the class. In the Doctors Office program, for example, the clsAppointment class displays the frmInput form. This is the form filled in by the user with the various appointment fields. What if one of the procedures in frmInput needs to call a clsAppointment method? Calling a method requires a variable that references a class object. In Visual Basic, the keyword **Me** represents the current object.

For this programming project, make a copy of the Doctor's Office program and modify it according to the following steps:

1. Add the following statements to frmInput. The variable **apptP** is a reference to the object that displayed this form:

    ```
    Private apptP As Object      'current appointment

    Public Property Get Appt() As Object
      Set Appt = apptP
    End Property

    Public Property Let Appt(obj As Object)
      Set apptP = obj
    End Property
    ```

2. Add the following statement to clsAppointment.InputFromUser, just before showing the frmInput form. It assigns the current appointment object to the frmInput property called **Appt**:

    ```
    frmInput.Appt = Me
    ```

3. Remove the following statement from InputFromUser:

    ```
    DoctorID = frmInput.DoctorID
    ```

4. In frmInput, when the user selects a doctor, assign a value to the DoctorID property of the current appointment:

    ```
    Private Sub cboDoctors_Click()
    ```

```
        Appt.DoctorID = cboDoctors.Text
End Sub
```

4.6.2 Student Collection: Searching for Names

In the clsStudentCollection class, the FindByLastName method locates only the first student in the collection matching the requested name. Revise this method so that it returns a collection containing all students having the same name. Run and test the revised program.

4.6.3 Student Collection: Saving in a File

Modify the Student Collection Class program so that it saves the collection in a file before the program exits. When the program starts up, load the collection from the same file. Use either a sequential or random-access file.

4.6.4 Student Collection: Completed Courses

Add a collection of college courses to the instance variables in the clsStudent class. When the program starts, read the course data for each student from a file. When the user searches for a student by either ID or name, display a list of all courses completed by the student. The members of the course collection should be objects containing the following data:

```
'clsCourse Class:
Dim numberP As String
Dim yearSemP As String
Dim creditsP As Integer
Dim gradeP As Integer
```

Table 3 displays some sample records.

Table 3. Sample Courses, Student Collection.

Student ID	Course Number	Year/Sem (yyss format)	Credits	Grade (A=4, F=0)
2342432	ENG 1001	9601	3	4
2342432	BIO 1050	9601	4	3
2342432	MTH 1022	9602	3	4
2342432	FRE 2051	9602	3	2
4392002	PHY 1010	9601	3	4
4392002	GEO 1702	9602	4	3
4392002	GER 1051	9603	3	4
4392002	CHM 1021	9603	4	3

4.6.5 Student Collection: The clsCourse Class

Using the program written for the previous exercise, improve the clsCourse class by adding properties called CourseNumber, YearSemester, Credits, and Grade. Add the following methods, and find a way to demonstrate each one by calling it from your program:

- AsString: Return a string representation of the course.
- SetFields(crsNum, yearSem, cred, grd): Assign values to all four class properties.
- Input: Let user input a new course.

4.6.6 Doctors Office: Appointments by Doctor

Enhance the Doctors Office Scheduling program from Section 4.4 by letting the user search for all appointments scheduled for a particular doctor. Activate the corresponding button in the main window. You will probably want to create a class called clsDoctor, and provide similar properties and methods as those in the clsPatient class.

4.6.7 Doctors Office: Sorted Appointment List

The Doctors Office Scheduling program currently displays appointments in the order that they were added to the file. Find a way to display the appointments in order by date. You might want to use a collection to sort the appointments; if so, review the programming exercise from Chapter 3 that related to sorting a collection.

4.6.8 Object-Oriented Glossary Program

Convert the Glossary program from Chapter 3 into an object-oriented application. The glossary itself can be a class. Provide methods that load the glossary from a file, save it in a file, search for keywords, and so on. Write a test program that creates two instances of the glossary class and displays each one in a separate MDI child window.

4.6.9 ButtonCollection Class

Using the Button Array program from Chapter 3 as a basis, create a class that encapsulates a collection of command buttons. Provide properties that let the user set the number of buttons per row, the number of rows, the button height and width, and the button captions. Provide methods that let the user modify the Visible properties of individual buttons. Write a short test program that lets the user test each of the properties and methods of your class.

4.6.10 IndexedFile Class

Using the Indexed Random-Access File chapter exercise from Chapter 3 as a basis, create an IndexedFile class. The class should be general enough to work with different types of objects. For example, there can be RecordLength property that is used by the class when opening the random-access file. The index itself should be stored in a collection while in memory, and saved to disk as a separate file when the program exits.

4.6.11 Mozart Music: InvoiceItem Class

In the Chapter Exercises for Chapter 3, you were asked to create a user-defined type called InvoiceItem for the Mozart Music Sales program. In this program, you will extend that idea by creating a class called clsInvoiceItem. It should have the following properties: skuNumber, Title, and Price.

Also, create a class that represents an entire invoice. It will contain a collection of clsInvoiceItem objects. Here are the suggested properties: InvoiceID, InvoiceDate, SalesPerson, TotalAmount, Tax, NetAmount, ItemCount, and ItemList (a collection of clsInvoiceItem objects).

4.6.12 Object-Oriented Time Clock

Using the Time Clock program from the exercises at the end of Chapter 2 as a guide, create an easy-to-use class called **clsTimeClock** that encapsulates the various calculations that were used in the earlier program. Here is a suggested list:

- Read-Only properties: StartTime, StopTime, ElapsedMinutes
- Read-Write property: ClientName
- Public Methods: StartClock, StopClock

The StartTime and StopTime properties contain Date/Time values. The ElapsedMinutes property contains a long integer representing the number of minutes between the starting and ending times. The StartClock and StopClock methods begin and end the timing sequence, respectively.

In the program's main form, declare a variable of type clsTimeClock; in Form_Load, create an instance of the class:

```
Dim clock As clsTimeClock
  .
  .
Set clock = New clsTimeClock
```

When the user clicks on the Start button, call the StartClock method and pass it the current time:

```
clock.StartClock Now
```

Similarly, when the use clicks on Stop, call the StopClock and ElapsedMinutes methods:

```
clock.StopClock Now
lblElapsed.Caption = clock.ElapsedMinutes
```

4.6.13 E-Mail Address Book

Write a program that lets the user display and modify an address book containing names, e-mail addresses, and phone numbers. The program should contain two classes: clsAddress, and clsAddressList. The clsAddress class contains the following information about one person: name, e-mail address, phone, and comments. The clsAddressList class encapsulates a collection of clsAddress objects. It contains operations that let the user add, remove, display, and edit individual address entries.

The main window displays the names from the address book in a list box (see Figure 12). The names can be loaded from a text file, random-access file, or database, depending on your preference.

Figure 12. E-Mail Address Book, Main Window.

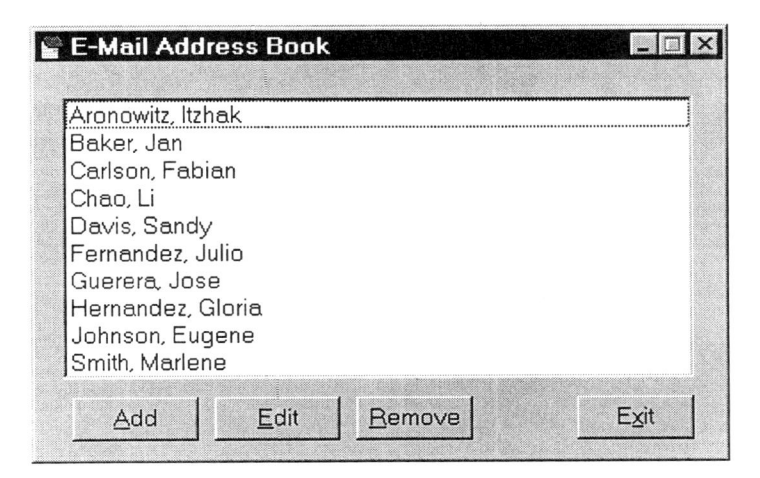

The user should be able to input new names and addresses, using a form similar to the one shown in Figure 13.

Figure 13. Adding a New Name and Address.

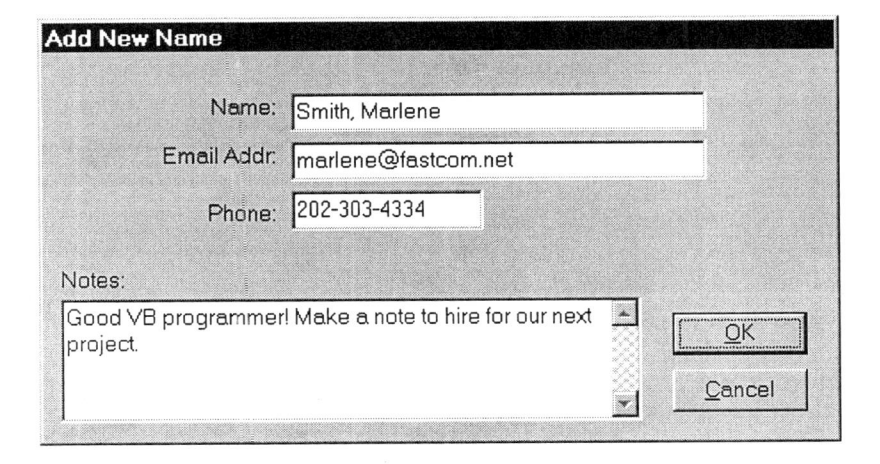

The clsAddress Class. The following is a suggested list of instance variables, properties, and methods for the clsAddress class. Notice that some properties and methods are designated *private* because they should only be accessed from within the class:

```
Private keyP As String          'key field, for collection
Private modifiedP As Boolean    'True if fields were modified

'The following fields are saved in a file:
Private personalNameP As String
Private emailP As String
Private phoneP As String
Private commentsP As String

'********************* PUBLIC PROPERTIES **********************

Public Property Get Modified() As Boolean
' Return True if the current address has been
' modified.
End Property

Public Property Get Email() As String
' Return the e-mail address.
End Property

Public Property Let Email(newval As String)
' Set the e-mail address
End Property

Public Property Get Phone() As String
' Return the phone number.
End Property

Public Property Get PersonalName() As String
' Return the personal name field.
End Property

Public Property Let PersonalName(newval As String)
' Set the personal name field.
End Property

Public Property Let Phone(newval As String)
' Set the phone number.
End Property

Public Property Get Comments() As String
' Return the comments field.
End Property

Public Property Let Comments(newval As String)
' Set the comments field.
End Property

'********************* PUBLIC METHODS **********************

Public Sub ClearAll()
' Clear all fields in the current address.
```

Chap 4: Object-Oriented Programming

```
    End Sub

    Public Sub EditFields()
    ' Display the current address and let the user
    ' modify the fields. Displays the frmAddress form.
    End Sub

    Public Function InputNew() As Boolean
    ' Let the user input a new address. Displays the
    ' frmAddress form. Return True if the user wants to
    ' save it.
    End Function

    Public Function IsBlank() As Boolean
    ' Return True if the current address is blank.
    End Function

    Public Property Get Key() As String
    ' Return the value of the Key field.
    End Property

    Public Function ReadFromFile(fileNum As Integer) As Boolean
    ' Read a single address from a text file that is
    ' already open. Return True if the record is not blank.
    End Function

    Public Sub SaveToFile(fileNum As Integer)
    ' Save the current address to a text file that is
    ' already open.
    End Sub

    '********** PRIVATE PROPERTIES AND METHODS *************

    Private Property Let Modified(newval As Boolean)
    ' Set the modifiedP boolean flag (private).
    End Property

    Private Property Let Key(newval As String)
    ' Set the value of the Key field (private).
    End Property
```

The clsAddressList Class. The following is a list of suggested instance variables, properties, and methods for the clsAddressList class:

```
    Private allAddrP As Collection
    Private fileNameP As String
    Private modifiedP As Boolean
    Private currentNdxP As Integer

    '********************* PUBLIC PROPERTIES **********************
```

```vb
Public Property Get addressList() As Collection
' Return a copy of the entire address collection. (read-only)
End Property

Public Property Get CurrentIndex() As Integer
' Return the current position, as an integer. (read-only)
  CurrentIndex = currentNdxP
End Property

Public Property Get FileName() As String
' Return the current file name.
End Property

Public Property Let FileName(newval As String)
' Set the current file name.
End Property

Public Property Get Modified() As Boolean
' Return True if the list has been modfied. (read-only)
End Property

'******************** PUBLIC METHODS **********************

Public Function AddNew(addr As clsAddress) As Boolean
' Add a new address to the collection.
' If a duplicate key is found, display
' an error message and return False.
End Function


Public Sub ClearCollection()
' Delete all members of the collection.
End Sub

Public Function Clone() As clsAddressList
' Create and return a new copy of this object.
End Function

Public Sub FillNameListBox(lbox As ListBox)
' Fill a list box with the names of the people
' in the address list.
End Sub

Public Function Find(Key As String) As Boolean
' Search for the address identified by "key". If
' successful, set Current to the target position in
' the collection, and return True. Otherwise, do not
' modify Current, and return False.
End Function

Public Function GetCurrentAddr(addr As clsAddress) As Boolean
' If CurrentIndx is valid, retrieve the address object
```

Chap 4: Object-Oriented Programming

```
' at the current position and return True; otherwise,
' return False.
End Function

Public Function ReadFromFile(aFile As String) As Boolean
' Clear the current collection, open a new
' file for input and fill the collection from
' the file. Return True if successful.
End Function

Public Function Remove() As Boolean
' Remove the address at the current position.
End Function

Public Sub SaveToFile(aFile As String)
' Save the collection of addresses to the text file
' identified by aFile.
End Sub

'********** PRIVATE PROPERTIES AND METHODS **************

Private Sub Class_Terminate()
' If the list was modified, ask the user if it
' should be saved, and save it to the same file
' if requested. Clear the list and deallocate all
' the address objects.
End Sub

Private Sub Class_Initialize()
   Set allAddrP = New Collection
End Sub

Private Property Let CurrentIndex(n As Integer)
' Set the current index position.
   currentNdxP = n
End Property

Private Property Let Modified(newval As Boolean)
' Set the modified property.
End Property

Private Function AskToSave() As Boolean
' Ask the user if the collection should be saved;
' return True if the user says Yes.
End Function
```

5 Introducing Databases

Chapter Contents

Tables and Databases
    Introduction
    Defining Tables
    Recordset Objects
    Field Types in Databases
    Using Data Controls
    Using Data-Bound Controls
Using Microsoft Access
    Creating a Database
    Creating the SalesStaff Table
    Creating Indexes
    Entering Table Data
Viewing the SalesStaff Table
    The Database Table
    Display the Table
    Adding New Records
    Changing the Record Order
Moving the Recordset Pointer
    Example: SalesStaff Table
Data-Bound List, Combo, and Grid
    Data-Bound List Control
    Data-Bound Combo Control
    Data-Bound Grid Control
Mozart Music Sales - 4
    Program Specifications
    Program Design
    Program Implementation
Mail-Order Computer Sales
    Program Specifications
    Program Design
    The Computer Database
    Program Implementation
Searching for Records (SalesStaff 3)
    Table Seek Method
    Using an SQL Search
    Example: A Simple Query Program
    FindFirst, FindNext, and Other Search Methods
Review Questions
Chapter Exercises

5.1 Tables and Databases

5.1.1 Introduction

Companies looking for Visual Basic programmers usually expect the applicants to know how to use Microsoft Access databases. Experience with a number of other database products are often desired, also. For this reason, it is critically important for you to develop good database skills as you learn to write Visual Basic applications.

In this chapter, we begin to address the need to use databases by showing how to use Data controls to display, move through, update, and search for records in databases. We also use Access to create database tables with indexes. In Appendix B, you can read about Visual Basic add-on utilities such as Data Manager, VisData, and Form Designer that may be used to create databases and data-bound forms. Upcoming chapters will explore databases in more depth, building on what you have learned here.

5.1.2 Defining Tables

A *table* is a sequence of rows, each containing related information in a consistent format. For example, a table might contain a list of names and addresses. Or, it might contain the ID numbers and names of sales staff members:

ID	Name
1	Adams, Adam
2	Baker, Barbara
3	Colson, Charles
4	Del Terzo, Daniel
5	Easterbrook, Erin

Each row in a table may also be called a *record*. Each column is called a *field*. In our sample table, the fields are called **id** and **name**, and the table is called **SalesStaff**.

A *database* is a collection of tables containing related information. In addition to the SalesStaff table, for example, a store database might contain a table called **Invoices** containing information about sales invoices:

invoiceID	date	staffId	netAmount
00001	01/02/97	3	55.25
00240	01/03/97	2	36.92
00301	01/05/97	1	14.05
00322	01/07/97	4	89.34
00329	01/07/97	2	128.26
00335	01/10/97	5	4.50

One reason why these tables belong in the same database would be that an implied relationship exists between them. Each different **staffId** in the Invoices table would match an ID in the SalesStaff table because they refer to the same employee.

5.1.3 Recordset Objects

Visual Basic accesses database tables via *recordset* objects. A recordset object contains properties and methods that provide power to the Visual Basic programmer when dealing with an Access database. Recordset objects are made available through the DAO library (data access objects) that is supplied with Visual Basic. There are three types of recordset objects: table, dynaset, and snapshot.

- A *table*-type recordset is a direct reference to the physical storage of data in one table of a database. A table is *updatable,* meaning that records can be added, changed, and deleted.
- A *dynaset*-type recordset is a collection of records that can be created at runtime, from one or more database tables. A dynaset is updatable.
- A *snapshot*-type recordset is a copy of data pulled from one or more database tables. A snapshot is *read-only,* meaning that it cannot be modified.

There are advantages and disadvantages to using each of these types:

Table:
- **Advantages:** A table can be indexed on any of its fields, making it possible to quickly vary the sequence of records at runtime. Also, an index provides a quick way of searching for specific records.
- **Disadvantages:** Methods such as FindFirst and FindNext cannot be used, so it is difficult to search for a range of values, or search a column that is not indexed.

Dynaset:
- **Advantages:** The FindFirst and FindNext methods may be used to search for all records matching search criteria. A dynaset can be constructed from multiple fields in different tables, and you can select which records you want (called *filtering*).
- **Disadvantages:** Indexes cannot be used, so searching and sorting is slower than with tables. Dynasets consume more memory than tables or snapshots.

Snapshot:
- **Advantages:** A snapshot can contain information from multiple tables. The FindFirst and FindNext methods can be used to search for records. Snapshots can usually be created faster than Dynasets, and they use less memory.
- **Disadvantages:** Indexes cannot be used, and snapshots cannot be updated. Large recordsets must be kept in memory, limiting the practical size of a snapshot to a few hundred rows.

In a multi-user database environment, there are additional differences between tables, dynasets, and snapshots. But we will defer that discussion until Chapter 6, when we discuss multiuser database processing.

5.1.4 Field Types in Databases

A database can contain the following types of fields:

- **Text:** Text and numbers, such as names and addresses, phone numbers and postal codes. A Text field can contain from 0 to 255 characters.

- **Memo:** Lengthy text and numbers, such as comments or explanations. A Memo field can contain up to 1.2 billion characters.

- **Number:** Numerical data on which you intend to perform mathematical calculations, except calculations involving money. The Number data types are: Byte, Integer, Long Integer, Single, and Double.

- **Date/Time:** Dates and times. The same field can store both a date and a time. All dates are stored in U.S. format.

- **Currency:** Used where a field contains monetary values. Don't use the Number data type for currency values, because numbers to the right of the decimal are rounded off during calculations. The Currency data type maintains a fixed number of digits to the right of the decimal.

- **Counter (Autonumber):** Sequential numbers automatically inserted by the Microsoft Jet database engine. Numbering begins with 1. The Counter data type makes a good primary key field.

- **Yes/No:** Holds values of Yes/No, True/False, On/Off. Corresponds to Visual Basic's Boolean type.

- **OLE Object:** Objects created in other programs using the OLE protocol. Managed by OLE, Image or PictureBox controls.

Table 1. Comparison of MS-Access and Visual Basic Types.

Access Field Type (numeric type)	VBasic Data Type
Yes/No	Boolean
Number(Byte)	Byte
AutoNumber	Long
Currency	Currency
Date/Time	Date
Number (Double)	Double
Number (Long Integer)	Long
OLE Object	String
Memo	String
Number (Single)	Single
Number (Integer)	Integer
Text	String
Hyperlink	String

Chap 5: Introducing Databases 169

5.1.5 Using Data Controls

The easiest way to manipulate data from a database table in Visual Basic is to use a **Data** control. When the form containing a data control loads, the data control automatically opens a database table. A useful list of specific data control properties appears in Table 2.

A data control has two properties that must be set before the control can be used with a database table: DatabaseName and RecordSource. The **DatabaseName** property contains the database filename. For a Microsoft Access database, the name has an extension of mdb. When you click on the property, a browse button appears, and you can search for the filename. A complete path name is inserted into the property, terminating with the database filename. For example:

```
c:\Vbprograms\recent\mozart.mdb
```

When you move your program to a different directory, however, the program will display an error when it starts up. One solution is to remove the path from the filename, and place the database file in the same directory as the program. Another solution is to save the database path in the system registry (See Section 2.5), and initialize the DatabaseName property at run time.

The **RecordSource** property is the name of a single table in the database. This determines that a data control may only be tied to a single table at any given time. For example, we might set the RecordSource property to SalesStaff. As a general habit, it is useful to set the Name property of the data control to a name that is similar to the RecordSource. For example, a good name might be datSalesStaff. (In Chapter 1, we listed Microsoft's preferred prefixes for controls, and **dat** is the prefix for data controls.)

Table 2. Useful Data Control Properties.

Property	Description
DatabaseName	Filename of the database.
RecordSource	Name of recordset attached to the data control. May be a database table or result of a query.
RecordsetType	Values are Table, Dynaset, Snapshot.
BOFAction	Values are MoveFirst, BOF.
EOFAction	Values are Last, EOF, Add New.
Exclusive	Values are True, False. If True, no other user may access the recordset at the same time.
ReadOnly	Values are True, False. If True, the recordset may not be modified.

Moving Through the Table. At run time, the user can move forward and backward through the records in the attached database table by clicking on the arrows on the data control (Figure 1).

Figure 1. Description of a Data Control.

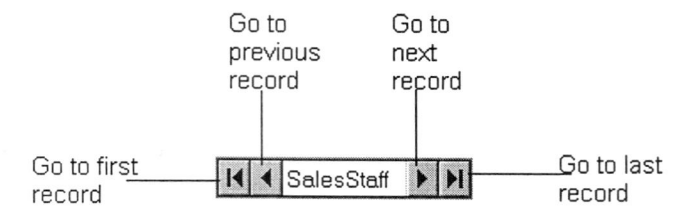

```
                    Go to         Go to
                    previous      next
                    record        record
                         |          |
    Go to first         |K| |◄| SalesStaff |►| |►I|        Go to last
    record                                                 record
```

5.1.6 Using Data-Bound Controls

By itself, a data control is not very useful because it cannot display data. But other controls, called *data-bound controls,* can be attached to a data control while in design mode. When the form is loaded at runtime, the data control opens the recordset (usually a database table) and fills all bound controls with data from the first record of the recordset. When the user clicks on the data control to move forward and backward through the recordset, the data-bound controls are updated automatically.

Linking the Data Control. In a bound control, the **DataSource** property holds the name of the data control that links to a database table. The **DataField** property holds the name of the field in the table that will be attached to this control. It can only be set after the DataSource property because the Properties window needs to collect a list of fields from the recordset object.

It might be helpful to think of a data control as a communication link between a database table and one or more fields on a Visual Basic form. The data control knows where to find the data; it makes the data available at run time to any other controls that request the data. As shown in Figure 2, these controls use the DataSource property to connect to the data control, and the DataField property to name the field from the database table supplying the data.

Figure 2. Connecting a Data Control to a Database and Data Field.

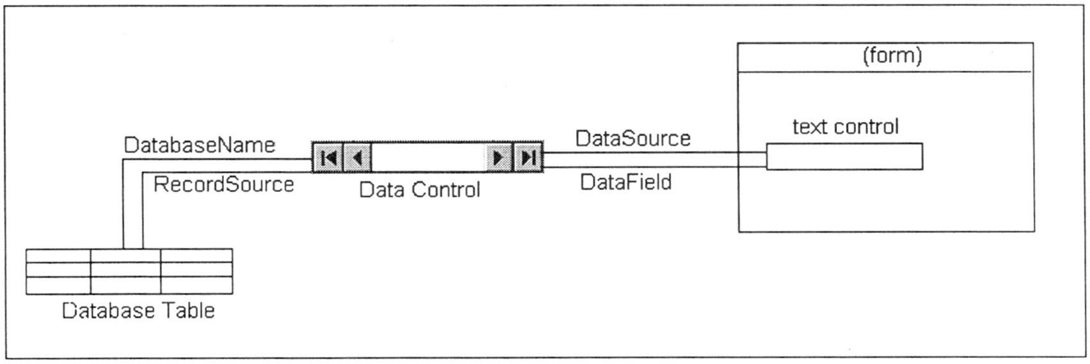

The RecordSource property may also refer to a recordset created purely in memory, usually by a statement written in SQL. For the moment, however, we will only connect to database tables.

Sales Staff Example. The mozart.mdb database has a table called **SalesStaff**, and the attached data control is called **datSalesStaff**. We can create two text controls called **txtID** and **txtName**:

Control	Property	Value
datSalesStaff	Databasename	staff.mdb
	RecordSource	SalesStaff
txtID	DataSource	datSalesStaff
	DataField	id
txtName	DataSource	datSalesStaff
	DataField	name

Any control having DataSource and DataField properties can be data-bound, including: label, text box, check box, combo box, list box, image control, OLE container, and picture box. Many of the custom controls also can be data-bound; you can consult the Visual Basic help documentation on each custom control.

Controls That Cannot Be Bound. Notably missing from the list of data-bound controls are option buttons and scroll bars. These controls must be updated manually, which usually turns out to be a fair amount of coding. It helps to use the Reposition event handler, which is activated whenever the data control's record pointer is moved. Here, for example, we set one of two option buttons based on a recordset field called gender:

```
Private Sub datMembers_Reposition()
  Select Case datMembers.Recordset!gender
  Case "M"
    optMale.Value = True
  Case "F"
    optFemale.Value = True
```

```
    Case Else         'unknown value
      optMale.Value = False
      optFemale.Value = False
  End Select
End Sub
```

When the user has modified an option button and wants to update the recordset, you can use the option button settings to update the corresponding field. The following code might be placed in a procedure that updates the current record:

```
'Update the gender field with the option buttons.
If optMale.Value = True Then
   datMembers.Recordset!gender = "M"
ElseIf optFemale.Value = True Then
   datMembers.Recordset!gender = "F"
Else
   datMembers.Recordset!gender = "?"
End If
```

This source code, incidentally, can be applied to one of the chapter exercises dealing with the Karate School Program.

5.2 Using Microsoft Access

If you have Microsoft Access, you will find it to be an easy-to-use and powerful tool for creating databases and tables. We will take you through a brief tutorial here and show how to create a table containing the names of the sales staff at the Mozart Music store. We assume that you are using Access 97, but there are similar tutorials in Appendix B for the Data Manager and VisData programs supplied with Visual Basic.

5.2.1 Creating a Database

Launch Microsoft Access. Select the Database Wizard option, and click the OK button. When the "Blank Database" icon appears, click on OK. You will then see a dialog box with the title "File New Database". In the upper window, move to the directory where you would like to save the database, and enter the database name as **staff.mdb**. Then click the Create button. You should now see the window shown in Figure 3.

Figure 3. The Database Window.

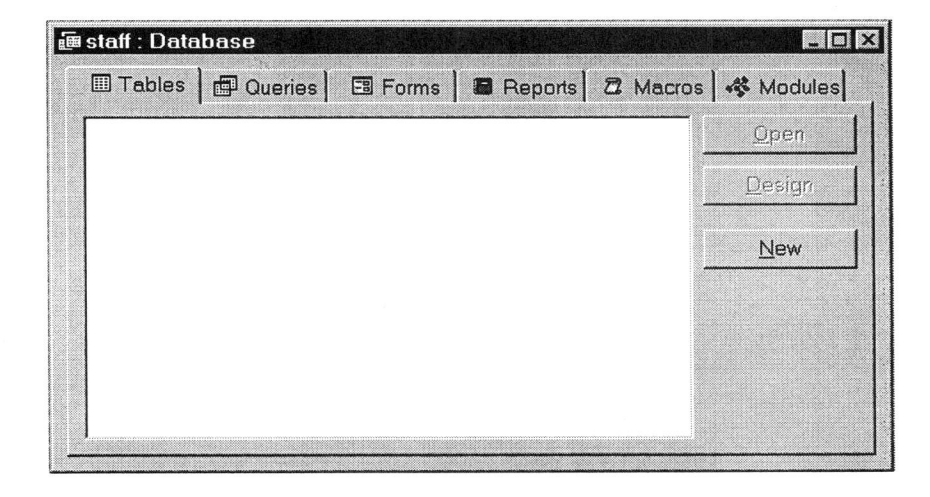

5.2.2 Creating the SalesStaff Table

Notice that the **Tables** panel has been selected in the database window. By clicking on any of these tabs, you bring another panel to the front. The Tables panel is the correct one to use when creating, deleting, viewing, or editing the design of a table.

Click the New button. Select Design View in the list box, and click the OK button to continue. The Table Design window appears, where you can enter the name and data type of each field in the table. Initially the table is called **Table1**, but we will soon give it a more meaningful name:

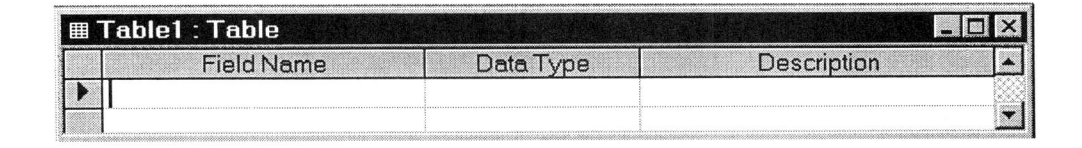

For the first field name, type **id** and press the Tab key to move to the Data Type column. For the data type, select **Number;** the specific type will default to Long Integer. In the Description column, type "Unique identification number". If you need to, you can drag the right side of this window in order to make more room for the description.

Press the Tab key to move to the next row. Enter **name** as the second field name, select **Text** as its data type. Notice the Field Size option in the lower half of the window. By default, the length of a Text field is 50 characters, but you can always enter any integer between 0 and 255. Finally, enter "Last, First" in the description column. The upper portion of the Table Design window should look like Figure 4.

Figure 4. SalesStaff Table Definition.

Field Name	Data Type	Description
id	Number	Unique identification number
name	Text	Last, First

Click on the **File/Save As** menu command and name the table **SalesStaff**. When you click on OK, Access will ask you about creating a primary key. Answer No, because we're about to do that as a separate step.

5.2.3 Creating Indexes

At this point, it would be possible to begin adding data to the table and using it in programs. But we can improve the usefulness of the table if we create table indexes. A *table index* (or simply *index*) is a mechanism built into a table definition that does two things: It permits records to be processed in a certain order, and it allows efficient searches for individual records in the table.

Let's create an index that will be based on the **id** field. Click on the View/Indexes menu command. Notice that the **id** field has already been filled in for you. Change the name of the index to **idNdx**. As a general habit, it's easy to just add an **Ndx** suffix to the name of a field when creating a matching index. Double-click on the box at the bottom of the window labeled **Primary Key** so that **Yes** appears. A *primary key* is a special type of index that guarantees that each value in that field is unique. Figure 5 shows how the Indexes window should look.

Figure 5. The Indexes Window.

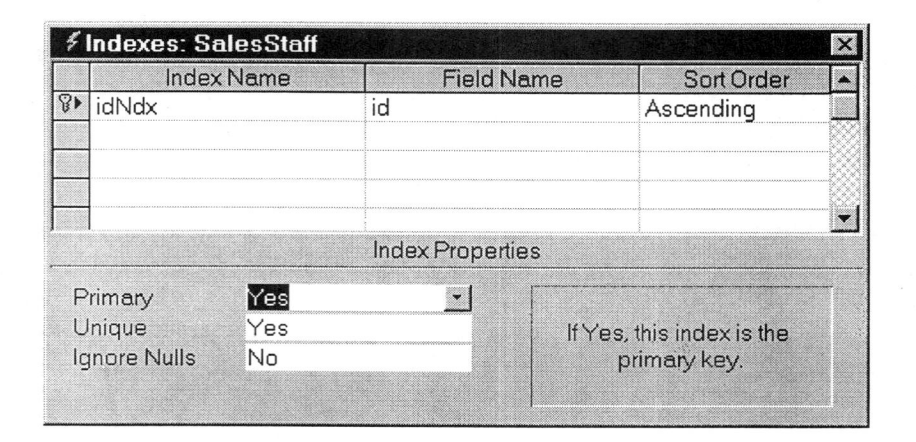

Index Name	Field Name	Sort Order
idNdx	id	Ascending

Index Properties

Primary: Yes
Unique: Yes
Ignore Nulls: No

If Yes, this index is the primary key.

Chap 5: Introducing Databases 175

Create a second index based on the **name** field, called **nameNdx**. This permits the table to be arranged in ascending order according to the names of the sales staff. Figure 6 shows the Indexes window after adding the second index. Close the Indexes window, close the Table Design window, and answer **Yes** when asked about saving changes. This will take you back to the Database window.

Figure 6. Indexes Window, Two Indexes.

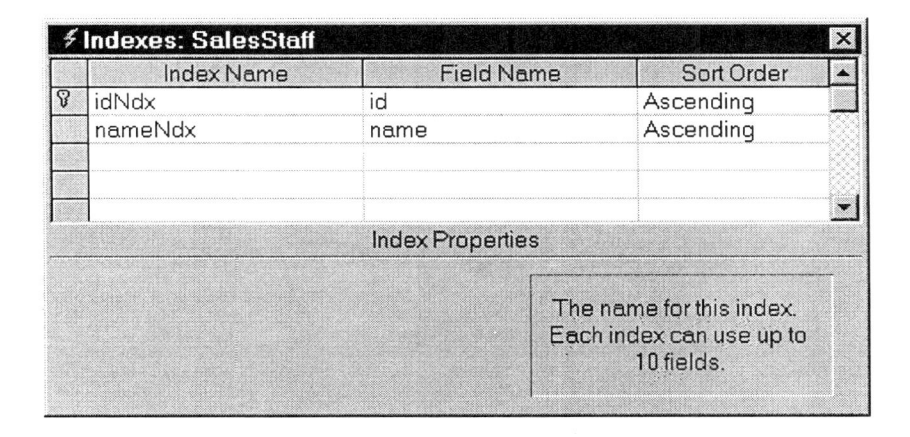

Index Name	Field Name	Sort Order
idNdx	id	Ascending
nameNdx	name	Ascending

Index Properties

The name for this index. Each index can use up to 10 fields.

5.2.4 Entering Table Data

Add some sales staff names to the table. From the Database window, click the Open button enter the following ID numbers and names, and add a few of your own:

101	Adams, Adrian
404	Del Terzo, Daniel
120	Baker, Barbara
114	Franklin, Fay
302	Easterbrook, Erin

The names are purposely not in alphabetical order, so we can later show how an index on the name field affects the record order. Click the Save button on the menu bar to save the changes you've made to the table. You're all done.

5.3 Viewing the SalesStaff Table

SlsStaff\
staff1.vbp

The easiest way to see how data controls and database tables work together is to create a short program that displays the SalesStaff table. When the user moves the data control forward and backward, the bound text controls will automatically be filled with the ID and name of the current record.

5.3.1 The Database Table

We will use an existing database called staff.mdb, which contains a table called SalesStaff, shown in Figure 7. **id** is a long integer, **name** is a Text field, **fullTime** is True/False, **hireDate** is Date/Time, and **salary** is type Currency. Figure 8 lists the indexes that have been defined for this table.

Figure 7. SalesStaff Table Data.

id	name	fullTime	hireDate	salary
101	Adams, Adrian	☑	5/20/95	$35,000.00
120	Baker, Barbara	☑	4/22/93	$32,000.00
404	Del Terzo, Daniel	☑	7/9/94	$37,500.00
302	Easterbrook, Erin	☐	7/9/94	$22,000.00
114	Franklin, Fay	☑	8/22/95	$56,000.00
821	Gomez, George	☐	1/1/90	$12,000.00
135	Heller, Henry	☑	1/1/90	$57,000.00
426	Irvine, Ian	☐	3/1/92	$18,300.00
813	Jackson, James	☑	3/1/92	$29,000.00
305	Johnson, Samuel	☑	10/20/87	$42,000.00
694	Kenwood, Kelsey	☑	6/1/89	$22,000.00
773	Lam, Lawrence	☐	6/1/89	$9,000.00
721	Molina, Marcos	☐	10/20/87	$15,000.00
396	Zabaleta, Maria	☑	11/1/85	$29,000.00

Figure 8. SalesStaff Table Indexes.

Index Name	Field Name	Sort Order
idNdx	id	Ascending
nameNdx	name	Ascending
hireDateNdx	hireDate	Ascending
salaryNdx	salary	Ascending

5.3.2 Display the Table

The main form is called **frmMain**, containing data-bound text controls and a check box to display the database fields (Figure 9). Table 3 lists the special property values that have been set in the form. When you run the program, you should be able to move forward and backward through the database table. If you modify any of the fields, the change will be saved when you move to the previous or next record.

Chap 5: Introducing Databases 177

Figure 9. SalesStaff Program, Main Window.

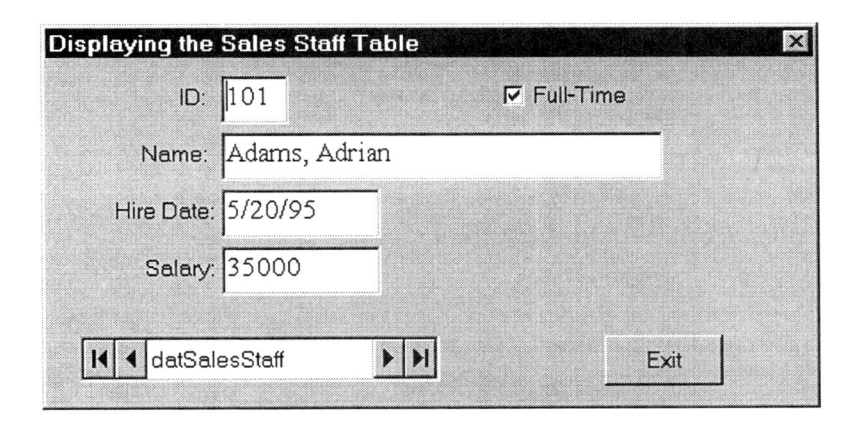

Table 3. Main Window Properties.

Control	Property	Value
datSalesStaff	Databasename RecordSource RecordSetType	staff.mdb SalesStaff 0 - Table
txtId	DataSource DataField	datSalesStaff id
txtName	DataSource DataField	datSalesStaff name
txtHireDate	DataSource DataField	datSalesStaff hireDate
txtSalary	DataSource DataField	datSalesStaff salary
chkFullTime	DataSource DataField	datSalesStaff fullTime

5.3.3 Adding New Records

The recordset object contained in the data control has three methods used by our program. The **AddNew** method creates a new, blank record. The **Update** method saves the current record into the database. The **Delete** method removes the current record from the database. With the program we've created so far, it's easy to allow the user to add new records. We will add three new buttons to the form: Add, Update, and Delete. Figure 10 shows how the main form looks when the program starts. The Update button is temporarily disabled.

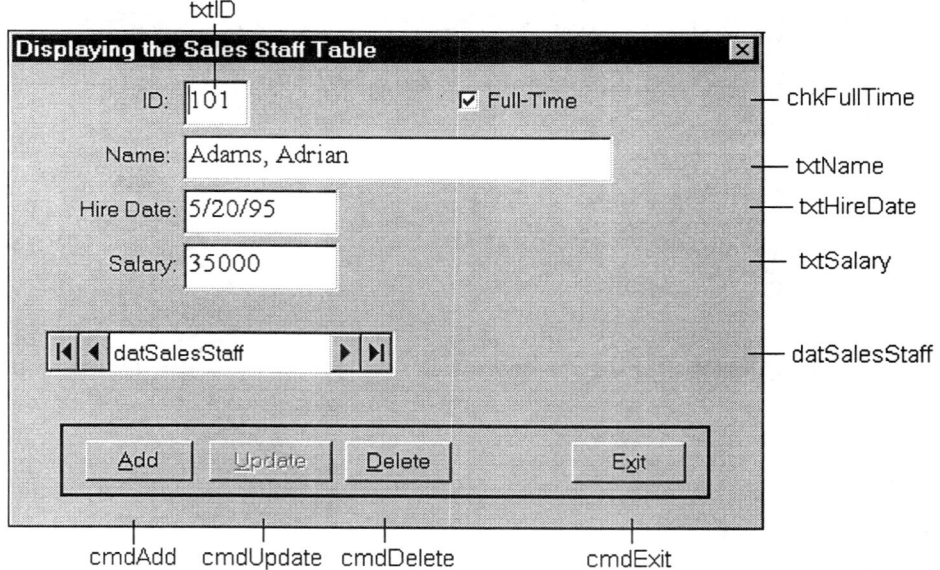

Figure 10. Displaying the SalesStaff Table.

> txtID — chkFullTime — txtName — txtHireDate — txtSalary — datSalesStaff
>
> cmdAdd   cmdUpdate   cmdDelete   cmdExit

To add a new record, the user clicks on the Add button and enters data in all of the fields. The Update button will be enabled, allowing the record to be saved.

AddNew Method. When the Add button is clicked, it is immediately disabled—this prevents the user from clicking on Add twice in a row and generating an error. We call the Recordset.AddNew method to create a new blank record:

```
Private Sub cmdAdd_Click()
  On Error GoTo cmdAdd1
  datSalesStaff.Recordset.AddNew
  cmdUpdate.Enabled = True
  cmdAdd.Enabled = False
  cmdDelete.Enabled = False
  txtID.Text = "000"
  txtID.SetFocus
  Exit Sub
cmdAdd1:
  MsgBox Error$, vbCritical, "Error"
End Sub
```

Notice that On Error Goto is very important here and in other database-related procedures, to trap potential runtime errors.

Update Method. If either the Edit or AddNew method has been called, the Update method can be used to save the values typed by the user. In the sample program, when the user clicks on the Update button, the following statements save the record in the database, disable the Update button, and enable the Add and Delete buttons:

```
Private Sub cmdUpdate_Click()
  On Error GoTo cmdUpdate1
  datSalesStaff.Recordset.Update
  cmdUpdate.Enabled = False
  cmdAdd.Enabled = True
  cmdDelete.Enabled = True
  Exit Sub
cmdUpdate1:
  MsgBox Error$, vbCritical, "Error"
End Sub
```

If you try to call the Update method without first calling either AddNew or Edit, a runtime error is generated.

Delete Method. When the Delete button is clicked, we call the Recordset.Delete method and immediately refresh the data control. This is necessary to prevent the data control from being positioned on a nonexistent record:

```
Private Sub cmdDelete_Click()
  On Error GoTo cmdDelete1
  datSalesStaff.Recordset.Delete
  datSalesStaff.Refresh
  Exit Sub
cmdDelete1:
  MsgBox Error$, vbCritical, "Error"
End Sub
```

When the program starts, we disable the Update button because the recordset's Update method cannot be called unless either an Add or Edit operation is in progress:

```
Private Sub Form_Load()
  cmdUpdate.Enabled = False
End Sub
```

5.3.4 Changing the Record Order

Next, let's add a combo box called cboIndex that lets the user select one of several predefined indexes that determine the ordering of records (Figure 11). Indexes are available for the ID, name, hireDate, and salary fields. A requirement is that the data control's recordset has to be a table-type recordset.

Figure 11. Selecting a Different Index.

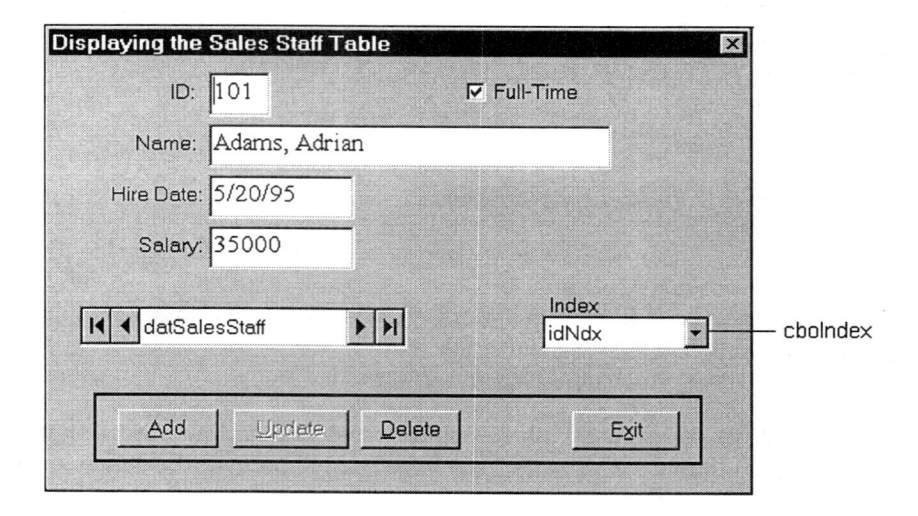

While in design mode, set the following properties for the cboIndex combo box:

Property	Value
List	idNdx, nameNdx, hireDateNdx, salaryNdx
Style	Dropdown List

The SetIndex procedure gets the index name from the combo box and assigns it to the Recordset.Index property of the data control:

```
Public Sub SetIndex()
  On Error GoTo SetIndex1
  datSalesStaff.Recordset.Index = cboIndex.Text
  Exit Sub
SetIndex1:
  MsgBox Error$, vbCritical, "Error"
End Sub
```

The click event procedure for the combo box modifies the index property of the Recordset:

```
Private Sub cboIndex_Click()
  SetIndex
End Sub
```

In Form_Activate, we select the first index name in the combo box by setting ListIndex to zero and call SetIndex:

```
Private Sub Form_Activate()
  cboIndex.ListIndex = 0
  SetIndex
End Sub
```

Chap 5: Introducing Databases   181

> *Visual Basic Tip:* We didn't set the ListIndex property inside the Form_Load procedure because setting the ListIndex property of a combo box or list box automatically triggers a Click event. Our cboIndex_Click procedure modifies the Index of the recordset, but this cannot be done until the recordset in datSalesStaff has been opened. By the time the Form_Activate event occurs, the recordset is open and ready to accept calls to its methods.

When you run the program, switch between indexes and notice that the order of records changes.

5.4   Moving the Recordset Pointer

A recordset always maintains an internal pointer to the current record, which we also call the *current position*. When a recordset is opened, refreshed, or created, the current position is at the first record. The following recordset properties return information about the current position:

Property	Description
BOF	Set to True if the current position is just before the first record in the recordset. BOF means "beginning of file".
EOF	Set to True if the current position is just after the last record in the recordset. EOF means "end of file".
PercentPosition	Returns a number between 0 and 100 indicating the approximate location of the current record in relation to the total number of records.

The following Recordset methods modify the current position:

Method	Description
Move *n*	If n > 0, move n rows forward from the current position; if n < 0, move n rows backward from the current position.
MoveFirst	Move to the first record
MoveLast	Move to the last record
MoveNext	Move forward one record
MovePrevious	Move backward one record

The following statement moves to the beginning of datInvoices.Recordset:

```
datInvoices.Recordset.MoveFirst
```

The following statement skips the next record and moves to the one after it:

```
datInvoices.Recordset.Move 2
```

In some cases, these methods will move the position to a nonexistent record. For example, if you follow MoveLast with MoveNext. This will generate a *trappable error*, meaning that you can handle it with On Error GoTo.

5.4.1 Example: SalesStaff Table

When you use the arrow buttons on a data control, it is not possible to move beyond the end of the recordset to a nonexistent record. But if you implement your own Previous and Next buttons, you have to handle errors in program code. Let's revisit the SalesStaff program. In this new version, we will add buttons that move to the first, last, previous, and next records. In doing so, we will have to check the BOF and EOF properties. Figure 12 shows the new program's main window, shown in design mode.

Figure 12. Adding Navigation Buttons to the SalesStaff Program.

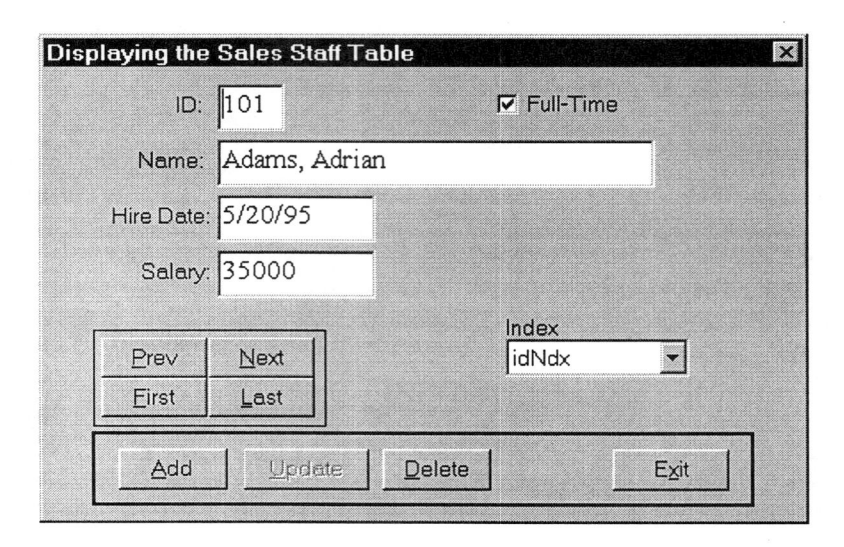

Next, we place code in the button event procedures. The cmdFirst and cmdLast buttons are simple because no error checking is required:

```
Private Sub cmdFirst_Click()
    datSalesStaff.Recordset.MoveFirst
End Sub

Private Sub cmdLast_Click()
    datSalesStaff.Recordset.MoveLast
End Sub
```

It would be tempting to write the cmdNext and cmdPrev event handlers the same way. For example:

```
Private Sub cmdNext_Click()
    datSalesStaff.Recordset.MoveNext
End Sub

Private Sub cmdPrev_Click()
    datSalesStaff.Recordset.MovePrevious
End Sub
```

Chap 5: Introducing Databases

But the user might move to the last record and then click on the "Next" button. A "No current record" error message would display when the current position was beyond the last record. The same error would appear if the user moved to the first record and clicked on the **Prev** button. When moving forward, the solution is to check the EOF property: if the position pointer has moved past the last record, back up:

```
Private Sub cmdNext_Click()
  datSalesStaff.Recordset.MoveNext
  If datSalesStaff.Recordset.EOF Then
    datSalesStaff.Recordset.MovePrevious
  End If
End Sub
```

Similarly, we check for BOF when moving to the previous record, and move forward if necessary:

```
Private Sub cmdPrev_Click()
  datSalesStaff.Recordset.MovePrevious
  If datSalesStaff.Recordset.BOF Then
    datSalesStaff.Recordset.MoveNext
  End If
End Sub
```

5.5 Data-Bound List, Combo, and Grid

5.5.1 Data-Bound List Control

The data-bound list control (DBList) fills itself automatically when linked to a data control. The recordset attached to the data control provides the data. This is a great convenience, sparing us from having to explicitly code a loop to do the same thing.

The two essential properties that need to be set in the data-bound list control are RowSource and ListField. **RowSource** is the name of a data control on the current form that is already attached to a database table. **ListField** is the name of the recordset field that we want to display.

To illustrate, let's create a form containing a data control and a data-bound list box. The data control is attached to the Publishers table in the **biblio.mdb** database supplied with Visual Basic (Figure 13).

Figure 13. Data-Bound List Box Example.

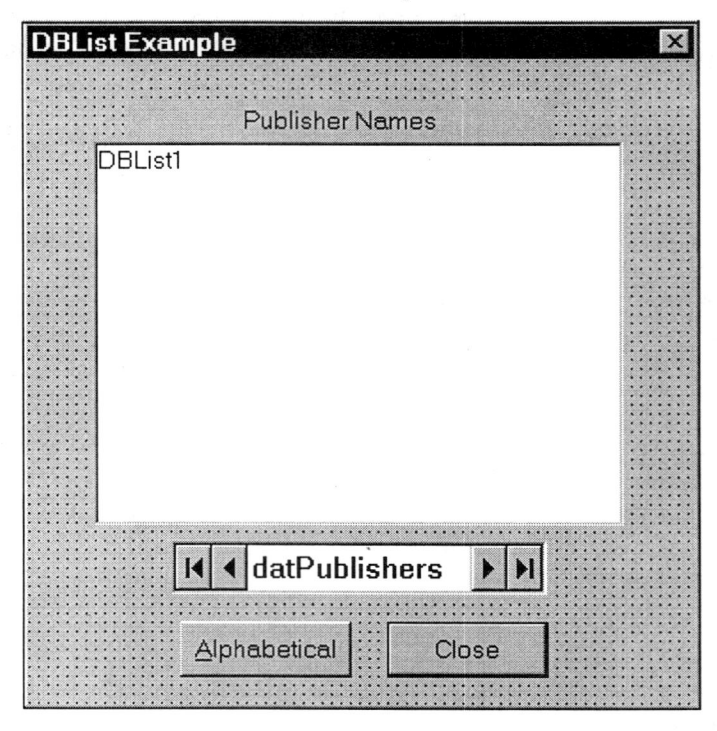

[DBList Example form showing "Publisher Names" label, DBList1 list box, datPublishers data control with navigation arrows, Alphabetical and Close buttons.]

The **datPublishers** and **DBList** properties are set to the following values:

datPublishers	
Recordsource	Publishers
RecordsetType	Snapshot
Visible	False
DBList1	
RowSource	datPublishers
ListField	Name
MatchEntry	dbExtendedMatching

The data control's Visible property is False because it is not manipulated by the user. Figure 14 shows what the form looks like while running.

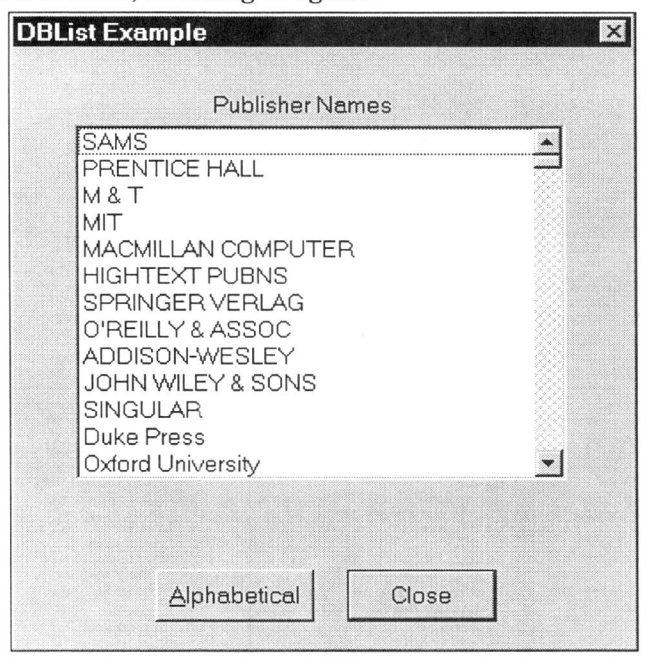

Figure 14. DBList, Running Program.

By default, the publisher names are displayed in the same physical order as the records in the database. The code behind the **Alphabetical** button uses an SQL (*structured query language*) command to select just the **name** field from the Publishers table, order the records alphabetically by name, and assign the result to the RecordSource property of the data control:

```
datPublishers.RecordSource = "SELECT name FROM Publishers " _
     + "ORDER BY name"
datPublishers.Refresh
```

Whenever you modify the RecordSource property of a data control, the **Refresh** method must be called to reload the data control. SQL will be discussed in Sections 5.8.2, 7.2, and 7.3.

MatchEntry Property. A data-bound list control has a property called MatchEntry that may be set to one of two values: dbBasicMatching or dbExtendedMatching. *Basic matching*, the default, causes the box to scroll to the first entry that matches a character pressed at the keyboard. For example, if you press the letter "N", the box will find the first publisher name in the list box beginning with N. *Extended matching* lets the user type in multiple characters that will be used in the search for the first matching entry. This mode takes a little getting used to. If you pause for three seconds or more, the matching string is discarded and the search starts over with the next character entered.

For example, run the sample program, which has MatchEntry equal to dbExtendedMatching. Click on the Alphabetical button, press the Tab key until the list box has the focus, and try the following input:

Input	Expected Result
na	Scrolls to "National Assn of Insurance"
(wait 3 seconds)	Matching mechanism resets.
b	Scrolls to "Baker & Taylor"

5.5.2 Data-Bound Combo Control

The data-bound combo control, like the data-bound list box, is able to automatically display one column of a recordset. But it is even more useful when it links two recordsets, allowing the user to pick a value from a list and use that value to update another recordset.

For example, in the **Biblio.mdb** database supplied with Visual Basic, the **Titles** and **Publishers** tables are related by the pubID field. By this, we mean that a publisher ID in the Titles table must match one of the publisher IDs in the Publishers table:

Titles: PubID, AU_ID, Title, Year_Published, ISBN
Publishers: PubID, Name

The publisher name is not stored in the Titles table, but the publisher ID is. The publisher name can always be found in the Publishers table along with its matching ID.

Sample Program. We will create a form on which there are two data controls called datTitles and datPublishers. There will be a data-bound combo box called DBCombo1.

Each database table will be attached to a separate data control. The **Titles** table is attached to datTitles, and the **Publishers** table is attached to datPublishers. The following properties of DBCombo1 are set:

RowSource	datPublishers
ListField	Name
BoundColumn	PubID
DataSource	datTitles
DataField	PubID

RowSource and ListField attach the combo box to the Publishers.Name field. BoundColumn shows that PubID will be the linking field between the two tables. The DataSource and DataField properties indicate that the Titles.PubID field will be updated. The DataField and BoundColumn fields should contain the same value.

When the user clicks on the datTitles data control to move from one record to the next, the book title and publisher names change. The user can then select a different publisher name. Here is a sample of the program's main form, shown in Figure 15.

Chap 5: Introducing Databases 187

Figure 15. Selecting a Different Publisher.

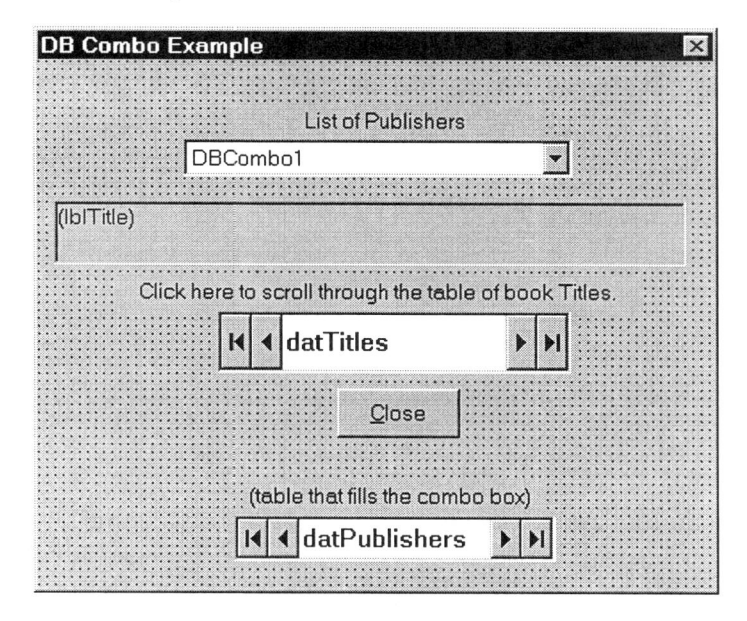

The same form is also shown at run time in Figure 16. As the user clicks on the data control to move to each new record in the Titles table, the publisher name in the combo box and the book title in the label both change automatically.

Figure 16. Displaying the Titles Table.

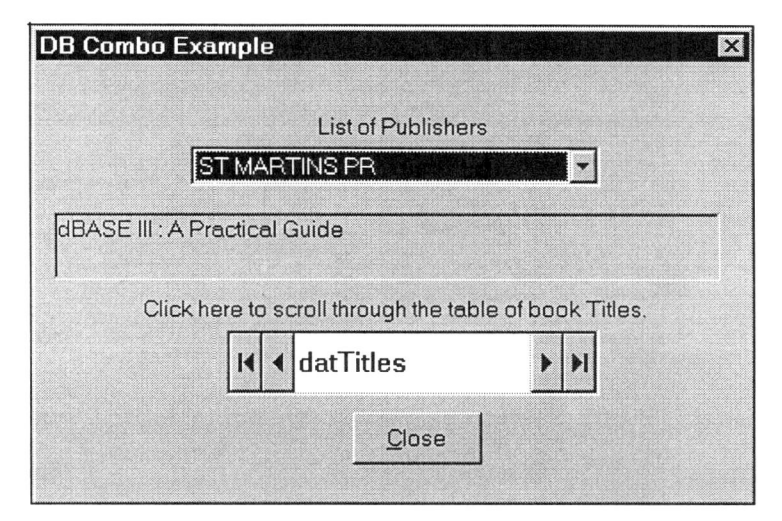

If you select another publisher from the combo box and click on the data control to move to another record, the new publisher ID will be saved in the Titles table. When you move back to the modified record, the new publisher name will appear.

5.5.3 Data-Bound Grid Control

The Apex Data-Bound Grid control, called **DBGrid**, is able to display a recordset in a spreadsheet-like format, where each row is a separate record and each column is a field. When attached to a data control, the grid is filled automatically when its form loads, and column headers contain the recordset's field names. An easy way to demonstrate the DBGrid control is to create a form with a data control and a grid, and set the following properties (some are defaults):

datPublishers	
Databasename	c:\...\Biblio.mdb
Recordsource	Publishers
RecordsetType	Dynaset (default)
DBGrid1	
DataSource	datPublishers
AllowUpdate	True (default)

Figure 17 displays the form as it appears in design mode.

Figure 17. DBGrid Attached to the Publishers Table.

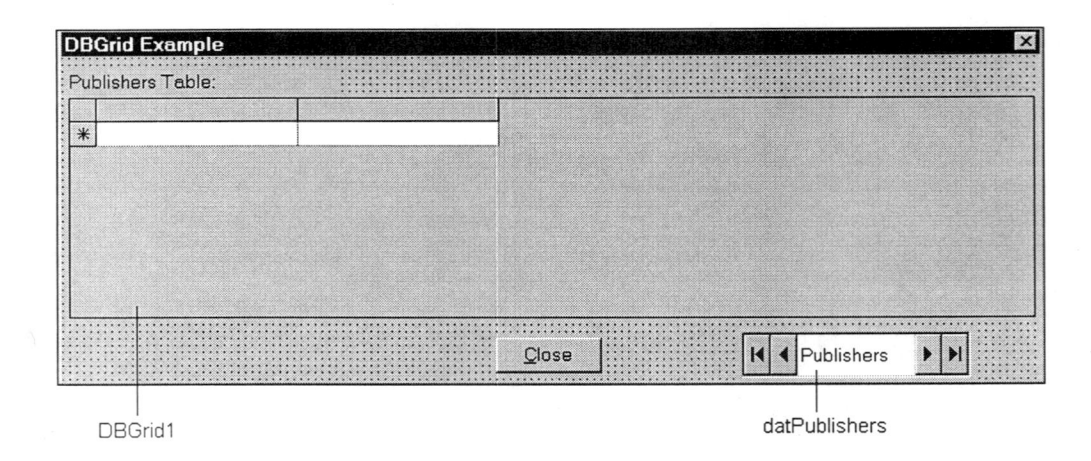

Figure 18 shows the same form as it appears while the program is running.

Figure 18. Publishers Table in Run Mode.

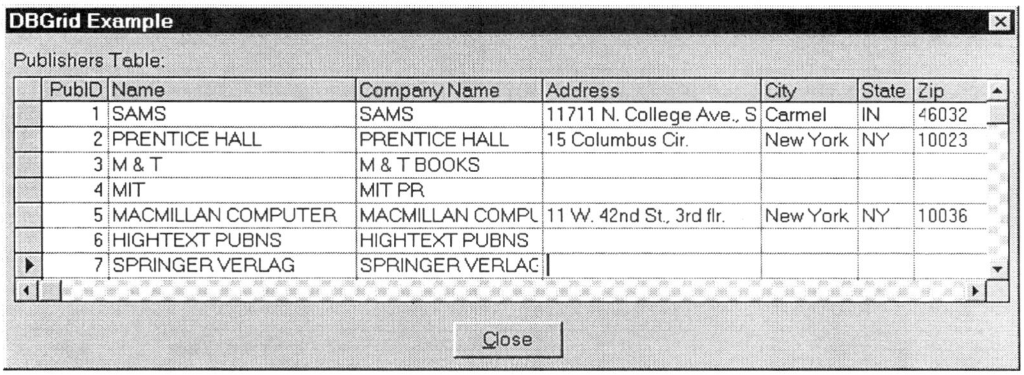

The user can adjust the widths of the columns by dragging the dividers between the field names to the right and left. If the attached recordset is updatable and the AllowUpdate property of the DBGrid is True, the user can also click and edit an individual cell, and the changes will be saved when the user moves to a new row.

Updatable Recordset. The recordset attached to a data control is considered updatable if all of the following are true:

- The data control's RecordsetType property is either *Dynaset* or *Table*.
- The data control's ReadOnly property is False.
- The Updatable property of the recordset named in the data control's Recordsource property is True.

One other factor to consider when deleting or modifying records is that the database itself may contain built-in error checking, called *referential integrity* checking. This refers to the links between common fields in different tables. If deleting or modifying a record would invalidate one of those links, the database will produce a runtime error that is displayed by Visual Basic.

Some other interesting DBGrid properties are listed in Table 4. There are a great many other properties in the DBGrid control, which are explained in the Visual Basic help system.

> ***Programming Tip.*** To add the DBGrid control to your VB5 project, use the Project / Components menu command, and place a check next to "Microsoft Data-Bound Grid Control". In VB4, the same control can be selected from the Options / Custom Control menu.

Table 4. Selected DBGrid Properties.

Property	Description
Columns	Collection of column objects.
Columns.Count	Number of columns.
Column.Width	Width of a single column.
Columns.ColIndx	Current column index.
ColumnHeaders	Values are: True, False. If True, the field names will display in the grid columns.
AllowAddNew	Values are: True, False. If True, when the user moves to the last row, a blank row will open up and the user may enter a new record.
AllowDelete	Values are: True, False. If True, the user can interactively delete records from the underlying recordset.
AllowUpdate	Values are: True, False. If True, the user can interactively update records from the underlying recordset.

5.6 Mozart Music Sales - 4

Let's do a minor revision of the Mozart Music Sales program from Chapter 2, by loading the list of salespeople from a database, and saving each invoice in the same database. We will use a data-bound combo box to display the list of salespeople.

5.6.1 Program Specifications

- The names of the sales staff will be read from a database table.
- Each invoice will be saved in a database table for later use. An invoice will contain an invoice number, date, total amount, tax, and net amount.
- To the user, the program will appear identical to Mozart Music Sales Version 3.

5.6.2 Program Design

We have added a data control to the form called **datSalesStaff**, which provides access to the SalesStaff table in the **mozart.mdb** database. Another data control, **datInvoices**, provides access to the Invoices table in the same database. Figure 19 shows the form in design mode.

Figure 19. Main Sales Program.

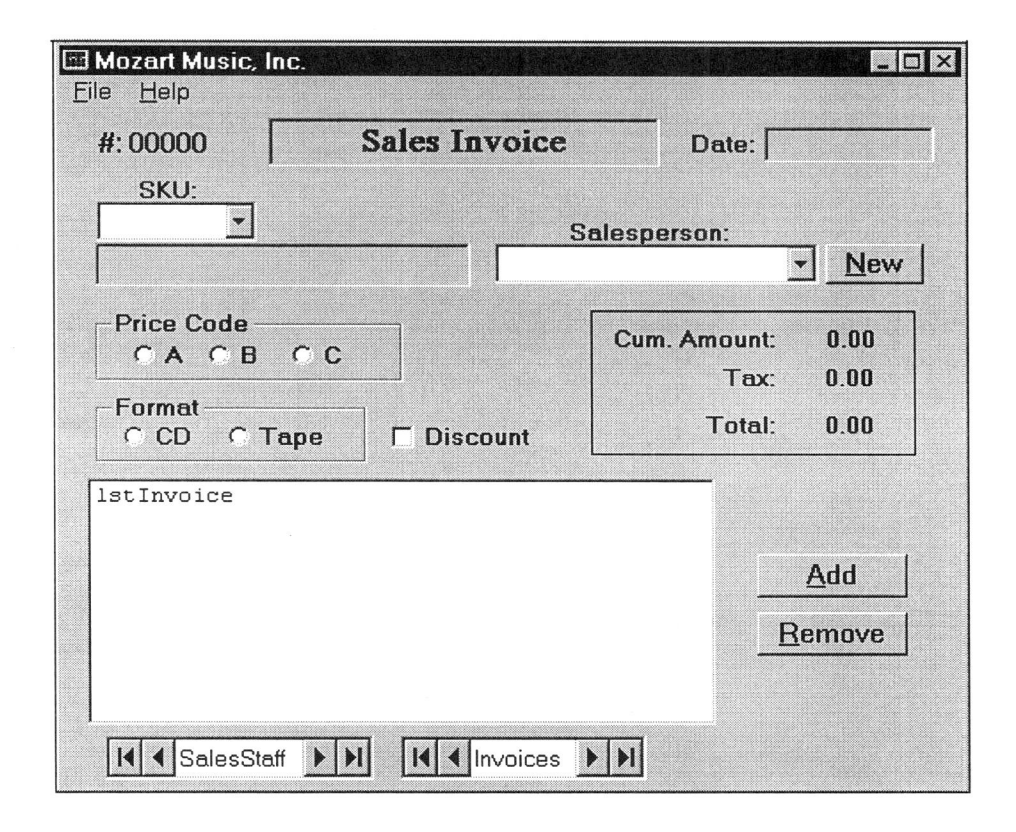

The Visible property of both data controls is set to False because the user will not manipulate them directly. There has also been a minor rearranging of controls on the form. The combo box holding the salesperson names is now a data-bound combo box, still called cboSalesPerson.

5.6.3 Program Implementation

Because this program is a continuation of Mozart Music Sales 3, we will show only the changes implemented here. The following control properties must be set:

```
cboSalesPerson
    RowSource           datSalesStaff
    ListField           name
datInvoices
    DatabaseName        mozart.mdb
    RecordSource        Invoices
datSalesStaff
    DatabaseName        mozart.mdb
    RecordSource        SalesStaff
    RecordsetType       Table
```

In the declarations area of frmMain, the SalesPerson filename has been removed. In **Form_Load,** it is no longer necessary to call LoadSalesStaff because the data-bound combo box loads the table automatically:

```
Private Sub Form_Load()
  frmSplash.Show vbModal
  ChDrive App.Path
  ChDir App.Path
  lblDate.Caption = Date$
  GetNewInvoiceNumber
  LoadTitles
  optPriceA.Value = True
  optCD.Value = True
End Sub
```

In Form_Activate, we select the Index of the recordset attached to datSalesStaff so the names can be displayed in alphabetical order:

```
Private Sub Form_Activate()
  datSalesStaff.Recordset.Index = "nameNdx"
End Sub
```

The **mnuFileSave_Click** procedure has been revised because the invoice is now saved in a database table. We use the Recordset property of the datInvoices data control. The AddNew method creates a blank record and the Update method saves the changes:

```
Private Sub mnuFileSave_Click()
  '...
  On Error GoTo FileSave1
  With datInvoices
    .Recordset.AddNew
    .Recordset!id = Format$(invoiceNum, "00000")
    .Recordset!Date = Date
    .Recordset!amount = Val(lblAmount.Caption)
    .Recordset!tax = Val(lblTax.Caption)
    .Recordset!netAmount = Val(lblNetTotal.Caption)
    .Recordset.Update
  End With
  (etc.)
```

Notation. The notation datInvoices.Recordset!id needs some explanation. A more verbose way to reference the value of the id field in the current record of the Invoices table would be the following:

```
datInvoices.Recordset.Fields("id").Value
```

This says, beginning with the current recordset object, get its Fields property, which is a collection; index into the collection using "id" as a lookup value; when the appropriate field is found, access its Value property. But the following notation is more efficient at runtime, and is recommended in the Visual Basic documentation:

```
datInvoices.Recordset!id
```

Chap 5: Introducing Databases

Or, if the **With..End With** block already includes the Recordset property, the Fields property is still useful:

```
With datInvoices.Recordset
  .AddNew
  .Fields!id = Format$(invoiceNum, "00000")
  .Fields!Date = Date
  .Fields!amount = Val(lblAmount.Caption)
  '(etc.)
End With
```

Adding a New Salesperson. The cmdNew_Click event handler also has to be updated, because the person's name is now saved in the database:

```
Private Sub cmdNew_Click()
  On Error GoTo cmdNew1
  If Len(Trim$(cboSalesPerson.Text)) = 0 Then
    MsgBox "The salesperson name cannot be blank.", _
           vbInformation, "New Salesperson"
  Else
    With datSalesStaff
      .Recordset.AddNew
      .Recordset!Name = cboSalesPerson.Text
      .Recordset.Update
    End With
  End If
  Exit Sub
cmdNew1:
  MsgBox Error$, vbCritical, "Error"
End Sub
```

5.7 Mail-Order Computer Sales

Whenever ordering a computer from a mail-order company, it's easy to be amazed at how quickly a salesperson can mix and match various options, quote prices, and check inventory stock levels. Clearly, their programmers and designers have worked hard to design software that allows instant access to a lot of information. With that idea in mind, the **Mail-Order Computer Sales** program represents the first step toward such an online system.

5.7.1 Program Specifications

- When the program starts, display the date and time in the upper right corner of the main form.
- When a customer calls, the salesperson (the user) needs to look up information about standard computer models sold by the company. Each model has a set price and a standard configuration.
- When the user selects a system, its price and configuration are displayed immediately.

- The user can also select one or more add-on options such as more memory, a larger video display, and so on. As each feature is selected, the total system price is recalculated and displayed.

5.7.2 Program Design

When the user selects the base system from the combo box in the upper left corner, a description of the system's basic configuration appears on the right side of the form, as in Figure 20. At the same time, a list of add-on options (for all computer models) appears in a multiselect listbox. Here, for example, is the configuration for a base system called MP-150, with one option added:

Figure 20. Mail-Order Computer Purchase.

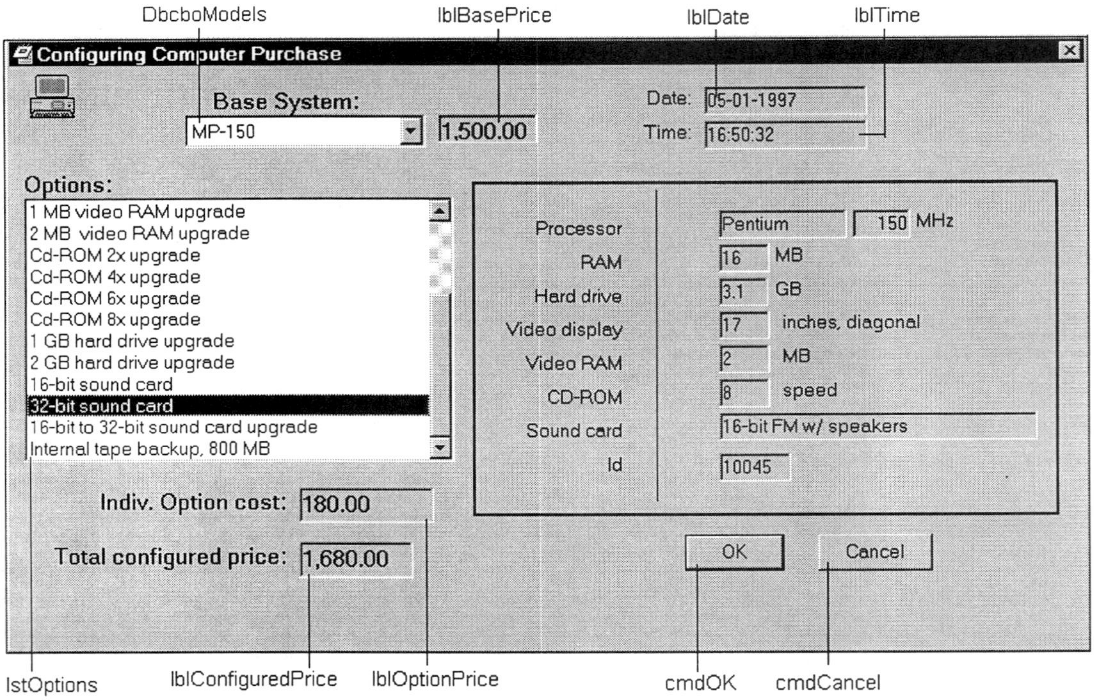

The user selects options to be added to the system by clicking on their descriptions in the listbox. As each option is selected, its individual cost appears below the listbox and its cost is added to the configured price of the system. If the user clicks on one of the selected options again, the option is deselected and the option price is subtracted from the configured price.

5.7.3 The Computer Database

Models Table. On the diskette accompanying this book, there is a database file called **computer.mdb.** In this database, there is a table called **Models** that contains information about different models of computers sold by a computer company. The following fields are integers: id, cpuSpeed, ram, displaySize, videoRam, cdROMspeed. The driveSpace field is type Single; the price field is type Currency, and the name, processor, and soundCard fields are type Text. Sample data for this table appears in Figure 21.

Figure 21. The Models Table.

	id	name	processor	cpuSpeed	price	ram	driveSpace	displaySize	videoRAM	cdROMspeed
1	10021	MDX4	80486	100	$600.00	8	1.2	14	1	4
2	10024	MP-180	Pentium	180	$1,900.00	16	2.2	17	2	8
3	10031	MP-133	Pentium	133	$1,200.00	16	2.4	15	1	6
4	10045	MP-150	Pentium	150	$1,500.00	16	3.1	17	2	8
5	10312	MP-200	PentPro	200	$2,500.00	32	3.6	17	2	10
6	10456	MP-75	Pentium	75	$1,000.00	16	2.2	14	1	4
7	10726	ZX-100	Pentium	100	$900.00	8	1.2	15	1	6

	soundCard
1	none
2	32-bit wave table w/ speakers
3	16-bit FM w/ speakers
4	16-bit FM w/ speakers
5	32-bit wave table w/ speakers
6	16-bit FM w/ speakers
7	none

The Models table has two indexes: The primary key is **idNdx**, based on the id field; a second index, called **nameNdx**, is based on the name field.

Options Table. The database also contains a table called **Options**, shown in Figure 22. Each record contains a description of an add-on option that may be purchased by a customer. The description field is type Text and the price field is type Currency. The id field provides a convenient way to sort the records so that similar types of options can be grouped together.

Figure 22. The Options Table.

id	description	price
1	8 MB RAM upgrade	$75.00
2	16 MB RAM upgrade	$150.00
3	32 MB RAM upgrade	$280.00
10	Video display 14 to 15 upgrade	$150.00
12	Video display 15 to 17 upgrade	$350.00
14	Video display 17 to 20 upgrade	$1,000.00
20	1 MB video RAM upgrade	$50.00
22	2 MB video RAM upgrade	$100.00
30	Cd-ROM 2x upgrade	$25.00
32	Cd-ROM 4x upgrade	$50.00
34	Cd-ROM 6x upgrade	$77.00
36	Cd-ROM 8x upgrade	$160.00
40	1 GB hard drive upgrade	$150.00
42	2 GB hard drive upgrade	$250.00
60	16-bit sound card	$100.00
61	32-bit sound card	$180.00
62	16-bit to 32-bit sound card upgrade	$80.00
70	Internal tape backup, 800 MB	$300.00

5.7.4 Program Implementation

The program contains a main form and a code module: frmMain.frm, and module1.bas. The following properties are assigned to frmMain:

```
frmMain
   BorderStyle            Fixed Dialog
   Caption                "Configuring Computer Purchase"
```

The following controls are on frmMain:

```
lblBasePrice                   (Label)
   DataSource                  datModels
   DataField                   price
datOptions                     (Data control)
   DatabaseName                computer.mdb
   ReadOnly                    True
   RecordsetType               Table
   RecordSource                Options
   Visible                     False
datModels                      (Data control)
   DatabaseName                computer.mdb
   ReadOnly                    True
   RecordsetType               Table
   RecordSource                Models
   Visible                     False
lstOptions                     (List Box)
   MultiSelect                 Simple
cmdCancel                      (Command Button)
```

Chap 5: Introducing Databases   197

```
       Cancel                          True
    cmdOK                              (Command Button)
       Default                         True
    DbcboModels                        (Data-Bound Combo)
       ListField                       name
       RowSource                       datModels
```

Each field in the Models table is attached to a data-bound label that appears on the right side of the form. The field names are: id, name, processor, cpuSpeed, price, ram, driveSpace, displaySize, videoRAM, cdROMspeed, and soundCard.

Module1.bas. The optionPrice array is loaded from the Options database table:

```
Const MaxPrices = 30
Public optionPrice(0 To MaxPrices) As Currency
```

The following procedures are in module1: Main, LoadOptions, and CalculatePrice:

```
Public Sub Main()
  ChDrive App.Path
  ChDir App.Path
  frmMain.Show vbModal
  End
End Sub
```

The **CalculatePrice** procedure gets the base price from the Models table, loops through the lstOptions list box, and checks for any items that have been selected. The corresponding price for each selected item is obtained from the optionPrice array and added to the price:

```
Public Sub CalculatePrice()
  Dim j As Integer, price As Currency
  On Error GoTo CalcPrice1
  price = frmMain.datModels.Recordset!price
  frmMain.lblBasePrice.Caption = Format$(price, _
     "standard")
  For j = 0 To frmMain.lstOptions.ListCount - 1
    If frmMain.lstOptions.Selected(j) Then
      price = price + optionPrice(j)
    End If
  Next j
  frmMain.lblConfiguredPrice.Caption = _
     Format$(price, "standard")
  Exit Sub
CalcPrice1:
  MsgBox Error$, vbInformation, "CalculatePrice"
End Sub
```

The **LoadOptions** procedure reads the Options table and fills the lstOptions list box. It also fills an array called optionPrice with the prices of all options:

```
Public Sub LoadOptions()
  Dim j As Integer, R As Recordset
  On Error GoTo LoadOptions1
```

```
      Set R = frmMain.datOptions.Recordset
      j = 0
      R.MoveFirst
      Do While Not R.EOF
         frmMain.lstOptions.AddItem R!Description
         optionPrice(j) = R!price
         j = j + 1
         R.MoveNext
      Loop
      Exit Sub
LoadOptions1:
      MsgBox Error$, vbInformation, "LoadOptions"
End Sub
```

The frmMain Form. In frmMain, the Form_Load procedure gets the current date and time:

```
Private Sub Form_Load()
   lblDate.Caption = Date$
   lblTime.Caption = Time$
End Sub
```

The **Form_Activate** handler executes when the form becomes visible, initializing the indexes of each data control and calculating the price of the current computer configuration:

```
Private Sub Form_Activate()
   datModels.Recordset.Index = "nameNdx"
   datOptions.Recordset.Index = "idNdx"
   DBcboModels.Text = datModels.Recordset!name
   CalculatePrice
End Sub
```

DBcboModels is a data-bound combo box that fills itself automatically from the Models database table. When the user selects a computer model from this list, we use the Seek method to search for the model name in the Models table, and if found, calculate the computer's price:

```
Private Sub DBcboModels_Click(Area As Integer)
   If Area <> 2 Then Exit Sub
   datModels.Recordset.Seek "=", DBcboModels.Text
   If datModels.Recordset.NoMatch Then
      MsgBox "Model information not found", _
         vbInformation, "Error"
   Else
      If lstOptions.ListCount = 0 Then LoadOptions
      CalculatePrice
   End If
End Sub
```

This procedure has a parameter called **Area** that equals 2 when the user has clicked on one of the combo box choices. Other Area values are returned when the user clicks elsewhere on the combo box.

Options List Box. In frmMain, when the user clicks on one of the options, we display the cost of the option and recalculate the total cost of the system. The optionPrice array was initialized when the list box was filled:

```
Private Sub lstOptions_Click()
  Dim n As Integer
  n = lstOptions.ListIndex
  lblOptionCost.Caption = Format$(optionPrice(n), "standard")
  CalculatePrice
End Sub
```

Closing the Form. The user can click on either the OK or Cancel button, and in each case, the program confirms the choice with a message box:

```
Private Sub cmdCancel_Click()
  Dim choice As Integer
  choice = MsgBox("Cancel this order?", _
          vbYesNo + vbQuestion, "")
  If choice = vbYes Then
    'User has decided to cancel the order.
    Unload Me
  End If
End Sub

Private Sub cmdOK_Click()
  Dim choice As Integer
  choice = MsgBox("Process this order?", _
          vbYesNo + vbQuestion, "")
  If choice = vbYes Then
    'User has decided to processs the order,
    'so code to save the invoice would be here.
    Unload Me
  End If
End Sub
```

Of course, future versions of this program should provide the user a way to save the order information, print invoices, and display a list of invoices on the screen.

5.8 Searching for Records (SalesStaff 3)

SlsStaff\
Staff3

There are two common ways of searching for records in a recordset. One way is to use the **Seek** method; another is to use **FindFirst** and **FindNext**. The Seek method can only be used with a table-type recordset, whereas the FindFirst and FindNext methods can only be used with snapshot and dynaset-type recordsets. In this section we will build a simple program that is a continuation of the Sales Staff table program. The last version was SalesStaff2; this one will be called SalesStaff3.

5.8.1 Table Seek Method

Before calling the Seek method (Figure 23), the recordset's Index property must be assigned the name of an index. In our discussions, we will refer only to indexes that have been predefined in the database. The RecordsetType property of the datSalesStaff data control is *Table*.

Figure 23. Using the Table Seek Method.

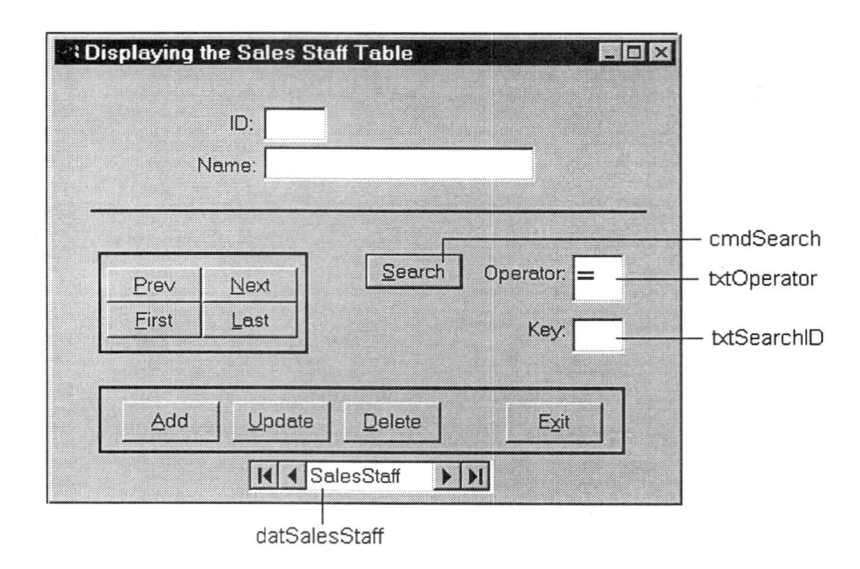

A button called **Search** has been added to the form, along with two text controls that hold a search operator and a search key. The Search button activates the search, looking for the ID number entered in the text control marked "Key". The user can modify the search operator.

cmdSearch Button. When we designed the SalesStaff table, we created indexes on each of the fields, including **idNdx** on the ID field:

```
datSalesStaff.RecordSet.Index = "idNdx"
```

The Seek method has two parameters: the first, a string, contains the comparison operator that will be used when searching:

```
recordSetName.Seek comparison, key
```

The *comparison* parameter must be a string containing one of the following operators: =, <, >, <= , or >=. The *key* parameter is the value being used for the search. Its data type has to match the data type of the current table index. For example, we might want to search for the record having ID = 5:

```
datSalesStaff.RecordSet.Seek "=", 5
```

If the index defines a field that has duplicate values, Seek stops as soon as it finds the first match.

Using Relational Operators. If the comparison operator is =, >, or >=, Seek starts at the beginning of the index and searches in a forward direction. If the comparison operator is < or <=, Seek starts at the end of the index and searches backward. For example, if the ID numbers in the SalesStaff table are indexed in ascending order, the following call to Seek will start at the beginning of the table, and stop when it locates the record with ID 6:

```
datSalesStaff.RecordSet.Seek ">", 5      'finds ID = 6
```

The following statement will start at the end of the table, and stop when it locates the record with ID 4:

```
datSalesStaff.RecordSet.Seek "<", 5      'finds ID = 4
```

If the table is indexed in descending order, however, the results are quite different. The following examples show this:

```
datSalesStaff.RecordSet.Seek ">", 5      'finds ID = 4
datSalesStaff.RecordSet.Seek "<", 5      'finds ID = 6
```

This is not quite intuitive, so the diagram in Figure 24 shows two sets of 10 ID numbers, sorted in ascending and descending order, along with the effect of searching for ID < 5 and ID > 5.

Figure 24. Seek Method, using < and > Operators.

Indexed in Ascending Order	Indexed in Descending Order
id < 5 1 2 3 4 [5] 6 7 8 9 10	id < 5 10 9 8 7 6 [5] 4 3 2 1
id > 5 1 2 3 4 [5] 6 7 8 9 10	id > 5 10 9 8 7 6 [5] 4 3 2 1

Modifying cmdSearch_Click. Returning to the current program, let's search for an ID number that was entered by the user. We retrieve it from a text box, convert it to a numeric value, and pass it to the Seek method. The search operator is taken from the txtOperator text control:

```
Private Sub cmdSearch_Click()
  Dim idNum As Integer
  datSalesStaff.Recordset.Index = "idNdx"
  idNum = Val(txtSearchId.Text)
  datSalesStaff.RecordSet.Seek txtOperator.Text, idNum
  If datSalesStaff.RecordSet.NoMatch Then
    MsgBox "Unable to locate Id = " & idNum, vbInformation,""
```

```
        End If
End Sub
```

The NoMatch property is set to True if the Seek method was unable to locate the record, so you should always check for this and handle the problem appropriately.

If the program fails to find a match, a message box lets the user know, but the data control is left pointing to a nonexistent record. If the user should click on the "Delete" button, for example, a "No Current Record" error message would appear. A better approach is to set a bookmark at the current location before searching, and if the search fails, restore the current position to the bookmark.

Setting Bookmarks. Just as you might mark a particular page in a book so you can return to the page later, you can do the same with recordsets. A *bookmark* is a unique string value that identifies each record in a recordset when it is created or opened. To save the current position, assign the Bookmark property to a string variable; to move back to that position later, just assign the same string to the recordset's Bookmark property. To demonstrate this in the current program, we modify cmdSearch_Click by saving a bookmark:

```
Private Sub cmdSearch_Click()
  Dim idNum As Integer, bmark As String
  bmark = datSalesStaff.Recordset.Bookmark
  datSalesStaff.Recordset.Index = "idNdx"
  idNum = Val(txtSearchId.Text)
  datSalesStaff.Recordset.Seek txtOperator.Text, idNum
  If datSalesStaff.Recordset.NoMatch Then
    MsgBox "Unable to locate Id = " & idNum, _
          vbInformation, "cmdSearch"
    '(return to bookmarked location)
    datSalesStaff.Recordset.Bookmark = bmark
  End If
End Sub
```

5.8.2 Using an SQL Search

A powerful way to search for database records is to assign an SQL query string to a data control's RecordSource property. To find a particular id number in the Models table of the computer.mdb database, for example, we could write the following query:

```
datModels.RecordSource = "SELECT * FROM Models WHERE id = 10045"
```

This would create a new dynaset-type recordset and assign it to the data control. Only records matching the given criteria would be placed in the recordset. The string containing the query must be formatted according to the rules of a SELECT statement in SQL (*Structured Query Language*). SQL is an industry-standard language for manipulating and searching databases; it works on many different computer systems and with different database software.

Assuming that we want the new recordset to contain all fields from the Models table (Figure 25), the SQL statement begins with the phrase "SELECT * FROM Models". This is

Chap 5: Introducing Databases

followed by the keyword WHERE and the search criteria. Each of the following sample SQL criteria are followed by a list of the record numbers that would be selected:

```
SELECT * FROM Models WHERE id = 10045
    (finds 4)
... id >= 10031
    (finds 3,4,5,6,7)
... price < 2000
    (finds 1,2,3,4,6,7)
... price < 2000 AND RAM >=16
    (finds 2,3,4,6)
... processor LIKE 'Pent*' AND cpuSpeed > 100 AND ram >= 16
    (finds 2,3,4,5)
... soundCard LIKE '*wave*'
    (finds 2,5)
```

Figure 25. Data From the Models Table.

	id	name	processor	cpuSpeed	price	ram	driveSpace	displaySize	videoRAM	cdROMspeed
1	10021	MDX4	80486	100	$600.00	8	1.2	14	1	4
2	10024	MP-180	Pentium	180	$1,900.00	16	2.2	17	2	8
3	10031	MP-133	Pentium	133	$1,200.00	16	2.4	15	1	6
4	10045	MP-150	Pentium	150	$1,500.00	16	3.1	17	2	8
5	10312	MP-200	PentPro	200	$2,500.00	32	3.6	17	2	10
6	10456	MP-75	Pentium	75	$1,000.00	16	2.2	14	1	4
7	10726	ZX-100	Pentium	100	$900.00	8	1.2	15	1	6

	soundCard
1	none
2	32-bit wave table w/ speakers
3	16-bit FM w/ speakers
4	16-bit FM w/ speakers
5	32-bit wave table w/ speakers
6	16-bit FM w/ speakers
7	none

Comparisons to Text fields are always enclosed in single quote marks. All of the standard relational operators may be used: <, >, <=, >=, =, <>. Also, the LIKE operator can be used to find a substring inside a Text field. In the last example, the criteria **LIKE '*wave*'** returns a match whenever the string "wave" appears anywhere within the soundCard field. The character * is called a *wildcard*.

The logical operators are NOT, AND, and OR. The statements are not case-sensitive, so you can use any combination of upper and lower case letters.

5.8.3 Example: A Simple Query Program

Let's look at a short program that displays all fields from the Models table in the computer.mdb database, and lets the user type in and test various SQL query statements.

frmMain. First, we create frmMain and add a data control named datModels with the following properties:

```
datModels
    DatabaseName            computer.mdb
    RecordSource            Models
    RecordsetType           Dynaset
```

There is a text control for each field in the Models table, and for each, the DataSource property equals "datModels". Each DataField property contains the name of the matching field from the database table. At run time, the user inputs a query string and clicks on the "Search" button. Two records (2, 4) are found and attached to the data control (Figure 26).

Figure 26. Results of the Search.

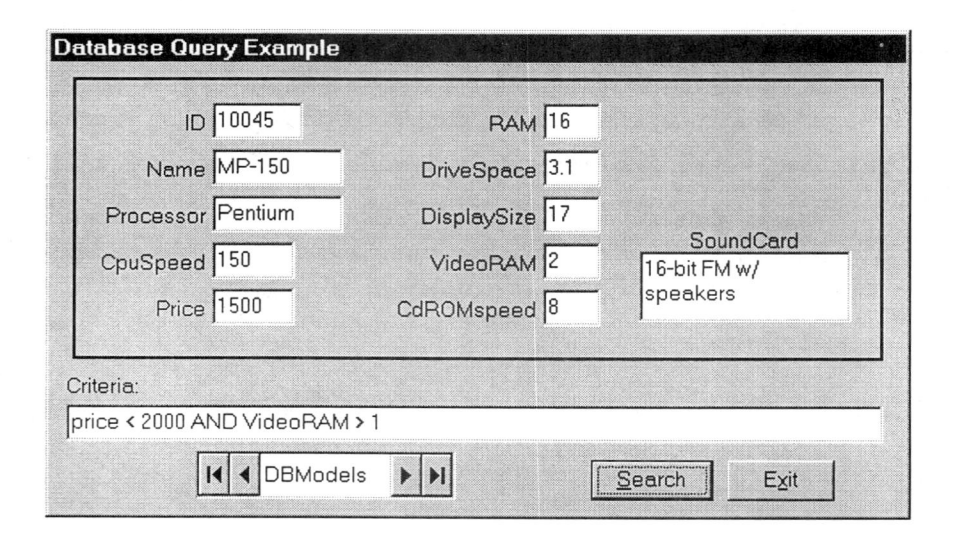

Very little code is needed in this program. When the user clicks on the Search button, the following event handler executes:

```
Private Sub cmdSearch_Click()
   datModels.RecordSource = "SELECT * FROM " + _
        "Models WHERE " + txtCriteria.Text
   datModels.Refresh
End Sub
```

We take the criteria typed by the user (stored in txtCriteria), concatenate it to the SELECT...WHERE statement, and assign it to the RecordSource property. The Refresh method causes the data control to read the new dynaset and load its first record into the data-bound controls.

5.8.4 FindFirst, FindNext and Other Search Methods

For dynaset and snapshot-type recordsets, you can use the **FindFirst, FindLast, FindPrevious,** and **FindNext** methods to search for records. The syntax for the four *Find* methods is the same:

```
recordset.FindFirst criteria
recordset.FindLast criteria
recordset.FindNext criteria
recordset.FindPrevious criteria
```

One of the nicest things about the Find methods is that the fields being searched do not have to be indexed. This flexibility is helpful in programs that search on different fields, and search for a range of records. This contrasts with the Seek method, which requires an active index and only searches for a single match.

Usually, the *Find* methods are placed in a loop that finds all records matching certain criteria. The criteria is a string that conforms to the WHERE clause of an SQL statement. Suppose, for example, that we would like to search for all names beginning with letters K-Z in the SalesStaff table, and insert the names in a list box called List1. The search begins at the first physical record in the table and continues searching until no more matches can be found:

```
Dim criteria As String
criteria = "name >= 'K'"
datSalesStaff.Recordset.FindFirst criteria
Do While Not datSalesStaff.Recordset.NoMatch
   List1.AddItem datSalesStaff.Recordset!name
   datSalesStaff.Recordset.FindNext criteria
Loop
```

Using the SalesStaff table developed earlier in this chapter, we would find "Kenwood", "Lam", "Molina", "Johnson", and "Zabaleta", but not necessarily in that order. The order would be determined simply by their physical order in the table.

The criteria for searching could also involve using the LIKE operator. For example, this searches for any name containing the string "George":

```
criteria = "name LIKE '*George*'"
```

Sample Program (Staff4). If you would like to experiment further with the FindFirst and FindNext methods, look at the Staff4 program (Figure 27). It presents two ways of searching the SalesStaff database, using either LIKE or the >= operator.

SlsStaff\
Staff4

Figure 27. The Staff4 Program.

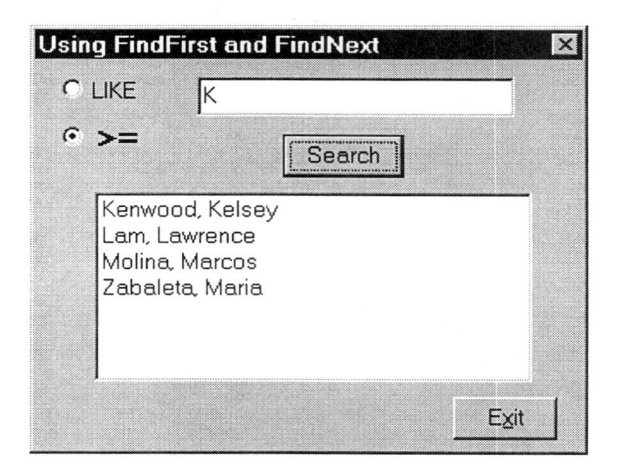

Programming Tip: When using a FindFirst statement to search for a specific concert date, remember to surround the date with date delimiter (#) characters. For example:

```
Dim theDate as Date
theDate = "1/5/98"
FindFirst "ConcertDate = #" & theDate & "#"
```

5.9 Review Questions

1. What are the names of the add-on utilities supplied with Visual Basic for creating databases and data-bound forms?

2. How is a table different from a database?

3. Each row of a table is also called a _____.

4. Each column of a table is also called a _____.

5. In the Invoice table presented in Section 5.1, how is the staffId field important in relating Invoices to sales staff?

6. Compare the terms *recordset* and *table*.

7. How is it that Visual Basic programs are able to use recordset objects?

8. How is a table-type recordset different from a dynaset-type recordset?

9. How are snapshot-type recordsets different from dynasets?

10. Is it possible to update a snapshot-type recordset?

11. Which types of recordsets can use the FindFirst and FindNext methods?

12. Which type of recordset can use the Seek method?

13. For looking up an employee's ID number, which type of recordset would probably be the fastest? Why?

Chap 5: Introducing Databases

14. Which types of recordsets would be used when you want to combine information from several tables?
15. In Access databases, how is the Text field type different from the Memo field type?
16. What type of field is used when you want new values for this field to be automatically generated when records are added to a table?
17. What type of field would be best for storing graphic images?
18. What special action is needed by the programmer to make a data control open a database table?
19. Which two properties of a data control must be set before it is connected to a database?
20. How many database tables can be attached to a data control at the same time?
21. What is the recommended name prefix for a data control?
22. Explain the RecordsetType property of the data control.
23. Explain the Exclusive property of the data control.
24. Explain the BOFAction and EOFAction properties of the data control.
25. Which standard VB controls can be bound to a data control?
26. Which two properties must be set in a data-bound control before it can be automatically updated by its attached data control?
27. How many text boxes can be linked to the same data control via the DataSource properties?
28. Can a check box be bound to a data control? If so, what type of database field can it represent?
29. To make it possible for a data control to automatically update a set of option buttons, which event must be handled?
30. In what ways are indexes useful when creating and using database tables?
31. What are the requirements of a primary key field?
32. Would a person's last name make a good primary key? Explain.
33. When using a data control with bound text boxes, how are changes saved when the user enters new values into the text boxes?
34. Which method must be called before the user can begin typing data for a new database record?
35. Which method guarantees that all changes typed by the user are saved immediately?
36. Before calling the Update method, which method(s) must be called?
37. What happens if a program assigns a misspelled index name to the Index property of a recordset?
38. Can the Index property of a recordset be assigned in either the Form_Load procedure or the Form_Activate procedure? Explain.
39. Does the BOF property point to the first row of a recordset?

40. Does the MoveLast method move to the same position as EOF?
41. What is the statement that would move the recordset pointer five rows forward from the current position?
42. If MoveNext is called and the recordset is empty, how can you prevent a runtime error?
43. What are the two properties of a data-bound list control that must be set before the list can be filled with the data from a recordset?
44. In the data-bound list control example (Section 5.5.1), how did we display the publisher names in alphabetical order?
45. Which property of a data-bound list control must be set before the user can enter a multi-character string from the keyboard that repositions the list pointer?
46. Which data control method should be called immediately after modifying the Recordsource property?
47. Which properties of a data-bound combo control must be set to fill the list with values from a recordset?
48. Which properties must be set before a data-bound combo control can update the fields in a recordset?
49. What special property must be set in a data-bound grid before the names of the recordset fields will be displayed?
50. Which property of a data-bound grid allows the user to edit individual cells?
51. Which property of a data-bound grid allows the user to append new rows to the recordset?
52. What is the preferred way to notate the following statement?
    ```
    datSalesStaff.Recordset.Fields("Name").Value = "Jones"
    ```
53. Show an example of setting a bookmark at the current position of a recordset attached to the datComputerModel data control.
54. Show an example of returning to the location of the bookmark set in the previous question.
55. Code a SELECT statement in SQL that builds a recordset from all fields in the SalesStaff table.
56. Code a SELECT statement in SQL that builds a recordset from all fields in the Models table whose price is less than $2,000.00 and cpuSpeed is greater than 180.
57. Code a SELECT statement in SQL that builds a recordset from all fields in the SalesStaff table in which the letters "JON" occur somewhere within the lastName field.

5.10 Chapter Exercises

5.10.1 E-Mail Address Book

Exercise 4.6.12 at the end of Chapter 4 was to create an E-Mail Address Book program, using class modules. For the current exercise, improve this program by using a database table to store all of the address records. Because the program is object-oriented, the required changes will be confined to just a few methods.

```
clsAddress Class:
   ReadFromFile
   SaveToFile
clsAddressList Class:
   ReadFromFile
   SaveToFile
```

Also, add two properties to the clsAddressList class that allow the main program to set the names of the database file and table: DbaseName property, TableName property.

5.10.2   Mozart Music Sales - Titles Table

Revise the Mozart Music Sales - 4 program from this chapter in the following ways:

- Create another table in the mozart.mdb database called **Titles**. It should have the following fields: sku (Text, 5), Title (Text, 50). Create an index called titleNdx, based on the Title field.
- Add another data control to the form, called datTitles; it's RecordSource property will equal "Titles", and its DatabaseName property will be "mozart.mdb".
- Load the SKU numbers and album titles from the new **Titles** database table, and place the SKU numbers in a DBCombo control.

When the user selects a SKU number, the title of the album should appear in a label, as it did in previous versions of the program.

5.10.3   Mozart Music Sales Wizard

The Mozart Music Sales main window is rather complicated, and a new user of the program might not know exactly how to fill out the invoice. Your task is to write a wizard that will guide the user through the required steps:

1. Let the user select an existing salesperson name or enter a new person's name.

2. The user starts to input the first item by selecting a SKU number from a combo box.

3. The user selects the price code and format. Explain the meanings of price codes A, B, and C to the user on this panel. The user clicks the Add button to continue.

4. Ask the user if there are any more items. If the answer is yes, return to Step 2; otherwise, proceed to step 5.

5. Display the cumulative invoice amount, tax, and total amount. Ask the user to either save the invoice, or cancel.

6. Ask the user if they want to create another invoice. If the answer is yes, return to step 1; if the answer is no, end the program.

Each step should be a separate panel (form), similar to the one shown in Figure 28.

Figure 28. Sample Wizard Panel.

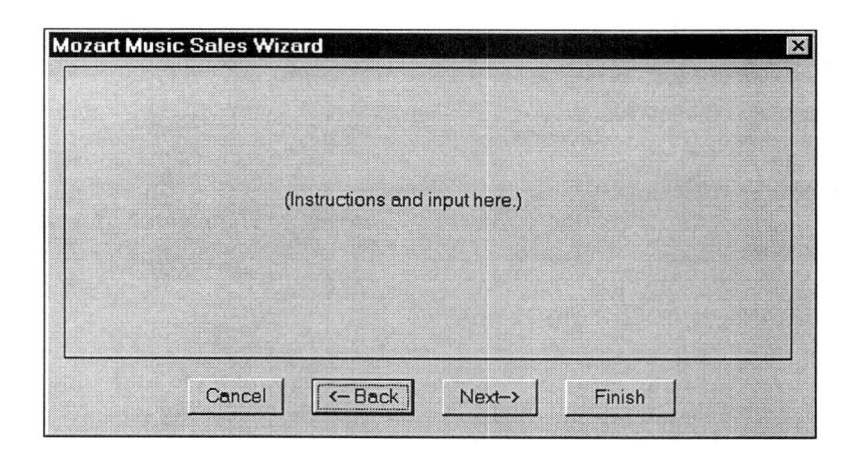

5.10.4 Computer Mail-Order Customer Data

Use the Mail-Order Computer Sales program from this chapter and make the following improvement: When the configuration is complete, display a separate form and let the salesperson enter the customer's name, phone, address, and credit card number. Create a database table called **Customer** that will hold all of the customer information, and assign a unique ID number to each customer.

5.10.5 Computer Mail-Order Invoice

Using the Mail-Order Computer Sales program from the previous exercise, make the following improvements:

- Add a text box into which the user can enter a customer ID.
- Create a table called **Invoice** with the following fields: customerId, date, invoiceNumber, configured price, model ID, options. The options field can be type Text, containing a comma-delimited list of option ID numbers.
- When the user confirms the computer configuration by clicking on the OK button, save the current information in a new Invoice record.
- Add a command button called "Invoices" to the main form that causes a separate form to display all data in the Invoice table. Use a DBGrid control to display the table in a spreadsheet-like format.

5.10.6 Computer Selection Wizard

One of the most difficult tasks facing a new computer buyer is knowing which type of system is most appropriate. Of course, given an unlimited budget, one could simply buy the best—but is the price worth it? Your task is to write a *computer selection wizard* in Visual

Basic that will assist the user in selecting the right system based on their needs. Use the following information, which you will store in a database:

Processor	Application	Price
166 MHz Pentium	Ordinary home use	400
200 MHz Pentium	Business use, high volume	600
200 MHz Pentium/MMX	Multimedia-Intensive	800

Hard Drive	Application	Price
2.2 GB, 12 ms	Average home use	300
4.2 GB, 10 ms	Business use	450
6.0 GB, 8 ms	High volume/ Network server	650

Video Display	Application	Price
15-inch	Low graphics usage	450
17-inch	Intensive graphics usage	600
20-inch	Group Presentations	1200

Video Card	Application	Price
2 MB, 32-bit	Average home / business use	100
4 MB, 32-bit	2-D graphics, computer games	175
6 MB, 64-bit	3-D games, desktop publishing, 3-D image rendering	350

Printer	Application	Price
8 ppm b/w laser	Low-volume business / programming	600
12 ppm b/w laser	Medium-volume business / programming	850
16 ppm b/w laser	High-volume business / network shared	1200
4 ppm color inkjet	Home usage, graphics pictures	300
8 ppm color inkjet	Home / business, med-quality graphics	500
large size color inkjet	Desktop publishing, advertising	1200
color laser	Commerical advertising	3000

In other words, you will have five different categories of components for the system that you are configuring. You may assign default prices to the other system components, such as the CD-ROM drive, modem, and backup storage. Try to keep the price reasonable for the target system, but make sure that the computer is at least powerful enough to serve the user's needs. As the user is making each selection, display a description of the configured system up to that point, along with the price. The user must be allowed to back up through previous steps and re-enter the choices.

5.10.7 Kyoshi Karate School - 1

Write a simple membership tracking system for a martial-arts school called Kyoshi Karate School. Kyoshi *Sensei* (*teacher*) has determined that he wants the program to manage a list of students, containing their personal data and dues payments. There will be four windows: Main, Membership, Edit/Add Members, and Dues Collection.

Database Design. Create an Access database named karate.mdb with the following tables:

Payments
memberName	Text	50
paymentDate	Date	
amount	Currency	

Members
id	Long		required
lastName	Text	30	required
firstName	Text	20	required
phone	Text	15	
street	Text	30	
city	Text	20	
zip	Text	10	
gender	Text	1	
birthDate	Date		required

For all non-required fields, be sure to set the "Allow zero length" option to Yes. Otherwise, Visual Basic will report an error when appending a record with blank fields to the file. Add at least five records to the Members table.

Main Window. The program starts with a main window that has a menu. Display the school name, program name and version, revision date, and so on. The sample in Figure 29 may serve as a general guide.

Figure 29. Kyoshi Karate Program, Main Window.

The menu commands are as follows:

```
&File
   E&xit
&Window
   &Membership
```

Membership Window. The menu in the Membership window contains commands to edit and add members, remove a member, display/edit the member's dues payments, and close the window:

```
&Member
   &Edit/Add
   &Remove
   &Dues Payments
   &Close
```

The Membership window has a hidden data control that is attached to the Members table in the karate.mdb database. Figure 30 shows a sample of the window.

Figure 30. Kyoshi Karate, Membership Window.

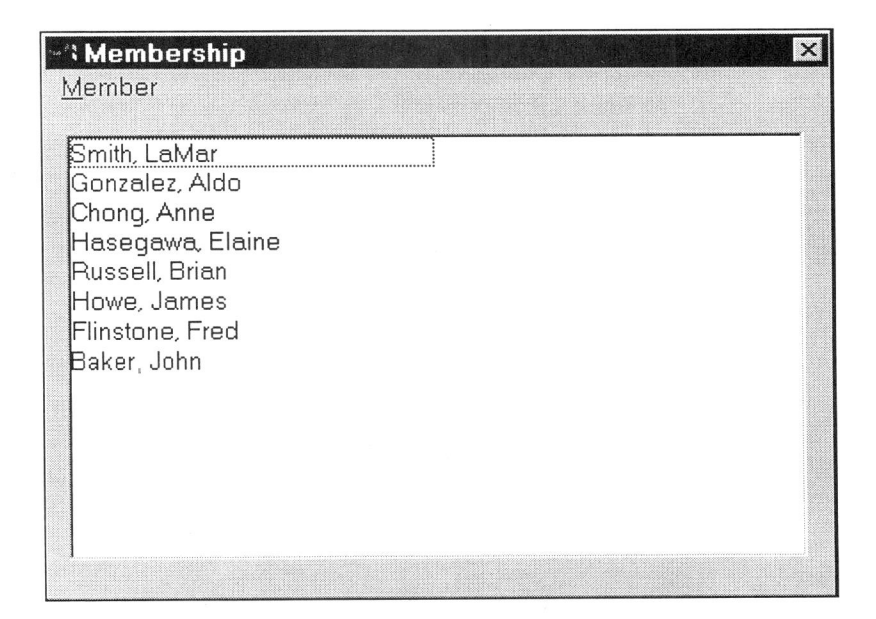

[Screenshot of Membership window with Member menu and a list box containing: Smith, LaMar; Gonzalez, Aldo; Chong, Anne; Hasegawa, Elaine; Russell, Brian; Howe, James; Flinstone, Fred; Baker, John]

The *Remove* and *Dues Payments* menu choices should be disabled until a member's name has been selected from the list box.

Edit/Add Members Window. When the user clicks on "Edit/Add" from the Member menu, display a form into which the user can enter membership data (Figure 31).

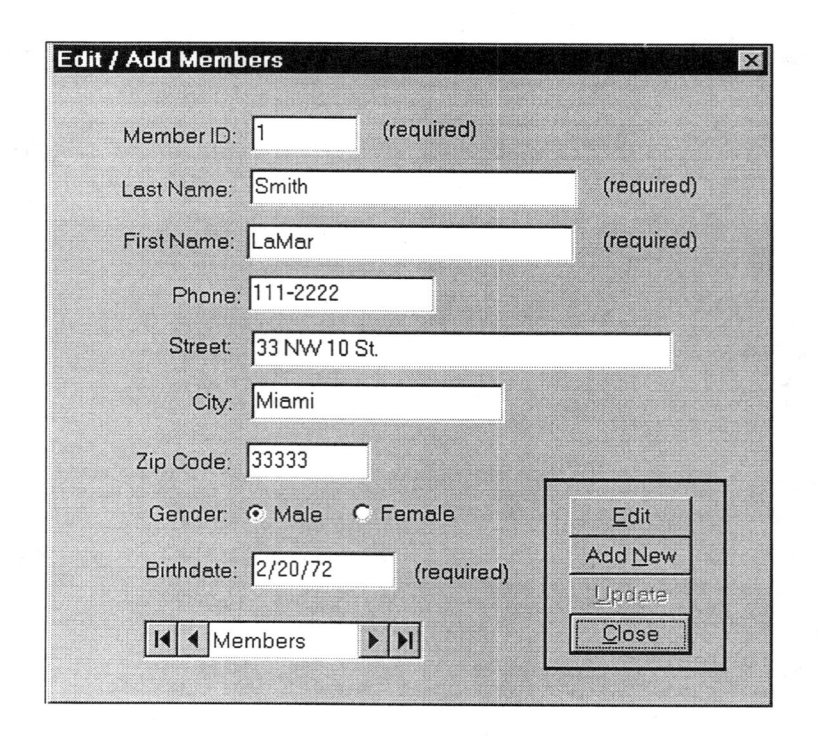

Figure 31. Add a New Member or Edit an Existing One.

[Edit / Add Members dialog: Member ID: 1 (required); Last Name: Smith (required); First Name: LaMar (required); Phone: 111-2222; Street: 33 NW 10 St.; City: Miami; Zip Code: 33333; Gender: ● Male ○ Female; Birthdate: 2/20/72 (required); buttons: Edit, Add New, Update, Close; navigation: Members]

There should be a data control attached to the Members table. If the user has selected a member name in the Membership window, then the current window should display that member's record (*hint:* in Form_Activate, use the FindFirst method to position the record pointer). Otherwise, the first member in the table will be displayed.

Notice that option buttons are used for the member's gender. Earlier in this chapter, we presented the program code to interpret these buttons.

Update Operations. In the Edit/Add Members window, the user can add new members or edit the records of existing members. Either the Edit or the Add New button must be clicked before the user can make any changes to the fields. You might want to initially set the Enabled property of all text boxes to False, then enable the boxes when either Edit or Add New is clicked. When the user clicks on the Update button, the program must make sure that the required fields are not blank before calling the Recordset.Update method. The Close button unloads the form.

Dues Collection Window. From the Membership Window, the user can select Dues Collection. The resulting window (Figure 32) displays the member name and a list of all previous payments in a two-column list box.

Figure 32. Dues Collection Window.

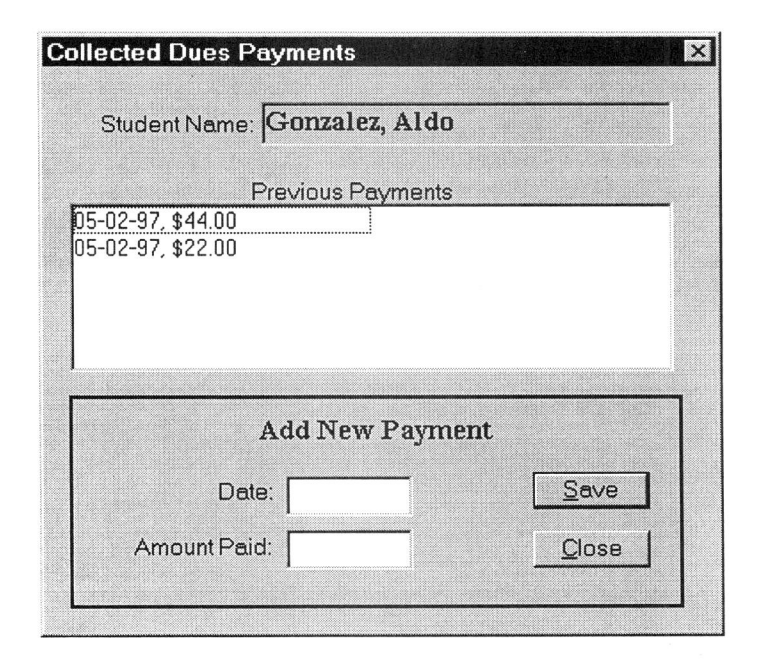

```
┌─ Collected Dues Payments ────────────────── [X] ─┐
│                                                   │
│        Student Name: │Gonzalez, Aldo         │   │
│                                                   │
│                 Previous Payments                 │
│        ┌─────────────────────────────────┐       │
│        │05-02-97, $44.00                 │       │
│        │05-02-97, $22.00                 │       │
│        │                                 │       │
│        │                                 │       │
│        └─────────────────────────────────┘       │
│                                                   │
│        ┌──── Add New Payment ──────────────┐     │
│        │                                   │     │
│        │   Date:   [        ]   [ Save  ]  │     │
│        │                                   │     │
│        │   Amount Paid: [   ]   [ Close ]  │     │
│        │                                   │     │
│        └───────────────────────────────────┘     │
└───────────────────────────────────────────────────┘
```

The user can add a new payment by filling in the date and amount paid, and clicking on the Save button. If the date is blank, the program should fill in the current system date automatically. If the amount is blank, display an error message and let the user try again. This window should stay open as long as the user keeps entering payments, and close only when the Close button is clicked.

5.10.8 MDI Kyoshi Karate School

Enhance the Karate School program written for the previous exercise in the following ways:

Make the program an MDI application. The program name and related information that was previous displayed in the main window should be placed on a separate splash window. The Main window will be the MDI parent, and all others except the splash window should be MDI child windows.

Have the program start with the Main procedure inside a code module. Show the splash window modally, and the MDI main window modelessly. Figure 33 shows the main window, containing the Membership, Dues Payments, and Edit/Add Members windows.

Figure 33. Karate School, MDI Application.

5.10.9 Kyoshi Karate Class Schedule

Enhance the Kyoshi Karate School program written for the previous exercise. This version of the Karate School program should allow the user to view a schedule of instructors and classes. Create a database table called **Schedule** containing the following fields:

Name	Type	Description
classId	Long	Identifies the class (primary key)
dayNum	Integer	0 = mon, 1 = tues, etc.
startTime	Date/Time	Class starting time
stopTime	Date/Time	Class ending time
instructorId	Long	Identifies the instructor

All fields are required, and the **classId** field is the primary key. Fill the table with at least ten records, taking care not to create any times that would overlap on the same day. For example:

Chap 5: Introducing Databases

classID	dayNum	startTime	stopTime	instructorId
1	0	16:00	16:59	142
2	0	17:00	18:29	151
3	0	18:30	19:59	126
4	1	09:30	11:29	115
5	3	09:30	11:29	115
6	2	16:00	16:59	142
7	2	17:00	18:29	151
8	2	18:30	19:59	104
9	3	17:00	18:59	101
10	4	17:00	19:29	101

Create a combined index out of the dayNum and startTime fields, and call it dayTimeNdx.

Create another database table named **Instructors**, with the following fields:

Name	**Type**	**Description**
id	Long	Identifies the instructor (primary key)
lastName	Text	30 character last name

Create an index on the **id** field, which can be used with the Seek function to look up an instructor. Use the following data, or substitute other names if you prefer:

```
101    Kyoshi Sensei
115    Jackson
104    Gonzalez
126    Kowalski
142    La Ferriere
151    Davies
```

Schedule Window. Display the class schedule in an MDI child window called frmSchedule; the schedule details will appear in a list box. Make sure that it is sorted first by day number, then by starting time. Set the Index property of the data control's recordset to "dayTimeNdx" before loading the list box. Remember, the data control's RecordsetType property must be equal to *Table* before you can set the recordset's Index property.

Show the day of the class as a three-letter abbreviation ("Mon", "Tue", etc.), and display the instructor's name for each class. Be sure to format the strings containing the beginning and ending class times, so the columns will line up in the list box. It also helps to use a fixed-width font such as *Courier New*. Figure 34 shows a sample of the class Schedule window.

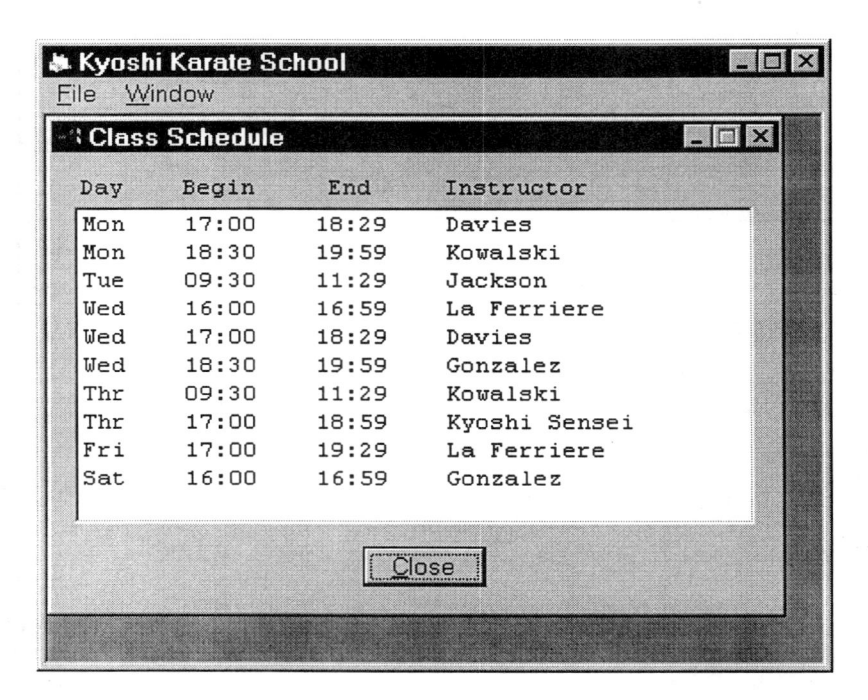

Figure 34. Kyoshi Karate Class Schedule.

```
Kyoshi Karate School
File  Window

  Class Schedule
  Day    Begin    End      Instructor
  Mon    17:00    18:29    Davies
  Mon    18:30    19:59    Kowalski
  Tue    09:30    11:29    Jackson
  Wed    16:00    16:59    La Ferriere
  Wed    17:00    18:29    Davies
  Wed    18:30    19:59    Gonzalez
  Thr    09:30    11:29    Kowalski
  Thr    17:00    18:59    Kyoshi Sensei
  Fri    17:00    19:29    La Ferriere
  Sat    16:00    16:59    Gonzalez

               [ Close ]
```

Looking up the instructor name is the trickiest part of the program. Inside the loop that fills the list box with the class schedule, you might want to call a function that looks up the instructor ID in the Instructor table and retrieves the matching instructor name.

5.10.10 Kyoshi Karate: Editing the Class Schedule

Enhance the Karate Program from the previous exercise by allowing the user to edit individual class schedule records (see Figure 35). The user can edit in one of the following ways:

- By double-clicking on a class in the list box.
- By single-clicking on a class, and clicking the Edit button.

When the user begins editing a single class, the text and data-bound combo controls at the bottom of the form are filled with the current values.

Figure 35. Editing the Karate Class Schedule.

```
Class Schedule                              _ □ ×
    Day      Begin     End       Instructor
    Mon      17:00     18:29     Davies
    Mon      18:30     19:59     Kowalski
    Tue      09:30     11:15     Davies
    Wed      16:30     16:59     Davies
    Wed      18:30     19:59     Kowalski
    Thr      17:00     18:29     Gonzalez
    Thr      17:00     18:59     Kyoshi Sensei
    Fri      17:00     19:29     Kyoshi Sensei
    Sat      09:30     11:29     Gonzalez
    Sat      16:00     16:59     La Ferriere

      Day         Begin          End          Instructor
    [Thr  ▼]  [5:00:00 PM]  [6:29:00 PM]  [Gonzalez     ▼]

           [ Edit ]  [ Save ]  [ Cancel ]  [ Close ]
```

Data-bound combo boxes are used for the Day and Instructor fields, so when the user selects a different day or instructor and clicks the Save button, the database record in the Schedule table is updated. The Edit button calls the Recordset.Edit method. The Save button calls the Recordset.Update method. The Cancel button cancels the current edit by moving to a different record (and back again, if you use a bookmark).

Buttons. Be sure to coordinate the Enabled properties of the command buttons. When the form is first displayed, only the Close button is enabled. When the user selects a class in the list box, the Edit button is enabled. When the Edit button is clicked, only the Save and Cancel buttons are enabled (as in the example shown above). When the user clicks on Save or Cancel, only the Edit and Close buttons are enabled.

6 Data Access Objects

Chapter Contents

Using the Data Access Object Library
    Workspaces
    OpenRecordset Method
    TableDefs Property
Project: Personal Contact Manager - 1
    Program Specifications
    Program Design
    Implementation: module1
    Implementation: frmMain
    Implementation: frmSplash
    Implementation: frmEdit
    Conclusion
Project: Personal Contact Manager - 2
    Program Specifications
    Program Design
    Program Implementation
Project: Doctors Office Appointments - 2
    Program Specifications
    Program Design
    Implementing the Appointment Program
    The Main Form: frmMain
    Implementing the clsAppointment Class
    The clsApptCalendar Class
    Implementing the clsPatient Class
    The frmDisplay and frmInput Windows
    Conclusion
Multiuser Database Processing
    Example: Record-Locking Program
    Program Implementation
    BeginTrans, CommitTrans, and Rollback
Review Questions
Chapter Exercises

6.1 Using the Data Access Object Library

In the previous chapter, we used data controls to access databases. As you may have noticed, data controls operate on the principle that "one size fits all"; meaning that we give up some flexibility in return for convenience when using data controls. For example, a data control opens its recordset as soon as the form loads, and closes the recordset when the form unloads.

But now it's time to move on to a more advanced and flexible way of dealing with databases, by directly programming database and recordset objects. Microsoft's library of database objects are officially called *Data Access Objects* (DAO). They can be used by all Microsoft Office applications. Currently, Visual Basic 5 began shipping with the DAO version 3.5 library.

At the root of DAO is *DbEngine* (also called the *Jet* database engine), which contains the methods and properties that make it possible to program database objects. Before using DbEngine for the first time, you might have to load it into the default setup for Visual Basic. In VB 4, from the Tools/References menu, select "Microsoft DAO 3.0 Object Library". In VB 5, use the Project/References menu, and select "Microsoft DAO 3.5 Object Library".

6.1.1 Workspaces

DbEngine contains a collection called **Workspaces,** in which every member is a **Workspace** object. A workspace contains a collection of open databases, and provides for transaction processing and database security within a group of users. The default workspace is **Workspaces(0),** which is the one we will use. **OpenDatabase** is the only workspace method we will use in this chapter. When opening an Access database, the syntax of the OpenDatabase method is:

```
Set database = workspace.OpenDatabase (dbname, exclusive, readOnly,
connect)
```

Database referes to the Database object returned by the method, *workspace* is a Workspace object. *Dbname* is the only required parameter: it is a string containing the name of a database file. *Exclusive* is True if the database is to be opened in exclusive mode, *readOnly* is True if the database is to be opened only for reading and no updating, and *connect* contains database type and password information. (For databases other than Access, the exclusive parameter contains various options that are not mentioned here.)

Example. The following statements open a database called **pcm.mdb** in non-exclusive, read-only mode and assign it to a variable named **Dbase**:

```
Dim Dbase as Database
Set Dbase = Workspaces(0).OpenDatabase("pcm.mdb", False, True)
```

This creates a database object and adds it to the **Databases** collection in Workspaces(0). The name **Dbase** will refer to the database object used by this program, particularly when opening and closing recordsets.

6.1.2 OpenRecordset Method

A database object can invoke the **OpenRecordset** method, which opens a table in the current database and assigns it to a recordset object. Here is the syntax of the OpenRecordset method:

```
object.OpenRecordset( source, recordsetType, options, lockEdits )
```

Only the first parameter is required, it is highly recommend that you also include the *recordsetType. Object* is a database object, *source* is either a table name or an SQL query string, *options* is a combination of constants that determine recordset characteristics, and *lockEdits* determines the type of record locking. *RecordsetType* can be one of the following constants: dbOpenTable, dbOpenDynaset, or dbOpenSnapshot.

LockEdits is an integer constant that can be one of the following predefined values: dbReadOnly, dbPessimistic (the default), or dbOptimistic. *Pessimistic* locking means that the 2,048-byte data area (called a *page*) containing the current record is locked while the Edit method is in effect. *Optimistic* locking means that the page containing the record is not locked until the Update method is executed.

Customer Table Example. For example, let's open the **customer** table and assign it to the recordset called Persons:

```
Dim Persons As Recordset
Set Persons = Dbase.OpenRecordset("customer", dbOpenDynaset)
```

Before a program ends, be sure to close all recordsets associated with a database before closing the database itself. Also, it is a good idea to set object variables to *Nothing* to make sure their memory is released:

```
Persons.Close
Dbase.Close
Set Persons = Nothing
Set Dbase = Nothing
```

> ***Programming Tip:*** You may want to use an "rs" prefix on all recordset names to more easily identify them in code. In our example, the recordset variable would be declared as:
>
> ```
> Dim rsPersons As Recordset
> ```

6.1.3 TableDefs Property

Every database object has a **TableDefs** property, which is a collection containing a description of every table in the database. You can use this collection, for example, to display the names of the tables:

```
Dim Td As TableDefs, i As Integer
Set Td = Dbase.TableDefs
For i = 0 To Td.Count - 1
  frmMain.cboTablenames.AddItem Td(i).Name
Next i
```

Accessing Fields in a TableDef. You can also use the **Fields** property of a single TableDef object to retrieve the name, data type, and size of each field. In the following program, when the user clicks on the Table Names button, we see a list of table names stored in the database (Figure 1).

Figure 1. TableDef Field Collection.

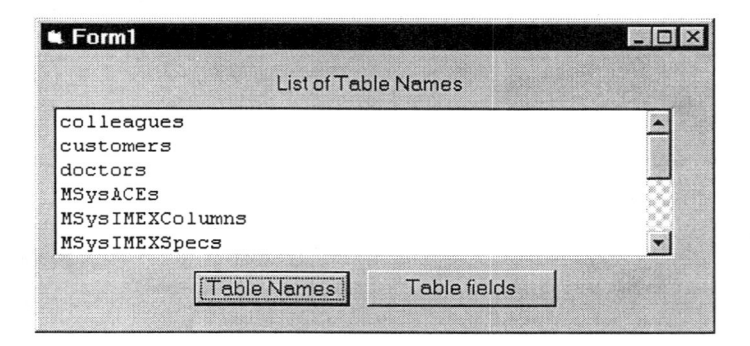

[Form1 window showing "List of Table Names" with entries: colleagues, customers, doctors, MSysACEs, MSysIMEXColumns, MSysIMEXSpecs, and buttons "Table Names" and "Table fields"]

The user selects a table name from the list, and clicks on the Table Fields button. The program displays the name, size, and data type of each field from the table. For example, this is the list of fields from the customers table, in Figure 2. Text fields have data type 10 and memo fields have data type 12.

Implementation. In Form_Load, we open the database and table:

```
Private Sub Form_Load()
  ChDrive App.Path
  ChDir App.Path
  Set Dbase = Workspaces(0).OpenDatabase("pcm.mdb")
End Sub
```

Figure 2. Field Properties.

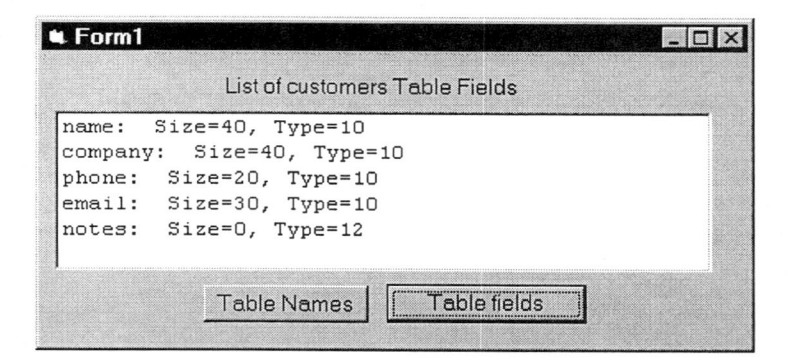

[Form1 window showing "List of customers Table Fields":
name: Size=40, Type=10
company: Size=40, Type=10
phone: Size=20, Type=10
email: Size=30, Type=10
notes: Size=0, Type=12
with buttons "Table Names" and "Table fields"]

In the Click event for the Table Names button, we loop through the TableDefs collection and get the table names:

```
Private Sub cmdNames_Click()
  Dim i As Integer, Td As TableDefs
  List1.Clear
  Label1 = "List of Table Names"
  For i = 0 To Dbase.TableDefs.Count - 1
    List1.AddItem Dbase.TableDefs(i).Name
```

```
    Next i
End Sub
```

The following statements loop through the Fields collection in the table selected by the user and display the name, size, and data type of each field:

```
Private Sub cmdTablefields_Click()
  Dim tableName As String, j As Integer, M As Field, T As TableDef
  tableName = List1.Text
  List1.Clear
  Set T = Dbase.TableDefs( tableName )
  Label1 = "List of the " + tableName + " Table Fields"
  For j = 0 To T.Fields.Count - 1
    Set M = T.Fields(j)
    List1.AddItem M.Name + ":  Size=" & _
       M.Size & ", Type=" & M.Type
  Next j
End Sub
```

6.2 Project: Personal Contact Manager - 1

Almost everyone needs a telephone/email list, particularly if they have a wide range of friends and acquaintances. Computerized address book programs have existed by the thousands, of course, but it's always nice to tailor one to your own needs. The program that we are about to create, called **Personal Contact Manager** (PCM), is just a starting point—it lets the user keep multiple lists of contact persons. It will offer valuable practice in reading, editing, and updating databases using database objects. It might also be valuable as an add-on, or supplement to existing programs.

6.2.1 Program Specifications

- The Personal Contact Manager program stores and retrieves the following information about individual persons: first and last name, company, phone number, e-mail address, and comments.
- In this first version of the program, the user is only able to view and modify existing records; new records will not be added to the database.
- The user selects the database to be opened from a File/Open dialog box. Once a database has been opened, the user selects the table to be opened from a list of available table names.
- Once the database and tables are open, the names of all people in the table are displayed in a listbox. The user selects a person's name and views the record.
- While viewing a record, the user is able to modify all fields except the person's name.
- A splash window displays the name of the program, version number, and date of last revision.

6.2.2 Program Design

The PCM Database. Let's begin by designing the database tables that hold personal information. All of the tables have the design shown in Table 1.

Table 1. PCM Table Description.

Field Name	Data Type	Length
name	Text	40
phone	Text	40
company	Text	20
email	Text	30
notes	Memo	(varies)

Each table has a unique index based on the name field, called **nameNdx**. We will use this index with the Seek method to look up names at run time. For each field except **name,** we set the AllowZeroLength option to Yes, and the name field should allow duplicates.

We are going to use separate tables for each group of persons, so we can create the first table and copy the structure to the remaining tables. To copy a table structure in Access, design and save the first table. Select the table name in the database window, click on the Edit/Copy command, and click on the Edit/Paste command. Make sure you select the "Structure Only" button if the table being copied already contains some records. Give the new table a name and click on OK. Do the same for all remaining tables. Here is a suggested list of tables for the program; you may want to rename these tables, or add new tables to the list:

- colleagues
- customers
- doctors
- newContacts
- relatives

Splash Window. When the program starts, it displays a splash window (Figure 3). The window has a timer control that closes it automatically in two seconds, or the user can close it immediately by clicking on it with the mouse.

Figure 3. PCM Splash Window.

Chap 6: Data Access Objects 227

Main Window. The main window, called frmMain, is the starting point for the program. From here, the user can open a database by clicking on the File/Open Database command. Figure 4 shows the main window in design mode. A common dialog control must be added to the form.

Figure 4. PCM Main Window.

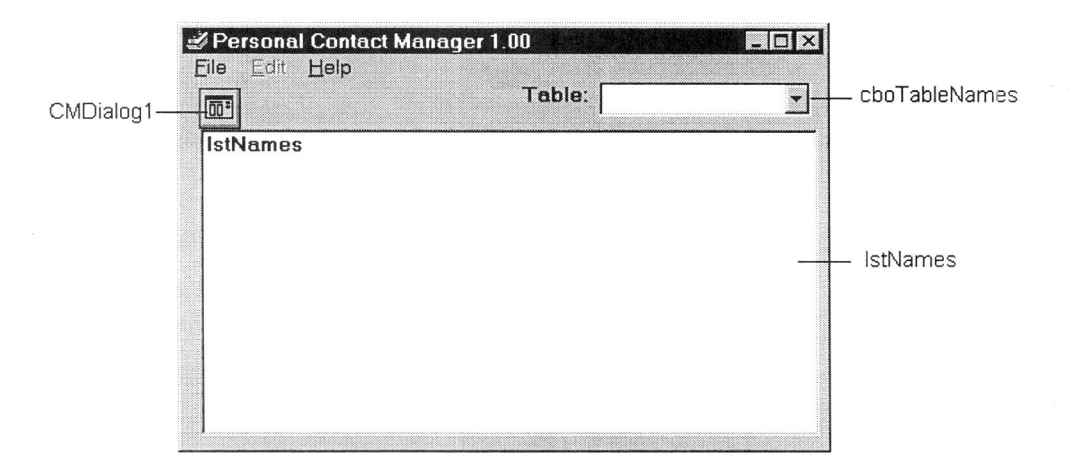

Table 2 displays the menu structure in frmMain. Notice that the Edit menu is disabled when the program begins.

Table 2. The Menu in frmMain.

&File	mnuFile
&Open Database	mnuFileOpen
E&xit	mnuFileExit
&Edit	mnuEdit (disabled)
&Modify Record	mnuEditModify
&Help	mnuHelp
&About PCM	mnuHelpAbout

Let's run the program: After selecting a database with the File / Open Database command, the user selects from one of the available tables whose names were placed in the combo box (Figure 5).

Figure 5. PCM - Selecting a Table.

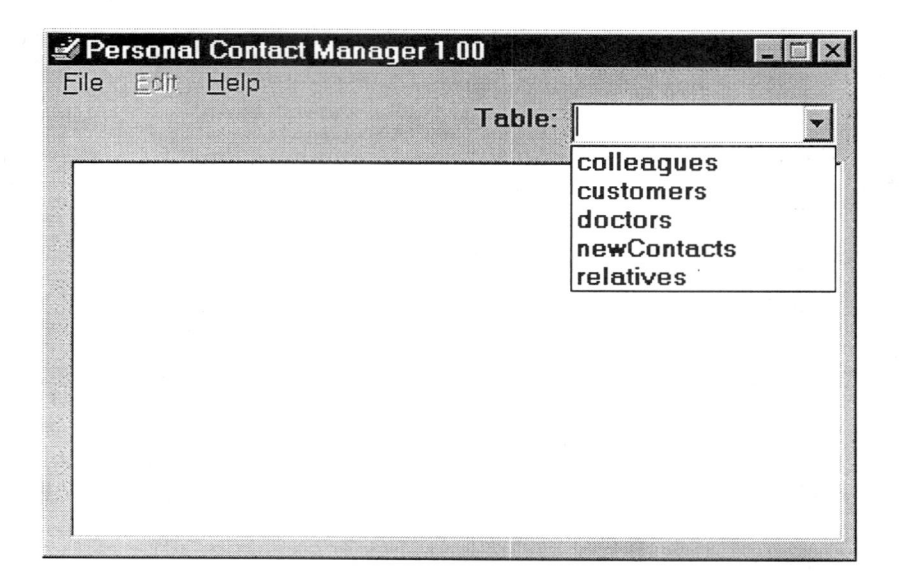

When the user selects a table, the table is opened and the names of people appear in a list box. The user can edit a record in one of two ways:

- Click on a person's name and select the Edit/Modify command.
- Double-click on a person's name.

The Colleagues table shown in Figure 6 is an example.

Figure 6. Listing of the Colleagues Table.

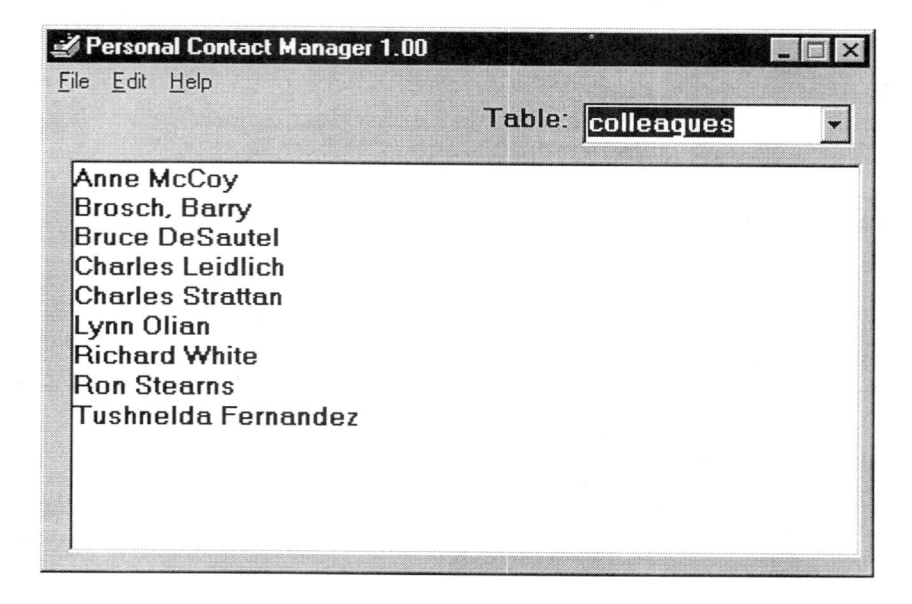

Chap 6: Data Access Objects 229

When the user selects a name to be modified, the Edit Window (frmEdit) appears (Figure 7). Any changes we make here are saved in the database when the Save button is clicked.

Figure 7. The Edit Window.

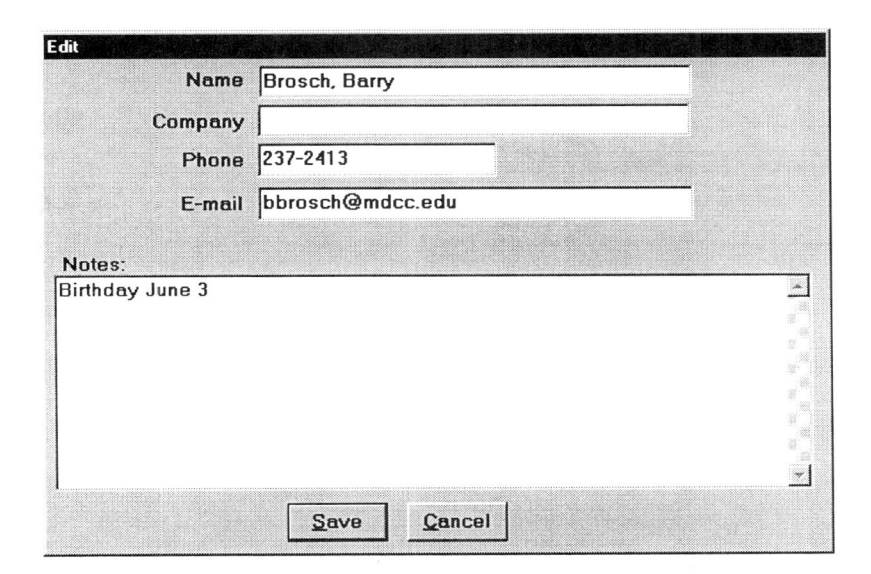

The controls on this form are not bound controls, and there is no data control on the form. We set txtName.Locked = True to prevent the user from modifying the person's name. If the user clicks on Cancel, the program confirms before abandoning changes to the record (Figure 8).

Figure 8. Cancel Confirmation Message.

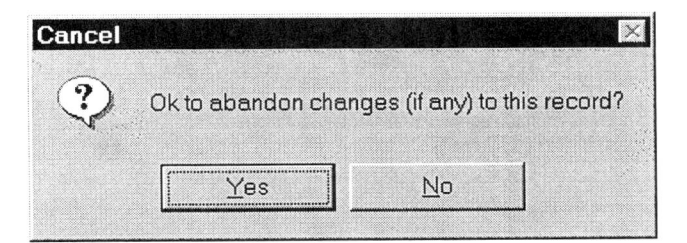

Using Identical Tables. Finally, a comment should be made about the fact that the database contains several tables having the same structure. We might have, for example, loaded all of the records into a single table, and provided an indicator field that identified the person as a colleage, customer, relative, doctor, and so on. On the other hand, the approach taken here was that each table might have been created at a separate location, or at a different point in time, or it might be kept for archival purposes. In short, the way this decision is handled depends on how the database will be used. As a chapter exercise, you will be asked to take the first approach and combine all records into a single table.

6.2.3 Implementation: module1

This program contains the following modules: frmSplash, frmMain, module1, and frmEdit. The program starts from the Main() subroutine. Because the program opens databases and tables separately, the **databaseOpen** and **tableOpen** flags let us know if a table or database must be closed before opening a new one. Here are the declarations in module1:

```
Public Const ReleaseDate As String = "06-01-1997"
Public Persons As Recordset
Dim databaseOpen As Boolean
Dim tableOpen as Boolean
Dim Dbase As Database
```

The Main procedure is very simple—it shows the splash window, followed by the main window, and closes the table and database:

```
Public Sub Main()
   databaseOpen = False
   tableOpen = False
   frmSplash.Show vbModal
   frmMain.Show vbModal
   CloseTable
   CloseDatabase
End Sub
```

Opening a Database. The OpenDatabase procedure displays a File/Open dialog box (using the common dialog control) and lets the user select a database:

```
Public Sub OpenDatabase()
   Dim dbaseFileName As String
   On Error GoTo OpenDatabase1
   With frmMain.CMDialog1
      .CancelError = True
      .DialogTitle = "Open PCM Database"
      .Filter = "PCM databases|pcm.mdb|All files|*.*"
      .ShowOpen
      dbaseFileName = .filename
   End With
'Close table and database if already open.
   CloseTable
   CloseDatabase
   On Error GoTo OpenDatabase2
   Set Dbase = Workspaces(0).OpenDatabase(dbaseFileName)
   databaseOpen = True
   LoadTableNames
   Exit Sub
OpenDatabase1:    'User clicked on Cancel
   Exit Sub
OpenDatabase2:
   MsgBox Error$, vbInformation, "OpenDatabase"
End Sub
```

Loading the Table Names. The LoadTablenames procedure retrieves the table names from the TableDefs collection. This is better than trying to hard code the table names into the combo box, because different databases might have different table names:

```
Public Sub LoadTableNames()
  Dim Td As TableDefs, i As Integer
  Set Td = Dbase.TableDefs
  frmMain.cboTablenames.Clear
  For i = 0 To Td.Count - 1
    If (Td(i).Attributes And dbSystemObject) = 0 Then
      frmMain.cboTablenames.AddItem Td(i).Name
    End If
  Next i
End Sub
```

If the dbSystemObject bit is equal to a 1 in the **Attributes** property, we skip the table because it is a system table. When we ANDing the Attributes property and the constant together, the result is equal to zero for every non-system table.

OpenTable Procedure. This is a complete listing of the OpenTable procedure:

```
Public Sub OpenTable()
  Dim tableName As String
  tableName = frmMain.cboTablenames.Text
  If Len(tableName) = 0 Then Exit Sub
  On Error GoTo OpenTable1
  CloseTable
  Set Persons = Dbase.OpenRecordset(tableName, dbOpenTable)
  Persons.Index = "NameNdx"
  tableOpen = True
  LoadListbox
  frmMain.mnuEdit.Enabled = True
  frmMain.mnuEditModify.Enabled = False
  Exit Sub
OpenTable1:
  MsgBox Error$, vbInformation, "OpenTable"
End Sub
```

Now let us go through it step-by-step. When the user selects a table to be opened, we retrieve the name from the cboTablenames combo box and continue if the name is not blank:

```
Dim tableName as String
tableName = frmMain.cboTablenames.Text
If Len(tableName) = 0 Then Exit Sub
```

We call CloseTable to close any table that might already be open:

```
On Error GoTo OpenTable1
CloseTable
```

The **OpenRecordset** method opens the table. We use the dbOpenTable constant here because we plan to search for names in the table using the Seek method. This also requires setting the Index property:

```
Set Persons = Dbase.OpenRecordset(tableName, dbOpenTable)
Persons.Index = "NameNdx"
tableOpen = True
```

We call LoadListBox to fill the list box with the names of all persons in the table:

```
LoadListbox
```

We enable the **Edit** menu, but disable the Edit/Modify command because the user must not modify a record until a person's name has been selected in the list box:

```
frmMain.mnuEdit.Enabled = True
frmMain.mnuEditModify.Enabled = False
```

The **LoadListbox** procedure loops through the table with MoveFirst and MoveNext, loading each person's name. The table index sets the order, so the list box will be loaded in alphabetical order:

```
Public Sub LoadListbox()
  On Error GoTo LoadListBox1
  frmMain.lstNames.Clear
  Persons.MoveFirst
  Do While Not Persons.EOF
    frmMain.lstNames.AddItem Persons!name
    Persons.MoveNext
  Loop
  Exit Sub
LoadListBox1:
  MsgBox Error$, vbInformation, "LoadListbox"
End Sub
```

Modifying Individual Records. The **ModifyRecord** procedure retrieves the name selected by the user in the lstNames list box, locates it in the Persons table, copies the database record into the frmEdit window, and displays the window:

```
Public Sub ModifyRecord()
  FindPerson frmMain.lstNames.Text
  On Error Resume Next   'skip null fields
  Load frmEdit
  With frmEdit
    .txtName = Persons!name
    .txtCompany = Persons!company
    .txtPhone = Persons!phone
    .txtEmail = Persons!email
    .txtNotes = Persons!notes
    .Caption = "Edit"
    Persons.Edit
    .Show vbModal
  End With
End Sub
```

The **On Error Resume Next** statement is used here because some of the fields in the database are empty and will return a value of Null. Assigning Null to a text control causes a runtime error, so we tell the program to ignore the problem and continue.

The **FindPerson** procedure performs a Seek operation on the Persons table, using the name selected in the list box. Calling the FindFirst method would also be acceptable, but the Persons recordset would have to be opened as a dynaset:

```
Public Function FindPerson(aName as string) As Boolean
   FindPerson = True
   Persons.Seek "=", aName
   If Persons.NoMatch Then FindPerson = False
End Function
```

Before the program ends, the table must be closed. We must check the value of tableOpen so we don't accidentally try to close a table that is already closed:

```
Public Sub CloseTable()
   On Error GoTo CloseTable1
   If tableOpen Then
     Persons.Close
     tableOpen = False
   End If
   Exit Sub
CloseTable1:
   MsgBox Error$, vbInformation, "CloseTable"
End Sub
```

Similarly, the database must be closed:

```
Public Sub CloseDatabase()
   On Error GoTo CloseDatabase1
   If databaseOpen Then
     Dbase.Close
     databaseOpen = False
   End If
   Exit Sub
CloseDatabase1:
   MsgBox Error$, vbInformation, "CloseDataBase"
End Sub
```

6.2.4 Implementation: frmMain

A number of event procedures need to be coded in frmMain. When the user clicks on the combo box containing the names of the available tables in the database, we call the OpenTable procedure:

```
Private Sub cboTablenames_Click()
   OpenTable
End Sub
```

When the user either double-clicks on the name of a person in the list box or clicks on the Edit/Modify menu, we call ModifyRecord:

```
Private Sub lstNames_DblClick()
  ModifyRecord
End Sub

Private Sub mnuEditModify_Click()
  ModifyRecord
End Sub
```

When the user clicks on a name in the lstNames list box, we enable the Edit/Modify menu choice:

```
Private Sub lstNames_Click()
  mnuEditModify.Enabled = True
End Sub
```

When the user clicks on the File/Exit menu choice, we unload the form:

```
Private Sub mnuFileExit_Click()
  Unload Me
End Sub
```

When the user clicks on the File/Open menu, we call OpenDatabase, which displays a File/Open dialog:

```
Private Sub mnuFileOpen_Click()
  OpenDatabase
End Sub
```

When the user clicks on Help/About, we show the splash window (you can substitute a different window for Help/About if you wish):

```
Private Sub mnuHelpAbout_Click()
  frmSplash.Show vbModal
End Sub
```

6.2.5 Implementation: frmSplash

The App.Major and App.Minor properties hold the program version number:

```
Private Sub Form_Load()
  Label3 = "Version " & App.Major & "." & App.Minor & _
    ", Released " + ReleaseDate
End Sub

Private Sub Form_Click()
  Unload Me
End Sub
```

6.2.6 Implementation: frmEdit

The user clicks on the Save button to retain changes made to the record displayed by frmEdit. The following code copies the data in the text controls to the database record and saves it in the database:

```
Private Sub cmdSave_Click()
  On Error GoTo CmdSave1
  Persons!company = txtCompany
  Persons!phone = txtPhone
  Persons!email = txtEmail
  Persons!notes = txtNotes
  Persons.Update
  Unload Me
  Exit Sub
CmdSave1:
  MsgBox Error$, vbInformation, "Error"
End Sub
```

If by any chance you forgot to set the AllowZeroLength attribute of each field except "name" to True, you will encounter a runtime error when a field is empty.

If the user clicks on the Cancel button while editing a record, we confirm before abandoning changes to the record:

```
Private Sub cmdCancel_Click()
  Dim ans As Integer
  ans = MsgBox("Ok to abandon changes (if any) to" _
    + " this record?", vbYesNo + vbQuestion, "Cancel")
  If ans = vbYes Then Unload Me
End Sub
```

6.2.7 Conclusion

Notice that most of the code in this program is placed inside module1.bas rather than in forms. An advantage to this approach is that it makes program maintenance a lot easier. You don't have to hunt through the various event handlers in the different forms for a given procedure, because the procedures are all listed alphabetically in the code module. If the name of a control should change, it is easier to rename all references to it in general procedures than it is to rename the names of event handlers associated with the control. On the other hand, a drawback to this appriach is that many procedure names are global, which works agains the object-oriented principle of encapsulation.

This first version of the Personal Contact Manager leaves a lot of room for improvement. We really need to write a new version of the program, and finish some of the features that were left out.

> ***Programming Tip: Incremental Development.*** Programs should be constructed and tested in steps, for several reasons: First, it's easier to debug a program incrementally rather than try to find all bugs in a finished program. Second, the sheer size and complexity of a large program seems less overwhelming when viewed as a set of evolutionary steps. Third, the user can give better input into the design process if early versions of the program are up and running.
>
> At each stage, be sure to test and evaluate the work you have done so far. Always design your programs with future expansion and improvement in mind. Even when a program is debugged, good programmers will often tinker with its design to make it more adaptable to future improvements. Any program that cannot be revised and improved is in danger of becoming extinct.

6.3 Project: Personal Contact Manager - 2

Let's create an improved version of the Personal Contact Manager program that allows the user to add, modify, copy, and delete records. On the surface, this doesn't sound too difficult, but there is quite a bit of extra coding involved.

6.3.1 Program Specifications

- The user will be able to delete records from the database.
- The user will be able to add new records to the database.
- The user will be able to modify all fields in a record, including the person's name.
- The user will be able to copy and move records from one table to another.
- Menu commands will be automatically disabled when their use would not be appropriate.

6.3.2 Program Design

We will add new choices to the Edit menu to allow the copying, deleting, and moving of records (Table 3).

Table 3. Edit Menu in PCM - 2.

&Edit	mnuEdit
&Add New	mnuEditAdd
&Modify Record	mnuEditModify
-	separator1
Cu&t Record	mnuEditCut
&Copy Record	mnuEditCopy
&Paste Record	mnuEditPaste

When the user has opened a database and selected a table name from the combo box, the Edit/Add menu command is activated so the user can add new records to the table.

When the user clicks on "Add New", a blank input form appears. This is the same frmEdit we used in the first version of the program, except that the txtName.Locked property must be set to False in design mode. Figure 9 shows a sample of the form.

Figure 9. The Add New Entry Window.

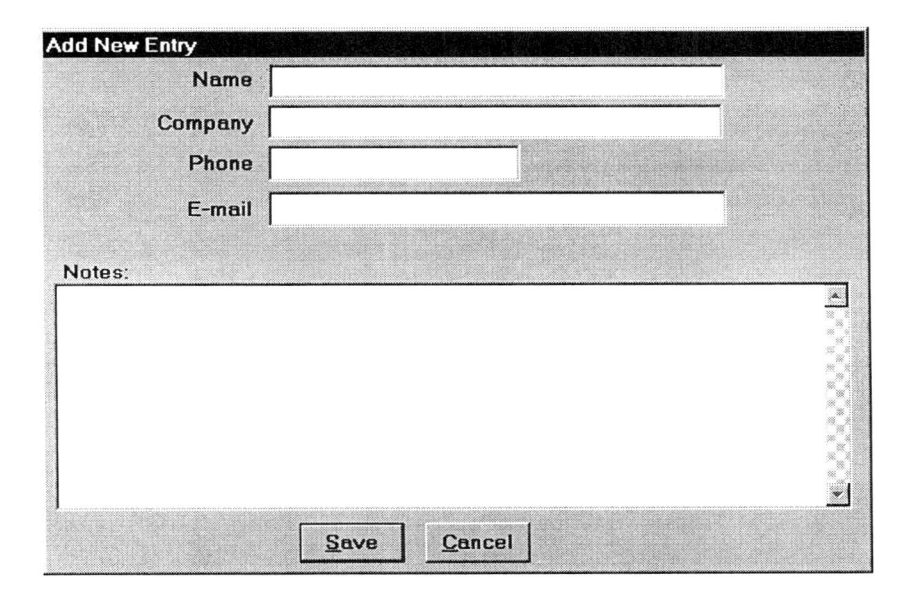

Once a name has been selected in frmMain, the Modify, Cut, and Copy menu commands are enabled. If we select the **Copy** command, a copy of the current record is made, and the **Paste** command is enabled. The user can then switch to another table and paste the copied record into it. Of course, you can't paste the same record into a table that already contains the record, or an error message appears (Figure 10).

Figure 10. Error Message: Duplicate Record.

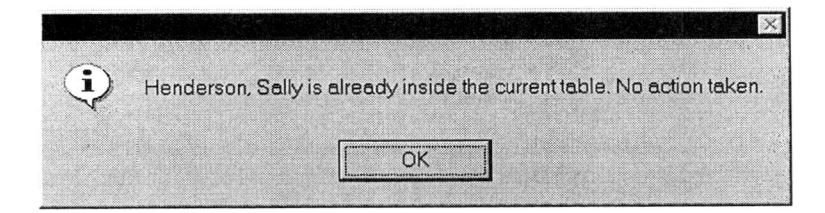

When the Edit/Cut command is used, the record is removed from the current table and held in memory. The record can then be pasted into a table.

6.3.3 Program Implementation

The following declarations appear at the beginning of Module1. **PersonRec** is a user-defined type that describes the fields stored in each database record, and **aPerson** is a variable, or *instance,* of type PersonRec. We use this to save the current record when performing the Edit/Cut, Copy, and Paste commands:

```
Type PersonRec
  name As String
  company As String
  phone As String
  email As String
  notes As String
End Type

Public Const ReleaseDate As String = "07-01-1997"
Public Persons As Recordset
Dim databaseOpen As Boolean
Dim Dbase As Database
Dim tableOpen As Boolean
Dim aPerson As PersonRec
```

The **OpenTable** procedure has been expanded slightly. When a new table is opened, we disable the Modify, Copy, and Cut operations:

```
Public Sub OpenTable()
  Dim tableName As String
  tableName = frmMain.cboTablenames.Text
  If Len(tableName) = 0 Then Exit Sub
  On Error GoTo OpenTable1
  Set Persons = Dbase.OpenRecordset(tableName, dbOpenTable)
  Persons.Index = "NameNdx"
  LoadListbox
  tableOpen = True
  frmMain.mnuEdit.Enabled = True
  frmMain.mnuEditModify.Enabled = False
  frmMain.mnuEditCopy.Enabled = False
  frmMain.mnuEditCut.Enabled = False
  Exit Sub
OpenTable1:
  MsgBox Error$, vbInformation, "Open Table"
End Sub
```

These commands will be enabled again when the user clicks on a person's name.

The **ModifyRecord** procedure is identical to the previous version of the program, except that we now call LoadListbox after frmEdit closes because the person's name may have changed:

```
Public Sub ModifyRecord()
  FindPerson (frmMain.lstNames.Text)
  On Error Resume Next   'skip null fields
  Load frmEdit
  With frmEdit
    .txtName = Persons!name
    .txtCompany = Persons!company
```

```
            .txtPhone = Persons!phone
            .txtEmail = Persons!email
            .txtNotes = Persons!notes
            .Caption = "Edit"
            Persons.Edit
            .Show vbModal
        End With
        LoadListbox          'reload the list box
    End Sub
```

The **AddNewRecord** procedure sets the caption of frmEdit, adds a new record to the current table, and displays frmEdit:

```
    Public Sub AddNewRecord()
        frmEdit.Caption = "Add New Entry"
        On Error GoTo AddNewRecord1
        Persons.AddNew
        frmEdit.Show vbModal
        LoadListbox
        Exit Sub
    AddNewRecord1:
        MsgBox Error$, vbInformation, "Add New"
    End Sub
```

After frmEdit closes, we reload the list box so the new name will appear. On the other hand, we could have just directly added the new name to the list box, but we would have to know whether or not the user clicked on the Cancel button when closing frmEdit.

The **CopyRecord** procedure finds the person's name in the table, makes a copy of the current record in the Persons table, and stores it in **aPerson,** a PersonRec variable:

```
    Public Sub CopyRecord()
        FindPerson frmMain.lstNames.Text
        On Error Resume Next
        aPerson.name = Persons!name
        aPerson.company = Persons!company
        aPerson.phone = Persons!phone
        aPerson.email = Persons!email
        aPerson.notes = Persons!notes
        frmMain.mnuEditPaste.Enabled = True
    End Sub
```

The Edit/Paste command is enabled, showing that a record is waiting to be pasted into some other table.

> ***Programming Tip:*** By carefully enabling and disabling menu commands at different times, you greatly reduce the amount of error checking required by a program. For example, if we left the Edit/Copy command enabled all the time, the CopyRecord procedure would have to make sure 1) the database was open, 2) the table was open, 3) a name had been selected in the list box.

The **CutRecord** procedure makes a copy of the current record before removing it from the table. We start by retrieving the name from the list box and asking the user if she really wants to remove the name:

```
Public Sub CutRecord()
  Dim msg As String, aName As String
  aName = frmMain.lstNames.Text
  msg = "Are you sure you want to remove " _
      + aName + " from this table?"
  If MsgBox(msg, vbYesNo + vbQuestion, _
    "CutRecord") = vbNo Then Exit Sub
```

CopyRecord makes a copy of the current record in the Persons table and enables the Edit/Paste menu command:

```
  CopyRecord  'make a copy of the record
```

We also delete the current database record and remove the person's name from the list box:

```
  On Error GoTo CutRecord1
  Persons.Delete
  frmMain.lstNames.RemoveItem frmMain.lstNames.ListIndex
  Exit Sub
CutRecord1:
  MsgBox Error$, vbInformation, "Cut Record"
End Sub
```

The **PasteRecord** procedure takes **aPerson** and adds it both to the current table and the list box. First, it makes sure the name is not already in the table:

```
Public Sub PasteRecord()
  If FindPerson(aPerson.name) Then
    MsgBox aPerson.name + " is already inside " _
      + "the current table. No action taken.", _
      vbInformation, ""
    Exit Sub
  End If
```

Next, a new record is added and initialized from **aPerson**, the PersonRec variable. The person's name is appended to the list box:

```
  On Error GoTo PasteRecord1
  Persons.AddNew
  Persons!name = aPerson.name
  Persons!company = aPerson.company
  Persons!phone = aPerson.phone
  Persons!email = aPerson.email
  Persons!notes = aPerson.notes
  Persons.Update
  frmMain.lstNames.AddItem aPerson.name
  Exit Sub
PasteRecord1:
  MsgBox Error$, vbInformation, "Paste Record"
End Sub
```

The frmMain Form. There is now a **lstNames_Click** event handler in frmMain. When the user clicks on the list box and selects a name, we enable the Edit/Modify, Edit/Cut, and Edit/Copy menu commands:

```
Private Sub lstNames_Click()
  mnuEditModify.Enabled = True
  mnuEditCut.Enabled = True
  mnuEditCopy.Enabled = True
End Sub
```

We also include event handlers for the new Edit menu commands:

```
Private Sub mnuEditAdd_Click()
  AddNewRecord
End Sub

Private Sub mnuEditCopy_Click()
  CopyRecord
End Sub

Private Sub mnuEditCut_Click()
  CutRecord
End Sub
```

The frmEdit Form. We also make a small addition to the cmdSave_Click procedure in frmEdit. Because the user can add new records and modify the name field, we have to assign txtName to Persons!name:

```
Private Sub cmdSave_Click()
  On Error GoTo CmdSave1
  Persons!name = txtName.Text
  (etc...)
```

> ***Programming Tip:*** When adding even a few new features to a program, the number of lines of code increases dramatically. The important thing is to let the program expand in an orderly fashion. Make sure no single procedure is too long or complex, and procedures call each other in a logical sequence.

6.4 Project: Doctors Office Appointments - 2

In this section, we revisit the object-oriented Doctors Office Appointments program from Chapter 4. The original version of the program allowed the user to schedule and display appointments made by patients at a medical office. The appointment objects were added to a collection. The improvement we make in the current version is to store all information in a database, and directly manipulate Data Access objects in program code.

6.4.1 Program Specifications

- A patient may request an appointment with a specific doctor at a specific date and time.

- When an appointment is scheduled, the program stores the appointment data in a database for easy retrieval. For each appointment, we need to identify the patient, the doctor, the date and time, and the purpose of the appointment.
- The program will let the user view all appointments currently scheduled, or all appointments scheduled for a chosen patient. The appointments are ordered by date and time.

(A future version of the program will allow the user to view all appointments scheduled for a single doctor.)

6.4.2 Program Design

We will use a database table called **Appointments** to save information such as the following. The doctorID field is a unique six-letter abbreviation of the doctor's last name:

```
doctorID    patientID    date        time          purpose
CHONG       1001         10/20/97    8:00:00 AM    Broken Leg
ROBINS      2030         10/20/97    3:00:00 PM    Yearly check-up
```

Table 4 lists the Appointment table fields.

Table 4. Appointment Table.

Name	Type	Size
doctorId	Text	6
patientId	Long Integer	
date	Date/Time	
time	Date/Time	
purpose	Text	30

The program first displays the main window, in which each button describes the major operations (Figure 11).

Figure 11. Adding New Appointments.

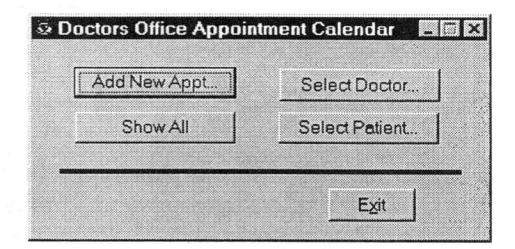

When the user clicks on "Add New Appt...", the Add Appointment window appears (Figure 12). The user selects a doctor ID, a patient name, the date and time of the appointment, and enters a description of the purpose of the appointment.

Figure 12. Adding a New Appointment.

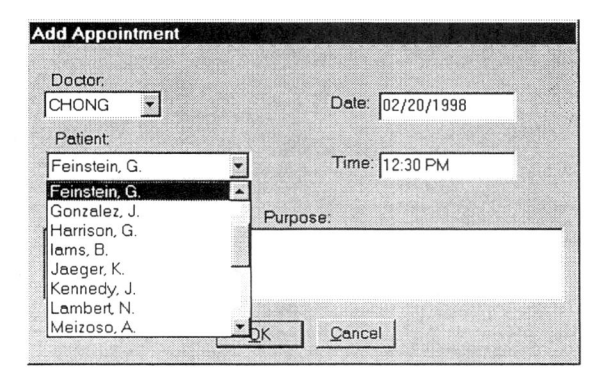

If the user clicks the OK button, the appointment is saved in the database. If the user clicks the Cancel button, the appointment is discarded.

Main Window. Back in the main window, the user can also view a list of all appointments in the calendar by clicking the **Show All** button. The list box uses a fixed-width font (Courier New, 8 pt) so the columns can be lined up (Figure 13). The project consists of the modules listed in Table 5.

Figure 13. List of All Appointments.

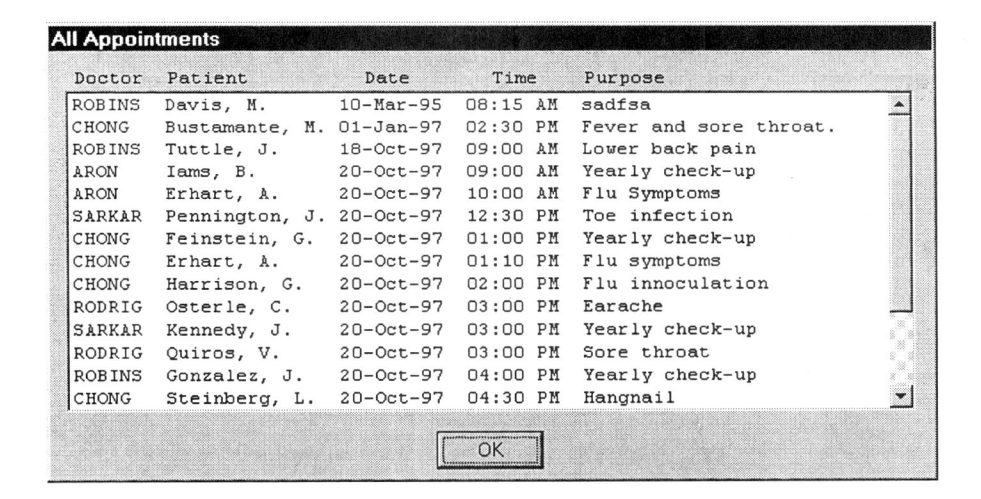

The user can also view all appointments made by a single patient, shown in Figure 14. A combo box lists all available patient names; once a name has been selected, a window displays the appointments.

Figure 14. One Patient's Appointments.

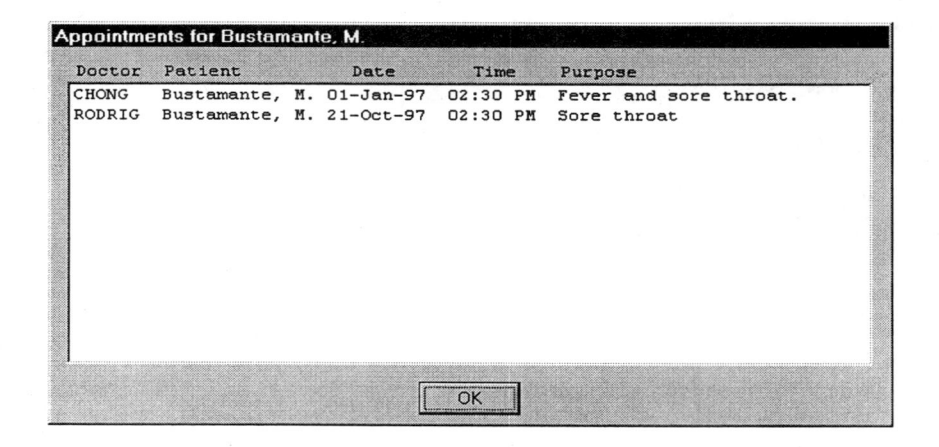

```
Appointments for Bustamante, M.
  Doctor  Patient         Date       Time      Purpose
  CHONG   Bustamante, M.  01-Jan-97  02:30 PM  Fever and sore throat.
  RODRIG  Bustamante, M.  21-Oct-97  02:30 PM  Sore throat

                              [ OK ]
```

Table 5. Modules in the Doctors Office Appointments Program.

Name	Description
modMain	Startup procedure
frmMain	Main form
frmInput	User inputs a new appointment
frmDisplay	Display list of appointments
frmSplash	Splash window
frmSelectPatient	Select a patient from a list
clsAppointment	Class module
clsApptCalendar	Class module
clsPatient	Class module

6.4.3 Implementing the Appointment Program

This program declares DBase *public* because it will be used when opening recordsets in individual classes and modules. Here is the code stored in the program's code module:

```
Public DBase As Database
Const DBaseFilename = "schedule.mdb"
Public Sub Main()
  ChDrive App.Path
  ChDir App.Path
  Set DBase = Workspaces(0).OpenDatabase(DBaseFilename)
  frmMain.Show vbModal
  DBase.Close
  End
End Sub
```

6.4.4 The Main Form: frmMain

The code in the program's main form, frmMain, is quite simple. It creates a clsApptCalendar object (an appointment calendar), and calls each of the program's main tasks. The user can display all appointments, add a new appointment to the calendar, and display appointments relating to one patient:

```
Option Explicit
Dim calendar As clsApptCalendar

Private Sub Form_Load()
  Set calendar = New clsApptCalendar
  calendar.TableName = "Appointments"
End Sub

Private Sub cmdShowAll_Click()
  calendar.ShowAllAppointments
End Sub

Private Sub cmdAddNew_Click()
  calendar.AddAppointment
End Sub

Private Sub cmdSelPatient_Click()
  calendar.ShowPatientAppointments
End Sub

Private Sub cmdExit_Click()
  Unload Me
End Sub

Private Sub Form_QueryUnload(Cancel As Integer, _
  UnloadMode As Integer)
    Set calendar = Nothing
End Sub
```

6.4.5 Implementing the clsAppointment Class

In the clsAppointment class, we declare the instance variables and constants relating to a single appointment:

```
Const EarliestApptTime As Date = #8:30:00 AM#
Const LatestApptTime As Date = #4:45:00 PM#
Private doctorIdP As String
Private patientIdP As Long
Private apptDateP As Date
Private apptTimeP As Date
Private purposeP As String

Private Sub Class_Initialize()
  DoctorID = ""
  PatientID = 0
  Purpose = ""
End Sub
```

The Property procedures are identical to those shown in the Chapter 4 version of this program, so they will not be repeated here.

The **InputFromUser** method allows the user to input all necessary data for an appointment. The form (frmInput) is used by this program to act as a user interface. The frmInput.SaveAppt property equals True if the user closed the window by clicking the OK button, and False if the user clicked the Cancel button:

```
Public Function InputFromUser() As Boolean
  On Error GoTo InputFromUser1
  With frmInput
    .FillComboBoxes
    .EarliestApptTime = EarliestApptTime
    .LatestApptTime = LatestApptTime
    .Show vbModal
  End With

  'Save input data in database.
  If frmInput.SaveAppt Then
    DoctorID = frmInput.DoctorID
    PatientID = Val(frmInput.PatientID)
    ApptDate = frmInput.txtDate.Text
    ApptTime = frmInput.txtTime.Text
    Purpose = frmInput.txtPurpose.Text
    InputFromUser = True
  Else
    InputFromUser = False
  End If
  Unload frmInput
  Exit Function
InputFromUser1:
  MsgBox Error$, vbCritical, _
    "Cannot Input Appointment"
  Unload frmInput
End Function
```

The **AsString** method concatenates the appointment's data into a single string. First, it looks up the patient's name by calling GetpatientName. Next, it formats the appointment date and time:

```
Public Function AsString() As String
  Dim D As New clsPatient
  Dim doctor As String * 8
  Dim patient As String * 15
  doctor = DoctorID
  patient = D.GetpatientName(PatientID)
  AsString = doctor & patient & _
    Format$(ApptDate, "Medium Date") + " " + _
    Format$(ApptTime, "Medium Time") + " " + _
    Purpose
  Set D = Nothing
End Function
```

The **AsRecordset** method copies the appointment into a RecordSet object, as defined in the Appointments table:

```
Public Sub AsRecordset(R As Recordset)
  On Error Resume Next
  R!DoctorID = DoctorID
  R!PatientID = PatientID
  R!Date = ApptDate
  R!Time = ApptTime
  R!Purpose = Purpose
End Sub
```

The **ReadRecord** method copies the data from a RecordSet object into the current appointment. It is the converse of the AsRecordset method:

```
Public Sub ReadRecord(R As Recordset)
'Transfer data from current database record to
'this object.
  On Error Resume Next
  DoctorID = R!DoctorID
  PatientID = R!PatientID
  ApptDate = R!Date
  ApptTime = R!Time
  Purpose = R!Purpose
End Sub
```

> *Programming Tip:* Many experienced object-oriented programmers avoid direct references to private instance variables, even in class methods. Instead, all access to the data is through property procedures. This may seem somewhat strict, but it offers a distinct advantage: You can enforce error checking on input values in the property/Let procedures, and you can do output processing or formatting in the property/Get procedures.

6.4.6 The clsApptCalendar Class

The clsApptCalendar class encapsulates (surrounds) the database table holding all appointments for all doctors in the schedule. The best part about the class is that it provides a simple interface, so details regarding database access are neatly hidden inside the class methods. Let's go through the complete listing of clsApptCalendar:

```
Option Explicit
'Uses the following Forms:  frmDisplay, frmSelectpatient

Private apptTable As Recordset
Private tableNameP As String     'Name of Appointments table
Private tableIsOpen As Boolean

Public Property Get TableName() As String
  TableName = tableNameP
End Property
```

```
Public Property Let TableName(tname As String)
    tableNameP = tname
End Property

Private Sub Class_Initialize()
    tableNameP = "Appointments"    'default name
End Sub

Private Sub Class_Terminate()
    If tableIsOpen Then apptTable.Close
    Set apptTable = Nothing
End Sub
```

OpenTable attempts to open the Appointments table and reports any errors:

```
Public Sub OpenTable()
'Open the Appointments table.
    On Error GoTo OpenTable1
    Set apptTable = DBase.OpenRecordset(TableName, _
        dbOpenDynaset)
    tableIsOpen = True
    Exit Sub
OpenTable1:
    MsgBox Error$, vbCritical, "Error"
    tableIsOpen = False
End Sub
```

AddAppointment opens the database table if necessary, creates a clsAppointment object, inputs an appointment from the user, and adds it to the calendar:

```
Public Sub AddAppointment()
    If Not tableIsOpen Then OpenTable
    If Not tableIsOpen Then Exit Sub
    On Error GoTo AddAppt1
    Dim anAppt As New clsAppointment
    If anAppt.InputFromUser Then
        apptTable.AddNew
        anAppt.AsRecordset apptTable
        apptTable.Update
        Set anAppt = Nothing
        Exit Sub
    End If
    Exit Sub
AddAppt1:
    MsgBox Error$, vbCritical, "Error"
    Set anAppt = Nothing
End Sub
```

ShowAllAppointments clears the list box, sets the form caption, executes an SQL query that returns a list of appointments sorted by date and time, and displays the resulting recordset:

Chap 6: Data Access Objects

```
Public Sub ShowAllAppointments()
  Dim R As Recordset, query As String
  frmDisplay.List1.Clear
  frmDisplay.Caption = "All Appointments"

'Use an SQL query to create a temporary recordset
'containing appointments ordered by date and time.
  query = "SELECT * from Appointments ORDER BY date + time"
  Set R = DBase.OpenRecordset(query, dbOpenDynaset)
  ShowRecordset R
  Set R = Nothing
End Sub
```

ShowPatientAppointments lets the user select a patient from a combo box. It also creates and executes an SQL query string that creates a temporary recordset containing appointments for a single patient, sorted by date and time:

```
Public Sub ShowPatientAppointments()
  Dim aPatient As New clsPatient
  aPatient.SelectByName
  If aPatient.PatientID = 0 Then Exit Sub   'cancelled

  frmDisplay.List1.Clear
  frmDisplay.Caption = "Appointments for " + aPatient.PatientName

'Use an SQL query to create a temporary recordset
'containing appointments for the selected patient's
'appointments, ordered by date and time.

  Dim R As Recordset, query As String

  On Error GoTo ShowPatientAppts1
  query = "SELECT * from Appointments WHERE patientId = " _
    & aPatient.PatientID & " ORDER BY date + time"

  Set R = DBase.OpenRecordset(query, dbOpenDynaset)
  ShowRecordset R
  Set R = Nothing
  Exit Sub
ShowPatientAppts1:
  MsgBox Error$, vbInformation, "Error"
End Sub
```

ShowRecordset loops through a recordset and formats appointment objects for display in a list box. This is called by ShowAllAppointments and ShowPatientAppointments:

```
Private Sub ShowRecordset(R As Recordset)
'Loop through the recordset and format the records
'for display in a list box.
  Dim anAppt As New clsAppointment
  Do While Not R.EOF
    anAppt.ReadRecord R
```

```
        frmDisplay.List1.AddItem anAppt.AsString
        R.MoveNext
    Loop
    R.Close
    frmDisplay.Show vbModal
End Sub
```

Because ShowRecordset calls ReadRecord from clsAppointment class, ShowRecordset doesn't have to know the appointment record structure.

6.4.7 Implementing the clsPatient Class

In our program, every patient has an ID number and name; the clsPatient class also keeps track of the name of the database table holding the list of patients. The class uses one form, frmSelectpatient, that lets the user select the name of a patient before searching the list of appointments. Here is the class listing:

```
Option Explicit
'Forms used:  frmSelectpatient
Dim patientIDp As Long
Dim patientNamep As String
Dim tableNamep As String
Dim Patients As Recordset
```

The **SelectByName** method lets the user select a patient name from a combo box. It fills the combo box with names from the Patients table, shows the frmSelectPatient form, and retrieves the name selected by the user:

```
Public Sub SelectByName()
    Dim j As Integer
    On Error GoTo SelectByName1
    Load frmSelectPatient
    frmSelectPatient.cboPatient.Clear
    j = 0
    Do Until Patients.EOF
        frmSelectPatient.cboPatient.AddItem Patients!Name
        frmSelectPatient.cboPatient.ItemData(j) = Patients!id
        Patients.MoveNext
        j = j + 1
    Loop
    frmSelectPatient.Show vbModal
    patientIDp = frmSelectPatient.PatientID
    patientNamep = frmSelectPatient.cboPatient.Text
    Exit Sub
SelectByName1:
    MsgBox Error$, vbInformation, "Error"
End Sub
```

The ItemData property of the cboPatient combo box stores each of the patient ID numbers. This will make it easier to locate the database record that corresponds to a name found in the combo box, when the user selects a patient.

The **GetPatientName** method takes an ID number and looks up the patient name that matches the ID:

```
Public Function GetPatientName(id As Long)
  Patients.FindFirst "id = " & id
  If Patients.NoMatch Then
    GetpatientName = ""
  Else
    GetpatientName = Patients!Name
  End If
End Function
```

The remaining methods perform general housekeeping:

```
Public Sub OpenTable()
  Set Patients = DBase.OpenRecordset( _
    TableName, dbOpenDynaset)
End Sub

Private Sub Class_Initialize()
  tableNameP = "Patients"
  OpenTable
End Sub

Private Sub Class_Terminate()
  Patients.Close
  Set Patients = Nothing
End Sub
```

The various Property procedures get and set the patient ID, name, and database table name:

```
Public Property Get PatientID() As Long
  PatientID = patientIdP
End Property

Public Property Get patientName() As String
  patientName = patientNameP
End Property

Public Property Get TableName() As String
  TableName = tableNameP
End Property

Public Property Let TableName(tname As String)
  tableNameP = tname
End Property
```

frmSelectPatient. The following code is placed inside the **frmSelectPatient** form. Its main purpose is to let the user choose a patient name from a combo box, and to return a long integer holding the patient's ID number:

```
Dim patientIDp As Long
```

```
Private Sub cboPatient_Click()
  Dim n As Integer
  n = cboPatient.ListIndex
  If n >= 0 Then
    patientIDp = cboPatient.ItemData(n)
  End If
  Me.Hide
End Sub

Public Property Get PatientID()
  PatientID = patientIDp
End Property

Private Sub cmdCancel_Click()
  patientIDp = 0
  Unload Me
End Sub
```

6.4.8 The frmDisplay and frmInput Windows

Code in the **frmDisplay** form:

```
Private Sub cmdOk_Click()
  Unload Me
End Sub
```

The **frmInput** form is displayed by clsAppointment when the user wants to create a new appointment. The property procedures are identical to the previous version of the program, so they will be omitted here. There are two new module-level variables that refer to the Doctor and Patient tables:

```
Private saveApptp As Boolean            'read-only
Private earliestApptTimeP As Date       'write-only
Private latestApptTimeP As Date         'write-only
Private doctorIDP As String             'read-only
Private patientIDp As String            'read-only
Dim Doctors As Recordset
Dim Patients As Recordset
```

FillComboBoxes has changed because it now reads the doctor and patient names from two database tables:

```
Public Sub FillComboBoxes()
  Dim j As Integer
  Set Doctors = DBase.OpenRecordset("Doctors", dbOpenDynaset)
  Set Patients = DBase.OpenRecordset("Patients", dbOpenDynaset)
  Do While Not Doctors.EOF
    cboDoctors.AddItem Doctors!id
    Doctors.MoveNext
  Loop
  j = 0
  Do While Not Patients.EOF
```

```
         cboPatients.AddItem Patients!Name
         cboPatients.ItemData(j) = Patients!id
         Patients.MoveNext
         j = j + 1
    Loop
    Doctors.Close
    Patients.Close
    Set Doctors = Nothing
    Set Patients = Nothing
End Sub
```

Other functions such as ValidateFields and the button click event handlers have not changed, so they will not be shown here.

6.4.9 Conclusion

As always, many improvements can be made to this program. For example, it should be possible for the user to modify existing appointments, view all appointments for a particular doctor, and remove appointments. The program could check for schedule conflicts before making appointments, to prevent any doctor from having to see two patients at the same time. More information relating to each patient should be stored, including their insurance company name, policy number, and phone. Appointments could all be billed at the same rate at first, but it should later be possible to enter a fee for each visit. As each office visit takes place, the user should be able to transfer each appointment record to a history file that would provide some of the information needed to prepare each patient's bill. Each patient record should include a billing history that contains records of office visits, payments, and a running balance.

6.5 Multiuser Database Processing

In this section we will show how to use the Jet database engine to handle multiple users. The Jet database engine is designed for a small number of users; estimates vary, but ten or fewer users is a safe estimate. For larger numbers of users, the Microsoft SQL server is recommended.

Each user can easily run their own copy of the program because it loads into memory on the user's workstation. The main issue that affects programs with multiple users is their shared access to data. When one user is in the process of modifying a record, the record is automatically locked; this prevents other users from simultaneously updating the same record. The record might be locked for only a fraction of a second, or it might be locked for several minutes, depending on how the application program is designed.

Record updates in a multiuser environment can follow several different scenarios. In this discussion, we interpret an *update* as an AddNew, Edit, or Delete operation:

1. Two or more users access the same record simultaneously, but only one user modifies the record.
2. Two or more users update different records within the same table.
3. Two or more users try to update the same record simultaneously.

Scenario 1 does not involve record locking, but creates a situation in which the actual record has been modified and the other users are viewing an obsolete copy of the record. Scenario 2 may create a conflict, because the Jet database engine locks the 2,048-byte memory block containing the record being updated. Any records unfortunate enough to be within the same block as the record being updated will also be locked. Scenario 3, where multiple users try to simultaneously update the same record, will always cause the record to be locked by the first user who starts to update the record.

Optimistic and Pessimistic Record Locking. With the Jet database engine, there are two methods of record locking. *Pessimistic locking*, the default, prevents other users from updating a record from the time an AddNew or Edit method is executed, until Update is executed. *Optimistic locking*, on the other hand, allows other users to update a record even while an AddNew or Edit operation is under way; the only locking that occurs is from the time the Update method begins to execute, until the database engine is able to free the lock on the record.

LockEdits Property. The Recordset.LockEdits property sets or returns a value indicating the locking that is in effect during editing. It can be used with either table-type or dynaset-type recordsets. Syntax:

```
object.LockEdits [= value]
```

Where value is True or False. True indicates *pessimistic* locking, and False indicates *optimistic* locking.

Shared Database Processing. Many database applications involve the operation where a user will open a record for viewing and editing, modify the record in some way, and save the modified record. In any application involving a shared database, record updates require some strategic decisions on the part of the designer.

Suppose, for instance, two users are viewing/editing hotel reservation records, and both happen to notice that room 2120 is available. User-1 makes a reservation for room number 2120 and confirms. User-2, thinking that the room is still available, reserves the same room and confirms. User-2 is issued an error message stating that room 2120 is no longer available. In this scenario, the first user to begin viewing and editing the record for room 2120 could be given exclusive use of the record. Otherwise, a customer on the phone with a reservations agent might be told that a particular room is available, only to find out seconds later that the room in question had just been given to another customer.

6.5.1 Example: Record-Locking Program

Let's create a short program that demonstrates the differences between optimistic and pessimistic record locking. The program itself is almost trivial: it displays the ID and salary

Chap 6: Data Access Objects   255

of a single person from the **SalesStaff** table in the staff.mdb database (the database was demonstrated in Section 5.3). Figure 15 displays the main window, shown with identifier names.

Figure 15. Multi-User Database Example.

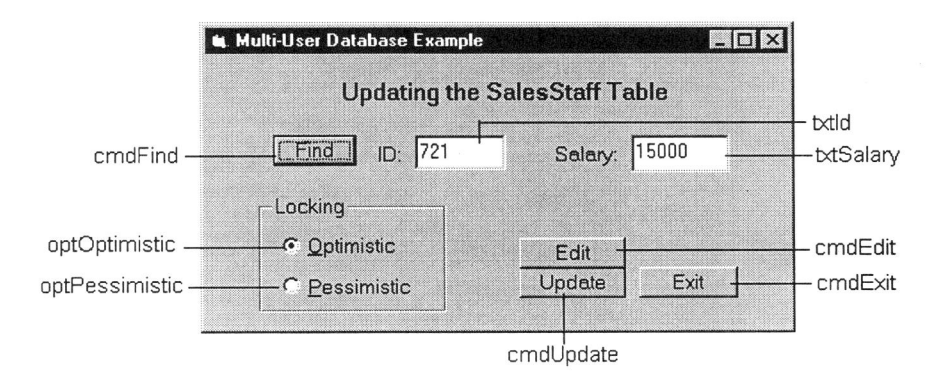

```
                    Multi-User Database Example
                    Updating the SalesStaff Table
                                                                        — txtId
    cmdFind ——————[ Find ]  ID: 721    Salary: 15000 ——————— txtSalary
                    ┌─ Locking ─────────┐
  optOptimistic ——— ⊙ Optimistic           [ Edit   ] ————— cmdEdit
  optPessimistic ——— ○ Pessimistic          [ Update ] [ Exit ] ——— cmdExit
                    └───────────────────┘
                                          cmdUpdate
```

The user enters an ID number and clicks the **Find** button; if a matching record is found, the employee's salary appears. If the user wants to change the salary, he clicks the **Edit** button, types in a new salary, and clicks on **Update**. For now, the **Optimistic** record locking option is selected.

Two Users. This program has been compiled to an executable file called locking.exe, so we can run two instances at the same time. For this discussion, we will call the instances *user-1* and *user-2*.

Example 1: Separate Edit Operations. Let's demonstrate a situation in which the edit operations do not overlap. Each user searches for ID 721 and displays the salary. User-1 clicks the Edit button, enters a new salary, and clicks on Update. User-2's program still displays the old salary, so she clicks on the Find button and retrieves the new salary.

Example 2: Overlapping Edits, Optimistic Locking. Each user searches for ID 721. User-1 clicks on **Edit**, and user-2 clicks on **Edit**. User-1 modifies the salary and clicks on **Update**. User-2 modifies the salary and clicks on **Update**. Figure 16 shows the runtime error generated by the database engine.**Figure 16. Runtime Error, Data Changed.**

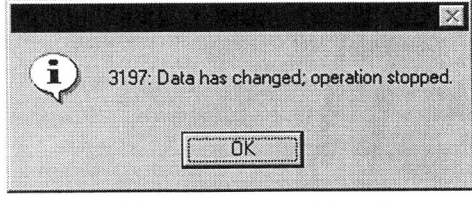

```
                    ┌─────────────────────────────────────┐
                    │  (i)  3197: Data has changed; operation stopped. │
                    │              [    OK    ]           │
                    └─────────────────────────────────────┘
                    Message seen by User-2:
```

User-2, however, can persist by clicking on **OK** to repeat the operation; the error message does not appear a second time and the update is successful. Alternatively, some programs might display the salary that was set by user-1 and ask user-2 to restart the edit operation. We suggest this approach in the chapter exercises for this program.

Example 3: Pessimistic Locking. In this example, both user-1 and user-2 select pessimistic locking. User-1 clicks on **Edit** to begin an edit operation. When user-2 clicks on **Edit**, the runtime error shown in Figure 17 is generated by the Jet engine because the record was locked by user-1. If user-2 had selected optimistic locking, this message would not have appeared until he clicked on the **Update** button.

Figure 17. Record Locked Message.

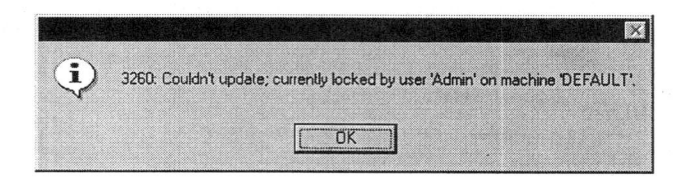

[Dialog box: "3260: Couldn't update; currently locked by user 'Admin' on machine 'DEFAULT'."]

6.5.2 Program Implementation

Here is the complete source code for the Record Locking program. The Form_Load procedure opens the database and recordset, and sets the record locking to *optimistic*:

```
Option Explicit
Dim dbase As Database
Dim staff As Recordset

Private Sub Form_Load()
   ChDrive App.Path
   ChDir App.Path
   Set dbase = Workspaces(0).OpenDatabase("staff.mdb")
   Set staff = dbase.OpenRecordset("SalesStaff", dbOpenDynaset)
   staff.LockEdits = False    'default: optimistic locking
End Sub
```

The user can select one of the two option buttons relating to record locking, and the **LockEdits** property is set accordingly:

```
Private Sub optOptimistic_Click()
   staff.LockEdits = False
End Sub

Private Sub optPessimistic_Click()
   staff.LockEdits = True
End Sub
```

FindFirst searches for a matching ID number. If one is found, the procedure retrieves the person's salary:

```
Private Sub cmdFind_Click()
   staff.FindFirst "id = " & Val(txtId)
   If staff.NoMatch Then
      MsgBox "Cannot find matching record", , ""
      txtSalary = ""
   Else
      txtSalary = staff!salary
   End If
End Sub
```

When the user clicks on **Edit** to begin an edit operation, the record might be pessimistically locked by another user, so On Error GoTo is required:

```
Private Sub cmdEdit_Click()
   On Error GoTo Edit1
   staff.Edit
   Exit Sub
Edit1:
   MsgBox Err.Number & ": " & Error$, vbInformation, ""
End Sub
```

When the user clicks on **Update** to save a record, the record might have been modified by another user, or it might be locked. In either case, an error would result:

```
Private Sub cmdUpdate_Click()
   On Error GoTo update1
   staff!salary = Val(txtSalary)
   staff.Update
   DBEngine.Idle dbFreeLocks
   Exit Sub
update1:
   MsgBox Err.Number & ": " & Error$, vbInformation, ""
End Sub
```

The event handlers for the Exit button and Form_Unload complete the implementation:

```
Private Sub cmdExit_Click()
   Unload Me
End Sub

Private Sub Form_Unload(Cancel As Integer)
   staff.Close
   dbase.Close
   Set staff = Nothing
   Set dbase = Nothing
End Sub
```

Using DBEngine.Idle. If the network is quite busy, the Jet database engine might not have enough free time to unlock the region containing the record immediately after the program has executed an Update operation. Freeing locked records is a background task which is often delayed in a multiuser environment where there is a great deal of database activity. But a call to the **DBEngine.Idle** method suspends other data processing and enables the Jet database engine to complete any pending tasks such as memory optimization and freeing memory locks. Data in memory is flushed to disk. The Idle method is usually called just after an Update:

```
staff.Update
DBEngine.Idle dbFreeLocks
```

6.5.3 BeginTrans, CommitTrans, and Rollback

A *transaction* is defined as a series of changes made to all databases in a workspace, where the changes are treated as a single unit. There are three workspace methods that may be used:

- **BeginTrans** begins a new transaction.
- **CommitTrans** ends the current transaction and saves the changes.
- **Rollback** ends the current transaction and restores the databases in the workspace object to the state they were in when the current transaction began.

Here are examples of calls to these three methods:

```
Dim ws as Workspace
Set ws = Workspaces(0)
ws.BeginTrans
' (database modified in here...)
If (changes are accepted)
  ws.CommitTrans
Else
  ws.Rollback
End If
```

A good application of transaction processing is when you update two or more tables, and all tables must be updated correctly. If any error occurs, you need to be able to roll back the changes and restore the database to its original state. For example, the Visual Basic help documentation points out that when transferring financial amounts between accounts, if an error occurs in one table and not the other, the entire transaction can be rolled back.

Batch Transaction Example. Using the same SalesStaff database from the record locking example, suppose that we wanted to give each employee hired after Jan. 1, 1994, a 10-percent raise. This would be an ideal use for transaction processing, because we could give the user the option to either commit (save) the transaction or to roll it back (cancel). The first step would be to invoke the BeginTrans method in the current WorkSpace object:

```
Private Sub cmdRaiseSalaries_Click()
   Dim count As Integer, amt As Currency
   Dim total As Currency, choice As Integer
   Workspaces(0).BeginTrans
```

The program uses a Do-Until loop to check each person's hire date. If the person was hired prior to 1/1/94, we call Edit, raise the salary by 10 percent, and call Update:

```
      staff.MoveFirst
      count = 0
      Do Until staff.EOF
```

```
        If staff!hireDate < #1/1/94# Then
          staff.Edit
          amt = staff!salary * 0.1
          staff!salary = staff!salary + amt
          staff.Update
          count = count + 1
          total = total + amt
        End If
        staff.MoveNext
    Loop
```

But these changes are not permanent. When the loop ends, a message box displays the number of salaries affected, the total dollar amount of the raises, and asks the user to confirm the changes:

```
    choice = MsgBox(count & " salaries will be increased, for a total " _
        & "cost to the company of " & vbCrLf & Format$(total, "currency") _
        & ". Do you want to keep these changes? ", vbYesNo, "Salary Raise")
    If choice = vbYes Then
       Workspaces(0).CommitTrans
    Else
       Workspaces(0).Rollback
    End If
    Exit Sub
```

If an error should occur during the loop, the On Error GoTo transfers to an error handler that informs the user that the transaction will be rolled back:

```
RaiseSalaries1:
    MsgBox Error$ & ". Batch transaction will be rolled back.", _
            vbInformation, "Error"
    Workspaces(0).Rollback
End Sub
```

When the user clicks on the cmdRaiseSalaries button, a confirmation messsage appears (Figure 18).

Figure 18. Confirmation Message.

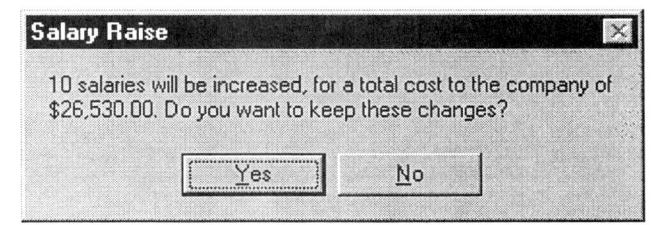

6.6 Review Questions

1. What operation does a data control have to perform when a form is loaded? Does this help explain why a form with several data controls seems to load slowly?

2. What is Microsoft's official name for the library of database objects? Which version number shipped with the first versions of Visual Basic 5?

3. What is the *Jet* engine, as applied to database objects?

4. In your version of Visual Basic, what is the menu command to enable the DAO library?

5. *Fill in the blank:* A DBEngine contains a collection of _____ objects that provide for transaction processing and database security within a group of users.

6. Code a complete statement that opens an Access database file called **accounts.mdb** and stores a reference to a database object in the variable **MyDb.**

7. What are the four parameters for the OpenRecordset method, and which ones are required?

8. What are some of the values for the *options* parameter in the OpenRecordset method?

9. Does OpenRecordset only open existing database tables?

10. What are the three constants that may be used for the recordsetType parameter, and what do each of them specify?

11. What is meant by pessimistic record locking?

12. If a table contains forty 50-byte records and record number 1 is locked, can other users access records 30-40?

13. Which should be closed first, a database, or one of its recordsets (tables)?

14. Which property of a database object allows you to access the names of the tables in the database?

15. Code an example of a statement that retrieves the name of the first field in a table called **Schedule** attached to a database object called **MyDb.**

16. Code a loop that displays the names of all fields in a table called Employees attached to a database object called **CompanyDb**.

The following questions refer to Version 1 of the Personal Contact Manager:

17. How does the PCM program keep the lists of individuals separated from other? Can you suggest another way to implement this program that would not involve the use of so many tables?

18. After selecting a database to be opened, what is the next action carried out by the user?

19. What special precaution does OpenDatabase have to take before opening a new database?

20. In the Attributes property of a TableDef object, what does the constant dbSystemObject indicate?

21. Why is the Allow Zero Length attribute useful in the table definitions used by this program?

The following questions refer to Version 2 of the Personal Contact Manager:

22. What important improvements does this version have over Version 1?
23. How are the Copy and Paste commands used in this program?
24. How does the PersonRec user-defined type make programming easier?
25. In the CopyRecord procedure, why is the variable **aPerson** not declared inside the procedure?
26. Why does the CutRecord procedure make a copy of the record being removed?

The following questions refer to the Doctors Office Appointments - 2 program from Section 6.4:

27. What is the major difference between the first version of this program (Chapter 4) and the current one?
28. What is the purpose of the AsRecordset method in the clsAppointment class?
29. How has the clsAppointment.ReadRecord method changed from the first version of this program?
30. In what way has the clsApptCalendar.AddAppointment method been simplified in this version of the program?
31. What is the SQL statement used by the clsApptCalendar.ShowAllAppointments method that fills the list box?
32. What is the SQL statement used by the clsApptCalendar.ShowPatientAppointments method that fills the list box?
33. In what way do the clsApptCalendar.ShowRecordset and clsAppointment.AsString methods work together?
34. What actions does the frmSelectPatient form carry out?
35. In frmSelectPatients, what is placed in the ItemData property of the cboPatients combo box? Why is this necessary?
36. Which class methods will have to be modified if the program prevents a doctor from having two appointments scheduled at the same time?
37. Suppose we add a method to the clsAppointment class that returns True when two appointment objects have equivalent dates and times. We might call this the "SameTimeAs" method. Can you write the implementation of the method? Here is a sample call to the method:

```
If appt1.SameTimeAs( appt2 ) Then
  msgBox "Time Conflict"
  Exit Sub
End If
```

The following questions refer to multiuser database processing:

38. Which three scenarios were described in Section 6.5 that involved two users and record locking?
39. Which Microsoft database product is recommended for more than ten simultaneous users?
40. What happens when a record is locked, and another user tries to update the record?
41. If two users want to display the same record at the same time, and only one user updates the record, will there be a conflict between them for access to the record?
42. What is meant by *pessimistic locking?*
43. What is meant by *optimistic locking?*
44. If two users implement optimistic locking, and each calls the Edit method for the same record at about the same time, will a runtime error result?
45. If you were an airline ticket agent, would you prefer the database software to use optimistic or pessimistic locking on the seat records for each flight?
46. If you lengthened the SalesStaff record by adding more fields, how long would it have to be so the Jet database engine could lock just one record at a time?
47. If a program generates a runtime error when it calls the Update method, do you think that optimistic or pessimistic locking is in effect?
48. If a program generated a runtime error when calling the Update method, what do you think would be the best course of action?
49. Explain the use of the LockEdits property.
50. Suppose that your program is running on a busy network, and even after Update has been called, it seems as if your database records are locked. What is the remedy for this situation?
51. Describe a *transaction*, in terms of the Jet database engine.
52. Explain the CommitTrans method.
53. Explain the Rollback method.
54. How would a transaction be useful when transferring data from one table to another?
55. In the batch transaction example in Section 6.4.3, what type of batch transaction was carried out on the SalesStaff table?
56. Can you think of any other applications where batch transaction processing would be useful?

Chap 6: Data Access Objects

6.7 Chapter Exercises

6.7.1 Record-Locking Program

In the Record-Locking Program presented in Section 6.5.1, an error message is displayed when the user attempts to update a record that has already been modified by another user. Error 3197 is the error code generated by this operation. Modify this program so that it explains to the user what has happened, refreshes the employee salary, and lets the user restart the editing operation. An example is shown in Figure 19.

Figure 19. Data Changed Message.

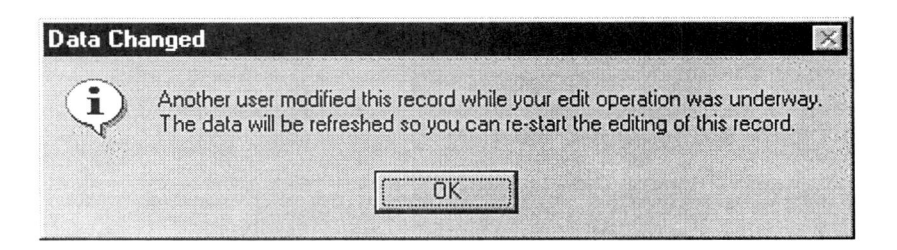

6.7.2 Personal Contact Manager - Using Categories

Add another field called **category** to the database table design that indicates the type of person stored in each record. This can be an integer, with values such as the following:

```
1          Relative
2          Colleague
4          Customer
8          Doctor/Dentist
16         PersonalFriend
255        All
```

Make up your own categories, and assign a different power of 2 to each one. By far the best way to do this would be to add another table to the database, containing the category numbers and descriptions. This table could be loaded into a multiselect list box by Form_Load. When the user selects from this list, limit the display of records to the selected group, or in the case of "All", display all records.

Because the category values are powers of 2, we can combine categories by adding the numbers together. To search for relatives and personal friends, for example, we could use a value of 17 (16 + 1):

```
Dim searchVal as Integer
searchval = Relative + PersonalFriend    'For testing only!

Persons.MoveFirst
Do While Not Persons.EOF
    If (Persons.Fields("category").Value And searchVal) > 0 Then
```

```
    lstNames.AddItem Persons!name
    Persons.MoveNext
Loop
```

This works because the **And** operator returns a value greater than zero if the category field contains either 16 or 1, or both. (This is called a *bitwise* operation, and is a common operation in languages such as 'C' and assembly language.)

6.7.3 Personal Contact Manager - Cut and Paste

In Version 2 of Personal Contact Mangager, a record that is cut or copied cannot be pasted into other Windows program. Modify the program so that such records can be pasted into Word documents, Excel spreadsheets, and so on. Insert a Tab character between the fields whenever a record is cut or copied.

6.7.4 Personal Contact Manager - MDI

Start with either Version 2 of the Personal Contact Manager or one of the versions generated in the previous two exercises. Make the program an MDI application. This will allow two or more database tables to be open at the same time. It also leaves open the possibility of opening the same table in two different child windows, but be aware that a change made to the data in one window should be immediately copied to all other windows holding the same table. Perhaps you might store the names of all open tables in a collection, and search the collection for a matching name before opening the new table. Or, you could search the Forms collection, checking the name of the recordset currently displayed in that form.

6.7.5 Personal Contact Manager - Multi-User

Make any necessary changes so that the Personal Contact Manager program can be run by multiple users. Use pessimistic record locking. Take note that the current program (Version 2) calls the Edit method in ModifyRecord, and it calls the AddNew method in AddNewRecord. In both cases, the current record and those around it will be locked for as long as it takes the user to input all data for the record. The Update method is not executed until the user clicks the OK button in the frmEdit form. If a record is locked, be sure to alert the user and provide a graceful way to recover from the problem.

6.7.6 Object-Oriented Personal Contact Manager

Make the Personal Contact Manager program fully object-oriented. Use Version 2 as the starting point for your program, or use one of the versions created from the previous two exercises. You can start with the PersonRec data type, and convert it into a class (clsPerson). Another useful class would be a list of PersonRec objects.

6.7.7 Doctors Office Appointments - 1

Use the Doctors Office Appointments from this chapter as a starting point. Make the following modification: All appointments are ten minutes long, and may start only on even multiples of 10 minutes after the hour. The first appointment is at 9:00 a.m., the next ones are at 9:10, 9:20, 9:30, and so on, up to 4:50 p.m. Select the hour and minute values from combo boxes. For example, you might want to use a separate combo box for the Hour, Minute, and AM/PM values (Figure 20).

Figure 20. Appoinment Input Form.

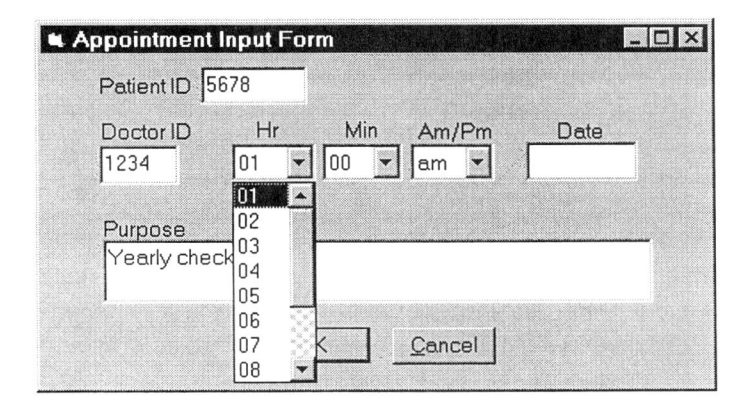

6.7.8 Doctors Office Appointments - 2

Continue the program you wrote for the previous Doctors Office Appointment project. Add the following feature: when the list of appointments for a single doctor is displayed, the appointments must be sorted by date and time (Figure 21).

Figure 21. Listing of One Doctor's Appointments.

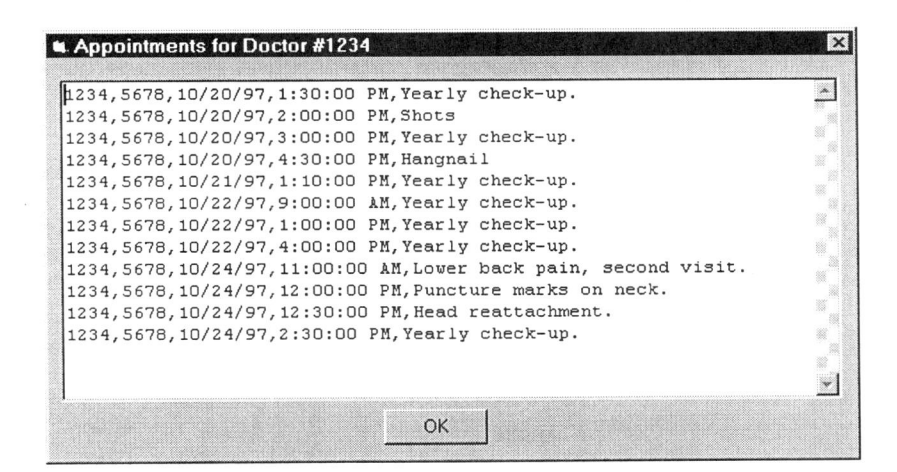

The best way to do this is to create a snapshot-type recordset in the FindDoctor method of the clsApptCalendar class. Use the OpenRecordset method, with an SQL query:

```
Dim R As Recordset, query As String
query = "Select * from Appointments " _
    + " WHERE doctorId = '" + id + "'" _
    + " ORDER BY date, time "
Set R = Dbase.OpenRecordset(query, dbOpenSnapshot)
```

The query searches for all records from the Appointments table that match the doctor ID, and sorts them by date and time. Once the snapshot has been created, just use the MoveFirst and MoveNext methods to loop through the recordset and concatenate them to a string.

6.7.9 Doctors Office Appointments - 3

Continue the program from the previous exercise. In the current program, let the user display and modify existing appointments using a shared database. Use optimistic record locking, so records are locked only while the Update method is executing. Compile the program to an EXE file and run three instances at the same time, either on the same computer or on a network. When another user has modified the current record, your program must notify the current user and display the modified record.

6.7.10 Doctors Office Appointments - 4

Continue the program from the previous exercise. In the current program, do not permit two appointments to be scheduled with the same doctor at the same date and time. Display a message box notifying the user of the conflict. Figure 22 shows an example of an attempt to schedule an appointment, along with the resulting message box that notifies the user of the conflict. *Hint:* You might want to use the FindFirst method to search the Appointments table for specific values in the DoctorId, Date, and Time fields.

Figure 22. Example of Appointment Schedule Conflict.

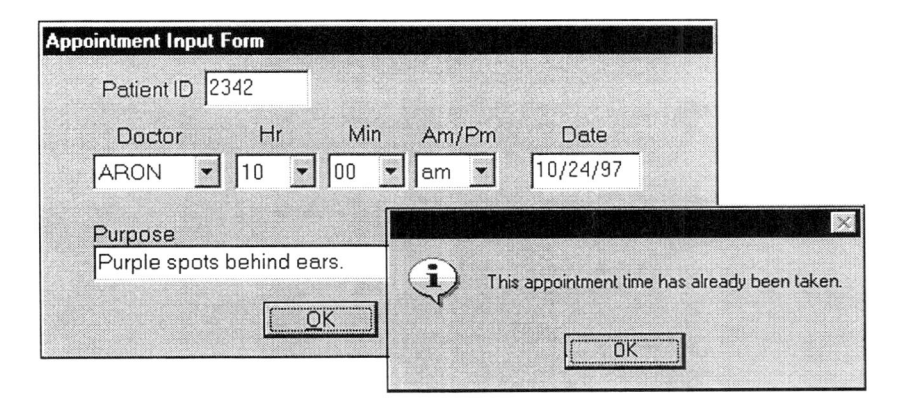

6.7.11 Concert Hall Ticketing - 1

Specifications. Write a program that could be used in the box office of a concert hall. The easiest way to describe the program's operations is to construct a scenario, or sequence of events:

- When a customer calls in and requests a particular concert, the box office attendant (the user of our program) verifies the concert's date and time.
- The customer asks for the ticket prices in each section of the hall.
- The customer asks for a certain number of tickets, in a particular section of the hall. The attendant verifies that the requested seats are available, and notifies the customer of the total price including tax.
- The customer pays for the tickets and the box office attendant issues the tickets.
- The program updates a database containing counts of the number of available tickets in each section of the concert hall. When tickets are sold, the appropriate count must be reduced.

Assumptions. Tickets purchased for a particular seating section can be used anywhere within that section. Customers cannot return tickets. Only one concert is scheduled per date. There will always be four sections in the concert hall: Orchestra1, Orchestra2, Balcony1, and Balcony2.

Other Specifications. Your program must do the following:

- Provide a way of looking up a concert's title, date, time.
- Retrieve the price per seat in each section of the concert hall for a particular concert.
- Retrieve the number of available seats in a given section, for a given concert.

Figure 23 shows the main window after the user has selected a concert and section and has entered the customer name and number of tickets. The program automatically recalculates the price, tax, and total when the number of tickets is changed or a different section is chosen.

Figure 23. Selecting a Concert and Section.

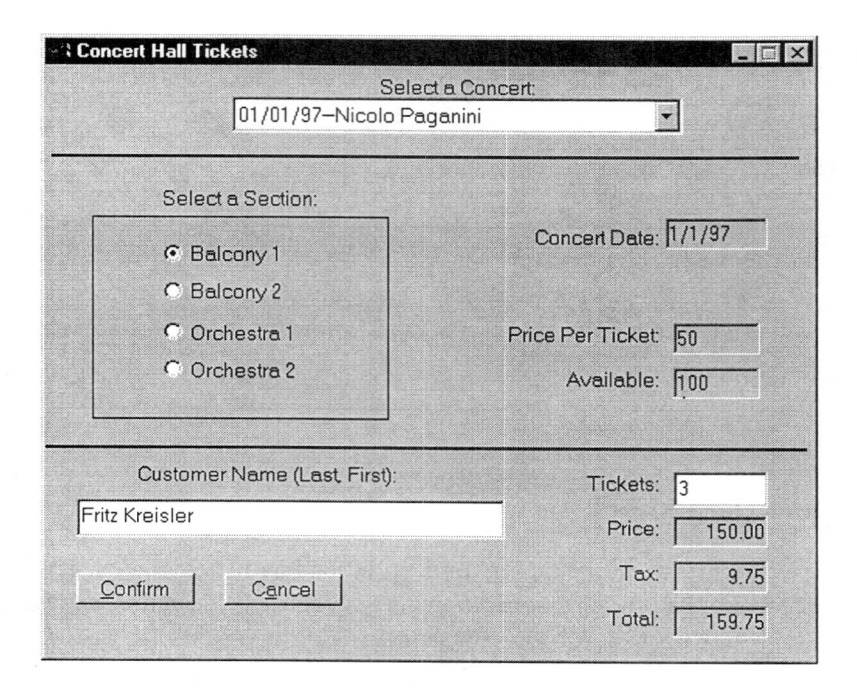

Database Definitions. The following tables are defined inside concert.mdb; a sample database file is provided on the student disk.

Table: Concerts
    ConcertDate - the date and time of the concert. (key, called *dateNdx*)
    Title - description of the concert.

Table: Seats
    ConcertDate
    B1Price - price per seat in the Balcony1 section.
    B1Avail - Number of seats that are still available in the section.
    B2Price - price per seat in the Balcony2 section.
    B2Avail - Number of seats that are still available in the section.
    O1Price - price per seat in the Orchestra1 section.
    O1Avail - Number of seats that are still available in the section.
    O2Price - price per seat in the Orchestra2 section.
    O2Avail - Number of seats that are still available in the section.

Table: Reservations
    ConcertDate - date and time of the concert.
    CustomerName
    SectionNumber (0 - 3)
    NumberOfTickets

The Reservations table contains a log of all reservations made by all customers. This is a useful reference for both printing tickets and confirming reservations. The SectionNumber field contains a value between 0 and 3, implying 0 = Balcony1, 1 = Balcony2, 2 = Orch1, and 3 = Orch2.

Hint: When using a FindFirst statement to search for a specific concert date, remember to surround the date with date delimiter (#) characters. For example:

```
Dim theDate as Date
theDate = "1/5/98"
FindFirst "ConcertDate = #" & theDate & "#"
```

6.7.12 Concert Hall Ticketing - 2

In this updated version of the Concert Hall Ticketing System, you must collect payment information from the customer, which is assembled into an invoice. A record of each transaction is saved in a database. The required payment information is:

- Customer name, address, phone, payment method.
- Amount paid.
- Type of payment (cash, check, or credit card).
- For credit card payments, the credit card type, number and expiration date are required.
- For payments by check, the customer's driver license number is required.

6.7.13 Concert Hall Ticketing - 3

In this updated version of the Concert Hall Ticketing System, you must reserve a specific seat for each ticket when it is purchased. No other customer can buy a ticket for that seat.

Let the program show a list of available seats in each section of the concert hall. This may be shown in text format (as in a list box), or in graphical format using a diagram of the hall and color coding to differentiate between seats that are available or reserved.

Ticket prices for each performance may vary, so your database must specify the ticket price for each seating section for each concert.

6.7.14 Concert Hall Ticketing - 4

Using any previous version of the concert hall ticketing program, make it suitable for a multiuser environment. Implement pessimistic locking, because you don't want a user to find that available seats were sold to another customer before the current transaction could be completed. To prevent a user from leaving a record locked for too long a time, use a Timer control to monitor the amount of time the record was locked, and automatically free it after a 2-minute time interval. Notify the user, of course, that the record has been released.

7 Relational Databases

Chapter Contents

Database Design
    Terminology
    Designing a Database
Using the SQL Language
    Structure of an SQL Statement
    A Sample Database
    SELECT Statement
    WHERE Clause
    Selecting from Multiple Tables
    JOIN Clause
    Creating Queries in Microsoft Access
SQL Action Queries
    UPDATE Statement
    DELETE Statement
    INSERT INTO Statement (Append Queries)
Creating Tables and Indexes
    Creating Indexes
    Creating Tables
    Removing Tables and Indexes
Application: Stellar Car Rental
    Overview
Table Descriptions
    Vehicle Inventory
    Vehicle Descriptions, Types, and Status
    Rental Prices
    Customers, Reservations, and Invoices
Validation Rules
    Creating Validation Rules in Access
Table Relationships
    Creating Table Relationships
Designing the Interface
    Vehicle Reservations
Reservation Implementation
    Module1
    The clsVehicleType Class
    The clsReservation Class
    The frmReserv Form
    The frmCustomer Form
    The frmFindFile Form
    The frmPrices Form
Review Questions
Chapter Exercises

7.1 Database Design

7.1.1 Terminology

A *relational database management system* (RDMS) is a collection of data that is organized so that you can look at it in different ways. It contains tables, index, queries, filters, views, and validation capabilities. RDMS's are able to maintain links, or relationships between tables and to ensure that the links are consistent.

As we have already seen, a *table* is a collection of data that pertains to a single topic, organized into rows and columns. Each row is called a *record,* and each column is called a *field.*

An *index* is a tool that orders a table according to one or more of the table's fields, called *keys*. The index contains all the values of the key field(s). For each key value, the index stores a pointer to the table row in which the key value was found. We use an index to present a table in a particular order, and to efficiently search for a single record in the table.

A *query* is a command written in the SQL language that either retrieves a set of records according to some criteria, or performs some action on the table. In past chapters, we used queries to build recordsets. In one case, we assigned a query string to the Recordsource property of a data control, and in another, we passed a query as an argument to the OpenRecordset method. Many database management systems, Microsoft Access included, let you create queries and store them in a database.

A *filter* is a tool that lets you limit the number of records displayed by a query or recordset. The filter represents a condition that must be true before a record can be displayed. In SQL, a filter is expressed by a WHERE statement, such as: "WHERE Salary > 12000".

A *view* of a database is usually a subset of the entire collection of data, determined by filters and indexes. A particular view might be limited to only certain fields from a table, or it might combine fields from different tables. We might create a view of an employee table, for instance, that excludes the social security number and salary fields so that other employees cannot see this information.

Database validation can take several forms: Automatic checks can be made for missing field values, values whose type is inconsistent with their declared field types, values that are out of range, and values that do not correlate correctly with other field values. We create *validation rules* to perform some of these checks, and the database system can perform checks between tables to make sure that table relationships are preserved correctly. These *relationships*, called *one-to-one* and *one-to-many*, are described later in this chapter.

7.1.2 Designing a Database

There are two general approaches to designing a database: one is *application-driven*, and the other is *application-independent*. In the first case, a database is designed around a single application program; the input/output needs of the program determine the way tables and relations are set up. In the second case, a database is designed in a more general way, with the intent that multiple application programs will share the data. This type of database is harder to design, because one has to anticipate the data needs of programs that have not yet been written.

We will use the application-driven approach to database design in this chapter, because it enables us to rapidly build an application program that uses the database.

There are a number of steps involved in designing an application-driven database:

- *Create a model* of the application. Decide which operations will be most critical. Try to determine what data the program will need for input and output. Some data that you thought you needed may later prove to be unecessary. In a more general design, you might keep the data just in case it might be needed by other programs. But in an application-driven design, you eliminate extra data.
- *Determine the data sources*. Once you know what the program's inputs and ouputs are, you need to know the sources and destinations of specific data. Will some data be from user input, from a shared database, or from other programs? Will the program's output be placed on a form, transmitted to another program, or sent to a database table for further processing or printing?
- *Organize the data into tables* so that it can be easily retrieved. Data relating to a single entity should probably be kept in the same table. For example, in a student records program, we might have a table called Transcript that contains all courses and grades completed by students. On the other hand, mixing information about this semester's courses with information about room scheduling would not be appropriate. There is a process called *normalization* which is used when building tables in a way that reduces the amount of redundant or hard-to-reach data.
- *Establish relationships between tables* to allow for automatic checking and updating of records. If the college course registration table contains a studentId number, for example, that Id number can be used to look up information about the student.
- *Create indexes and establish validation rul*es for the data in your tables. Indexes greatly speed up access to data and provide an easy way to order the data in tables. Validation rules help to ensure that table data is consistent within certain restraints. Bounds checking, set membership, data type checking, and referential integrity checking are some of the more common types of data validation.

To be, or not to be Object-Oriented. Another factor in the design of data that will be used by an application program is that the program itself is likely to be object-oriented. By this, we mean that objects, with properties and methods, are likely to be the important players in a program's design. Microsoft Access databases follow a Relational model rather than object-oriented, but it can be helpful to keep in mind that database tables can be encapsulated inside classes, providing a program "layer" between the users of the database and the database itself. For an example of this, see the Doctor's Office Schedule program in Chapter 6.

7.2 Using the SQL Language

The name SQL stands for *Structured Query Language*, the most widely used language for defining and manipulating relational databases. Nearly all databases produced in recent years support SQL, which greatly helps anyone learning to use a new database program. Generally, SQL statements can be used to create new databases, add and modify tables, search for data, build new tables from existing ones, and to remove tables and data.

SQL statements can also be used by programs that select and retrieve data from databases. SQL statements can be used by end users to perform interactive *ad-hoc queries* that retrieve database data.

The Jet database engine directly interprets SQL statements. Some database operations are more efficient when written in SQL than if explicitly coded using DAO methods. If you need to delete all the records in a dataset, for example, a single statement in SQL can do the job. Without SQL, you would have to set up a loop that iterates through all records and removes them one by one.

There are actually two languages within SQL: The *data definition language* (DDL) is used for defining databases, tables, and indexes. The *data manipulation language* (DML) is used for searching, retrieving, modifying, inserting, deleting, and updating table data.

Terminology. Because SQL queries often refer to recordsets in memory rather than in a physical database file, records are usually called *rows,* and fields are called *columns*. We will use the terms interchangeably.

Queries. The most common type of SQL statement is called a *query*. It defines the fields to be used when retrieving data, the tables that contain the fields, selection criteria for the records, and the ordering of the retrieved data. The data is usually returned in a dynaset-type recordset object. Queries can be processed interactively, or they can be stored in the database for later use.

7.2.1 Structure of an SQL Statement

An SQL statement consists of the following:

- Parameter declarations: Optional parameters that can be passed to the query by a program.
- Manipulative statement: Indicates what type of action will be taken, such as INSERT, DELETE, SELECT, or UPDATE (see Table 1).
- Options: Conditions for selecting records, grouping, ordering, and totaling of records. Some keywords used here are WHERE, ORDER BY, and SUM (see Table 2).

- Aggregate functions that process multiple records, possibly a subset of the entire table (see Table 3).

Table 1: Data Manipulation Statements.

Statement	Operation
DELETE	Deletes rows from a table.
INSERT	Inserts rows into a table.
SELECT	Retrieves a group of records from a table and places them in a separate recordset.
UPDATE	Modifies the values of table fields.

Table 2: SQL Clauses.

Clause	Description
FROM	Names the table(s) from which records are selected.
WHERE	Conditions for selecting records.
GROUP BY	Groups records together and provides summary information.
HAVING	Condititon to be satisfied by each group.
ORDER BY	Sorts records on one or more fields, in a selected order.

Table 3: Aggregate Functions.

Function	Description
AVG	Calculates the average of values in a field.
COUNT	Counts the number of selected records.
SUM	Sums, or totals the selected records.
MAX	Returns the highest value in a certain field.
MIN	Returns the lowest value in a certain field.

7.2.2 A Sample Database

The best way to learn SQL is by example, so we will use a small database containing two tables, called Employee and Payroll. Each social security number in the Payroll table matches a social security number in the Employee table:

```
Employee (ssn, lastName, firstName, phone)
Payroll (ssn, paymentDate, hoursWorked, payRate )
```

Figure 1 contains some sample records in the Employee table. Notice that each social security number occurs only once in the table. It is the table's primary key field.

Figure 1. Sample Records, Employee Table.

ssn	lastName	firstName	phone
111-22-3333	Jones	Sam	222-3333
111-30-3000	Baker	Bob	333-2222
111-44-3232	Davidson	Anne	444-3232
200-10-5000	Gonzalez	Arturo	543-1234
222-32-4444	Chong	Helen	522-5678
300-56-9999	Franklin	Bill	677-5432
333-22-5555	Jackson	Deke	877-2424
400-33-2555	Robinson	Diane	888-4444

Some social security numbers appear more than once in the Payroll table (Figure 2) because the same employee receives paychecks on different payment dates. Therefore, the **ssn** field cannot be a primary key. All of the social security numbers in the Payroll table match records in the Employee table, except for ssn = 425-55-4444. The **ssn** field is called a *foreign key*.

Figure 2. Sample Records, Payroll Table.

ssn	paymentDate	hoursWorked	payRate
111-22-3333	1/15/98	40	$12.50
111-44-3232	2/15/98	38.5	$14.00
111-44-3232	1/15/98	38.5	$14.00
222-32-4444	2/15/98	42	$12.50
222-32-4444	1/15/98	42	$12.50
300-56-9999	2/15/98	45	$14.50
300-56-9999	1/15/98	45	$14.50
425-55-4444	1/15/98	37.5	$18.00
		0	$0.00

7.2.3 SELECT Statement

SELECT is by far the most commonly used SQL statement because it provides a way to select only certain rows from a table and build a new data set. The basic syntax for SELECT appears here. Keywords are capitalized, and italicized names are definitions of programmer-supplied information:

```
SELECT fieldlist
  FROM tablelist
  IN databasename
  WHERE search-conditions
  GROUP BY fieldlist
  HAVING group-criteria
  ORDER BY fieldlist
  WITH OWNERACCESS OPTION
```

SQL is not case-sensitive, so capitalization is unimportant when writing actual statements. Only the SELECT and FROM clauses are required. *fieldlist* is a list of field names, separated by commas. *tablelist* is a list of table names from the current database, separated by commas. Field names may optionally be qualified by its table name. Examples are: Employee.ssn, Payroll.payRate, and Student.credits.

The following SELECT statement creates a data set containing a single column (lastName) from the Employee table:

```
SELECT lastName FROM Employee
```

If you use a wildcard character (*) for the field list, all fields are selected:

```
SELECT * FROM Employee
```

In general, runtime processing is faster if you specify only fields that are actually needed.

> *Programming Tip:* If a field or table name contains embedded spaces or punctuation characters, the name must be enclosed in brackets:
>
> ```
> SELECT [pay rate] FROM [January Payroll]
> ```

Queries in Visual Basic. In Visual Basic, one way that we use SQL queries is when calling the OpenRecordset method. For example, assuming that DBase is a Database object that is already open, we can build a new recordset object using a query:

```
Dim temp As Recordset
Dim query As String
query = "SELECT lastName, firstName FROM Employee"
Set temp = DBase.OpenRecordset( query, dbOpenDynaset )
```

Now **temp** can be used like any other dynaset. Here, we use it to fill a list box:

```
Do Until temp.EOF
   List1.AddItem temp!lastName
   temp.MoveNext
Loop
temp.Close
```

7.2.4 WHERE Clause

The WHERE clause uses selection criteria to determine which rows of a table are selected. Table 4 shows a list of the comparison operators that may be used.

Table 4. Comparison Operators in SQL.

Operator	Description
<	Less than
>	Greater than
<=	Less than or equal to
>=	Greater than or equal to
=	Equal to
<>	Not equal to
BETWEEN	Compares a range of values
LIKE	String pattern matching
IN	Specify records in a database

In the following query, only rows from the Payroll table in which the hours worked are greater than 40 are selected:

```
SELECT ssn, paymentDate, hoursWorked
   FROM Payroll
   WHERE hoursWorked > 40
```

The following query selects rows in which the hourly pay rate of each employee falls within a certain range:

```
SELECT ssn, payRate FROM Payroll
   WHERE payRate Between 14 AND 30
```

The following query selects rows in which the **ssn** field begins with the digits '111':

```
SELECT ssn, lastName, firstName from Employee
   WHERE ssn LIKE '111*'
```

If a date or time literal is being compared to a date/time field, the literal must be enclosed in # delimiters:

```
SELECT ssn, payRate FROM Payroll
   WHERE paymentDate < #02/01/98#
```

> *Programming Tip:* The date in an SQL statement must be in standard U.S. format, even when Windows has been set up for another country's date representation. For example, many South American countries represent February 1, 1998 as 01/02/1998. The simplest workaround to this problem is to let the DateValue function convert a date from a country-specific format to the one recognized by SQL:
>
> ```
> SELECT ssn, payRate FROM Payroll
>    WHERE paymentDate < DateValue('01/02/1998')
> ```

Calculated Columns. It is often useful to add a new column to the recordset created by an SQL statement, using calculated values. Suppose we wanted to calculate the amount of pay for each employee, using the hoursWorked and payRate fields. This would create a new column:

```
SELECT ssn, hoursWorked * payRate
   FROM Payroll
```

Figure 3 shows the data set generated by this query.

Figure 3. Calculating a New Column.

ssn	Expr1001
111-22-3333	525
111-44-3232	565.95
111-44-3232	565.95
222-32-4444	551.25
222-32-4444	551.25
300-56-9999	685.125
300-56-9999	685.125
425-55-4444	708.75

Calculated fields can also be used as criteria for selecting records:

```
SELECT ssn, hoursWorked * payRate
   FROM Payroll
   WHERE hoursWorked * payRate > 500
```

SQL assigns a default name to the calculated field, such as "EXPR1001". We can optionally assign a specific name such as payAmount to the calculated field, using the AS clause:

```
SELECT ssn, hoursWorked * payRate AS payAmount
   FROM Payroll
```

The + operator can be used to create a string expression. In the following query, we display the combined first and last names of all employees:

```
SELECT lastName+ ", " + firstName
   FROM Employee
```

Logical Operators. The AND and OR logical operators can be used to combine expressions, and the NOT operator reverses an expression's meaning. Usually, the operators appear in the WHERE clause. The following statement selects rows in which the hourly pay rate is between 14 and 30, and the payment date is less than February 1, 1998:

```
SELECT ssn, payRate, paymentDate FROM Payroll
   WHERE payRate Between 14 AND 30
   AND paymentDate < #02/01/98#
```

The following selects all rows in which the calculated pay amount is greater than 500, as well as all rows in which the hourly pay rate is greater than 20:

```
SELECT ssn, payRate, hoursWorked, hoursWorked * payRate
   FROM Payroll
   WHERE hoursWorked * payRate > 500
   OR payRate > 20
```

7.2.5 Selecting from Multiple Tables

Most databases consist of more than one table with relationships between the tables. SQL statements can select individual fields from more than one table at a time. Here, again, is the structure of the Employee and Payroll tables that we have used in examples so far:

```
Employee (ssn, lastName, firstName, phone)
Payroll (ssn, paymentDate,  hoursWorked, payRate )
```

Notice that the field **ssn** occurs in both tables: It is the *primary key* in the Employee table, and it is called a *foreign key* in the Payroll table. This means that we have a *one-to-many* relationship between Employee and Payroll. For every *one* social security number in the Employee table, there can be *many* instances of the same number in the Payroll table.

When we write a SELECT statement using the **ssn** field, we have to use the notation table.field to clarify which table's **ssn** value is being referenced. The following statement pulls data from the Employee and Payroll tables:

```
SELECT Employee.ssn, lastName, paymentDate
   FROM Employee, Payroll
      WHERE Employee.ssn = Payroll.ssn
```

For readability, it is often a good idea to supply table names for all fields, whether they are required or not:

```
SELECT Employee.ssn,Employee.lastName,Payroll.paymentDate
   FROM Employee, Payroll
      WHERE Employee.ssn = Payroll.ssn
```

The DISTINCTROW option eliminates any duplicate rows in the resulting data set:

```
SELECT DISTINCTROW Employee.ssn,Employee.lastName,Payroll.paymentDate
   FROM Employee, Payroll
      WHERE Employee.ssn = Payroll.ssn
```

When we create a new data set from two or more tables and match the records using the WHERE clause, there is one drawback: the data set cannot be updated. The preferred way to combine tables is by using the JOIN clause.

Avoiding Redundant Queries. A common mistake made by someone learning SQL is to select records from two or more tables without using the WHERE or JOIN clauses. The database will create a *cartesian product* of the tables. Suppose, for example, that one table contained three members (10,20,30) and another table contained three members (A,B,C). Then the cartesian product would consist of all possible member pairs:

(10,A), (10,B), (10,C), (20,A), (20,B), (20,C), (30,A), (30,B), (30,C)

If we produced a cartesian product between two tables having 1000 records each, the resulting data set would contain one million records. In a network environment, most database administrators are reluctant to let general users run ad-hoc SQL queries on multi-user databases because queries of this type could bring the system to a standstill.

Let's create such a cartesian product with the Employee and Payroll tables. Remembering that each table contains eight records, we will process the following query:

```
SELECT lastName, firstName, hoursWorked
FROM Employee, Payroll
```

The resulting data set contains 64 records, some of which are shown in Figure 4.

Figure 4. Cartesian Product Example.

lastName	firstName	hoursWorked
Jones	Sam	40
Baker	Bob	40
Davidson	Anne	40
Gonzalez	Arturo	40
Chong	Helen	40
Franklin	Bill	40
Jackson	Deke	40
Robinson	Diane	40
Jones	Sam	38.5
Baker	Bob	38.5
Davidson	Anne	38.5
Gonzalez	Arturo	38.5
Chong	Helen	38.5
Franklin	Bill	38.5
Jackson	Deke	38.5
Robinson	Diane	38.5
Jones	Sam	38.5
Baker	Bob	38.5
Davidson	Anne	38.5
Gonzalez	Arturo	38.5
Chong	Helen	38.5
Franklin	Bill	38.5

7.2.6 JOIN Clause

The JOIN clause indicates how the rows from two or more tables are to be related together. There are three types of joins: *inner, left,* and *right:*

- INNER JOIN: Only include rows where the joined fields from Table1 and Table2 are equal.
- LEFT JOIN: All rows from Table1 and only rows from Table2 where the joined fields are equal.
- RIGHT JOIN: All rows from Table2 and only rows from Table1 where the joined fields are equal.

To illustrate the three types of join methods, we will start with the tables shown in Figure 5.

Figure 5. Employee and Payroll Tables.

Employee Table

ssn	lastName	firstName	phone
111-22-3333	Jones	Sam	222-3333
111-30-3000	Baker	Bob	333-2222
111-44-3232	Davidson	Anne	444-3232
200-10-5000	Gonzalez	Arturo	543-1234
222-32-4444	Chong	Helen	522-5678
300-56-9999	Franklin	Bill	677-5432
333-22-5555	Jackson	Deke	877-2424
400-33-2555	Robinson	Diane	888-4444

Payroll Table

ssn	paymentDate	hoursWorked	payRate
111-22-3333	1/15/98	40	$13.13
111-44-3232	1/15/98	38.5	$14.70
111-44-3232	2/15/98	38.5	$14.70
222-32-4444	1/15/98	42	$13.13
222-32-4444	2/15/98	42	$13.13
300-56-9999	1/15/98	45	$15.23
300-56-9999	2/15/98	45	$15.23
425-55-4444	1/15/98	37.5	$18.90

Inner Join. The following INNER JOIN includes only records having the same social security numbers in both tables:

```
SELECT DISTINCTROW Employee.ssn, Employee.lastName,
   Payroll.paymentDate, Payroll.hoursWorked
FROM Employee
INNER JOIN Payroll
ON Employee.ssn = Payroll.ssn
```

The data set created by this query appears in Figure 6.

Figure 6. Inner Join Example.

ssn	lastName	paymentDate	hoursWorked
111-22-3333	Jones	1/15/98	40
111-44-3232	Davidson	1/15/98	38.5
111-44-3232	Davidson	2/15/98	38.5
222-32-4444	Chong	1/15/98	42
222-32-4444	Chong	2/15/98	42
300-56-9999	Franklin	1/15/98	45
300-56-9999	Franklin	2/15/98	45

Left Join. The following LEFT JOIN includes all rows from Employee, and only rows in Payroll that match the social security numbers of rows in Employee:

```
SELECT DISTINCTROW Employee.ssn, Employee.lastName,
   Payroll.paymentDate, Payroll.hoursWorked
   LEFT JOIN Payroll
   ON Employee.ssn = Payroll.ssn
```

The resulting data set (Figure 7) contains four rows from the Employee table that have no matching rows in the Payroll table.

Figure 7. Left Join Example.

ssn	lastName	paymentDate	hoursWorked
111-22-3333	Jones	1/15/98	40
111-30-3000	Baker		
111-44-3232	Davidson	1/15/98	38.5
111-44-3232	Davidson	2/15/98	38.5
200-10-5000	Gonzalez		
222-32-4444	Chong	1/15/98	42
222-32-4444	Chong	2/15/98	42
300-56-9999	Franklin	1/15/98	45
300-56-9999	Franklin	2/15/98	45
333-22-5555	Jackson		
400-33-2555	Robinson		

Right Join. The following RIGHT JOIN includes all rows from Payroll, and only the rows from Employee where the social security numbers are equal. Notice that the first field in the SELECT list is now Payroll.ssn:

```
SELECT DISTINCTROW Payroll.ssn, Employee.lastName,
   Payroll.paymentDate, Payroll.hoursWorked
   RIGHT JOIN Payroll
   ON Employee.ssn = Payroll.ssn
```

The resulting data set (Figure 8) contains one row from the Payroll table that did not have a matching row in the Employee table. The row is called an *orphan*.

Figure 8. Right Join Example.

ssn	lastName	paymentDate	hoursWorked
111-22-3333	Jones	1/15/98	40
111-44-3232	Davidson	1/15/98	38.5
111-44-3232	Davidson	2/15/98	38.5
222-32-4444	Chong	1/15/98	42
222-32-4444	Chong	2/15/98	42
300-56-9999	Franklin	1/15/98	45
300-56-9999	Franklin	2/15/98	45
425-55-4444		1/15/98	37.5

7.2.7 Creating Queries in Microsoft Access

Microsoft Access has a Query Wizard that greatly simplifies the writing of SQL queries. From the database window, you can select the Queries tab and click the New button. Select the Simple Query Wizard, which will display the following window. In this window (Figure 9), you select the tables and fields that you want to be displayed in the data set produced by the query.

Figure 9. Query Wizard, Microsoft Access.

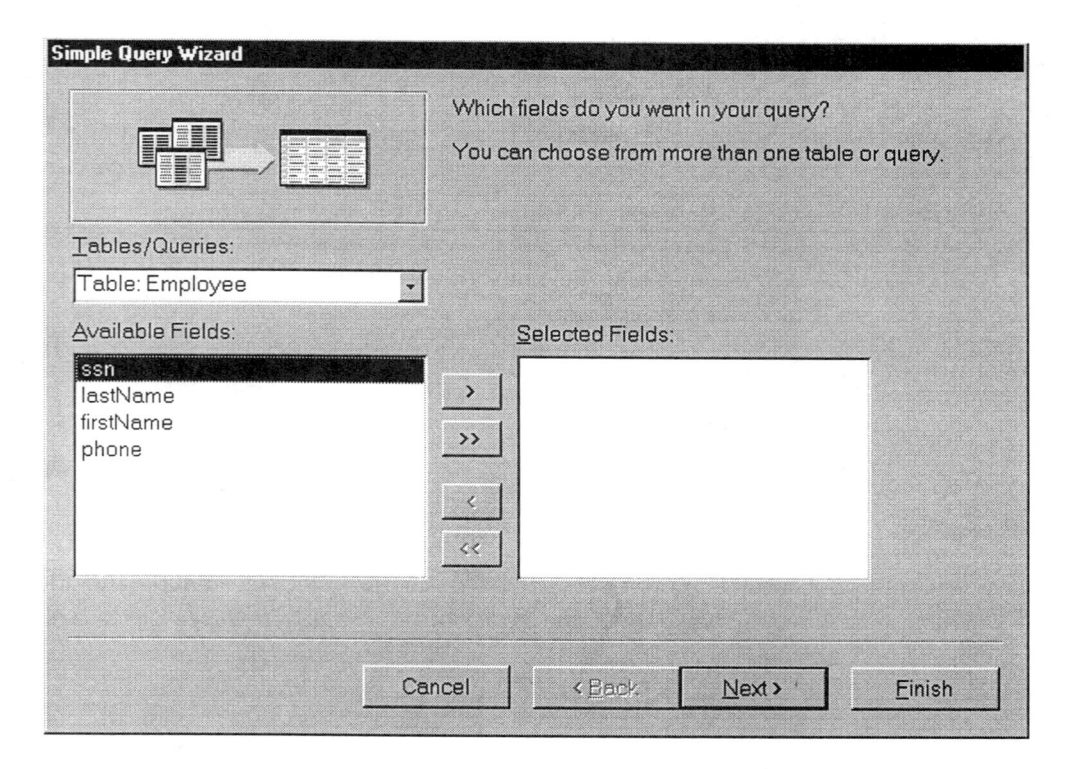

For example, we could select ssn, lastName, and firstName from the Employee table, along with paymentDate and hoursWorked from the Payroll table. After the wizard has finished, click the View/SQL menu to see the query's SQL source code. For example, this query was generated when we selected the ssn, lastName, firstName, paymentDate, and hoursWorked fields from the two tables:

```
SELECT DISTINCTROW [Employee].[ssn], [Employee].[lastName],
    [Employee].[firstName], [Payroll].[paymentDate],
    [Payroll].[hoursWorked]
FROM Employee
INNER JOIN Payroll
ON [Employee].[ssn] =[Payroll].[ssn]
```

By default, Access places brackets around the field names, which is only necessary when field names contain embedded spaces or punctuation. This query can be pasted directly into a Visual Basic program, or the query can be given a name and saved in the database itself.

Database Tip: Microsoft Access will not let you use the Query Wizard to create a query that involves two tables unless you set table relationships first (one-to-one, or one-to-many). Later in this chapter, we show you how to create these relationships.

7.3 SQL Action Queries

SQL action queries carry out some immediate action on a database. They are: DELETE, INSERT INTO, UPDATE, and MAKE-TABLE.

7.3.1 UPDATE Statement

The UPDATE statement is used to create what is called an *update* query. This type of query changes values in one or more fields in one or more tables, based on given criteria. The syntax is:

```
UPDATE table
SET fieldname = newvalue
WHERE criteria
```

With this statement, you can update many records at the same time, modifying one or more fields. The updated records can also be in different tables.

The following statement increases the pay rate in all rows of the Payroll table by 5%:

```
UPDATE Payroll
SET payRate = payRate * 1.05
```

We will introduce a new table called **Sales**, shown in Figure 10.

Figure 10. The Sales Table.

ssn	Jan	Feb	percIncrease
111-22-3333	50	65	
111-30-3000	75	95	
111-44-3232	550	620	
200-10-5000	22	48	
222-32-4444	250	55	
300-56-9999	400	350	
333-22-5555	475	425	
400-33-2555	827	890	

The following SQL statement calculates the percent increase for each employee between January and February:

```
UPDATE Sales
SET percIncrease = (Feb - Jan) / Jan
```

7.3.2 DELETE Statement

The DELETE statement can be used to delete entire rows from a table. The WHERE clause can be used to select the rows. The syntax is:

```
DELETE [table.*]
FROM tablelist
WHERE criteria
```

The table argument is only required when deleting from multiple tables. Be careful: Once a row has been deleted, it cannot be recovered.

For example, we might want to delete all rows from the Payroll table in which the payment date was earlier than January 1, 1998:

```
DELETE FROM Payroll
WHERE paymentDate < #1/1/98#
```

If we wanted to delete all rows but retain the Payroll table structure, we would use the following:

```
DELETE FROM Payroll
```

One-to-Many Relationships. If you specify more than one table, none of the tables can contain the primary key of a one-to-many relationship. You can, however, remove rows from the *many* side of a one-to-many relationship.

Using Action Queries in Visual Basic. In a Visual Basic program, use the Execute method to execute action queries. If Dbase was an open database object, for example, the following statement would delete all the rows from the Payroll table:

```
Dbase.Execute "DELETE FROM Payroll"
```

In a multiuser environment, it is a good idea to include the **dbFailOnError** option to tell the database to roll back (undo) the update if an error occurs. A record might locked by another user, for example, generating a trappable error:

```
Dbase.Execute "DELETE FROM Payroll", dbFailOnError
```

7.3.3 INSERT INTO Statement (Append Queries)

The INSERT INTO statement can be used to add new records to a table. This is also called an *append* query. You can add a single record by supplying all of its field data, or records can be appended from another table, using an append query.

Single-Record Append. A single-record append query has the following syntax:

```
INSERT INTO target
[(field1[,field2[,...]])]
VALUES(value1,[,value2[,...]])
```

The single-record append can be used if you want to add a single record to a table. You have to specify all of the field values. For example, the following appends a new record to the Payroll table:

```
INSERT INTO Payroll (ssn, paymentDate, hoursWorked, payRate)
VALUES('400-33-2555', #1/15/1998#, 47.5, 17.50)
```

The following is an alternate syntax for the same operation:

```
INSERT INTO Payroll (ssn, paymentDate, hoursWorked, payRate)
SELECT '400-33-2555', #1/15/1998#, 47.5, 17.50
```

Multiple-Record Append. A multiple-record append query has the following syntax:

```
INSERT INTO target
SELECT [source.]field1[,field2[,...]
FROM tablename
```

The following statement copies all records from the Payroll table to the **PayTemp** table:

```
INSERT INTO PayTemp
  SELECT *
  FROM Payroll
```

The following statement selects and appends only full-time employees:

```
INSERT INTO PayTemp
  SELECT *
  FROM Payroll
  WHERE hoursWorked >= 40
```

7.4 Creating Tables and Indexes

SQL is also a powerful data definition language (DDL), that can create and delete tables, indexes, and views. Although a complete description of this language is outside of our discussion here, we can show some useful examples that you might want to incorporate into Visual Basic programs.

7.4.1 Creating Indexes

The CREATE INDEX statement creates a new index for an existing table. The syntax is:

```
CREATE [ UNIQUE ] INDEX indexname
ON tablename (field1 [ASC|DESC][, field2 [ASC|DESC], ...])
[WITH { PRIMARY | DISALLOW NULL | IGNORE NULL }]
```

The following creates a non-unique index called **ssnNdx**, on the **ssn** field in the **PayTemp** table (there are duplicate social-security numbers in this table):

```
CREATE INDEX ssnNdx
   ON PayTemp(ssn)
```

The following creates a unique index called **pKey** on the **ID** field in the **Depts** table, and makes it the primary key:

```
CREATE UNIQUE INDEX pKey
   ON Depts(ID)
   WITH PRIMARY
```

The default order for indexes is ascending, but you can specify descending order by following the field name with DESC. The following creates an index called **salesNdx** on the **Sales** field of the **Depts** table, arranging the values in descending order:

```
CREATE INDEX salesNdx
   ON Depts(Sales DESC)
```

7.4.2 Creating Tables

The CREATE TABLE statement creates a new database table. You have to supply field descriptions. Leaving out constraints and indexes, the basic syntax is:

```
CREATE TABLE tablename
(field1 type [(size)] [NOT NULL]
[, field2 type [(size)] [NOT NULL]
[, ...]]
)
```

where *tablename* is the name of a table that does not already exist, *type* is the field type, and *size* is only relevant for Text and Binary fields. The NOT NULL field option specifies that new records must have valid data in the field—in Access, the *required* option is set to True. A comparison of Access, Visual Basic, and SQL type descriptors is shown in Table 5.

The following SQL statement creates a table called **Depts** that contains a variety of field types. The table and field names are in bold type:

```
CREATE TABLE Depts
  (ID Long NOT NULL,
   Name Text(20) NOT NULL ,
   Active YesNo NOT NULL,
   NumMembers Short,
   Sales Currency,
   Created DateTime,
   Comments Memo)
```

Note that a **Short** field type in SQL is the same as an **Integer** type in Access.

Table 5. Comparison of Access, Visual Basic, and SQL Types.

Access Field Type (numeric type)	VBasic Data Type	Jet SQL Type (synonym)[1]
AutoNumber	Long	COUNTER
Currency	Currency	CURRENCY
Date/Time	Date	DATETIME
Hyperlink	String	LONGTEXT (MEMO)
Memo	String	LONGTEXT (MEMO)
Number (Double)	Double	DOUBLE
Number (Integer)	Integer	SHORT
Number (Long Integer)	Long	LONG
Number (Single)	Single	SINGLE
Number (Byte)	Byte	BYTE
OLE Object	String	LONGBINARY
Text	String	TEXT (CHAR)
Yes/No	Boolean	BOOLEAN (YESNO)

Note: The CREATE TABLE statement is not supported by the Jet Database Engine for non-Microsoft Jet Engine databases. For those, you have to use the DAO *Create* methods instead.

7.4.3 Removing Tables and Indexes

The **DROP** statement removes either a table or an index. There are two variations:

---

[1] There are additional SQL synonyms for field types not show here that may be found in MS-Access help.

```
DROP TABLE tablename
DROP INDEX indexname ON tablename
```

For example, we can drop the PayTemp table:

```
DROP TABLE PayTemp
```

Or, we can drop the salesNdx index from the Depts table:

```
DROP INDEX salesNdx ON Depts
```

This does not affect any data in the table. Of course, a table must be closed before it can be dropped, or before any of its indexes can be dropped.

7.5 Application: Stellar Car Rental

7.5.1 Overview

Let's create a database and accompanying application program for the imaginary **Stellar Car Rental Company**. We will call this the Rentals database. The general types of service that our program will offer are:

- Make advance reservations for car rentals.
- Create and store an invoice when a car is rented.
- Keep track of all cars in the company inventory.
- Update an invoice when a car is returned by the customer.

We know the database will contain a number of tables, each related to a topic or grouping in the application. The best way to design the tables is to think about what information will be required for each step in the rental process: Reservations, Rentals, Returns, and Inventory.

Reservations. For example, when a customer calls to reserve a Stellar vehicle, the reservations clerk needs to collect and store the following information:

- A reservation confirmation number.
- The customer's name, phone, address, and credit card information.
- The dates the vehicle will be rented and returned.
- The requested vehicle type (economy, midsize, etc.).
- The daily and weekly rental rate quoted to the customer.
- Miscellaneous notes or comments.

That sounds easy enough. We can simply create a database table with all of the above information and add a record to the table when the reservation is made. But we also see that rental rates require information from another source, most likely a table containing daily and weekly rental rates for each type of vehicle. Further, we can assume that rental rates change all the time for competitive reasons—this means that the reservations clerk will have to lock in a price for the customer that is unaffected by rate changes that might occur before the actual rental takes place.

Rentals. When a Stellar vehicle is rented by a customer, an invoice must be prepared and saved in the database. The invoice should contain the following information:

- An invoice number.
- The date and time the car was rented.
- The expected return date.
- The vehicle ID number.
- The customer's name, phone, address, and credit card information.
- The total amount due.
- The amount paid.
- Notes or comments.

We can already see the potential for duplication of data. The customer's name, phone, and address are needed for both reservations and invoices. This will be a factor in our database design, causing us to separate the customer information and make it available to both invoices and reservations.

Returns. When a vehicle is returned, the return date is filled in and the invoice is completed. At that time, the invoice could be moved to a history file and kept for future reference.

Inventory. At the time a vehicle is rented, the clerk will have to search for an available vehicle that matches the size stated on the reservation. Rental agencies rarely reserve specific vehicles for customers, but they do try to guarantee a certain size or style when a reservation is made. We want to store the following information about each vehicle:

- The vehicle's ID number
- A description of the vehicle, such as "Mercury Sable, 4-door".
- The vehicle's size classification, such as "Luxury", "Midsize", or "Economy".
- The vehicle's status, such as "Available", "Rented", or "Maintenance".

At this point, there is enough available information to begin designing the tables for a database. In nearly every table, there will be a record key that makes it possible to locate individual records.

7.6 Table Descriptions

The Rentals database contains the following tables:

- **Customer:** Information about each customer who has either made a reservation or rented a vehicle.
- **Invoice:** The rental invoice that is created at the time a vehicle is rented.
- **Price:** Daily and weekly rental rates for each type of vehicle, based on the date of the rental.
- **Reservation:** Information that is saved when each customer calls to reserve a vehicle for an upcoming rental.
- **Vehicle:** Information about each vehicle in the company's inventory.

- **VehicleDescription:** A lookup table containing standard vehicle description codes and their explanations.
- **VehicleStatus:** A lookup table containing standard vehicle status codes and their descriptions.
- **VehicleType:** A lookup table containing standard vehicle type codes and their descriptions.

7.6.1 Vehicle Inventory

To keep track of Stellar's inventory, let's create a table called **Vehicle.** We need to know the vehicle's description, type (Economy, Compact, etc.), and its status (available or not). Each record contains a unique vehicle ID number. Table 6 shows a preliminary version of the Vehicle table, with a few sample records that have intentionally misspelled text values. It is clear from this sample that there would be a lot of duplicate data. Most disturbing is the fact that a data entry clerk might misspell the text fields, making it very difficult to perform a reliable search for specific values. What if we wanted to locate all vehicles having a "Minivan" vehicle type? Only one of the vehicles in Table 6 would be found.

Table 6. Preliminary Design for Vehicle Table.

VehicleId	Description	VehicleType	Status
100	Chevy Geo	Economy	Available
101	VB Rabbit	Economi	Rentd
106	Plymouth Voyager	Minivan	Availabl
107	Ford Aerostar	Mnivan	Rented
108	Lincoln Town Car	Luxury	Available
115	Ford Aeorostar	Minvian	Maintenence

A preferred design for the Vehicle table would be to convert all text fields into short codes (Table 7). This design greatly reduces the possibility of misspelling, and minimizes the amount of redundant data.

Table 7. The Vehicle Table.

VehicleId	DescriptionId	VehicleTypeId	StatusId
100	1	EC	A
101	4	EC	R
102	5	MV	A
103	6	MV	R
104	3	LX	A
105	6	MV	M

If a customer wants to rent a Lincoln Town Car, we can just search for descriptionId = 3. Or, if the customer wants a luxury car, we can search for vehicleTypeId = LX.

Alphanumeric codes such as these can usually be understood by employees who are familiar with the company's operations.

7.6.2 Vehicle Descriptions, Types, and Status

When printing reports or when asking for input from inexperienced users, we need to make the full descriptions of the codes available in separate tables. The best way to do this is to create *lookup tables,* each of which contains a list of codes and their matching descriptions. The table of vehicle descriptions could be called **VehicleDescription** (Table 8), the table of vehicle types would be **VehicleType** (Table 9), and the table of status values would be **VehicleStatus** (Table 10). These lookup tables fit neatly into combo box controls, making their use almost effortless.

Table 8. The VehicleDescription Table.

id	description
1	Chevy Geo
2	Toyota Tercel
3	Lincoln Town Car
4	VW Rabbit
5	Plymouth Voyager
6	Ford AeroStar

Table 9. The VehicleType Table.

id	description
EC	Economy
CM	Compact
MS	Midsize
LX	Luxury
MV	Minivan

Table 10. The VehicleStatus Table.

id	description
M	Maintenance
A	Available
R	Rented

7.6.3 Rental Prices

When a reservation is made or a rental invoice is processed, the clerk and the customer need to know how much it costs to rent the vehicle. Rental rates are typically determined by types of vehicles and seasonal changes in prices. Each record in the **Price** table (see Table 11) holds a vehicle type, a date range, and the applicable daily and weekly rental rates. Table 12 displays sample records for the Price table, with rental rates for economy and compact vehicles. The date ranges for each type of vehicle do not have to be the same, giving us some degree of flexibility. If it were possible to calculate the weekly rate directly from the daily rate, we would not have to place the weekly rate in this table. But at Stellar Rentals, the weekly rate is asssumed to be independent of the daily rate. Both rates would ordinarily be determined by external factors such as marketing and competition.

Table 11. The Price Table.

Field Name	Type	Comments
vehicleType	Text (2)	Foreign key (VehicleType)
startDate	Date	Date the price takes effect.
endDate	Date	Date the price ends.
dailyRate	Currency	Rental rate, per day.
weeklyRate	Currency	Rental rate, per week.

Table 12. Sample Records in the Price Table.

vehicleType	startDate	endDate	dailyRate	weeklyRate
EC	01-01-1998	03-31-1998	19.95	110.00
EC	04-01-1998	07-31-1998	24.95	125.00
EC	08-01-1998	12-31-1998	18.95	105.00
CO	01-01-1998	03-31-1998	24.95	125.00
CO	04-01-1998	07-31-1998	30.95	155.00
CO	08-01-1998	11-30-1998	26.95	131.00
CO	12-01-1998	01-15-1999	28.95	131.00

7.6.4 Customers, Reservations, and Invoices

Customer information must be accessible to both reservations and rentals. We might want to keep track of customers past and present, send out sales literature, or collect on unpaid rentals. This information will be in the **Customer** table (Table 13).

Table 13. The Customer Table.

Field Name	Type	Comments
customerId	Long	Unique key
lastName	Text (30)	
firstName	Text (20)	
street1	Text (40)	
street2	Text (40)	Not required
city	Text (20)	
stateOrProvince	Text (15)	
zip	Text (10)	
country	Text (20)	Not required
phone	Text (20)	

The **Reservation** table (Table 14) contains data collected by a clerk when a customer reserves a car. The **Invoice** table (Table 15) contains data collected by a clerk when the vehicle is rented and returned. When the vehicle is rented, we save the date and time in **rentalDate**. When the vehicle is returned, the date and time are saved in **actReturnDate**.

Table 14. The Reservation Table.

Field Name	Type	Comments
reservationId	Long	Unique key
customerId	Long	Foreign key
rentalDate	Date/Time	
returnDate	Date/Time	
vehicleTypeId	Text (2)	Foreign key
dailyRate	Currency	
weeklyRate	Currency	
creditCardNum	Text (30)	
notes	Memo	Not required

Table 15. The Invoice Table.

Field Name	Type	Comments
invoiceId	Long	Unique key
vehicleId	Long	Foreign key
customerId	Long	Foreign key
rentalDate	Date/Time	Date/time rented
expReturnDate	Date/Time	Expected return date/time
actReturnDate	Date/Time	Actual return date/time
amountDue	Currency	Amount to be paid
amountPaid	Currency	Amount paid so far
creditCardInfo	Text (30)	Card number, expiration date
notes	Memo	Not required

7.7 Validation Rules

An Access database is able to store and evaluate *validation rules* for tables and fields. If you violate a rule when inserting data into a field or record, a trappable runtime error is generated. This is a great convenience, because it means that programs sharing the same database do not have to employ nearly as much validation code as they would for databases that have no validation rules.

Both tables and fields can have validation rules, but there are fundamental differences between the two:

- A *field-level* validation rule can only make references to built-in functions and itself.
- A *record-level* (or *table-level*) validation rule can call built-in functions, and it can also make references to various fields within the same record.

Each validation rule is accompanied by a corresponding *validation text* property. It contains a message that is automatically displayed when a validation error is triggered.

Field-Level Validation Rules. Table 16 contains a list of field-level validation rules that have been placed in the Rentals database. This is provided as a sample, but no doubt there are many other validation rules that would be useful.

Table 16. Field-Level Validation Rules for the Rentals Database.

Field Name	Validation Rule
Vehicle.vehicleId	Between 1 And 9999
Customer.customerId	Between 1 And 9999
Reservation.reservationId	Between 1 And 9999
Invoice.invoiceId	Between 1 And 9999
Price.dailyRate	Between 1 And 200
Price.weeklyRate	Between 1 And 1000
Reservation.dailyRate	Between 1 And 200
Reservation.weeklyRate	Between 1 And 1000
Invoice.amountDue	> 0

Record-Level Validation Rules. You can create a validation rule that applies to an entire record. For example, in the Price table, we have a rule that makes sure the starting date of each record is less than or equal to its ending date:

Validation rule: `[startDate]<=[endDate]`
Validation text: `StartDate must be less than endDate.`

In a validation rule, field names must be enclosed in square brackets. Table 17 contains several record-level validation rules for the Rentals database. Each rule compares two fields in the same record for reasonable and consistent values.

Table 17. Record-Level Validation Rules.

Table	Validation Rule
Reservation	[returnDate] >= [rentalDate]
Invoice	[expReturnDate] >= [rentalDate]
Price	[startDate] <= [endDate]

7.7.1 Creating Validation Rules in Access

To create validation rules in Microsoft Access[2], open the database, select a particular table, and click the Design button. To create a field-level rule, click on the field name and look at the listing of field properties at the bottom of the window. Enter the validation rule here, and add the corresponding validation text in the box just below it. For example, in the Price table, the properties of the dailyRate field are shown in Figure 11.

---

[2] If you use the VisData program, see the tutorial in Appendix B.

Figure 11. Validation Rule for DailyRate Field.

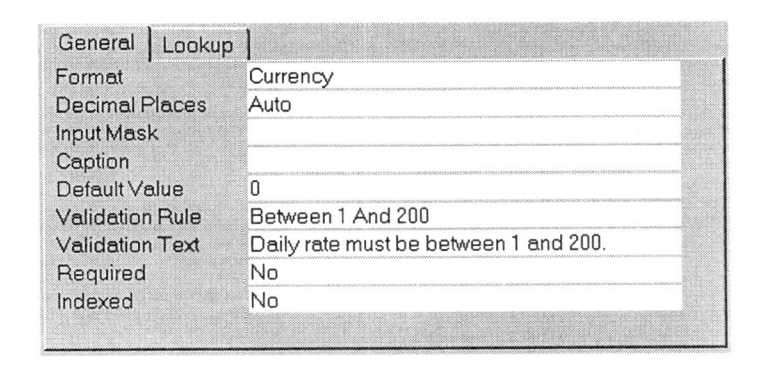

General	Lookup	
Format	Currency	
Decimal Places	Auto	
Input Mask		
Caption		
Default Value	0	
Validation Rule	Between 1 And 200	
Validation Text	Daily rate must be between 1 and 200.	
Required	No	
Indexed	No	

Microsoft Access provides an *expression builder* tool that activates when you enter a validation rule for a field or record. This tool provides a list of all available built-in functions, which are also explained in the Functions Reference help topic. The built-in functions are grouped into five categories: Conversion, Date/Time, General, Math, and Text.

To create a record-level validation rule, select Properties from the View menu. Figure 12 shows a validation rule for the Price table that compares the startDate and endDate fields whenever a record is inserted or modified. You can also enter a table description in this window.

Figure 12. Record-Level Validation Rule.

Table Properties	
General	
Description	
Validation Rule	[startDate]<=[endDate]
Validation Text	StartDate must be less than EndDate.
Filter	
Order By	

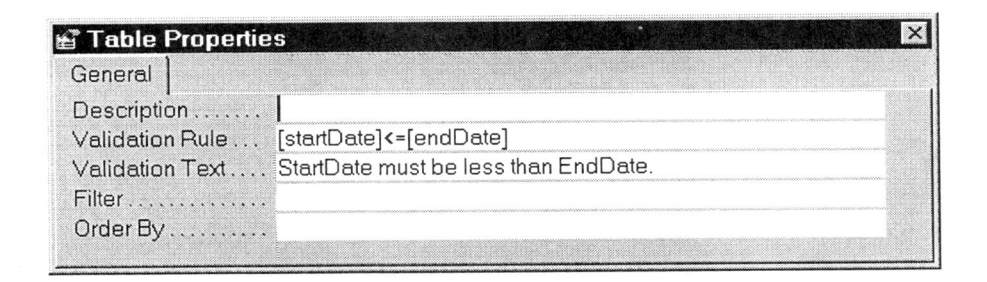

7.8 Table Relationships

The Invoice and Reservation tables both contain ID numbers that relate to other tables. For example, the Reservation table contains a customerId and a vehicleId. These are called *foreign keys* because they match the primary key fields of other tables. In the Customer table, customerId is the primary key, a unique identifying number for each record. In the Vehicle table, vehicleId is the primary key (Figure 13).

Figure 13. Relation Between Invoice and Vehicle Tables.

Invoice Table

invoiceId	vehicleId
1001	105
1002	101
1003	104
1004	102
1005	103

Vehicle Table

vehicleId	descriptionId	vehicleTypeId
100	1	EC
101	4	EC
102	5	MV
103	6	MV
104	3	LX
105	6	MV
106	5	MV
107	5	MV
108	3	LX
109	1	EC

There are two common types of relations between database tables, determined by the fields that link the tables together. Let's call the tables *table-x* and *table-y*:

- **One-to-one:** Each record in *table-x* matches only one record in *table-y*. This relation might be created when part of an existing table is split away and assigned a more restrictive security level.

- **One-to-many:** Each record in *table-x* can match one or more records in *table-y*. This is probably the most common type of table relation. In the Rentals database, for example, in the Vehicle table, each vehicleId is unique; but in the Invoice table, the same vehicleId may appear many times.

Table 18 lists the various relations we have created in this database. In the Primary Table column, the record key field is always the link. For example, each customerId in the Invoice table matches only one customerId in the Customer table. When a new reservation is created, we create a corresponding customer record. When an invoice is created, we use the same customer ID from the reservation, which has to match a record in the Customer table.

Table 18. Relationships in the rentals.mdb Database.

Primary Table.Field	Secondary Table.Field
Customer.customerId	Invoice.customerId
Vehicle.vehicleId	Invoice.vehicleId
VehicleDescription.id	Vehicle.descriptionId
VehicleType.id	Vehicle.vehicleTypeId
VehicleStatus.id	Vehicle.vehicleStatusId
VehicleType.id	Reservation.vehicleTypeId
Customer.customerId	Reservation.customerId

Joining Tables. Table relationships also make it easy to display reports and forms containing joined information from different tables. Suppose we were to create a report based on information from the Invoice table. The **Rental Date** column is from the Invoice table, **lastName, firstName,** and **phone** are from the Customer table:

```
Rental      Customer          Customer         Vehicle
Date        Name              Phone            Description
-----------------------------------------------------------
02/01/98    Jackson, Robert   (305)233-4444    Ford Taurus
02/05/98    Chong, Anson      (202)333-1234    Toyota Camry
```

Retrieving the **Vehicle Description** involves a two-step process: First, the vehicleId from the Invoice table forms a link to the Vehicle table. Then, the descriptionId in the Vehicle table forms a link to the VehicleDescription table.

Referential Integrity Rules. Microsoft Access can enforce referential integrity rules that check for consistency between related tables. Checks of this type happen when a record in a table is added, modified, or deleted. For example, there is a one to many relationship between Customer.id and Invoice.customerId. This means that for every value of Invoice.customerId, there must be a matching value in the Customer table.

The one-to-many relationship between Vehicle and Invoice requires that every vehicleId in the Invoice table exist in the same field in the Vehicle table. If this rule is not enforced, a record could be inserted into the Invoice table having an unknown or erroneous vehicle ID. This problem would show itself as soon as we tried to print reports, search the database, or join two tables.

7.8.1 Creating Table Relationships

In Microsoft Access, use the Tools/Relationships menu command to set a relationship between any two tables in the current database. For example, let's create a relationship between the Vehicle table and the Invoice table using the vehicleId as the linking field. As shown in Figure 14, select the Vehicle table first because vehicleId is its primary key, and click on the Add button.

Figure 14. Selecting Tables for a Relation.

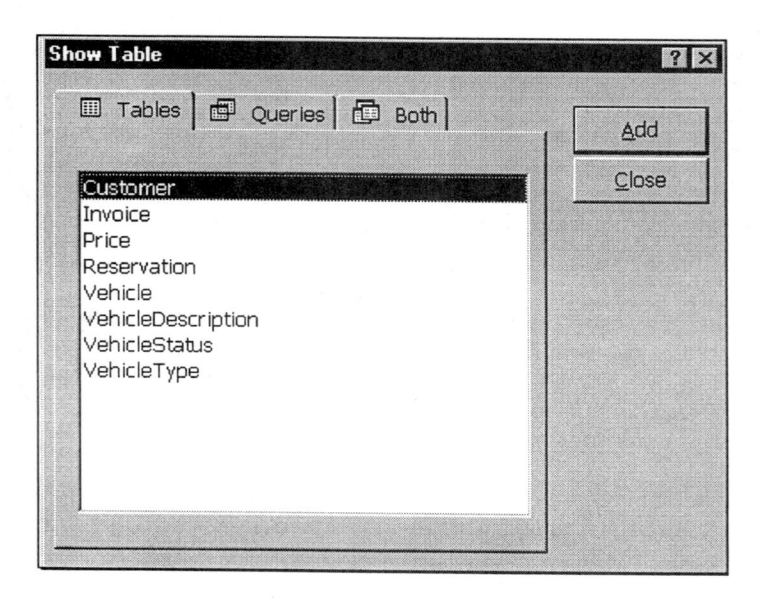

We also insert the Invoice table. Now the two tables appear in the Relationships window, shown in Figure 15.

Figure 15. The Relationships Window (Access).

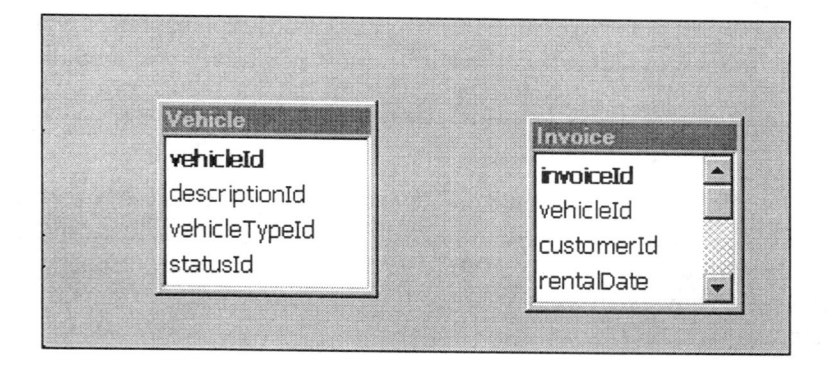

All we have to do now is create a connection between the two. Drag the mouse from the Vehicle.vehicleId field to the Invoice.vehicleId field. Figure 16 shows the dialog window that appears. Place a check next to "Enforce Referential Integrity".

Figure 16. Choosing the Type of Relation.

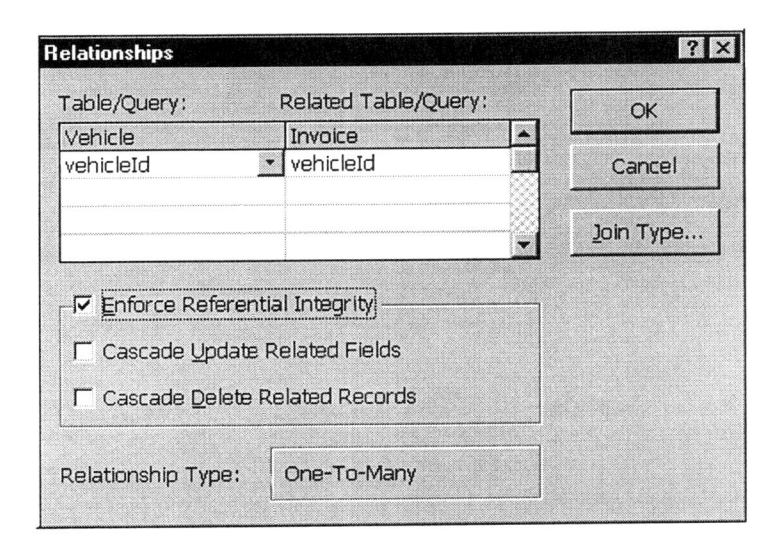

Click on OK, then on Create. In Figure 17, the line between the tables shows that a one-to-many relationship exists between the two tables (the ∞ symbol indicates "many"). The Vehicle table has vehicleId as its *primary key,* and the Invoice table has vehicleId as a *foreign key*.

Figure 17. Relationship Window, Showing Joined Tables.

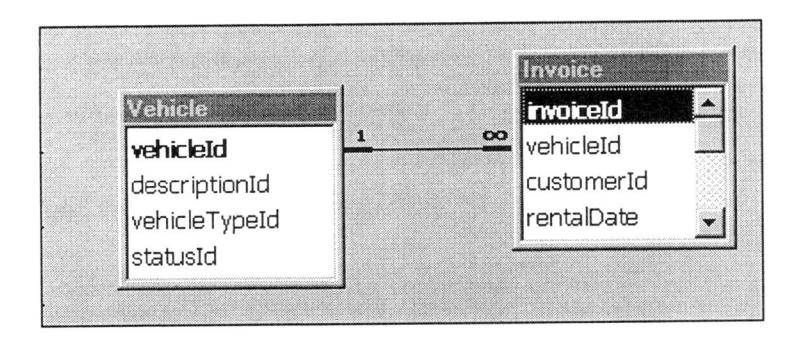

Design Tip: When you clicked on the Create button, you may have received an error message saying that the data in your tables violates the database's referential integrity. This probably means that some of the vehicleId values in the Invoice table did not have matching values in the Vehicle table. To fix the problem, open both tables, inspect the values, and correct the vehicleId fields until they match. After doing this, try to save the table relationship again.

Similarly, we would create all of the relationships listed in Figure 18.

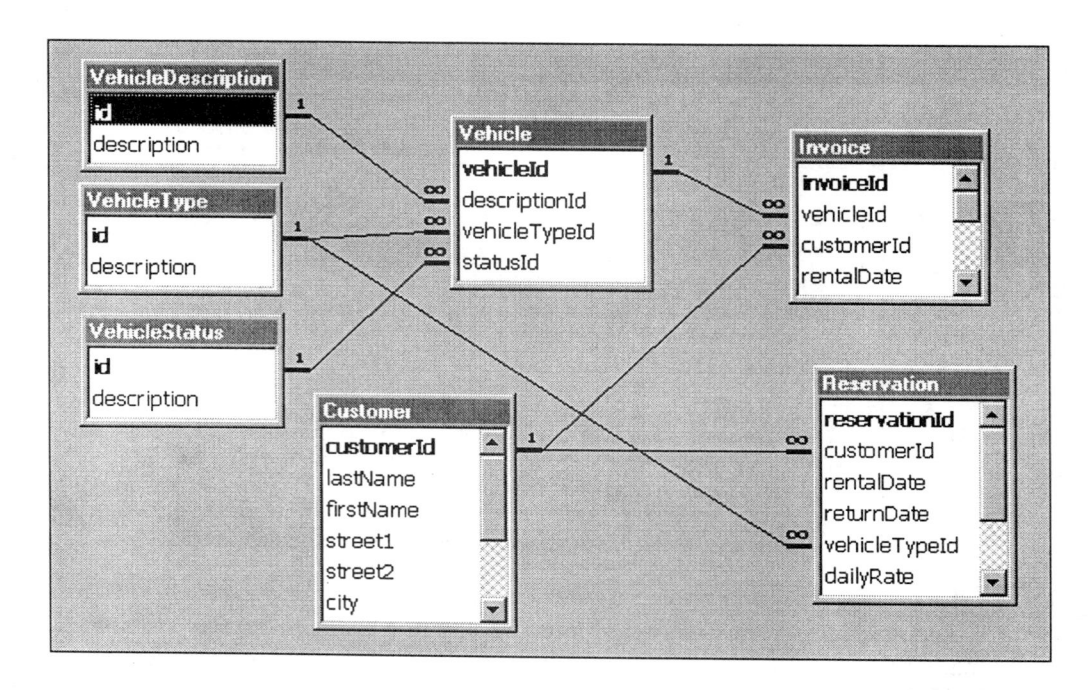

Figure 18. All Relations in Rentals Database.

7.9 Designing the Interface

Now that we have a reasonably good database design and some sample data for the Stellar Car Rental application, it's time to begin working on the visual interface. Designing a good visual interface is a tricky business, because software users have widely varying opinions about how they want the program to look and behave.

Users will have different levels of expertise. Making the software easy to use for beginners should not prevent expert users from working efficiently. The software should be easy to use at all levels.

When we create the user interface for the rental reservation system, we will stick to a fairly standard Windows interface and attempt to make the program easy to use. The reservations agents who use this program will be on the phone with customers, so we will keep in mind the following design goals:

- Keep the amount of typing to a minimum. Because they will be using the software almost continuously, we will try to provide keystrokes that provide command shortcuts.
- They will need to be able to look up information quickly when a customer asks questions about rental rates and availability of vehicles.
- The user might want to display and manage multiple reservation windows at the same time. In that case, we should try to create a reservation object that keeps track of its current state.

7.9.1 Vehicle Reservations

Let's create a form that lets the user create a reservations record. When a customer calls and requests a rental reservation, we can provide lookup information to the user, who is the reservations agent.

Reservation Window. After the database has been located and opened, the Reservation window appears. The user clicks on the **New** button to create a new reservation. A randomly generated reservation ID number is inserted in the first combo box (Figure 19).

Figure 19. The Reservation Window.

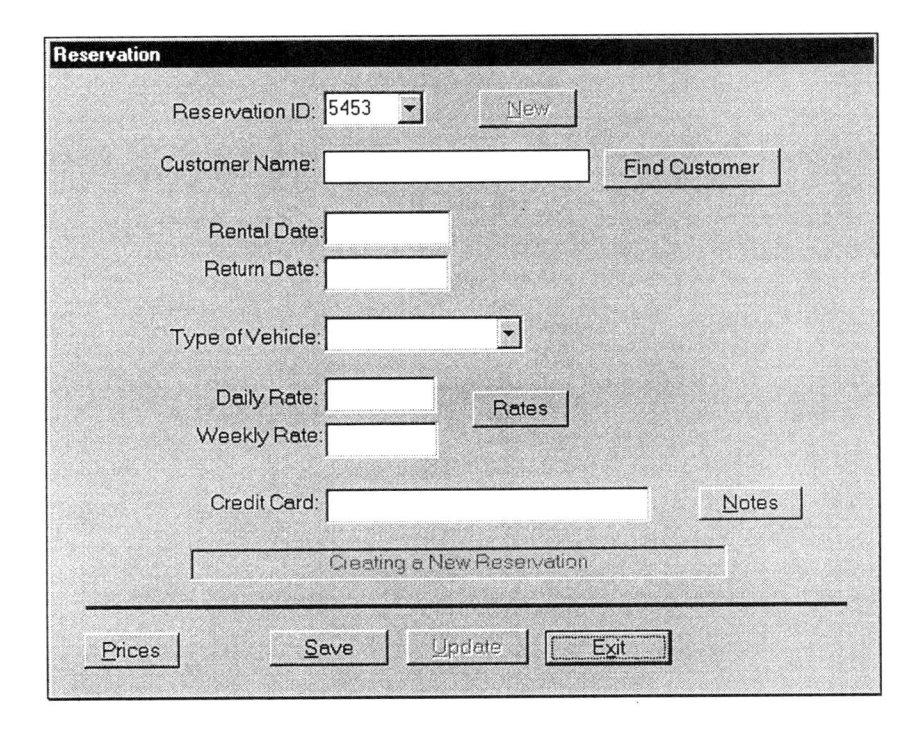

To get the customer name, the user clicks on the **Find Customer** button. This displays the Customer Information window.

When the program starts up, it tries to find the database (rentals.mdb) in the current directory. If the file is not found, the dialog in Figure 20 appears, in which the user can either type the complete path to the database, or click on the Browse button to search for the file.

Figure 20. Database Not Found Message.

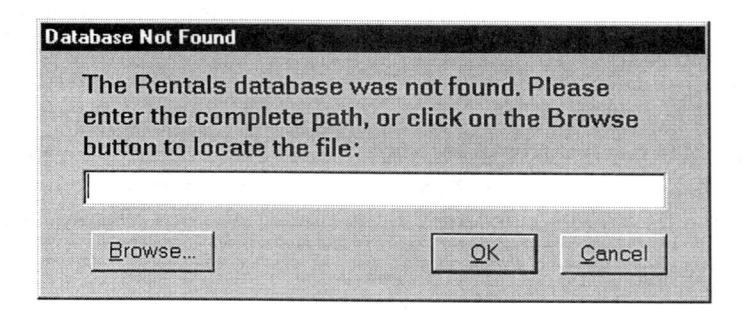

The Browse button uses the common dialog control to display the standard Windows File/Open dialog.

Customer Information Window. In the Customer Information window, the user types in an area code and phone number in the box at the top of the window, which the program uses to search for a matching database record. Figure 21 shows a sample of the Customer Information window.

Figure 21. The Customer Information Window.

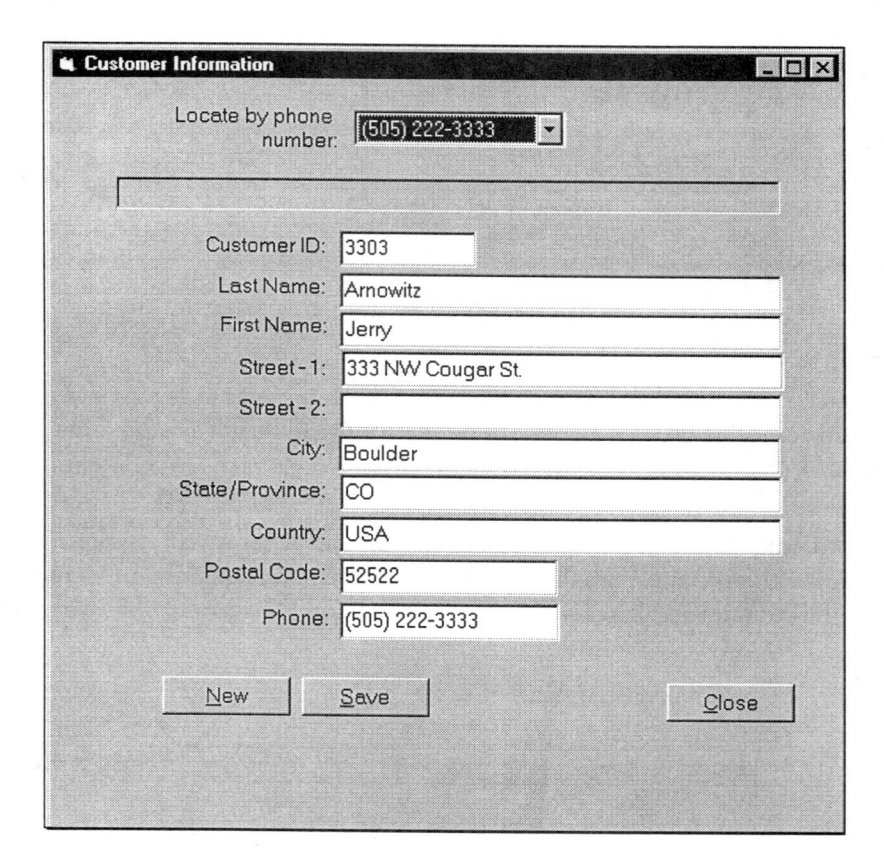

The user can also create, modify, and save a new customer record in this window. When the user clicks on **Close**, the customer name is copied into the Reservation window. To get the rental rates, the user must enter the rental date and select the type of vehicle to be rented. For example, we want to rent an economy vehicle on 6/1/1998. After entering this information, we click the Rates button. This fills in the daily and weekly rental rates, shown in Figure 22.

Figure 22. Rental Rates Displayed.

If the user enters a rental date that is not listed in the Price table, a status message appears, indicating that rental rates are not available for that date.

Clicking the Notes button displays a popup window into which the user can type supplemental information (Figure 23).

Figure 23. The Notes Window.

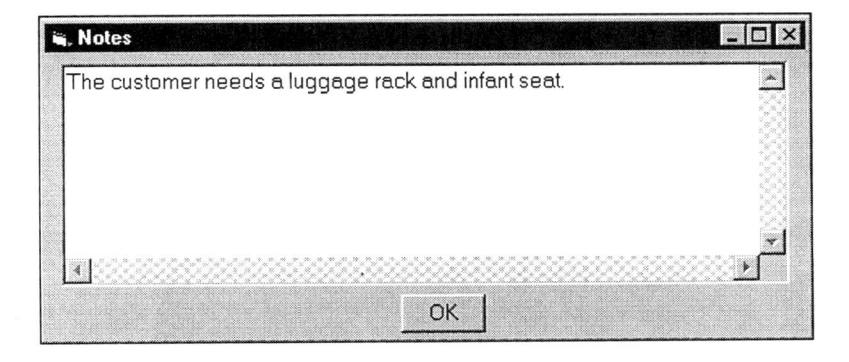

After the user clicks on the Save button, the program verifies that all fields have been filled in and a new record is added to the Reservation table in the database (Figure 24).

Figure 24. Saving a Reservation.

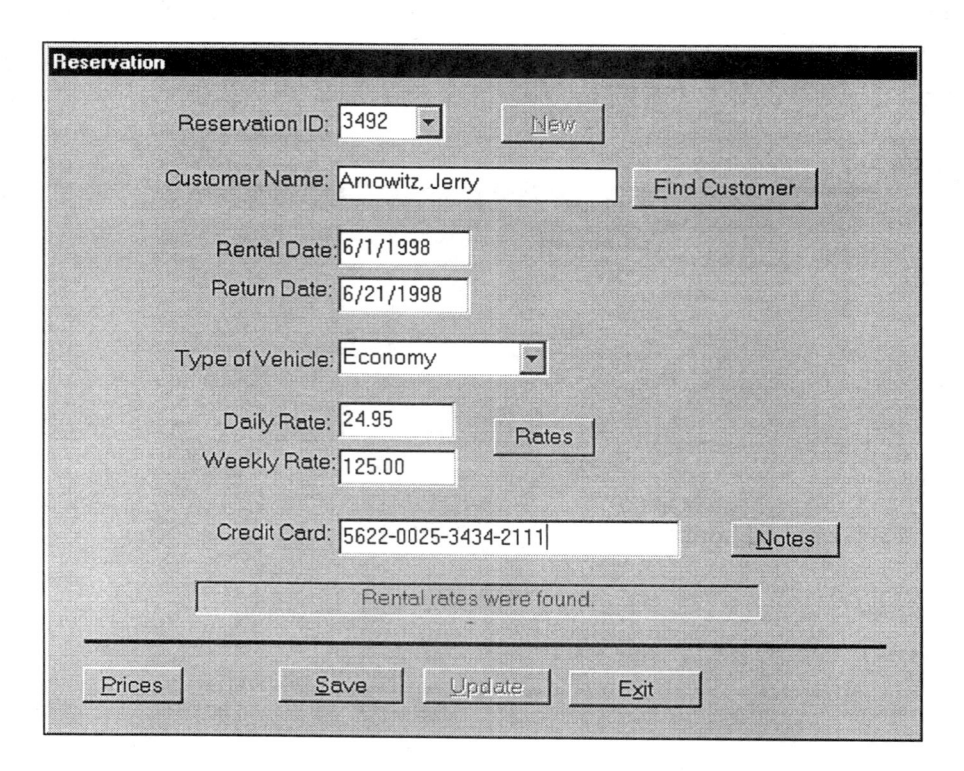

Rental Prices. The Reservation window also has a button called **Prices** that provides a quick way for the reservation agent to view a list of rental prices for each type of car and date range. The Rental Prices window (Figure 25) contains a Data control tied to the Price table, and a DBGrid control to display the data.

Figure 25. Rental Prices Window.

vehicleType	startDate	endDate	dailyRate	weeklyRate
EC	1/1/98	3/31/98	19.95	110
EC	4/1/98	7/31/98	24.95	125
EC	8/1/98	12/31/98	18.95	105
CM	1/1/98	3/31/98	24.95	125
CM	4/1/98	7/31/98	30.95	155
CM	8/1/98	12/31/98	26.95	131
MS	1/1/98	3/31/98	29.95	140

7.10 Reservation Implementation

The Stellar Car Reservations program is implemented as an object-oriented application, so the structure revolves around the interactions between classes and forms.

7.10.1 Module1

The following code is in module1.bas. It contains global declarations, the startup procedure, a procedure that opens the database, and two very useful procedures that set and retrieve field values from recordsets:

```
Const DefDbasename = "rentals.mdb"
Const ErrorNoFile As Long = 3024    'Jet engine error code
Public Const PriceTablename = "Price"
Public Const ReservationTablename = "Reservation"
Public Const VehicleTablename = "Vehicle"
Public Const VehicleTypeTablename = "VehicleType"
Public DBasename As String
Public DBase As Database
Dim reserv As clsReservation
```

The clsReservation class describes a reservation object; a reservation object will display various windows and interact with the Reservation database table.

In Sub **Main**, the startup procedure, we select a default database name and call OpenDatabase. If this succeeds, we create and display a reservation object:

```
Public Sub Main()
  ChDrive App.Path
  ChDir App.Path
  DBasename = DefDbasename    'set the global database name
  Randomize                   're-seed the random number generator
  If OpenDatabase Then
    Set reserv = New clsReservation
    reserv.Display vbModal
    DBase.Close
  End If
  End
End Sub
```

OpenDatabase attempts to open the database using the default filename. If it fails, the program jumps to the OpenDbase1 label. There, we display a separate window that informs the user of the problem and prompts for a new filename. The Resume statement returns to the beginning of the procedure and tries to open the database again:

```
Public Function OpenDatabase() As Boolean
'Open the database used by this program. Return True if successful,
'False if not.
```

```
OpenDbase1A:
  OpenDatabase = True
  On Error GoTo OpenDbase1
  Set DBase = Workspaces(0).OpenDatabase(DBasename)
  Exit Function
OpenDbase1:
  If Err.Number = ErrorNoFile Then
    frmFindFile.Show vbModal
    If frmFindFile.Continue Then
      DBasename = frmFindFile.Filename
      Resume OpenDbase1A
    End If
  Else
    MsgBox Err.Number & ": " & Err.description
  End If
  OpenDatabase = False
End Function
```

GetTableFields is a generic procedure that retrieves fields from a recordset and copies them to a TextBox control array. Errors caused by null fields are ignored. This procedure can be used with any database table, because there is no specific mention of the number of fields or their types:

```
Public Sub GetTableFields(R As Recordset, txtFields As Variant)
  Dim j As Integer
  On Error Resume Next
  For j = 0 To R.Fields.Count - 1
    txtFields(j).Text = R.Fields(j).Value
  Next j
End Sub
```

SetTableFields is a generic function procedure that copies the contents of an array of text boxes to a recordset. If an error is caused by a data type mismatch, the name of the field and the data being assigned to it are both displayed:

```
Public Function SetTableFields(R As Recordset, _
    txtFields As Variant) As Boolean
  Dim fieldNum As Integer
  On Error GoTo SetTableFields1
  For fieldNum = 0 To R.Fields.Count - 1
    R.Fields(fieldNum).Value = txtFields(fieldNum).Text
  Next fieldNum
  SetTableFields = True
  Exit Function
SetTableFields1:
  Dim fld As String
  fld = R.Fields(fieldNum).Name
  MsgBox "Trying to assign '" + txtFields(fieldNum).Text + _
      "' to the " + fld + " field.", vbCritical, Error$
  SetTableFields = False
End Function
```

To display the field name in the SetTableFields error handler, we used the Name property of the recordset's Fields collection.

7.10.2 The clsVehicleType Class

The clsVehicleType class acts as a shell that encapsulates the VehicleType database table. It has two public properties:

- Description: Returns a string description of the vehicle's type, such as "Lincoln Town Car" (read-only).
- VehicleId: Returns the vehicle's ID number (read-only).

The class has several public methods:

- DescriptionOf: Given an ID number, searches the table of vehicle types and returns the matching vehicle description.
- VehicleIdOf: Given a description, finds the matching vehicle ID.
- FillComboBox: Fills a combo box argument with descriptions of vehicle types.
- OpenTable: Opens the VehicleType database table.

Here is the clsVehicleType class source code:

```
'The clsVehicleType class.
Option Explicit
Private vtable As Recordset
Private tableIsOpen As Boolean

'************ PUBLIC PROPERTIES ********************

Public Property Get Description() As String
  If Not tableIsOpen Then Exit Property
  Description = vtable!Description
End Property

Public Property Get VehicleId() As String
  If Not tableIsOpen Then Exit Property
  VehicleId = vtable!id
End Property

'************** PUBLIC METHODS **********************

Public Function DescriptionOf(searchId As String) As String
'Given a vehicle description ID, search for a matching
'description. If not found, return an empty string.
  DescriptionOf = ""
  If Not tableIsOpen Then Exit Function
  vtable.FindFirst "id = '" + searchId + "'"
  If Not vtable.NoMatch Then
    DescriptionOf = vtable!Description
  End If
End Function
```

```
Public Sub FillComboBox(box As ComboBox)
'Fill the combo box argument with the list of
'vehicle descriptions.
  vtable.MoveFirst
  Do While Not vtable.EOF
    box.AddItem vtable!Description
    vtable.MoveNext
  Loop
End Sub

Public Sub OpenTable(DB As Database)
  If tableIsOpen Then Exit Sub
  Set vtable = DB.OpenRecordset(VehicleTypeTablename, _
      dbOpenSnapshot)
  tableIsOpen = True
End Sub

Public Function VehicleIdOf(Description As String) As String
'Given a vehicle description, search for a matching ID
'string. If not found, return an empty string.

  If Not tableIsOpen Then Exit Function
  vtable.FindFirst "description = '" + Description + "'"
  If vtable.NoMatch Then
    VehicleIdOf = ""
  Else
    VehicleIdOf = vtable!id
  End If
End Function

'**************** EVENT HANDLERS ********************

Private Sub Class_Initialize()
  tableIsOpen = False
End Sub

Private Sub Class_Terminate()
  If tableIsOpen Then vtable.Close
End Sub
```

7.10.3 The clsReservation Class

The **clsReservation** class encapsulates all operations dealing with creating, displaying, modifying, and searching for rental reservations. Its main window is the frmReserv form, but it also displays the frmCustomer form, the frmNotes form, and the frmPrices form. This class also creates an instance of the clsVehicleType class, which provides access to the VehicleType database table. The frmPrices form provides a listing of the Price database table, and frmCustomer provides access to the Customer table.

Chap 7: Relational Databases

There is a close interactive relationship between the clsReservation class and the frmReserv form (which is also a class). The clsReservation object creates a frmReserv object, shows it, and accesses its properties. At the same time, the event handlers in frmReserv have to call methods and set properties in the clsReservation class. This situation arises often in object-oriented programs, because class modules in VB4 cannot contain event handlers. This situation has been remedied in VB5 with ActiveX controls, as we shall see in Chapter 11. For the moment, however, we will have the clsReservation object pass itself as an argument to a method in the frmReserv form. Using this backward reference, the form can refer to methods and properties in the clsReservation class.

Here is the source code for the **clsReservation** class:

```
'The clsReservation class.
Option Explicit
Const DisplayMode As Integer = vbModal

'Field positions within the database record, which also
'match the Index property of the txtFields control array:
Const reservationId = 0, customerId = 1, rentalDate = 2, _
      returnDate = 3, vehicleTypeId = 4, dailyRate = 5, _
      weeklyRate = 6, creditCardNum = 7, Notes = 8

Private Vehicles As clsVehicleType
Private reservTableP As Recordset    'Reservation table
Private reservWin As frmReserv       'Reservation window
Private notesP As String             'the Notes field
Private modifiedP As Boolean         'True if record modified

Public Sub Display()
'Display the reservation window.
  Set reservWin = New frmReserv
  frmReserv.SetReservObject Me
  frmReserv.Show DisplayMode
End Sub

'******************** EVENT HANDLERS ***********************
```

The **Initialize** event handler for this class opens the Reservation database table, fills a combo box with all of the reservation IDs, and retrieves a list of vehicle types from another table:

```
Private Sub Class_Initialize()
  Set Vehicles = New clsVehicleType
  Set reservTableP = DBase.OpenRecordset(ReservationTablename, _
      dbOpenTable)
  reservTableP.Index = "reservationIdNdx"
  FillReservationList
  reservTableP.MoveFirst
  Vehicles.OpenTable DBase
  Vehicles.FillComboBox frmReserv.cboVehicleType
  modifiedP = False
```

```
    End Sub
```

The **Terminate** event handler closes the Reservation table and frees the memory used by the Reservation table, reservation window, and the Vehicles table:

```
    Private Sub Class_Terminate()
      reservTableP.Close
      Set reservTableP = Nothing
      Set reservWin = Nothing
      Set Vehicles = Nothing
    End Sub
```

The **Modified** property is set to True when the current record has been altered, so we can remind the user to save the changes:

```
    Public Property Get Modified() As Boolean
      Modified = modifiedP
    End Property

    Public Property Let Modified(mval As Boolean)
      modifiedP = mval
    End Property

    Public Property Get ReservTable() As Recordset
    'Database table (read-only property)
      Set ReservTable = reservTableP
    End Property

    '********************* PUBLIC METHODS *************************
```

GetRentalRates opens the Price table and looks up the daily and weekly rental rates for the type of car listed in the combo box. It displays a status message indicating success or failure. First, we verify that a rental date was entered and a vehicle type was selected:

```
    Public Sub GetRentalRates()
      If Not IsDate(frmReserv.txtFields(rentalDate).Text) Then
        frmReserv.lblStatus.Caption = "A rental date must be entered."
        Exit Sub
      End If
      If frmReserv.txtFields(vehicleTypeId).Text = "" Then
        frmReserv.lblStatus = "A vehicle type must be selected."
        Exit Sub
      End If
```

Then we open the Price table and pass it a query string that searches for a table row that contains a matching vehicle type and range of dates that includes the requested rental date:

```
    Dim dt As String, query As String
    Dim R As Recordset
    On Error GoTo GetRates1
    Set R = DBase.OpenRecordset(PriceTablename, dbOpenSnapshot)
    On Error Resume Next
    dt = frmReserv.txtFields(rentalDate).Text
```

Chap 7: Relational Databases

```
        query = "vehicleType = '" & frmReserv.txtFields _
           (vehicleTypeId).Text _
           & "' AND #" & dt & "# Between startDate And endDate"
        R.FindFirst query
```

If a matching row is found, the rates are displayed on the reservations form:

```
        If R.NoMatch Then
           frmReserv.lblStatus.Caption = "No rental rates available."
        Else
           frmReserv.txtFields(dailyRate).Text = Format$(R!dailyRate, _
               "fixed")
           frmReserv.txtFields(weeklyRate).Text = Format$(R!weeklyRate, _
               "fixed")
           frmReserv.lblStatus.Caption = "Rental rates were found."
        End If
        R.Close
        Exit Sub
    GetRates1:
        MsgBox Error$, vbCritical, "GetRentalRates"
    End Sub
```

SaveRecord saves the current reservation record. If the user clicks on the Save button after creating a new reservation, the addingNewRecord parameter is True. If the user clicks on Update to save changes to the current record, addingNewRecord is False:

```
    Public Function SaveRecord(addingNewRecord As Boolean) _
        As Boolean
        SaveRecord = False
        On Error GoTo SaveRecord1
        If addingNewRecord Then
           reservTableP.AddNew
        Else
           'Search for the record, to make sure the record
           'pointer is positioned correctly.
           reservTableP.Seek "=", Val(frmReserv.txtFields _
               (reservationId).Text)
           If reservTableP.NoMatch Then
              MsgBox "No matching id"
              Exit Function
           Else
              reservTableP.Edit
           End If
        End If
```

We call **SetTableFields** to copy all values from the array of text boxes (txtFields) on the reservation form, into the current database record. The Modified flag is reset, indicating that the record no longer has any pending modifications:

```
        If SetTableFields(reservTableP, frmReserv.txtFields) Then
           reservTableP.Update
           frmReserv.lblStatus = "Reservation saved."
           Modified = False
```

```
      SaveRecord = True
   End If
   Exit Function
SaveRecord1:
   MsgBox Error$ & "  Cannot save record in database.", _
         vbCritical, "SaveRecord"
End Function
```

The **ShowReservation** method retrieves an existing reservation record after the user has selected a reservation ID from a combo box. First, if the current record has changed, we ask the user to save it:

```
Public Sub ShowReservation()
   If Modified Then PromptSaveCurrent  'save current?
   With frmReserv
   'Look for the reservation.
     If Not FindReservation(id:=Val(.cboReservationID.Text)) Then
       .lblStatus = "Reservation not found."
       Exit Sub
     End If
```

Assuming that the reservation was found, we call GetTableFields to copy all data from the current database record into the array of text boxes on the reservation form:

```
'Fill in the text boxes with recordset data.
   GetTableFields ReservTable, .txtFields
```

We use the Vehicles object to look up the description, using the vehicleTypeId:

```
'Note: Style property must be equal to Dropdown Combo.
  .cboVehicleType.Text = Vehicles.DescriptionOf _
     (.txtFields(vehicleTypeId))
```

The frmCustomer object looks up the customer name, given an ID number:

```
'Look up the customer's name.
  If frmCustomer.FindCustomerById(Val(.txtFields _
    (customerId))) Then
      .lblCustomerName = frmCustomer.GetCustomerName
  Else
      .lblStatus = "Customer name not found."
  End If
```

The command buttons are adjusted so the user can either add a new reservation or update the current one:

```
    'Adjust the command buttons.
    .cmdAddNew.Enabled = True
    .cmdSave.Enabled = False
    .cmdUpdate.Enabled = True
  End With
  Modified = False
End Sub
```

The **GetVehicleId** method is called when the user selects a different vehicle type from the combo box on the reservation form. We also blank the daily and weekly rate boxes:

```
Public Sub GetVehicleId()
  With frmReserv
    .txtFields(dailyRate).Text = ""
    .txtFields(weeklyRate).Text = ""
    .txtFields(vehicleTypeId) = _
    Vehicles.VehicleIdOf(.cboVehicleType.Text)
  End With
End Sub
```

AddNewReservation is called when the user clicks on the New button to create a new reservation. The text boxes are cleared, a new unique reservation ID is randomly generated, and the command buttons are adjusted:

```
Public Sub AddNewReservation()
'Create a brand-new reservation record.
  Dim j As Integer
  With frmReserv
    For j = 0 To .txtFields.Count - 1
      .txtFields(j).Text = ""
    Next j
    .lblCustomerName.Caption = ""
    .cboVehicleType.Text = ""

    CreateReservationId
    .cmdAddNew.Enabled = False
    .cmdSave.Enabled = True
    .cmdUpdate.Enabled = False
    .lblStatus = "Creating a New Reservation"
    Modified = False
  End With
End Sub
```

When the user clicks on the Find button, the **FindCustomer** method locates the name of a customer using their phone number. The frmCustomer form performs the actual search:

```
Public Sub FindCustomer()
'Display the customer form, let user enter a phone
'number; get the customer's name.
  With frmReserv
    frmCustomer.Show vbModal
    If frmCustomer.txtFields(reservationId).Text <> "" Then
      .lblCustomerName = frmCustomer.GetCustomerName
      .txtFields(customerId) = frmCustomer.GetCustomerId
    End If
  End With
End Sub
```

The **SaveNewReservation** method is called when the user saves a new reservation. The record is saved, the reservation ID is added to the combo box, and the command buttons are adjusted:

```
Public Sub SaveNewReservation()
'Save a new reservation for the first time.
  If SaveRecord(addingNewRecord:=True) Then
    FillReservationList
    With frmReserv
      .cboReservationID.Text = .txtFields(reservationId).Text
      .cmdAddNew.Enabled = True
      .cmdSave.Enabled = False
      .cmdUpdate.Enabled = True
    End With
  End If
End Sub
```

Using a named argument when calling SaveRecord is helpful here, because the value True indicates that we are adding a new record to the database:

```
If SaveRecord(addingNewRecord:=True) Then ...
```

GetNotes is called when the user clicks on the Notes button (previously shown in Figure 23). It displays a form with a text box, and saves the text in the appropriate member of the txtFields array:

```
Public Sub GetNotes()
'Let the user enter and edit notes about
'the reservation.
  With frmReserv
    frmNotes.txtNotes.Text = .txtFields(Notes)
    frmNotes.Show vbModal
    .txtFields(Notes) = frmNotes.txtNotes.Text
  End With
End Sub
```

PromptSaveCurrent is called when the user is about to lose changes made to the reservation that is currently being displayed:

```
Public Sub PromptSaveCurrent()
  Dim ans As Integer
  ans = MsgBox("Save changes (if any) that were made to the " _
    + "current reservation?", vbQuestion + vbYesNo, "")
  If ans = vbYes Then
    SaveRecord addingNewRecord:=False
    Modified = False
  End If
End Sub
```

```
'********************* PRIVATE METHODS ********************
```

CreateReservationId is called when we create a new reservation record. It creates a random integer, checks for its existence in the reservation table, and keeps it if it is unique:

```
Private Sub CreateReservationId()
  Dim anId As Long, bmark As String
  Dim finished As Boolean
```

```
  'Create a random reservation ID, and make sure
  'that it is not already in the database.
   bmark = reservTableP.Bookmark    'save current position in bookmark
   finished = False
   Do While Not finished
     anId = CreateRandomId
     reservTableP.Seek "=", anId
     If reservTableP.NoMatch Then
       frmReserv.cboReservationID.Text = anId
       frmReserv.txtFields(reservationId) = anId
       finished = True
     End If
   Loop
   reservTableP.Bookmark = bmark    'return to previous position
End Sub
```

CreateRandomId, **FillReservationList**, and **FindReservation** are the remaining class methods:

```
Private Function CreateRandomId() As Long
'Create and return a random integer between 1000 and 9999.
   CreateRandomId = Int(Rnd() * 9000) + 1000
End FunctionEnd Function

Private Sub FillReservationList()
'Fill the cboReservationID combo box from the
'Reservation table.
   frmReserv.cboReservationID.Clear
   reservTableP.MoveFirst
   Do While Not reservTableP.EOF
     frmReserv.cboReservationID.AddItem reservTableP!reservationId
     reservTableP.MoveNext
   Loop
End Sub

Private Function FindReservation(id As Long) As Boolean
'Search for the reservation ID number; if found, set the
'current position in the Reservation table to the matching
'record and return True. If not found, return False.
   reservTableP.Seek "=", id
   FindReservation = Not reservTableP.NoMatch
End Function
```

7.10.4 The frmReserv Form

The **frmReserv** source code is shown here. The instance variable called **reserv** holds a reference to the reservation object that displays this form. The code in this form consists almost entirely of event handlers that call methods in the clsReservation module:

```
Option Explicit
Const dailyRate = 5, weeklyRate = 6, rentalDate = 2   'field identifiers
Dim reserv As clsReservation   'the object that controls this form
```

```
Private Sub cmdAddNew_Click()
  reserv.AddNewReservation
End Sub

Private Sub cmdExit_Click()
  Unload Me
End Sub

Private Sub cmdFind_Click()
  reserv.FindCustomer
End Sub

Private Sub cmdGetRates_Click()
  reserv.GetRentalRates
End Sub

Private Sub cmdNotes_Click()
  reserv.GetNotes
End Sub

Private Sub cmdPrices_Click()
  frmPrices.Show vbModal
End Sub

Private Sub cmdSave_Click()
  reserv.SaveNewReservation
End Sub

Private Sub cmdUpdate_Click()
  reserv.SaveRecord addingNewRecord:=False   'not adding new record
End Sub

'******************* OTHER CONTROLS ********************

Private Sub cboReservationId_Click()
  reserv.ShowReservation
End Sub

Private Sub cboVehicleType_Click()
  reserv.GetVehicleId
End Sub

Private Sub txtFields_Change(Index As Integer)
'Set a flag showing that a field was modified.
  reserv.Modified = True

'If the rental date changes, erase the rental rates.
  If Index = rentalDate Then
    txtFields(dailyRate).Text = ""
    txtFields(weeklyRate).Text = ""
```

```
      End If
End Sub

Public Sub SetReservObject(R As clsReservation)
'Set the current reservation object.
   Set reserv = R
End Sub
```

7.10.5 The frmCustomer Form

The frmCustomer form implements the Customer Information window (previously shown in Figure 21) encapsulates properties, event handlers, and methods associated with customer information. It provides an interface for the Customers database table. This form uses a data control called Data1, and a data-bound combo box called dbcPhones that contains the phone numbers of customers. Here is the form's source code:

```
Option Explicit
Const PhoneNumberSize = 10
'Constants that match Customer field positions:
Const customerId = 0, lastName = 1, firstName = 2, street1 = 3, _
      street2 = 4, city = 5, stateOrProvince = 6, zip = 7, _
      country = 8, phone = 9

Private Sub Form_Load()
   'Get global name of database file.
   Data1.DatabaseName = DBasename
End Sub

Private Sub cmdNew_Click()
'Create a new customer record.
   lblStatus.Caption = "Creating New Customer Record"
   Dim j As Integer
   For j = 0 To txtFields.Count - 1
     txtFields(j).Text = ""
   Next j
   Data1.Recordset.AddNew
   cmdSave.Enabled = True
End Sub

Private Sub cmdClose_Click()
   Hide
End Sub

Private Sub cmdSave_Click()
'The user wants to save the customer record.
   On Error GoTo cmdSave1
   SetTableFields Data1.Recordset, txtFields
   Data1.Recordset.Update
   lblStatus.Caption = "Customer Record Saved"
   Exit Sub
cmdSave1:
```

```
    MsgBox Error$, vbCritical, "Save"
End Sub

Private Sub dbcPhones_Click(Area As Integer)
'User has selected a phone number, so we search
'for a matching customer record. If found,
'the record is displayed.
  If Area = 0 Then Exit Sub   'exit if list item not selected
  If FindCustomerByPhone(phoneNum:=dbcPhones.Text) Then
    GetTableFields Data1.Recordset, txtFields
  Else
    lblStatus.Caption = "Customer Record Not Found"
  End If
End Sub

Public Property Get GetCustomerId() As Long
  GetCustomerId = Val(txtFields(customerId).Text)
End Property

Public Property Get GetCustomerName() As String
  With Data1.Recordset
    GetCustomerName = .Fields!lastName & ", " & _
      .Fields!firstName
  End With
End Property

Public Function FindCustomerById(searchId As Long) As Boolean
'Attempt to locate a customer by the ID number; return True if
'successful, False if not.
  Data1.Recordset.Index = "customerIdNdx"
  Data1.Recordset.Seek "=", searchId
  FindCustomerById = Not Data1.Recordset.NoMatch
End Function

Public Function FindCustomerByPhone(phoneNum As String) As Boolean
'Attempt to locate a customer by phone number; return True if
'successful, False if not.
  Data1.Recordset.Index = "phoneNdx"
  Data1.Recordset.Seek "=", phoneNum
  FindCustomerByPhone = Not Data1.Recordset.NoMatch
End Function
```

7.10.6 The frmFindFile Form

The frmFindFile form is displayed by the main module (module1.bas) if the database filename cannot be found in the current directory. This window was previously shown in Figure 20. The user is prompted for a new path, or he/she can click on a Browse button. The source code appears here:

```
Private continueP As Boolean    'property
Private filenameP As String     'property
```

Chap 7: Relational Databases

```
Private Sub cmdBrowse_Click()
'The user wants to look for the file.
  On Error GoTo cmdBrowse1
  dlgOpen.ShowOpen
  filenameP = dlgOpen.Filename
  txtFilePath.Text = filenameP
  Exit Sub
cmdBrowse1:   'user clicked on Cancel
End Sub

Private Sub cmdCancel_Click()
  continueP = False
  Me.Hide
End Sub

Private Sub cmdOK_Click()
  continueP = True
  Me.Hide
End Sub

Public Property Get Continue() As Boolean
  Continue = continueP
End Property

Public Property Get Filename() As String
  Filename = filenameP
End Property

Private Sub txtFilePath_Change()
  filenameP = txtFilePath.Text
End Sub
```

7.10.7 The frmPrices Form

The frmPrices form implements the Rental Prices window (previously shown in Figure 25). It displays a DBGrid control with car rental dates and rates from the Prices table. The default column width is calculated based on the number of fields in the table so all columns will be displayed:

```
Private Sub cmdOK_Click()
  Unload Me
End Sub

Private Sub Form_Load()
  Const numberOfFields As Integer = 5
  datPrice.DatabaseName = DBasename
  DBGrid1.DefColWidth = (DBGrid1.Width * 0.92) / numberOfFields
End Sub
```

7.11 Review Questions

1. Describe a relational database management system, including the names of its various components.
2. What is the relationship between a table and a row?
3. What is the relationship between a column and a field?
4. An *index* orders a table according to one or more of the table's fields; these fields are called _____.
5. Can a query be used to update the Recordsource property of a data control?
6. How is a filter similar to a query?
7. Why would one want to create a *view* of a database?
8. What types of rules can be created and saved with a database to help ensure that its data is consistent?
9. What does *one-to-many* mean in relation to a database structure?
10. Describe the application-driven approach to designing a database.
11. What advantages does an application-independent design have over an application-driven design?
12. Which database design step suggests that you try to determine which operations will be most critical?
13. Once you have determined the data sources, which database design step follows?
14. What is the name of the process used when creating tables to eliminate redundant data?

The following questions relate to the SQL Database Query Language:

15. What do the letters "SQL" stand for, in terms of databases?
16. What is an *ad-hoc query*?
17. What are the two languages that are part of SQL? Which one would involve the use of queries?
18. What does the WHERE clause do?
19. What does the ORDER BY clause do?
20. Name at least two *aggregate* functions.
21. In the Employee and Payroll tables that appeared in Section 7.2.2, which field was common to both tables?
22. Write a SELECT statement that displays all last and first names from the Employee table.
23. Write a SELECT statement that displays fields called **soc sec num** and **hourly pay** from a table called **EmplData**.

Chap 7: Relational Databases 323

24. Show an example of using an SQL query to create and open a recordset in Visual Basic.

25. Write a SELECT statement that displays only rows of the Payroll table in which the **payRate** field contains a value between 20 and 30.

26. Write a SELECT statement that displays only rows of the Payroll table in which the **payRate** field contains a value between 20 and 30, and **hoursWorked** field is greater than 40.

27. Write a SELECT statement that displays only rows of the Employee table in which the **phone** field contains the digits "2222".

28. Write a SELECT statement that calculates and displays a student's social security number and grade point average (GPA) using the data in the table called **Transcript.** Divide the totalPoints by credits to get the overall GPA:
    ```
    Transcript(ssn,totalPoints,credits)
      ("111-44-3232",80,25)
      ("222-32-4444",120,42)
    ```

29. Write a SELECT statement that displays the ssn and lastName from the Employee table, along with the paymentDate and payRate from the Payroll table. Use the WHERE clause.

30. Which option in the SELECT statement guarantees that all resulting rows will be different from each other?

31. Why is it necessary to use either a WHERE or JOIN clause when selecting records from two or more tables?

32. What is a *cartesian product*?

33. What are the three types of joins between a pair of tables?

34. Which type of join only includes rows where the joined fields from both tables are equal?

35. What is the general syntax of the UPDATE statement?

36. Write an UPDATE statement for the Payroll table that increases each employee's pay rate by 10%.

37. For the following Department table, write a statement that calculates the percent increase in the credits field between Fall (earlier) and Spring (later):
    ```
    Department(FallCredits, SpringCredits, percentChange)
     ( 480, 560, 0)
     ( 840, 720, 0)
     ( 670, 710, 0)
     (etc.)
    ```

38. Write a statement that deletes the Payroll table.

39. Write a statement that deletes an index called ssnNdx from the Payroll table.

40. Write a statement that copies all records from a table called Transcript to a table called Temp.

41. Write a statement that appends a new record to an existing recordset.

42. Write a statement that creates an index for the Transcript table that orders records in descending order by the student last names.
43. Write a statement that creates a new table with the following structure: (id - Long, lastName – Char(30), totalCredits - Integer)

7.12 Chapter Exercises

7.12.1 Stellar Car Rental - Inventory

The Stellar Car Rental branch manager needs to view a daily listing of the complete vehicle inventory. When a customer arrives to pick up a car, the rental agent must be able to search for a list of vehicles that match the type requested on the rental reservation. Because specific vehicles are rarely assigned to customers ahead of time, the agent will locate the next available car that fits the reservation requirements.

7.12.2 Stellar Car Rental – Customers

Add the following changes to the Stellar Car Rental program:

- Display an alphabetical listing of all customer names and phone numbers. When the user clicks on a name, display a window containing all customer fields. Allow the user to edit and save changes to fields.
- Let the user search for customers by ZIP code, last name, phone, or customer ID. Display a list of all customers that match the criteria.

7.12.3 Stellar Car Rental – Invoices

When a vehicle is rented, the user should be able to make a copy of the record that was saved when the reservation was originally booked. Save the invoice in the Invoices database table. Let the user search for invoices by Invoice ID.

7.12.4 Stellar Car Rental – Prices

Let the manager display and edit the Price table. The program should prevent the insertion of overlapping dates in the table.

7.12.5 Stellar Car Rental – SQL Queries 1

Create SQL queries for each of the following, and activate the queries from a Visual Basic program:

- List all customers who have rented a vehicle between two given dates. Let the user enter the two dates.
- List all invoices where the return date is less than today's date.

Chap 7: Relational Databases   325

- List all reservations where the rental date is equal to today's date.

7.12.6 Stellar Car Rental – SQL Queries 2

Stellar6

Create SQL queries for each of the following, and activate the queries from a Visual Basic program:

- List all customers who rent luxury cars.
- Count all reservations for a given type of vehicle.
- List all vehicles whose status is *maintenance*.
- List all reservations for a given date, in which their status is *available*.

7.12.7 Yachting Regatta Program, Revisited - 1

Yacht1

You may recall the Yachting Regatta Program from the Chapter 3 exercises. Rather than storing the RaceInfo objects in a collection, convert the collections to database tables, using DAO objects. The original description of the program, slightly modified for databases, follows:

The SeaWind Yacht Club keeps track of the results of multiple sailboat races that together make up a single regatta. Write an MDI application that lets the user display and modify information for several races and several sailboats. Create separate MDI child windows for **clsRaceInfo** and **clsBoatInfo**, both user-defined types. Store the RaceInfo objects in a database table that has an index built from the boat number and race number fields. Store the BoatInfo objects in a database table whose primary key is the boat number. Create the database tables first. The RaceInfo table's structure is described in Table 19.

Table 19. Description of the RaceInfo Table Fields.

Field	Data Type	Description
Boat Number	Integer	Identifies the boat. Matches one of the boat numbers in the *BoatInfo* file.
Race Number	Integer	Unique for each race (1..10).
Starting Time	Date/Time	Time when the race started.
Finishing Time	Date/Time	Time when the race ended.
Handicap Minutes	Integer	Number of minutes to be added to the boat's actual completion time.
Adjusted Time	Integer	Length of time taken to complete the race, adjusted by the boat's handicap.
Comments	Memo	Notes concerning special race conditions or pending protests involving this boat.

For now, the Handicap Minutes and Adjusted Time fields should be set to zero. Create a database table called **BoatInfo** that contains the fields shown in Table 20. Create a class called **clsBoatInfo** that acts as a "shell" around the database table.

Table 20. BoatInfo Table Description.

Field	Data Type	Description
Boat Number	Integer	Matches boat numbers in the *RaceInfo* file.
Boat Name	Text	The boat's name.
Owner Name	Text	Last name, first initial.
Handicap Factor	Single	0.0 to 2.00, used when calculating the Handicap Minutes in the *RaceInfo* table.

7.12.8 Yachting Regatta Program, Revisited - 2

Continue the the Yachting Regatta program from the previous exercise. Provide the following additional features:

1. When displaying the window containing the race information (RaceInfo records), let the user quickly display information about a single boat by double-clicking on the boat number.

2. Create a database table called **RaceInfo** that contains the fields shown in Table 21.

Table 21. The RaceInfo Table.

Field	Data Type	Description
Race number	Integer	Matches boat numbers in the *Races* table.
Race date/time	Date/Time	Date and time when the race began.
Scratch Boat Time	Long	Number of minutes estimated for completion of the race by a pre-selected boat, called the "scratch boat".

3. Calculate the *handicap minutes* and *adjusted time* for each boat in each race, using the formula described in the next paragraph. Display these values in the *RaceInfo* window (these two fields were originally left empty.)

Handicap. In sailboat races involving boats of different sizes and configurations, boats vary greatly in their speed. Therefore, a handicapping system is used that will give each boat a more or less equal chance of winning the race. In this program, we will calculate the handicap minutes (HCM) for a boat in a particular race by multiplying the scratch boat time (SBT) by the boat's handicap factor (HCF). A fast sailboat would have a large handicap factor, and a slow boat would have a small one. Table 22 contains some examples of calculations. For the same boat, more handicap minutes are applied to a longer race than a shorter one.

Table 22. Sample Handicaps.

Race #	Boat #	SBT	HCF	HCM
1	1	180	.8	144
1	2	180	.5	90
1	3	180	.1	18
2	1	60	.8	48
2	2	60	.5	30
2	3	60	.1	6

7.12.9 Yachting Regatta - 3

Using the Yachting Regatta programs from the previous exercises, calculate and display the ranking of each boat for each race. For each race, the boat in first place will have the lowest adjusted time. The adjusted time (AT) is calculated from the starting time (ST), finishing time (FT) and handicap minutes (HCM) as follows: AT = (FT - ST) + HCM. For each race, produce a database table such as the one shown in Table 23.

Table 23. Results for Race 1.

Boat Name	Rank	Adjusted Time
Blue Star	1	220
Windward Passage	2	270
Ticonderoga	3	275
Kialoa II	4	280
Queen Mab	5	310
Novia del Mar	6	400

8 Reports and Online Help

Chapter Contents

Crystal Reports
    Creating a Columnar Report
    Dividing a Report Into Groups
    Adding Selection Criteria
    Creating a Cross-Tab Summary Report
    Using the Crystal Reports Custom Control
    Sample Application: Concert Ticket Reports
    Program Implementation
Creating Online Help
    The User Assistance Model
    StatusBar Control
    Creating Online Help Files
    VB/HelpWriter Lite
    Example: Stellar Car Rental Reservations
    Adding Help Commands to the Menu
    Expanding the Help File
    Adding Jumps
Review Questions
Chapter Exercises

8.1 Crystal Reports

Crystal Reports is a great report generator tool that is supplied free with Visual Basic. You can use it to create professional-looking reports directly from database tables and text files. Crystal Reports has an interactive editor that lets you specify report parameters, drag and drop fields, titles, and labels into position, and view a preview of a finished report. You can save database data inside the report, or indicate that the report is to be refreshed with new data from a database. Summaries and totals can be generated by grouping data according to criteria, and records can be filtered according to user-defined criteria. Finally, the Crystal Reports custom control, when placed on a form, allows a predefined report to be displayed from a running Visual Basic program.

This chapter introduces you to some basic techniques for creating reports that can be attached to Visual Basic programs. We will show only a subset of what the report generator is capable of doing, but you are encouraged to read the complete Crystal Reports documentation that is supplied with Visual Basic. There is also a Crystal Reports Professional product that is sold separately.

A useful database for these examples is **tickets.mdb**, a database similar to the one used in the Chapter 6 *Concert Hall Ticketing* exercises. The database contains three tables with information about concerts and ticket sales for a concert hall:

- **Concerts:** A list of concert dates and descriptions.
- **Seats:** A count of available seats and prices for each concert, in each section of the concert hall.
- **Reservations:** Tickets that have been sold for specific concerts. A reservation record consists of a concert date, customer name, seating section, and the number of tickets purchased.

This section has been designed as a series of hands-on exercises that help you learn Crystal Reports more quickly by experimenting and reviewing the results.

8.1.1 Creating a Columnar Report

Crystal sales1.rpt

Let's create a simple tabular report that lists all ticket sales for the concert dates in the Reservations table. The following steps will guide you through the process:

1. Select Report Designer from Add-Ins menu. This launches Crystal Reports.
2. Enter product registration information, if necessary. Proceed to Crystal Reports, then maximize the main window.
3. Select from the menu: File/New/Report (Figure 1). As you can see, there are three basic types of reports you can create here: Report, Cross-Tab, and Labels. The Report button has already been selected, so just click on OK.

Figure 1. Creating a New Report.

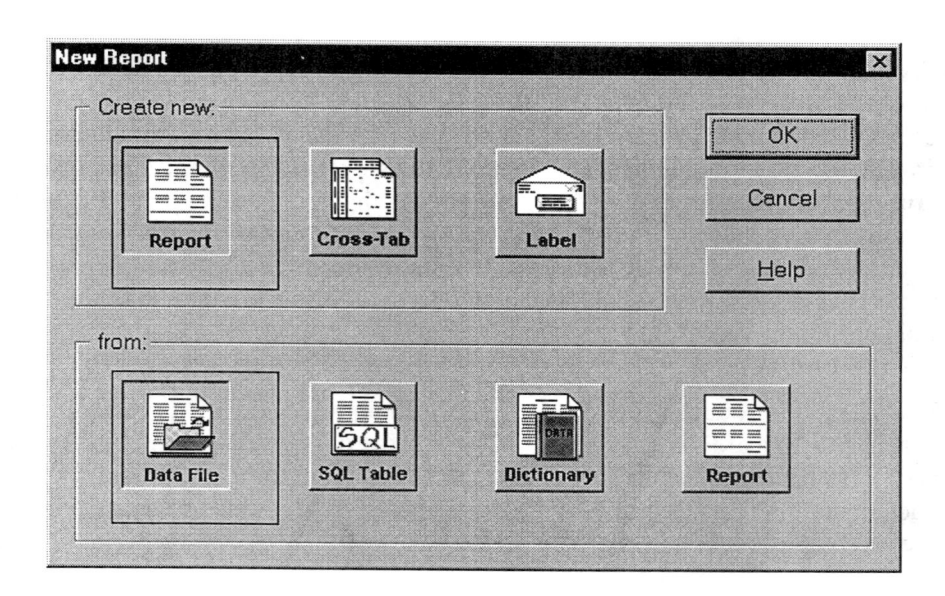

Chap 8: Reports and Online Help 331

4. A **Choose Database File** dialog will appear. Locate the tickets.mdb database in the \Crystal directory, and click on OK.

5. The **Report Design** window will appear (Figure 2). On top of this, the Insert Database Field dialog will list all tables and fields belonging to the database.

Figure 2. Report Design Window, Inserting Fields.

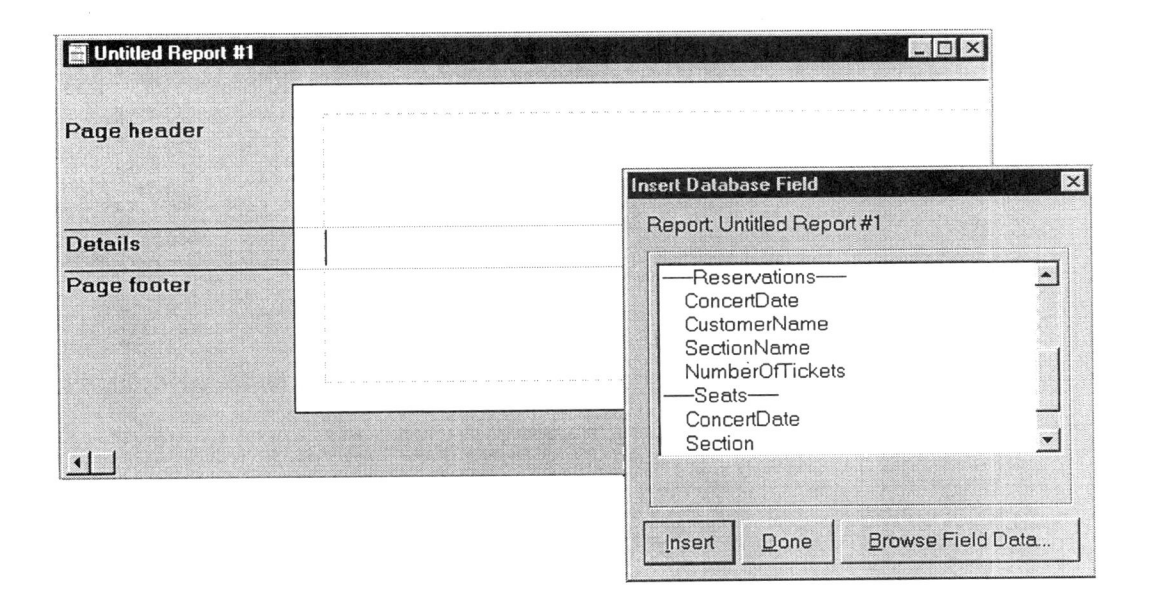

6. Double-click on the ConcertDate field in the Reservations table. The mouse cursor will become a rectangle.

7. Drag and drop the rectangle at the left side of the section marked Detail on the report design. The column title will appear above the line, in the Page Header area.

8. Drag and drop the following fields from the Reservations table, in order from left to right: CustomerName, SectionName, NumberOfTickets.

9. Shorten the CustomerName column by selecting it with the mouse, and dragging the handle on its right side. Do the same with the column's title. Use the mouse to drag the SectionName and NumberOfTickets fields into position.

Changing Field Properties. Whenever you want to change the properties of a column heading or report field, select the item and right-click the mouse. A pop-up menu will offer choices such as those shown in Figure 3.

Figure 3. Changing Field Properties.

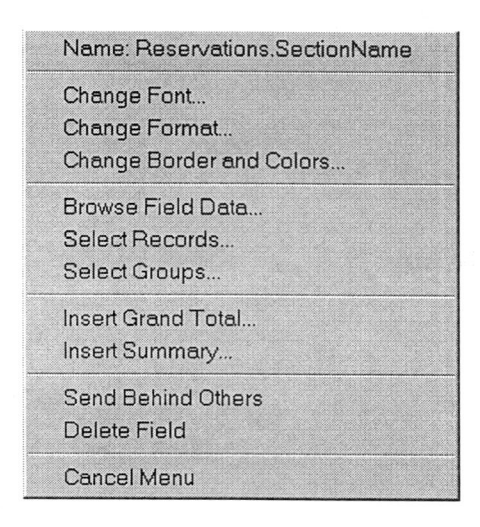

```
Name: Reservations.SectionName
Change Font...
Change Format...
Change Border and Colors...
Browse Field Data...
Select Records...
Select Groups...
Insert Grand Total...
Insert Summary...
Send Behind Others
Delete Field
Cancel Menu
```

10. Select the ConcertDate field with the mouse; right-click on the field and select the Change Format option. Change the date to a 99-99-99 format.

11. Using the File/Save As menu, save the report as sales1.rpt, in the same directory as the database.

12. Select Print Preview from the File menu and view the report. The following is a sample:

ConcertDate	CustomerName	Section	NumberOfTickets
01-01-1997	Johnson, Paul	LOGE	2
01-01-1997	Baker, Susan	ORCH1	5
01-02-1997	Rosenblatt, Zak	BALC	5
01-05-1997	Gonzalez, Julio	BALC	6
01-08-1997	McAfee, Susan	ORCH1	3

Adding a Title. To insert a title in the caption bar of the report window, select Report Title from the Report menu. To insert a title into the Page header area of the report, select Text Field from the Insert menu. Then drag the title to the report's page heading area.

13. For the report title on the caption bar, enter "Concert Ticket Sales (sales1.rpt)". For the title in the Page header, enter "Ticket Sales". Right-click on the title and change the font to 18 point bold. Figure 4 shows a sample.

Figure 4. Ticket Sales Report.

Adding a Grand Total. To add a total to a column, you have to select the field that will be totaled by clicking it once with the mouse (see Figure 5). You then right-click the field and select the **Insert Grand Total** option; a list of types of totals will be shown, such as sum, average, maximum, minimum, count, and sample variance.

Figure 5. Window: Insert Grand Total.

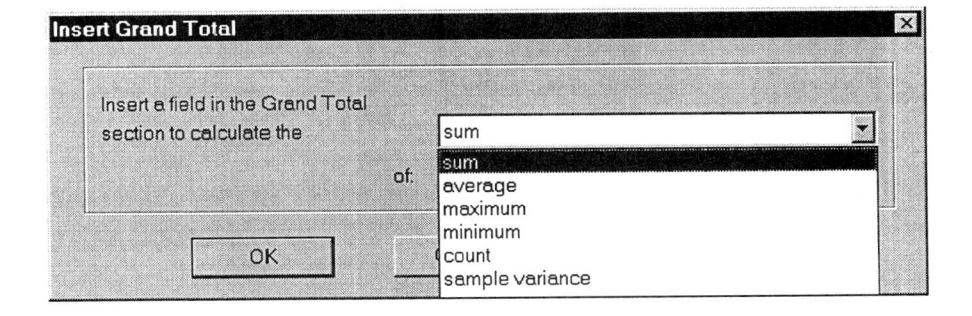

14. Add a grand total to the NumberOfTickets column, and make it a sum. Notice that a Grand Total section has been added to the report design window. Insert a text field just to the left of the total tickets, with the caption "Total Tickets Sold:". Figure 6 shows the report design.

Figure 6. Ticket Sales Report with Grand Total.

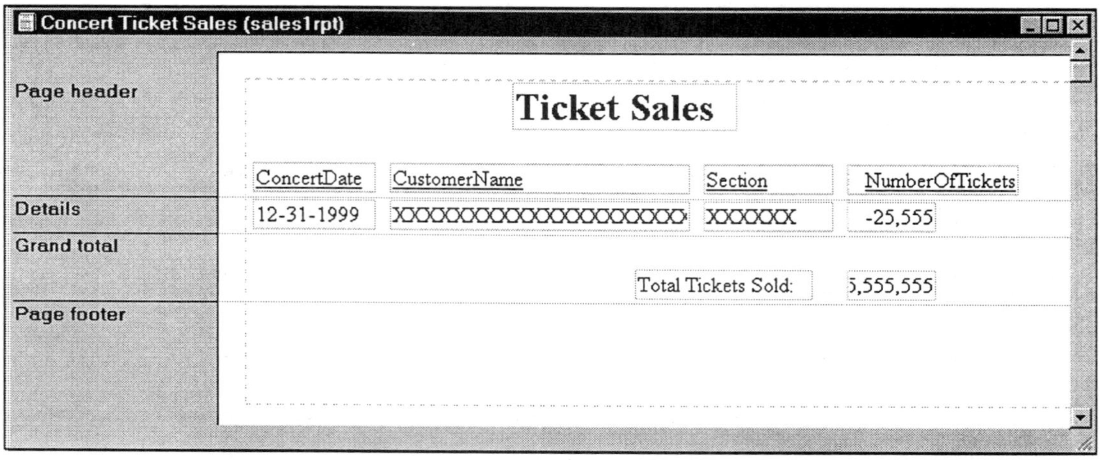
Concert Ticket Sales (sales1rpt)
Page header
Ticket Sales
ConcertDate
CustomerName
Section
NumberOfTickets
Details
12-31-1999
XXXXXXXXXXXXXXXXXXXXX
XXXXXX
-25,555
Grand total
Total Tickets Sold:
5,555,555
Page footer

15. Run the print preview again. Figure 7 shows a sample of the report.

Figure 7. Print Preview, Ticket Sales Report.

Ticket Sales

ConcertDate	CustomerName	Section	NumberOfTickets
01-01-1997	Baker, Susan	ORCH1	5
01-01-1997	Johnson, Paul	LOGE	2
01-01-1997	Mahler, Susan	ORCH1	4
01-01-1997	Chopin, Paul	LOGE	3
01-02-1997	Rosenblatt, Zak	BALC	5
01-02-1997	Liszt, Zak	BALC	7
01-05-1997	Gonzalez, Julio	BALC	6
01-05-1997	Beethoven, Harold	BALC	2
01-05-1997	Paganini, Julio	BALC	2
01-05-1997	Berlioz, Harold	BALC	4
01-08-1997	McAfee, Susan	ORCH1	3
01-08-1997	Schumann, Susan	ORCH1	1
		Total Tickets Sold:	44

16. Add a count to the Grand totals area of the report that displays the number of customers.

Chap 8: Reports and Online Help   335

17. If you plan to print the report on the printer, you may prefer to increase the page margins and use a larger font. To set the margins, select Page Margins from the File menu, and set the top, left, right, and bottom margins to 1.0 inches each.

18. To change the font sizes, select each of the fields on the report with the mouse. Hold down the Ctrl key as you select each field, and right-click the mouse to change the font size of all fields to 12 points.

8.1.2 Dividing a Report Into Groups

Crystal sales2.rpt

One of the most powerful features of Crystal Reports is its ability to divide records into groups and print subtotals. To illustrate, let's add more records to the reservations table, sort the records in order by concert date, and provide a subtotal on the **ConcertDate** field.

1. Right-click the ConcertDate field and select **Insert Summary** from the popup menu. Set each of the options as in Figure 8.

Figure 8. Inserting a Summary Line.

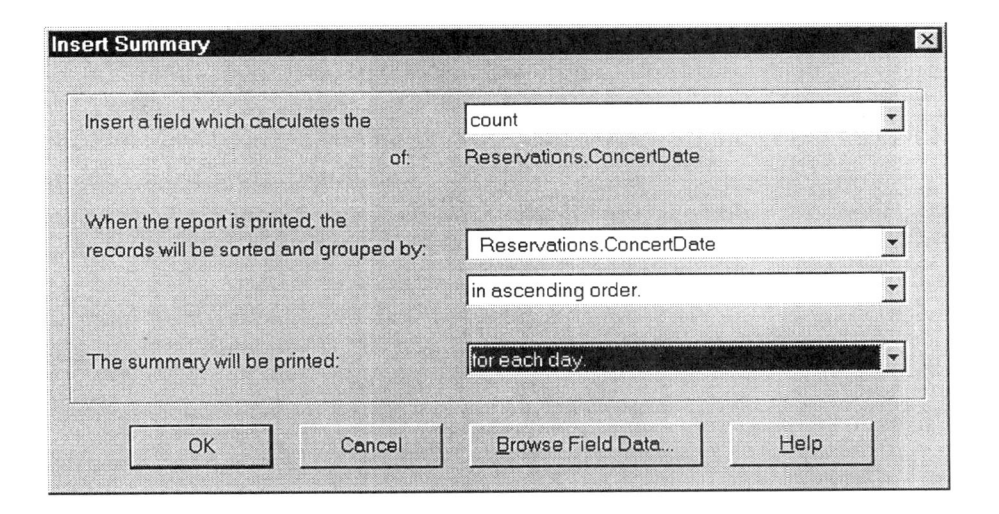

2. Drag the concertDate field from the detail line up to the summary header line. This is the section labeled "#1 ConcertDate - A" section.

3. Insert a text field next to the count in the summary line containing the word "Customers". Move the counter field and the text field under the Customer Name column.

4. Drag the line below the group summary downward to create a blank line after each summary line. Figure 9 shows the report design window:

Figure 9. Report Design with Group Summary and Grand Total.

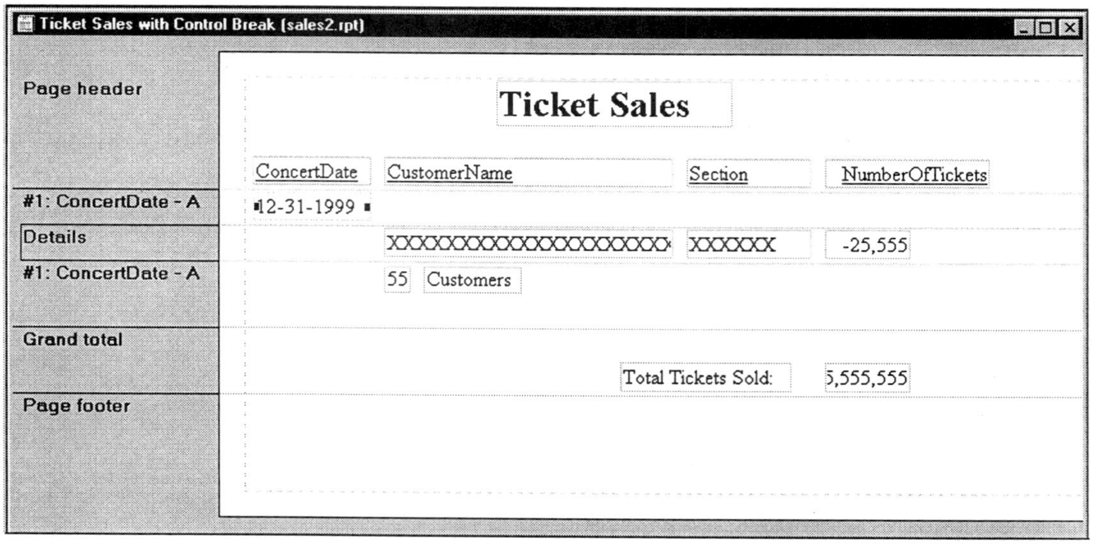

Page header		**Ticket Sales**		
	ConcertDate	CustomerName	Section	NumberOfTickets
#1: ConcertDate - A	12-31-1999			
Details		XXXXXXXXXXXXXXXXXX	XXXXXX	-25,555
#1: ConcertDate - A		55 Customers		
Grand total			Total Tickets Sold:	5,555,555
Page footer				

Figure 10 contains a sample of the preview report.

Figure 10. Sample Preview Report with Subtotals.

Ticket Sales

ConcertDate	CustomerName	Section	NumberOfTickets
01-01-1997			
	Baker, Susan	ORCH1	5
	Johnson, Paul	LOGE	2
	Mahler, Susan	ORCH1	4
	Chopin, Paul	LOGE	3
	4 Customers		
01-02-1997			
	Rosenblatt, Zak	BALC	5
	Liszt, Zak	BALC	7
	2 Customers		

5. Add a subtotal that displays the number of tickets sold for each concert date. Right-click on the numberOfTickets field on the detail line, and select the **Insert Subtotal** command. Save the report again.

8.1.3 Adding Selection Criteria

Reports often become more useful if they are selective in the information they print. In particular, managers often request reports that screen out certain data, because it makes it easier for them to focus on essential information. *Exception reports*, for example, focus on information that could be considered exceptional, or different from the rest of the data. In the case of our Concert Hall ticket sales report, a detail listing of all ticket purchases by all customers for all concerts in the coming year might generate several hundred pages or more. Most of this information would probably be useless, so the concert hall manager might request a report for only concerts for the coming month, or a report listing only concerts having low ticket sales, and so forth.

It's very easy to select only certain detail lines or groups to appear on a report. *Selection criteria* make it possible to include only records or groups that satisfy given constraints. Crystal Reports lets you create a *record selection formula* to select only certain records, or a *group selection formula* to select only certain groups.

Crystal sales3.rpt

Record Selection Formula Example. Let's insert a formula that only prints detail lines for customers sitting in the Balcony section of the concert hall.

1. From the Report menu, choose Edit Record Selection Formula. This displays the Edit Formula window.

2. In the Fields option box, double-click the field Reservations.SectionName. This adds the field to the Formula text box.

3. Type an = sign into the Formula text box, followed by 'BALC'. The entire fomula should be

   ```
   {Reservations.SectionName}='BALC'
   ```

4. Click on the Check button to check the formula for errors. If there were no errors, click on the Accept button to save the formula.

5. Choose Print Preview from the File menu. In Figure 11, the report only lists customers who bought tickets in the section called "BALC".

Figure 11. Report Using Record Selection Formula.

Ticket Sales

ConcertDate	CustomerName	Section	NumberOfTickets
01-02-1997			
	Rosenblatt, Zak	BALC	5
	Liszt, Zak	BALC	7
	2 Customers	Total:	12
01-05-1997			
	Gonzalez, Julio	BALC	6
	Beethoven, Harold	BALC	2
	Paganini, Julio	BALC	2
	Berlioz, Harold	BALC	4
	4 Customers	Total:	14
		Total Tickets Sold:	26

For practice, modify the record selection formula so it only displays records in which the number of tickets purchased is greater than 2.

Crystal sales4.rpt

Group Selection Formula Example. Let's insert a formula that only prints concerts occurring after January 2, 1997.

1. From the Report menu, select Edit Group Selection Formula. Enter the following formula in the Formula text box:

    ```
    {Reservations.ConcertDate} > Date(1997,01,02)
    ```

2. Notice that you have to use a function called Date to place a date into a formula. Click on the Check button to check for errors, and click on Accept to save the formula.

3. Remove the Grand Total line because it does not help the user to interpret this report.

4. Display the report preview again, as in Figure 12.

Chap 8: Reports and Online Help

Figure 12. Report Using Group Selection Formula.

Ticket Sales

ConcertDate	CustomerName	Section	NumberOfTickets
01-05-1997	Gonzalez, Julio	BALC	6
01-05-1997	Beethoven, Harold	BALC	2
01-05-1997	Paganini, Julio	BALC	2
01-05-1997	Berlioz, Harold	BALC	4
	4 Customers	Total:	14
01-08-1997	McAfee, Susan	ORCH1	3
01-08-1997	Schumann, Susan	ORCH1	1
	2 Customers	Total:	4

Another Group Selection. What if you only wanted to display concerts in which the total number of tickets sold was less than 10? (Of course, our database contains rather small numbers of customers compared to those in a real concert hall.) Here are the steps:

1. Return to the Edit Group Selection Formula window and delete the existing formula.

2. From the Fields box, select the field called "Sum of NumberOfTickets" listed after the Group Footer #1 entry, and click the Select button.

3. Add "< 10" to the formula, so the entire formula is the following:

   ```
   Sum ({Reservations.NumberOfTickets},
        {Reservations.ConcertDate}, "daily")<10
   ```

4. This indicates that the sum is calculated for each grouping of the ConcertDate field.

5. Click the Check button to check for errors, click on Accept.

6. Preview the report again, shown in Figure 13.

Figure 13. Another Group Selection.

Ticket Sales

ConcertDate	CustomerName	Section	NumberOfTickets
01-08-1997	McAfee, Susan	ORCH1	3
01-08-1997	Schumann, Susan	ORCH1	1
	2 Customers	Total:	4

8.1.4 Creating a Cross-Tab Summary Report

A *cross-tab* report is one that summarizes information more conveniently than the detail reports we have created so far. Company management often prefers summary reports to detail reports, because the former is able to reduce the amount of information presented to the reader. The concert hall manager, for instance, might want to know how many tickets remain in each of the sections of the hall, for each concert date. We could provide this information in a tabular report, but there would be an excessive number of detail lines. Each section of the concert hall would be printed on a separate line, producing four report lines for each concert date (Figure 14).

Crystal seats.rpt

Figure 14. Report of Available Seats.

Available Seats, by Section

ConcertDate	Section	Available
01-01-97	BALC	0
01-01-97	LOGE	48
01-01-97	ORCH1	145
01-01-97	ORCH2	50
01-02-97	BALC	73
01-02-97	LOGE	134
01-02-97	ORCH1	147
01-02-97	ORCH2	50
01-05-97	ORCH1	150
01-05-97	ORCH2	40
01-05-97	BALC	70
01-05-97	LOGE	150
01-08-97	ORCH1	147
01-08-97	ORCH2	50
01-08-97	BALC	80
01-08-97	LOGE	150
01-15-97	BALC	80

Further, if we wanted to print the total seats for each concert, we would have to specify report subtotals. On the other hand, if we created a cross-tab report as in Figure 15, each section of the concert hall would print as a separate column. This would make a more concise report, and totals for each concert date would be generated automatically.

Figure 15. Cross-Tab Report of Available Seats.

Available Seats, by Section

	BALC	LOGE	ORCH1	ORCH2	Total
01-01-97	0	48	145	50	243
01-02-97	73	134	147	50	404
01-05-97	70	150	150	40	410
01-08-97	80	150	147	50	427
01-15-97	80	150	150	50	430
Total	303	632	739	240	1,914

The following steps will guide you through the process of creating a cross-tab report:

1. Run Crystal Reports.
2. Select from the menu: File/New/Cross-Tab, and click on OK.
3. Locate the tickets.mdb database in the \Crystal directory, and click on OK.
4. The Cross-Tab setup window will appear. From the Fields list box in the lower left corner, drag each of the following fields with the mouse:

   Drag Seats.ConcertDate to the **Rows** textbox.
   Drag Seats.Section to the **Columns** textbox.
   Drag Seats.Available to the **Summarized Field** textbox.

Figure 16 shows how the window will look.

Figure 16. Cross-Tab Field Selection Window.

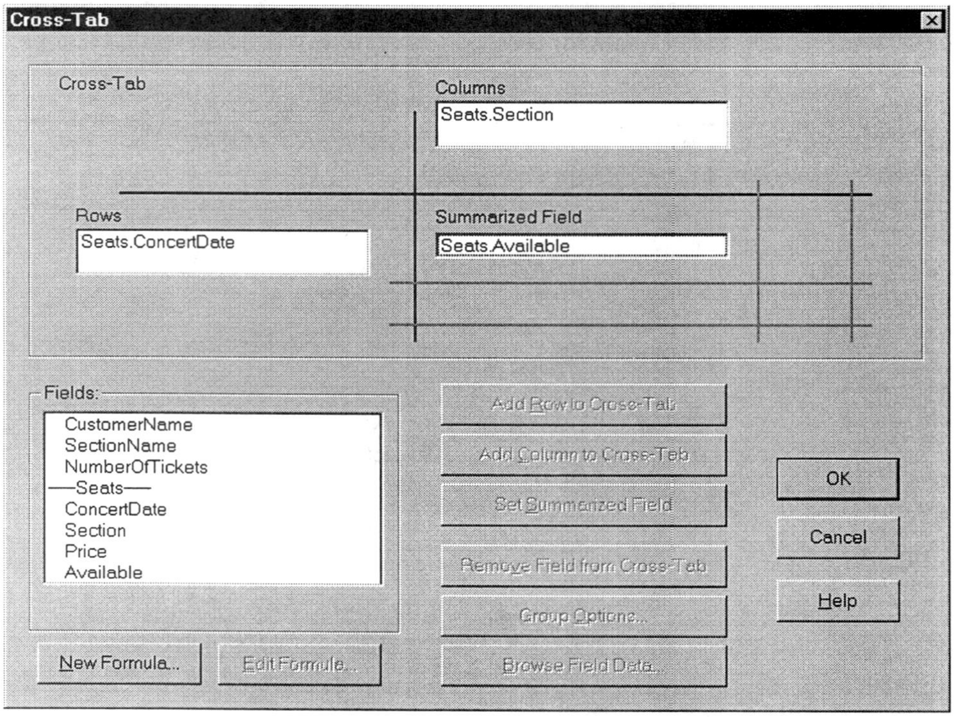

5. Click on OK to close this window. When the report design window appears, close the Insert Database Field window. Figure 17 shows the report design window so far, containing the Cross-Tab section. The concert dates will print along the left side, the section names will print along the top, and a column will appear on the right side with the total available seats for each concert.

Figure 17. Cross-Tab Report Design Window.

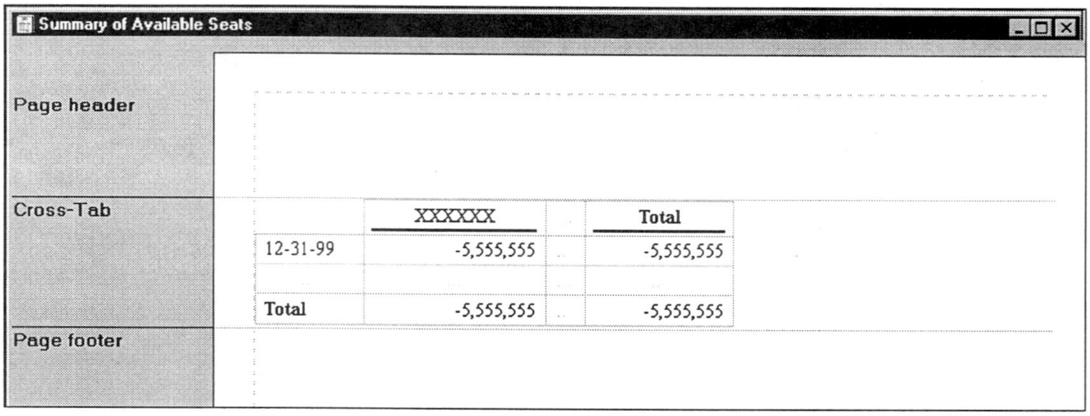

Chap 8: Reports and Online Help   343

Formatting and Titles. Click on the Report/Report Title menu selection, and make the title "Summary of Available Seats". In the page heading area, insert a text field with the caption "Available Seats, by Section". Choose a 16-point bold font.

6. Select all four numeric fields with the mouse, right click, and change the format option to zero decimal places so the number of available seats will print as integers. Change the date format to 99-99-99. Drag the vertical separator between the date column and the second colum to the right. This will widen the date field slightly. Figure 18 contains a new sample of the report design.

Figure 18. Available Seat Report, Final Formatting.

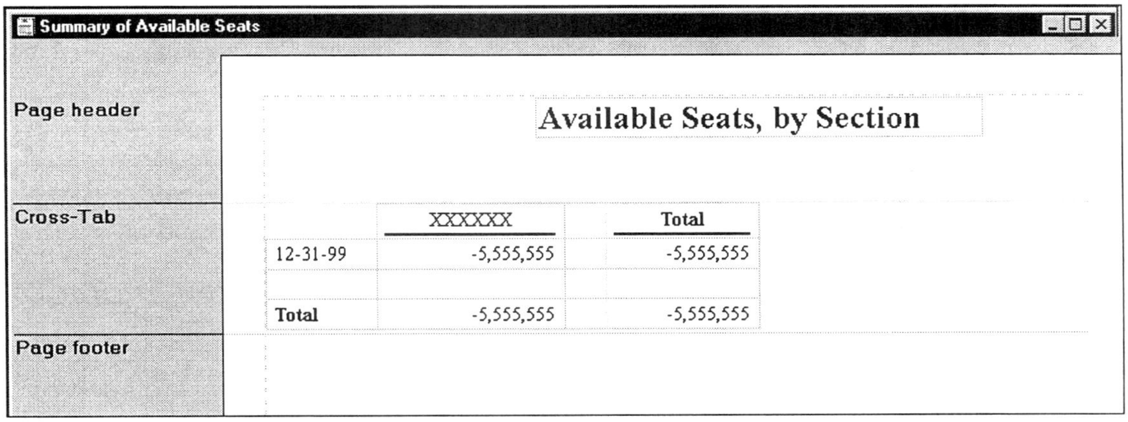

7. From the File menu, select Print Preview. The report will appear as it did at the beginning of this section.

8. Save the report under the filename seats.rpt in the same directory as the tickets.mdb database.

8.1.5 Using the Crystal Reports Custom Control

Visual Basic includes the Crystal Reports custom control, which is required if you want to display a report from your program. We have created four reports in the previous sections of this chapter, so we now need to create a program that will launch those reports. The Crystal Reports control does not appear in the default Visual Basic toolbox, so it must be added.

A number of important properties associated with Crystal Reports Custom Control Version 4.6 are shown in Table 1. Table 2 contains selected output formats available when a report is printed to a file. In particular, note that it is easy to create HTML output suitable for Internet Web pages.

PrintReport is the most important method associated with this control, as it launches the report. If an error occurs, PrintReport returns a non-zero value, and you can query the **LastErrorNumber** and **LastErrorString** properties to find out what went wrong. For example, we can display the error in a message box:

```
Dim result As Integer
With CrystalReport1
  result = .PrintReport
  If result <> 0 Then
    MsgBox .LastErrorNumber & ": " & .LastErrorString, _
      vbInformation, "Error"
  End If
End With
```

Table 1. Crystal Reports Custom Control Properties.

Property	Description
ReportFileName	Name of the Crystal Report file, with extension .rpt.
DataFiles(0)	The first database file used by the report.
DataFiles(1..n)	Other database files, if any, used by the report.
Destination	The output for the report will go to one of the following: 0 = Window, 1 = Printer, 2 = File.
PrintFileName	Name of the print output file, if Destination = File.
PrintFileType	Type of print output file, if Destination = File. See Table 2 for a description of the possible values.
CopiesToPrinter	Number of copies to be printed, if Destination = Printer.
SelectionFormula	Selection criteria for detail records, based on Crystal Reports Record Selection Formula syntax.
GroupSelectionFormula	Selection criteria for group fields, based on Crystal Reports Group Selection Formula syntax.

Table 2. Selected PrintFileType Definitions.

Predefined Constant	Description (value)
crptCharSep	Character-Separated (5)
crptCSV	Comma-Separated values (4)
crptDIF	Data-Interchange Format (3)
crptExcel50	Excel 5.0 XLS (19)
crptHTML30	HTML 3.0 Draft (20)
crptNetscape	Netscape HTML (22)
crptRecord	Fixed-Length Columns (0)
crptRTF	Rich-Text Format (15)
crptTabSep	Tab-Separated Fields (1)
crptText	Text File (2)
crptWinWord	Word for Windows (17)

Chap 8: Reports and Online Help 345

8.1.6 Sample Application: Concert Ticket Reports

Crystal
tickets.vbp

Let's create a Visual Basic program that displays the reports created earlier in this chapter. This program will have a single window called frmMain, containing a Tab control that leads the user through the steps to select a report, choose the output mode, and if the report is written to a file, the output file type.

Figure 19 contains a sample of frmMain with the first tab selected. The user selected the second report, and the program displays the corresponding report filename.

Figure 19. Concert Hall Reports, Main Window.

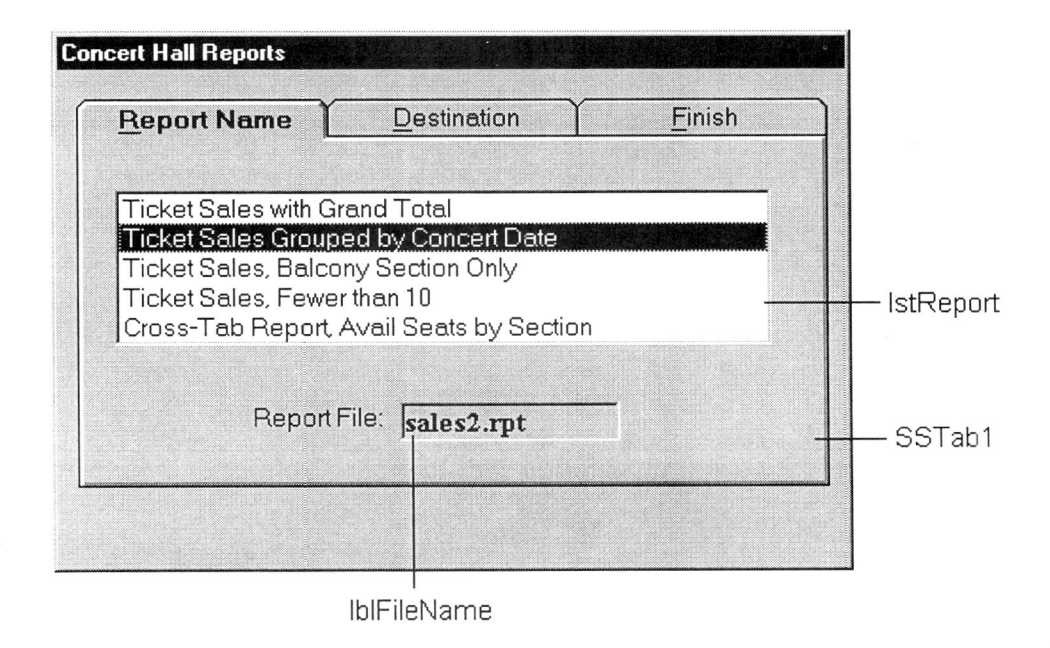

Next, the user selects the report destination, which can be window, printer, or file (Figure 20).

Figure 20. Selecting the Report Destination.

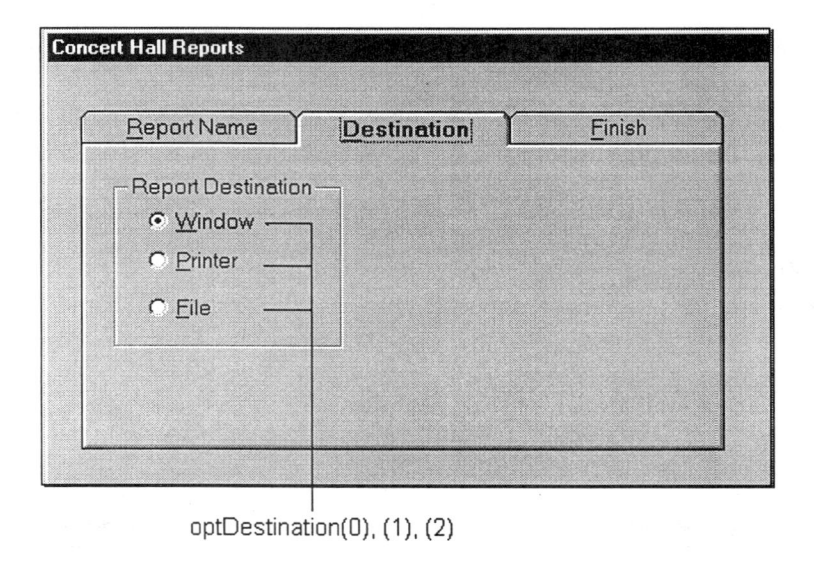

[Screenshot of Concert Hall Reports dialog with Destination tab selected, showing Report Destination options: Window (selected), Printer, File. Labeled: optDestination(0), (1), (2)]

If the user selects printer output, the program asks for the number of copies to print:

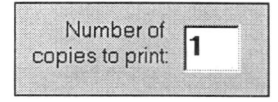

[Screenshot showing "Number of copies to print: 1"]

If the user selects file output, the program prompts for the filename and output file format. In Figure 21, for example, the user has decided to produce a report in HTML format for a Web page. Finally, the user clicks on the **Finish** tab to begin printing the report.

Figure 21. Selecting the Report File Type.

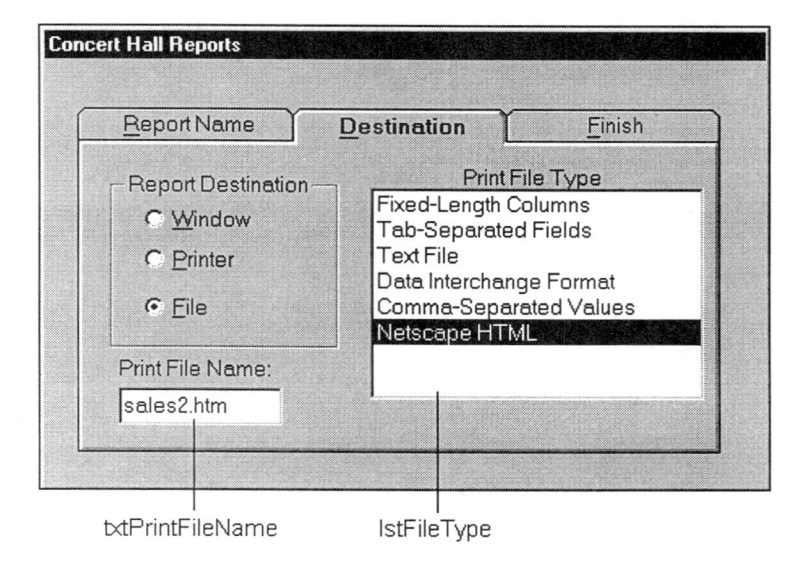

[Screenshot of Concert Hall Reports dialog with Destination tab selected, Report Destination: File selected, Print File Name: sales2.htm, Print File Type list showing: Fixed-Length Columns, Tab-Separated Fields, Text File, Data Interchange Format, Comma-Separated Values, Netscape HTML (selected). Labeled: txtPrintFileName, lstFileType]

Chap 8: Reports and Online Help

When the user clicks on the Finish panel, the **Start Printing** button generates the report and the Exit button quits the program (Figure 22).

Figure 22. Generating the Report.

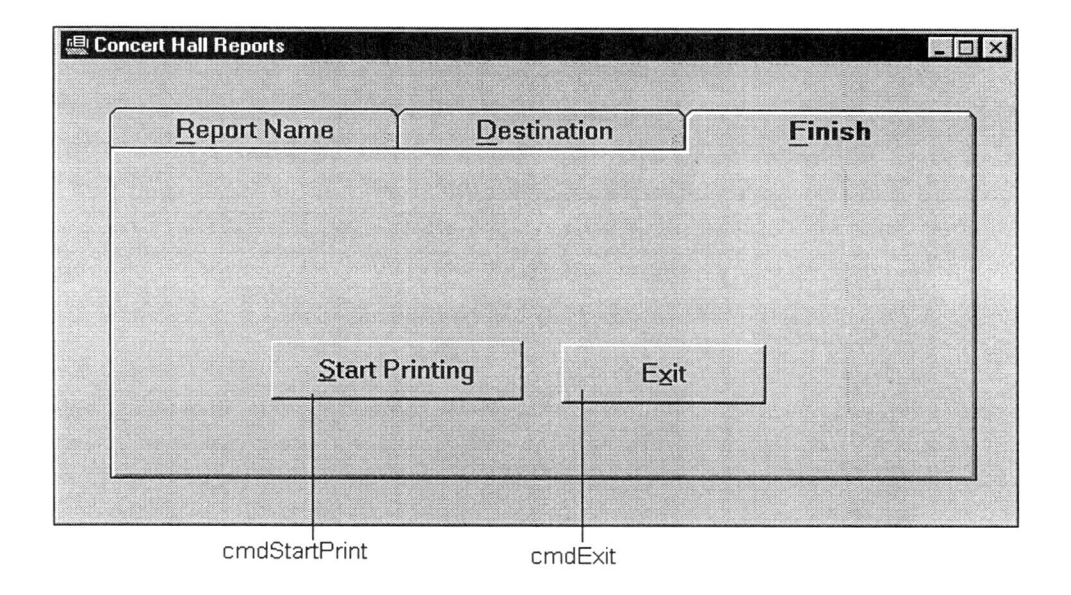

8.1.7 Program Implementation

Most of this program could easily be inserted in other application programs, because the techniques are common to all programs that use the Crystal Reports custom control. First, we make the database filename a constant, with the understanding that in a future version, we could allow the user to select the database from a File/Open dialog box. The fileName array contains all of the predefined report filenames:

```
Const DatabaseName As String = "tickets.mdb"
Dim fileName(0 To 10) As String
```

In **Form_Load**, we let PrepareReportNames load the list box with report names. In this procedure, we fill a list box with a variety of report file types and set the ItemData array to the corresponding Crystal Reports constants:

```
Private Sub Form_Load()
   ChDrive App.Path
   ChDir App.Path
   PrepareReportNames
   'List the report file types:
   With lstFileType
      .AddItem "Fixed-Length Columns"
      .AddItem "Tab-Separated Fields"
      .AddItem "Text File"
      .AddItem "Data Interchange Format"
      .AddItem "Comma-Separated Values"
```

```
      .AddItem "Netscape HTML"
   'And the corresponding constants:
      .ItemData(0) = crptRecord
      .ItemData(1) = crptTabSep
      .ItemData(2) = crptText
      .ItemData(3) = crptDIF
      .ItemData(4) = crptCSV
      .ItemData(5) = crptNetscape
   End With
End Sub
```

The **PrepareReportNames** procedure builds an array of filenames and fills a list box with corresponding report titles:

```
Public Sub PrepareReportNames()
'Prepare the report file names:
   fileName(0) = "sales1.rpt"
   fileName(1) = "sales2.rpt"
   fileName(2) = "sales3.rpt"
   fileName(3) = "sales4.rpt"
   fileName(4) = "seats.rpt"
'And the corresponding descriptions:
   With lstReport
      .AddItem "Ticket Sales with Grand Total"
      .AddItem "Ticket Sales Grouped by Concert Date"
      .AddItem "Ticket Sales, Balcony Section Only"
      .AddItem "Ticket Sales, Fewer than 10"
      .AddItem "Cross-Tab Report, Avail Seats by Section"
   End With
End Sub
```

The **lstReport_Click** event handler responds when the user has selected one of the report titles; we retrieve the corresponding filename and display it in a label:

```
Private Sub lstReport_Click()
   lblFileName.Caption = fileName(lstReport.ListIndex)
End Sub
```

Report Destinations. When the user clicks on an **optDestination** button array, we use the Index parameter to set the Destination property of the custom control, and coordinate the display of filename options or printer options on the same panel. Unfortunately, this type of coding tends to be rather long:

```
Private Sub optDestination_Click(Index As Integer)
'Coordinate the display of destination options.
'The Index parameter in this procedure corresponds
'exactly to the three numeric values for the Destination
'property of the Crystal Reports control.
   CrystalReport1.Destination = Index
   Select Case Index
   Case crptToWindow:
      txtPrintFileName.Visible = False
      lstFileType.Visible = False
```

```
        Label2.Visible = False
        Label4.Visible = False
        txtNumCopies.Visible = False
        Label5.Visible = False
      Case crptToPrinter:
        txtPrintFileName.Visible = False
        lstFileType.Visible = False
        Label2.Visible = False
        Label4.Visible = False
        txtNumCopies.Visible = True
        Label5.Visible = True
      Case crptToFile:
        txtPrintFileName.Visible = True
        lstFileType.Visible = True
        Label2.Visible = True
        Label4.Visible = True
        txtNumCopies.Visible = False
        Label5.Visible = False
    End Select
End Sub
```

The Click event of the **lstFileType** list box uses the ListIndex property to index into the ItemData array and retrieve the crystal reports constant that determines the PrintFileType property:

```
Private Sub lstFileType_Click()
'User has selected the type of print file from a
'list box. The ItemData array contains matching
'constants that set the PrintFileType property.
  CrystalReport1.PrintFileType = lstFileType.ItemData _
      (lstFileType.ListIndex)
End Sub
```

PrintReport. When the user clicks on the **Print** button to begin printing the report, the event handler for this button sets a number of essential custom control properties and calls the PrintReport method:

```
Public Sub PrintReport()
'Initalize report properties and start printing the
'report. If an error occurs, display the error number
'and error string.

  Dim result As Integer, choice As Integer
  On Error GoTo PrintReport1
  With CrystalReport1
    .ReportFileName = lblFileName.Caption
    .DataFiles(0) = DatabaseName
    .PrintFileName = txtPrintFileName.Text
    .CopiesToPrinter = Val(txtNumCopies.Text)
    result = .PrintReport      'start printing...
    If result = 20514 Then
      choice = MsgBox("Report file already exists. Overwrite?", _
```

```
            vbYesNo + vbQuestion, "")
      If choice = vbYes Then
        Kill .PrintFileName    'delete the old file
        .PrintReport           'try again...
      End If
    ElseIf result <> 0 Then
      MsgBox .LastErrorNumber & ": " & .LastErrorString, _
        vbInformation, "Error"
    End If
  End With
  Exit Sub
PrintReport1:
  MsgBox Error$, vbInformation, "Error"
End Sub
```

Still discussing the **PrintReport** procedure, we notice that the PrintReport method returns a status code. For example, if a print filename already exists by the same name, the report control will refuse to print and issue code 20514. Our reponse is to prompt the user, and if agreed, delete the existing print file. Of course, other errors may occur, and they are handled by displaying the LastErrorNumber and LastErrorString properties of the custom control.

Two more event handlers complete the code for this program:

```
Private Sub cmdExit_Click()
  Unload Me
End Sub

Private Sub cmdStartPrint_Click()
  PrintReport
End Sub
```

8.2 Creating Online Help

8.2.1 The User Assistance Model

There are several ways you can add help to your Visual Basic applications. The VB5 documentation defines a *user assistance model* as being the complete package of assistance that may be provided by a program to help the user: *online help, printed documentation, tool tips, status bars, what's this help,* and *wizards*.

Online help refers to a help file (extension .hlp) installed by your application, that may be accessed by pressing the F1 key or clicking on the Help menu in your program. This file is a document originally created in *rich-text format* (rtf) which has been compiled by the Windows *help compiler*. This compiler is supplied with the Professional version of Visual Basic.

Printed documentation is becoming increasingly rare today. Because of the expense of printed manuals, and because manuals need to be updated frequently, software suppliers often prefer to provide electronic manuals. Some manuals are supplied via the Internet and may be viewed with web browsers such as *Netscape* or *Internet Explorer*.

Tool tips are small labels that display below menu items and controls when the user positions the mouse over the controls. Most Windows applications, including Visual Basic use tool tips. In VB5, you can add a tool tip to a control simply by placing text inside the control's ToolTipText property. For VB4 users, there is a shareware utility called VBTips that does the same thing.

A *status bar* is a horizontal strip, usually placed at the bottom of a window, which is divided into rectangular sections called *panels*. Each panel can display a string, a graphic, or both.

What's this help provides a link to a pop-up help topic that is displayed when the user selects *What's This Help* from a menu or toolbar and clicks on a control. This requires a *context ID* number in the **WhatsThisHelpID** property of a control. This context ID activates a particular help topic in an online help file (.hlp).

Wizards are step by step instructions and assistance for tasks that would otherwise be difficult for the user to master. A wizard will ask the user to enter information and make decisions that often direct the sequence of questions that follow. VB5 contains a *Wizard Manager* tool that simplifies creating wizards.

8.2.2 StatusBar Control

The **StatusBar** control displays a status bar on a form. It can be divided into a maximum of sixteen separate sections, called *panels*. Usually, a StatusBar appears at the bottom of a window. A panel can contain text, a picture, or both. A program can update the status bar when it detects that the user has either clicked on or moved the mouse over a particular panel. You can set the properties easily by clicking on **Custom** in the Properties window.

The Style Property. The Style property of the StatusBar control affects the number of panels. The **sbrSimple** style indicates that there will be only one panel and its text will be shown in the SimpleText property. The **sbrNormal** style indicates that multiple panels will be used, and each will have a separate Caption property.

The Panels Collection. Most of the work in setting up a status bar control is involved with the Panels property, a collection of Panel objects. Figure 23 shows the custom properties dialog for the Panels collection, and Table 3 describes properties of the Panels collection, and Table 4 describes constants that refer to panel styles.

Figure 23. StatusBar Properties for the Panels Collection.

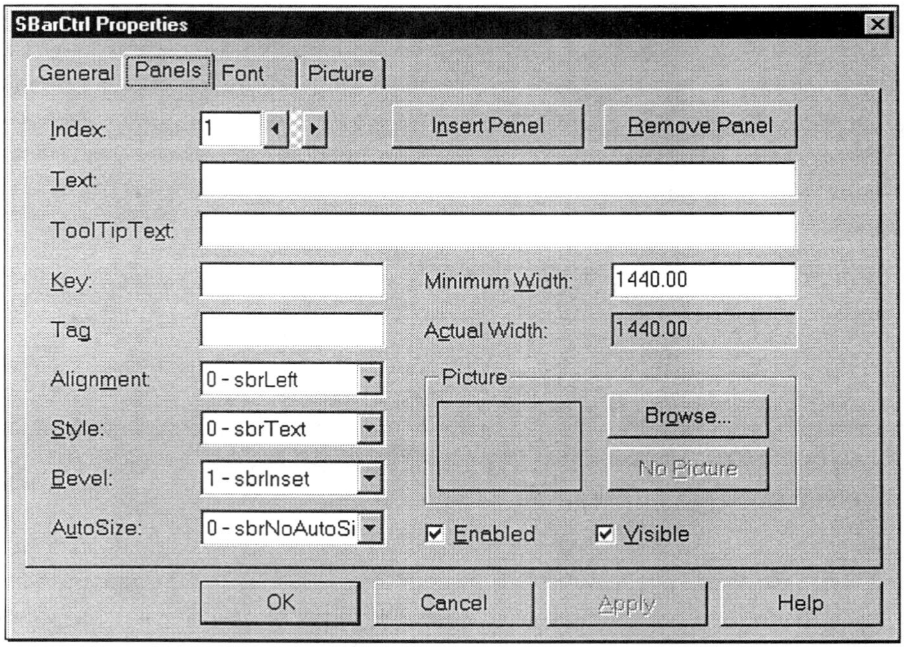

Table 3. Panel Object Properties.

Property	Description
Alignment	Alignment of its text. Settings: sbrLeft, sbrCenter, and sbrRight.
AutoSize	Controls whether the width of a Panel is resized when its contents change or the parent form is resized. Settings: sbrNoAutoSize, sbrSpring (grow if space is available), sbrContents (resize to contents).
Bevel	Controls the border, or bevel around the panel. Settings: sbrNoBevel, sbrInset, sbrRaised.
Text	The text appearing inside a panel.
Key	A unique string for each panel that identifies it in the collection. You can search for a particular panel using its key.
Picture	A bitmap, metafile, or icon return by the LoadPicture function.
Style	Affects the panel's appearance. See Table 4.
MinWidth	The minimum width that the panel can have.
Width	The width of a single panel. Cannot be smaller than MinWidth.

Table 4. Panel Style Constants.

Constant	Object(s) Displayed
sbrText	Text and/or bitmap
sbrCaps	Caps Lock status
sbrNum	Number Lock status

Table 4 (continued).

sbrIns	Insert Key status
sbrScrl	Scroll Lock status
sbrTime	Time of day
sbrDate	Today's date

Sample StatusBar Program. Let's write a short program containing a window with two status bars. The first bar has its style property set to sbrSimple (single panel), and its SimpleText property contains "Reservations file open." The second status bar has its style set to sbrNormal (multiple panels), and its Panels collection contains four panels. The properties of each panel are shown in Table 5.

Table 5. Second StatusBar Panel Properties.

Index	Alignment	Style	AutoSize
1	sbrCenter	sbrText	sbrContents
2	sbrCenter	sbrDate	sbrContents
3	sbrCenter	sbrTime	sbrContents
4	sbrCenter	sbrCaps	sbrNoAutoSize

When the program runs, the current date and time are automatically filled in, and the CAPS label is highlighted when the Caps Lock key is pressed. See Figure 24 for a sample.

Figure 24. Window with Two Status Bars.

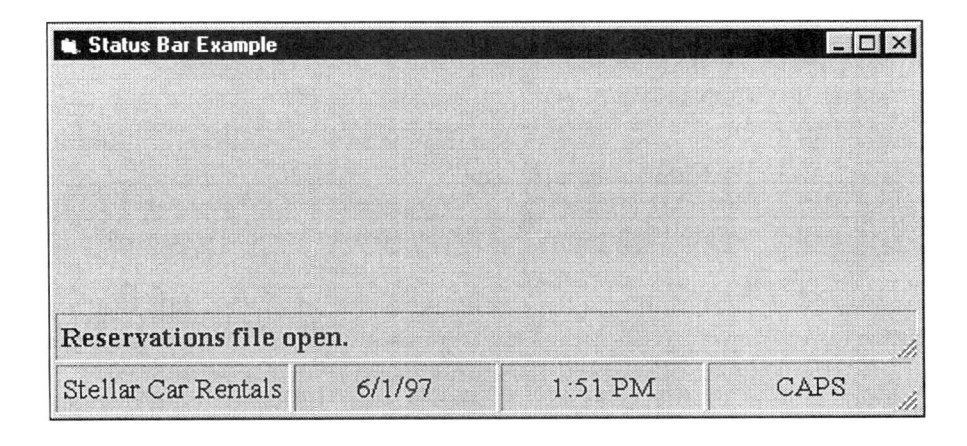

Status bar panels also respond to mouse click events. In the following example, a Select Case statement checks the Index property of the panel object that was clicked. If the user clicks on either the date or time, a message box prompts for replacement values:

```
Private Sub staDateTime_PanelClick(ByVal Panel As Panel)
  Dim temp As String
  Select Case Panel.Index
  Case 2
```

```
        temp = InputBox("Enter a new date:", "Current Date", _
            Format$(Now, "mm/dd/yyyy"))
      If temp <> "" Then
        Date = temp
        Panel.Style = sbrDate   'force refresh
      End If
    Case 3
      temp = InputBox("Enter a new time:", "Time of Day", _
         Format$(Now, "hh:mm"))
      If temp <> "" Then
        Time = temp
        Panel.Style = sbrTime   'force refresh
      End If
  End Select
End Sub
```

8.2.3 Creating Online Help Files

Creating an online help files "from scratch" is a daunting task because a document must be prepared that contains special formatting codes for topic names, jumps between topics, keyword search lists, graphics, and so on. This document is compiled by the Windows *help compiler* (hc.exe, hc30.exe, hc31.exe, or hcp.exe) that is supplied with Visual Basic. After the help file is compiled, it must be displayed by your program when the user presses **F1** or clicks on the program's Help menu. This is done by a Windows library function called **WinHelp**. One of the WinHelp parameters is a command that indicates the action to be taken. Table 6 lists the command constants.

Table 6. WinHelp Command Constants.

Constant	Description
HELP_CONTEXT	Display a numbered topic.
HELP_QUIT	Terminate help.
HELP_INDEX	Display a keyword index.
HELP_HELPONHELP	Display help on using help.
HELP_SETINDEX	Set an alternate index for a help file that has more than one index.
HELP_KEY	Look up and display a single help topic by keyword.
HELP_MULTIKEY	Look up keyword in the alternate table and display its topic.

Fortunately, there are easier ways to create online help: Use one of the many online help creation utility programs such as **RoboHelp**, **DocToHelp**, or **VB/HelpWriter**. New products appear regularly, so search for them on the Web and read product reviews in computer magazines. Often these companies offer a shareware or introductory version that you can download for free. In this chapter, we have selected a product called **VB/HelpWriter Lite** as an example, which can currently be downloaded for free from their Web site.

8.2.4 VB/HelpWriter Lite

The VB/HelpWriter Lite program is available for download on the Internet from Teletech Systems, Inc. (**www.teletech-systems.com**). The file you download will be a self-extracting archive file—just run it and it will launch its own setup program. After installing the program, run VB/Helpwriter for the first time and view its on-line tutorial (we will just nickname it *HelpWriter*).

Before you can create help for your programs, you must have a copy of the Windows help compiler. The file name might be one of the following: (hcp.exe) The help compiler is automatically supplied with the Visual Basic Professional and Enterprise editions, but it may not have been installed when VB was installed. Look for the \HC directory in the Visual Basic home directory; if it is missing, the help compiler was probably not installed.

Before generating a help file for a Visual Basic application, it's helpful to add short help descriptions to the Tag properties of the controls on your program's forms. In the help windows that HelpWriter generates, each control with a non-blank tag is automatically assigned a help topic.

HelpWriter also generates a source code module containing declare statements for Windows API calls, as well as simple Visual Basic procedures that can be called by your program. This source code module must be included in your project before the help window can be activated.

Before running HelpWriter, add a short help text description in the Tag property (or ToolTipText property in VB5) of each control that will be assigned a help file topic. Also, in the Menu Editor, each menu item has a property called the **Help Context ID.** We have not used this ID before, but its purpose is to provide context-sensitive help for users of your applications. HelpWriter will use any existing context IDs when generating help files.

8.2.5 Example: Stellar Car Rental Reservations

Let's create a simple set of help topics for the Reservations window in the Stellar Car Rental program. First, enter topic names into the Tag properties of the form's controls. Open the **stellar.vbp** project file in Visual Basic and display the frmReserv form. Enter a description into the **Tag** property (VB4) or **ToolTipText** property (VB5) of each control. Table 7 lists the control names and suggested descriptions.

Table 7. Tag or ToolTipText Property Values in frmReservations.

Control	Tag/ToolTipText Value
frmReserv	Reservations Window
cboReservationID	Reservation ID Number
cmdAddNew	Adding a New Reservation ID
lblCustomerName	Customer Name
cmdFind	Finding an Existing Customer
txtFields(2)	Rental Date
txtFields(3)	Return Date
cboVehicleType	Type of Vehicle (combo box)
txtFields(5)	Daily Rental Rate
txtFields(6)	Weekly Rental Rate
cmdGetRates	Getting Rental Rates (button)
txtFields(7)	Credit Card Number
cmdNotes	Reservation Notes
lblStatus	Displaying Status Messages
cmdPrices	Viewing all Prices
cmdSave	Saving the Reservation
cmdUpdate	Updating the Reservation
cmdExit	Closing the Window

1. Save the **frmReserv** form and run the VB HelpWriter program; its main window is shown in Figure 25.

Figure 25. VB/HelpWriter Main Window.

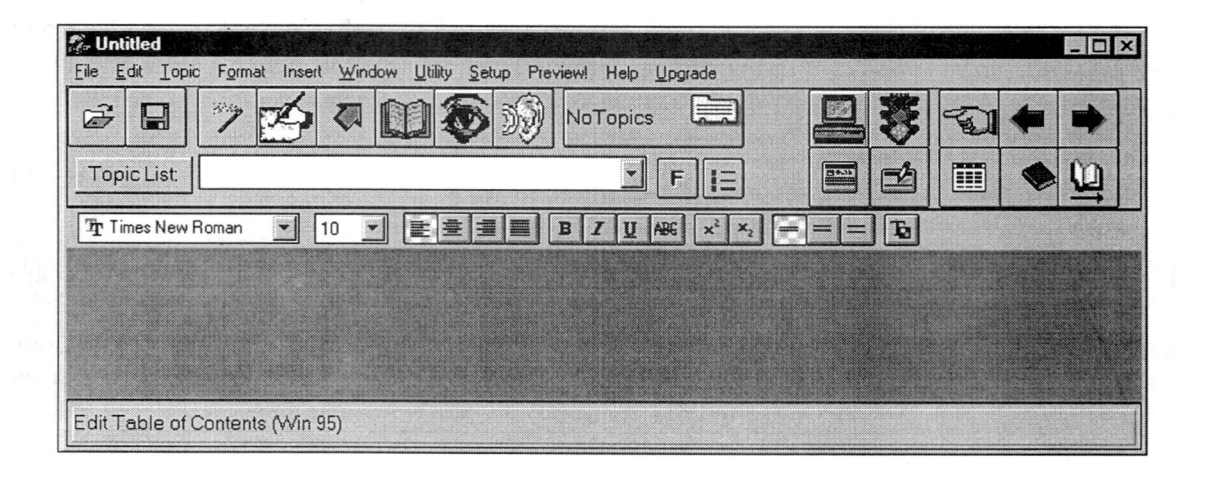

In VBHelpWriter, select **New** from the File menu. Answer **Yes** when asked if you want to create help for a Visual Basic program.

Chap 8: Reports and Online Help

2. When the **Autogenerate Helpfile** window appears, click on the "Select Source Files" button. Select the stellar.vbp project file.

3. When asked if this is the main form of your project, answer **Yes**.

4. You will see a list of all form files in the project. (We have only modified the Tag properties of one of these forms, reserv.frm, so the other forms will be ignored.)

5. Click on the **Next** button.

6. In the **Control Selection** pane of this window, make sure that "Controls with non-empty TAG property" has been checked. Un-check the "Interactive Selection" check box.

7. Click on the **Create Helpfile** button.

8. The following text should appear inside an edit window entitled "Reservation". Each line contains the caption or name of a control, followed by the Tag or ToolTipsText property:

```
Reservation
  Prices              Viewing all Prices
  cboReservationID    Reservation ID Number
  cboVehicleType      Type of Vehicle (combo box)
  txtFields           Weekly Rental Rate
  txtFields           Daily Rental Rate
  txtFields           Return Date
  txtFields           Rental Date
  Update              Updating the Reservation
  Rates               Getting Rental Rates (button)
  Find Customer       Finding an Existing Customer
  Notes               Reservation Notes
  Exit                Closing the Window
  New                 Adding a New Reservation ID
  txtFields           Credit Card Number
  Save                Saving the Reservation
  lblCustomerName     Customer Name
  lblStatus           Displaying Status Messages
```

You may now add additional descriptive text on the lines following each of these topics. The control names themselves are not useful so they can be deleted. The following is a sample paragraph for the **Reservation ID** Number topic:

Reservation ID Number

The reservation ID number is a unique 5-digit number that identifies each reservation saved in the database. When you select an existing reservation number from the combo box, the reservation record will be found in the database and displayed in the Reservation Window.

Select "Run Helpfile Compiler" from the Utility window, or click on the button. The compiler will run in a DOS window, and close automatically. A new button will appear on the Windows 95 task bar (or as an icon in Windows 3.1) with the caption "Windows Help". Click on the button to display your new help file. The Windows help file created in this step is named **reserve.hlp.**

The help file must be linked to the Reservations program. HelpWriter automatically generates a module called **contxtid.bas** containing code that makes it possible for the program to launch the help window.

Open the **stellar.vbp** project file in Visual Basic and notice that the **contxtid.bas** module has already been added to your project. View the code portion of the frmReserv form, and note that the following statement has been added to the Form_Load event handler:

```
SetAppHelp Me.hWnd
```

The following statement has been added to the Form_Unload event handler:

```
QuitHelp
```

Run the program, and while it is running, press **F1** to see the new help file. Right now, you just see a single page of help entitled Reservation Window. In the sections coming up, you will be able to expand this into a help system with jumps between topics.

8.2.6 Adding Help Commands to the Menu

We would also like to launch the help window from the Reservation form's menu. Using the menu editor, create the following definitions:

&File	mnuFile
&New Reservation	mnuFileNew
&Save New Reservation	mnuFileSave
&Update Current Reservation	mnuFileUpdate
&View	mnuView
&Price Table	mnuViewPrice
&Help	mnuHelp
&Contents	mnuHelpContents
&About Stellar Reservations	mnuHelpAbout

Code Implementation. In the Help/Contents menu item's click event, the following statement loads the help file and displays the main help window. This event is also activated when the user presses the **F1** key:

```
Private Sub mnuHelpContents_Click()
    ShowHelpContents
End Sub
```

ShowHelpContents is one of the procedures that were generated by HelpWriter, located in contextid.bas, a code module:

```
Sub ShowHelpContents()
```

Chap 8: Reports and Online Help 359

```
        Dim Result As Variant
        Result = WinHelpByNum(m_hWndMainWindow, App.HelpFile, _
                HELP_CONTENTS, CLng(0))
End Sub
```

WinHelpByNum is an *alias* (alternate name) for the standard WinHelp procedure in the Windows API libarary.

8.2.7 Expanding the Help File

Returning to the help file, it would be a good idea to add more topics to the help file. First, we need a table of contents; from there, we can branch to other topics. Let's create a new topic called **Contents**. Selecting **New Topic** from the Topic menu displays the Create New Topic window (Figure 26). Enter the topic name and select *Contents* as the topic style.

Figure 26. Create New Topic Window.

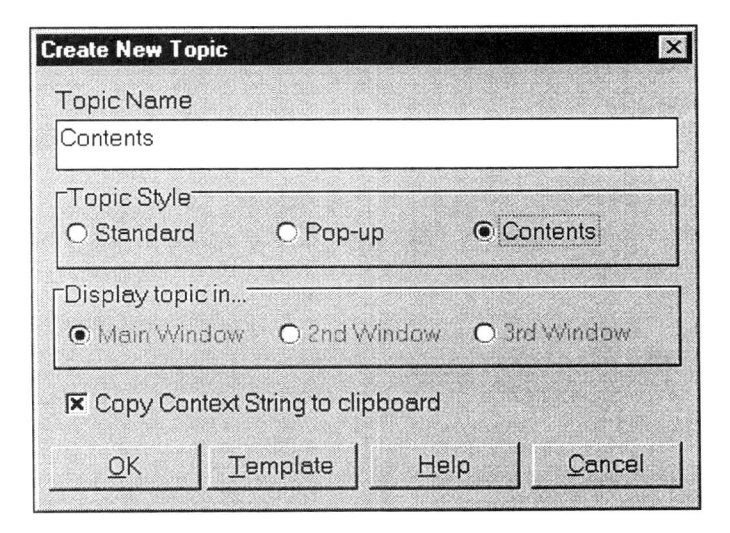

Place the following text in the Contents topic window. To insert the bitmap file, choose Insert Bitmap Graphic from the Insert menu:

> Contents
> {bmc BAR.BMP}
>
> Program Overview
>
> Making Rental Reservations
>
> Processing Vehicle Rentals
>
> Processing Vehicle Returns
>
> Keeping Track of Vehicle Inventory

Create another topic called **Overview** and insert the following text. The same bitmap file has been inserted in this window:

> Overview
> {bmc BAR.BMP}
>
> This program is a database and accompanying application program for the Stellar Car Rental Company. The main program functions are:
>
> · Make advance reservations for car rentals.
> · Create and store an invoice when a car is rented.
> · Keep track of all cars in the company inventory.
> · Update an invoice when a car is returned by the customer.
>
> The database contains a number of tables, each related to a topic or grouping in the application.
>
> The rental process involves four main steps: Reservations, Rentals, Returns, and Inventory.

Project Tree Window. The Project Tree window lists all of the topics in your help project (Figure 27). Topics that contain jumps to other topics have a file folder icon next to them. From this list, you can display a topic's text window by double-clicking on the topic name. Or, you can bring up the topic's properties by right-clicking on the topic name.

Figure 27. Project Tree Window.

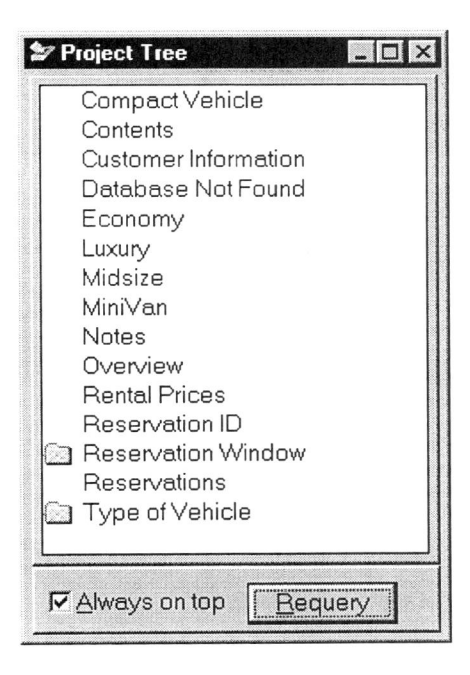

For example, to make the Contents window the startup window, display the topic's properties window (Figure 28). Place a check next to the Startup option, and click on the Close button.

Figure 28. Setting a Topic's Properties.

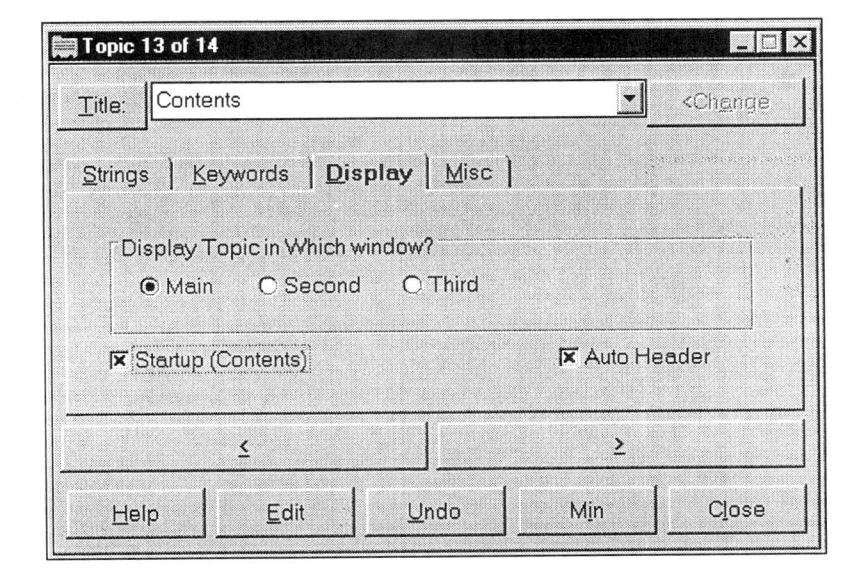

8.2.8 Adding Jumps

To insert a jump to another topic, highlight the word or phrase that will be the jump label, or hypertext button. Then select Insert Jump from the Insert menu. A list of topics will display—click on the topic that will be the target of the jump, click on the Add Jump button, and close the dialog. For example, in Figure 29 we create a jump from the Contents topic to the Overview topic.

Figure 29. Adding a Jump Destination (from Contents to Overview).

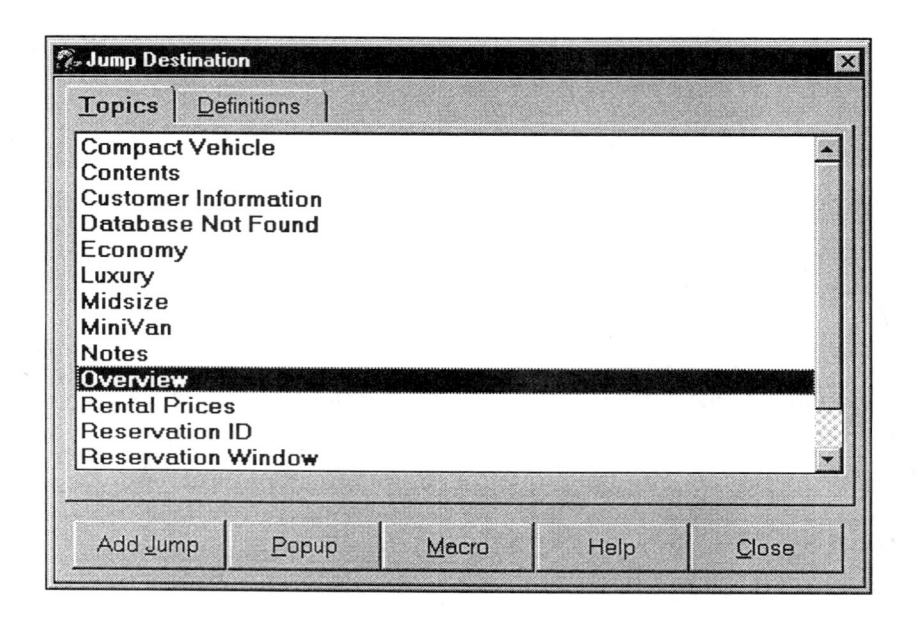

Figure 30 shows the **Contents** window, which the user sees first when clicking on Help. At present, it contains a single jump to the Overview window. Figure 31 shows the finished Overview window.

Figure 30. Help Topic: Table of Contents.

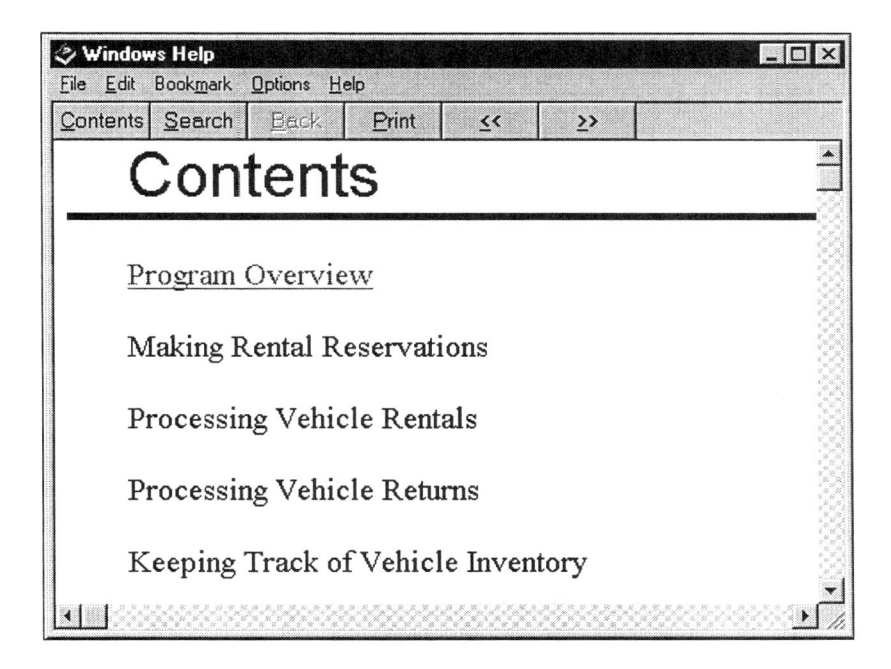

Figure 31. Help Topic: Overview.

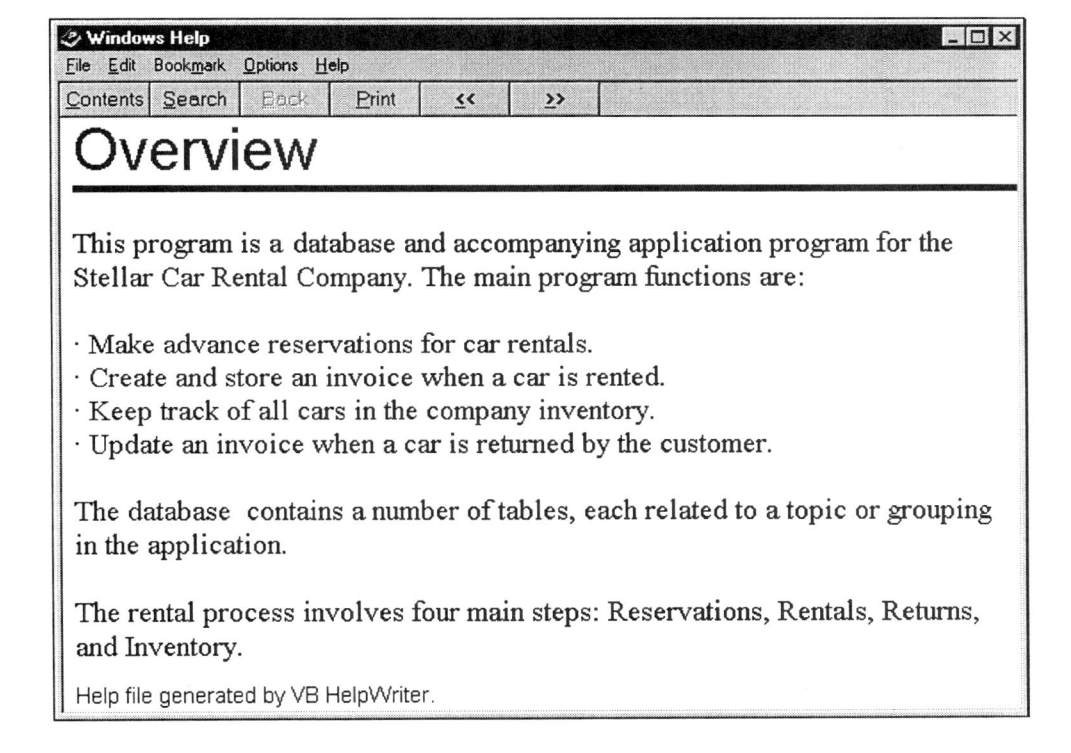

Figure 32 shows the Reservations Window topic, with jumps to images that display the reservations and prices windows. In this topic are headings relating to the various controls on the form. Many of these headings could become jumps to other help window topics.

Figure 32. Reservation Window Topic.

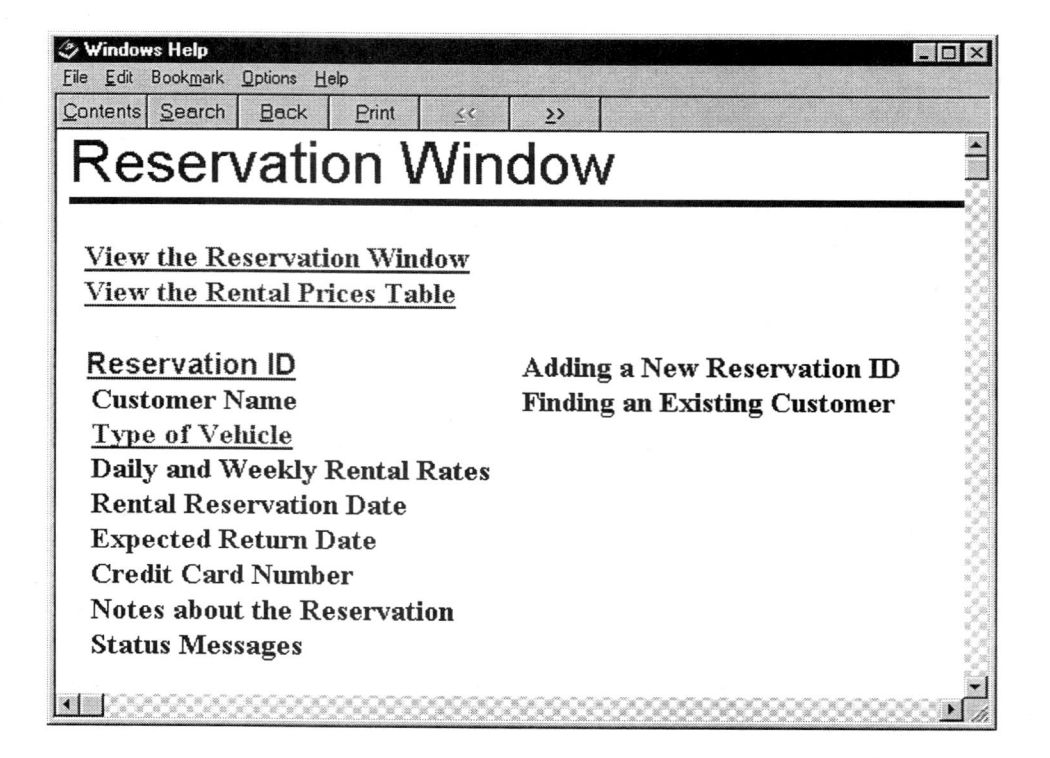

8.3 Review Questions

The following questions refer to Crystal Reports:

1. Which three types of reports may be created in Crystal Reports?
2. Can a report be created from an SQL table in Crystal Reports?
3. How do you insert a database field in a columnar report?
4. Is it possible to use fields from more than one table?
5. How do you add a second database to a report?
6. What is at least one way to change the properties of a field?
7. How do you change the format of a date field to *mm-dd-yyyy*?
8. Which two choices are presented when you click on the Print Preview command?
9. How do you add a title to the report window caption?

10. How do you place text in the report's Page Header area?
11. Name at least four sections of a report.
12. In the Sales report shown in Section 8.1, how did we insert a grand total for the NumberOfTickets column?
13. How do you change the page margins?
14. How do you create a group summary on the ConcertDate field?
15. What is an *exception report?*
16. How do you add record selection criteria to a report?
17. Code a selection formula that finds records having a value of 'ORCH' in the SectionName field of the Reservations table.
18. Code a selection formula that finds records whose ConcertDate field is earlier than January 8, 1997.
19. How do you add group selection criteria to a report?
20. In Section 8.1.3, when we created a group selection formula that selected only concert dates with ticket sales less than 10, what were the arguments passed to the Sum() function?
21. In what ways is a *cross-tab* report different from a columnar report?
22. In Section 8.1.4, which field was summarized by the cross-tab report?

The following questions refer to the Crystal Reports custom control:

23. At a minimum, which properties must be set before a report can be displayed from a Visual Basic program?
24. What are the three possible output formats, and which property must be set to determine the output format?
25. If the destination will be the printer, how do you determine the number of copies to be printed?
26. If the destination will be a file, which two special properties must be assigned values?
27. Which property holds a record selection formula?
28. Name at least six different types of file formats that are available when a report is printed directly to a file.
29. Which print file formats are suitable for Internet Web pages?
30. Is it possible to print a report directly to a Word for Windows document?
31. What happens when you print a report to a file, but the report filename already exists?
32. If an error occurs while printing a report, how can you retrieve the error number and a string containing an error message?

The following questions refer to the User Assistance Model:

33. Name six types of user assistance mentioned in the VB5 documentation.

34. How do you attach a tool tip to a command button?
35. How might a *wizard* be useful in a program that implements a cooking recipe?

The following questions refer to the StatusBar control:

36. How might you use a status bar in a Visual Basic program?
37. What are the names of the individual rectangles within a StatusBar control?
38. What two options are available for a StatusBar's Style property?
39. What can be stored in a Panel object?
40. Which panel property must be set before the panel can display the current date? What is the name of the constant that is assigned to this property?
41. Write a statement that will cause the first panel in a status bar to resize itself according to the length of the text placed in the panel.
42. Write a For-Next loop that will cause all five panels in a status bar to automatically adjust their widths to the enclosing form's width when the form is resized.
43. Is it possible to store a bitmap and some text within the same panel?
44. In the sample StatusBar program in Section 8.2.2, what actions are carried out when the user clicks on the panel containing the date?
45. Which StatusBar property could be set if you want the entire status bar to display just a single panel of text?

The following questions refer to creating online help files with VB/HelpWriter:

46. How does a document in rich-text format get translated into a Windows help file (*filename*.hlp)?
47. Which Windows library function loads and displays a help file?
48. In VB4, how does VB/HelpWriter use the Tag property? Which property should be used in VB5 to do the same thing?
49. What is the purpose of the contxid.bas file that is created by VB/HelpWriter?
50. What statement must be placed in Form_Load to identify the name of the help file used by your program?
51. What statement is placed in Form_Unload, to release the help file?
52. What is the name of the procedure in contxid.bas that displays the Help Table of Contents?
53. What is the use of the Project Tree Window in Figure 27?
54. How do you display the properties window for a help topic?
55. How do you insert a jump from the current help topic to another topic?
56. How do you insert a graphics bitmap in a help window?
57. When learning how to use a program, which type of Help would you rather use—the usual Windows HLP file, or a web browser such as Netscape or Internet Explorer?

58. What advantages would there be, if any, to placing application help files on the World Wide Web?

8.4 Chapter Exercises

8.4.1 Mail-Order Computer Sales

The Mail-Order Computer Sales program from Chapter 5 was designed to let a salesperson configure a computer system for a customer. One of the exercises at the end of Chapter 5 was to create an Invoice table containing the customer ID, date, invoice number configured price, model ID, and options.

Use Crystal Reports to produce a report showing all computer sales from the Invoice table.

8.4.2 Kyoshi Karate School - Member Report

The Kyoshi Karate School (from the Chapter 5 exercises) needs to have a membership report that lists the ID numbers, last and first names, birth dates, and phone numbers of its members. The records should be sorted in ascending order by last name (see a sample in Figure 33). Once you have designed this report, place a Crystal Reports control on the Membership window and use a menu command to launch the report. Let the user select the mode of output: disk, screen, or printer.

Figure 33. Membership Listing, Alphabetical.

Membership Listing

ID	lastName	firstName	phone	birthDate
10	Chong	Anne	232-2323	
32	Flinstone	Fred	809-8837	2/20/04
2	Gonzalez	Aldo	123-2345	6/ 6/76
12	Hasegawa	Elaine	313-34554	2/20/75
30	Howe	James	414-2345	
33	John	Baker		5/20/81
15	Russell	Brian	646-93873	5/20/74
1	Smith	LaMar	111-2222	2/20/72

8.4.3 Kyoshi Karate School - Member Report Enhancements

Improve the Membership Report completed in the previous exercise: Concantenate the first and last names into a single string, and display the report. Capitalize all of the column titles. Display the current date on the report.

8.4.4 Kyoshi Karate School - Dues Payments

The Kyoshi Karate School has been collecting dues payments from members for some time. The Payments table consists of three columns: member name, payment date, and payment amount. For this exercise, create a *cross-tab* report using Crystal Reports that summarizes the dues payments for each member. An example is shown in Figure 34. This type of report works best if there are a limited number of payment dates, because each payment date creates a new column. Place a Crystal Reports control on the Membership form and display the report. Give the user the choice of outputting the report to the screen, to a disk file, or directly to the printer. If the output goes to disk, store the file in HTML format, suitable for display by a Web browser.

Figure 34. Kyoshi Karate Dues Payments Report.

Membership Dues Payments

	10/20/97	11/20/97	12/20/97	1/16/98	2/16/98	Total
Baker, John	$0.00	$50.00	$150.00	$0.00	$0.00	$200.00
Gonzalez, Aldo	$0.00	$0.00	$0.00	$25.00	$35.00	$60.00
Smith, LaMar	$150.00	$200.00	$0.00	$45.00	$135.00	$530.00
Total	$150.00	$250.00	$150.00	$70.00	$170.00	$790.00

8.4.5 Kyoshi Karate School - Address Labels

Create a Mailing Labels report for the Kyoshi Karate School, using Crystal Reports. The Membership table will provide the data.

8.4.6 Kyoshi Karate Class Schedule

Create a report listing the class schedule table from the Karate Exercises in Chapter 5. The primary sort should be by the day number, and the secondary sort should be by the class start time. Give the user the option of printing the report to a window, to the printer, or to a file in any of the formats that were shown in Figure 21 in the section dealing with concert ticket reports.

9 Object Linking and Embedding (OLE)

Chapter Contents

OLE Fundamentals
    Embedding and Linking
    Insertable Objects
    Example: Creating a WordPad Document
OLE Container Control
    Example: Creating an Embedded Word Object
    Example: Creating an Embedded Excel Worksheet
    CreateLink Method
OLE Container Program
    Program Specifications
    Creating a New Excel Worksheet
    Creating a New Word Document
    Inserting an Excel Worksheet
    Inserting a Word Document
    Program Implementation
OLE Automation
    Visual Basic for Applications
    Example: Creating a Word Document
    Word Classes, Properties, and Methods
    OLE Automation with Excel
    Excel: Statistical Score Analysis
College Admissions Program
    Program Specifications
    Program Design
    Program Implementation
    Conclusion
Review Questions
Chapter Exercises

9.1 OLE Fundamentals

Object linking and embedding (OLE) allows data created by different programs to be interconnected. An *OLE container* is a program or application that contains links and/or embedded copies of objects created by other programs. Both the *compound document*, as it is often called, and the other programs must support a protocol known as *OLE*.

OLE is a direct descendant of DDE (*Dynamic Data Exchange*), which allows two or more running programs to pass data back and forth as strings. DDE is nearly obsolete because of its slow execution speed, instability, and severe restrictions.

OLE History. OLE 1.0, introduced a few years ago, was a major improvement over DDE because it allowed copies of documents, spreadsheets, and other data to be inserted, displayed, and modified inside OLE containers. But OLE 1.0 was somewhat slow and used a great deal of memory, so it was only gradually accepted by the programming community, while DDE continued to be used.

OLE 2.0, the newest incarnation of OLE, runs faster and uses less memory than Version 1.0. Most important, it supports *OLE automation*, the ability of programs to expose their objects, properties, and methods to other programs. The Microsoft DAO database object, for example, is an OLE 2.0 server. That is why Visual Basic programs can create Database, TableDef, QueryDef, and Recordset objects, and can call methods such as CreateDatabase, OpenRecordset, and CreateQueryDef.

Applications. Imagine that you are writing a Visual Basic program that displays a company's quarterly sales summary that includes the following elements: an Excel spreadsheet containing the sales data, a piechart that graphically displays the sales, a popup calendar for scheduling the next sales meeting, and several paragraphs that summarize the sales results. Finally, you might like to let the user click on an icon and attach a short note in response to your sales summary. The text portion of the memo would be created by Microsoft Word; the spreadsheet and chart would be created by Excel, the calendar could be created by the Calendar program, and the short response note could be created by WordPad.

Similarly, when creating a multimedia tutorial, you might like to include text, pictures music, a video clip, and sound effects. A database could be used to store all these elements as OLE objects, and SQL statements could be used to search the database for relevant keywords. All of the objects mentioned in these two examples can be incorporated into Visual Basic programs, using OLE containers.

Using OLE Objects. There are three ways to use OLE objects in a Visual Basic program:
- Select a custom control from the Toolbox window that supports the type of object you wish to create. The control is also called an *insertable object*.
- Select the OLE container control from the Toolbox window and place a copy of it on a form. This control can hold various types of OLE objects such as Word documents, Visio drawings, Excel worksheets, sound files, and movie clips.
- Using programming code, call the CreateObject and GetObject procedures that activate applications and create the objects you need. For example, you could use CreateObject to activate Microsoft Excel, which would create a new worksheet object. In this role, Excel would be called an *OLE automation server*.

An *OLE object* is a discrete unit of data supplied by an application. The application *exposes* the object, meaning that it makes the object available to other programs. The Windows Paint program, for example, exposes a bitmap picture. Excel exposes charts, worksheets, and named ranges of cells within worksheets.

9.1.1 Embedding and Linking

The two basic types of OLE objects that can be manipulated by an OLE container application are *embedded objects* and *linked objects*.

An *embedded object* stores all of its data inside the container application. In other words, if a Visual Basic program is a container for a Word document, the entire document is stored inside the Visual Basic program, along with the name of the program that created the object, Microsoft Word. When the user selects the embedded object, Word is activated and the user can edit the document. Embedded objects can be created in Visual Basic either with the OLE container control or as *insertable objects,* which are custom controls that activate applications such as Word or Excel.

A *linked object* stores its data outside the container application, in a separate file that was created by the program that supplied the object. For example, a worksheet file created by Excel can be a linked object. The container application stores only an image of the data, along with link references to the file containing the actual object. Any application containing a link to the same object can display and update the data. The modified file will be displayed in all applications that are linked to it. You must use an OLE container control to create a linked object.

One factor to be taken into consideration is this: whether or not the user of a OLE container application has copies of the necessary software on their system that would allow them to edit the contents of an OLE container. The examples in this chapter require Word 97 and Excel 97; the remaining programs mentioned are already supplied with Windows.

9.1.2 Insertable Objects

Using custom controls, you can create *insertable objects* and place them directly on Visual Basic forms. The available list of insertable objects can be found by selecting the Tools/Custom controls menu command in VB4. Using the checkboxes in this dialog box, select only "insertable objects" (Figure 1).

To add any of these objects to the Visual Basic toolbox, place a check next to their names and click the OK button. For example, an object called "Microsoft Excel 8.0 Object Library" appears in the list. Each one of these objects has been made available by an application program. Naturally, the list of available insertable objects varies from one system to another, depending on which applications are installed.

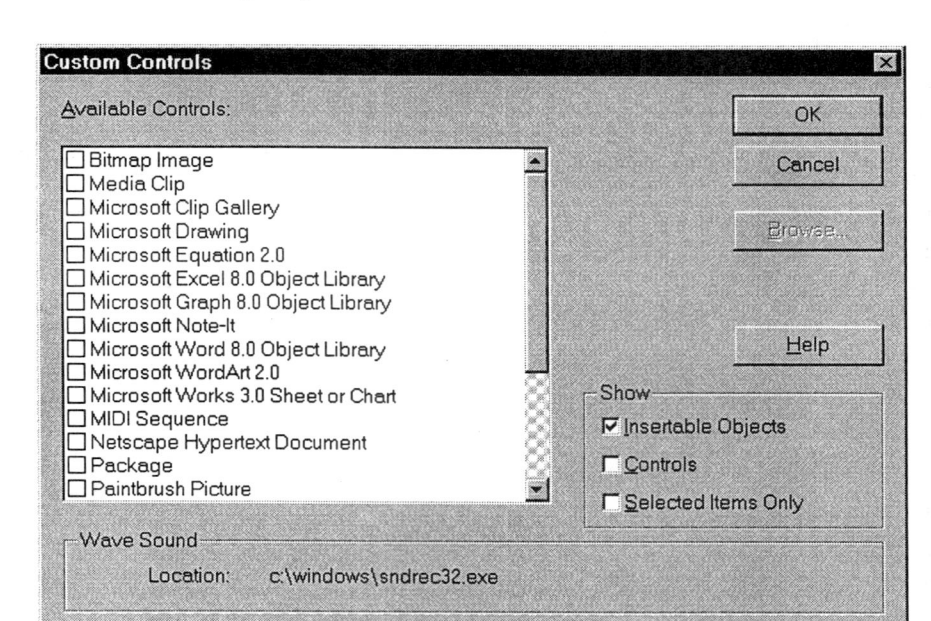

Figure 1. Insertable Objects, Custom Controls in VB4.

You can view the object properties and methods of any installed object or custom control with the **Object Browser**. In Figure 2, for example, the Excel 8.0 object library has been selected.

Figure 2. Excel 8.0 Classes and Modules.

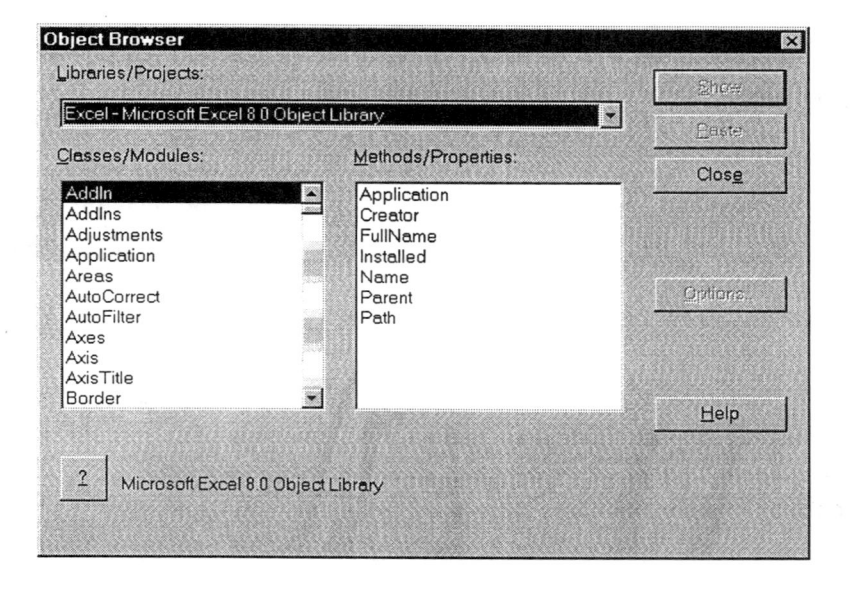

9.1.3 Example: Creating a WordPad Document

We're going to insert an embedded WordPad document (WordPad.exe is part of Windows 95, usually in the **C:\Program Files\Accessories** folder). WordPad is a simple text editor that handles text files, Word 6.0 documents, Windows Write, and rich text (RTF) files.

Create a new project and add a WordPad control to the Visual Basic toolbox. Click on the control and place it on the main form. As soon as you do this, WordPad is activated, and its menu appears on the form's menu bar. Type in the line of text shown in Figure 3. After typing in some text, run the program and observe that the text you typed is displayed directly on the form.

Figure 3. Creating a WordPad Document.

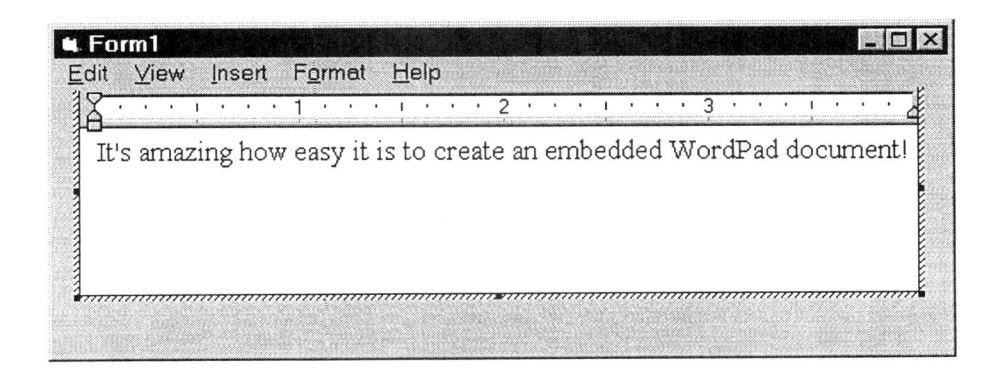

Activating an Object. In run mode, the user can double-click on the text to *activate* the embedded object. This starts up the WordPad program, allowing the object to be modified. But when the program terminates, any modifications made by the user are not saved. There is no standard way of saving objects in custom controls, and the WordPad Document control has no methods for doing so. This provides a good reason for us to learn how to use the OLE container control, because it has easy to use methods that load and save OLE objects in a standard file format.

9.2 OLE Container Control

The OLE container control was introduced in Visual Basic 4.0 as a general-purpose tool for inserting any type of registered OLE object. The OLE container comes with an extensive set of properties and methods. Objects can be either linked or embedded, and the OLE container can be bound to a data control. This means that OLE objects can be stored in databases.

9.2.1 Example: Creating an Embedded Word Object

The easiest way to create an embedded object is to name the object's type in design mode at the same time the OLE container is placed on the form. The following steps show how to do this:

Step 1. Create a new form called frmWord and add the following menu:

```
&File       mnuFile
  E&xit     mnuFileExit
```

Set the NegotiatePosition property of mnuFile to 1 (Left). Drag an OLE container control onto the form so that it fills most of the form. It will resemble a text box (Figure 4).

Figure 4. OLE Container, Word Document.

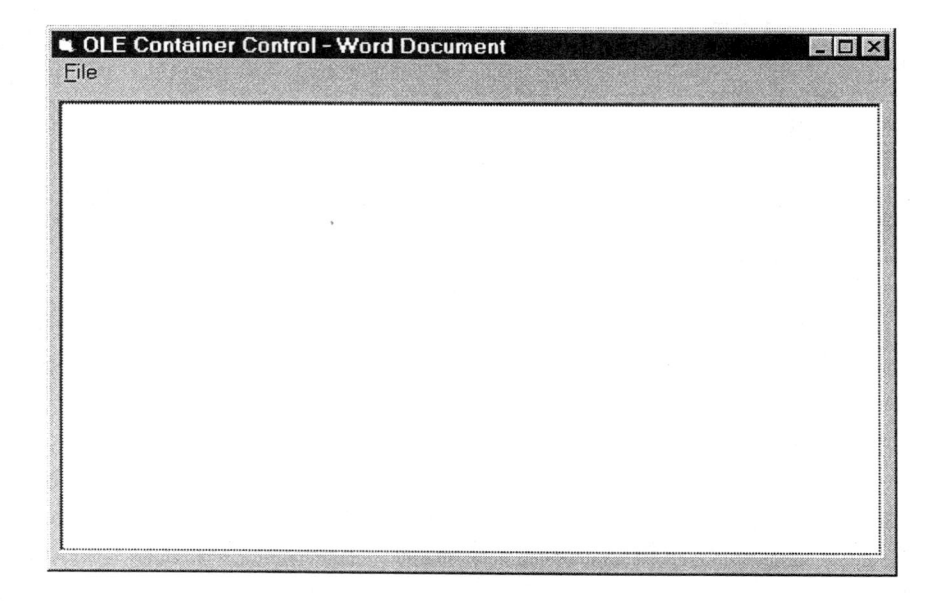

Immediately, the **Insert Object** window pops up; select **Microsoft Word Document** and click OK (Figure 5).

Figure 5. Insert Object Dialog (VB 4).

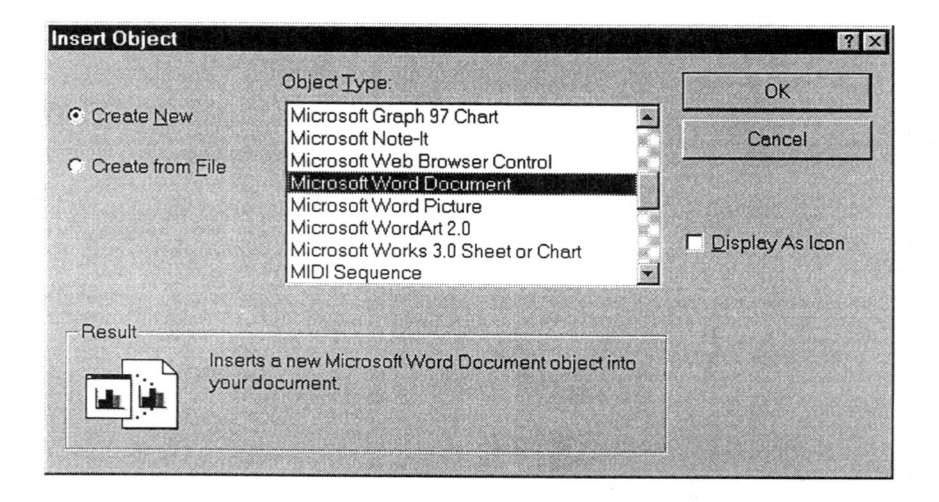

The **Create New** option creates an embedded object; the **Create From File** option creates a linked object. When you click OK, Word is immediately activated, and a simplified Word menu is displayed.

Step 2. Write a short note, shown in Figure 6.

Figure 6. Editing the OLE Word Document.

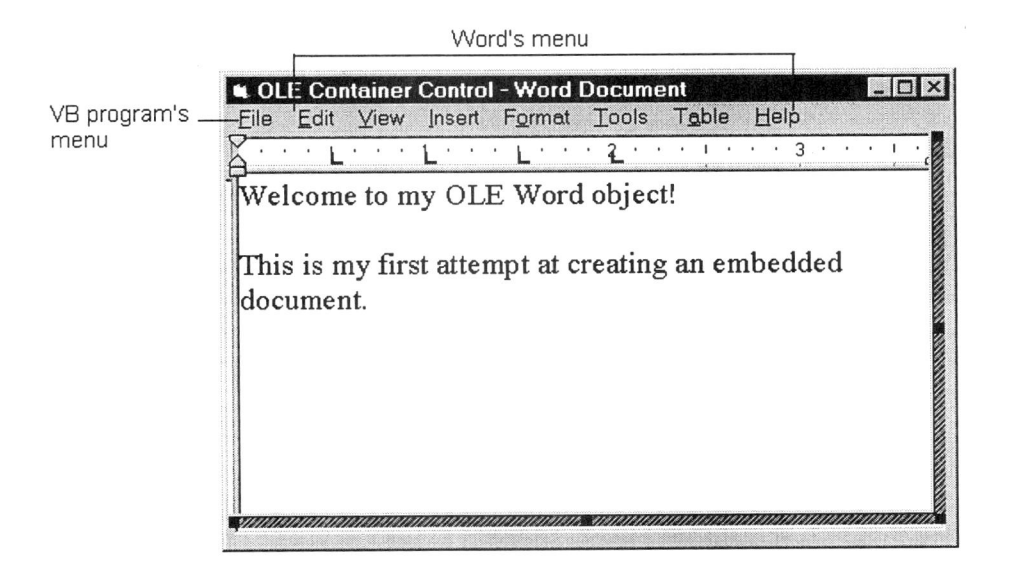

Step 3. Set the Name property of the OLE container control to **oleWord**. Run the program and observe in Figure 7 that the Word menu has disappeared, leaving only the OLE container's text on the form. Or, you can make the container a little less obvious by setting the OLE container's BorderStyle to none and BackColor to the same color as the form's background. When the user double-clicks on the text, the object is activated and the text can be modified.

Figure 7. Editing OLE Word Document at Run Time.

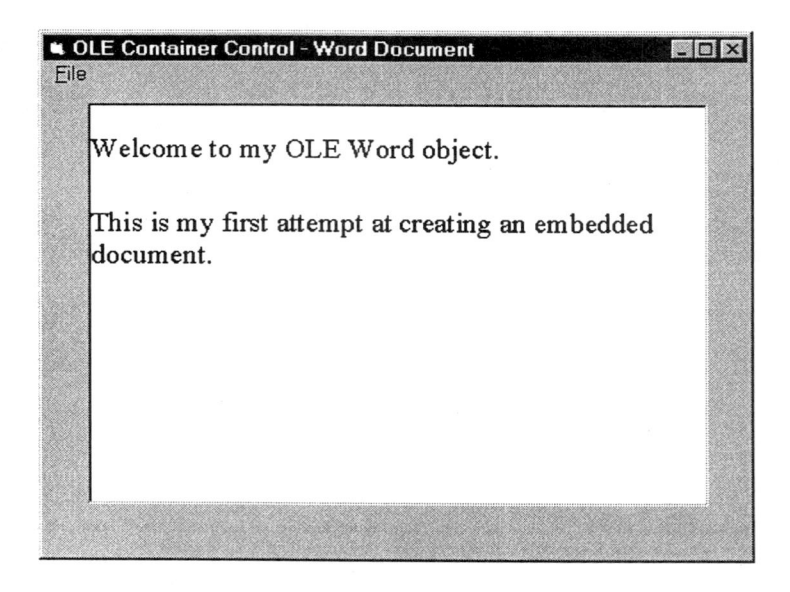

NegotiateMenus Property. Notice that the Word menu does not appear when the user edits the document. If you want an embedded object's menu to appear at runtime when the user activates the object, you must set the form's NegotiateMenus property to True.

NegotiatePosition Property. If you create a menu on the enclosing form of an OLE control, you can use the **NegotiatePosition** property of individual submenus to determine whether or not they will be displayed along with the activated object's menu. By default, the NegotiatePosition property equals 0 (none); if you change it to 1 (Left), 2 (Middle), or 3 (Right), the submenu will remain on the menu bar when the OLE object is activated.

Step 4. Set the NegotiateMenus property to True on the main form. Create the following menu on the form and set the NegotiatePosition property of mnuFile to 1 (left):

```
    &File       mnuFile
      &Save     mnuFileSave
      &Open     mnuFileOpen
      E&xit     mnuFileExit
```

Run the program, activate the OLE object, and notice that the File menu appears at the left side of Word's menu.

NegotiateToolbars Property. The NegotiateToolbars property on an MDI form is useful because it lets you choose whether the OLE object's tool bars will appear on the parent window. The MDI parent form is not required to already have a tool bar. Toolbars are usually contained in a picture box on the parent form. The NegotiateToolbars property of the picture box determines whether the existing parent tool bar is completely replaced by the OLE object's toolbar.

Saving an OLE Container Object. The OLE control's SaveToFile method saves the embedded object to a binary file in OLE 2.0 format. Here, the object is saved in a file called sample.bin:

```
Private Sub mnuFileSave_Click()
  Open "sample.bin" For Binary As #1
  oleWord.SaveToFile 1
  Close 1
End Sub
```

An OLE container control may also be bound to a Data control, and OLE objects can be stored in databases.

Loading an OLE Container Object. The OLE control's LoadFromFile method loads an embedded object from an OLE 2.0 binary file called sample.bin:

```
Open "sample.bin" For Binary As #1
oleWord.LoadFromFile 1
Close 1
```

Right-Clicking the Mouse. Either in design mode or run mode, you can edit an embedded document by right-clicking the mouse on the object. This activates a pop-up menu with at least two choices: Edit and Open. Select the Open command, and a copy of Word will run, with the document displayed in it. Best of all, Word's complete **File** menu will be available, so you can save or print the object.

9.2.2 Example: Creating an Embedded Excel Worksheet

You can also create an embedded object inside an OLE control at runtime, by using the CreateEmbed method. This is a flexible approach because it allows the same OLE container to hold different types of objects, although it can only hold one object at a time.

CreateEmbed Method. There are two basic forms of the CreateEmbed method. You can either specify a filename which will be used as a template for the embedded object, or you can specify a class name:

```
oleControl.CreateEmbed sourceFilename
oleControl.CreateEmbed "",class
```

This method can be used in lieu of setting the Class and SourceDoc properties.

For example, using a Word document called memo.doc as a template, the following statement would place a copy of the document inside the OLE control:

```
OLE1.CreateEmbed "memo.doc"
```

The OLE control would immediately display memo.doc.

Using a Class Name. The second form of the CreateEmbed method takes a class name as a parameter. Class names are placed in the Windows registry by installation programs for

OLE-aware programs. To view a list of available class names, select the OLE control, display the properties window, and click the button next to the Class property. A listbox will display a list of all registered class names (Figure 8).

Figure 8. Registered Class Names (sample).

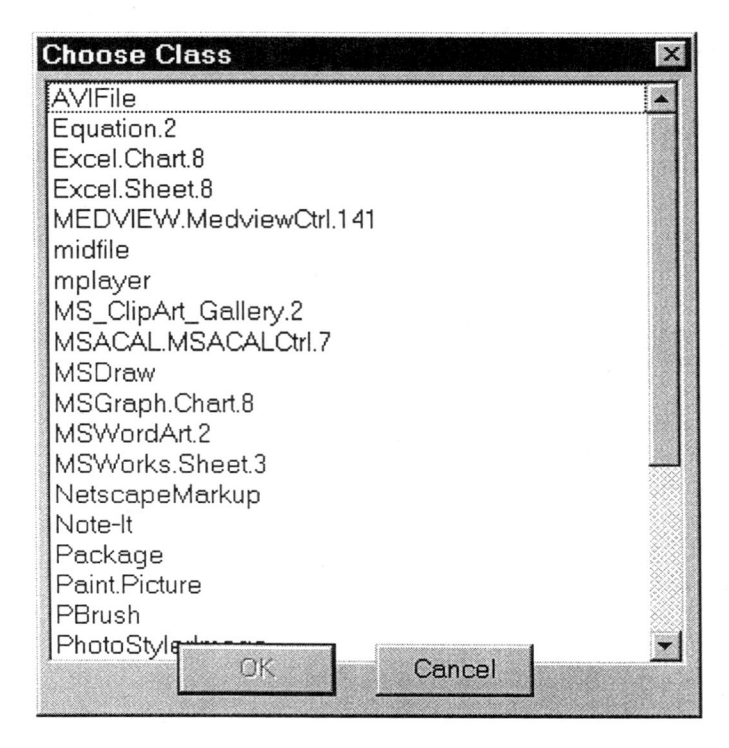

```
Choose Class
AVIFile
Equation.2
Excel.Chart.8
Excel.Sheet.8
MEDVIEW.MedviewCtrl.141
midfile
mplayer
MS_ClipArt_Gallery.2
MSACAL.MSACALCtrl.7
MSDraw
MSGraph.Chart.8
MSWordArt.2
MSWorks.Sheet.3
NetscapeMarkup
Note-It
Package
Paint.Picture
PBrush
PhotoStyle
        OK          Cancel
```

The following statement would create a new Word document:

```
OLE1.CreateEmbed "", "Word.Document.8"
```

The following statements would create an Excel chart and an Excel worksheet:

```
OLE1.CreateEmbed "", "Excel.Chart.8"
OLE1.CreateEmbed "", "Excel.Sheet.8"
```

Sample Chart. Try the following hands-on example: Create a new form and place two OLE containers on it. When the Insert Document window appears, click on the Cancel button. Place the following statements inside Form_Load:

```
OLE1.CreateEmbed "", "Excel.Chart.8"
OLE2.CreateEmbed "", "Excel.Chart.8"
```

Set the SizeMode property of both controls to AutoSize. This will make the controls automatically size themselves to the embedded chart.

Run the program. The same chart, with sample data, will appear in both OLE containers (Figure 9). Activate the container on top, and click on the tab labeled "Sheet 1".

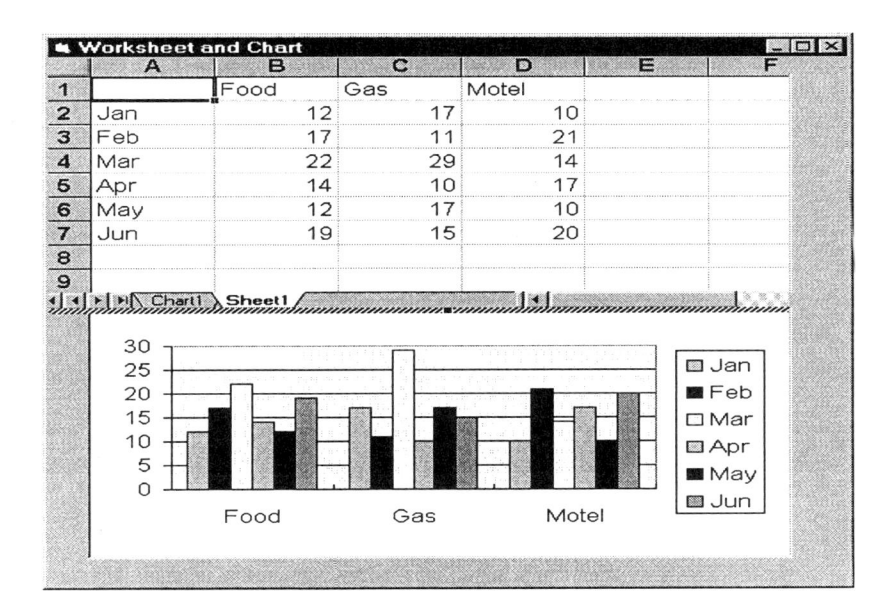

Figure 9. Worksheet and Chart Containers.

Click once on the lower OLE control to deactivate the worksheet. The form will display the worksheet and the chart that graphically represents the data.

The Windows clipboard can easily be used to transfer objects between OLE controls and between other Windows applications that support OLE. For example, add a command button to the current form and write the following statements in its click event that copy the chart in OLE1 to the clipboard and paste the clipboard into OLE2:

```
OLE1.Copy
OLE2.Paste
```

To test this, modify one of the numbers in the worksheet in OLE1. Click the command button, and notice that OLE2 now has the same change that you made to OLE1.

SizeMode Property. The SizeMode property contains an integer that determines how the OLE container is sized, or how its image is displayed when it contains an object. In our examples, the SizeMode property was set to AutoSize. The property can be set either in design mode or at run time to one of the values shown in Table 1.

Table 1. SizeMode Property Values.

SizeMode	Description
Clip	The object, displayed in actual size, is clipped to the control's borders. (vbOLESizeClip)
Stretch	The object is sized to fill the control, which may alter the object's proportions. (vbOLESizeStretch)
Autosize	The control is resized to display the entire object. (vbOLESizeAutoSize)
Zoom	The object is resized to fill the container as much as possible, while still retaining its original proportions. (vbOLESizeStretch)

In general, the Autosize mode is best when inserting an existing spreadsheet or document, because the user can expand the form holding the OLE control at runtime. The OLE control expands automatically as far as it needs to, up to the right and bottom borders of the enclosing form.

AutoActivate Property. The AutoActivate property controls the way in which the user can activate an OLE object for editing. It can be set in either design mode or run mode. The default is vbOLEActivateDoubleclick, meaning that the user can double-click the mouse to activate the object. If you set the property to vbOLEActivateManual, the user cannot activate the object.

DoVerb Method. The DoVerb method can be used to open an OLE object for some action, usually editing. The main reason for using DoVerb is if the AutoActivate property is set to *manual*, the program can open the object with a statement such as the following:

```
OLE1.DoVerb vbOLEShow
```

The vbOLEShow constant specifically opens the object for editing. The vbOLEPrimary constant, on the other hand, opens the object for its default action:

```
OLE1.DoVerb vbOLEPrimary
```

Loading an Existing Worksheet. The following statements load an Excel worksheet and set the SizeMode property to Clip:

```
ole1.SizeMode = vbOLESizeClip
ole1.CreateEmbed "budget.xls"
```

Before the control is activated by the user, it appears as ordinary text (Figure 10).

Figure 10. Embedded Expenses Worksheet Example.

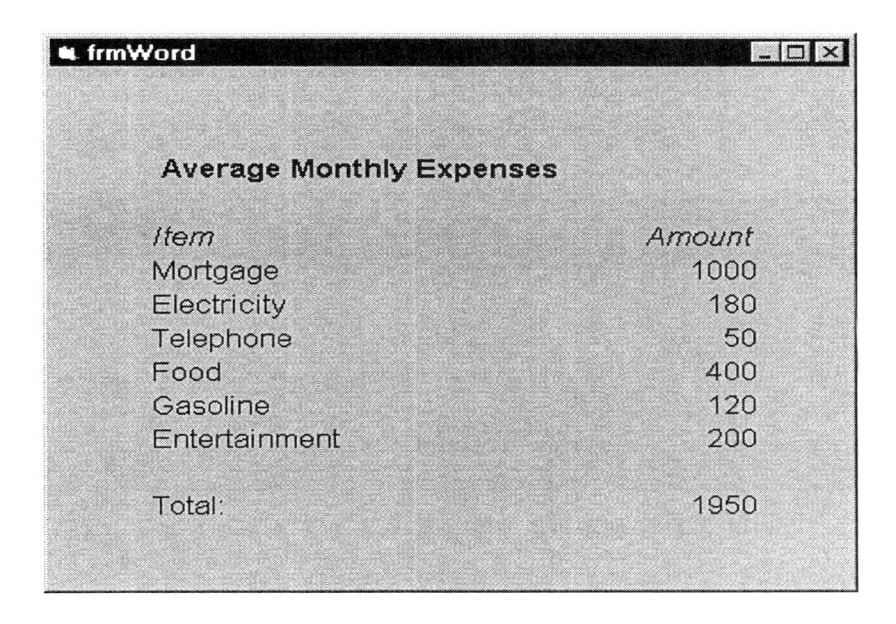

When activated by the user, it appears as a spreadsheet that can be modified (Figure 11). The user can change the spreadsheet's size by dragging the handles along the sides. Individual numbers can be changed, causing the total to recalculate.

Figure 11. In-Place Editing of the Expenses Worksheet.

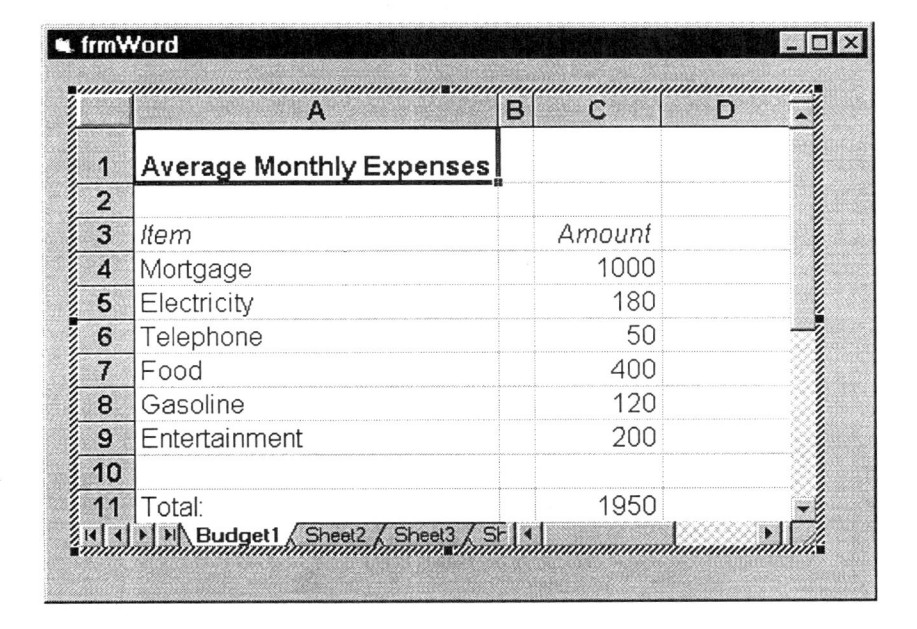

9.2.3 CreateLink Method

The CreateLink method creates a linked object from the contents of a file. The general syntax is:

```
oleControl.CreateLink sourceDoc [,sourceItem]
```

where *sourceDoc* is the filename from which the OLE control will be linked, and *sourceItem* names the data within the file that will be linked; *sourceItem* is optional. The values placed in the sourceDoc and sourceItem parameters override the properties by the same names in the OLE control.

When an object is created with this method, the OLE container control displays an image of the file specified by the SourceDoc property. If the OLE object is saved, only the link references are saved, because the original document is saved by its own application.

For example, the following statement creates a link to the budget.xls worksheet file:

```
OLE1.CreateLink "budget.xls"
```

This displays the worksheet on the OLE control as if it were an embedded object, but the difference becomes clear when the user activates the object. The Excel program itself starts up, allowing the user full access to its menus and toolbars (Figure 12).

Figure 12. Linked Worksheet Example.

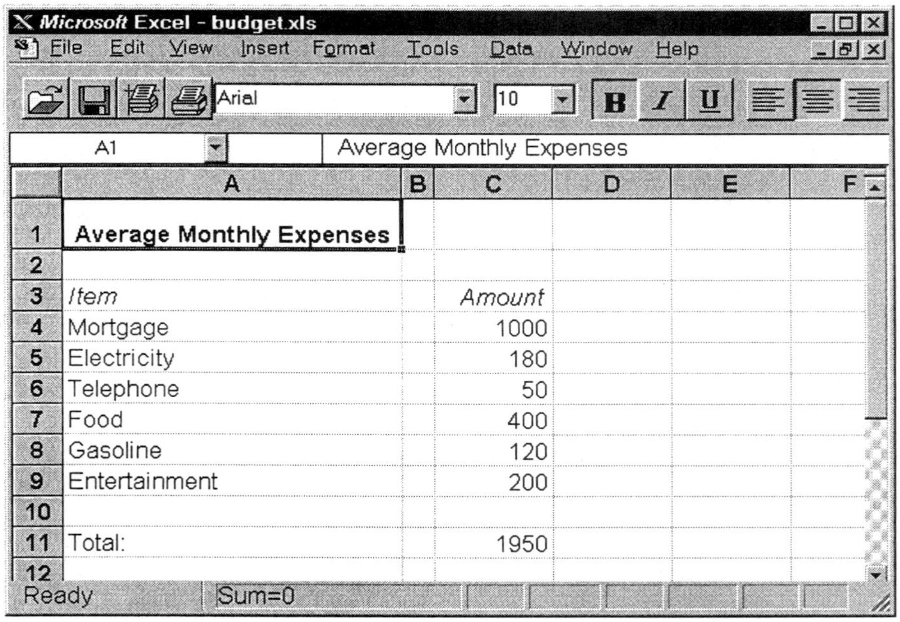

Chap 9: Object Linking and Embedding (OLE) 383

If the user makes any changes to the sheet and saves it in Excel, the link to the Visual Basic program is updated. Any other OLE links that exist between the source document and other containers are also updated.

Update, Delete, and Close. If another application should modify the linked object at the same time that our program is displaying it, it would be necessary to call the **Update** method to display the most recent version of the object. For example:

```
OLE1.Update
```

The **Delete** method immediately deletes the object and frees the memory used by it. Otherwise, an OLE object would be deleted automatically when the form was closed or when replaced by another object (using CreateLink or CreateEmbed).

The **Close** method, useful only with embedded objects, terminates the connection to the application that created the object. From the user's point of view, the Close method simply deactivates the OLE control. If the object is inactive already, Close has no effect.

9.3 OLE Container Program

9.3.1 Program Specifications

Let's write a simple program with an OLE container control that lets the user do the following:

- Create a new Excel Worksheet or Chart.
- Create a new Word Document.
- Open an existing Excel Worksheet.
- Open an exsiting Word Document.

Each of the objects will be embedded, not linked.

9.3.2 Creating a New Excel Worksheet

The main window contains only an OLE container control and a File menu. To create a worksheet, the user selects the File/New/Worksheet menu command (Figure 13). After the user clicks on File/Close, the embedded worksheet displays only its data.

Figure 13. Creating a New Worksheet.

9.3.3 Creating a New Word Document

To create the following document, the user selects the File/New Document menu command (Figure 14).

Figure 14. Creating a New Word Document.

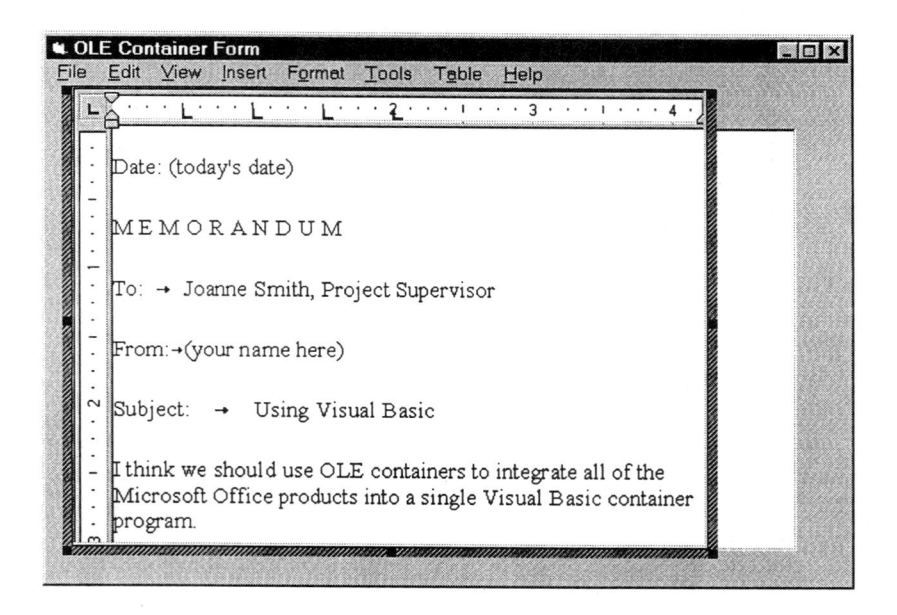

9.3.4 Inserting an Excel Worksheet

To insert an existing worksheet, the user selects the File/Insert/Worksheet command. This brings up a File/Open dialog box, in which the user selects a worksheet file to insert. The selected file is embedded in the OLE control, and is not activated until the user double-clicks (Figure 15).

Figure 15. The Embedded Budget Worksheet.

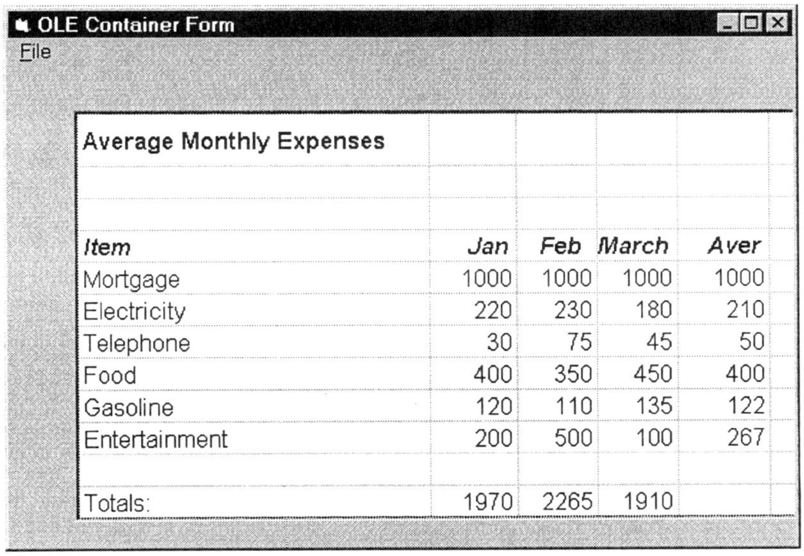

Average Monthly Expenses				
Item	*Jan*	*Feb*	*March*	*Aver*
Mortgage	1000	1000	1000	1000
Electricity	220	230	180	210
Telephone	30	75	45	50
Food	400	350	450	400
Gasoline	120	110	135	122
Entertainment	200	500	100	267
Totals:	1970	2265	1910	

9.3.5 Inserting a Word Document

To insert an existing Word document, the user selects the File/Insert/Document command. Again, a File/Open dialog box lets the user select a document file, and the file is embedded in the OLE control. Word automatically selects the "Page" view, shown in Figure 16 holding Chapter 1 from this book. Because the SizeMode of the OLE control is set to AutoSize, the OLE control expands as much as it is able to without going beyond the edge of the form. When the user resizes the form, the OLE control automatically resizes itself. When the user double-clicks on the document, the Word menu activates and the document may be edited.

Figure 16. Resizing a Form Containing a Document.

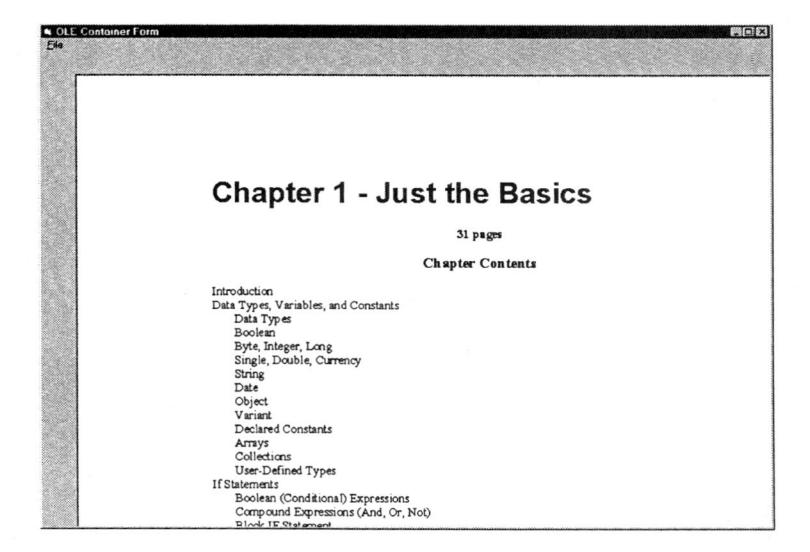

9.3.6 Program Implementation

The project contains one form, called frmOLE. The OLE container control is named OLE1, and the common dialog control is named dlgInsert.

Form_Load initializes the CancelError and Filter properties of dlgInsert, the dialog used for opening files:

```
Private Sub Form_Load()
  ChDrive App.Path
  ChDir App.Path
  dlgInsert.CancelError = True
  dlgInsert.Filter = "Excel file (*.xls)|*.xls|" _
  + "Word Document (*.doc)|*.doc|All files (*.*)|*.*"
End Sub
```

The user closes the application associated with the OLE control by selecting the File/Close menu command:

```
Private Sub mnuFileClose_Click()
'Close the OLE object's application.
  OLE1.Close
End Sub

Private Sub mnuFileExit_Click()
  Unload Me
End Sub
```

When the user wants to insert a worksheet, a File/Open dialog is displayed, and the selected filename is passed to the CreateEmbed method of the OLE control:

```
Private Sub mnuInsertWorksheet_Click()
'Let user select a worksheet to embed.
  On Error GoTo InsertWorksheet1
  dlgInsert.DialogTitle = "Select a Worksheet to Insert"
  dlgInsert.FilterIndex = 1
  dlgInsert.ShowOpen
  OLE1.CreateEmbed dlgInsert.filename
  Exit Sub
InsertWorksheet1:
End Sub
```

Inserting a Word document is nearly identical to inserting a worksheet, except that different values are assigned to the DialogTitle and FilterIndex properties:

```
Private Sub mnuInsertDocument_Click()
'Let user select a document to embed.
  On Error GoTo InsertDocument1
  dlgInsert.DialogTitle = "Select a Document To Insert"
  dlgInsert.FilterIndex = 2
  dlgInsert.ShowOpen
  OLE1.CreateEmbed dlgInsert.filename
  Exit Sub
InsertDocument1:
End Sub
```

The user clicks on the File/New/Chart command to create a new embedded Excel chart. The DoVerb method activates Excel automatically:

```
Private Sub mnuNewChart_Click()
'Create and activate a new Excel chart.
  OLE1.CreateEmbed "", "Excel.Chart.8"
  OLE1.DoVerb vbOLEPrimary
End Sub
```

Similarly, the user clicks on File/New/Document to create and activate a new Word document:

```
Private Sub mnuNewDocument_Click()
'Create and activate a new Word document.
  OLE1.CreateEmbed "", "Word.Document.8"
  OLE1.DoVerb vbOLEPrimary
End Sub
```

The File/New/Worksheet command creates a new worksheet:

```
Private Sub mnuNewWorksheet_Click()
'Create a new Excel Worksheet.
  OLE1.CreateEmbed "", "Excel.Sheet.8"
  OLE1.DoVerb vbOLEPrimary
End Sub
```

9.4 OLE Automation

The major innovation of OLE Version 2.0 was that it added OLE automation, which meant that container applications could directly access classes, methods, and properties of other OLE-aware programs. All of the Microsoft Office applications support OLE 2.0. A Visual Basic program can create an invisible Excel worksheet or Word document in the background, for example. Using programming code, the program can call methods and set properties within the applications. The concept of objects as "plug-in" components is fundamental to OLE, giving the programmer the option of constructing applications from a wide range of OLE-compatible tools.

9.4.1 Visual Basic for Applications

One of the most popular uses of OLE automation in Visual Basic is the use of objects exposed by the suite of Microsoft applications. Excel, Word, Access, Visual Basic, PowerPoint, and Project all support a common language, called Visual Basic for Applications (VBA). You may have noticed that VBA is one of the object types available in Visual Basic, displayed by the Object Browser. For example, Figure 17 shows a list of methods and properties from the VBA Financial class.

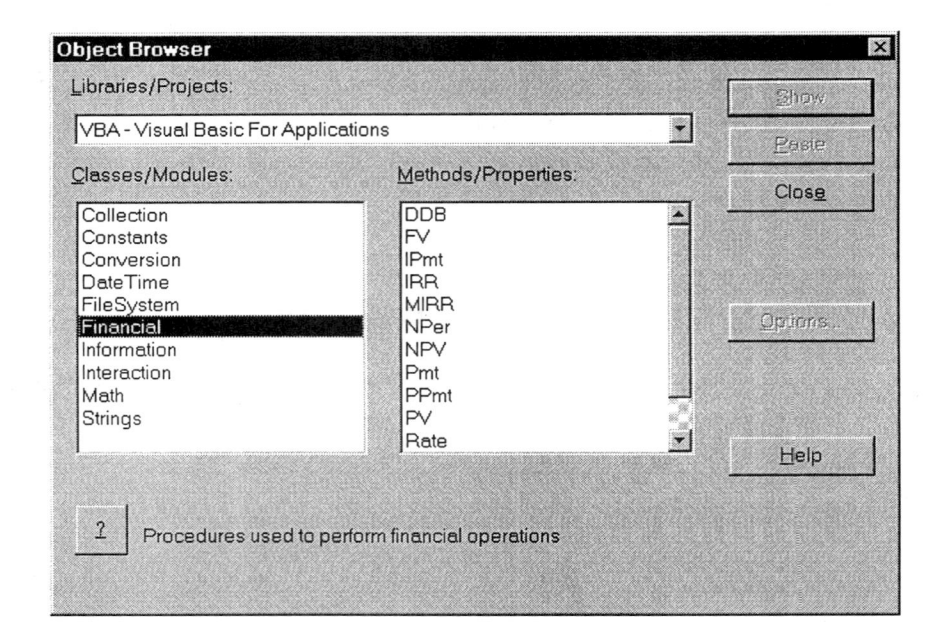

Figure 17. The VBA Financial Class (Object Browser).

In other words, one can call VBA methods and access VBA constants and properties within Visual Basic as if they were part of the native Visual Basic language. For example, the **DateDiff** function returns the number of time intervals between two dates. The following sets n to 151, the number of days between 1/1/97 and 6/1/97:

```
n = DateDiff("d", #1/1/97#, #6/1/97#)
```

9.4.2 Example: Creating a Word Document

To create a document using OLE automation with Microsoft Word 8.0, call the CreateObject function, passing it the class name for a Word application:

```
Dim word As Object
Set word = CreateObject("Word.Application")
```

This creates an invisible running instance of Microsoft Word. The variable **Word** now holds an Application object. At least one Document object must be created and added to the application's Documents collection:

```
word.Documents.Add
```

A new variable, **doc**, refers to the application's currently active document:

```
Dim doc As Object
Set doc = word.ActiveDocument
```

Every document has a **Range** property, which is a portion of a document. Here, the Range.InsertBefore method is called, passing it some text to be inserted into the document:

```
doc.Range.InsertBefore "Insert this text." + vbCrLf
```

Finally, the Word application is displayed with the document in an edit window:

```
word.Visible = True
```

The user can modify and save the document, and close Word itself. In case Word is still running, the Quit method terminates it. The single argument, False, indicates that the user will not be prompted to save the document:

```
word.Quit False
Set word = Nothing
```

Complete Program. The following program creates a Word 8.0 document and uses OLE automation to insert text and display the document:

```
Option Explicit
Dim word As Object

Private Sub cmdCreate_Click()
  Dim sampleText As String
    sampleText = "This text was passed to the " _
      + "Microsoft Word OLE Automation Server."

  Dim doc As Object
  Set word = CreateObject("Word.Application")
  word.Documents.Add
  Set doc = word.ActiveDocument
  doc.Range.InsertBefore sampleText
  word.Visible = True
End Sub
```

```
Private Sub cmdCloseDoc_Click()
  word.Quit False
  Set word = Nothing
End Sub
```

The program's main window, frmMain (Figure 18), has only two operations, Create Document and Close Document.

Figure 18. OLE Automation Program, Main Window.

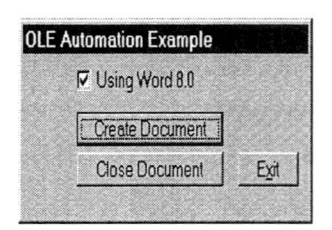

Figure 19 shows the window displayed by Microsoft Word when the user clicks on Create Document.

Figure 19. Create Document Window.

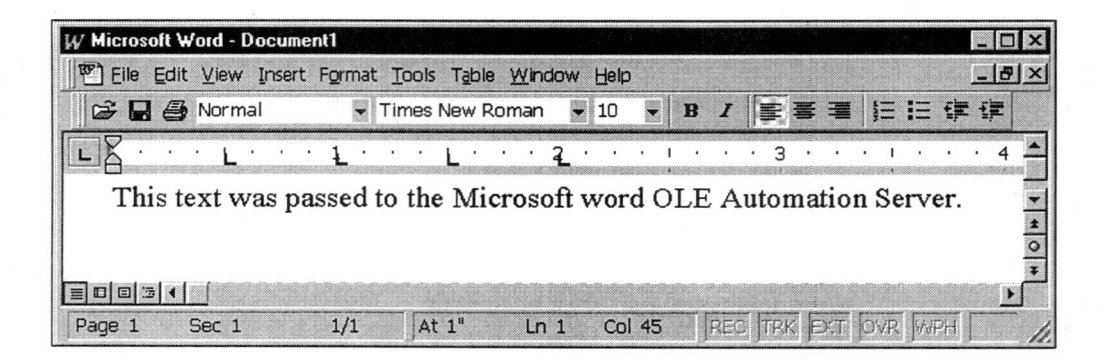

The user can directly modify the document, save it, and close Word. In case the user does not close Word, clicking on the Close Document button in frmMain will also terminate Word.

9.4.3 Word Classes, Properties, and Methods

Some useful Word 8.0 classes, properties, and methods are listed in Table 2. This is only a minimal list, compared to the complete set of objects listed in the object browser under Word 8.0.

Table 2. Word 8.0 Classes, Properties, and Methods.

Class	Property / Method	Description
Application	Documents	Collection of documents, starting with index 1; index may also be a string containing the document name.
	ActiveDocument	The currently active document.
	Selection	Selected range or insertion point in a document. Useful in search and replace operation.
	Visible	If True, Word is displayed on the screen. By default, Visible is False.
Document	PageSetup	A PageSetup object.
	Paragraphs	Collection of paragraphs, starting with index 1.
	Close	Close the document. Optionally, changes may be saved.
	CheckSpelling	Perform a spell-check of this document.
Documents	Add	Add a new document to the collection. A template name may optionally be specified.
	Save	Save the current document.
	SaveAs	Save the current document. May optionally supply a filename and format type.
PageSetup	TopMargin	Integer, measured in points.
	LeftMargin	Integer, measured in points.
	RightMargin	Integer, measured in points.
	BottomMargin	Integer, measured in points.
	Orientation	wdOrientLandscape or wdOrientPortrait.
Paragraph	Alignment	Can be assigned wdAlignParagraphLeft, wdAlignParagraphCenter, wdAlignParagraphRight, or wdAlignParagraphJustify.
	Format	Returns the ParagraphFormat object associated with the paragraph.
	LeftIndent, RightIndent	Amount of indent on left and right, measured in points.
	Range	The Range object returned by all characters between the beginning and end of the paragraph.
	Style	Set or return the formatting style of the paragraph.
Range	Start	Starting point of a range; integer ≥ 0.
	End	Ending point of a range.
	Font	The current font (a Font object).
	InsertBefore	Insert text at the beginning of a range.

Table 2 (continued)

	InsertAfter	Insert text at the end of a range, causing it to expand.
	MoveStart	Move the starting point of a range.
	SetRange	Modify Start and End values in the range.
Font	Bold	True/False
	Italic	True/False
	Underline	True/False
	Name	A string, such as "Times New Roman".
	Size	Point size, as an integer.

Tip: Word 8.0 (Word 97) is the first version that uses Visual Basic for Applications. Previous versions of Word used a similar language called WordBasic.

Using the Macro Recorder. A practical way to learn how to accomplish simple tasks in Word is to run the macro recorder from within Word itself. Use the following steps:

- Use the mouse to select any text that will be affected by the macro.
- Choose the Tools/Macro/Record New Macro command from the menu.
- Click on the macro recorder's start button.
- Carry out the actions you wish to record.
- Click on the macro recorder's stop button.

The cursor could be placed on a paragraph, for example, the macro recorder started, and the left and right margins indented by 1/2 inch. The following statements would be generated:

```
Selection.ParagraphFormat.LeftIndent = InchesToPoints(0.5)
Selection.ParagraphFormat.RightIndent = InchesToPoints(0.5)
```

From this, it is clear that the **ParagraphFormat** property of a paragraph has properties called LeftIndent and RightIndent, measured in points. The following is an example of a macro recording made when the File/Page Setup command was executed:

```
With ActiveDocument.PageSetup
    .LineNumbering.Active = False
    .Orientation = wdOrientPortrait
    .TopMargin = InchesToPoints(1.5)
    .BottomMargin = InchesToPoints(1)
    .LeftMargin = InchesToPoints(1.5)
    .RightMargin = InchesToPoints(1)
    .Gutter = InchesToPoints(0)
    .HeaderDistance = InchesToPoints(0.5)
    .FooterDistance = InchesToPoints(0.5)
    .PageWidth = InchesToPoints(8.5)
    .PageHeight = InchesToPoints(11)
    .FirstPageTray = wdPrinterDefaultBin
    .OtherPagesTray = wdPrinterDefaultBin
```

```
    .SectionStart = wdSectionNewPage
    .OddAndEvenPagesHeaderFooter = False
    .DifferentFirstPageHeaderFooter = False
    .VerticalAlignment = wdAlignVerticalTop
    .SuppressEndnotes = False
    .MirrorMargins = False
End With
```

One would never have to modify all of these properties, of course, but some might be selectively changed. The following example sets the margins in the page setup:

```
Dim Word As Object
Set Word = CreateObject("Word.Application")
Word.Documents.Add
'...
With Word.ActiveDocument.PageSetup
    .TopMargin = InchesToPoints(1.5)
    .BottomMargin = InchesToPoints(1)
    .LeftMargin = InchesToPoints(1.5)
    .RightMargin = InchesToPoints(1)
End With
```

Finding and Replacing Text. It is possible to find and replace text inside a Word document. The following code, recorded by the Macro recorder in Word, can be used by a Visual Basic program to search for "frog" and replace it with "prince":

```
Selection.Find.ClearFormatting
Selection.Find.Replacement.ClearFormatting
With Selection.Find
    .Text = "frog"
    .Replacement.Text = "prince"
    .Forward = True
    .Wrap = wdFindContinue
    .Format = False
    .MatchCase = False
    .MatchWholeWord = False
    .MatchWildcards = False
    .MatchSoundsLike = False
    .MatchAllWordForms = False
End With
Selection.Find.Execute Replace:=wdReplaceAll
```

Because **Selection** is a property in Word's Application class, it must be qualified by the name of the Word application object:

```
Dim Word As Object
Set Word = CreateObject("Word.Application")
'Create a document, insert some text...
'
'Search and replace:
Word.Selection.Find.ClearFormatting
Word.Selection.Find.Replacement.ClearFormatting
With Word.Selection.Find
```

```
        .Text = "frog"
        .Replacement.Text = "prince"
        .Forward = True
        .Wrap = wdFindContinue
        .Format = False
        .MatchCase = False
        .MatchWholeWord = False
        .MatchWildcards = False
        .MatchSoundsLike = False
        .MatchAllWordForms = False
    End With
    Word.Selection.Find.Execute Replace:=wdReplaceAll
```

9.4.4 OLE Automation with Excel

Excel 5.0 was the first Microsoft product that introduced Visual Basic for Applications, and continues to be an excellent implementation of the language. To use it in Visual Basic, you must select *Microsoft Excel 8.0 Object Library* from the Tools/References menu (or Excel 5.0). After doing this, view the rather large set of Excel classes in the Object Browser.

Creating an Excel worksheet using OLE automation involves a few simple steps:

- Create an Excel Application object.
- Add a Workbook object to the application.
- Locate the active worksheet and assign it to an object variable.
- Assign formulas and values to specific worksheet cells.

For example, three object variables must be declared: one to hold Excel, one to hold a workbook, and one for the worksheet:

```
    Dim Excel As Object, wbook As Object, wsheet As Object
    Set Excel = CreateObject("Excel.Application")
    Set wbook = Excel.Workbooks.Add
    Set wsheet = Excel.ActiveWorkbook.ActiveSheet
```

The following statements assign values to cells in the first two rows of column 1:

```
    wsheet.Cells(1, 1).Value = 20
    wsheet.Cells(2, 1).Value = 40
```

Table 3 and Table 4 list some important methods and properties that you will likely use when accessing Excel as an OLE automation server.

Table 3. Some Useful Excel Methods.

Class.Method	Description
Workbook.Close	Close the current Workbook.
Application.Quit	Quit the Excel application.
Workbooks.Add	Add a new Workbook to the Workbooks collection.

Table 4. Some Useful Excel Properties.

Class.Property	Description
Worksheet.Cells(r,c).Value	The value stored in a single cell.
Worksheet.Cells(r,c).Formula	The formula stored in a single cell.
Application.ActiveWorkbook	The currently active Workbook.
Workbook.ActiveSheet	The currently active Worksheet.

9.4.5 Excel: Statistical Score Analysis

To demonstrate a simple example of OLE automation with Excel, let's write a short program that performs the following steps, in order:

1. Generate an array of 50 random test scores.
2. Place the scores in a list box.
3. Create a hidden worksheet object.
4. Insert the scores into a column of worksheet cells.
5. Insert formulas into worksheet cells that calculate the standard deviation, median score, and mean of the column containing the scores.
6. Retrieve the formula results from the worksheet and display them in the Visual Basic program.

Visual Basic does not have built-in functions that compute the mean, median, and standard deviation function of a list of values. These functions are, however, available in Excel, so this provides some motivation to use Excel as an OLE automation server.

Figure 20 shows a sample of the program's output, showing the list of scores and the calculated values returned by Excel.

Program Implementation. Let us go through the program's code in some detail. In the declarations section of the main form, the following variables are declared: ScoreCount (the number of scores), the Score array, and three object variables used to control Excel: Excel, wbook, and wsheet:

```
Const ScoreCount As Integer = 50
Dim Score(0 To ScoreCount - 1) As Integer
Dim Excel As Object, wbook As Object, wsheet As Object
```

Figure 20. Excel OLE Automation - Statistics.

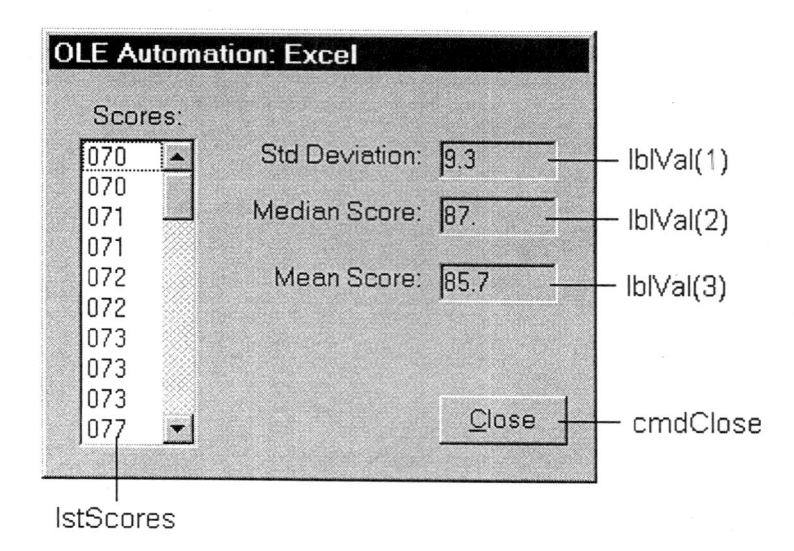

[Screenshot of dialog "OLE Automation: Excel" showing Scores listbox (lstScores) with values 070, 070, 071, 071, 072, 072, 073, 073, 073, 077; Std Deviation: 9.3 — lblVal(1); Median Score: 87. — lblVal(2); Mean Score: 85.7 — lblVal(3); Close button — cmdClose.]

CreateScores fills the Score() array with fifty random integers between the values 70 and 100. The scores are also displayed in a list box:

```
Private Sub CreateScores()
  Dim j As Integer
  For j = 0 To ScoreCount - 1
    Score(j) = (Rnd() * 30) + 70
    lstScores.AddItem Format$(Score(j), "000")
  Next j
End Sub
```

Form_Load calls CreateScores and it creates the necessary Excel objects—Application, Workbook, and WorkSheet:

```
Private Sub Form_Load()
  CreateScores
  Set Excel = CreateObject("Excel.Application")
  Set wbook = Excel.Workbooks.Add
  Set wsheet = Excel.ActiveWorkbook.ActiveSheet
  FillCells
  CalcStatistics
End Sub
```

The **FillCells** procedure fills a column of spreadsheet cells with the array of scores. Because OLE automation can be slow, an hourglass cursor is assigned to the mouse:

```
Private Sub FillCells()
```

```
    Screen.MousePointer = vbHourglass
    Dim j As Integer
    For j = 0 To ScoreCount - 1
      wsheet.Cells(j + 1, 1).Value = Score(j)
    Next j
    Screen.MousePointer = vbDefault
End Sub
```

CalcStatistics inserts formulas that calculate the standard deviation, median, and average value of the column containing the scores. To provide some flexibility, the formulas will work with up to 100 scores in column A:

```
Private Sub CalcStatistics()
    Screen.MousePointer = vbHourglass
    wsheet.Cells(1, 2).Formula = "=STDEV(A1:A100)"
    wsheet.Cells(2, 2).Formula = "=Median(A1:A100)"
    wsheet.Cells(3, 2).Formula = "=Average(A1:A100)"
```

CalcStatistics also retrieves the values calculated by the three formulas and inserts them into labels on the current form:

```
    (continued...)
    Dim row As Integer
    For row = 1 To 3
      lblVal(row).Caption = Format$(wsheet.Cells _
        (row, 2).Value, "####.#")
    Next row
    Screen.MousePointer = vbDefault
End Sub
```

The **Form_Unload** event handler calls the Close method to close the current workbook, and the Quit method to quit Excel. Failing to do so would leave a copy of Excel in memory:

```
Private Sub Form_Unload(Cancel As Integer)
    Set wsheet = Nothing
    wbook.Close False
    Set wbook = Nothing
    Excel.Quit
    Set Excel = Nothing
End Sub

Private Sub cmdClose_Click()
    Unload Me
End Sub
```

This program example only begins to show the potential for using Excel as an OLE server. Aside from creating a worksheet from scratch, another useful technique is to plug values into an existing worksheet and perform a series of calculations that would be awkward if done in Visual Basic. This will be suggested in the Chapter exercises.

9.5 College Admissions Program

9.5.1 Program Specifications

Let's write a program that simplifies the job of an admissions officer at a fictitious college called the "Better Business College". An important task given to such a person is to answer inquiries by prospective students. The inquiries might be general, or they might be specific. Some specific questions might be related to the following:

- Business degrees
- Computer degrees
- Courses in computer applications
- Courses in computer programming
- Information about faculty
- Tuition and fees

Naturally, it is a lot of work to generate letters that specifically answer the questions asked by each applicant. But our program can speed up the process by pulling paragraph topics and applicant information from a database and generating the response letters automatically. An important goal of our program is flexibility and expandability. It must be easy for the admissions officer to add new applicants and topics to the database.

> ***Programming Tip:*** Before your Visual Basic programs can use Microsoft Word as an OLE automation server, a reference to the Microsoft Word 8.0 Library must be added to your project. In VB4, select *References* from the Tools menu. In VB5, select *References* from the Project menu. Then place a check in the box next to Microsoft Word.

9.5.2 Program Design

The college is assumed to already have two database tables, one containing response paragraphs relating to each admissions topic, and another containing the names and addresses of students who have contacted the college. Using the database information, OLE automation will be used to create a Microsoft Word document and fill it with the student's name and response paragraphs. The document will be displayed, and the user will have the opportunity to modify, print, and save the document.

The program will consist of a single main window (Figure 21) with an SSTab custom control. One of the tab panels will consist of information on applicants, and the other panel will contain paragraph topics for the form letters. When the program starts up, no database has been opened yet.

Figure 21. Better Business College, Main Window.

The user clicks on the File/Open menu command, bringing up an Open Document Database dialog box. There is one database in the current directory, called inquiries.mdb.

Select the Applicant. After the database has been opened, the user uses the mouse to select the name of the applicant who will receive the letter. Upon selecting a name, the person's address appears on the same form (Figure 22).

Figure 22. Selecting an Applicant.

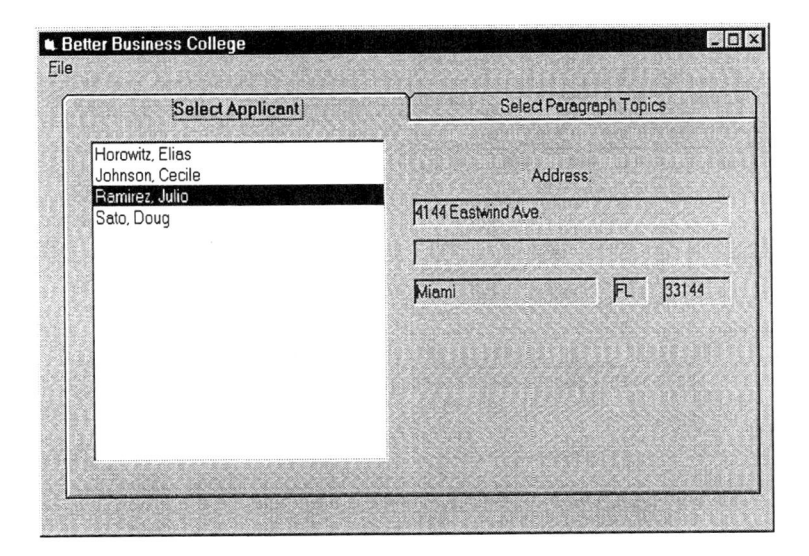

Select the Topics. After an applicant has been selected, the user selects the paragraph topics to be inserted in the letter. In Figure 23, for example, a letter is being generated as a response to an initial inquiry about the college. It includes a discussion of business degrees, an explanation of the tuition plan, and the names of faculty.

Figure 23. Select Response Topics.

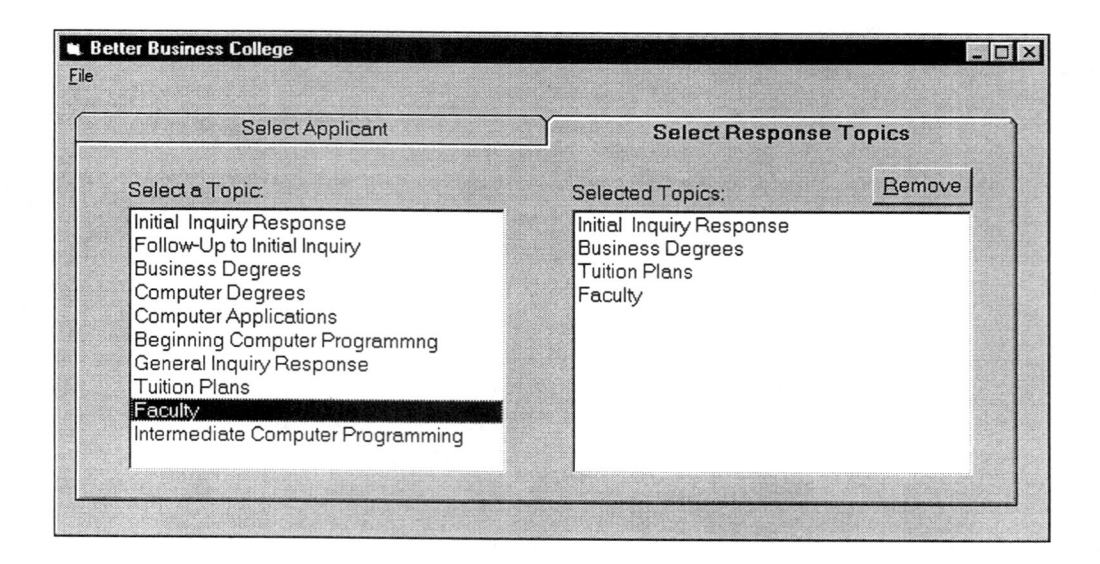

The user can also view the text of the topic paragraphs by double-clicking on individual topics, as in Figure 24.

Figure 24. Sample Topic Paragraph.

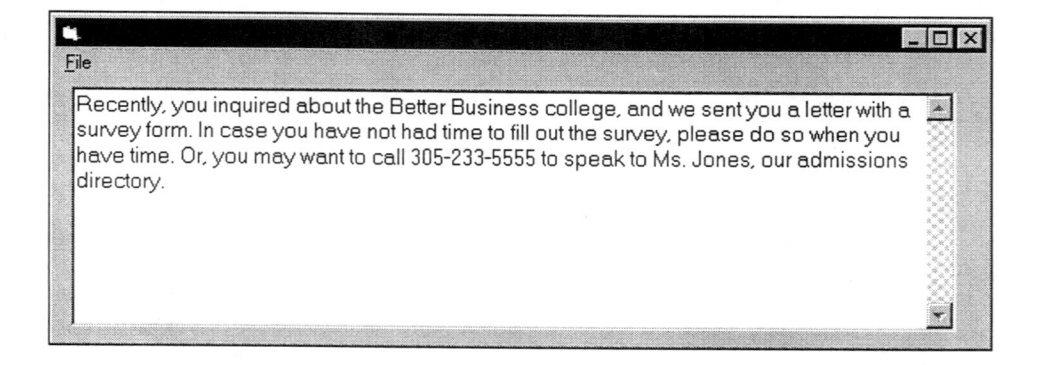

When the user has selected all topics and clicks the File/Generate Letter command, the program creates and fills a Word document. Figure 25 shows a sample letter that was generated and displayed by the program. Some fonts were directly modified by the user. Of course, this letter is only one among many that could be generated from list of available response topics.

Figure 25. Generated Response Letter.

Better Business College
111 NorthWind Way, Miami, Florida, 33133

Tuesday, March 25, 1997

Dr. Julio Ramirez
4144 Eastwind Ave.
Miami, FL 33144

Dear Julio:

Thank you for your inquiry about the Better Business College. We offer a number of business and computer degrees designed to help you to enter the job market quickly, at a high starting salary. On the survey form accompanying this letter, please indicate your interest areas, and return the survey to us. If you would like to speak to one of our staff, please call our office at 305-233-5555, or visit our web site at www.BetterBus.com.

Our graduates have been placed in many Fortune-500 companies, starting at competitive salaries. The major degree areas for business at our college are: Marketing, Finance, Accounting, and International Banking.

The following faculty serve as department heads at the Better Business College:

Marketing:	John Adams
Finance:	Susan Bennington
Accounting:	Jerry Highsmith
Systems Analysis:	Brenda Brown
Computer Applications:	Itzhak Leibowitz

To better suit your needs, we offer four different tuition plans at the Better Business College:

- By paying the entire year's tuition in advance, you receive a 20% discount off the standard rate.
- By paying the year's tuition in two installments, one at the beginning of the year and another halfway through the year, you receive a 10% discount off the standard rate.
- By paying the year's tuition in four equal installments, you receive the standard rate.
- If you wish to pay tuition in monthly installments, there is a 3% surcharge to cover processing costs.

Sincerely,

Dr. John Q. Smyth, Director

9.5.3 Program Implementation

The main window's menu consists of the following items:

File	mnuFile
Open	mnuFileOpen
Create Letter	mnuFileCreate
Exit	mnuFileExit

Let's take a careful look at the program's source code. In the general declarations section are the database variable, two recordset variables for the applicants and the paragraph responses, and a Word object that will be used later:

```
Const DirectorName As String = "Dr. John Q. Smyth"
Dim dbase As Database
Dim Applicants As Recordset
Dim Responses As Recordset
Dim Word As Object
```

The following code displays a File/Open dialog box that lets the user select the database name to be loaded. Two procedures fill list boxes with response topics and applicant names:

```
Private Sub mnuFileOpen_Click()
    On Error GoTo Open1
    dlgOpen.ShowOpen
    OpenDatabase dlgOpen.fileName
    FillResponseList
    FillApplicantList
    Exit Sub
Open1:
End Sub
```

The **OpenDatabase** procedure closes the Applicants and Responses tables, before closing the database. The On Error Resume next lets the program skip any statement that causes a runtime error, because the tables might already be closed:

```
Private Sub OpenDatabase(fileName As String)
    On Error Resume Next
    Applicants.Close
    Responses.Close
    dbase.Close
```

The database, Responses table, and Applicants table are all opened:

```
    (continued...)
    On Error GoTo OpenDatabase1
    Set dbase = Workspaces(0).OpenDatabase(fileName)
    Set Responses = dbase.OpenRecordset("Responses", dbOpenTable)
    Responses.Index = "idNdx"
    Set Applicants = dbase.OpenRecordset("Applicants", dbOpenTable)
    Applicants.Index = "idNdx"
    Exit Sub
OpenDatabase1:
```

```
    MsgBox Error$, vbCritical, "OpenDatabase"
End Sub
```

The **FillResponseList** procedure, called from FileOpen_Click, fills the Responses list box with all available topics. The topic's ID number is stored in the ItemData array:

```
Private Sub FillResponseList()
  On Error GoTo FillResponse1
  Dim j As Integer
  lstResponses.Clear
  Responses.MoveFirst
  j = 0
  Do Until Responses.EOF
    lstResponses.AddItem Responses!Description
    lstResponses.ItemData(j) = Responses!id
    Responses.MoveNext
    j = j + 1
  Loop
  Exit Sub
FillResponse1:
  MsgBox Error$, vbInformation, "FillResponseList"
End Sub
```

Similarly, the **FillApplicantList** procedure fills the applicant list box with first and last names:

```
Public Sub FillApplicantList()
  On Error GoTo FillApplicant1
  Dim j As Integer
  lstApplicants.Clear
  Applicants.MoveFirst
  j = 0
  Do Until Applicants.EOF
    lstApplicants.AddItem Applicants!lastName + _
       ", " + Applicants!firstName
    lstApplicants.ItemData(j) = Applicants!id
    Applicants.MoveNext
    j = j + 1
  Loop
  Exit Sub
FillApplicant1:
  MsgBox Error$, vbInformation, "FillApplicantList"
End Sub
```

When the user selects an applicant from the list box, the record containing his/her address is located. Some fields may be Null, so the *On Error Resume Next* statement skips them:

```
Private Sub lstApplicants_Click()
  On Error Resume Next   'skip Null fields
  Dim id As Long
  id = lstApplicants.ItemData(lstApplicants.ListIndex)
  Applicants.Seek "=", id
  If Not Applicants.NoMatch Then
```

```
      lblField(0).Caption = Applicants!street1
      lblField(1).Caption = Applicants!street2
      lblField(2).Caption = Applicants!city
      lblField(3).Caption = Applicants!state
      lblField(4).Caption = Applicants!zip
   End If
End Sub
```

When one of the response topics is clicked, the topic name is copied to the list box on the right side of the form, called lstSelected. It is the lstSelected list box that will be used when building the form letter:

```
Private Sub lstResponses_Click()
   lstSelected.AddItem lstResponses.Text
   lstSelected.ItemData(lstSelected.ListCount - 1) = _
      lstResponses.ItemData(lstResponses.ListIndex)
End Sub
```

If the user double-clicks on a response topic, the program displays the topic's entire paragraph in a separate form called frmSample. This was previously shown in Figure 24:

```
Private Sub lstResponses_DblClick()
   Dim id As Long
   id = lstResponses.ItemData(lstResponses.ListIndex)
   Responses.Seek "=", id
   frmSample.txtSample.Text = Responses!body
   frmSample.Show vbModal
End Sub
```

The **cmdRemove** button removes any selected topic from the lstSelected list box:

```
Private Sub cmdRemove_Click()
   Dim n As Integer
   n = lstSelected.ListIndex
   If n >= 0 Then
      lstSelected.RemoveItem n
   End If
End Sub
```

A utility function called **ToString** converts any expression, numeric or otherwise, to a string. It calls the standard CStr function, which adapts to the locale setting in Windows. This affects the display of dates and numbers, for example. Unfortunately, CStr generates a runtime error when trying to convert Null, and Null is frequently found in empty database fields. ToString specifically converts Null to an empty string:

```
Public Function ToString(val As Variant) As String
   If IsNull(val) Then
      ToString = ""
   Else
      ToString = CStr(val)
   End If
End Function
```

The **CreateLetter** procedure builds a Word document, using OLE automation. The student's name and address are pulled from the Applicants table. The **ToString** function is used here to prevent any runtime errors from Null database fields:

```
Public Sub CreateLetter()
   Dim j As Integer, st As String, txt As String
   If Not Check_Selections Then Exit Sub
   On Error GoTo CreateLetter1

   st = Format$(Now, "Long Date") + vbCrLf + vbCrLf _
      + ToString(Applicants!Title) + " " _
      + ToString(Applicants!firstName) _
      + " " + ToString(Applicants!lastName) + vbCrLf _
      + ToString(Applicants!street1) + vbCrLf

   txt = ToString(Applicants!street2)
   If txt <> "" Then st = st + txt + vbCrLf
   st = st + ToString(Applicants!city) + ", " _
      + ToString(Applicants!State) + " " _
      + ToString(Applicants!zip) + vbCrLf + vbCrLf _
      + "Dear " + ToString(Applicants!firstName) _
      + ":" + vbCrLf + vbCrLf
```

Also, CreateLetter uses a loop to go through the selected topics list box, locate the matching database record containing the topic paragraph, and build a string containing the paragraphs:

```
(continued...)
 For j = 0 To lstSelected.ListCount - 1
   Responses.Seek "=", lstSelected.ItemData(j)
   If Not Responses.NoMatch Then
      st = st + ToString(Responses!body) + vbCrLf + vbCrLf
   End If
 Next j
```

A closing statement is added to the string that will be inserted in the document:

```
(continued...)
st = st + vbCrLf + "Please let me know if there is " _
   + "any other way we can help you. " + vbCrLf + vbCrLf _
   + "Sincerely," + vbCrLf + vbCrLf + vbCrLf _
   + DirectorName + ", Director" + vbCrLf
```

The string **st** is inserted into a new Word document:

```
(continued...)
Dim doc As Object, range As Object
Set Word = CreateObject("Word.Application")
Word.Documents.Add
Set doc = Word.ActiveDocument
doc.PageSetup.TopMargin = InchesToPoints(2.5)
Set range = doc.Range(Start:=0, End:=0)
```

```
    CreateHeading range           'company name, etc.
    doc.Paragraphs(1).Alignment = wdAlignParagraphCenter
    doc.Paragraphs(2).Alignment = wdAlignParagraphCenter

    range.InsertBefore st         'body of letter
    doc.SaveAs App.Path + "\temp.doc", wdFormatDocument
    Word.Visible = True
    Exit Sub
CreateLetter1:
    MsgBox Error$, vbInformation, "CreateLetter"
End Sub
```

The **CreateHeading** procedure inserts two heading lines containing the company name and address:

```
Public Sub CreateHeading(range As Object)
    range.InsertBefore "Better Business College" + vbCrLf
    range.Font.Bold = True
    range.Font.Italic = True
    range.Font.Size = 18
    'Move start of range to next paragraph.
    range.MoveStart Unit:=wdParagraph
    range.InsertBefore "111 NorthWind Way, Miami, FL 33133" _
        + vbCrLf
    range.Font.Size = 10
    range.MoveStart Unit:=wdParagraph
End Sub
```

Each range has a Font object with properties such as Bold and Italic. After a title line has been inserted, it counts as a paragraph because it ends with a hard return (vbCrLf). The **Range.MoveStart** method moves the input pointer beyond the current paragraph so more text can be added. After all text has been inserted in the letter, Word is shown on the screen, holding the new document. The user can edit, print, and save the document as needed.

A few miscellaneous procedures are also included here. The **Check_Selections** procedure verifies that an applicant name has been selected and that at least one response topic was chosen:

```
Public Function Check_Selections() As Boolean
    Check_Selections = True
    If lstApplicants.ListIndex = -1 Then
        MsgBox "An applicant must be selected before creating the " _
            + "letter. ", vbInformation, "Error"
        lstApplicants.SetFocus
        Check_Selections = False
        Exit Function
    End If
    If lstSelected.ListCount = 0 Then
        If MsgBox("No response topics were selected. Do you " _
            + "still want to create the letter?", vbYesNo, "") _
            = vbNo Then Check_Selections = False
        Exit Function
```

```
      End If
End Function

Private Sub mnuFileCreate_Click()
'Create the form letter.
   CreateDocument
End Sub

Private Sub Form_Load()
   ChDrive App.Path
   ChDir App.Path
End Sub

Private Sub Form_Unload(Cancel As Integer)
   On Error Resume Next
   Responses.Close
   Applicants.Close
   dbase.Close
   Set Word = Nothing
End Sub

Private Sub mnuFileExit_Click()
   Unload Me
End Sub
```

9.5.4 Conclusion

There are certainly many other improvements that could be made to this program. For example:

- Use OLE commands to name and save the document.
- Build other databases for this program for other types of businesses.
- Load a Word template file with formatting and fonts, and use it to build applicant letters.
- Allow new paragraphs to be added to the Responses table.
- Allow new applicant records to be added to the Applicants table.
- Allow existing applicant records to be modified.
- When a document is created, keep a copy of the document and assign it a date and applicant ID number for future reference.
- Provide a retrieval system for documents, accessible by applicant ID.

9.6 Review Questions

1. What is an *OLE container program*?
2. Is an OLE container also known as a *compound document*?
3. In what ways was OLE 1.0 a major improvement over dynamic data exchange?
4. How is OLE 2.0 different from OLE 1.0?
5. Does the DAO object library use dynamic data exchange?

6. Assuming that an OLE server exposes objects to other applications, how does that make it easy to use?
7. If you wanted to integrate text, pictures, and sound into the same Visual Basic form, which single control from the Toolbox window would be the most useful?
8. What are the three ways in which OLE objects can be used in Visual Basic programs?
9. What is the purpose of the CreateObject procedure?
10. What type of object does the Windows Paint program expose?
11. What are three types of objects exposed by Excel?
12. What are the differences between *linked* and *embedded* objects?
13. Is it necessary to own a copy of Microsoft Word when using the OLE container control to edit Word documents?
14. Where can you find a list of available insertable objects?
15. How can the Object Browser help you to locate exposed objects?
16. If a WordPad custom control is placed on a form, can the document created by the user be saved in a file?
17. If a Word document is opened inside an OLE container control, how can changes to this document be saved in a binary OLE file?
18. What is the purpose of the NegotiateMenus property in the Form class?
19. If you want the OLE application menu to share space with the enclosing Form's File menu, which property should be set?

The following questions refer to the OLE container control:

20. Which OLE method allows you to create an embedded object at run time? Show a sample call to this method.
21. How can you locate a list of class names in the properties list of an OLE control?
22. What are the four possible values for the SizeMode property?
23. What is the effect of setting SizeMode = Autosize?
24. What is the purpose of the AutoActivate property?
25. Under which conditions is the DoVerb method useful?
26. Show an example of using the CreateEmbed method to load an existing Excel worksheet file into an OLE control.
27. Which OLE method creates a linked object from an existing worksheet file? Show an example.
28. When a linked object is activated by the user, are the menus and toolbars of the host application program displayed? (For example, if the linked object is a worksheet, the host application would be Microsoft Excel.)
29. Which programming language is the native language for Microsoft Excel, Word, Access, PowerPoint, and Project?

The following questions refer to the Word and Excel Object libraries:

30. Name at least three classes exposed by the Word 8.0 object library.

31. Using the Word 8.0 object library, how would you set the top margin of the page setup to 1.5 inches? (Assume that the variable **doc** already contains a reference to the active document.)

32. Write statements in Visual Basic that would create a Word application object and add a new document object to the Documents collection.

33. Show an example in Visual Basic that creates an Excel application object, adds a new worksheet to the Workbooks collection, and obtains a reference to the active worksheet.

34. Assuming that the variable currWorksheet contains a reference to the active worksheet in an Excel object, write statements that place the number 100 in cell "A2" (column A, row 2).

The following questions refer to the College Admissions Program in Section 9.5:

35. When the user clicks on an applicant name, how does the program retrieve the applicant's address?

36. When the user clicks on a paragraph topic in the list box, how is the matching topic retrieved from the database?

37. How does the program allow the user to browse through specific response topic paragraphs before generating a letter?

38. What is the purpose of the following statement in the CreateHeading procedure?
    ```
    range.MoveStart Unit:=wdParagraph
    ```

39. Which procedure verifies that an applicant name was selected, and that at least one response topic was selected?

9.7 Chapter Exercises

9.7.1 Mozart Music Instruments - 1

In the Chapter 2 exercises (2.7.2), there is a specification for a program that reads a file containing instrument names, purchase prices, and rental prices. Complete the solution to that exercise first, and add the following enhancement: Generate the customer invoice as a Microsoft Word document, using OLE automation. Use the College Admissions program in Section 9.5 as a guide.

9.7.2 Mozart Music Instruments - 2

Create an Excel spreadsheet detailing quarterly sales and rentals for the current year. Each row should be represented by a different type of instrument; each column will be a different quarter of the year. Use an OLE control to link the spreadsheet shown in Figure 26 to your program. Use the CreateLink method, so the complete Excel menu will be displayed. The user will be able to display, edit, and save the spreadsheet.

Figure 26. Excel Worksheet, Mozart Music.

	A	B	C	D	E	F	G
1	Mozart Music Inc., Quarterly Rental Income						
2							
3			Rentals by Quarter				
4	Instrument	Jan-Mar	Apr-Jun	Jul-Aug	Sep-Dec	Total	Average
5	Flute	500	350	500	475	1,825	456
6	Alto Saxophone	800	675	640	825	2,940	735
7	Tenor Saxophone	600	500	425	335	1,860	465
8	Bb Clarinet	400	425	450	475	1,750	438
9	Oboe	250	225	175	265	915	229
10	Bassoon	125	100	95	85	405	101
11	Violin	94	190	125	94	503	126
12	Viola	72	72	50	72	266	67
13	Cello	228	200	355	475	1,258	315
14	Electric Guitar	670	620	610	750	2,650	663
15							
16	Quarterly Totals:	3,739	3,357	3,425	3,851	14,372	

9.7.3 Hardbodies Health Club

In Chapter 2, there were a series of exercises relating to the Hardbodies Health Club application. The program managed a membership list, for example. For the current program, create an Excel spreadsheet that lists the dues collections for each member, on a monthly basis. Each row will be a different member, and each column will be a month in the current year. Then create a new form in the Visual Basic program that contains an OLE container control, and link the control to the Excel spreadsheet. Allow the user to display, edit, and save changes to the spreadsheet.

Extra: Ask the user to enter a user ID and password; look up the ID and password in a database table, determine the person's security level (1, 2, or 3) and restrict their access to the Excel spreadsheet according to the following scheme:

- Level 1 security: Display, edit, and save the spreadsheet.
- Level 2 security: Display the spreadsheet only.
- Level 3 security: Cannot display the spreadsheet.

9.7.4 Depreciation Schedule

In the exercises at the end of Chapter 2, the *Depreciation Schedule* program calculated the depreciation of computer and office equipment over a five-year period. Now that we know how to use OLE automation, we can take advantage of the power of Excel. For example, Excel's *fixed-declining balance* depreciation function has the following syntax:

```
DB(cost, salvage, life, period, month)
```

Where *cost* is the initial cost of the asset, *salvage* is the value at the end of the depreciation, *life* is the number of periods over which the asset is being depreciated, *period* is the period for which you want to calculate the depreciation, and *month* is the number of months in the first year. If *month* is omitted, it is assumed to be 12. The value for *period* must use the same units as *life*. For example, Table 5 shows the result of using this function with the following values: cost = 10000, salvage = 1000, life = 5, period (1..5), month = 7.

Table 5. Fixed-Declining Balance Example.

Year	Depreciation
1	$2,152.50
2	$2,895.73
3	$1,827.20
4	$1,152.97
5	$727.52

Therefore, your job is to rewrite the Depreciation Schedule program using an OLE container control (or use OLE automation), and make use of Excel's fixed-declining balance function.

9.7.5 Family Photo Album

Write a program that stores and displays names and photographs of your friends and/or family in a database. The photographs can be taken with a digital camera or scanned from snapshots, and can be in GIF, TIFF, JPEG, BMP, or other graphical formats.

Step 1. Create an Access database, and create a table with a Text field that describes each photo, and an OLE field that will store the photo itself.

Step 2. Open the table, insert a description of the first photo, and move to the OLE field. Select Object from the Insert menu, and click on the "Insert From File" option. Select the graphic file name containing the picture.

Repeat steps 1 and 2 for all pictures that will be stored in the database.

Step 3. Create a Visual Basic program and place the following objects on the main form:
- A label that will hold the photo's description.
- A data control. Set the Databasename and Recordsource properties to the database and table containing the photos.
- An OLE container control. Set the Datasource property to the data control name, and set the Datafield property to the name of the database field containing the graphic images.
- A command button that will let the user decide when to display the picture.

Set the following properties for the OLE container:

    Visible = False, AutoActivate = Manual.

In the Command button click event procedure, the following statement activates the OLE control and displays its contents:

    OLE1.DoVerb vbOLEShow

A sample of the main window as the program is running is shown in Figure 27. When the user clicks on the command button, the type of graphic file will determine how the file is displayed.

Figure 27. Picture Database, Main Window.

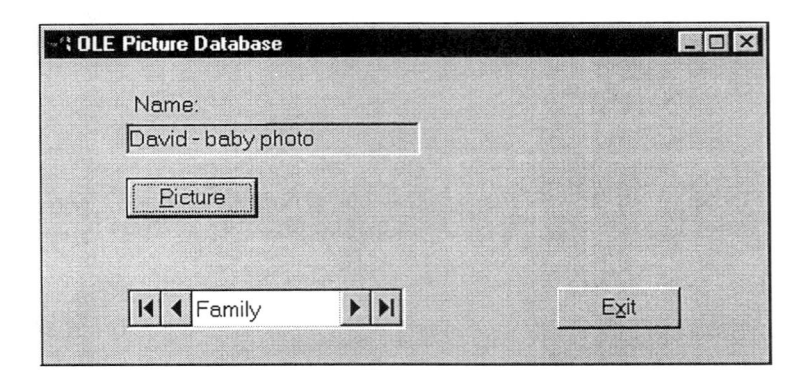

For example, on my system, the *LView Pro* program is associated with files having a GIF, JPG, or TIF extension. This application activates automatically when the OLE control is activated (Figure 28).

Figure 28. Sample Photo (OLE field).

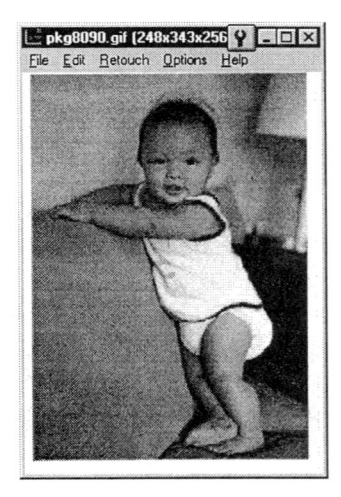

9.7.6 Personal Stock Portfolio - 1

Write a program that helps the user manage a personal stock portfolio. First, create a worksheet that shows the name of each stock or mutual fund along with its initial purchase information (see Figure 29). Display the purchase date, number of shares, price per share, and amount invested (number of shares * price per share). Name this worksheet as **InitialPurch**, and save the Excel file under the name **stock.xls.**

Then write a Visual Basic program that uses the worksheet in the following two ways:

- As a linked object in an OLE container control. The user can view and edit the worksheet using Excel.
- As an OLE automation server. The user cannot see the worksheet, but your program displays certain information such as the amount invested for each asset, or the total initial investments.

Figure 29. Personal Stock Portfolio (the InitialPurch worksheet).

	A	B	C	D	E	F
1	**Personal Stock Portfolio**					
2	Initial Purchases					
3						
4		Purchase	Num	Price Per	Amount	
5	**Asset Name**	Date	Shares	Share	Invested	
6						
7	Merlin Futures	01/01/94	450	35.72	16,074	
8	Oz Foreign Travel	03/01/94	225	22.50	5,063	
9	Aladdin Technology	05/05/95	1024	75.20	77,005	
10	Narnia Cap. Growth	03/01/93	965	22.40	21,616	
11	Star Fleet Medical	06/20/96	895	62.10	55,580	
12						
13	Total Initial Investments:				175,337	
14						

9.7.7 Personal Stock Portfolio - 2

Using the Excel worksheet and program written in the previous exercise, provide some additional features: create a database file called stocks.mdb and create a table called **Performance**. This table will contain the name of each stock or fund, the initial purchase price (per share), the number of shares purchased, and the price per share for the first day of each quarter of the year, as well as for the last day of the year (see Table 6).

Table 6. Performance Table Description.

Field Name	Field Type
stockName	Text, 30
initShares	Number, Single
initPurchPrice	Number, Single
price_Jan	Number, Single
price_Apr	Number, Single
price_Jul	Number, Single
price_Oct	Number, Single
price_Dec	Number, Single

Next, write a Visual Basic program that uses Excel as an OLE automation server. Use Excel object methods to add a new worksheet to the stocks.xls file, and fill it with the fields from the Performance table in the database that you created for this project (the worksheet is displayed in Figure 30). Insert formulas in the worksheet that calculate the market value of each stock for each quarter. Each formula multiplies the price per share by the number of shares purchased. For example, Aladdin Technology on 4/1/97 is 74.3 dollars per share and we own 1024 shares, so the market value on that date is $76,032 (74.3 * 1024).

Finally, display the worksheet for the user.

Figure 30. Excel: Personal Stock Portfolio.

	A	B	C	D	E	F	G	H
1	**Personal Stock Portfolio**							
2	Performance, 1997							
3				Price Per Share				
4	**Asset Name**		Initial	1/1/97	4/1/97	7/1/97	10/1/97	12/31/97
5	Merlin Futures		35.72	34.0	34.8	34.0	36.0	38.0
6	Oz Foreign Travel		22.50	21.2	23.0	24.5	25.7	28.1
7	Aladdin Technology		75.20	75.1	74.3	78.2	82.1	88.4
8	Narnia Cap. Growth		22.40	25.2	22.1	25.1	27.6	29.9
9	Star Fleet Medical		62.10	64.0	67.0	69.0	75.0	82.0
10								
11				Market Value				
12			Shares	1/1/97	4/1/97	7/1/97	10/1/97	12/31/97
13	Merlin Futures		450	15,300	15,638	15,300	16,200	17,100
14	Oz Foreign Travel		225	4,770	5,175	5,513	5,787	6,325
15	Aladdin Technology		1,024	76,902	76,032	80,097	84,081	90,522
16	Narnia Cap. Growth		965	24,318	21,355	24,250	26,653	28,854
17	Star Fleet Medical		895	57,280	59,965	61,755	67,125	73,390
18								

10 Tapping Into the Windows API

Chapter Contents

The Need for External Procedures
    Static and Dynamic Linking
Declaring and Calling DLL Procedures
    The Declare Statement
    The API Viewer Utility Program
    First Example: Flashing a Window Caption
Parameters in DLL Procedures
    String Parameters
    Numeric Parameters
    User-Defined Types
    Example: GetWindowsDirectory
Reading and Writing Application INI Files
    Maintaining a Program's INI File
Example: The clsIniFile Class
    Class Description
    A Short Test Program
Review Questions
Chapter Exercises

10.1 The Need for External Procedures

Visual Basic is optimized for a straightforward, easy to learn approach to Windows application programming. One of the great things that it does is to shield us from the low-level details of Windows programming. It is almost impossible to write a Visual Basic program, for example, that will abnormally terminate because of a memory boundary violation. But this "safe" approach creates some limitations to what your programs can do, if they are restricted only to the objects, methods, and properties that exist in Visual Basic. If you want to go beyond these and tap into the full power of Windows programming, the way to do it is by calling external procedures, whether the procedures are supplied by Windows, are written by third-party vendors, or are procedures that you write yourself. In short, external procedures are used for a variety of reasons:

- Many Windows and system-level progamming tasks cannot be accomplished purely by writing Visual Basic code. External procedures provide a way to do this.

- Specific details about hardware devices can be hidden inside external libraries of procedures, allowing only an "interface" or accepted range of messages to be sent to the libraries by application programs.
- Tasks that are performance-critical, such as graphics, calculations, and file I/O, can be coded in languages such as C, C++, and Assembly Language. The code that handles these tasks can be placed in external procedures and called from Visual Basic.

10.1.1 Static and Dynamic Linking

Nearly all programming languages let you write programs that call *external procedures,* that is, procedures that are not part of the original program. External procedures are often written in another language, sometimes part of a library purchased from a third-party vendor. There are many custom controls and libraries for Visual Basic that enhance its power and range of applications. External procedures must be linked to their calling program. There are two general ways to do this, by either static or dynamic linking.

Static linking is a way of binding external procedures to a program in such a way that the program and the procedures it calls are stored in the same executable file. An advantage to this approach is that all of a program's executable code is in the same place, so it is not necessary to guess which files are required in order for the program to run. On the other hand, there is a major disadvantage: If more than one program has to link to the same procedure, each will contain a separate copy of the procedure. This results in large executable programs and considerable use of memory at run time.

Dynamic linking allows compiled procedures to be stored in a separate file from the calling program; this file is called a *dynamic link library,* or *DLL.* There are distinct advantages to this approach:

- The same DLL procedures can be shared by multiple programs without their needing to have their own copies.
- A DLL procedure does not usually have to be loaded into memory until a program actually requests it. When the procedure is no longer needed, it can be removed from memory. This results in smaller programs and more efficient use of memory.
- A DLL library can be modified and improved without having to recompile the programs that use it. Windows, for example, undergoes regular upgrades in which internal details of its DLLs are modified.

DLL filenames can have a variety of extensions, such as DLL, VBX, OCX, DRV, and EXE. Visual Basic custom controls and *ActiveX* controls are also DLLs.

Application Programmer's Interface (API). The best examples of DLL procedures are in Windows itself. The complete collection of external procedures supplied by Windows is called the *Windows API library,* where API stands for *application programmer's interface.* The API library contains procedures, constants, and data structures that let you hook into the full power of Windows programming. The API library is spread out over a number of different DLL files. The most common ones are:

- Windows 3.1: user.dll, gdi.dll, and kernel.dll contain only 16-bit DLLs.

- Windows 95 and Windows NT: kernel32.dll, user32.dll, gdi32.dll, and comdlg32.dll contain 16-bit and 32-bit DLLs.

The 16-bit version of Visual Basic can only call 16-bit DLLs; the 32-bit version of Visual Basic can only call 32-bit DLLs.

Passing parameters and getting return values from the API procedures can be tricky because the API data types are based on the 'C' programming language. Some translation is necessary to pass and return data to Visual Basic programs.

> *Differences Between VB4 and VB5.* Visual Basic 4 programs are only partially compiled, so a VB4 application must be accompanied by a number of runtime DLLs when installed on a user's machine. In other words, VB4 implements its own language as a set of DLLs. For example, the file vb40032.dll must be in the Windows\System directory before a 32-bit VB4 program can be executed. Numerous other DLLs are also required. VB4 does not provide a way to create DLL procedures, so DLLs are typically created in C, C++, Assembly Language, and Borland Delphi.
>
> Visual Basic 5 programs can be compiled into native code executable programs, providing for improved performance. VB5 can also be used to create DLLs called *ActiveX components* and *ActiveX controls*.

10.2 Declaring and Calling DLL Procedures

There are two basic steps to calling a DLL: First, it must be declared, using the **Declare** statement. Next, it is called in the same way that you call ordinary Visual Basic procedures.

10.2.1 The Declare Statement

The **Declare** statement identifies the procedure's name, DLL filename, and parameter list. The syntax is:

```
[Public | Private ] Declare Sub name Lib "libname"
    [Alias "aliasname" ] [([paramlist])]
```

Elements enclosed in brackets [. . .] are optional: *name* is the name of the procedure, *libname* is the name of the DLL file containing the procedure, *aliasname* indicates that the procedure being called has another name inside the DLL, and *paramlist* is the procedure's parameter list, which has the same syntax as all Visual Basic procedures. By default, Declare is Public.

The syntax for declaring a function procedure is almost the same, except that it uses the **Function** keyword and returns a data type:

```
[Public | Private ] Declare Function name Lib "libname" [Alias
   "aliasname" ] [([arglist])][As type]
```

A Declare statement that is qualified as **Public** can only be placed in the declarations section of a code module (.bas) file. Declare statements in forms and class modules must be declared **Private**, and must be located in the declarations section.

Using an Alias. Sometimes, the name of a DLL procedure is the same as a Visual Basic keyword, or the name contains characters that would not be allowed in a Visual Basic identifier. In either case, an alias is used in the Declare statement. Windows API functions having an alias name ending with the letter "A" are 32-bit functions.

> *Getting the Right Declaration.* Most programmers who use the Windows API to any great extent borrow or purchase a reference book on Windows API procedures. One well-known source is Daniel Appleman's *Visual Basic Programmer's Guide to the Win32 API*. Fortunately, Visual Basic is supplied with text files containing the Declare statements for all API procedures, for both 16-bit and 32-bit platforms. Some of the filenames are Win30api.txt, Win31api.txt, and Win32api.txt. VB4 also ships with the file vb4dll.txt, which contains helpful information on how to create your own DLLs in C or C++ and call them from Visual Basic.

10.2.2 The API Viewer Utility Program

VB4 also ships with a useful utility program called apilod32.exe, which reads a text file containing Windows API declarations and creates an Access database (Figure 1). You can then browse the various categories of data types, constants, and Declare statements for all API procedures. When you run the program for the first time, select the **File/Load Text File** command, and select the Win32api.txt file (for Windows 95 or Windows NT users). The program will build a database called Win32api.mdb.

Figure 1. The API Viewer Program.

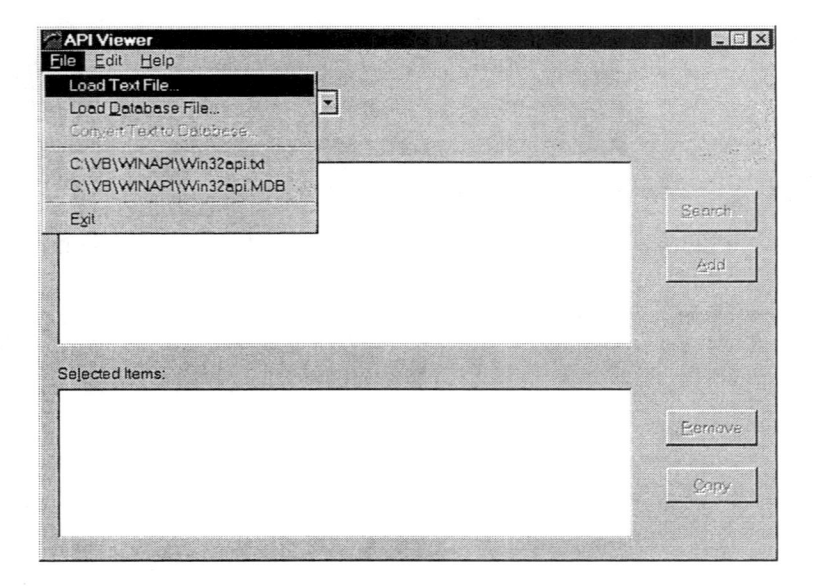

Chap 10: Tapping into the Windows API   419

The next time you run the program, select the **File/Load Database File** command, and open the Win32api.mdb file. Then select either Constants, Declares, or Types from the combo box. For example, if we select **Declares**, we then see a list of API procedures. In Figure 2 we have selected the **GetSystemInfo** procedure and clicked the **Add** button to add its name to the list at the bottom.

Figure 2. Selecting API Functions.

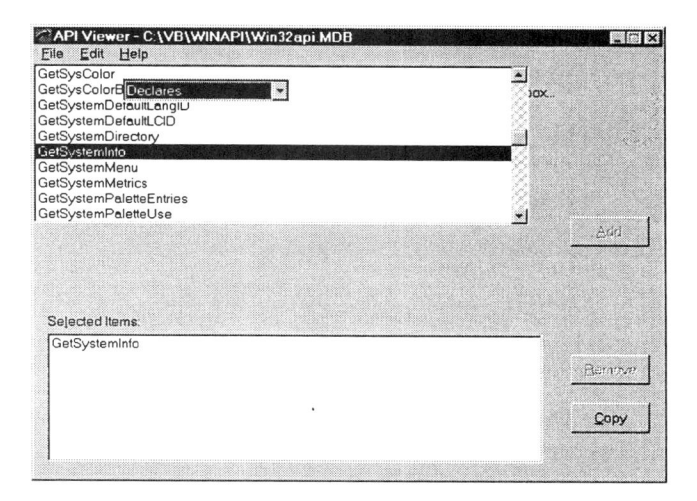

When the lower box contains all the items you want, click the **Copy** button to place the declarations on the Windows clipboard. You can then paste the clipboard contents into the declarations section of a module or form.

10.2.3 First Example: Flashing a Window Caption

For a quick introduction to DLLs, let's write a short program that calls two API functions: **FlashWindow**, a Windows API function procedure that flashes the caption area of a window, and **Sleep**, a procedure that creates a delay in a program's execution. The program will flash a window's caption off and on at regular intervals.

Create a new program and name its startup form **frmMain**. Create a code module named **Module1** and place the following in the declarations area:

```
Declare Sub Sleep Lib "kernel32" _
        (ByVal dwMilliseconds As Long)

Declare Function FlashWindow Lib "user32" Alias "FlashWindow" _
        (ByVal hwnd As Long, ByVal bInvert As Long) As Long
```

In **FlashWindow**, the first parameter, **hwnd**, is a handle to the window that will be flashed. The second parameter, **bInvert**, must be non-zero if we want to toggle the window's caption bar, and zero if we want to return the caption bar to its original state.

Next, create a command button on frmMain, set its caption to "Flash", and place the following code inside its Click event procedure. It toggles the form's caption off and on, with a 100 millisecond delay between calls to FlashWindow:

```
Private Sub Command1_Click()
  Dim j As Integer
  For j = 1 To 4
    FlashWindow Me.hWnd, 1
    Sleep 100
  Next j
End Sub
```

The **hWnd** property is only available at run time. It is called a *window handle*, and is a unique long integer that identifies a window or a control. We have used hWnd in any programs in this book before. But hWnd was designed for just this situation, when a window handle is passed to a DLL procedure.

Run the program and observe the flashing caption area of the main window.

A Modular Design. Rather than call a DLL function directly, a better approach is to create a procedure "wrapper" around the DLL function that simplifies its use. In the following example, **FlashCaption** has two parameters: a Form object, and a count of the number of times the caption should be flashed:

```
Public Sub FlashCaption(F As Form, count As Integer)
'Flash the caption bar of a form, <count> times.
  Dim j As Integer
  For j = 1 To count
    FlashWindow F.hWnd, 1    'DLL call
    Sleep 100                'DLL call
  Next j
End Sub
```

A procedure wrapper like this can provide both simplicity and flexibility to its callers. In this case, we allowed the caller to decide how many times the caption should be flashed. It is unnecessary for the calling procedure to worry about using a loop or calling the Sleep procedure. Now we can flash the current window's caption with a single statement:

```
FlashCaption Me, 4
```

FlashWindow has only two parameters, but most Windows API procedures are more complex. Using a Visual Basic procedure as an interface layer surrounding DLL calls can help prevent runtime errors caused by passing invalid arguments to DLLs.

Differences Between Win32 and Win16. *Win32* is the name of the full 32-bit API for the Windows NT operating system. *Win32c*, used by Windows 95, is a subset of Win32. Using Win32c, you can call all of the Win32 functions, but some of them are not yet implemented under Windows 95. Windows 3.1, the older version of Windows, uses the *Win16* API. There are a few important differences between the two APIs that you need to be aware of when calling DLL procedures:

- The names of functions in the two libraries are not always the same.
- Win32 has support for *Unicode* characters, in which each character is stored in 16 bits and can have a value between 0 and 65,535. Unicode makes it possible to represent character sets from all world languages. Win16 supports only the 8-bit ANSI character set, not Unicode.
- There are many new procedures in Win32 that did not exist in Win16.
- Under Win32, DLL function names are case-sensitive, but under Win16, they are not.

It should be mentioned that Unicode is the native character set for both Visual Basic and Windows NT, but is not supported by Windows 95. Therefore, when Visual Basic programs pass Unicode strings to the Win32 API, the strings are automatically translated to 8-bit ANSI so they can be processed by Windows 95.

10.3 Parameters in DLL Procedures

Because DLL procedures have traditionally been written in the C language, DLL declarations ordinarily use C data types. It is important to understand how Visual Basic data types compare to C data types so arguments can be correctly passed to DLL procedures. The examples we use will assume that the DLLs use 32-bit integers, which is true in the Win32 API. In Table 1, all Visual Basic parameters require the ByVal qualifier. In addition, Table 2 lists a number of Windows API data types that must also be translated to Visual Basic. Fortunately, the hard work of translating the Windows API procedure parameters into Visual Basic has already been done for you, so you can copy and paste them from the from the Win32api.txt file into your programs. If you use DLL procedures from another source (your own DLLs or those written by another party), you will still need to know how to translate C parameter types to Visual Basic types.

Table 1. C and Visual Basic Parameter Types.

C Parameter Type	VB Parameter Type	Comments
char, unsigned char	Byte	Do not use String * 1, because VB Strings use 16-bit Unicode characters.
short, unsigned short	Integer	VB Integer is always signed.
int, unsigned, long, unsigned long	Long	VB Long is always signed.
float	Single	
double	Double	
NULL	String	Use the vbNullString constant.
char *	String	Always pass ByVal.

Passing by Value or Reference. By default, Visual Basic passes arguments by reference. DLL procedures, on the other hand, follow the C/C++ default of passing arguments by value. This means that in the Declare statement for DLL functions, Visual Basic programs have to explicitly use the ByVal qualifier, unless the DLL parameter is a pointer.

We use the terminology that refers to *parameters* as the identifiers in a procedure declaration, and *arguments* as the values that are passed to a procedure.

Table 2. Windows API and Visual Basic Parameter Types.

Windows API Parameter Type	Visual Basic Parameter Type	Comments
BYTE	Byte	Unsigned in C, signed in VB.
WORD	Integer	Unsigned in C, signed in VB.
BOOL	Long	Boolean (True <> 0, False = 0)
DWORD	Long	32-bit address, unsigned in C, signed in VB.
HWND, HPEN, HGLOBAL	Long	Handle to a Windows object.
LPSTR	ByVal As String	Pointer to a character string.
FARPROC	(not supported)	32-bit pointer to a procedure.

10.3.1 String Parameters

When passing a String variable to an API function, the ByVal qualifier must be used in the parameter declaration. When ByVal is used, Visual Basic copies the string variable to a null-terminated ANSI string and passes the address of the string to the procedure. The procedure can modify the string if necessary. In other words, the usual meaning of ByVal does not apply when passing strings.

If a DLL procedure needs to insert characters into a string parameter, storage space for the characters must be reserved before the procedure is called. A String declaration such as the following, by itself, does not reserve any space, and a runtime error would result if a DLL tried to insert characters into the string:

```
Dim buffer As String
```

On the other hand, the following statement reserves sixty-one bytes of storage for **buffer** and fills it with null bytes. Now a DLL procedure can insert as many as sixty characters into the buffer and follow it with a null byte:

```
buffer = String$(61,0)
```

When reserving space for characters, remember that one additional character position must be reserved for the null byte appended to all strings by C language programs.

Passing NULL Rather Than a String Pointer. Some DLL functions allow a string parameter to be either a pointer to a string or the value NULL. The Visual Basic equivalent to NULL is the predefined constant **vbNullString**.

10.3.2 Numeric Parameters

Boolean Values. There is an important difference between the way the 'C' language and Visual Basic treat boolean values. In C, **True** equals any nonzero integer value, and **False** equals zero. In Visual Basic, True equals –1 and False equals 0. So if you pass True from Visual Basic to a DLL, everything is fine. But if a DLL returns a nonzero value, the Visual Basic program will not interpret it as being True unless by coincidence the value happens to be equal to –1.

A Visual Basic program can use a simple boolean expression to convert the long integer result of a DLL function to a boolean value. For example, if MyDLL returns zero, **result** will equal False; otherwise, **result** will equal True:

```
Dim result As Boolean
result = MyDLL() <> 0
```

Or, a less cryptic way of converting the result would be the following:

```
Dim n as Long, result As Boolean
n = MyDLL()
If n = 0 Then
   result = False
Else
   result = True
End If
```

Unsigned Integers. Windows API procedures and other DLLs often have unsigned integer parameters. All Visual Basic integers are signed, which potentially creates an overflow problem. An unsigned long in C, for example, holds a value between 0 and 4,294,967,295. But the range for a Long in Visual Basic is –2,147,483,648 to +2,147,483,647.

Floating-Point Numbers. The Single and Double data types in Visual Basic are compatible with the single and double types in C, as long as the C compiler uses the IEEE floating-point standard and the Microsoft calling convention for floating-point numbers.

Handles. Handles are 32-bit integers that identify objects such as forms and controls. Handles are compatible with Visual Basic's Long data type. They are never used for calculations, so the difference between a signed value versus an unsigned one is irrelevant.

10.3.3 User-Defined Types

When a DLL procedure parameter is a pointer to a structure, the equivalent in Visual Basic is to create a user-defined type and declare the parameter with the ByRef qualifier. For example, RECT is a user-defined type that is used in many Declare statements for API procedures:

```
Type RECT
  Left As Long
  Top As Long
  Right As Long
  Bottom As Long
End Type
```

For example, the DrawText API function names **lpRect** as one of its parameters, where "lp" indicates that the parameter is a long (32-bit) pointer to a RECT structure:

```
Declare Function DrawText Lib "user32" ...
    (..., ByRef lpRect As RECT, ...) As Long
```

By default, Visual Basic passes parameters by reference, so the **ByRef** qualifier is often omitted from the Declare statement.

Character Arrays. If a C structure contains a string (also known as a character array), the Visual Basic program must declare this as an array of bytes.

10.3.4 Example: GetWindowsDirectory

Sometimes it is useful to know the full path of the Windows directory. It is there, for example, that the win.ini file is stored. The GetWindowsDirectory procedure returns the path in **winPath**, along with the length of the string in **count**:

```
Declare Function GetWindowsDirectory Lib "kernel32" Alias _
    "GetWindowsDirectoryA" (ByVal winPath As String, _
    ByVal count As Long) As Long
```

Before calling GetWindowsDirectory, prepare the **winPath** parameter by padding the string with null bytes. The following example uses the String$ function to allocate 128 bytes of storage for winPath:

```
Dim winPath As String, count As Long
winPath = String$(128, Chr$(0))
count = GetWindowsDirectory(winPath, 128)
WindowsDirectory = Left$(winPath, count)
```

After GetWindowsDirectory is called, **count** equals the number of bytes placed inside **winPath**, and the Left$ function extracts only **count** characters from winPath. The following program listing is a simple demonstration of this procedure:

```
Private Declare Function GetWindowsDirectory Lib "kernel32" _
    Alias "GetWindowsDirectoryA" (ByVal winPath As String, _
```

```
    ByVal count As Long) As Long

Private Function WindowsDirectory() As String
  Dim winPath As String, count As Long
  winPath = String$(128, Chr$(0))
  count = GetWindowsDirectory(winPath, 128)
  WindowsDirectory = Left$(winPath, count)
End Function

Private Sub Form_Load()
  lblWinDir = WindowsDirectory()
End Sub
```

The main window displays the Windows directory path in Figure 3. There are many Windows API procedures that can prove useful to Visual Basic programmers. A few of these are listed in Table 3.

Figure 3. Windows Directory Path.

Table 3. Some Useful Windows API Procedures.

API Procedure	Description
BitBlt	Copy a bitmap from one device context to another.
BringWindowToTop	Activate a window.
CreateCompatibleBitmap	Create a device-independent bitmap.
ExtractIcon	Find and extract icons from an executable file or DLL.
FindExecutable	Find the executable program that is associated with a specified filename. For example, a filename such as myfile.txt is usually associated with the Notepad editor because of the .txt extension.
GetLogicalDrives	Determine which logical drive letters exist.
GetSystemDirectory	Get the full path name of the Windows system directory.
GetSystemInfo	Get information about the computer's hardware.
GetSystemMetrics	Get information about the Windows environment.
GetWindowsDirectory	Get the full path name of the Windows directory.
SetActiveWindow	Activate a window.
IsWindow	Determines if a window handle is valid. Can be called before using the handle for other operations.
SendMessage	Send a message to a window. The procedure does not return until the message is processed.

10.4 Reading and Writing Application INI Files

For a long time, Windows applications have used INI files to store information about their location and configuration options. At first, programs tended to clutter up the win.ini file that is shared by all other Windows applications. But the preferred method is to store an application's setup information in a private INI file, usually named after the application itself, and usually located in the \Windows directory. Figure 4, for example, shows an abbreviated sample of the vb.ini file created by Visual Basic.

An INI file may contain any number of sections, each denoted by an identifier enclosed in square brackets [...]. In Figure 4, the sections are [Visual Basic], [Add-Ins32], and [VBX Conversions32] (for brevity, some sections were omitted). Within each section, there can be any number of keys, identified by the first word on a line, followed by the = sign. For example, in the [Visual Basic] section, some keys are: vbpath, ReportDesign, DataAccess, and so on. The string following the = sign is the key's value. If the value consists of multiple parts, they will be each separated by a space. When a value is 1 or 0, the 1 generally indicates True and 0 indicates False.

Figure 4. Sample VB.INI File (for VB4).

```
[Visual Basic]
vbpath=C:\vb
ReportDesign=1
DataAccess=1
DebugWindow=647 368 233 279 0
MainWindow=26 0 693 76 1
ToolBar=0
ProjectWindow=595 56 280 246 9
ToolBox=11 80 0 0 1
PropertiesWindow=737 11 233 689 9
ColorPalette=69 391 0 0 0
CustomColors=16777215 16777215 16777215 16777215 16777215 16777215
16777215 16777215 16777215 16777215 16777215 16777215 16777215 16777215
16777215 16777215
(etc...)

[Add-Ins32]
DataFormDesigner.DFDClass=1

[VBX Conversions32]
msoutlin.vbx={BE4F3AC8-AEC9-101A-947B-
00DD010F7B46}#1.0#0;C:\WINDOWS\SYSTEM\msoutl32.ocx
cmdialog.vbx={F9043C88-F6F2-101A-A3C9-
08002B2F49FB}#1.0#0;C:\WINDOWS\SYSTEM\comdlg32.ocx
grid.vbx={A8B3B723-0B5A-101B-B22E-
00AA0037B2FC}#1.0#0;C:\WINDOWS\SYSTEM\grid32.ocx
crystal.vbx={00025600-0000-0000-C000-
000000000046}#1.0#0;C:\WINDOWS\SYSTEM\crystl32.ocx
(etc...)
```

10.4.1 Maintaining a Program's INI File

Any Visual Basic program can create an INI file and place configuration information in it that will be retained from one runtime session to another. It is the program's responsibility to load the values from the INI file on startup, and to save any changes to the values when the program exits.

The only difficulty is, Visual Basic does not provide any standard procedures for reading and writing INI files. One could, of course, open an INI file as an ordinary sequential text file, search for the sections and keys, and update the information manually. But this is where the Windows API comes to the rescue: functions such as GetProfileString and WriteProfileString automatically read and write the strings associated with keys.

Table 4 contains a list of API procedures that greatly simplify the reading and writing of strings to WIN.INI, and Table 5 lists procedures that interact with an application's INI file.

Table 4. API Procedures that Read and Write the WIN.INI File.

Procedure Name	Description
GetProfileSection	Retrieve a list of all key names and values for a specified section. Returns a string in which each name is terminated by a single null byte and the string is terminated by two null bytes.
GetProfileString	Retrieve the string associated with a particular key name.
GetProfileInt	Retrieve the integer associated with a particular key name.
WriteProfileSection	Set all of the key names and associated values for a specified section.
WriteProfileString	Set the string value that is associated with a specified key name.

Table 5. API Procedures that Read and Write a Private application.INI File.

Procedure Name	Description
GetPrivateProfileSection	Retrieve a list of all key names and values for a specified section. Returns a string in which each name is terminated by a single null byte and the string is terminated by two null bytes.
GetPrivateProfileString	Retrieve the string associated with a particular key name.
GetPrivateProfileInt	Retrieve the integer associated with a particular key name.
WritePrivateProfileSection	Set all of the key names and associated values for a specified section.
WritePrivateProfileString	Set the string value that is associated with a specified key name.

Example: GetPrivateProfileString. Let's take a closer look at the parameters and return value of GetPrivateProfileString.

Table 6 contains a description of each parameter listed in the following declaration:

```
Declare Function GetPrivateProfileString Lib "kernel32" Alias _
    "GetPrivateProfileStringA" (ByVal lpApplicationName As String, _
    ByVal lpKeyName As Any, ByVal lpDefault As String, ByVal _
    lpReturnedString As String, ByVal nSize As Long, ByVal _
    lpFileName As String) As Long
```

Table 6. Description of GetPrivateProfileString Parameters.

Parameter	Description
lpApplicationName	The name of the section in which the key name is located. If this parameter is equal to vbNullString, lpReturnedString will be filled with a list of all the sections in the INI file.
lpKeyName	The key name or entry to retrieve. If this parameter is equal to vbNullString, lpReturnedString will be filled with a list of all the key names in the section specified by lpApplicationName.
lpDefault	The default value to return if the specified entry is not found.
lpReturnedString	A string buffer preallocated to at least nSize bytes.
nSize	Maximum number of characters to load into lpReturnedString.
lpFileName	The name of the private INI file. If a full path is not given, the Windows directory will be assumed.
(return value)	A count of the number of bytes copied into the lpReturnedString buffer, not counting the final null byte.

Calling **GetPrivateProfileString** from a Visual Basic program involves some preparation of the arguments that will be passed to the function. For example, it is necessary to create a string to hold the function's return value and pad it with null characters:

```
Const BufSize = 128
Dim buffer As String, count  As Long
buffer = String$(BufSize, Chr$(0))
```

The function returns an integer that indicates the number of characters in the buffer, so we use the Left$ function to keep only the significant part of the string. For example, the following retrieves the string associated with the **LastRunDate** key inside the section called **History**:

```
count = GetPrivateProfileString("History", "LastRunDate", _
        "", buffer, BufSize, "sample.ini" )
buffer = Left$(buffer, count)
```

This is an example of the corresponding entry in the private INI file:

```
[History]
LastRunDate=12-05-1997
```

ReadPrivateString. To avoid repeating all of these statements each time an API procedure is called, the ReadPrivateString procedure acts as a wrapper around the API call:

```
Public Function ReadPrivateString(sectionName As String, _
   keyName As String, FileName As String) As String
   Const BufSize = 128
   Dim buffer As String, count  As Long
   buffer = String$(BufSize, Chr$(0))
   count = GetPrivateProfileString(sectionName, keyName, _
            "", buffer, BufSize, FileName)
   ReadPrivateString = Left$(buffer, count)
End Function
```

Now a program can get a key value from an INI file with just a single statement:

```
lblLastDate = ReadPrivateString("History","LastRunDate","sample.ini")
```

Most Visual Basic programmers either create or purchase a library of such procedures, which are designed to simplify API calls.

WritePrivateString. The following WritePrivateString procedure simplifies the writing of a key string to an INI file, and allows us to do some useful error trapping if the INI file is write-protected:

```
Public Function WritePrivateString(sectionName As String, _
      keyName As String, strValue As String, _
      FileName As String) As Boolean
   Dim buffer As String, status As Long
   WritePrivateString = False
   If FileName = "" Then Exit Function
   buffer = strValue + Chr$(0)   'append null byte
   status = WritePrivateProfileString(sectionName, keyName, _
            buffer, FileName)
   WritePrivateString = status <> 0
End Function
```

The following statements save the current date as the **LastRunDate** key value:

```
WritePrivateString "History", "LastRunDate", Date$, "sample.ini"
```

10.5 Example: The clsIniFile Class

Creating wrapper procedures around Windows API calls is a good step toward making the procedures easier to use. But you can improve them further by grouping together related API functions into a class. All of the low-level details related to the API functions can be kept in a single class module, and this module can easily be plugged into any program we wish. All you have to do is create an instance of the clsIniFile class and begin setting properties and calling methods. As you discover new capabilities to add to the class, it can easily be expanded. A program using the **clsIniFile** class must include the class module file in the current project, create an instance of the class, and set its FileName property:

```
Dim iniFile As clsIniFile
...
Set iniFile = New clsIniFile
iniFile.FileName = "sample.ini"
```

10.5.1 Class Description

There are two public methods in the clsIniFile class: **ReadPrivateString** and **WritePrivateString**. All other methods are private and are hidden from the class user. There is one read/write property, **FileName**.

Properties:

- *FileName.* Set and get the name of the private INI file. If a complete path is not given, the file will be assumed to be in the Windows directory. If the user forgets to set the FileName property before calling one of the class methods, an error message will display.

Public Methods:

- *ReadPrivateString.* Inputs to the ReadPrivateString function are a section name and a key name to be found in the specified section of the INI file. If the section and key are found, this method returns the string value associated with the key; otherwise, an empty string is returned:

```
Public Function ReadPrivateString(sectionName As String, _
    keyName As String) As String
```

- *WritePrivateString.* Inputs to the WritePrivateString function are a section name, a key name, and a string value to be associated with the key. The method returns True if the key and string were successfully written to the INI file. This is the function declaration:

```
Public Function WritePrivateString(sectionName As String, _
    keyName As String, strValue As String) As Boolean
```

Private Methods:

- *IsValidFilename.* Returns True if the FileName property has been initialized to a non-blank string; otherwise, returns False and displays an error message box.
- *GetPrivateProfileString.* Windows API function declaration. Reads a profile string from a private INI file.
- *WritePrivateProfileString.* Windows API function declaration. Writes a profile string to a private INI file.

10.5.2 A Short Test Program

To test the clsIniFile class, let's create a simple form with two combo boxes and a text box (Figure 5). As the user switches between sections and keys, the program attempts to get the matching key values from the INI file. The user can also modify a key value by typing into the text box and clicking the Write button. Each of the named controls are labeled.

Figure 5. Testing the clsIniFile Class.

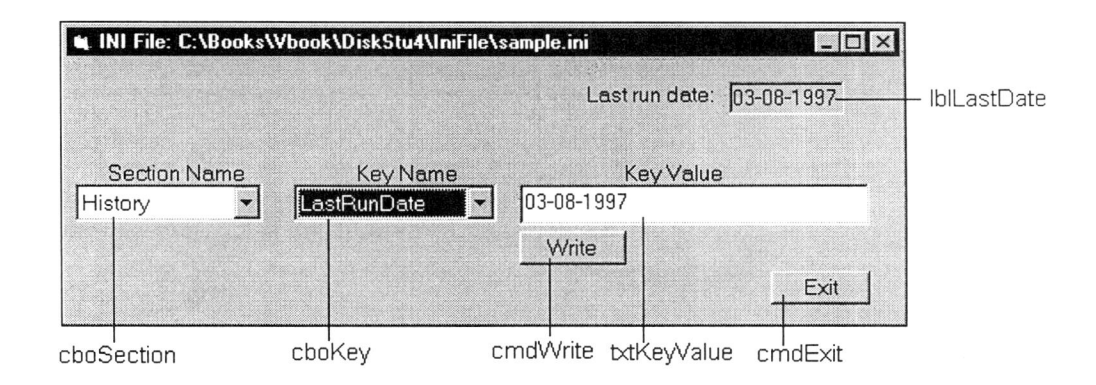

A complete listing of the test program follows:

```
Option Explicit
Private fileNameP As String

Private _
Declare Function GetPrivateProfileString Lib "kernel32" Alias _
    "GetPrivateProfileStringA" (ByVal lpApplicationName As String, _
    ByVal lpKeyName As Any, ByVal lpDefault As String, ByVal _
    lpReturnedString As String, ByVal nSize As Long, ByVal _
    lpFileName As String) As Long

Private _
Declare Function WritePrivateProfileString Lib "kernel32" Alias _
    "WritePrivateProfileStringA" (ByVal lpApplicationName As String, _
    ByVal lpKeyName As Any, ByVal lpString As Any, ByVal lpFileName _
    As String) As Long

Public Function ReadPrivateString(sectionName As String, _
    keyName As String) As String
'Return the string associated with keyName, or "" if not found.
    Const BufSize = 128
    Dim buffer As String, count  As Long
    If Not ValidFilename Then Exit Function
    buffer = String$(BufSize, Chr$(0))
    count = GetPrivateProfileString(sectionName, keyName, _
            "", buffer, BufSize, fileName)
    ReadPrivateString = Left$(buffer, count)
End Function

Public Function WritePrivateString(sectionName As String, _
        keyName As String, strValue As String) As Boolean
'Write a string value to the INI file, return True if successful.
'If the INI file cannot be modified, display an error message
```

```
'and return a value of False.

    Dim buffer As String, status As Long
    If Not ValidFilename Then Exit Function
    buffer = strValue + Chr$(0)   'append null byte
    status = WritePrivateProfileString(sectionName, keyName, _
         buffer, fileName)
    WritePrivateString = status <> 0
End Function

Public Property Get FileName() As String
  FileName = fileNameP
End Property

Public Property Let FileName(vNewValue As String)
   fileNameP = vNewValue
End Property

Private Function ValidFilename()
'Return true if the FileName property has been set
'to a non-blank string.

  If Len(FileName) > 0 Then
    ValidFilename = True
  Else
    MsgBox "The INI file name was not initialized.", _
      vbInformation, "clsIniFile Class"
    ValidFilename = False
  End If
End Function
```

The source code for the test program is listed here:

```
Option Explicit
Const IniFilename = "sample.ini"
Dim iniFile As clsIniFile

Private Sub Form_Load()
' Create an instance of the clsIniFile class, set the
' form's caption, initialize the FileName property,
' get the program's last run date from the INI file.

  Set iniFile = New clsIniFile
  iniFile.FileName = App.Path + "\" + IniFilename
  Me.Caption = "INI File: " + iniFile.FileName
  lblLastDate.Caption = iniFile.ReadPrivateString( _
                    "History", "LastRunDate")
  cboSection.ListIndex = 0
  cboKey.ListIndex = 0
End Sub

Private Sub cboKey_Click()
```

```
      txtKeyVal.Text = iniFile.ReadPrivateString( _
        cboSection.Text, cboKey.Text)
   End Sub

   Private Sub cboSection_Click()
      txtKeyVal.Text = iniFile.ReadPrivateString( _
        cboSection.Text, cboKey.Text)
   End Sub

   Private Sub cmdExit_Click()
      iniFile.WritePrivateString "History", "LastRunDate", _
        Date$
      Unload Me
   End Sub

   Private Sub cmdRead_Click()
      txtKeyVal = iniFile.ReadPrivateString(cboSection.Text, cboKey.Text)
   End Sub

   Private Sub cmdWrite_Click()
     If Not iniFile.WritePrivateString(cboSection.Text, cboKey.Text, _
        txtKeyVal.Text) Then
        MsgBox "Could not modify the following INI file, probably " _
           + "because the file is marked as read-only: " & _
           iniFile.FileName, vbInformation, "Error"
     End If
   End Sub
```

10.6 Review Questions

1. What are some *low-level* programming tasks? What are some *high-level* tasks?

2. What three letters are the acronym for the Windows DLL procedure library?

3. Name at least two reasons for calling DLL procedures from Visual Basic.

4. What is static linking? What is its primary advantage?

5. What is dynamic linking? In particular, how is it different from static linking?

6. Does a custom control (ActiveX control) use static linking or dynamic linking?

7. Why is the sharing of a single DLL procedure by several programs useful?

8. Name at least three well-known file extensions for DLL files.

9. How is the 'C' programming language related to DLL procedures?

10. Can a DLL procedure be created in VB 4?

11. In what way is an ActiveX component like a DLL? How is it different?

12. How is the Declare statement important when calling a DLL from a Visual Basic program?

13. What is the purpose of an alias name in the Declare statement?

14. What does the sample FlashWindow procedure do?
15. How can you make a program pause for one second?
16. Describe the API Viewer utility program.
17. What is a window handle?
18. What is the equivalent, in Visual Basic, of the C language's pointer to a string?
19. Should a string created by a DLL procedure be assigned directly to a Visual Basic variable, or should it be assigned to an array of characters?
20. What is the Visual Basic equivalent to a LPSTR data type when passed by the Windows API?
21. When passing an integer argument to a DLL procedure, should it be passed by value or by reference?
22. Which API function returns the path to the directory where Windows is installed?
23. Which API functions obtain information from the Windows 95 System Registry?
24. When Visual Basic passes an empty string to an API function, why is it important to fill the string first?
25. How can an API function be used to set tab stops in list boxes?

10.7 Chapter Exercises

10.7.1 Expanding the ClsIniFile Class

Expand the clsIniFile class introduced in this chapter to include two more operations: GetKeyValueList and GetSectionList.

GetKeyValueList. The GetKeyValueList function should fill an array of key names and its corresponding array of key values with all of the keys in a given section of an INI file:

```
Public Function GetKeyValueList(sectionName As String, _
    keyNames() As String, keyVals() As String) As Long
' Given a section name, fill an array of key names, fill
' an array of key values, and return a count of the number
' of keys found. Calls the GetPrivateProfileSection
' API function. Sample call to this function:

'   Dim keyNames(50) As String, keyVals(50) As String
'   Dim numKeys as Long
'   numKeys = GetKeyValueList("Colors", keyNames, keyVals)
```

This is the API function declaration:

```
Private Declare Function GetPrivateProfileSection Lib _
    "kernel32" Alias "GetPrivateProfileSectionA" (ByVal _
    sectionName As String, ByVal lpReturnedString As String, _
```

```
           ByVal nSize As Long, ByVal lpFileName As String) As Long
```

GetSectionList. The GetSectionList function should fill an array with the names of all sections in the INI file and return a count of the number of sections found:

```
Public Function GetSectionList(sectionNames() As String) As Long
' Fill an array with the names of the sections and return a count
' of the number of sections found. Sample call to this function:

'   Dim sectionNames(20) As String, count As Long
'   count = GetSectionList( sectionNames )
```

There is a trick to implementing this function. When you call the GetPrivateProfileString API function, if the first argument (lpApplicationName) is null, then lpReturnedString will be filled with all of the section names in the INI file. To pass a null argument to the function, use the predefined constant, vbNullString:

```
Const BufSize = 1024
Dim buffer As String, count As Long
buffer = String$(BufSize, Chr$(0))
count = GetPrivateProfileString(vbNullString, "", _
      "", buffer, BufSize, FileName)
```

At this point, **buffer** contains all of the section names, each terminated by a single null byte. The last section name is terminated by two null bytes. All you have to do, then, is set up a loop that looks for the null bytes and copies each section name into a separate element of the sectionNames array.

10.7.2   Setting Tab Stops in a List Box

A frequent problem that Visual Basic programmers have when trying to display more than one column in a list box is that the columns do not line up when a proportional font is used. This happens because each character has a different width. A solution used earlier in this book was to use a monospace font such as Courier New. But it is still possible to use proportional fonts, given a knowledge of Windows API functions—use the **SendMessage** API function to send an LB_SETTABSTOPS message to the list box.

Your task is to write a program that demonstrates the setting of tab stops in a list box. Allow the user to interactively move the tab stop positions, using a separate scroll bar to control each tab stop. Add several lines of text to the list box, with four columns in each line.

Here is the declaration of the SendMessage function. The first parameter is a handle to the list box, the second parameter is the message to be sent, the third parameter counts the number of tab stops to be set, and the fourth parameter is a pointer to the first element of an array of tab stop values:

```
Declare Function SendMessage Lib "user32" Alias "SendMessageA" _
    (ByVal hwnd As Long, ByVal wMsg As Long, ByVal wParam As Long, _
    lParam As Any) As Long
```

The following is an example of declaring and initializing the necessary procedure arguments before calling SendMessage:

```
Const LB_SETTABSTOPS = &H192
Dim numTabs As Long, tabArray(0 to 5) As Long
numTabs = 3
tabArray(0) = 48
tabArray(1) = 96
tabArray(2) = 144
SendMessage List1.hwnd, LB_SETTABSTOPS, numTabs, tabArray(0)
```

When calling SendMessage, the last parameter is tabArray(0). Because Visual Basic passes by reference, this is the same as passing a pointer to the first element of the array. After this message has been sent, it is necessary to call the list box's Refresh method to force it to redraw itself:

```
List1.Refresh
```

As in other examples of API procedures shown in this chapter, it is a good idea to create a function that acts as a wrapper around SendMessage. The parameters would be a list box, an array of tab positions, and the number of tabs:

```
Sub SetTabStops(lbox As ListBox, tabArray() As Long, numTabs As Long)
    SendMessage lbox.hwnd, LB_SETTABSTOPS, numTabs, tabArray(0)
End Sub
```

Sample Program. Figure 6 shows a sample of the program when it starts. The user may now click on the three horizontal scroll bars to change each of the three tab stops.

Figure 6. Tab Stop Program at Startup.

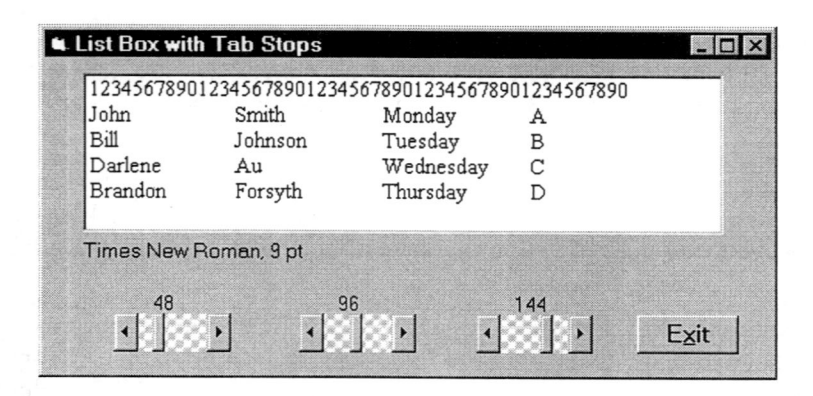

A label just below the list box should display the Font.Name and Font.Size properties of the list box.

Moving the Tab Stops. When the user clicks on a scroll bar, the number just above it (a label) is updated, and the appropriate tab column in the list box moves. In Figure 7, for example, the user has scrolled the first tab stop backward from 48 to 29.

Figure 7. Tab Stop Program.

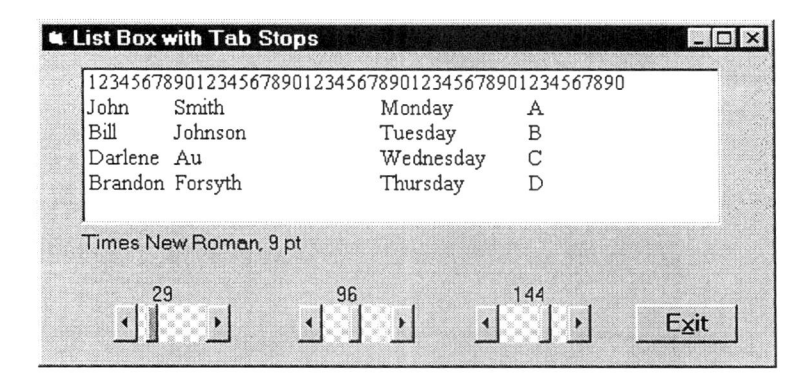

Figure 8 show the main form shown in design mode, with suggested control names. Notice that control arrays were used for the scroll bars and labels. When the user clicks on a scroll bar, the Index parameter of the Click event procedure can be used as an subscript into an array of tab stops.

Figure 8. Tab Stop Program in Design Mode.

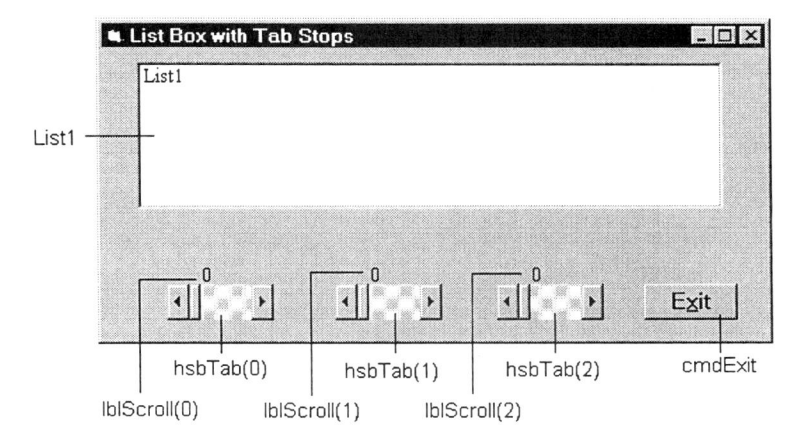

The final step in getting this program to work is to implement the Change event procedure of the hsbTab array (the horizontal scroll bars). The basic steps are as follows:
- Set the appropriate tabArray element to the current scroll bar value.
- Set the label caption above the scroll bar with the scroll bar's Value property.
- Call SetTabStops to change the tab stops in the list box.
- Redraw the list box, using the list box Refresh method.

10.7.3 Getting a List of INI Files

Write a program that does the following tasks:

- Calls the GetWindowsDirectory API procedure to get the directory path where Windows has been installed.
- Uses a FileListBox control to display all filenames in the Windows directory that have an INI extension.
- After the user has selected a file from the FileListBox, the program should display the file in a Text control.

11 Creating ActiveX Controls

This Chapter Requires Visual Basic Version 5.0

Chapter Contents

ActiveX Components
    Types of Objects Provided by Components
    ActiveX Controls
Creating a Student ID Number Text Box
    Creating a Test Program
    Adding an Event to the Control
    Comments
AddAppointment ActiveX Control
    Program Specifications
    User Interface
    Saving and Restoring Properties
    Raising Events in ActiveX Controls
    Implementing Property Procedures
    AddAppointment Control Source Listing
    Client Program Listing
Creating an ActiveX DLL
    The DoctorSchedule ActiveX DLL
    Client Program Implementation
    Instancing Property
    DoctorSchedule Implementation
    The clsSchedule Class
    The clsAppointment Class
    The clsPatient Class
    Testing the Compiled Component
Creating an Out-Of-Process Component
    Converting DoctorSchedule to ActiveX EXE
Where To Go From Here
Review Questions
Chapter Exercises

11.1 ActiveX Components

Component software development is the assembling of programs from tested, standardized components. Microsoft has created an open standard called the *component object model* (COM) that permits software components to interact with each other. Programs can be assembled from components that you create, components that are part of standard libraries, and existing programs that support COM.

An *ActiveX component* is a unit of executable code such as an .exe, .dll, or .ocx file, that follows the ActiveX specification for providing objects. ActiveX components use object-oriented programming techniques to define the classes, methods, and properties that make up the component source code. But ActiveX is more than just object-oriented programming—it provides the mechanism so that objects can work together. It is a natural process to build ActiveX components from a group of existing controls. When combined in a control, the existing controls are called *constituent controls.*

Before ActiveX was created, programs could expose objects, methods, and properties using a technique known as *OLE automation*. Programs that provide objects are called *OLE servers*. ActiveX is an extension of the same process, so OLE servers are being replaced with ActiveX components.

Microsoft has promoted ActiveX components as a way of enabling cross-platform program development. This means that you can write the same programs that will work in Windows 95, Windows NT, or on Internet browser pages. ActiveX components can also be used with Microsoft applications such as Word, Excel, and Access. One area that is particularly exciting is using ActiveX components as connections to database servers on the Internet. This allows an ActiveX component running on a Web page to communicate with a database and pass data back to the user's Web browser.

11.1.1 Types of Objects Provided by Components

Components can provide three general types of objects: ActiveX Controls, ActiveX Documents, and Code Components.

ActiveX Controls. ActiveX controls are user interface components that can be assembled on a form in an application program. These controls can be created and tested within the VB development environment, then exported to OCX files for other applications to use. The term *UserControl* is another name for an ActiveX control. Literally thousands of ActiveX controls are available, through both shareware and commercial sources. It is often easier and faster to obtain existing controls and add them to your programs than to code similar routines yourself.

ActiveX Documents. ActiveX documents are applications that can appear within Internet browser windows. They can be designed in the same way as Visual Basic forms.

Code Components. A code component may be thought of as a library of classes. Programs using a code component create object instances at runtime, using the classes provided by the component. The objects often do not have a visual component, but they provide some functionality used by other applications. A good example of a code component is Microsoft Excel, which can export objects such as worksheets and charts. Similarly, the Microsoft DAO library exports objects such as recordsets and fields.

11.1.2 ActiveX Controls

An ActiveX control, or *UserControl*, is a component that can be placed in a Visual Basic toolbox window and used by developers. When saved as an OCX file, an ActiveX control can be used in development environments such as C++ and Delphi. If you are using Visual Basic 5, you have already used a number of ActiveX controls. ActiveX controls have replaced what were called *custom controls* in earlier versions of Visual Basic. In those versions you could use custom controls in programs, but there was no way to create them—that had to be done in programming languages such as C, C++, or Delphi.

Visual Basic 5 creates ActiveX components and controls that can be used either within a single project or by external programs. This means, for example, that the same ActiveX component can interact with multiple client programs at the same time.

The Visual Basic *Control Creation Edition* (CCE) appeared before Visual Basic 5, and is distributed by Microsoft at their Web site (www.microsoft.com). The CCE lets you create and test ActiveX controls. The main limitation is that stand-alone executable controls cannot be created. Visual Basic 5 *Professional* integrates the features from the CCE with the ability to create EXE and DLL files, use database controls, and use data access objects.

Class modules, which appeared first in Visual Basic 4, may contain properties and methods, but no visual elements or event handlers. The only way to produce a visual component of a class is to display it on a separate form. As we learned in Chapter 4, the link between a class module and other forms is somewhat awkward. An ActiveX control, on the other hand, integrates a class module with a user interface. It can define event types, raise events at run time, display visual controls, and still encapsulate instance variables, properties, and methods.

Properties, Methods, and Events. We have already created class modules with properties and methods, so much of the conceptual groundwork has already been laid for using ActiveX. The user of an ActiveX control can read and write its properties in either design mode or run mode. When you place a text box on a form, for example, properties can be set in design mode that are saved along with the form. At run time, your program code can also modify the text box properties.

An ActiveX control can respond to events generated by its constituent controls, and it can also generate events. When designing an ActiveX control, you define specific events that the control can generate. A user of your control will have the option of writing specific event handlers.

Now it's time to be practical. The best way to understand ActiveX components is to create them yourself. In the coming sections of this chapter, we will create two different ActiveX controls. We will also create a code component that acts as a database server. Finally, we will create a program that loads and searches Web pages for links to other pages.

11.2 Creating a Student ID Number Text Box

StudentIdx

Let's follow a simple sequence of steps to create an ActiveX control that contains a text box into which the user can enter a Student ID number. We will make some assumptions about the length and format of the number. It is suggested that you try these steps at the computer.

1. Run VB5, select the *New Project* command, and choose *ActiveX Control* as the project type.

   ActiveX Control

2. The *User Control Form* is the rectangular gray window containing a grid in the middle of the screen. This is where controls are designed. Bring up the Properties window (F4) and change the name of the form to **StudentIdText.** Set the form's BorderStyle property to fixed single.

3. Place a label on the design form, as in Figure 1. Set its caption to **Student ID,** and set its alignment to right-justified. Place a text box on the form just to the right of the label, set its Text property to blank, set Name to **txtID**, and set MaxLength to 7.

Figure 1. Designing the StudentIdText Control.

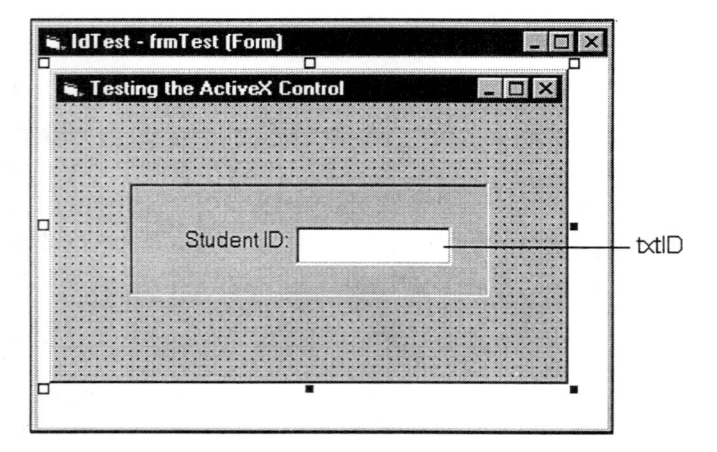

4. In the **Project Explorer** window, right-click the project name to bring up its **Project Properties** window (Figure 2). Set the project name to **ActiveXSource** and type in a short project description. Click OK to close this window.

Figure 2. Project Properties Window.

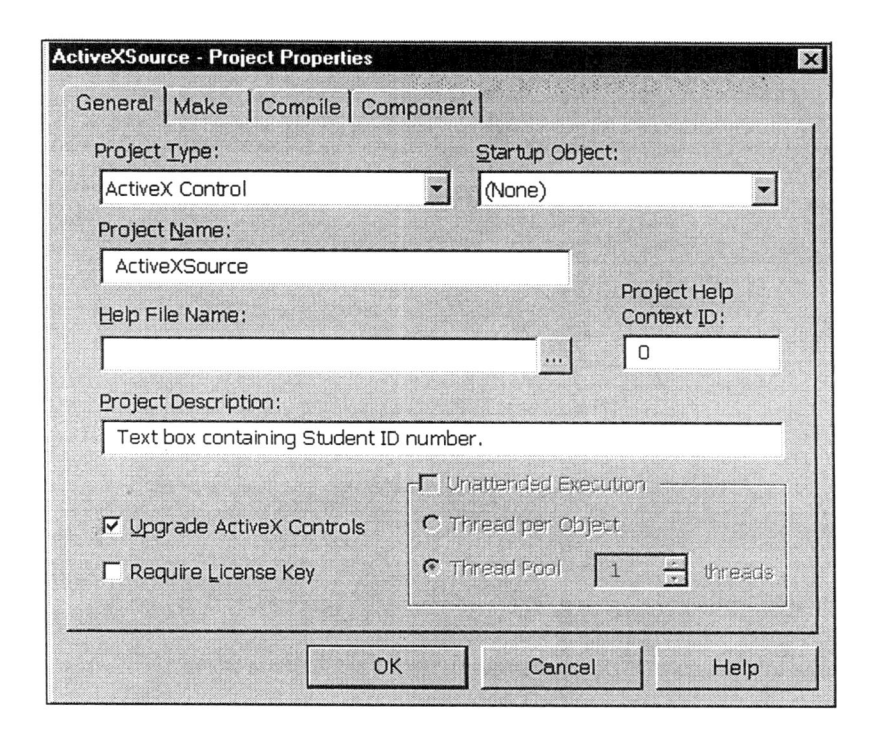

4. Double-click the text box to bring up its **Change** event handler. Write the following code:

```
Private Sub txtID_Change()
  If Not IsNumeric(txtID.Text) Then
    txtID.SelStart = 0
    txtID.SelLength = Len(txtID.Text)
  End If
End Sub
```

If the characters in the text box are nonnumeric, all text in the box will be highlighted as if someone had dragged a mouse over it.

5. Save the project. We are ready to create a short test program that displays the control we just created.

11.2.1 Creating a Test Program

1. Select the **Add Project** command from the File menu; select **Standard EXE** as the project type. Figure 3 shows the contents of the Project Group, viewed in the *Project Explorer* window.

Figure 3. Project Group for the StudentIdText Control.

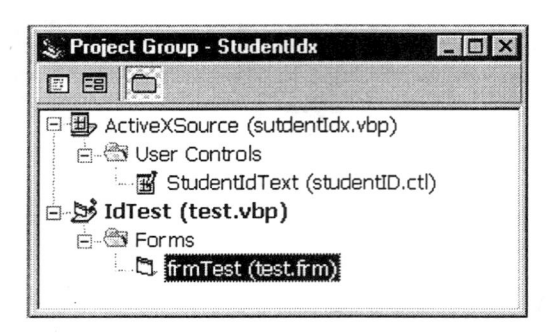

Notice that our new control appears in the toolbox as the following icon: ▣ . The control has also been registered as a new component type. To see this, select **Components** from the **Project** menu, click on the Controls tab, and scroll through the list until you find the description *Text box containing Student ID number* (Figure 4).

Figure 4. The VB5 Components Window.

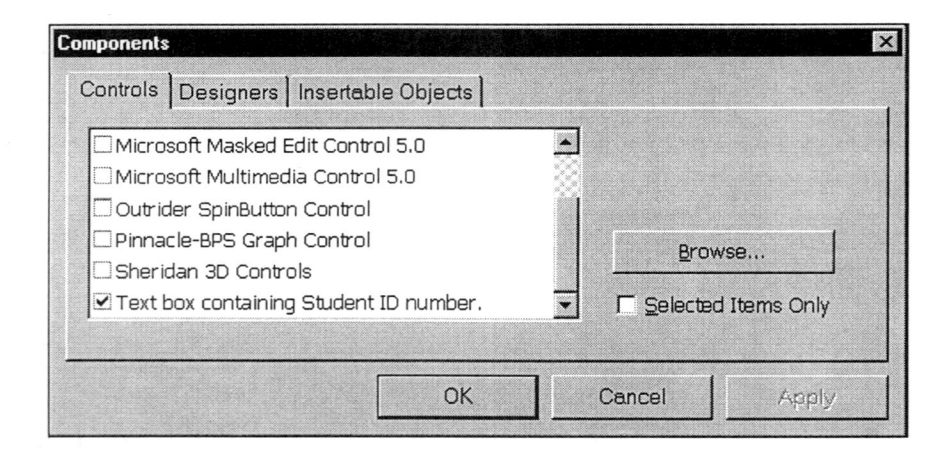

2. Close the Components window. Double-click the new ActiveX control's icon in the Toolbox window, causing an instance of the control to be inserted in the test program's form. Notice that the control is the same size as when we saved it. The border around the edge appears because we set the Borderstyle property to fixed single (Figure 5).

Figure 5. The Test Program.

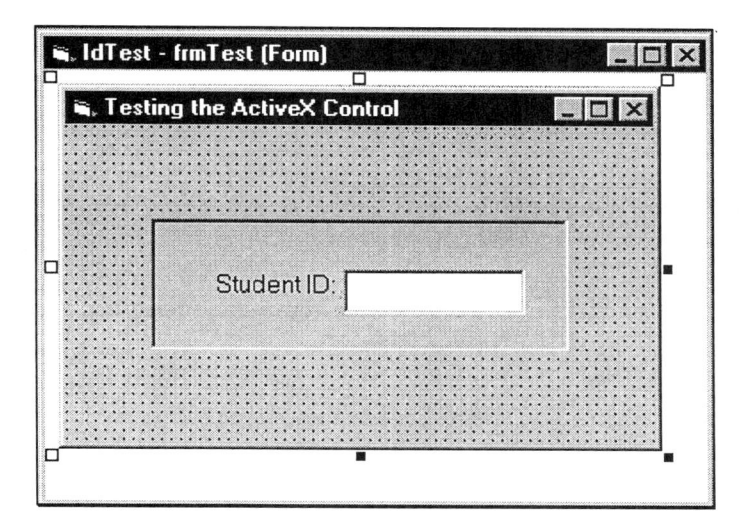

3. Run the test program and type in a numeric student number, up to seven digits long. If you try to enter any more digits, they will be refused. Backspace over some of the digits and enter a letter. Oops! The entire field is automatically highlighted as in Figure 6, signaling to the user that a nonnumeric character was entered.

Figure 6. Running the Client Program.

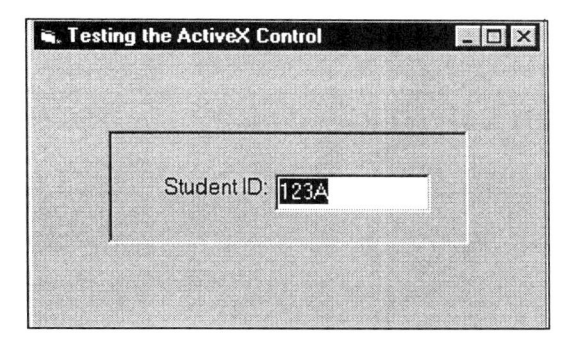

11.2.2 Adding an Event to the Control

One of the most powerful features of ActiveX controls is their ability to define specific events that can be raised (activated) at runtime. We will define an event for this control called **InvalidData**, which will be raised when the Change event handler for the text box determines that non-digit characters have been entered.

1. Stop the test program if it is still running, and select the ActiveXSource project from the Project Group Window. Right-click on the **StudentIdText** form within this project and select **View Code** from the popup menu.

2. In the declarations section of the module, add the following line:

   ```
   Public Event InvalidData()
   ```

This announces that an **InvalidData** event can be raised (signaled) by procedures in this class. We will add a statement to the txtID_Change procedure that raises the InvalidData event when a non-digit is entered into the text box. The complete source code is listed here, with the new lines shown in bold type:

```
Option Explicit
Public Event InvalidData()

Private Sub txtID_Change()
  If Not IsNumeric(txtID.Text) Then
    txtID.SelStart = 0
    txtID.SelLength = Len(txtID.Text)
    RaiseEvent InvalidData
  End If
End Sub
```

3. Switch to the **IdTest** project and double-click on the frmTest module name. The main form still contains the StudentIdText control; double-click on the control. Notice that if you select the control name from the combo box on the left, an InvalidData event handler is automatically created, as in Figure 7.

Figure 7. The InvalidData Event Handler.

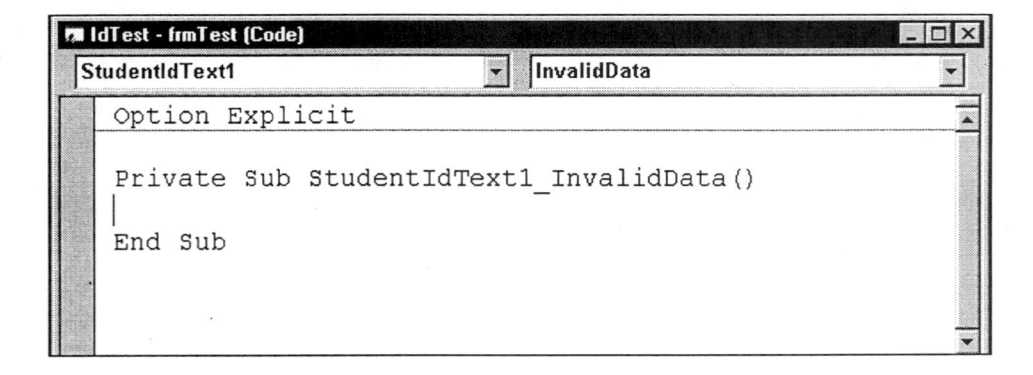

```
IdTest - frmTest [Code]
StudentIdText1                          InvalidData
  Option Explicit

  Private Sub StudentIdText1_InvalidData()

  End Sub
```

4. Write statements in this event handler that display a message box:

```
Private Sub StudentIdText1_InvalidData()
  MsgBox "A student number may contain only digits.", _
    vbExclamation, "Error"
End Sub
```

Run the test program again, enter a non-digit character, and view the new message box. The program is complete, so save the project one more time.

11.2.3 Comments

Let us not give the false impression that ActiveX controls are trivial to create. Ordinarily, a considerable amount of thought goes into designing a useful control. Perhaps a good challenge is to make the control flexible and useful enough to justify the effort expended in its creation.

To keep things simple, this first control sidesteps a number of issues. For example, there is no way for the control to be resized when placed on the test program's form. There are no custom properties to be set in design mode. Our next ActiveX control, related to the Doctor's Office Appointment program from Chapter 4, will incorporate some important features that make it more powerful.

11.3 AddAppointment ActiveX Control

11.3.1 Program Specifications

In Chapter 4, the Doctors Office Scheduling program contained several classes, including clsAppointment. This class encapsulated properties, methods, and a form relating to individual appointment objects. Let's recreate the visual component of that class, frmAppointment and adapt it into an ActiveX control called **AddAppointment**. The AddAppointment control will input all information from the user regarding a single appointment.

Design Mode, Run Time. When discussing any of the ActiveX controls in this chapter, we will distinguish between what happens in design mode and what happens at run time. The user of our control is able to place an instance of the control on a form while in design mode. We will call the program created by this person the *client program*. When the client program runs, there will again be a user who will be able to retrieve runtime properties.

Design Mode Properties. When the control is placed on a form, the user can set the **BackColor** property, which affects the background color of the control, as well as that of the combo boxes and text boxes on the control. The designer can also set the control's **Caption** property. When the container form is saved, the controls' properties will automatically be saved in the form.

Run Time Properties. The AddAppointment control contains the following read-only properties that can only be accessed at run time: DoctorName, PatientName, ApptDate, ApptTime, and Purpose. Each property returns a string.

User Actions. At run time, the user selects the doctor and patient from combo boxes, and enters the date, time, and purpose of the appointment. When the **OK** button is clicked, the field contents are validated and the control displays a confirmation message. If the **Cancel** button is clicked, the control clears all of the input fields and informs the user that the appointment has been cancelled.

Error Trapping. Error trapping is handled by raising different events in the ActiveX control's methods. The client program handles these events by displaying message boxes.

Project Group Window. The Project Group window (Figure 8) shows the UserControl's project (AddAppointment), and the client program (TestProject). The test program contains a single form called frmMain.

Figure 8. The VB5 Project Group Window.

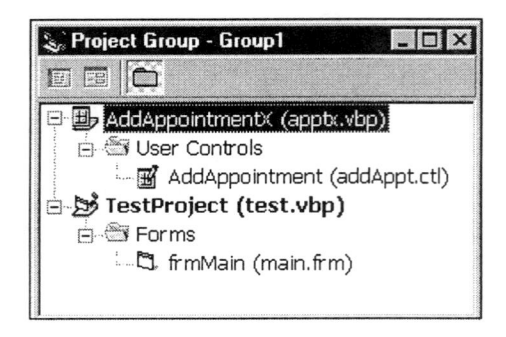

11.3.2 User Interface

Using Constituent Controls. Many ActiveX controls are created by combining existing controls in a useful way. The latter are called *constituent controls*. For example, your control might contain several text boxes, a frame, and some buttons. You can use any of the controls supplied with Visual Basic, except the OLE container control. Also, insertable objects such as Excel charts and Word documents cannot be constituent controls. Third-party ActiveX controls can be constiutent controls, but be aware of distribution restrictions in the license agreements for these controls before distributing your programs.

Component Design Window. The design window for the AddAppointment control contains all of the labels, buttons, text boxes, and combo boxes that belong to the control (see Figure 9). Any properties set at this time will be in effect when control instances are created.

Client Program. When our ActiveX control has been placed on a form in the client program and all supporting code written in the client program, the program may be tested. In run mode, Figure 10 shows the client program after the user has entered data into all fields. The

OK and Cancel buttons belong to the control, whereas the Clear and Exit buttons belong to the enclosing form.

Figure 9. Designing the AddAppointment UserControl.

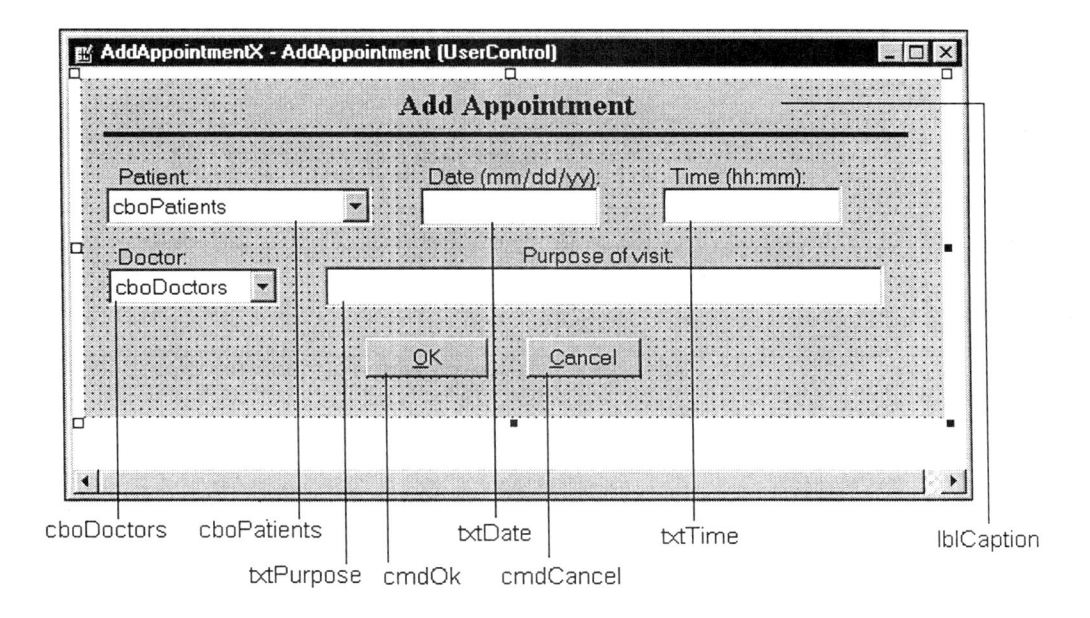

Figure 10. Running the Client Test Program.

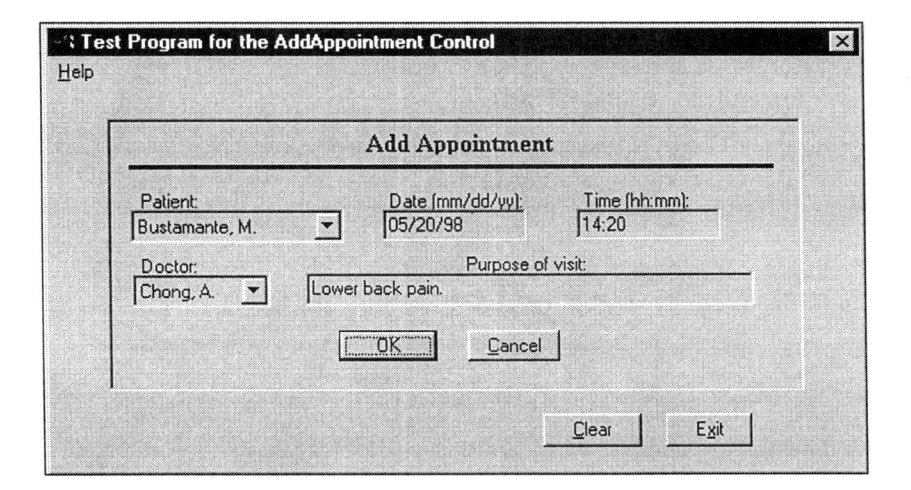

A confirmation message box (Figure 11) displays when the OK button is pressed. The names of the patient and doctor are obtained from the control's properties.

Figure 11. Message displayed by the CloseWindow Event Handler.

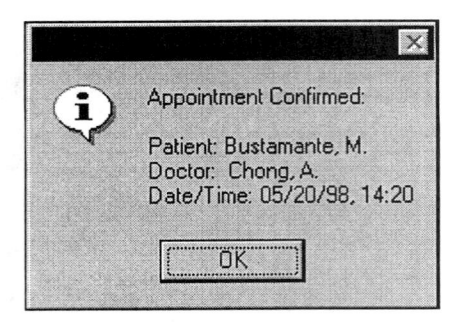

```
Appointment Confirmed:

Patient: Bustamante, M.
Doctor: Chong, A.
Date/Time: 05/20/98, 14:20

        OK
```

11.3.3 Saving and Restoring Properties

Initializing Properties. When an ActiveX control is first inserted into a container form, an **InitProperties** event is automatically generated. The event handler assigns default values to properties. For example, the following handler initializes the Caption and BackColor properties that belong to this control:

```
Private Sub UserControl_InitProperties()
  Caption = caption_default
  BackColor = backColor_default
End Sub
```

WriteProperties Event. The **UserControl_WriteProperties** event handler is responsible for writing the property values from your control to the container form. The properties are stored in a specialized type of collection called a **PropertyBag**. The following procedure saves the control's Caption and BackColor properties:

```
Private Sub UserControl_WriteProperties(PropBag As PropertyBag)
   PropBag.WriteProperty "Caption", Caption, caption_default
   PropBag.WriteProperty "BackColor", BackColor, backColor_default
End Sub
```

The syntax of the **WriteProperty** method is

*object.***WriteProperty***(dataName, value[, defaultVal])*

Where *object* is a PropertyBag object, *dataName* is a string that identifies the property to be placed in the bag, *value* is the data value to be saved, and *defaultVal* is the default value for this property. The last parameter is optional, but highly recommended because it reduces the size of the container file (usually .frm). Visual Basic only writes a property value to the container file if the property's value is different from the default value.

ReadProperties Event. The **UserControl_ReadProperties** event handler gets the saved property values stored in the form file. The following procedure restores the Caption and BackColor properties:

```
Private Sub UserControl_ReadProperties(PropBag As PropertyBag)
  On Error Resume Next
  Caption = PropBag.ReadProperty("Caption", caption_default)
  BackColor = PropBag.ReadProperty("BackColor", backColor_default)
End Sub
```

Notice that default property values are still used. Also, the On Error Resume statement is there to prevent the program from halting if the designer assigns an invalid property value while editing the form file with a text editor.

Properties Window. Figure 12 shows the properties window that appears when the AddAppointment control has been placed on the client program's main window.

Figure 12. AddAppointment Properties Window.

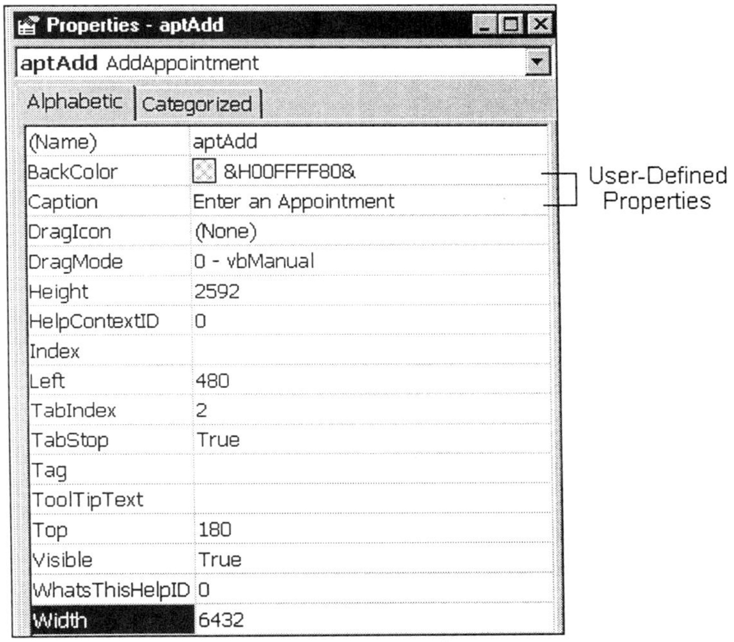

11.3.4 Raising Events in ActiveX Controls

An *event* is a signal that something has happened in a program. Examples of common events are Click, Resize, Load, Unload, Change, MouseMove, and so on. All controls, whether they are standard VB controls or UserControls, have the ability to raise events. Raising an event means sending a signal that can be received by a procedure known as an *event handler*.

An ActiveX control can define any events it wishes, with specific names. This capability allows the control to quietly pass messages to its client program. The latter can either respond to the messages or ignore them. The response to a message is achieved by writing code in a message handler procedure. This is exactly what we have done in the past with events such as Click or Change that were raised by controls such as command buttons and text boxes, respectively.

Defining Specific Events. Before a UserControl can raise a specific event, it must declare, or define the event's name. An event declaration looks a lot like the first line of a procedure declaration. Its syntax is:

```
[Public] Event eventName [(arglist)]
```

Where *eventName* is the name of the event that will be raised by the control. An event cannot return a value. Events can have the same types of arguments as ordinary procedures, except named arguments, optional arguments, and ParamArray arguments are not permitted.

AddAppointment Events. The AddAppointment control supports several user-defined events, declared in the declarations section of the module:

```
Public Event BadDateFormat(dt As String)
Public Event BadTimeFormat(tm As String)
Public Event MissingField(fieldName As String)
Public Event CloseWindow(save As Boolean)
```

In the client program we have written, the control instance is called **aptAdd**. This means that an empty event handler is available in frmMain whose name is a combination of the control name and the event name:

```
Private Sub aptAdd_MissingField(fieldName As String)
    .
    .
End Sub
```

MissingField Event. The following is the implementation of the **MissingField** event handler in the test program. It displays a message box with the name of the missing field:

```
Private Sub aptAdd_MissingField(fieldName As String)
  MsgBox "The following field is missing: " & fieldName, _
    vbInformation, "Error"
End Sub
```

Figure 13 shows an example of a message box displayed at run time by the MissingField event handler.

Figure 13. MissingField Event Message.

11.3.5 Implementing Property Procedures

You may recall that we created property procedures in Chapters 4 and 6. Property procedures in UserControls are nearly identical, except that the Let property should always include a call to **PropertyChanged**, which notifies Visual Basic that a property has been changed. The following is an example from the AddAppointment control:

```
Public Property Let Caption(st As String)
   lblCaption.Caption = st
   captionP = st
   PropertyChanged "Caption"
End Property
```

Unless PropertyChanged is called, Visual Basic cannot generate a WriteProperties event, and the control instance's properties cannot be saved. A person using your control in their program would lose any changes that were made to the control's properties the next time their project was loaded from disk.

Constituent Controls. Another consideration when creating property procedures is that some properties have to broadcast the same value to various constituent controls within the control. For example, the **Let BackColor** property in the AddAppointment control assigns the same color to the control's instance variable (backColorP), the control's BackColor property, and the BackColor property of each label, text box and combo box:

```
Public Property Let BackColor(ByVal color As OLE_COLOR)
   backColorP = color
   UserControl.BackColor = color
   On Error Resume Next
   Dim j As Integer
   For j = 0 To Controls.Count - 1
     Controls(j).BackColor = color
   Next j
   PropertyChanged "BackColor"
End Property
```

Fortunately, the task is made easier by looping through the built-in **Controls** collection. Just in case any control does not have a BackColor property, the **On Error Resume Next** statement is ready to step in and bypass runtime errors.

11.3.6 AddAppointment Control Source Listing

Let's take a look at the source code for the AddAppointment ActiveX control. This control inputs information from the user that can be used to schedule an appointment:

```
'The AddAppointment User Control.
Option Explicit

'Used for saving/restoring design properties:
Private backColorP As OLE_COLOR
Private captionP As String

'Default design property values:
Const backColor_default = vbButtonFace
Const caption_default = "Add Appointment"

'Custom Events raised by this control:
Public Event BadDateFormat(dt As String)
Public Event BadTimeFormat(tm As String)
Public Event MissingField(fieldName As String)
Public Event CloseWindow(save As Boolean)

'*********** Public Properties *************
'The following properties may be set at design
'time and/or run time.

Public Property Get Caption() As String
   Caption = lblCaption.Caption
End Property

Public Property Let Caption(st As String)
   lblCaption.Caption = st
   captionP = st
   PropertyChanged "Caption"
End Property

Public Property Get BackColor() As OLE_COLOR
   BackColor = backColorP
End Property

Public Property Let BackColor(ByVal color As OLE_COLOR)
   backColorP = color
   UserControl.BackColor = color
   On Error Resume Next
   Dim j As Integer
   For j = 0 To Controls.Count - 1
     Controls(j).BackColor = color
   Next j
   PropertyChanged "BackColor"
End Property
```

```vb
'*********** Runtime Properties *****************
'All properties are read-only.

Public Property Get PatientName() As String
  PatientName = cboPatients.Text
End Property

Public Property Get DoctorName() As String
  DoctorName = cboDoctors.Text
End Property

Public Property Get ApptDate() As String
  ApptDate = txtDate.Text
End Property

Public Property Get ApptTime() As String
  ApptTime = txtTime.Text
End Property

Public Property Get Purpose() As String
  Purpose = txtPurpose.Text
End Property

'*********** Public Methods *************

Public Sub Clear()
  cboPatients.ListIndex = -1
  cboDoctors.ListIndex = -1
  txtDate.Text = ""
  txtTime.Text = ""
  txtPurpose.Text = ""
End Sub

'*********** Private Event Handlers ********

Private Sub cmdCancel_Click()
  RaiseEvent CloseWindow(False)
End Sub

Private Sub cmdOk_Click()
  If ValidateFields Then
    RaiseEvent CloseWindow(True)
  End If
End Sub

'************ Private Methods *************

Private Function ValidateFields() As Boolean
  ValidateFields = True

  'Check for a doctor.
  If cboDoctors.ListIndex = -1 Then
```

```vb
      RaiseEvent MissingField("Doctor Name")
      ValidateFields = False
   End If

   'Check for a patient.
   If cboPatients.ListIndex = -1 Then
      RaiseEvent MissingField("Patient Name")
      ValidateFields = False
   End If

   If Trim$(txtPurpose.Text) = "" Then
      RaiseEvent MissingField("Purpose of Appointment")
      ValidateFields = False
   End If

   'Check for an appointment date.
   If Not IsDate(txtDate.Text) Then
      RaiseEvent BadDateFormat(txtDate.Text)
      ValidateFields = False
   End If

   ' Check the appointment time and look for a runtime
   ' error if an invalid time format was used.
   On Error GoTo BadTime
   TimeValue txtTime.Text
   Exit Function

BadTime:
   RaiseEvent BadTimeFormat(txtTime.Text)
   ValidateFields = False
End Function

'******** Save and Load the Bag of Properties *********

Private Sub UserControl_WriteProperties(PropBag As PropertyBag)
   PropBag.WriteProperty "Caption", Caption, caption_default
   PropBag.WriteProperty "BackColor", BackColor, backColor_default
End Sub

Private Sub UserControl_ReadProperties(PropBag As PropertyBag)
   On Error Resume Next
   Caption = PropBag.ReadProperty("Caption", caption_default)
   BackColor = PropBag.ReadProperty("BackColor", backColor_default)
End Sub

Private Sub UserControl_InitProperties()
   Caption = caption_default
   BackColor = backColor_default
End Sub
```

11.3.7 Client Program Listing

```vb
'Client program for the AddAppointment control.
Option Explicit

Private Sub aptAdd_BadDateFormat(dt As String)
    MsgBox "The appointment date " & dt & " is invalid. " _
      + "Please use mm/dd/yy format.', vbInformation, "Error"
End Sub

Private Sub aptAdd_BadTimeFormat(tm As String)
    MsgBox "The appointment time " & tm & " is invalid. " _
      + "Please use 24-hour hh:mm format.", _
        vbInformation, "Error"
End Sub

Private Sub aptAdd_CloseWindow(save As Boolean)
  If save Then
    With aptAdd
      MsgBox "Appointment Confirmed: " & vbCrLf & vbCrLf _
        & "Patient: " & .PatientName & vbCrLf _
        & "Doctor:  " & .DoctorName & vbCrLf _
        & "Date/Time: " & .ApptDate & ", " & .ApptTime, _
          vbInformation, ""
    End With
  Else
    MsgBox "Appointment Cancelled", vbInformation, ""
    aptAdd.Clear
  End If
End Sub

Private Sub aptAdd_MissingField(fieldName As String)
   MsgBox "The following field is missing: " & fieldName, _
      vbInformation, "Error"
End Sub

Private Sub cmdClear_Click()
  aptAdd.Clear
End Sub

Private Sub cmdExit_Click()
  Unload Me
End Sub

Private Sub Form_Load()
'The Caption and BackColor properties may also
'be set at run time.
  aptAdd.Caption = "Enter an Appointment"
End Sub

Private Sub mnuHelpAbout_Click()
```

```
frmAbout.Show vbModal
End Sub
```

11.4 Creating an ActiveX DLL

An *in-process component*, or *ActiveX DLL component*, shares the same address space with its client program. The component and its client are often part of the same application. An *out-of-process component*, or *ActiveX EXE component*, runs in its own address space. The client is usually another application. In this chapter, we will show how to create both types of components.

In-process components tend to run faster than out-of-process components, because the former can easily communicate with its client via the stack and pointer variables. An out-of-process component, on the other hand, requires a different, slower method of communication between component and client.

11.4.1 The DoctorSchedule ActiveX DLL

Let's borrow part of the Doctors Office Scheduling program from Chapter 6, simplify it, and turn it into an ActiveX DLL. The DLL is called **DoctorSchedule** and it contains the clsSchedule, clsPatient, and clsAppointment classes. The DLL does not have a visual element—instead, it is a database server, providing data to client programs on demand.

Type Library. The **DoctorSchedule** component exposes the **clsSchedule** class to other programs. DoctorSchedule is the name of the component's *type library*, which may be seen in the Object Browser window (Figure 14). If the name **clsSchedule** existed in more than one library, fully qualified references to the name would have to include their type library names:

```
DoctorSchedule.clsSchedule
CollegeSchedule.clsSchedule
```

Figure 14. DoctorSchedule Type Library, in Object Browser.

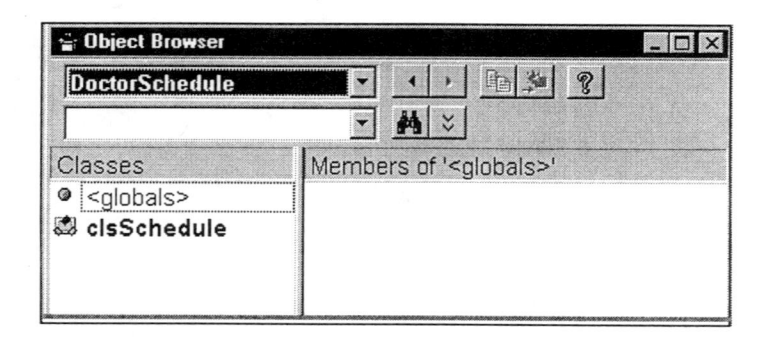

Chap 11: Creating ActiveX Controls

Project Group. Our project group contains two projects—one for the DLL, and one for a client program that demonstrates and tests the DLL. In Figure 15, the Project Group includes the DoctorSchedule project for the ActiveX component, and TestProgram, the client program's project.

Figure 15. The Project Group for the DoctorSchedule Component.

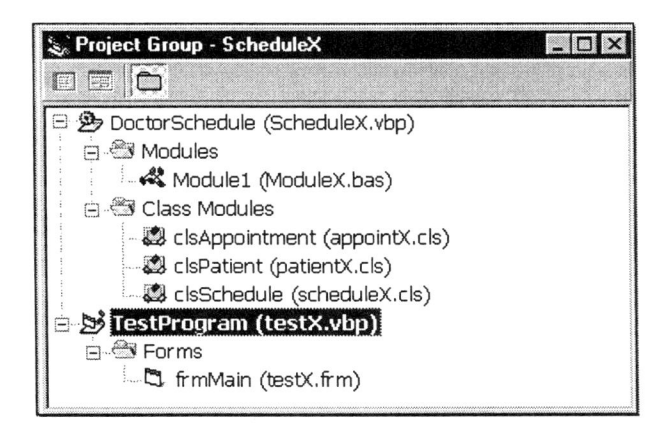

The client program prompts the user for a patient ID number, and when the Search button is clicked, retrieves a list of all appointments for the patient. Figure 16 shows the results of searching for patient 1001's appointments.

Figure 16. The Client Program, After Retrieving Appointments.

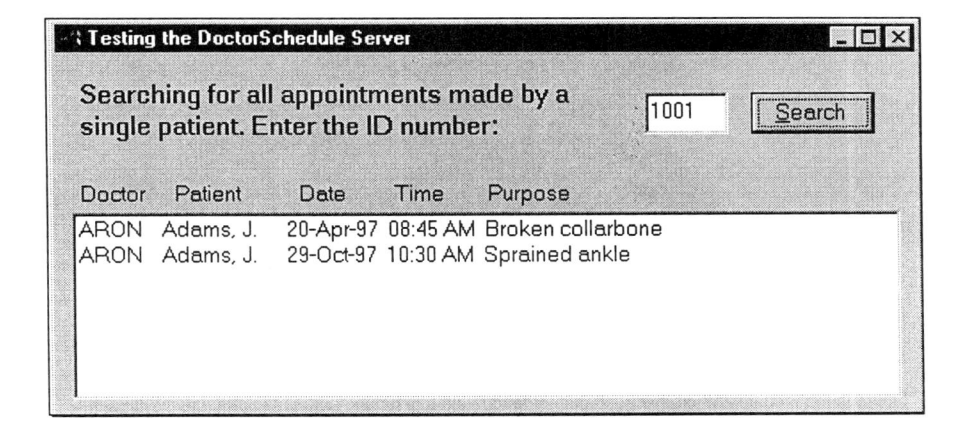

The DoctorSchedule Component. If the client program has no knowledge of the database structure or mechanics of retrieving appointment schedules from the database, clearly these tasks must be handled inside the DoctorSchedule component. Therefore, the clsSchedule class searches the database for records containing specific patient ID numbers. It creates instances of clsPatient and clsAppointment so methods in these classes can act as helpers.

From the DoctorSchedule project properties window, set the following options:

- Project Type: ActiveX DLL
- Project Name: DoctorSchedule

11.4.2 Client Program Implementation

The client program is remarkably simple. It creates a clsSchedule object, calls a method called **GetAppts** that returns a collection of appointments for a single patient, and displays the appointments in a list box. The following is the complete source code for this program. First, two objects are declared and created:

```
Option Explicit
Private schedule As clsSchedule
Private apptList As Collection

Private Sub Form_Load()
  Set schedule = New clsSchedule
  Set apptList = New Collection
End Sub
```

When the user clicks on the **Search** button, **cmdSearch_Click** calls **GetAppts**, passing it a patient ID number and an empty collection. The ActiveX server fills in the **apptList** collection with strings representing appointments, and the strings are inserted in a list box:

```
Private Sub cmdSearch_Click()
  Dim j As Integer
  On Error GoTo Search1
  List1.Clear
  ClearCollection apptList

  If schedule.GetAppts(Val(txtPatientId.Text), apptList) Then
    For j = 1 To apptList.Count
      List1.AddItem apptList(j)
    Next j
  Else
    MsgBox "No matching appointments were found."
  End If
  Exit Sub
Search1:
  MsgBox Error$, vbInformation, ""
End Sub
```

If an unhandled error should occur during the call to GetAppts, the error will be handled in cmdSearch_Click.

ClearCollection is a general-purpose loop that will remove all members of a Collection object:

```
Public Sub ClearCollection(coll As Collection)
  Dim obj As Variant
  For Each obj In coll
```

```
        coll.Remove 1
    Next obj
End Sub
```

In **Form_Unload**, the procedure sets the schedule and appointment list to **Nothing**, so their memory can be released:

```
Private Sub Form_Unload(Cancel As Integer)
    Set schedule = Nothing
    Set apptList = Nothing
End Sub
```

This clearly shows that the hard work has all been offloaded onto the ActiveX component. In particular, only the component has detailed knowledge about the database structure. This creates a clear separation of tasks. Any number of programs might use this ActiveX component to search for appointments in the doctor's office. The component needs to be written and debugged only once.

11.4.3   Instancing Property

The three classes in this component, clsSchedule, clsAppointment, and clsPatient, each have an **Instancing** property. This property controls the way in which client programs outside of the component's project may create instances of the class. There are six possible Instancing values: MultiUse, GlobalMultiUse, Private, PublicNotCreateable, SingleUse, and GlobalSingleUse.

MultiUse. For ActiveX DLL components, the default value for Instancing is *MultiUse*, meaning that one instance of the component can provide any number of objects to client applications. If the Instancing property were *GlobalMutiUse*, client programs could invoke class methods without explicitly declaring an instance of the class. In the DoctorSchedule component, for example, clsSchedule is *MultiUse*.

Private. If the Instancing property of a class is *Private*, other applications cannot access type library information about the class, and cannot create class instances. In the DoctorSchedule component, the clsAppointment and clsPatient classes are private. If the instancing property of clsSchedule were *Private*, however, the client program would not be able to create an instance of clsSchedule. The error message shown in Figure 17 would appear.

Figure 17. Error Message When Instancing = Private.

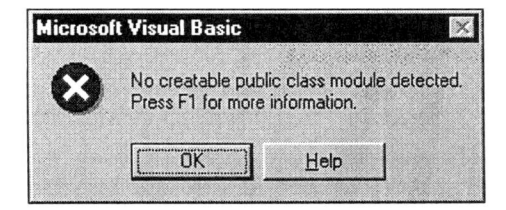

PublicNotCreateable. If the Instancing property is *PublicNotCreateable*, other applications can use instances of the class only if the component creates the objects first. In DoctorSchedule, for example, we could create a clsAppointment object and make the object available to the client program.

SingleUse, GlobalSingleUse. If the Instancing property is *SingleUse*, other applications can create objects from the class, but every created object starts a new instance of the component. If the Instancing property is *GlobalSingleUse*, it is similar to SingleUse except that class methods can be called as if they are global procedures.

Table 1 cross-references the types of components and programs created by Visual Basic 5, using an X to indicate which Instancing properties are permitted.

Table 1. Permitted Values of the Instancing Property.

Instancing Property	ActiveX Exe	ActiveX DLL	ActiveX Contol	Standard Exe
Private	X	X	X	X
PublicNotCreatable	X	X	X	
SingleUse	X			
GlobalSingleUse	X			
MultiUse	X	X		
GlobalMultiUse	X	X		

If you plan on creating multiple instances of a class, read Chapter 8 of the Visual Basic 5 *Component Tools Guide* manual. The chapter deals with the important issues of scalability and multithreading, which are beyond the scope of the current book. For example, the chapter explains what happens when two or more processes are simultaneously requesting services from the same component. The issues raised are important in any multitasking environment where programs are competing for the same resources.

11.4.4 DoctorSchedule Implementation

The DoctorSchedule component has a code module (moduleX.bas) with a **Main** procedure, which could be used for startup code if necessary. The database filename and its object variable are also declared here because they are shared by the different classes in the component:

```
Option Explicit
Public Const DBaseFileName As String = "schedule.mdb"
Public DBase As Database

Public Sub Main()
  ' Perform component initialization here, even before
  ' the Class_Initialize event occurs.

End Sub
```

Because Sub Main executes even before any objects are created by this component, you have the opportunity to perform any special initialization. The code should not take too long to execute, however, or the client program's request to create an object could time out.

11.4.5 The clsSchedule Class

Initialize Event. When a client program creates a clsSchedule class instance, the Class_Initialize event handler runs. The database is opened and a message is written to the Debug window:

```
Private Sub Class_Initialize()
  ChDrive App.Path
  ChDir App.Path
  Set DBase = Workspaces(0).OpenDatabase(DBaseFileName)
  Debug.Print "Server has just opened the database."
End Sub
```

> *Debugging Tip.* Any Debug.Print statements left in a program's source code are automatically dropped from the compiled program.

Terminate Event. Similarly, when the object reference is set to *Nothing* by the client program, the Class_Terminate event handler runs. You must use the On Error statement here, because applications that use this component cannot handle errors that might occur in the Terminate event handler:

```
Private Sub Class_Terminate()
  On Error Resume Next
  DBase.Close
  Debug.Print "Server has just closed the database."
End Sub
```

The GetAppts Method. Last, and most important, is the GetAppts method that a client program calls when it wants to get a list of appointments scheduled by a particular patient. The calling program passes a patient ID number, along with an empty collection object:

```
Public Function GetAppts(ByVal PatientID As Long, _
         ByRef apptList As Collection) As Boolean

'Get list of appointments for a single patient, specified by ID.
'Return True if some were found, False otherwise.

'Use an SQL query to create a temporary recordset
'containing appointments for the selected patient,
'ordered by date and time.

  Dim R As Recordset, query As String
  GetAppts = False
  query = "SELECT * from Appointments WHERE patientId = " _
        & PatientID & " ORDER BY date + time"

  Set R = DBase.OpenRecordset(query, dbOpenDynaset)
```

```
      Dim anAppt As New clsAppointment
      Do While Not R.EOF
        GetAppts = True
        anAppt.ReadRecord R
        apptList.Add anAppt.AsString
        R.MoveNext
      Loop
      R.Close
      Set anAppt = Nothing
      Set R = Nothing
   End Function
```

Error Handling. Notice that we perform no error trapping inside this method. If a runtime error should occur in this procedure, the error is automatically bounced back to the calling procedure. This gives the client program control over how the error should be handled and whether or not the user should be notified.

> ***Programming Tip:*** In the clsSchedule class, you might be tempted to handle errors inside the GetAppts method by displaying a message box. But this is considered poor style when writing ActiveX components. The VB5 manual says in no uncertain terms, "A well behaved component does not intrude on the client application's user interface by displaying message boxes containing error text."[1]

Besides turning off error handling inside GetAppts, we could have generated an error number of our own, by using the Err.Raise method. The error number should be an integer between 512 and 65535, added to the standard constant **vbObjectError**. Of course, any custom error numbers you generate should be documented in the program's online help.

Suppose we wanted to raise error number 1000 inside GetAppts when no matching patients were found. The following statements would do this:

```
    Set R = DBase.OpenRecordset(query, dbOpenDynaset)
    If R.EOF Then
      Err.Raise (vbObjectError + 1000), "DoctorSchedule.clsSchedule", _
          "No matching patients were found."
      Exit Sub
    End If
```

The three arguments passed to the Err.Raise method were the error number, the name of the project and class, and the error message.

---

[1] *Visual Basic Component Tools Guide*, Part 2, p.376.

> *VB5 Tip:* To prevent the program from halting when an unhandled error occurs inside the GetApps method, you must set one of the VB environment options. Select **Options** from the **Tools** menu, and click on the **General** tab. Select the option button labeled "Break on Unhandled Errors."

11.4.6 The clsAppointment Class

If you looked carefully at the code in the clsStudent.GetAppts method, you noticed that it creates an instance of the clsAppointent class. This means that we have to include clsAppointment in the project. This class is simpler than the original version in Chapter 6 because it includes only the instance variables and the AsString, AsRecordset, and ReadRecord methods:

```
'The clsAppointment class.
Option Explicit
Private doctorIdP As String
Private patientIdP As Long
Private apptDateP As Date
Private apptTimeP As Date
Private purposeP As String
```

The **AsString** method creates a string representation of the current appointment object. One of its tasks is to use the patient ID number to look up the patient's name. This involves creating an instance of clsPatient:

```
Public Function AsString() As String
  Dim D As New clsPatient
  Dim doctor As String * 8
  Dim patient As String * 15
  doctor = doctorIdP
  patient = D.GetpatientName(patientIdP)
  AsString = doctor & patient & _
    Format$(apptDateP, "Medium Date") + " " + _
    Format$(apptTimeP, "Medium Time") + " " + _
    purposeP
  Set D = Nothing
End Function
```

The **AsRecordset** method saves the object's instance variables in the current record of an open recordset object:

```
Public Sub AsRecordset(R As Recordset)
  On Error Resume Next
  R!DoctorID = doctorIdP
  R!PatientID = patientIdP
  R!Date = apptDateP
  R!Time = apptTimeP
  R!Purpose = purposeP
End Sub
```

The **ReadRecord** method copies data from the current record of an open recordset into the object's instance variables:

```
Public Sub ReadRecord(R As Recordset)
  On Error Resume Next
  doctorIdP = R!DoctorID
  patientIdP = R!PatientID
  apptDateP = R!Date
  apptTimeP = R!Time
  purposeP = R!Purpose
End Sub
```

11.4.7 The clsPatient Class

Last of all, the clsPatient class is needed in the DoctorSchedule component because the AsString method in the clsAppointment class creates an instance of clsPatient. The **Initialize** event opens up the Patients recordset, and the Terminate event closes the recordset:

```
Option Explicit
Dim Patients As Recordset

Private Sub Class_Initialize()
  Set Patients = DBase.OpenRecordset( "Patients", _
      dbOpenDynaset)
End Sub

Private Sub Class_Terminate()
  Patients.Close
  Set Patients = Nothing
End Sub
```

The **GetPatientName** method searches the table with a patient ID number, and if successful, returns the patient's name:

```
Public Function GetpatientName(id As Long)
  Patients.FindFirst "id = " & id
  If Patients.NoMatch Then
    GetpatientName = ""
  Else
    GetpatientName = Patients!Name
  End If
End Function
```

11.4.8 Testing the Compiled Component

Once you have run and tested an in-process component in the Visual Basic, you can compile the component into a DLL file:

- From the File menu, select the **Make ScheduleX.dll** to create the .dll file.
- Select the component in the Project Group window, and select the **Remove Project** command from the **File** menu.

- A warning message will appear: "The project is referenced from another project. Are you sure you want to remove it?". Click on **Yes** to remove the project.
- Run the test program. It will load and execute the saved DLL component automatically.

11.5 Creating an Out-Of-Process Component

Not all programs lend themselves to using in-process components, and it is not possible or practical to use an ActiveX DLL. The DoctorSchedule component, for example, might be more useful as a stand-alone executable program that could provide services to any number of applications that happen to be running at the same time. Out-of-process components can show both modal and modeless forms, and if designed as such, can be run as stand-alone programs.

Microsoft Word and Excel are good examples of out-of-process components. Any Windows application that supports OLE automation or ActiveX technology can create an instance of a Word document or Excel worksheet.

Client programs can also run *asynchronously* in relation to out-of-process ActiveX components. This means, for example, that a client program can make a request for data or services from a component, and then continue its own processing until notified by the ActiveX component that the requested data is ready or the service is completed. This involves the use of asnychronous call backs and events, which is thoroughly explained in Chapter 8 of the VB5 *Component Tools Guide*, Part 2.

11.5.1 Converting DoctorSchedule to ActiveX EXE

Converting the DoctorSchedule component into an out-of-process component (an ActiveX EXE) involves just two steps. First, in the project properties window, change the project type to **ActiveX EXE**. Second, select **Make ScheduleX.exe** from the **File** menu, to create a *reference executable*. This executable file does not have to be created again unless you modify the component.

Testing the Out-Of-Process DoctorSchedule Component. When you create an out-of-process ActiveX component, it is a good idea to run and debug it from within the Visual Basic environment. If you want, you can set breakpoints in the component's code and in the code of the test program. The component and the test program must run in two separate instances of Visual Basic. The following steps explain the process.

1. Load just the DoctorSchedule project file (scheduleX.vbp)

2. Run the DoctorSchedule project, while still in the VB development environment. Minimize Visual Basic while DoctorSchedule is still running.

3. Start a second instance of Visual Basic and load the test program's project (testX.vbp). Select **References** from the **Project** menu. Locate the entry for DoctorSchedule.vbp, and click on its check box.

> *Tip:* There might be two entries for the Doctor Schedule, one for the .vbp file, and the other for the .exe file. You can tell them apart by looking at the **Location** label at the bottom of the window. You must choose the .vbp file in order to debug the component in the VB5 development environment.

4. Run the test program and search for the appointments for one or more patients. When you halt the test program, always do so by closing its window. Do not halt the test program by clicking on Visual Basic's **End** button or by selecting **End** from the **Run** menu. Doing so would abort the program and prevent it from releasing memory used by objects.

5. Activate the original copy of Visual Basic, the one containing the DoctorSchedule component. Ordinarily, the ActiveX component would have halted and unloaded itself as soon as none of its objects were referenced by client programs. Because it is running in the VB environment, however, it does not halt as expected. The only way to stop it is to click on the **End** button in the VB toolbar.

You can, if you wish, modify the DoctorSchedule component, but just remember to recompile it and run it again before testing it.

To test DoctorSchedule.exe from outside Visual Basic, run the test program from either the VB Editor or from the Windows Explorer. The test program will automatically load and execute the DoctorSchedule component.

11.6 Where to Go From Here

The explanations given about concepts and techniques relating to creating ActiveX components that you find in this chapter are merely a brief introduction. (An upcoming release of this book will integrate ActiveX into most of the sample programs.) In the mean time, if you would like to dive wholeheartedly into this topic, here's what to do:

Read Part 2 of the *Component Tools Guide* manual that was supplied with VB5. The software is usually shipped without printed manuals, but you can send in an additional payment (about $8.00) and receive the printed manuals. This is *highly recommended*. Here are the topics in Part 2 of the manual:

- Chapter 1. ActiveX Components. A brief discussion of ActiveX concepts and definitions of terms.
- Chapter 2. Creating an ActiveX DLL. You get a chance to create a simple ActiveX DLL that reverses the characters in a string.

Chap 11: Creating ActiveX Controls 469

- Chapter 3. Creating an ActiveX EXE Component. This is an interesting program called the Coffee project, where you create an out-of-process ActiveX server that notifies the client program when the coffee is ready.
- Chapter 4. Creating an ActiveX Control. This chapter shows you how to create an ActiveX control called ShapeLabel, save and load its properties, raise events, and create a property page.
- Chapter 5. Creating an ActiveX Document. You build your first ActiveX document that contains a window and menu; it saves and loads its properties. This requires Internet Explorer 3.0 or later to run.
- Chapter 6. General Principles of Component Design. The topics in this chapter and in Chapter 7 contain background information that relate to all ActiveX component types.
- Chapter 7. Debugging, Testing, and Deploying Components. Besides debugging and testing, this chapter covers the generating and handling of errors, providing user assistance (Help), deploying ActiveX components.
- Chapter 8. Building Code Complements. Really advanced stuff regarding asynchronous call-backs, multithreading, binding, and marshaling.
- Chapter 9. Building ActiveX Controls. Continuation of Chapter 2: Adding properties and methods, raising events, named constants, setting up a test project, debugging, distributing, and localizing ActiveX controls.
- Chapter 10. Creating Property Pages for ActiveX Controls.
- Chapter 11. Building ActiveX Documents. Continuation of Chapter 5, using ActiveX pages on the Internet.

Of course, look for the many shareware ActiveX controls that are available on the Internet. Start with **www.microsoft.com** and follow their links to Visual Basic Web sites.

Don't forget about the web page devoted to this book! We provide lots of supplemental programs, ActiveX controls, and links to other Visual Basic locations on the Internet:

```
www.pobox.com/~irvinek/vbook
```

And if you are identified as a teacher or professor who has adopted this book, you can download improved and updated solutions to the programming exercises and new chapter exercises that are designed specifically for use with this book.

11.7 Review Questions

1. Define *component software development.*

2. What is the name of the model created by Microsoft that permits software components to interact with each other.

3. In what way is ActiveX more than just object-oriented programming?

4. What is the term that applies to a group of controls inside a single ActiveX control?

5. What relationship do OLE servers have with ActiveX components?

6. If an ActiveX component is created in Visual Basic, can it be used in an Excel application?

7. What are the three general types of objects provided by ActiveX components?
8. How are code components different from ActiveX controls?
9. What type of ActiveX component compiles into an OCX file?
10. What type of ActiveX component compiles into a DLL file?
11. Are in-process servers compiled into EXE files?
12. What is the primary limitation of the Control Creation Edition of Visual Basic?
13. What is the primary difference between a class module and an ActiveX component?
14. Show an example of declaring an event called FileError inside an ActiveX control's source code.
15. Show an example of raising the FileError event inside an ActiveX control's source code.
16. In the StudentIdText ActiveX control that was demonstrated in Section 11.2, what happens when the user enters a nonnumeric character?
17. Why doesn't the StudentIdText control allow itself to be resized by a developer who places the control on a form?
18. What relationship does a client program have to an ActiveX component?

The following questions refer to the AddAppointment ActiveX control:

19. Which design mode properties may be set in the AddAppointment control? (Section 11.3).
20. Which runtime properties may be accessed in the AddAppointment control? Are they read-write properties, or read-only?
21. How can a property be designated as read-only?
22. What happens when the user forgets to select a doctor from the combo box?
23. What happens when the user enters an invalid date?
24. Which event occurs when an ActiveX control is first placed on a form?
25. Which event occurs when the designer modifies either the Caption or BackColor property of the AddAppointment control?
26. Why is it important to supply default property values when calling the WriteProperty method?
27. What is a PropertyBag object?
28. Which event handler executes when a form file containing an ActiveX control is opened in design mode?
29. What are the four user-defined events declared in the AddAppointment component?
30. Why is it important to call PropertyChanged inside a *Property Let* procedure? In other words, what would happen if it were not called?
31. What is the difference between an *in-process component* and an *out-of-process component*?

32. Why is DoctorSchedule called a *type library?*
33. Is an ActiveX DLL an in-process or out-of-process component?
34. What does PublicNotCreateable mean when applied to the Instancing property?
35. Which Instancing property values are allowed for ActiveX DLLs?
36. Which Instancing property values are allowed for ActiveX Controls?
37. What special operation does clsSchedule perform when an instance of the class is first created? What is the name of the event handler where this happens?
38. Why is it important to use the On Error statement inside the Terminate event of an ActiveX component?
39. When procedure X calls procedure Y and no error handler exists in procedure Y, what happens to the error?
40. What special steps must be taken to debug an out-of-process component?
41. Is it possible to run an out-of-process component from the Windows Explorer? If so, how is it done?

11.8 Chapter Exercises

11.8.1 The StudentIdText Control

Using the StudentIdText control presented in Section 11.2, add another event to the control, called IdChanged. Raise this event during the txtID_Change event handler in the component's code. Also, add a Get Property procedure called IDNumber. Modify the client program so it handles the new event and retrieves the ID number.

11.8.2 The AddAppointment Control

Remove the OK and Cancel buttons from the AddAppointment control in Section 11.3. Let the main program carry out these tasks instead.

11.8.3 The clsSchedule Class

The Class_Initialize event handler in the clsSchedule class (Section 11.4.5) assumes that the database is in the current directory. But this may not always be practical. If the default filename location is not found, display a common dialog control and ask the user to select the file.

11.8.4 Stellar Car Rental Rates

In the Rental Reservations program from Chapter 7 (Section 7.9), we showed how the Rental Prices window could display a DBGrid control containing the daily and weekly rental rates of vehicles. For the current project, create an ActiveX control that encapsulates a Data control and DBGrid so the user can display price information (see Figure 18).

Make a copy of the Stellar car rental program from the Student disk, and add your new ActiveX control to the Rental Prices form.

Figure 18. Testing the Rental Prices ActiveX Control.

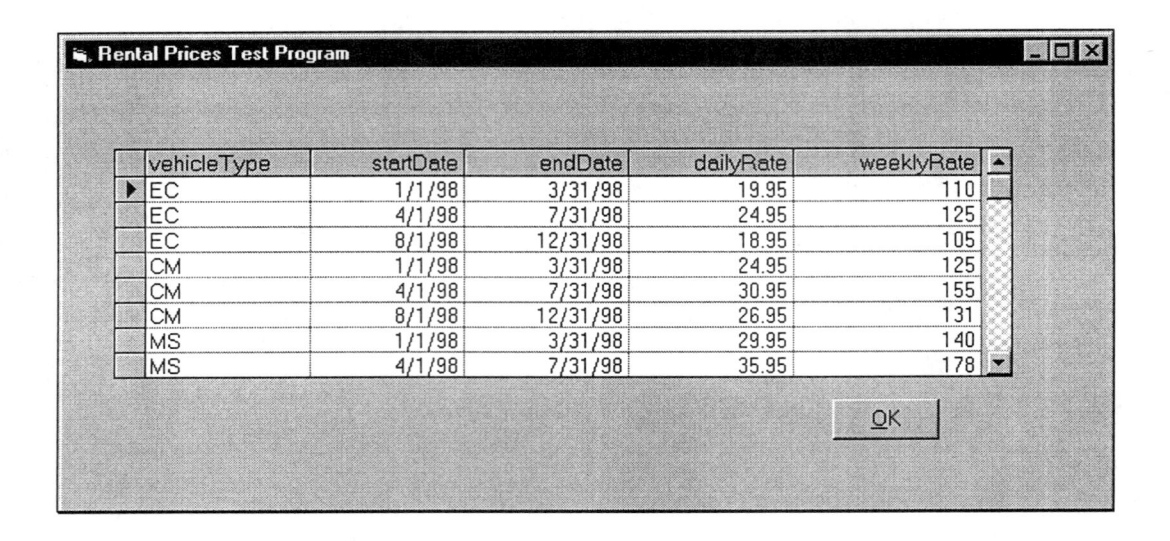

vehicleType	startDate	endDate	dailyRate	weeklyRate
EC	1/1/98	3/31/98	19.95	110
EC	4/1/98	7/31/98	24.95	125
EC	8/1/98	12/31/98	18.95	105
CM	1/1/98	3/31/98	24.95	125
CM	4/1/98	7/31/98	30.95	155
CM	8/1/98	12/31/98	26.95	131
MS	1/1/98	3/31/98	29.95	140
MS	4/1/98	7/31/98	35.95	178

11.8.5 The GetURLs ActiveX Control.

Create and test an ActiveX control called **GetURLs** that downloads the contents of a Web page over the Internet and lists all of the links found on the page (see Figure 19). Let the user enter any web page address and click on the **Go** button. The constituent controls will include the Internet Transfer Control, a Timer control, two Text box controls, and a command button. The large text box should have horizontal and vertical scroll bars. Write a test program that includes an instance of the GetURLs control.

Some **Internet Transfer** control methods and properties that you may find useful are:

- **OpenURL:** Opens a Web page and retrieves its text.
- **RequestTimeout:** The maximum number of seconds to wait before generating a trappable runtime error. Be sure to provide an error handler for this.
- **StillExecuting:** True if the control is in the process of downloading a Web page, False if it is finished.

Figure 19. URLs Found Using the GetURLs ActiveX Control.

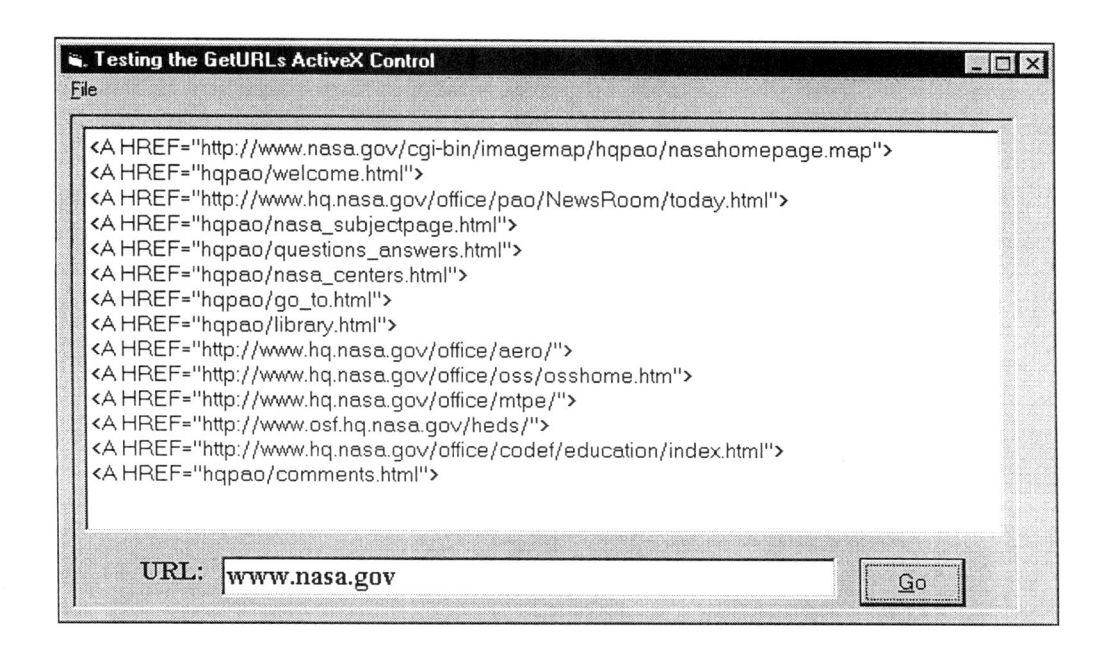

```
<A HREF="http://www.nasa.gov/cgi-bin/imagemap/hqpao/nasahomepage.map">
<A HREF="hqpao/welcome.html">
<A HREF="http://www.hq.nasa.gov/office/pao/NewsRoom/today.html">
<A HREF="hqpao/nasa_subjectpage.html">
<A HREF="hqpao/questions_answers.html">
<A HREF="hqpao/nasa_centers.html">
<A HREF="hqpao/go_to.html">
<A HREF="hqpao/library.html">
<A HREF="http://www.hq.nasa.gov/office/aero/">
<A HREF="http://www.hq.nasa.gov/office/oss/osshome.htm">
<A HREF="http://www.hq.nasa.gov/office/mtpe/">
<A HREF="http://www.osf.hq.nasa.gov/heds/">
<A HREF="http://www.hq.nasa.gov/office/codef/education/index.html">
<A HREF="hqpao/comments.html">
```

URL: www.nasa.gov

The Timer control is useful as a way of periodically checking the StillExecuting property of the Internet Transfer control. You can set the System.MousePointer to vbHourglass when you call OpenURL. The Timer control can set the MousePointer back to vbDefault when the StillExecuting property becomes False.

After downloading the HTML code from a page, you can use a loop to search for strings containing "<A HREF", and copy all text up to the ">" character. Append each string to the Text property of the Text Box. *Hint:* The **Instr** function is useful for searching for a substring within another string.

11.8.6 IniFileBrowser ActiveX Control

Use the clsIniFile class and program from Exercise 10.7.1 in Chapter 10 as a starting point for creating an ActiveX control that lets the user browse an INI file. Write a test program that demonstrates the control. The test program should also use a common dialog control to let the user select an INI filename.

Appendix A: Visual Basic Review

Chapter Contents

Competency Review Test
Data Types, Variables, and Constants
    Data Types
    Boolean
    Byte, Integer, Long
    Single, Double, Currency
    String
    Date
    Object
    Variant
    Declared Constants
    Static Arrays
    Dynamic Arrays
    Collections
    User-Defined Types
If Statements
    Compound Expressions (And, Or, Not)
    Block IF Statement
    Using ELSE
    Select Case
Loops
    For-Next Statement
    Do-While Statement
    Do-Until Statement
    While-Wend Statement
Procedures
    Declaring a Subroutine Procedure
    Procedure Parameters
    Declaring a Function Procedure
    Passing Arguments by Reference
    Passing Arguments by Value
    Private and Public
    Optional Parameters
    Parameter Arrays
String Handling
Forms
    Properties
    Methods
    Sample Form-Loading Program
    Events
Standard Visual Basic Controls

Label
Text
Command Button
Option Button
Frame
Check Box
Image
Line
Timer
Scroll Bars
List Boxes and Combo Boxes
Default Properties
Coding Guidelines
Naming Controls
Using General Procedures
Tools for Input-Output
Print Method
Format$ Function
MsgBox Procedure
MsgBox Function
InputBox Function
Printer Object
Screen Object
Application Object
Creating Menus
Common Menu Types
Creating a Simple Menu
Menu Properties
Sequential Files
Basic Syntax
Reading from an Input File
Writing to an Output File
Answers to the Competency Test Questions

A.1 Competency Review Test

Because this book is an advanced Visual Basic text, we assume that you already know the fundamentals of programming in Visual Basic. The following competency review test is designed to help you evaluate a basic level of competency in Visual Basic. If you have no trouble answering the questions on this test, there is a strong probability that you will be successful in understanding this book.

1. Name at least five standard data types.
2. Distinguish between variables that have module-level scope and procedure-level scope.
3. Visual Basic allows variables to be of type *object*. Give an example of two different types of objects that can be assigned to an object variable.
4. What is the role or purpose of a variable of type *variant*?
5. What is the primary feature or characteristic of Visual Basic's dynamic array?
6. Implement the following rules in Visual Basic:
   - All employees are paid overtime if hours worked are greater than 40.

Appendix A: Visual Basic Review 477

- Union members are paid at time and three-fourths for all hours over 40.
- Non-union members are paid at time and a half for all hours worked over 40.

Assume that HrsWrkd contains the number of hours worked, HrlyRate contains the hourly rate of the current employee, and that UnionMember is a Boolean variable which is true if the employee is a union member and false if not. Write the code segment to compute gross pay using the variables HrsWrkd, HrlyRate, and UnionMember.

7. The integer array *Score* contains 100 entries. Use a For-Next loop as part of a code segment to compute the average of the 100 scores. Store the computed average in the variable *Average*. You may need additional variables to complete the code.

8. A list of names are stored alphabetically in the array *Name*. There are 100 entries in the list. The variable *strName* contains a name known to be stored in the list. Write the code segment using a Do While-Loop structure to locate the first occurrence of the name stored in *strName*. Display the position in the list where the match occurred.

9. What is the purpose of a form's *Name* property?

10. Briefly describe the term *method*. Name at least two methods that are associated with a form.

11. What is the difference between "loading" a form and "showing" a form?

12. How do *labels* and *text boxes* differ with respect to how they are typically used?

13. For what purpose is the *command button* typically used?

14. What is the purpose of the command button's *Default* property?

15. How are option buttons and check boxes alike? not alike?

16. For what purpose is a *frame* typically used?

17. How are subroutines and functions alike? not alike?

18. What is the difference between passing arguments *by reference* and *by value*?

19. Procedures may be declared as either *Public* or *Private*. What is the difference?

20. The contents of the variable Net_Pay needs to the formatted to two decimal places with a comma and dollar sign. Use the *Format* function to print the formatted value on a form.

21. What is the purpose of the *MsgBox* procedure?

22. Including the *Option Explicit* command in your program serves what purpose?

23. What is the purpose of a control's *TabIndex* property?

24. What is the difference between the *MsgBox function* and the *MsgBox statement*?

25. A list box contains a *List* property. What values are contained in the *List* property?

26. In a list box, what is the difference between the *Clear* and *RemoveItem* methods?

27. Name the three different modes for which a sequential file can be opened.

28. For what purpose is the *On Error Goto* statement used?

29. For what purpose is the *Resume* statement used?
30. Briefly describe the use of the *Err* object with respect to error handling.

Answers to the Competency Test questions are at the end of Appendix A. The remainder of Appendix A is a general review of Visual Basic fundamentals.

A.2   Data Types, Variables, and Constants

A.2.1   Data Types

The standard data types are Boolean, Byte, Integer, Long, Single, Double, Currency, String, Date, Object, and Variant. To declare a non-array variable, we use the Dim statement in one of the following forms:

```
Dim varname As type
Dim varname
```

varname is a 1-255 character identifier, starting with a letter, containing any combination of letters, numbers, and the underscore character (_); *type* is a standard Visual Basic data type, user-defined type, or class module type. The following sections contain brief descriptions of the basic data types.

A.2.2   Boolean

A boolean variable only holds values of True and False, both of which are predefined identifiers in Visual Basic. Boolean variables are ideal for holding the values of logical expressions. The following are examples of declaring and assigning values to a boolean variable:

```
Dim contine As Boolean
continue = True
continue = score > 0
continue = (score > 0) AND (count < 20)
```

Internally, Visual Basic represents True as –1 and False as 0.

A.2.3   Byte, Integer, Long

Whole numbers can be stored in variables of type Byte, Integer, or Long. Each has a different range of possible values:

Byte	0 to 255
Integer	–32,768 to +32,767
Long	–2,147,483,648 to 2,147,483,647

The following are examples of declarations and assignments:

```
Dim age As Byte
Dim score As Integer
Dim miles as Long
age = 25
score = 25000
miles = -123456789
```

You can also use the following abbreviations when declaring Integer and Long variables:

```
Dim score%      'Integer
Dim miles&      'Long
```

A.2.4 Single, Double, Currency

Single, Double, and Currency variables hold non-integer values. The approximate range of each is shown:

Single	-3.4×10^{38} to -1.4×10^{-45}, and 1.4×10^{-45} to 3.4×10^{38}
Double	-1.8×10^{308} to -4.9×10^{-324}, and 4.9×10^{-324} to 1.8×10^{308}
Currency	$-922,337,203,685,477.5808$ to $922,337,203,685,477.5807$

The following are examples of declarations and assignments:

```
Dim budget As Currency
budget = 123456789012345.1234
Dim payRate As Single
payRate = 25.5
Dim velocity as Double
velocity = 1234.5678901234
```

Single variables have 7 digits of precision, so if you try to assign a more precise number, it is automatically rounded off. For example,

```
Dim temperature As Single
temperature = 1.2345678         'stored as  1.234568
```

Double variables have 15 digits of precision. Currency variables are ideal for financial calculations, because they can store 15 digits to the left of the decimal point and 4 digits to the right. The ! character can be used when declaring a Single, the # character can be used when declaring a Double, and the @ character can be used when declaring a Currency variable:

```
Dim payRate!        'Single
Dim velocity#       'Double
Dim budget@         'Currency
```

Real number literals can be expressed in either fixed-point or scientific (exponential) notation. For example,

```
Dim velocity As Double
velocity = 1.2E+15
```

A.2.5 String

The String data type in Visual Basic is, by default, a variable-length string. In the 32-bit version of Visual Basic, a String can be as long as 2^{31} characters. String literals must be surrounded by double quotes:

```
Dim lastName As String
lastName = "Frankenstein"
```

The + character concatenates two strings, whether they are literals or variables:

```
Dim fullName As String
fullName = lastName + ", " + firstName
```

The & character concatenates a string to a number or numeric variable, and can also concatenate two strings:

```
Print "You worked " & hoursWorked & " hours this week."
Print "Hello " & "there!"
```

Fixed-Length Strings. A fixed-length string, once declared, cannot change size. This type of string can be processed more quickly by Visual Basic than a variable-length string. Any extra characters assigned to the string are truncated, and if there are fewer characters than the length of the string, the string is padded with spaces at the end:

```
Dim zipCode As String * 5
zipCode = "33156"
zipCode = "33156-2364"       'stored as "33156"
zipCode = "33"               'stored as "33   "
```

A.2.6 Date

A Date variable holds both a date and a time as a single floating-point value. The value represents a date between January 1, 0100, to December 31, 9999, and a time of day between 0:00:00 and 23:59:59. Literal dates and times must be surrounded by # characters. For example,

```
Dim birthday As Date
Dim appointment As Date
birthday = #1/22/82#
appointment = #12:06:00 PM#
appointment = #4/6/98 14:00#
```

If you try to assign a date in a different format, such as #1982/01/22#, the Visual Basic editor will transform it to the format #1/22/82#.

IsDate Function. Visual Basic provides the IsDate function for validating times and dates. It returns True or False, depending on whether the input expression can be converted to a valid date or time. The general format is:

```
result = IsDate( expression )
```

The expression can be a string, the text property of a Text control, or a date literal. For example,

```
If Not IsDate( txtUserDate.Text ) Then
  Debug.Print "Invalid date: " & userDate
End If
```

A.2.7 Object

Object variables can hold forms, controls, or user-defined class objects. For example, you can assign Form1 to an object variable. The following does this, and prints "Hello" on Form1:

```
Dim F As Object
Set F = Form1
F.Print "Hello"
```

When assigning a value to an object variable, you have to use the **Set** statement.

A.2.8 Variant

A variable of type Variant can hold nearly any value except a fixed-length string or a user-defined type. When a value is assigned to it, the value implies its type. The following example demonstrates this:

```
Dim anything as Variant
anything = 1234
anything = "A big lobster"
anything = #7/4/96#
```

You can also declare a Variant by not specifying any type:

```
Dim anything
anything = 1234
(etc.)
```

Variants are useful in those rare situations when you cannot predict at design time what type of value will be assigned to a variable at run time. A Variant variable also takes a little more time to process than a typed variable, because the type of data inside the Variant has to be identified before the data can be used.

The **IsEmpty** function returns True if a Variant has not been intitialized:

```
If IsEmpty( anything ) Then anything = 0
```

A.2.9 Declared Constants

A declared constant is assigned a value when it is declared, and keeps this value throughout the program. The constant's type can be determined by the type of value assigned to it, but explicitly declaring the type is preferred:

```
Const WeekDays As Integer = 5
Const DaysInWeek As Integer = 7
Const Author As String = "Juan Gonzalez"
Const PI As Single = 3.14159
```

A.2.10 Static Arrays

There are two types of arrays in Visual Basic: static and dynamic. To declare a static array, provide the lower and upper bounds in the Dim (or Public) statement. The following all declare one-dimensional arrays:

```
Public NameTable(0 To 20) As String
Dim scores(1 To 50) As Single
Dim coordinate(-100 To 100) As Integer
Dim Customers(1 To 1000) As String
Dim payRates(1 To 50) As Single
Public statusFlags(0 to 9) As Boolean
```

The boundary values are integers in the range of a long data type (-2^{31} to $+2^{31} - 1$). It is possible to omit the lower bound, in which case it defaults to 0. The **Option Base** statement can be used to change the default to 1. The meaning of the array declaration is clearer if you provide both the lower and upper bounds.

A.2.11 Dynamic Arrays

A dynamic array is one that can be re-dimensioned at runtime. To declare a dynamic array, use Dim, Public, or Private with no array boundaries:

```
Public NameTable() As String
Dim coordinate() As Integer
Private scores() As Single
```

Then within a procedure, use the ReDim statement to give an explicit size to the array. Notice that the array's type is not included, and the boundaries can be specified by either variables or constants:

```
Private Sub MySub()
  ReDim NameTable(1 To NameCount)
  ReDim coordinate(xLow To xHigh)
  ReDim scores(0 to 99)
  '(etc.)
End Sub
```

You can ReDim an array only once in the same procedure, but you can ReDim an array throughout a program any number of times. If you need to preserve the current contents of the array, include the Preserve option with ReDim. Here, for example, we expand NameTable by 10 entries and preserve its contents:

```
ReDim Preserve NameTable(1 To NameCount + 10)
```

The standard UBound and LBound functions return the upper and lower boundary values of an array:

```
n = LBound(NameTable)
n = UBound(NameTable)
```

A.2.12 Collections

Visual Basic lets you create collections, which are both similar to, and more powerful than arrays. You can insert a list of names into a collection, for example:

```
Dim myFriends As New Collection
myFriends.Add "Tom"
myFriends.Add "Sue"
myFriends.Add "Dan"
myFriends.Add "Robert"
```

Visual Basic has a specialized loop statement for dealing with collections, called **For Each**. Here, for example, we iterate over **myFriends** and print each name:

```
Dim person As Variant
For Each person In myFriends
   Debug.Print person
Next person
```

You can also use a numeric index to refer to collection members. The indexes range from 1 to Count, where Count is a property stored in the collection itself. Again, we display all of the names:

```
Dim j As Integer
For j = 1 To myFriends.Count
   Debug.Print myFriends(j)
Next j
```

A.2.13 User-Defined Types

A user-defined type is a unique data type created by the programmer, using the **Type** and **End Type** keywords. For example, the following declaration creates a type called Student, consisting of two data members, an ID number and a last name:

```
Type Student
   id As Long
   lastName As String
End Type
```

The following statements declare a Student variable and assign values to its two data members:

```
Dim stu As Student
stu.id = 123456
stu.lastName = "Ramirez"
```

User-defined types provide an enormously useful way to collect related data inside a single variable, pass the variable to procedures, and write the variable to a file.

> *Programming Tip:* User-defined types cannot be inserted into Collection objects.

A.3 IF Statements

A.3.1 Compound Expressions (And, Or, Not)

No Short-Circuit Evaluation. When the AND operator is used to build a compound expression, VBasic does not use short-circuit evaluation. In the following compound expression, for example, we would like to verify that count is greater than zero before using it as a divisor. Unfortunately Visual Basic evaluates both expressions, resulting in a runtime error when count equals zero:

```
If (count > 0) And (TotalSales / count > 500) Then
   frmSales.Print "Average Sales Over 500"
End If
```

The expression must be rewritten as the following:

```
If count > 0 Then
  If (TotalSales / count > 500) Then
    frmSales.Print "Average Sales Over 500"
  End If
End If
```

A.3.2 Block IF Statement

An If statement always contains a boolean (True/False) expression. For example, we assign a value of True to OverTime when the hours worked are greater than 40:

```
If hours > 40 Then OverTime = True
```

This type of If statement is not too flexible because only a single statement can be executed after the If condition. In most cases, we prefer to use a block-If statement, which can be expanded to include any number of statements after the condition:

```
If hours > 40 Then
  OverTime = True
  Status = "Overtime hours worked"
End If
```

A.3.3 Using ELSE

Often, we insert an Else clause in the If statement to handle both true and false alternatives:

```
If hours > 40 Then
```

```
    OverTime = True
Else
    OverTime = False
End If
```

The If-ElseIf structure can be used when there are several alternatives. Be sure to make "ElseIf" a single word. Here, we determine the special fees paid by a student based on the number of enrolled credits:

```
If credits < 10 Then
    fees = 0
ElseIf credits < 15 Then
    fees = 100
Else
    fees = credits * 10
End If
```

If statements can be nested, but the result is often difficult to read. The following example calculates student fees based on both the credits taken and the state residency status. Use structures like this only when necessary, and be sure to indent them carefully:

```
If credits < 10 Then
    If stateResident Then
        fees = 0
    Else
        fees = 50
    End If
ElseIf credits < 15 Then
    If stateResident Then
        fees = 100
    Else
        fees = 150
    End If
Else
    If stateResident Then
        fees = credits * 10
    Else
        fees = credits * 15
    End If
End If
```

A.3.4 Select Case

The Select Case statement provides a convenient multiway selection structure. Its syntax is:

```
Select Case testexpression
[Case expressionlist-n
    [statements-n]] . . .
[Case Else
    [elsestatements]]
End Select
```

Where *testexpression* can be any numeric or string expression, *expressionlist* is a list of expressions in one of the following forms:

```
expression
expression-1 To expression-2
Is comparisonoperator expression
```

Student Credits. For example, a simple program that lets the user input the number of college credits taken by a student can use the Select Case statement to display an appropriate message. Each of the basic expression types is demonstrated here:

```
Private Sub cmdEvaluate_Click()
  Dim st As String
  Select Case Val(txtCredits.Text)
    Case 0
      st = "Student not enrolled"
    Case 1 To 11
      st = "Part-time student"
    Case Is > 11
      st = "Full-time student"
    Case Else
      st = "Credits cannot be negative!"
  End Select
  lblResult.Caption = st
End Sub
```

The user interface for this program consists of a text box, command button, and label:

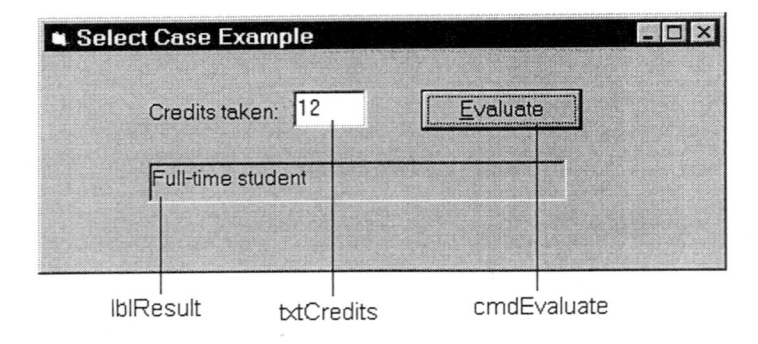

A.4 Loops

There are two basic types of loops: counting loops, and conditional loops. A *counting* loop is most effective when the number of times that a loop must repeat can be determined either at compile time or run time. A *conditional* loop is effective when the number of repetitions is determined by some input source and cannot be calculated before the loop begins. The For-Next statement is a counting loop; the Do-While, Do-Until, and While-Wend statements are conditional loops.

A.4.1 For-Next Statement

The For-Next statement creates a counting loop; it begins at *startval*, ends at *stopval*, and increments *counter* either by 1 or an optional value stored in increment:

```
For counter = startval To stopval [Step increment]
  '...
Next [counter]
```

For example, the following loop counts forward in the sequence: 0, 1, 2, ..., 48, 49, 50:

```
For count = 0 To 50
  Print "count = ";count
Next count
```

The following loop counts backward in the sequence: 20, 19, 18, ..., 1:

```
For j = 20 To 1 Step -1
  Print samples[j];
Next j
```

The following loop counts forward in the sequence -50, -48, -46, ..., 46, 48, 50:

```
For j = -50 To 50 Step 2
  Print j
Next j
```

A.4.2 Do-While Statement

There are two versions of the Do-While statement:

Pre-Test:
```
Do While condition
  loop body
Loop
```

Post-Test:
```
Do
  loop body
Loop While condition
```

If *condition* is True, the loop repeats; if *condition* is False, the loop stops. In the Pre-test version, the loop is never executed if the condition is initially False. In the Post-test version, the loop executes at least once before the condition is tested.

This type of loop is very useful when a value is input each time the loop repeats. For example, the following loop reads from a file until the end of the file has been reached:

```
Dim aRecord As String, fileNum as Integer
'(file is opened...)

Do While Not EOF(1)
  Input #fileNum, aRecord
```

```
Loop
```

The following loop iterates through an array of integers, adding each to a sum, until one of the values in the array is less than or equal to zero. If the first number equals zero, no numbers are added:

```
Dim j As Integer, sum as Integer
Dim aList(1 to 20) as Integer
j = 0
Do While aList(j) > 0
  j = j + 1
  sum = sum + aList(j)
Loop
```

A.4.3 Do-Until Statement

The Do-Until statement has two forms:

Pre-Test:
```
Do Until condition
   loop body
Loop
```

Post-Test:
```
Do
   loop body
Loop Until condition
```

If *condition* is False, the loop repeats; if *condition* is True, the loop stops. In the Pre-test version, the loop is never executed if the condition is initially True. In the Post-test version, the loop executes at least once before the condition is tested.

In the following example, we repeat the loop if the current number in the array is greater than zero, and the array subscript is <= 20:

```
Dim j As Integer, sum As Integer
Dim aList(1 to 20) As Integer
j = 1
Do
   sum = sum + aList(j)
   j = j + 1
Loop Until (aList(j) <= 0) Or (j > 20)
```

A.4.4 While-Wend Statement

The While-Wend loop was a part of the old Microsoft QuickBasic language, and was probably retained in Visual Basic for compatibility. It works exactly the same as a Do-While loop, in which the condition is tested before the loop body executes:

```
While condition
   '...
```

```
Wend
```

A.5 Procedures

Procedures are one of the fundamental building blocks of programs, because a procedure can perform a specific task as many times as the procedure is called. Visual Basic supports three types of procedures: subroutine, function, and property. A subroutine is a procedure that does not return a value. A function procedure always returns a value. A property procedure sets or returns the value of a property in a form or class (a topic that will be covered in detail in Chapter 3).

To insert a procedure into your program, open a code window for a form, code module, or class module. Use the **Insert / Procedure** menu command. The following dialog window will appear:

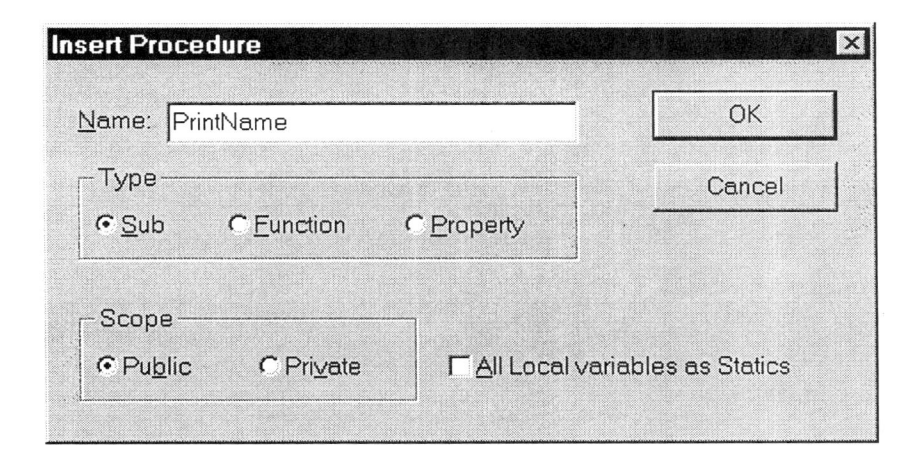

At this point, re-enter a name for the procedure, using the same rules for naming as we mentioned for variables. The three option buttons (Sub, Function, Property) let you determine which type of procedure is to be created. After you click on OK, an empty procedure will be inserted at the end of the code window.

A.5.1 Declaring a Subroutine Procedure

A *sub procedure* (or simply, *procedure*) is a procedure that carries out some action but does not return a value. The general syntax for declaring a sub procedure is

```
[ Public | Private ] Sub procedureName ( parameterList )
   (local variable and constant declarations)
   (zero or more statements)
End Sub
```

where *procedureName* follows the same rules as any Visual Basic identifier, and *parameterList* is an optional list of parameters. The parentheses after the procedure name are required, even if the parameter list is empty. Public and Private refer to the scope of the procedure: A public procedure can be called from anywhere in a program, whereas a private procedure can only be called from the same form or module.

A public sub procedure named SumArray with no parameters would be declared as follows:

```
Public Sub SumArray()

End Sub
```

The parentheses at the end of the procedure name hold the procedure parameters, if any. The same procedure declared as private would be:

```
Private Sub SumArray()

End Sub
```

A.5.2 Procedure Parameters

Procedure parameters are identifiers that appear in the header of a procedure definition that identify values that will be passed to the procedure. Most of the time, each parameter is assigned a data type, so the Visual Basic compiler can verify that the right types of values were passed to the procedure. A parameter list contains one or more parameters, separated by commas. Each parameter has the following syntax:

```
[Optional] [ByVal|ByRef] [ParamArray] varname[()] [As type]
```

Where *type* can be Byte, Boolean, Integer, Long, Currency, Single, Double, Date, variable-length String, Object, Variant, a user-defined type, or an object type. **ParmArray** can be used only as the last item in a parameter list to indicate that the parameter is an optional array of Variant elements.

Examples. The SumArray procedure is declared with a single parameter called **count**, of type Integer:

```
Public Sub SumArrray(count As Integer)

End Sub
```

Now SumArray is declared with several parameters: the array being summed, a counter, and a variable to hold the sum. Inside the procedure, we use a loop to add the array elements:

```
Public Sub SumArray(anArray() As Integer, _
      count As Integer, sum As Integer)
  Dim j As Integer
  sum = 0
  For j = 1 To count
    sum = sum + anArray(j)
  Next j
End Sub
```

When calling a subroutine procedure in Visual Basic, do not surround the argument list with parentheses. The following statements call SumArray and display the sum in a message box:

```
Dim array(1 To 3) As Integer
Dim sum As Integer
array(1) = 10
array(2) = 20
array(3) = 40
SumArray array, 3, sum
MsgBox sum
```

Terminology. Unfortunately, books and documentation are inconsistent in their use of the terms *parameter* and *argument*. In the Visual Basic documentation, procedure parameters are also called procedure arguments. In this book, we will consistently distinguish between parameters and arguments in the following way: A *parameter* appears in a procedure's declaration, whereas an *argument* is a value passed to a procedure. In the following example, **str** is a parameter, and **msg** is an argument:

```
                              parameter
                                 |
Public Sub ShowMe( str As String )
   MsgBox str
End Sub

Public Sub Main()
   Dim msg as String
   msg = "Passing an argument"
   ShowMe msg
End Sub      |
           argument
```

A.5.3 Declaring a Function Procedure

A *function procedure* (or simply, *function*) is a procedure that returns a value when the function is called. The general syntax is:

```
[ Public | Private ] Function procedureName ( parameterList )
   As returnType
   (local variable and constant declarations)
   (statements)
   (ProcedureName = returnvalue)
End Function
```

where *procedureName* and *parameterList* are the same as for subroutine procedures, and *returnType* is the type of value that will be returned by the function.

For example, we might have declared SumArray as a function. Rather than make the sum a parameter, we made it the function return value. The "As Integer" at the end of the line tells us that the function returns an Integer value:

```
Public Function SumArray(anArray() As Integer, _
    count As Integer) As Integer
  '...
End Function
```

When we implement the function, an extra variable called sum is declared locally, and at the end of the function, the variable is assigned to the function name itself. This is how the function returns a value:

```
Public Function SumArray(anArray() As Integer, _
    count As Integer) As Integer
  Dim j As Integer, sum As Integer
  sum = 0
  For j = 1 To count
    sum = sum + anArray(j)
  Next j
  SumArray = sum    '<--- returns the function result
End Function
```

When calling a function, surround the arguments with parentheses:

```
Dim array(1 To 3) As Integer, numVals As Integer
Dim sum As Integer
array(1) = 10
array(2) = 20
array(3) = 40
numVals = 3
sum = SumArray(array, numVals)
```

A.5.4 Passing Arguments by Reference

The **ByRef** keyword can be used before the name of a procedure parameter, indicating that the corresponding argument will be passed by reference. ByRef is the default method for parameter passing in Visual Basic. The parameter inside the procedure is just another name for the object that was passed to the procedure. Any change the procedure makes to the parameter will automaticallly modify the argument that was passed to the procedure. Suppose, for example, that SumArray assigned zero to **count**:

```
Public Function SumArray(anArray() As Integer, _
    count As Integer) As Integer
  '...
  count = 0
End Function
```

Assuming that the procedure was called with an argument named **numVals**, we would find after the procedure call that numVals had also been set to zero:

```
numVals = 3
MsgBox SumArray(array, numVals)
```

```
' now, numVals equals 0
```

Needless to say, this poses an obstacle to writing bug-free code, as it might be easy to forget that a parameter had been modified by a procedure. On the positive side, large objects such as arrays and Forms can be passed more efficiently by reference, because the compiler does not have to make a complete copy of the object before passing it to the called procedure.

A.5.5 Passing Arguments by Value

The ByVal keyword can be used before the name of a procedure parameter to assert that the corresponding argument will be passed by value. Passing arguments by value lets you avoid the side effects caused by passing by reference. When passing by value, any change to a parameter inside a procedure has no effect on the passed argument, because the procedure is only working with a copy of the original variable.

For example, count will be passed by value:

```
Public Function SumArray(anArray() As Integer, _
        ByVal count As Integer) As Integer
    '...
End Function
```

If you are unable or unwilling to use ByVal in a procedure declaration, another way to pass an argument by value is to surround it with parentheses:

```
Public Function SumArray(anArray() As Integer, _
        count As Integer) As Integer
    '...
End Function
                                    pass by value
numVals = 3
MsgBox SumArray(array, (numVals))
' numVals equals 3
```

Arrays and objects are always passed by reference. For example, if we try to pass Form1 by value, Visual Basic just ignores the ByVal qualifier:

```
Public Sub SetCaption(ByVal F As Form)
    F.Caption = "This is a New Caption"
End Sub

Public Sub Main()
    Load Form1
    SetCaption Form1
    Form1.Show vbModal
End Sub
```

The parameter F is a *reference* to Form1, meaning that any modification to F is also a modification to Form1.

A.5.6 Private and Public

A procedure declared as **public** can be called from anywhere in a program. If the procedure belongs to a form, the procedure name has to be attached to the form name when the call is made. For example, from the Main procedure in module1.bas, we call SumArray, located in frmMain:

```
sum = frmMain.SumArray(array, 3)
```

On the other hand, if a public procedure is located in a code module (such as module1.bas), it can be called just by using its name:

```
sum = SumArray(array, 3)
```

A procedure declared **private** can only be called from the same form or module. For example, all of the event procedures relating to a form or its controls are declared private by default:

```
Private Sub Command1_Click()
   MsgBox "Command1 button was pushed"
End Sub
```

You can always change private to public, however. If Command1_Click were declared Public, we could "push" this button from Main() in module1, although frmMain was not currently displayed:

```
Public Sub Main()
   frmMain.Command1_Click    '<-- "push" the button in frmMain
End Sub
```

A.5.7 Optional Parameters

Procedures can be declared with optional parameters; this means that one or more arguments can be omitted when the procedure is called. For example, we might have a procedure called OpenFile that can be called with or without a filename. If the filename is omitted, we display an InputBox and ask the user for a name:

```
Public Sub OpenFile(Optional filename As Variant)
   If IsMissing(filename) Then
      filename = InputBox("Name of file to open:", _
         "Opening File", "")
   End If
   '(etc...)
End Sub
```

Optional parameters must be type Variant. The standard **IsMissing** function returns True if the procedure argument has been omitted. The **InputBox** function is discussed at some length in Chapter 2. Optional parameters must be at the end of the parameter list.

A.5.8 Parameter Arrays

The **ParamArray** keyword in a parameter list indicates that the parameter is an array of Variant parameters. This is the way that a Visual Basic procedure can have a variable-length parameter list. For example, the **PrintItems** procedure has a parameter called **count** that indicates the number of parameters that will follow. The **items** array contains the rest of the parameters:

```
Private Sub PrintItems(count As Integer, ParamArray items())
  Dim j As Integer
  For j = 0 To count - 1
    Print items(j); ", ";
  Next j
End Sub
```

The procedure prints the items on the current form. Notice that the **items** array is zero-based, and the passed arguments can be of any type. The following are examples of calls to this procedure:

```
PrintItems 3, "One", 26, Caption
PrintItems 1, "Giraffe"
PrintItems 2, 126.35, 400.2
```

A.6 String Handling

Table 1 contains a list of standard Visual Basic statements, operators, and procedures that manipulate strings.

Table 1. String Statements, Procedures, and Operators.

Statement/Procedure/ Operator Syntax	Return Type	Description
+	String	Concatenate two strings (+).
&	String	Concatenate string to another string or numeric expression (&).
Asc(st)	Integer	Return the ASCII code of the first character in string <st>.
Chr$(n)	String	Return a string containing the character that matches ASCII code in <n>.
CStr(exp)	String	Convert expression <exp> to a string.
Format$(n, fst)	String	Format numeric value <n> using format string <fst>.
Instr([start,]st,srch)	Long	Find the character position of string <srch> inside string <st>, starting in position <start>. Return 0 if not found.
LCase$(st)	String	Return <st> in all lowercase letters.
Left$(st, n)	String	Copy <n> characters from the left side of string <st>.
Len(st)	Long	Find the length of string <st>.

result = st LIKE pattern	Boolean	Compare string <st> to <pattern>
LSet dest = source	String	Copy a <source> string to a <dest> string, left-aligned.
LTrim$(st)	String	Remove all leading spaces from string <st>.
Mid$(st, start, n)	String	Copy <n> characters from the middle of string <st>, starting in position <start>.
option compare Binary option compare Text	(none)	Set the default comparison method for strings to either binary or textual. Appears in module declarations.
Right$(st, n)	String	Copy <n> characters from the right side of string <st>.
RSet dest = source	String	Copy a <source> string to a <dest> string, right-aligned.
RTrim$(st)	String	Remove all trailing spaces from string <st>.
Space$(n)	String	Create a string containing <n> spaces.
Str$(n)	String	Convert numeric value <n> into a string.
StrComp(st1,st2)	Integer	Return -1 if string <st1> less than <st2>; return 0 if <st1> equal to <st2>; return 1 if <st1> greater than <st2>.
StrConv(st, conv)	String	Convert string <st>, based on the type of conversion specified by <conv>. Sample values are vbUpperCase, vbLowerCase, vbProperCase, etc.
String$(n, st)	String	Create a string containing <n> occurrences of character/string <st>.
Trim$(st)	String	Remove both leading and trailing spaces from string <st>.
UCase$(st)	String	Return <st> in all uppercase letters.
Val(st)	Number	Returns the numbers contained in string <st>.

Asc(). The Asc() function provides a simple way to convert a character into its corresponding numeric ASCII code. For example, we might want to inspect the first character of a text box to be sure it is a digit:

```
Dim n as Integer
n = Asc( txtSalary.Text )
```

Chr$(). The Chr$() function is useful for representing non-displayable keyboard characters. Certain common character sequences are assigned predefined constants, as shown in Table 2 They can be used in any Visual Basic program, as long as **Visual Basic for Applications** has been selected in the Tools/References menu. For example, we often add a carriage-return/linefeed to the end of each line when inserting a string in a text box:

```
Dim st As String
Dim totalSales As Currency
'...
st = vbTab + "Monthly Income Report" + vbCrLf + _
"----------------------------------------" + vbCrLf + _
"Sales of Computers...................." & totalSales & vbCrLf
'(etc.)
```

```
txtReport.Text = st
```

Or, when printing a report, we could advance the printer to the next page by appending a form feed character:

```
salesReport = salesReport + vbFormFeed
Printer.Print salesReport
```

Table 2. Predefined Character Sequences.

Predefined Constant	Character Sequence	Description
vbCrLf	Chr$(13)+Chr$(10)	Carriage-return/linefeed
vbNullChar	Chr$(0)	Null character
vbCr	Chr$(13)	Carriage return
vbLf	Chr$(10)	Linefeed
vbBack	Chr$(8)	Backspace
vbTab	Chr$(9)	Tab
VbVerticalTab	Chr$(11)	Vertical tab (not supported by Windows)
VbFormFeed	Chr$(12)	Form feed

CStr. The CStr function converts any expression to a string. The expression can be any valid numeric or string expression. CStr uses the international settings of Windows to perform conversions that recognize differences in numeric symbols such as decimal separators. For this reason, CStr is preferred to Str, which does not recognize international settings. The CStr function will generate a runtime error in one case: when trying to convert Null to a string.

A.7 Forms

In this section we will discuss only the more often-used properties, methods, and event handlers associated with forms. A *property* basically behaves like a variable, or data value enclosed in the form. A *method* is a procedure that carries out some action on the form. An *event handler* is a procedure that is activated because of some action by the user or the operating system.

A.7.1 Properties

Name. The Name property of a form is used when referring to the form in program code. For example, to print "Hello" on a form whose Name property equals **Form1**, we would write:

```
Form1.Print "Hello"
```

Appearance. The Appearance property of a form can be set to the following values:
- *Flat:* Changes the background color to the standard Windows background color.

- *3D:* A standard Windows button face color is the default

BorderStyle. The Borderstyle property can be set to one of the following values:
- *None:* The form will have no border.
- *Fixed single:* The form will have a thin single-line border, and the form cannot be resized by the user.
- *Sizable:* The border is a thick line, and the user can resize the form.
- *Fixed Dialog:* Appears as a Windows dialog box with thick borders, and cannot be resized. Has no minimize or maximize buttons by default, but you can add them back on.
- *Fixed ToolWindow:* Appears similar to the Toolbox window that contains all of the Visual Basic controls. Cannot be resized.
- *Sizable ToolWindow:* A ToolWindow that can be resized.

If you want to prevent the user from dragging the form, set the Caption to blank, and set the ControlBox, MinButton, and MaxButton properties to False.

Caption. The Caption property of a form contains the text that appears on the title bar at the top of the form. This also appears when the form is minimized, on the Windows 95 task bar.

Icon. This property lets you select an icon file that will be loaded into the form's title bar, alongside the caption.

ControlBox. If set to True, this displays a standard Windows control box at the right side of the form's title bar.

MinButton. If set to True, the user can minimize the form.

MaxButton. If set to True, the user can maximize the form.

BackColor, ForeColor. Select the background and foreground colors for the form. When you click on this property, a standard color pallete window will appear and you can select a color.

Font. Select the font and its properties (size, bold, underline, etc.) to be used when text is written to the Form.

Left, Top, Height, Width. Set the screen position for the left side or top of the form. Set the height and width of the form. The unit of measurement is determined by the ScaleMode property, which defaults to *Twips*. There are 1440 Twips per logical inch.

Visible. If set to True, the form will be visible to the user.

WindowState. The integer value of this property (0, 1, or 2) determines whether the form will be first be displayed as Normal (0), Minimized (1), or Maximized (2). Normal is the default.

A.7.2 Methods

A *method* is a procedure that is attached to a specific type of object. Because a form is a type of object, you can call form methods. Table 3 describes a number of methods that are important when dealing with forms.

Table 3. Frequently Used Form Methods.

Method	Description
Show	Display a form (load the form first if it is not already in memory.)
Load	Load the form's visual portion into memory, but do not show the form.
Unload	Unload the visual part of a form, but do not unload the form's properties and instance variables.
Hide	Remove the form from the display, but do not unload its visual portion.
Cls	Clear all text from the form.
Print	Display text on the form, starting at the upper-left corner. Each call to Print writes text on a separate line.
PrintForm	Print a snapshot of the form on the printer.
Move	Move the form to a specific screen location.

The following statements, for example, load a form called frmMain into memory, initialize one of its label controls, show the form, retrieve the contents of a text box on the form, and unload the form:

```
Load frmMain
frmMain.lblTitle = "Employee Payroll System"
frmMain.Show vbModal
employeeName = frmMain.txtLastName
Unload frmMain
```

This implies that when the form was closed, the form was simply hidden (with the Hide method), allowing us to access one of its controls. This can be a useful technique because a form may have a great deal of information that we want to use before the form is unloaded.

Automatic Loading. If a form is not currently loaded and you access one of its controls, the form will be loaded automatically. In the following example, the form is loaded exactly when the Caption property of the button is modified:

```
Unload frmMain
    .
    .
frmMain.cmdCalculate.Caption = "Calculate Pay"
```

Show (Modal and Modeless). The **Show** method displays the form as either a modal or modeless window. If a form is shown modally, the current sequence of statements cannot continue until the form is closed. The vbModal constant is predefined as the value 1. In the following example, frmStatus will not be shown until frmMain is closed (either by hiding it or unloading it):

```
frmMain.Show vbModal
frmStatus.Show vbModal
```

To show a form as a *modeless* window, pass the predefined constant vbModeless as an argument to the Show method. In the following example, both forms will display simultaneously:

```
frmMain.Show vbModeless
frmStatus.Show vbModeless
' execution continues here...
```

Hide. The Hide method makes a form disappear from the screen, but does not remove it from memory. This is useful when we still want to access data stored in the form's controls. The following statements hide frmMain and then access the form's Caption property:

```
frmMain.Hide
Debug.Print frmMain.Caption
```

Cls, Print, PrintForm. The Cls method clears all text from a form. The Print method lets one print a sequence of strings, variables, and numbers directly on a form. The form must be visible before the Print method is executed. The PrintForm method sends a snapshot of an entire form to the printer. The following statements, for example, might be placed in a form's Form_Activate event handler:

```
Private Sub Form_Activate()
   Print "Better Breakfasts, Inc."
   Print "Revision date: " & RevisionDate
   PrintForm            'print a snapshot of the entire form
End Sub
```

Unloaded, But Still There. Even when a form has been unloaded, its properties and instance variables are still kept in memory. This can be an advantage if you need to retain the values of variables inside the form, and do not want to lose them when the form has been unloaded. On the other hand, the form still uses up memory. The only way to completely remove a form from memory is to assign to it a predefined value called **Nothing**:

```
Unload frmMain          'variables are still there
Set frmMain = Nothing   'now it's really gone
```

A.7.3 Sample Form-Loading Program

To help clarify questions you might have regarding the loading and unloading of forms, their controls, and their properties, the program shown in Figure 1 provides a simple demonstration. The program consists of two forms: frmMain, the startup form, and Form2, the form displayed by frmMain. The command buttons on frmMain describe the various operations about to be performed.

Figure 1. Program That Loads and Shows Forms.

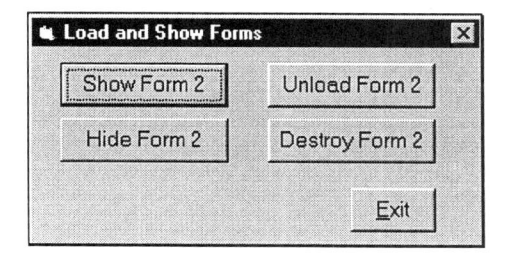

If the user clicks "Show Form 2", Form2 is displayed. On the form, we display two counters: One shows the number of times the form has been loaded, and the other displays the number of times the form has been activated (the Activate event was executed). Initially, the counters are both equal to 1:

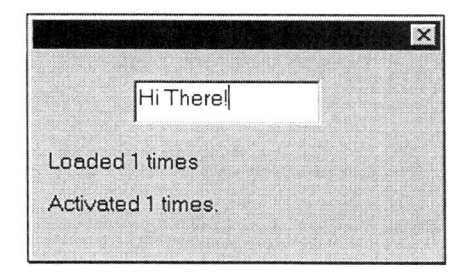

The user has also typed a short message into the form's text box. Now, what happens when we click on the "Hide Form 2" button, followed by "Show Form 2"? Form2 disappears and reappears, retaining the contents of the text box. All that has changed is that the Activated count now equals 2:

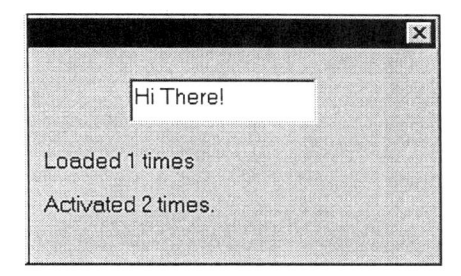

Now the user clicks on "Unload Form 2", followed by "Show Form 2". As we might anticipate, the text box has been cleared, and both counters have been incremented:

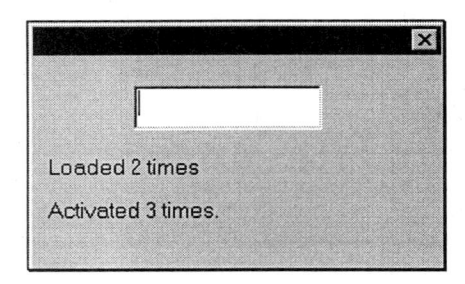

Loading and Unloading Forms. To load a form into memory without displaying it, use the Load statement. Once the form is in memory, its properties and the values of its controls may be accessed. For example, the following statements load frmMain, center it on the screen horizontally, and then display it:

```
Load frmMain
frmMain.Left = (Screen.Width - frmMain.Width) / 2
frmMain.show vbModal
```

The Unload statement removes a form from memory. If the form is currently being displayed, the form is removed from the screen and then unloaded. For example, the following statement unloads the current form (known in Visual Basic as **Me**):

```
Unload Me
```

A.7.4 Events

Load, Unload. A Load event occurs when a form is being loaded into memory, and an Unload event occurs when a form is unloaded. The Form_Load and Form_Unload procedures are automatically executed at these times. During Form_Load, you might want to initialize module-level variables, open files and databases, fill listboxes, and so on. During Form_Unload, you might want to close files and databases and do other types of cleanup work.

Activate, Deactivate. The *Activate* event occurs when a form becomes the active window. This can only happen while the form is visible. Conversely, the *Deactivate* event occurs when a form stops being the active window. The Form_Activate procedure is a good place to put statements that initialize a Data control. For example, the following statements move DBStudents to the end of a table, get the number of records, and reset the control to the beginning of the table:

```
DBStudents.RecordSetMoveLast
numRecs = DBStudents.RecordSet.RecordCount
DBStudents.RecordSet.MoveFirst
```

Resize. A *Resize* event occurs when the size of a form changes. The form might have been maximized, minimized, normalized, or the user may have resized it with the mouse. This often gives you the opportunity of adjusting other controls to match the size of the form. For example, every time the form is resized, the following statements set the width of Text1 to 95% of the width of Form1, and center Text1 on the form:

```
Private Sub Form_Resize()
  If WindowState <> 1 Then
    Text1.Width = Form1.Width * 0.95
    Text1.Left = (Form1.Width - Text1.Width) / 2
  End If
End Sub
```

> ***Programming Tip:*** You cannot change the position or size of a window that is currently minimized, so you must use an If statement that checks the WindowState property.

A.8 Standard Visual Basic Controls

A.8.1 Label

A label control is used strictly for output for characters and numbers. Any value to be displayed should be assigned to its Caption property. Its Font, ForeColor, and BackColor properties are often given specific values. In general, we rarely deal with event procedures in labels. The following statement, for example, displays the current date in lblDate:

```
lblDate.Caption = Date$
```

A.8.2 Text

A text control is used primarily for input of text and numbers. It may be used for output, and at the same time allow the user to modify its contents. The Text property holds the characters that are both input and displayed. For example, we can print the contents of a text control called txtLastName on the printer:

```
Printer.Print txtLastName.Text
```

The Change event alerts the program that the characters in the Text property have been modified. For example, we call the CalculatePay procedure when the contents of txtHoursWorked have changed and the value is greater than zero:

```
Private Sub txtHoursWorked_Change()
  If Val(txtHoursWorked.Text) > 0 Then
    CalculatePay
  End If
End Sub
```

> ***Programming Tip:*** It's not a good idea to try to do calculations using a number typed by the user into a Text control. If the text is blank, Visual Basic will not automatically convert it into a number, and your program will stop with a *type mismatch* error. Instead, use the Val function to convert the text to a number; blank text will convert to a value of zero, which at least will not generate an error.

You can use the MaxLength property to limit the number of characters typed by the user into a text control. The MultiLine property should be set to True if you want to allow the user to type multiple lines of text. The Locked property can be set to True if you want to lock the contents of the text box and prevent it from being modified by the user. To right-justify numbers in a text control, set Alignment = Right Justify, and MultiLine = True. Horizontal and vertical scroll bars can be added to a text control by setting the ScrollBars property.

A.8.3 Command Button

In all Windows programs, the user expects a command button to execute some action as soon as it is pressed. You can use the Caption property to change the text inside the button. If the Default property equals True, the button will be pressed when the user presses the Enter key. If the Cancel property equals True, the button will be pressed when the user presses the Esc key. We often use the Enabled property to temporarily enable and disable command buttons. For example, the following sets cmdCalculate.Enabled based on the value of payRate:

```
If payRate > 0 Then
   cmdCalculate.Enabled = True
Else
   cmdCalculate.Enabled = False
End If
```

> ***Programming Tip:*** If you like to be clever with boolean expressions, the foregoing can be simplified to the following:
>
> ```
> cmdCalculate.Enabled = (payRate > 0)
> ```

The Click event is the one we most often handle in program code. In the following, we call the CalculatePay procedure when the cmdCalculate button has been clicked by the mouse:

```
Private Sub cmdCalculate_Click()
   CalculatePay
End Sub
```

A.8.4 Option Button

Option buttons are used to represent mutually exclusive choices. The Value property of an option button may only be True or False. Within a group, only one option button can be True, while the others are False. The Click event is the one we usually handle in program code. The following example sets rentalRate to 50.00 when the user clicks on the optLuxuryCar button:

```
Private Sub optLuxuryCar_Click()
   rentalRate = 50.00
End Sub
```

To query an option button, we check its Value property:

```
If optLuxuryCar.Value = True Then
   rentalRate = 50.00
```

```
        End If
```

A.8.5 Frame

A frame control is useful for grouping other controls. For example, when option buttons are enclosed in a frame, they function as a single group. In the following form, buttons A and B form one group, while buttons X and Y form another group. This is why it is possible for both A and Y to be selected:

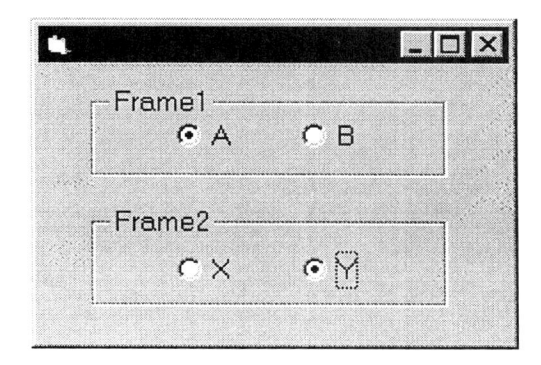

A.8.6 Check Box

Check boxes have a Value property that can be equal to vbUnchecked(0), vbChecked (1), or vbGrayed (2). They are ideal for expressing independent options that can be Yes or No. For example, each of the following check boxes can be checked or unchecked:

In program code we would query each check box separately. For example,

```
If chkMultiCar.Value = vbChecked then discount = 0.10
If chkSafeDriver.Value = vbChecked then discount = discount + 0.15
If chkTheftProtect.Value = vbChecked then discount = discount + 0.05
```

Programming Tip: evaluating a check box for a value of True or False will not work because Visual Basic represents True as -1 rather than 1.

A.8.7 Image

An image control displays a graphical picture on a form. The picture might be an icon, bitmap, or metafile. You can set the Picture property in design mode to the name of a file, or you can use the LoadPicture function to load a file into an image control at run time:

```
imgPortrait.Picture = LoadPicture("jones.bmp")
```

Another important property is the Stretch property—when set to True, this property allows the image control to expand to accommodate pictures of various sizes.

A.8.8 Line

A line control lets you place a line on a form at design time. The small blocks, or handles that appear at the ends of the line can be dragged by the mouse. The BorderWidth property affects the width of the line. There are no events tied to line controls. The BorderStyle property affects the line style, being solid, dashed, dotted, and so forth. However, any line with a BorderWidth greater than 1 always displays as a solid line, regardless of its style.

A.8.9 Timer

A timer control is ideal for controlling timed events, including animation. The Interval property measures (in milliseconds) the time between timer clicks. The timer starts counting when its Enabled property equals True. The only event is the Timer event, which permits you to take action each time the timer clicks. For example, we intialize a timer when the form is loaded:

```
Private Sub Form_Load()
   Timer1.Interval = 1000
   Timer1.Enabled = True
End Sub
```

The Time$ function returns the current time of day as a string:

```
Private Sub Timer1_Timer()
   lblTime.Caption = Time$
End Sub
```

A.8.10 Scroll Bars

The horizontal scroll bar and vertical scroll bar controls work the same way. Each limit the minimum and maximum values returned by the scroll bar to the values specified in the Min and Max properties. The Value property returns the relative position of the moving button on the scroll bar. The SmallChange property determines how much the button moves when the user clicks on a scroll arrow, and the LargeChange property determines how much the button moves when the user clicks between the button and the arrow. Here is an example of a horizontal scroll bar:

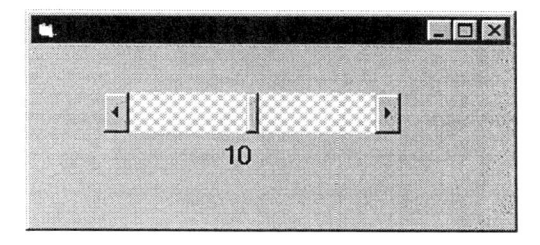

It is often useful to use the Change event to update a label on the form that displays the scroll bar's current value:

```
Private Sub hsbFirst_Change()
  Label1.Caption = hsbFirst.Value
End Sub
```

A.8.11 List Boxes and Combo Boxes

A List Box or Combo Box control holds a list of items. The items might be the names of people, a list of inventory items, prices, state abbreviations, and so on. The items in a list or combo box are usually related in some way. The user is expected to click on one or more items in the list, and when this happens, a Click event is generated. Table 4 contains a list of the list box and combo box properties that are used most often. For example, we could iterate through all of the list box choices and count the number of ones that are currently selected:

```
Dim j As Integer, count As Integer
count = 0
For j = 0 To lstNames.ListCount - 1
  If lstNames.Selected(j) Then
    count = count + 1
  End If
Next j
```

Table 4. List Box and Combo Box Properties.

Property	Usage
List	An array of strings containing the items in the list box.
ListCount	A count of the items in the list or combo box.
ListIndex	The row position (starting at 0) of the last item selected by the user.
ItemData	Array of long integers in which each element corresponds to an item in the list box.
MultiSelect	When True, the user can select multiple items.
Selected	When True, the user selected this item.
Sorted	When True, the items are in sorted order.
Text	A copy of the last item selected by the user.

The subscript is needed because the Selected property is an array in which each element corresponds to a different row of the list box. There are three commonly-used list/combo box methods, shown in Table 5. For example, let's clear the lstNames list box and add four names:

```
lstNames.Clear
lstNames.AddItem "Joe"
lstNames.AddItem "Sam"
lstNames.AddItem "Ann"
lstNames.AddItem "Bob"
```

When the user clicks on a name, we display the row number and delete the name:

```
Private Sub lstNames_Click()
  Dim row As Integer
  row = lstNames.ListIndex
  MsgBox "Row " & row & " was clicked."
  lstNames.RemoveItem row
End Sub
```

Table 5. List Box and Combo Box Methods.

Method	Usage
AddItem	Add a new line to a list or combo box.
Clear	Remove all lines from a list or combo box.
RemoveItem	Remove a line from a list or combo box.

Using the ItemData Property. The ItemData property provides a convenient way of associating a long integer with each item in a list box or combo box. For example, you might want to save an ID number for each person in a list box containing employee names:

```
lstEmployees.AddItem "Brooks. A."
lstEmployees.ItemData(0) = 1000
lstEmployees.AddItem "Meaney, C."
lstEmployees.ItemData(1) = 1111
lstEmployees.AddItem "Chao, R."
lstEmployees.ItemData(2) = 2000
```

Later, when the user clicks on a name, you can retrieve the employee's ID number and use it to look the person up in a database:

```
Private Sub lstEmployees_Click()
  Dim n As Integer, id As Long
  n = lstEmployees.ListIndex
  id = lstEmployees.ItemData(n)
  'search the database, using <id>...
End Sub
```

Combo Box Styles. There is one important combo box property that list boxes don't have. The Style property can have one of three values, listed in Table 6. A dropdown combo is useful if an unanticipated value must be entered from time to time. The vbComboSimple style is rarely used. A dropdown list is useful when all choices are predetermined.

Appendix A: Visual Basic Review

Table 6. Combo Box Styles.

Style Constant	Description
vbComboDropdown	Dropdown Combo: The user can select an item from the list or type a new value directly into the edit window of the combo box.
vbComboSimple	Simple Combo: The combo box does not drop down when clicked by the user. It is always visible.
vbComboDropdownList	Dropdown List: The user must select an existing item from the list; new values cannot be entered.

A.8.12 Default Properties

You will probably encounter other Visual Basic programs that rely on default properties of controls because these defaults allow statements to be shorter. In this book, we almost always use explicit property names, so the reader is not forced to remember the default property name. This also helps to make the source code more self-documenting. So that you can read other programs that use default properties, however, default properties of selected controls are shown in Table 7.

Table 7. Default Properties of Selected Controls.

Control	Default Property
Label	Caption
Frame	Caption
Text	Text
Image	Picture
Option Button	Value
Check Box	Value
Horizontal Scroll	Value
Vertical Scroll	Value

A.9 Coding Guidelines

A.9.1 Naming Controls

When possible, use standard prefixes for form, control, and menu names. Definitely do not want to use names that look like ordinary variables. Table 8 contains a list of standard identifier prefixes for forms, menus, and controls.

Table 8. Standard Identifier Prefixes for Forms, Menus, and Controls.

Type of Object or Control	Prefix	Example
Check box	chk	chkDiscount
Combo box	cbo	cboLocations
Command button	cmd	cmdExit
Common dialog	dlg	dlgOpenFile

Data control	db, dat	dbAuthors, datAuthors
Directory list box	dir	dirTextFiles
Form	frm	frmMain
Graph	gra	graSales
Horizontal scroll bar	hsb	hsbDate
Image	img	imgPortrait
Label	lbl	lblLastName
List box	lst	lstTitles
MDI child form	mdi	mdiCustomerProfile
OLE control	ole	oleSalesChart
Option button	opt	optPlanType
Picture box	pic	picButtonBar
Report	rpt	rptClasslist
Text box	txt	txtFirstName
Timer	tmr	tmrSeconds
Vertical scroll bar	vsb	vsbTemperature
Menu Item	mnu	mnuFileExit

A.9.2 Using General Procedures

When you have a lot of code to write in a program, store it in general procedures rather than in event handlers. It's very tempting, for example, to place all the statements that calculate the price on a sales invoice inside the command button called "Calculate". But problems occur later if the button is removed from the form. Instead, write a general procedure called something like CalculatePrice, and place all of your calculation statements inside of it. Then the command button's event handler can contain just a single statement:

```
Private Sub cmdCalculate_Click()
   CalculatePrice
End Sub
```

As it often turns out, you may decide later to call CalculatePrice whenever the user clicks on an option button or a check box, or enters information that may require the item's price to be recalculated. For example, when the "Discount" box is checked or unchecked:

```
Private Sub chkDiscount_Click()
   CalculatePrice
End Sub
```

Above all, remember that the final version of your program may be quite different from the one you started with. Anything you can do to make the program's code more flexible and easy to modify will end up saving you time in the long run.

A.10 Tools For Input-Output

A.10.1 Print Method

The Print method may be used on either a form or on the debug window. If you print multiple lines on a form, the lines begin at the top line and continue to the bottom of the form. For example,

```
For j = 1 To 20
  Form1.Print "This is line";j
Next j
```

In fact, most programs do not print directly on a form; instead, they use label and text controls to display output at specific locations on the form.

You can also print to the Debug window, which appears only in the Visual Basic development environment. Once a program is compiled and run as an EXE file, debug output does not appear. The following type of statement can greatly help when debugging complicated programs:

```
Debug.Print "Hours worked = "; hoursWorked
```

A.10.2 Format$ Function

The Format$ function offers a powerful, flexible tool for formatting data in Visual Basic. Most of the time, you can choose from a number of standard formats when displaying numbers, dates, and times. In addition, you can create user-defined formats for numbers, dates, times, and strings. We will not discuss them here, but you can look up the topic "Format Function" in the Visual Basic help system for more information.

Formatting Numbers. When formatting a number, pass a numeric expression as the first argument, and a format string as the second argument. The function returns a string containing the formatted number:

```
resultString = Format$( numExpression, "formatString" )
```

For the *formatString* parameter, you can choose among a set of predefined names. For each of the following formats shown in Table 9, we format the number n (containing 1234.5) and print it to the Debug window. Many of the formats are affected by the regional settings in effect on your machine. To view the current settings in Windows 95, click on the Start button, choose Settings/Control Panel and click on the Regional Settings icon.

The Yes/No format displays "No" if the number is zero, and "Yes" for any other value. The True/False format displays "False" if the number is zero, and "True" for any other value. The On/Off format displays "Off" if the number is zero, and "On" for any other value. The Percent format multiplies the number by 100 and appends a % sign.

Table 9. Format Function Examples.

Format Statement	Result
Format$(n, "General Number")	1234.5
Format$(n, "Currency")	$1,234.50
Format$(n, "Fixed")	1234.50
Format$(n, "Standard")	1,234.50
Format$(n, "Percent")	123450.00%
Format$(n, "Scientific")	1.23E+03
Format$(n, "Yes/No")	Yes
Format$(n, "True/False")	True
Format$(n, "On/Off")	On

Formatting Dates. You can also use predefined formats for dates with the Format$ function. The Now function returns the current system date and time. Table 10 shows a sample of the current date and time formatted in a variety of ways.

Table 10. Date and Time Formats.

Format Example	Result
Format$(Now, "General Date")	11/21/96 9:22:30 AM
Format$(Now, "Long Date")	Thursday, November 21, 1996
Format$(Now, "Medium Date")	21-Nov-96
Format$(Now, "Short Date")	11/21/96
Format$(Now, "Long Time")	9:22:30 AM
Format$(Now, "Medium Time")	09:22 AM
Format$(Now, "Short Time")	09:22

A.10.3 MsgBox Procedure

The MsgBox procedure lets you pop up a small window from anywhere in a program and display a message to the user. The user has to click on the OK button to close the window before going on with the program. The general syntax is:

```
MsgBox message, options, title
```

Where *message* is a string that appears inside the message box. *Options* is an integer that specifies the type of icon and/or buttons that will appear in the box. *Title* is a string that will appear in the message box's title bar.

At the very least, you would want to pass a string containing the message as an argument to the procedure. For example,

```
MsgBox "Hours worked must be greater than zero."
```

This would produce the following window. Notice that by default, the project name appears in the window's title bar:

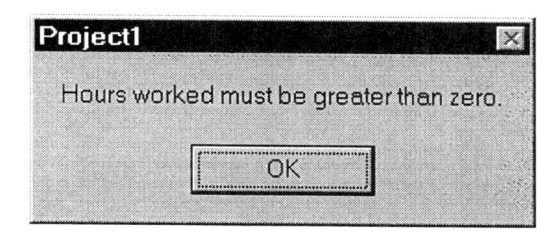

On the other hand, you might want to display an icon in the message box, as an attention-getter. The choices are:

vbCritical	Display a critical message (red circle with "X")
vbExclamation	Display a warning message (exclamation point)
vbInformation	Display an information message (letter i)
vbQuestion	Display a warning query (question mark)

For example, we will make our previous message a warning message:

```
MsgBox "Hours worked must be greater than zero.", _
    vbExclamation
```

Finally, we might want to change the title bar of the message box to the word "Error":

```
MsgBox "Hours worked must be greater than zero.", _
    vbExclamation, "Error"
```

> *Programming Tip:* Use a line continuation character (_) to break up long lines and make them more readable. The rules for using this character will be explained in the next section.

This is the final version of our message window:

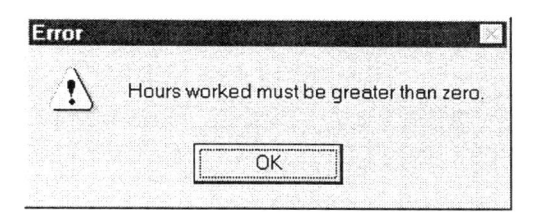

A.10.4 MsgBox Function

There are times when we also need to ask the user to confirm a question. In that case, MsgBox becomes a function and returns an integer that tells us which button the user clicked. The syntax is the same as the MsgBox procedure, except the function returns an integer value. For example, perhaps we would like to ask the user to confirm before exiting the program:

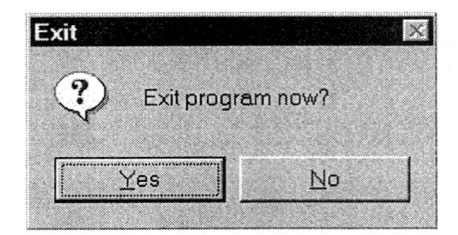

If the user clicks on the **Yes** button, the function returns a predefined integer constant called vbYes; if the **No** button is clicked, the value vbNo is returned. We can use this information in an If statement to decide whether or not the user wants to exit:

```
Private Sub cmdExit_Click()
  Dim choice As Integer
  choice = MsgBox("Exit program now?", vbYesNo _
        + vbQuestion, "Exit")
  If choice = vbYes Then Unload Me
End Sub
```

The possible return values of the MsgBox function are predefined constants, shown in Table 11. Each indicates a button pressed by the user. We also use constants to tell the function which buttons to display on the window.

Table 11. MsgBox Function Return Values.

Constant	Value	Description
vbOK	1	OK button pressed
vbCancel	2	Cancel button pressed
vbAbort	3	Abort button pressed
vbRetry	4	Retry button pressed
vbIgnore	5	Ignore button pressed
vbYes	6	Yes button pressed
vbNo	7	No button pressed

The predefined MsgBox button constants are shown in Table 12. You can combine button and icon constants by adding them together. In our sample window, we used vbYesNo + vbQuestion, for example.

Table 12. MsgBox Function Buttons.

Constant	Value	Buttons Shown
vbOKOnly	0	OK button only (default)
vbOKCancel	1	OK and Cancel buttons
vbAbortRetryIgnore	2	Abort, Retry, and Ignore buttons
vbYesNoCancel	3	Yes, No, and Cancel buttons
vbYesNo	4	Yes and No buttons
vbRetryCancel	5	Retry and Cancel buttons

A.10.5 InputBox Function

Visual Basic provides a simple function called InputBox, which is an easy way to input a string from the user. Its general format is:

```
retVal = InputBox( prompt, heading, default, xpos, ypos, helpfile,
   context )
```

where the parameters are the following:

- *prompt* is a string that displays inside the window.
- *heading* displays in the window's title bar.
- *default* is a string placed in the user's input line.
- *xpos* is the horizontal distance from the edge of the screen to the window's left side.
- *ypos* is the vertical distance from the edge of the screen to the top of the window.
- *helpfile* is the name of a help file containing context-sensitive help.
- *context* is the help topic number inside *helpfile*.

The function's return value is the string typed by the user when the window was closed. If the user clicked on the Cancel button, the return value is an empty string.

For example, let's ask the user for his/her last name. By default, the title bar contains the name of the project:

```
lastName = InputBox("What is your last name?")
```

The resulting input box is shown in Figure 2.

Figure 2. InputBox Function Example.

We might want to put a default string in an input box asking for the name of a file to be opened. If the user clicks on Cancel, the original file name is retained:

```
dim fileName As String, temp As String
fileName = "default.txt"
temp = InputBox("Enter the name of the file to be opened:", _
   "Open File", fileName)
if Len(temp) > 0 then fileName = temp
```

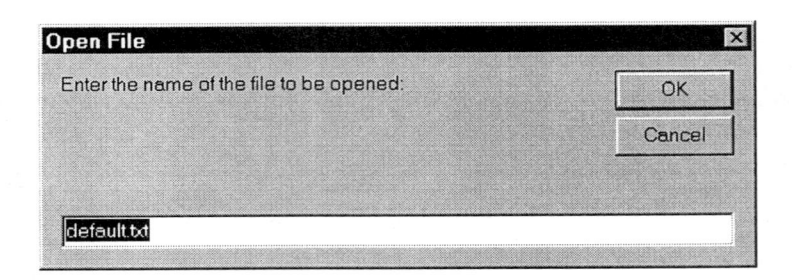

A.10.6 Printer Object

The Printer, Screen, and App objects are automatically created in a Visual Basic program. The Printer object lets you communicate with whichever printer is currently set as the default printer.

- The Orientation property orients the paper direction, and may be set to either vbPRORPortrait (vertical) or vbPRORLandscape (horizontal).
- The NewPage method ends the printing of the current page.
- The Print method prints text and numbers to the printer.
- The EndDoc method ends the printing of the current document.

The following statements, if placed inside a command button, will print the contents of a text control called txtAddress with a sideways orientation:

```
Printer.Orientation = vbPRORLandscape
Printer.Print txtAddress.Text
Printer.EndDoc
```

Of course, there are many other properties and methods. To find out about them, look under the topic "Printer Object" in the Visual Basic help system.

A.10.7 Screen Object

The Height and Width properties of the Screen object contain the height and width of the screen, measured in Twips. The following example uses these properties to center a form on the screen:

```
Dim top As Integer, left As Integer
top = (Screen.Height - Me.Height) \ 2
left = (Screen.Width - Me.Width) \ 2
Me.Top = top
Me.Left = left
```

First, we calculate the difference between the screen height and the form's height. Then, we calculate the difference between the screen width and the form's width. Using this information, we set the Top and Left properties of the form:

The MousePointer property can be used to change the mouse to an hourglass when the user has to wait for some operation to finish. For example,

```
Screen.MousePointer = vbHourglass
'  do something that takes time...
Screen.MousePointer = vbDefault
```

A.10.8 Application Object

The **App** object is a global identifier for the current program (called an *application*). You can use it to access information about the program's title, the path and name of its executable file and help files, and whether or not another instance of the application is running.

- The **PrevInstance** property equals True when another instance of the same program is currently running.
- The **Path** property equals the complete pathname of the program, from the drive letter through the directory where the program is stored.
- Version Information such as the major and minor version numbers, company name, product name, and copyright notice.

Use the Path property to reset the current drive and directory to the same location as the program's path. If your program uses Main Sub as the startup procedure, place the following statements in Main:

```
ChDrive app.Path
ChDir   app.Path
```

Or, if your program uses a startup form, place these statements in the Form_Load procedure.

A.11 Creating Menus

From the user's point of view, a command button is the simplest type of command interface. Most programs have a sufficient number of commands that it becomes impractical to activate all commands with buttons. Instead, programs generally use menus to provide a heirarchy of commands. Visual Basic provides the Menu control as the vehicle for displaying menus and responding to menu events. Any form having a caption bar may contain a menu. In design mode, we use the Tools/Menu Editor command to create menus.

A.11.1 Common Menu Types

If appropriate to the program, the first submenu on the left is the **File** menu. It contains commands such as New, Open, Close, Save, Save As, Delete, Import, Print, and Exit. If any of your program's commands relating to files or documents seem to fit into this list, you will probably want to create a File menu.

The next menu is the **Edit** menu. Some common commands on this menu relate to Windows clipboard operations: Cut, Copy, Paste, and Clear. Find, Replace, Go To, and Bookmark commands appear on the Edit menu. Any operations that modify the current document or file can be placed on this menu.

Many programs have a **Tools** menu, an **Options** menu, a **Window** menu, and a **Help** menu. In many cases, the Options menu is the last choice on the Tools menu. The Window menu is useful for resizing, arranging, and locating individual windows that might be open at the same time. The Help menu is generally the last menu on the right.

If you want to get a feel for well-designed menu structures, look at some of the Windows applications software from Microsoft and other leading companies.

A.11.2 Creating a Simple Menu

Let's try a simple hands-on example that demonstrates the process of creating a menu. Create a project with a single form, called **frmMain**. With frmMain displayed, click on the Tools menu and select **Menu Editor**. Each menu item must be assigned both a caption and name. For example, for the main File menu heading, we would enter the following property values:

```
Caption:    &File
Name:       mnuFile
```

The & before the letter F will cause the letter to be underlined when the menu appears. The user will be able to activate the File menu by pressing Alt-F. Figure 3 shows the menu editor as the File menu is being created.

Figure 3. Creating a File Menu.

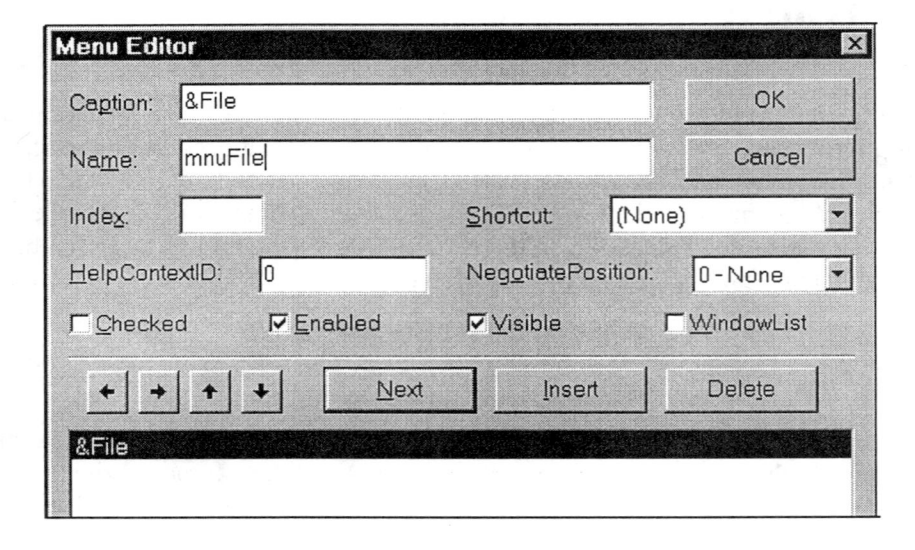

After entering the caption and name for a menu choice, click the **Next** button, and type the following menu choices:

```
Caption:    E&xit
Name:       mnuFileExit
```

Appendix A: Visual Basic Review 519

But this menu choice should appear only when the user clicks on the File menu. To make this work, click on the arrow pointing to the right—this will indent the word "Exit" to the right in the window in the lower half of the menu editor:

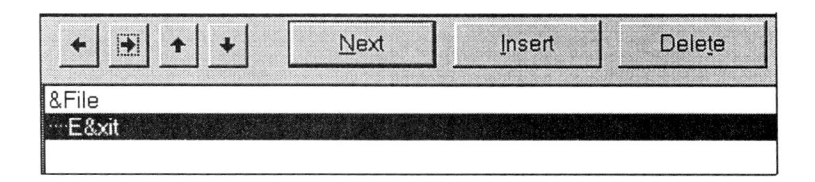

Finally, from the Shortcut combo box, select Ctrl-X as the shortcut key for the File/Exit command. This will allow the user to activate the command more quickly. Notice that the shortcut key appears in the menu next to its matching command:

A.11.3 Menu Properties

Notice that you can decide whether each menu choice will be checked, enabled, and visible when the program starts up:

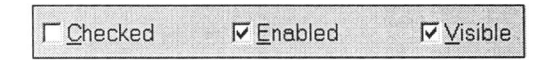

Programs typically disable or render invisible any menu choices that are not appropriate at a given time. If a file is not open, for example, most programs will disable the Edit menu. But making a menu disappear completely is an extreme step that could confuse the first-time user of a program. There are a number of other useful menu properties, shown in Table 13 which we will use in later chapters.

Table 13. Menu Properties.

Property	Description
Caption	**Required:** Text that appears in the user's menu at runtime.
Checked	If True, a check appears next to the menu item when the form is displayed.
Enabled	If True, user may click on the menu item; if False, the menu item is grayed and may not be selected by the user.
HelpContextID	An integer that refers to a matching help topic in the help file identified by the HelpFile property.
Index	Determines the item's position within a control array; not related to the item's position within the menu on the screen.
Name	**Required:** Identifier for menu item used in program code.
NegotiatePosition	Determines whether and how the menu appears when it is on a form that has an OLE container control.
Shortcut	A keyboard shortcut key (such as Ctrl-S) can be assigned to the menu item.
Visible	If True, the menu item will be visible at runtime; otherwise, the item will not appear.
WindowList	If checked, the menu will display a list of open MDI (*Multiple Document Interface*) child forms.

Menu Events. Menu controls respond to a mouse click event, and you will want to write code in the corresponding procedures. In the mnuFileExit_Click() procedure, for example, we might unload the current form:

```
Private Sub mnuFileExit_Click()
   Unload Me
End Sub
```

Checked Menu Choices. Menu choices that represent options can usually be checked or unchecked by the user. For example, we might let the user select which parts of the current program will be visible: the status bar, the button bar, and the toolbox:

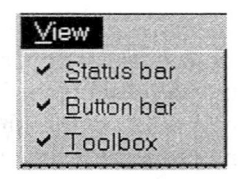

The actual checking and unchecking of these choices must be handled by code in the event handlers of these menu choices. For example, we could simply reverse the value of the Checked property for each menu choice:

```
Private Sub mnuViewStatusbar_Click()
   mnuViewStatusbar.Checked = Not mnuViewStatusbar.Checked
End Sub

Private Sub mnuViewButtonbar_Click()
```

```
    mnuViewButtonbar.Checked = Not mnuViewButtonbar.Checked
End Sub

Private Sub mnuViewToolbox_Click()
    mnuViewToolbox.Checked = Not mnuViewToolbox.Checked
End Sub
```

A.12 Sequential Files

For small amounts of information that must be used by your programs, sequential files are simple and convenient to use. Small sequential files may be read more quickly than databases, because the latter require the loading of a number of DLL libraries at run time. A "small" sequential file might be one containing only a few thousand characters or less. Another advantage to using sequential files is that they can be modified with almost any text editor, such as the DOS **Edit** program or the Windows **NotePad** program.

A.12.1 Basic Syntax

The Open Statement. The Open statement prepares a disk file for input or output. Informally, the syntax is

```
Open pathname For mode As [#] filenumber
```

where *pathname* is either a file name or a complete path and filename, starting with the drive letter. *Filenumber* is an integer that identifies the file for further input or output. *Mode* is one of the following:

- **Input**: Open an existing file for input only. Data may be read from the file, using the Input and Line Input statements.
- **Output**: Create a new file, truncating any existing file by the same name. Data may be written to the file, using the Write and Print statements.
- **Append**: Add data to the end of an existing file, or create a new file if the file does not already exist.

The file number is usually 1, 2, or 3, depending on whether or not other files are currently open, and two open files cannot share the same number. The following example opens a file called **names.txt** for input, a file called **scores.dta** for output, and a file called **logfile** for appending. Each must be assigned a different file number:

```
Open "names.txt" For Input As 1
Open "scores.dta" For Output As 2
Open "logfile" For Append As 3
```

Obtaining a File Number. The **FreeFile** function returns the next available file number, which guarantees that you will not accidentally try to use a file number that is already in use. In the following example, we call FreeFile, assign its result to fileNum, and use fileNum in the Open statement:

```
Dim fileNum as Integer
```

```
fileNum = FreeFile
Open "names.txt" for Input as fileNum
```

The Close Statement. To close a file, refer to its file number. The syntax is:

```
Close filenumber
```

If you forget to close an input file, the filenumber value cannot be used with another file, and memory used by the file is not released. If you forget to close an ouput file, data that your program has written to the file may not be saved in the file. This is because output data is written to a memory buffer and held there until the buffer is full, or the file is closed. At that time, the buffer is "flushed", meaning that the data in the buffer is physically written to disk.

A.12.2 Reading From an Input File

Example: Automobile Models File. In a car rental program, we might want to create a text file containing the names of available automobile models and their daily rental prices. This can easily be done with the Windows Notepad editor, placing each model name on a single line followed by its daily rental price on the next line:

```
Ford Aerostar
50
Mercury Villager
45
Chevrolet Cavalier
47
Dodge Aspen
50
Toyota Camry
55
Lincoln Continental
75
```

After typing this data into Notepad, we would select the File/Save As menu command and call the file **models.txt**. In a Visual Basic program, we would write the following statement to open the file for input:

```
Dim fileNum As Integer
fileNum = FreeFile
Open "models.txt" For Input As fileNum
```

To read a single model name from the file, we use the Input statement. This would be followed by a statement to read the corresponding price:

```
Dim modelName As String, price As Single
Input #fileNum, modelName
Input #fileNum, price
```

There are two general approaches used when opening and closing files:

- Open a file when the program starts, leave it open, and close it only when the program ends. This is an acceptable approach, unless an excessive number of files are left open at the same time. An advantage to this approach is that the current file pointer position is retained across procedure calls.

- Open and close a file within the same procedure. An advantage to this approach is that you will be more likely to remember to close the file. A disadvantage is that if the procedure is called repeatedly, some processing time is lost due to the opening and closing of the file, and the current file position is reset to the beginning of the file each time the file is opened. If the same file is being used for both input and output, the file must be closed and re-opened when switching between input and output modes.

Reading Multiple Variables. If an input file contains multiple variables, they must be separated by commas, and string values might have to be enclosed in quotation marks. The latter is particularly true when the strings contain embedded commas. In the following file, each record contains a complete customer name and an account balance. The quotes around each name tell Visual Basic to consider the name a single string value:

```
"Jones, Larry", 200.50
"Baker, Sam", 120.40
"Johnson, Susan", -50.00
(etc.)
```

The following Input statement reads a single record:

```
Input #fileNum, custName, acctBalance
```

Reading All Records. To read all records from an input file, use a looping statement that calls the EOF function to check for end of file. If each record is to be kept in memory, insert it in a list box, combo box, or array. The following procedure reads a customer name and account balance from an input file. The name is inserted in a list box, and the account balance is inserted in an array:

```
Dim balance(0 to 100) as Single    'declare at the Module level

Public Sub ReadNameFile()
  Dim fileNum As Integer, j As Integer, custName As String
  fileNum = FreeFile
  j = 0
  Open "names.txt" For Input As fileNum
  Do Until Eof(fileNum)
    Input #fileNum, custName, balance(j)
    List1.AddItem custName
    j = j + 1
  Loop
  Close fileNum
End Sub
```

Notice from the example that **balance**, the array of customer balances, would probably be declared at the module level—this would allow it to be accessed by other procedures. Also, be sure to increment the array subscript before reading each subsequent record. The array subscript in our example was **j**.

Line Input. The Line Input statement reads an entire record, including all commas and quotes, into a single string:

```
Dim rec As String
'...
Line Input #fileNum, rec
```

The Line Input statement is particularly useful when the data is not in a standard readable format, and you need to manually separate the record into individual fields. For example, each record might contain some other type of field delimiter:

```
Jones, Larry\200.50
Adams, Bill\325.20
```

A.12.3 Writing to an Output File

A file must already be open in the Output or Append mode before data can be written to the file. There are two statements that write to sequential files: Print and Write. The **Print** statement writes data to the file exactly as it would appear on the screen. For example:

```
name = "Bob Jones"
age = 54
Print 1, lastName;",";age
```

Would store data in the file as: `Bob Jones, 54`

The **Write** statement, on the other hand, automatically surrounds strings with quotation marks and places a comma separator between variables:

```
name = "Bob Jones"
age = 54
Write #1, lastName,age
```

Would store data in the file as: `"Bob Jones", 54`

Writing All Records. To write all records from an array or list box to a file, set up a loop with a subscript. The following procedure writes all names from a list box to a file, along with the contents of an array called balance. This is the counterpart to a procedure we showed earlier called ReadNameFile:

```
Dim balance(0 to 100) as Single   'declare at the Module level

Public Sub WriteNameFile()
  Dim fileNum As Integer, j As Integer
  fileNum = FreeFile
  Open "names.txt" For Output As fileNum
  For j = 0 To List1.ListCount - 1
    Write #fileNum, List1.List(j), balance(j)
  Next j
  Close fileNum
End Sub
```

> Programming Tip: If you are storing data in a file that will later be used as an input file, use the **Write** statement because it formats the data in a way that is easily readable by Visual Basic. On the other hand, if you are printing a report or some other document that will not be used as an input file for a Visual Basic program, use the **Print** statement.

A.13 Answers to the Competency Test Questions

1. Boolean, integer, byte, long, single, double, currency, string, date, object, and variant.

2. Variables that are declared in a module's general declaration section (module-level variables) have meaning (are visible) anywhere in the module. Variables that are declared within a procedure (procedure-level variables) have meaning (are visible) only within that procedure.

3. Forms, controls, and user-defined objects.

4. A variable of type Variant can hold a value of any data type with the exception of fixed-length strings and user-defined types.

5. The dynamic array may be resized to accommodate more or less data while the programming is executing.

6. Code Segment:

```
If HrsWrkd <= 40 Then
   GrossPay = HrsWrkd * HrlyRate
Else
   If UnionMember = True Then
      GrossPay = 40 * HrlyRate + (HrsWrkd - 40) * HrlyRate * 1.75
   Else
      GrossPay = 40 * HrlyRate + (HrsWrkd - 40) * HrlyRate * 1.50
   End If
End If
```

7. Code Segment:

```
Dim Score(1 to 100) as Integer
Dim Average as Single
Dim Tot as Integer, K as Integer
For K = 1 to 100
   Tot = Tot + Score(K)
Next K
Average = Tot / 100
```

8. Code Segment:

```
K = 1
Do While (strName <> Name(K)) AND (K <=100)
```

```
        K = K + 1
Loop
Form1.Print K
```

9. A form's Name property is used to identify the form from within a program, typically to execute a method; e.g., Form1.Show or Form1.Print "Hello World".

10. A method is a procedure or action that is associated with an object. Unlike an event, it is not initiated by the user. Examples of methods associated with a form include Show, Hide, Cls, and Print.

11. The *Load* statement directs Visual Basic to retrieve a form from disk and place it in memory (it is not necessarily displayed/shown). The *Show* method directs Visual Basic to actually display (and possibly load) a form.

12. A label's use is restricted to output only while a text box may be used for both input and output.

13. The command button is used to initiate an action, to cause something to happen.

14. When the command button's Default property is set to True, pressing the Enter key is equivalent to clicking the command button.

15. Both controls are alike in that they allow the user to make a choice from a finite list. They are not alike in that option buttons are mutually exclusive - selecting one deselects all others. The user may select none, one, all, or any combination of check boxes.

16. A frame is typically used to group a set of controls such as option buttons or check boxes.

17. Subroutines and functions are alike in that they are both building-block subprogram units. They are different in that the function always returns a value to the calling program unit whereas the subroutine may return no values, one value, or many values.

18. Passing arguments by reference allows the receiving program unit to alter and return that altered value/argument to the calling program unit. Passing arguments by value means that even though the receiving program unit may alter the argument, the altered value is not returned to the calling program unit.

19. A procedure declared with the Public keyword allows the procedure to be called from anywhere in the project. A procedure declared with the Private keyword restricts procedure calls to the form or module which contains the procedure.

20. Form1.Print Format$ (Net_Pay,"currency")

21. The MsgBox procedure creates a standard Windows pop up dialogue to display a message to the user.

22. Including the Option Explicit command in a program forces the explicit declaration of all variables (and their corresponding data types). This means that variables may not be used within the program unless they have been declared.

23. A control's tabindex property determines the order in which a control receives the focus when the user uses the tab key to move from control to control.

24. The MsgBox function's return value is assigned to a variable so that the program can determine, for example, which key was pressed by the user when responding to the MsgBox dialogue. The MsgBox statement does not assign a return value to a variable and is used primarily to halt program execution until the user responds to the dialogue.

25. The List property is an array which contains the contents of the list box.

26. The Clear method removes all entries from a list box whereas the RemoveItem method removes a single entry from the list box.

27. Input, Output, and Append.

28. The On Error Goto statement is used to direct program control to a location in the program where an error-handling routine can be found. When an error occurs, the code at that location is enabled.

29. The Resume statement is used to direct Visual Basic to resume processing at the line following the one that caused an error.

30. The Err object is created whenever a runtime error occurs. The Err object's *Number* and *Description* properties are used to identify and describe the runtime error. Use of both of these properties are typically placed in an error handler.

Appendix B: Standard VB4 Add-Ins

Chapter Contents

Using VisData
    Creating the Database
    Creating the SalesStaff Table
    Creating Indexes
    Entering Table Data
    Creating Validation Rules
    Setting Table Relationships
Using Data Manager
    Creating the Database
    Creating the SalesStaff Table
    Editing a Table Design
    Creating Indexes
    Entering Table Data
Using the Data Form Designer
    Code Modifications in the Author Form
    Create the Main Window
    Add Another Table

B.1 Using VisData

The **VisData** program is a particularly useful sample program that is supplied with Visual Basic versions 4 and 5. You can use it to create Access databases as well as Visual Basic forms that connect to your databases. VisData may already be accessible from your Visual Basic **Add-Ins** menu. If not, check the Visual Basic home directory for the file Visdata.exe.

To show how VisData works, let's create a simple database that contains a single table called **SalesStaff**. This table might hold the names of salespeople in a store. To get the most out of this discussion, it would be a good idea for you to perform all of the steps at the computer.

B.1.1 Creating the Database

From the VisData File menu, select New, and select Jet Engine MDB as the type of database to be created, and if you are using the 32-bit version of Visual Basic, select Version 3.0 MDB; for the 16-bit Visual Basic, select Version 2.0 MDB. A sample Main Menu is shown in Figure 1.

Figure 1. VisData Main Menu.

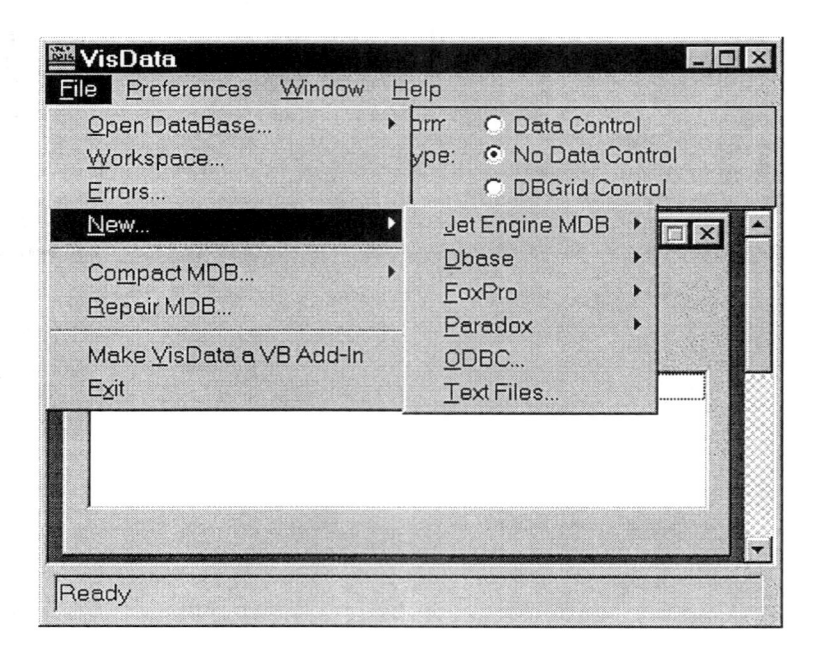

The name of the database file is **staff.mdb**, shown in Figure 2 at the top of the Tables/Queries window. Your display may look different from this, because the SQL Statement window has been closed to save space.

Figure 2. Tables/Queries Window.

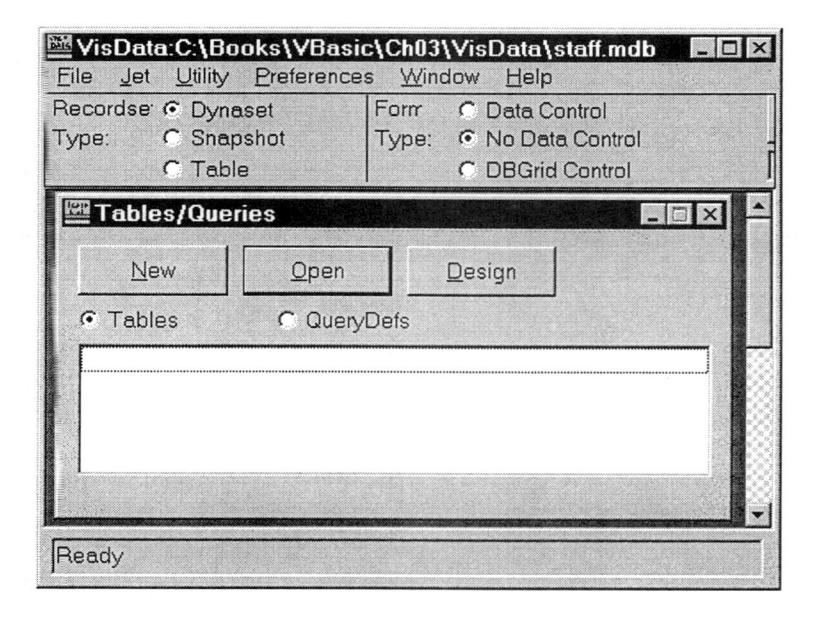

Appendix B: Standard VB4 Add-Ins

B.1.2 Creating the SalesStaff Table

We're going to create a table called **SalesStaff** that contains the ID number and name of each member of the sales staff of a store:

Field Name	Data Type
id	Long Integer
name	Text (Length = 30)

Click the New button to create a new table. This brings up the Table Structure window (Figure 3), where you will enter the name and characteristics of each field. First, type the name of the table, **SalesStaff**, in the Table Name box. Click the **Add Field** button to add the first field, called **id** (Figure 4). Check the **Required** option to ensure that a record will not be saved in the table without an ID number.

Figure 3. Table Structure Window.

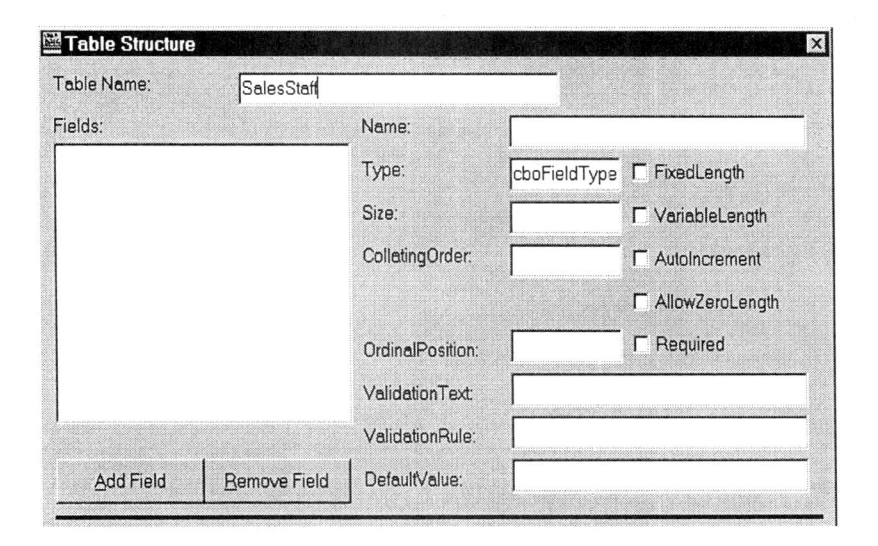

Figure 4. Add Field Window.

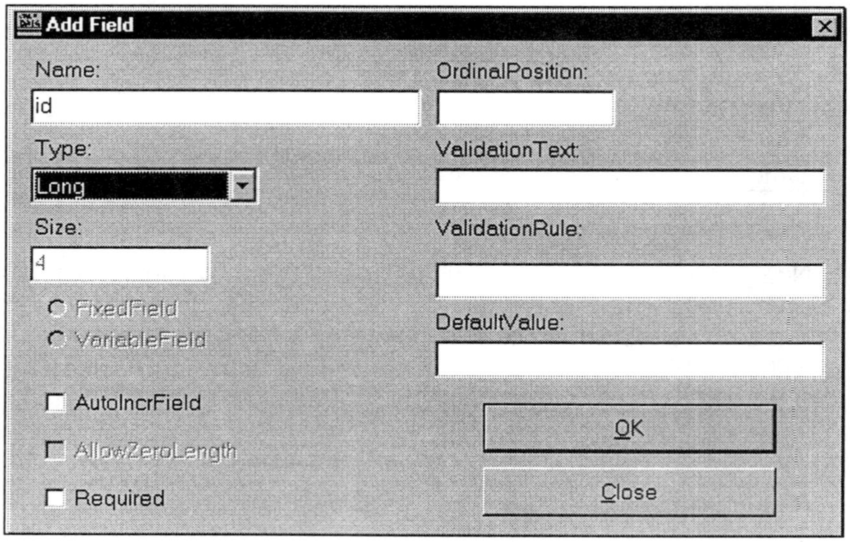

When you click the OK button, the field is saved and the window is prepared for you to specify another field. This time, the field is called name, and its length is 30. Select the AllowZeroLength and Required options, click on OK to save the field, and click the Close button. When you return to the Table Structure window, you will see the two field names.

B.1.3 Creating Indexes

Next, we will create two indexes. An index makes it easy for a program to search for specific records, because the physical position of each record was already calculated by the database when the index was created. Also, an index automatically orders the table records in either ascending or descending order based on one or more field values.

From the Table Structure window, click the **Add Index** button. The window shown in Figure 5 lets you enter a name for the index and identify the field(s) on which the index will be based. Our index will be called **idNdx**, and it is based on the **id** field. Notice that by default, the Primary and Unique options are already checked.

Figure 5. Adding an Index to SalesStaff.

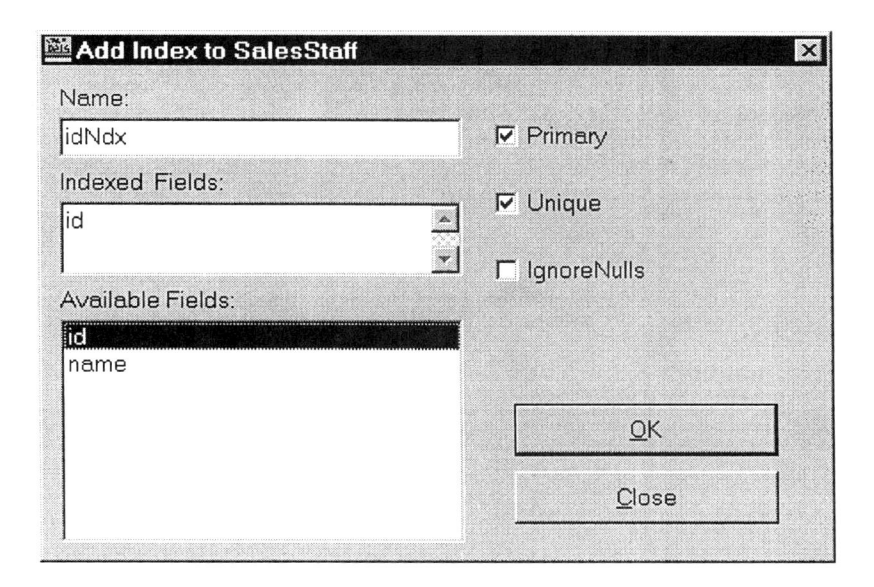

A *primary key* consists of one or more fields that are guaranteed to uniquely identify each table record. Click on OK to save the index. Let's create a second index called **nameNdx**, based on the **name** field. This index will be useful to programs that need to display the names of the sales staff in alphabetical order. There might be duplicate names in the table, so make sure that the Primary and Unique options are not selected (Figure 6).

Figure 6. Adding a Second Index to SalesStaff.

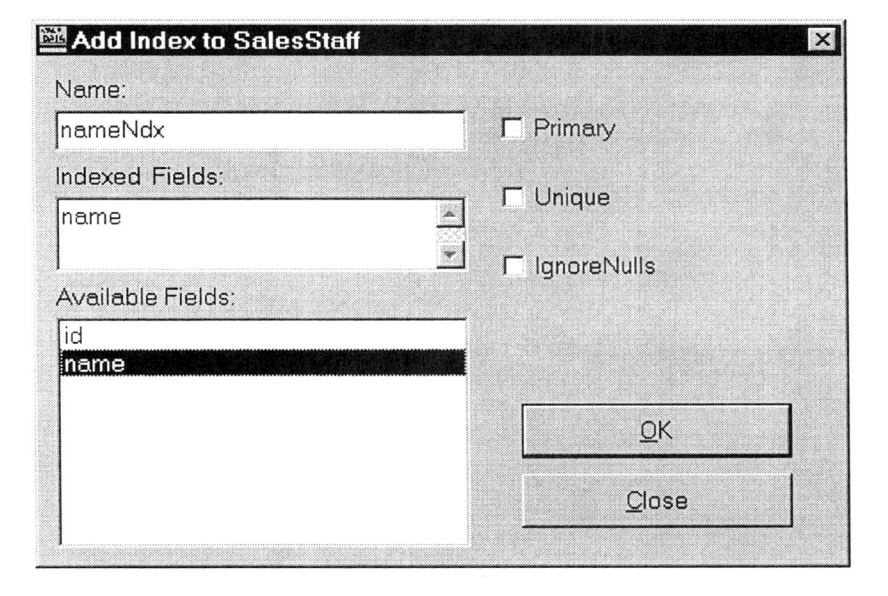

After clicking on **OK** to save the index, click on **Close** to return to the Table Structure window. Figure 7 contains the lower half of the window, showing both index names.

Figure 7. Table Structure Window: Indexes.

Finally, click the **Build the Table** button, causing the table to be built and saved in the database. Click the **Close** button. Now the table name appears in the Tables/Queries window.

If at any time you need to modify or edit a table's description, select the table in the Tables/Queries window and click the **Design** button. This will bring up the Table Structure window, which we used when specifying each of the fields in the table.

B.1.4 Entering Table Data

Now we're ready to enter some names into the SalesStaff table. From the Tables/QueryDefs window, select the table name and click the **Open** button. This brings up what we will call the **Table Data** window (Figure 8).

Figure 8. Entering Table Data into SalesStaff.

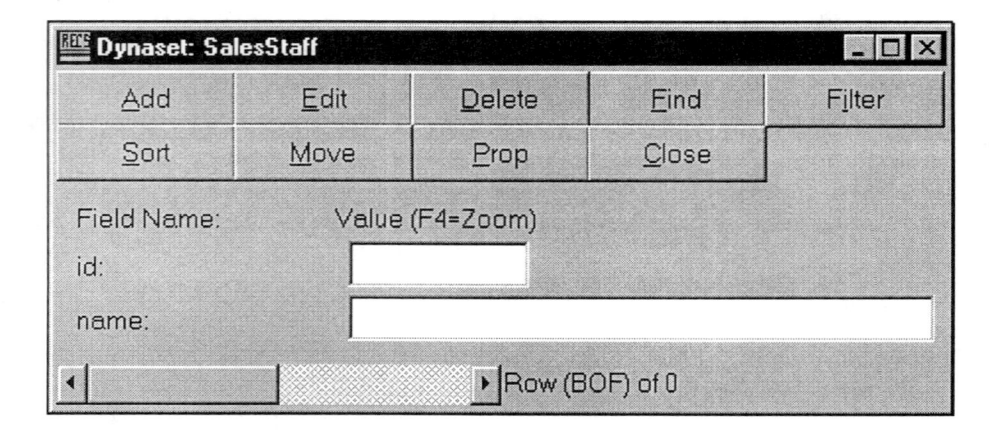

Click the **Add** button and enter the first person's ID number (1) and name ("Adams, Adrian"). Figure 9 shows what the window looks like.

Appendix B: Standard VB4 Add-Ins 535

Figure 9. SalesStaff Table, Adding First Record.

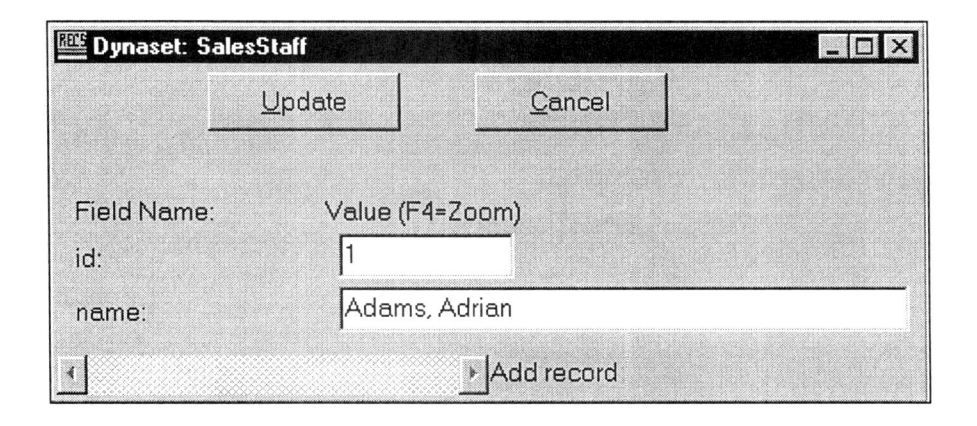

Click the **Update** button to save the record. Add five more records, using the following information. Remember to click the Update button after entering each record:

id	name
2	Baker, Barbara
3	Del Terzo, Daniel
4	Easterbrook, Erin
5	Franklin, Fay

Close this window; then close the VisData program—you're finished. We've only touched on a few of the basic operations in this program, but you can probably see that it has much more to offer. Later, when we create databases with multiple tables, we will extend our knowledge of this program further.

B.1.5 Creating Validation Rules

To create a field-level validation rule in VisData, open the database, select the desired table, click the Design button. This brings up the Table Structure window, where you can select the field and type the validation rule and validation text. In Figure 10, for example, we enter a rule for the dailyRate field in the Price table.

Figure 10. Price Table Structure.

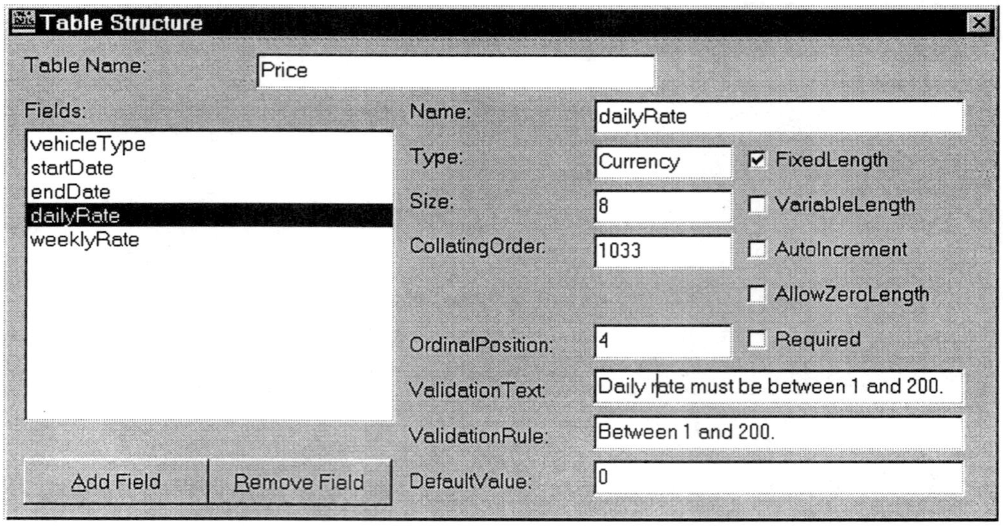

B.1.6 Setting Table Relationships

You can easily set table relationships in the Rentals database using the VisData program. To begin, run VisData and open the **rentals.mdb** database from the **File** menu. Then, select the **Relations** command from the **Jet** menu.

Let's create a relation called **VehicleInvoice** that links the Vehicle table and the Invoice table using their common **vehicleId** field. Vehicle.vehicleId is a primary key, so Vehicle is considered the *base table*. Invoice is the *foreign table*. Click the **New Relation** button to save the relation. When you use an SQL statement to joint two tables as part of a query, the type of join that is selected (by default) is the first option: Only rows where joined fields from both tables are equal are included in the joined table. In the same manner, we would create any other necessary relations.

B.2 Using Data Manager

The Data Manager program, supplied with Visual Basic, provides a straightforward way to create and modify Microsoft Access databases. Let's create the same database that was shown earlier in this chapter, containing the SalesStaff table. To get the most out of this discussion, it would be a good idea for you to perform all of the steps at the computer.

Appendix B: Standard VB4 Add-Ins　　　　　　　　　　　　　　　　　　　　　　　　537

B.2.1 Creating the Database

\SlsStaff

Run the Data Manager by selecting **Data Manager** from the **Add-Ins** menu in Visual Basic. You can also run the Data Manager as a stand-alone program: the 32-bit version is called **dataman32.exe** and the 16-bit version is called **datamgr.exe.** When Data Manager starts up, select **New Database** from the **File** menu. Figure 11 shows the dialog box that lets you locate the database.

Figure 11. Data Manager: New Database Window.

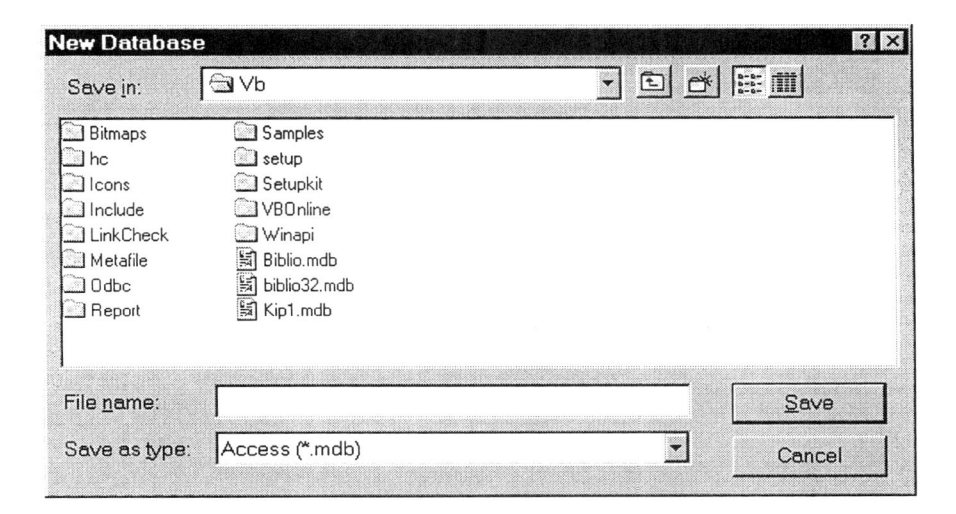

Let's name the database **staff.mdb.** Figure 12 shows the **Tables/QueryDefs** window, which is the starting point for creating and manipulating tables and queries. Because we haven't created a table yet, only the **New** and **Attached Tables** buttons are enabled.

Figure 12. The QueryDefs Window in Data Manager.

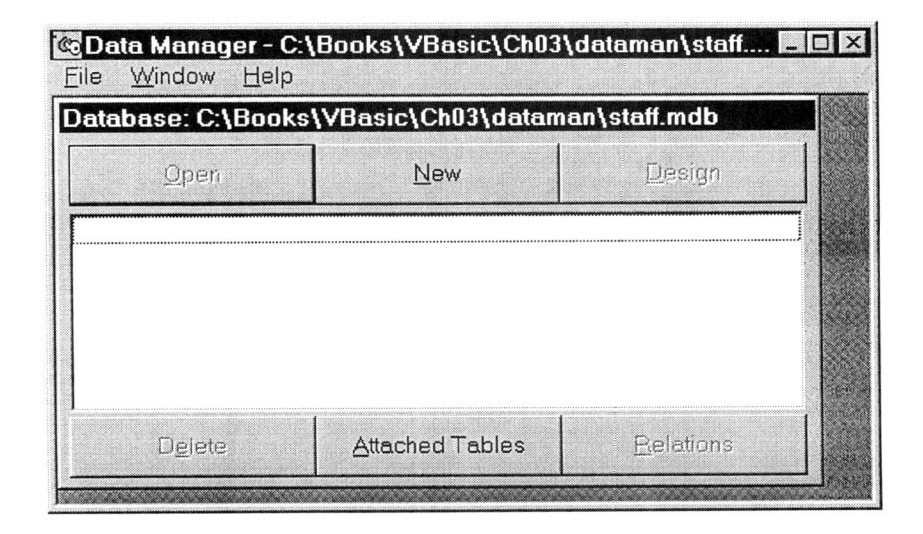

B.2.2 Creating the SalesStaff Table

The next step is to create a table called **SalesStaff**. Click the New button, which brings up the **Add Table** window. In the Name box, type SalesStaff. There will be two fields in this table, **id** and **name**:

Field Name	Data Type
id	Long Integer
name	Text (Length = 30)

To create the first field, type **id** into the Field Name box; select **Long Integer** as the Data Type; click the arrow > button—this copies the field name into the list box on the right side. Figure 13 shows the Add Table Window just before copying the **id** field.

Figure 13. The Add Table Window.

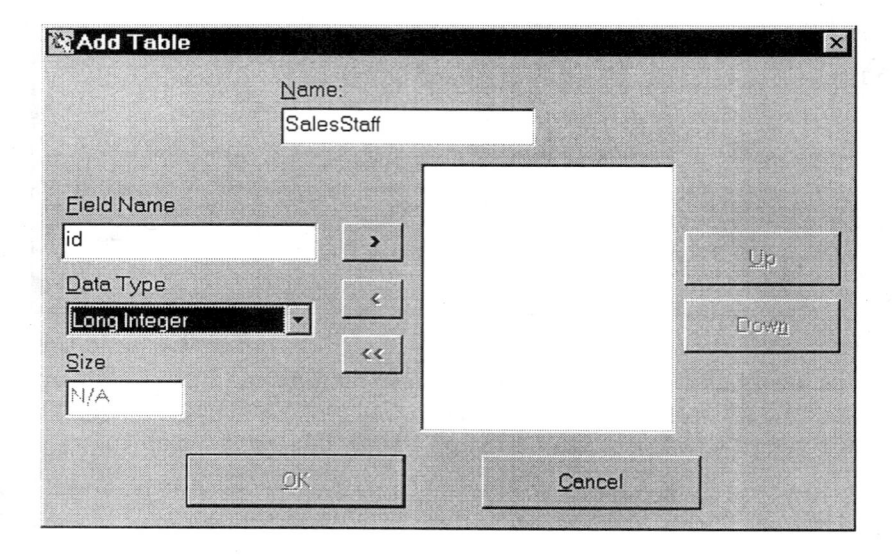

Now enter the second field, called **name**, with data type Text, and a size of 30. If necessary, you can use the < button to remove a field name from the list, and you can use the Up and Down buttons to change the field order. The << button removes all fields at once.

You're finished adding fields, so click the OK button to close this window. This returns you to the Tables/QueryDefs window, where the SalesStaff table name appears in the list box (Figure 14).

Appendix B: Standard VB4 Add-Ins

Figure 14. Tables/QueryDefs Window.

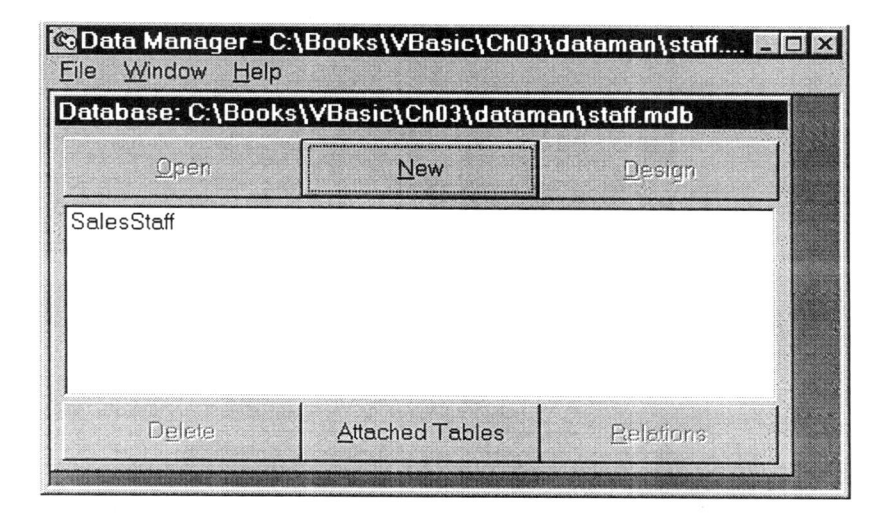

B.2.3 Editing a Table Design

You may have saved a new table design, only to discover that you left out a field, or that you need to delete or modify the table in some way. The **Table Editor** window allows you to do this. From the Tables/QueryDefs window, select the SalesStaff table and click the **Design** button. A list of the attributes of each field appears under the field's name (Figure 15).

Figure 15. Editing the Table Design.

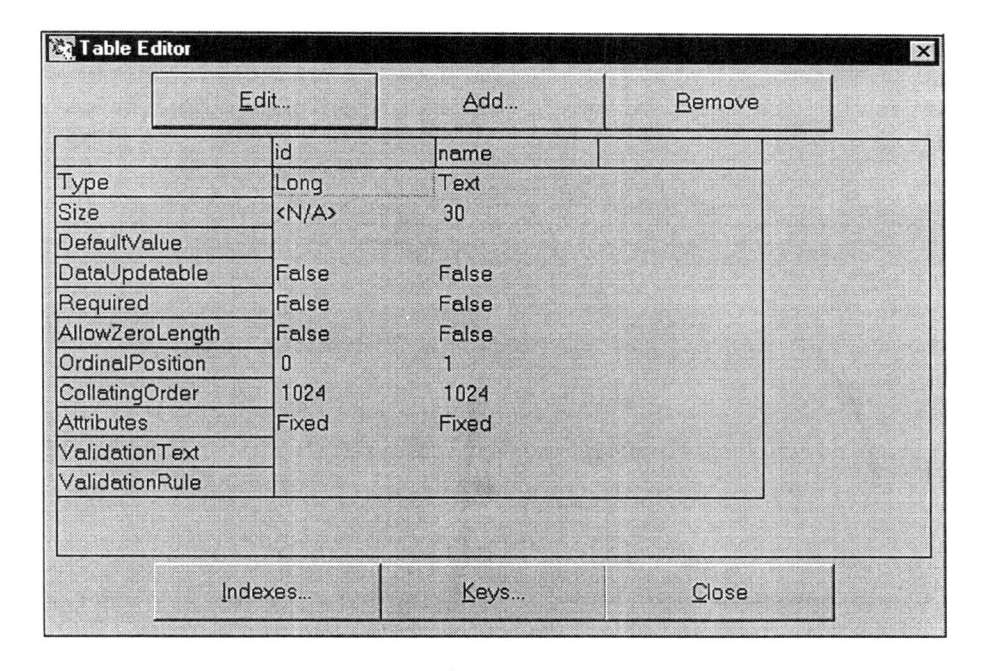

Table 1 describes each of the buttons from the Table Editor window.

Table 1. Editor Window Buttons.

Button	Action
Edit	Edit a single field definition.
Add	Add a new field to the table.
Remove	Remove a field from the table (all data in the field will be lost).
Indexes	Create indexes on any fields in the table.
Keys	Create primary and foreign keys. A primary key uniquely indentifies each record. A foreign key connects this table to the primary key of another table.
Close	Close the window and stop editing the table design.

To modify the description of the id field, click on the id column and click on the Edit button. When the Edit Field window appears (Figure 16), click on the **Required** option.

Figure 16. Edit Field Window.

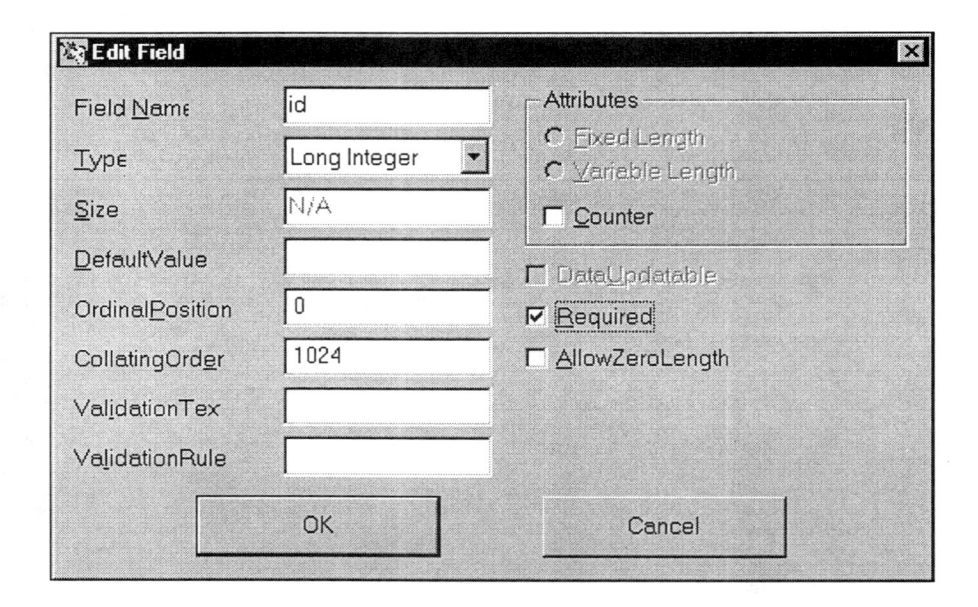

Click the **OK** button to save the change. From the Table Editor window, click the **Close** button to return to the Tables/QueryDefs window.

B.2.4 Creating Indexes

Next, we will create two table indexes. A table index makes it easy for a program to search for specific records, because the physical position of each record was already calculated by the database when the index was created. From the Tables/QueryDefs window, click the

Appendix B: Standard VB4 Add-Ins

Design button to bring up the Table Editor window. Then click the Indexes button to bring up the Indexes window (Figure 17).

Figure 17. Indexes Window.

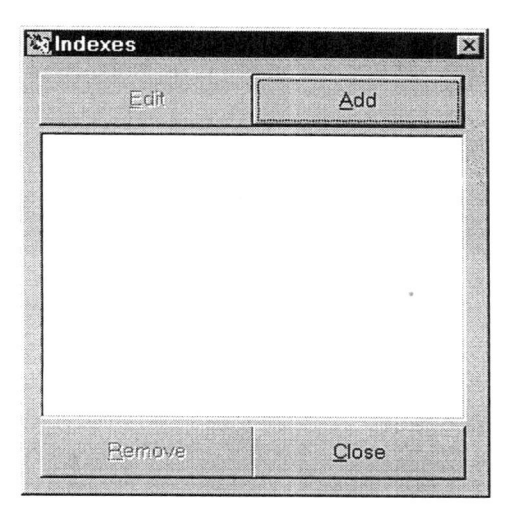

Click the Add button to add an index, which brings up the Add Index window. Enter the index name as **idNdx**, select the **id** field, check the Primary Index, Unique, and Required options. A *primary key* is one or more fields that are guaranteed to uniquely identify each table record. The window should appear as in Figure 18.

Figure 18. Add Index Window.

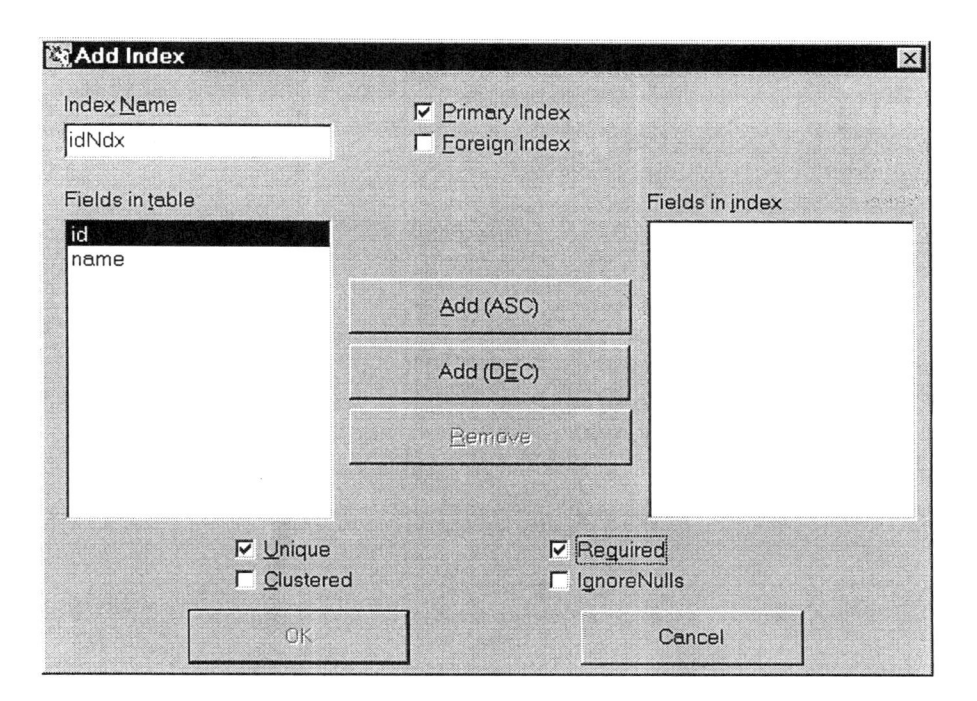

Click the **Add (ASC)** button to create the index, which will order the records in ascending order based in the id field. Click on OK to save the index and close this window.

Indexing the Name Field. Let's create a second index based on the name field. Programs can use this index when they want to arrange the records in alphabetical order by the name of the sales staff. From the Indexes window, click the Add button. In Figure 19 we call this index **nameNdx** and select only the **Required** option.

Figure 19. Adding the NameNdx Options.

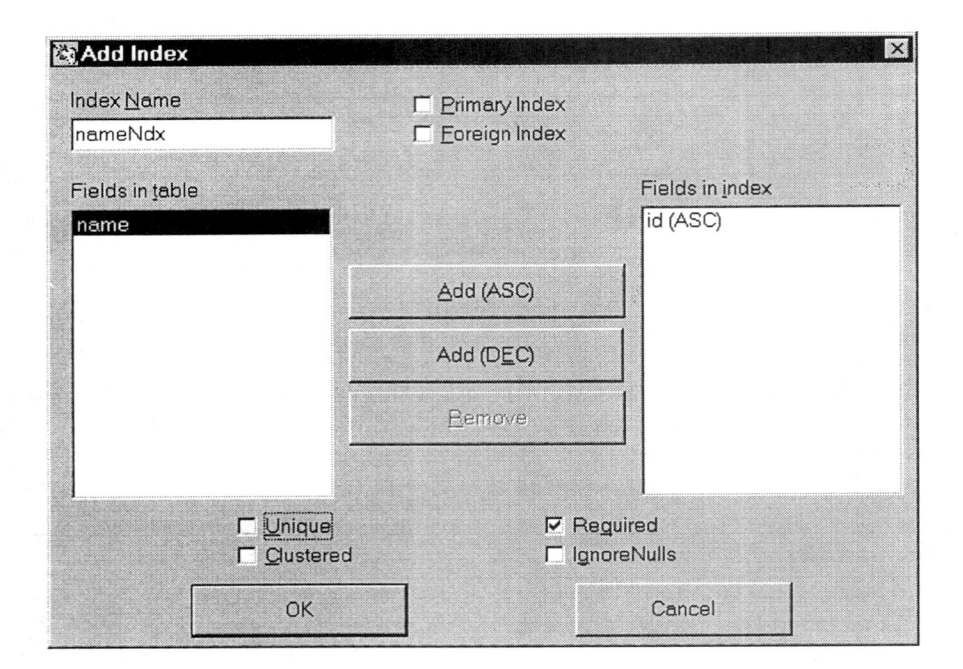

Click on OK to save the index and close this window, close the Indexes window, and close the Table Editor window.

B.2.5 Entering Table Data

Now we're ready to enter some names into the SalesStaff table. From the Tables/QueryDefs window, select the table name and click the Open button. This brings up what we will call the **Table Data** window (Figure 20). Click the Add button, enter 1 in the **id** field, and and enter "Adams, Adrian" in the **name** field. The Add button is automatically renamed to **Cancel**.

Figure 20. Entering Data into the SalesStaff Table.

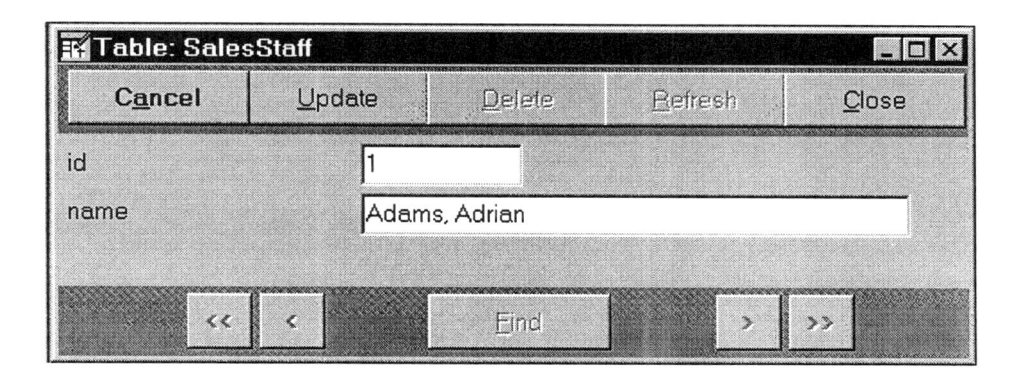

After inputting the first record, click the **Update** button to save the record. Then click the **Add** button and repeat these steps for the following records:

name
```
Del Terzo, Daniel
Baker, Barbara
Franklin, Fay
Easterbrook, Erin
```

When you're finished, close the Table Data window and close the database from the File menu.

B.3 Using the Data Form Designer

Create a new project. Run the **Data Form Designer** from the Add-Ins menu. In the main window (Figure 21), open the biblo.mdb database from the Visual Basic home directory. Enter **author** as the base form name, and select the **Authors** table as the RecordSource. Copy all three fields into the list box on the right side.

Figure 21. Data Form Designer Main Window.

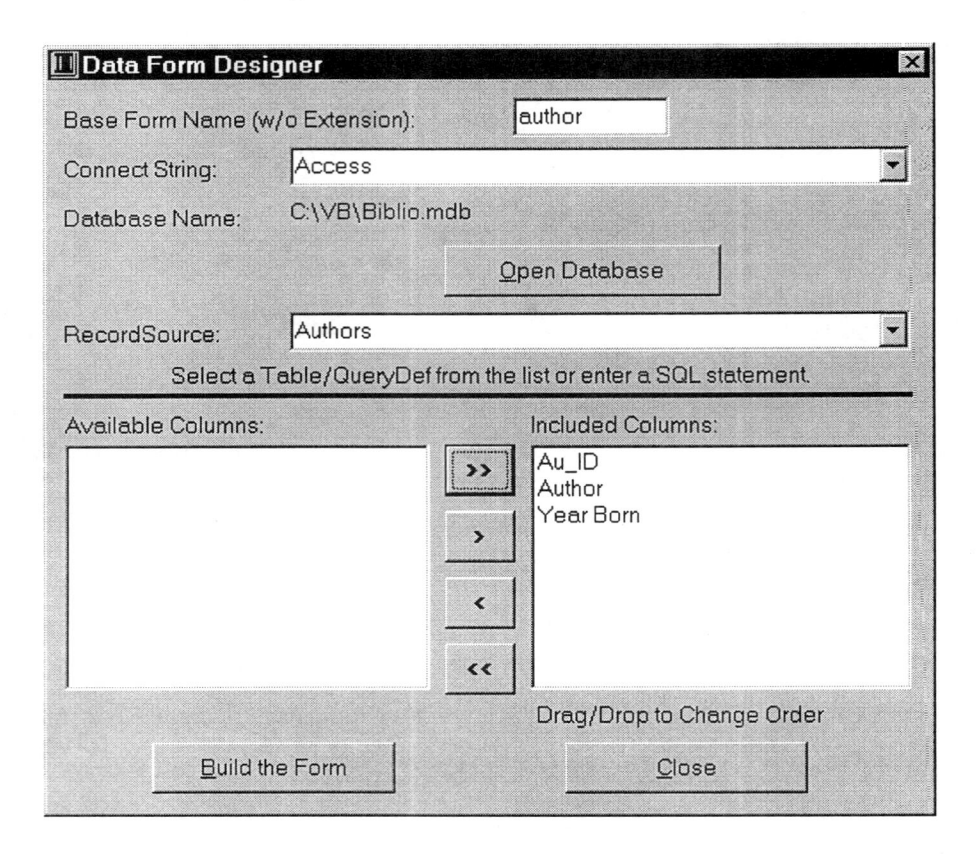

Click the **Build the Form** button. Click on **Close**. The form in Figure 22 will be created and displayed.

Figure 22. Form Created by Data Form Designer.

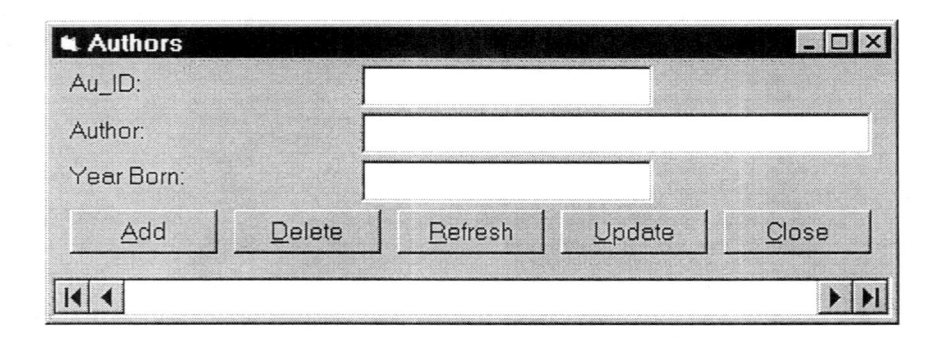

Remove the **Delete** button, because we do not want to delete any authors from the database; links to other tables would be violated. Name this form **frmAuthor** and save it. The data control has its Align property set to "bottom", so it sticks to the bottom of the form like glue. Stretch the edges of the form, reduce the sizes of the fields, and make the form slightly more attractive. You might also want to right-justify the field labels, as in Figure 23.

Appendix B: Standard VB4 Add-Ins   545

Figure 23. The frmAuthor Form, with Modifications.

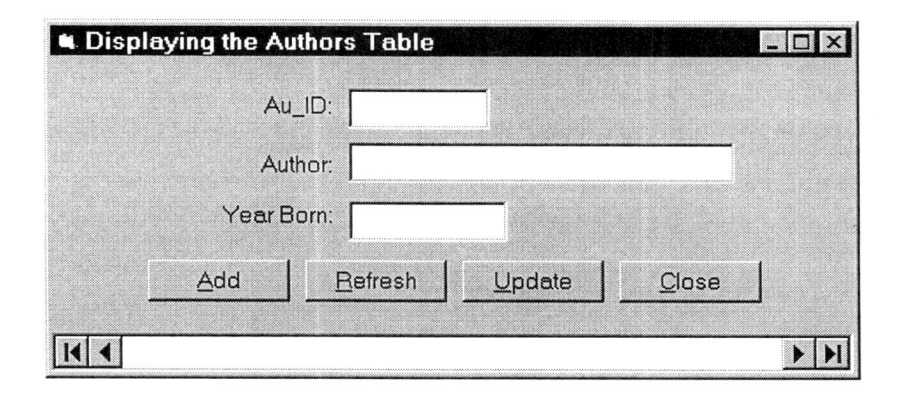

You might also decide to move the button commands to a menu.

B.3.1 Code Modifications in the Author Form

Data1_Validate. The following procedure was generated automatically inside frmAuthor. Ordinarily, you would customize this procedure to validate each of the standard database actions that could be performed by the user. For now, comment out the last line to prevent the mouse from becoming an hourglass when you close the window:

```
Private Sub Data1_Validate(Action As Integer, Save As Integer)
   'This is where you put validation code
   'This event gets called when the following actions occur
   Select Case Action
     Case vbDataActionMoveFirst
     Case vbDataActionMovePrevious
     Case vbDataActionMoveNext
     Case vbDataActionMoveLast
     Case vbDataActionAddNew
     Case vbDataActionUpdate
     Case vbDataActionDelete
     Case vbDataActionFind
     Case vbDataActionBookmark
     Case vbDataActionClose
   End Select
   'Screen.MousePointer = vbHourglass
End Sub
```

B.3.2 Create the Main Window

Create a main window for your program called frmMain; this will launch each of the other database table windows (Figure 24).

Figure 24. Data Form Designer Example.

The menu for this form should have the following structure:

```
&File              mnuFile
   E&xit           mnuFileExit
&Table             mnuTable
   &Authors        mnuTableAuthors
   &Titles         mnuTableTitles
```

Insert the following statement in the Table/Authors menu event handler:

```
frmAuthor.Show vbmodal
```

Insert the following statement in the File/Exit menu event handler:

```
Unload Me
```

Run the program. You should be able to nagivate between the main window and the author window, and scroll through the database records.

B.3.3 Add Another Table

Run the Data Form Designer again and create another window containing the **All Titles** table. The base form name is **titles** (Figure 25).

Appendix B: Standard VB4 Add-Ins 547

Figure 25. New Form Containing the All Titles.

The form shown in Figure 26 is created from **frmTitles.** As with the case of the titles form, you may want to place more space between fields, change the lengths of the text boxes, and so on.

Figure 26. AllTitles Window, Created by Data Form Designer.

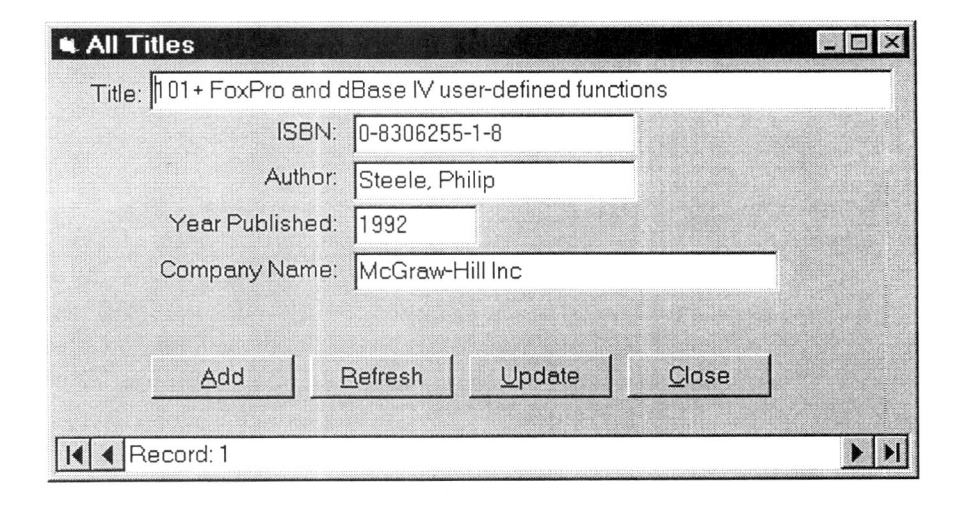

On the main form, revise the event handler for the mnuTableTitles menu selection:

```
frmTitles.show vbModal
```

Experiment with running the program from the main window, and test the author and title forms.

Appendix C: Answers to Odd-Numbered Review Questions

Chapter 1

1. During the Design step.

3. Because choices in the design will be affected by the available resources. The design should not attempt to do something which is not possible.

5. Prototyping is creating the visual part of the program (forms and controls) before writing any code.

7. Object-oriented design focuses on the physical entities that make up the application problem.

9. Doctor, Patient, Appointment, Schedule.

11. PayRate would be a property.

13. The addition of new features are possible without destroying the original program.

15. Special library software is used, such as SourceSafe, that requires modules to be checked out to only one person at a time.

17. Inadequate time and resources are devoted to testing and validation.

19. Because the process of fixing the bugs may have introduced new bugs.

21. KeyPress, KeyUp, and KeyDown.

23. File, Edit, Options, Help, Tools, View, Window, Format, Insert.

25. Choose descriptive names. Optionally, use prefixes that identify the scope and type of the variable.

27. Integer = int, Long = lng, String = str, Currency = cur, Single = sng, Boolean = bln.

29. Global, Module, Local.

31. A list is shown in Section 1.5.1.

33. A text box uses more memory.

35. Because VB loads modules on demand, less time will be spent loading if related procedures are in the same module.

37. code speed, display speed, and perceived speed.
39. It takes less processing time to set and get ordinary variable values.
41. Preloaded forms can be displayed more quickly, but they also use up a lot of memory.
43. Display a splash screen while the rest of the forms are loading.

Chapter 2

1. The price is determined by the format (media type) and the price code.
3. Using the ListIndex property as a subscript into the titles() array.
5. The album prices are numeric constants inside the CalcPrice procedure.
7. The sales tax rate would be different from state to state.
9. If itemPrice equals zero, we skip the calculations.
11. Five option buttons and one check box.
13. If the user forgets, itemPrice will be zero.
15. A message box displays the string returned by Error$ when there is a runtime error.
17. Version 2 lets the user purchase multiple items and add them to a list box representing an invoice.
19. Output file: invoices.txt. It contains each of the purchased items, the total sale amount, tax, and net total.
21. Ctrl-N = new invoice; Ctrl-S = file save; Ctrl-X = exit.
23. CalcPrice is only called when the user adds a new item to the invoice.
25. Open the file in Append mode.
27. Version 3 lets the user remove an item from the Invoice, and generates new invoice numbers.
29. It reads the most recent invoice number from a file.
31. Virtually any number, because itemPrices is a collection.
33. The itemPrices collection holds the prices of all items in the invoice, so when we remove an item, we can locate its price and delete that amount from the bill.
35. When CancelError is True, a trappable error will be generated when the user clicks on the Cancel button.
37. The FileTitle property contains just the filename with no path.
39. Assign the constant cdlOFNFileMustExist to the Flags property.
41. By assigning special constants to the Flags property.
43. A trappable runtime error is generated.
45. There is no known limit to the number of key values.

47. The return value is a two-dimensional array of strings containing all the keys and their respective values in the specified section.

Chapter 3

1. A control array makes it easy to process the controls with a loop, and assign the same properties to all members of the array.

3. The Load statement creates a new instance of an object that may be placed in a control array. The Buttons program from this chapter is a good example.

5. Code Example:
    ```
    Dim aForm As Form
    Set aForm = frmAuthor
    ```

7. Code Example:
    ```
    Dim F As Form
    Set F = New frmMain
    ```

9. Code Example:
    ```
    Dim j As Integer
    For j = 1 To 9
      Load btn(j)
      btn(j).Caption = "Button " & j
      btn(j).Visible = True
    Next j
    ```

11. No. The Picture property contains a unique integer, called a handle.

13. Because the program uses the command button index values to compare the appropriate elements in the array of Image controls.

15. When two images match, the Visible property of each image is set to False, and the user's score is incremented.

17. The Randomize statement.

19. The image1Index and image2Index variables identify the positions in the button array that were clicked by the user.

21. Disable the form.

23. The collection makes it easy to process all the forms without missing any. For example, you might want to close all of a program's forms.

25. Code Example:
    ```
    Dim frm As Form
    For Each frm in frm
      Unload Frm
    Next frm
    ```

27. The social security number, beause it is unique.

29. Randomly, using a subscript. Sequentially, using a loop that starts with the first collection member.

31. object.Add(member, key, before, after). Object is the collection object; member is the data value being inserted, key is a unique string identifier for the object, before and after determine the posiiton where the object will be inserted in the collection.

33. The Item method searches the collection, using an index or key. The syntax is shown here, where index may also be the key.
    ```
    Result = object.Item( index )
    ```

35. Because that ratio will determine the position and size of each control on the form.

37. A trappable runtime error is generated.

39. Random-access files let you select individual records for reading, in any order. The records can be modified and save in their original locations.

41. Record 1.

43. It's more difficult, because the program has to be able to switch data types after identifying the record type.

45. 5,000 bytes.

47. Because the MDI child windows are completely contained within the parent, and when the parent is closed or minimized, the child windows are also.

49. The menu on the MDI parent is replaced by the MDI child's window.

Chapter 4

1. Algol, SmallTalk, and C++. Object Pascal was available around that time also.

3. A class is a definition of a data type, with properties, methods, and events.

5. The toolbox icons are classes.

7. Yes, each instance has a separate copy of all event handlers.

9. No, unless the buttons are part of a control array.

11. Student, FirstDate, LastDate, Courses (a collection), major, gpa, credits, advisor.

13. Inheritance!

15. No, but a single class module can assist in creating separate instances of a class.

17. Code Example:
    ```
    Dim T As clsTranscript
    Set T= new clsTranscript
    ```

19. Code Example:
    ```
    Set T = Nothing
    ```

21. An instance variable is a variable defined inside a class module or form module. It is generally designated Private.

23. The Get Property procedure and the Let Property procedure.

25. Code Example:
    ```
    Public Property Let LastName()
        lastNameP = LastName
    ```

```
End Property
```

27. Inside the Property Let procedure for that property, check the range and notify the user about the problem.

29. The Class_Initialize event.

31. A class interface is composed of properties and methods.

33. The AsString method creates a user-friendly string representation of a class object.

35. One clsStudent object; the other is just a reference.

37. The frmMain form creates an instance of clsStudent.

39. The last name cannot be blank.

41. The clsStudentCollection class contains a Collection object.

43. It uses On Error GoTo to trap the runtime error generated by Visual Basic when an attempt to add a duplicate key is encountered.

45. FindById searches the collection for a matching ID number, using the collection's key field.

47. If users are allowed full access to the collection, they could modify it without the knowledge of clsStudentCollection.

49. clsPatient, clsAppointment, and clsApptCalendar.

51. Doctor ID, patient ID, date and time, purpose of appointment.

53. A link relationship.

55. No, it relates more closely to the clsPatient class.

57. They create instances of clsAppointment.

59. It compares the time against the predefined constants EarliestApptTime and LatestApptTime.

61. The frmInput form.

63. The appointment time must be in a valid range; a doctor must be selected, a patient must be selected; and the appointment date must be a valid date.

Chapter 5

1. VisData and Data Manager.

3. Record.

5. Each StaffID value matches the id number of an employee in the SalesStaff table.

7. Visual Basic can use Data Access Objects, through the Jet Database Engine, and indirectly, through the Data control (on a form).

9. Snapshots cannot be updated.

11. Dynasets and snapshots.

13. A table-type recordset, using the Seek method with a predefined index. No searching would be required.
15. A Text field is limited to 255 characters; a memo can be 1.2 billion characters.
17. An OLE container field.
19. The DatabaseName and RecordSource properties, in that order.
21. The prefix is "dat".
23. While opened in Exclusive mode, the recordset cannot be opened by any other users.
25. Label, Text box, check box, combo box, list box, OLE container, image control and picture box.
27. There is no practical limit.
29. The Reposition event.
31. It must be unique for all records in the table, and it must always be present.
33. When the data control is repositioned to another record, the new values are written to the database.
35. The Update method.
37. A trappable runtime error occurs.
39. No, it points just before the first row.
41. Move 5
43. The RowSource and ListField properties.
45. The MatchEntry property.
47. The RowSource and ListField properties.
49. The ColumnHeaders property.
51. The AllowAddNew property.
53. Code Example:
```
Dim bmark As String
bmark = datComputerModel.Recordset.BookMark
```
55. Code Example:
```
SELECT * FROM SalesStaff
```
57. Code Example:
```
SELECT * FROM SalesStaff
WHERE lastName LIKE '*JON*'
```

Chapter 6

1. It has to open the attached database and table. Yes.
3. The Microsoft Jet engine, also called DbEngine, provides OLE automation services for using Access databases.

5. Workspace

7. source, recordsetType, options, lockEdits. Only source is required.

9. No, OpenRecordset can create a dynaset or snapshot from an SQL query.

11. The block containing the record is locked as soon as the Edit method is called.

13. All of its recordsets must be closed first.

15. MyDb.TableDefs("Schedule").Fields(0)

17. It keeps each list in a separate table. You could put all records in the same table and include an indicator field that identifies the person's category.

19. It must close the existing database, if it is open.

21. AllowZeroLength lets the user omit certain nonessential fields.

23. A record can be copied from one table and pasted into another.

25. Because the value in aPerson must be available to two different procedures.

27. A database is used now, and we directly manipulate Data Access objects.

29. ReadRecord now reads from a database table.

31. "SELECT * FROM Appointments ORDER BY date + time".

33. The ShowRecordset method calls the AsString method just before displaying appointment objects in a list box.

35. The patient ID number. This value is copied into the patientID property when the user clicks on a patient name. The patientID is necessary for looking up a patient record.

37. Code Example:
```
Public Function SameTimeAs( A2 As clsAppointment ) As Boolean
  If ApptDate = A2.ApptDate And ApptTime = A2.ApptTime Then
    SameTimeAs = True
  Else
    SameTimeAs = False
  End If
End Function
```

39. The SQL Server program.

41. No conflict.

43. The record is only locked while the Update method is running.

45. Pessimistic locking, so no other agents could take seats that I had promised to a customer.

47. Pessimistic locking, probably.

49. The LockEdits property sets or returns a value that indicates whether pessimistic locking is in effect.

51. A transaction is a series of changes made to all databases in a workspace, where the changes are treated as a single unit.

53. Rollback ends the current transaction and restores the databases to the state they were in before the transaction began.

55. A 10% raise was given to each employee.

Chapter 7

1. A *relational database management system* (RDMS) is a collection of data that is organized so that you can look at it in different ways. It contains tables, index, queries, filters, views, and validation capabilities. It is able to maintain links, or relationships between tables and to ensure that the links are consistent.

3. A column is the same as a field, but *column* is a more familiar term in relational database discussions.

5. Yes.

7. To restrict access of users to sensitive data or columns that should not be updated.

9. One-to-many means that a single value in one table can match multiple values in another table.

11. An application-independent design is general so that that multiple application programs can share the data.

13. Organize the data into tables.

15. Structured Query Language.

17. Data-Definition Language, and Data-Manipulation Language.

19. The ORDER BY clause sorts the records.

21. The ssn field was common to both tables.

23. Code Example:
```
SELECT [soc sec num], [hourly pay]
FROM EmplData
```

25. Code Example:
```
SELECT * FROM PayRoll
WHERE payRate BETWEEN 20 AND 30
```

27. Code Example:
```
SELECT * FROM Employee
WHERE Phone LIKE '*2222*'
```

29. Code Example:
```
SELECT ssn,lastName,paymentDate,payRate
FROM Employee, Payroll
WHERE Employee.ssn = Payroll.ssn
```

31. To avoid generating a cartesian product of the two tables, with a large number of redundant rows.

33. Left Join, Inner Join, Right Join.

35. Code Example:

```
UPDATE table
SET newvalue
WHERE criteria
```

37. Code Example:
    ```
    UPDATE Department
    SET percentChange = (SpringCredits - FallCredits) / FallCredits
    ```

39. Code Example:
    ```
    DROP INDEX ssnNdx ON Payroll
    ```

41. Code Example:
    ```
    INSERT INTO Payroll (ssn, paymentDate, hoursWorked, payRate)
    VALUES('400-33-2555', #1/15/1998#, 47.5, 17.50)
    ```

43. Code Example:
    ```
    CREATE TABLE Student
    (lastName TEXT(30),
     totalCredits SHORT)
    ```

Chapter 8

1. Columnar, Cross-Tab, and Labels.

3. Using the Insert Database Field dialog, double-click on the field name.

5. From the Database menu, select Add Database to Report.

7. Right-click on the date in the detail line, select the Change Format command.

9. Select Report Title from the Report menu.

11. Page header, Details, Grand Total, Page Footer, Group Header, Group Summary.

13. Select Page Margins from the File menu.

15. An exception report focuses on data that is out of the ordinary.

17. Code Example:
    ```
    {Reservatins.SectionName] = 'ORCH'
    ```

19. From the Report menu, select Edit Group Selection Formula.

21. A cross-tab report automatically summarizes information in a matrix-like format, where totals and averages are inserted into each cell position.

23. ReportFileName and Destination.

25. The CopiesToPrinter property must be set.

27. The SelectionFormula property.

29. The crptHTML30 and crptNetscape formats.

31. A trappable runtime error results.

33. Online help, printed manuals, tool tips, status bar, what's this help, and wizards.

35. The wizard can lead you through each step and let you back up if you need to redo a step.

37. Panels.

39. Text, graphics, and predefined values such as key states, date, and time.

41. stsBar.Panels(0).AutoSize = sbrContents

43. Yes

45. Style = sbrSimple

47. The WinHelp function.

49. It reads the Tag property of each control and creates a topic header. In VB5, the ToolTipsText property is used.

51. QuitHelp

53. You can see all of the help topics, inspect the links between topics, and change topic properties.

55. Select the word or phrase with the mouse, then select the Insert Jump command from the Insert menu.

57. The Web browser (HTML) file format is becoming more universal, because it works on all types of computers. Some software companies use the Web to display online help in their programs that run on home computers. Netscape does this, for example.

Chapter 9

1. An *OLE container* is a program or application that contains links and/or embedded copies of objects created by other programs.

3. OLE 1.0, introduced a few years ago, was a major improvement over DDE because it allowed copies of documents, spreadsheets, and other data to be inserted, displayed, and modified inside OLE containers.

5. No, the DAO library uses OLE 2.0.

7. The OLE container control.

9. CreateObject creates an instance of an OLE object and returns a reference to the object, which you can assign to a variable.

11. Workbook, Worksheet, and Chart.

13. Yes, because Word is running in the background.

15. The object browser lists all of the class types that are available for OLE automation.

17. Yes, using the SaveToFile method.

19. Set the NegotiatePosition property of the enclosing form's menu.

21. Click on the Class property of the OLE container control.

23. This makes the controls automatically size themselves to the embedded object.

25. The main reason for using DoVerb is if the AutoActivate property is set to *manual*, the program can open the object by calling DoVerb.

27. The CreateLink method.

Appx C: Answers to Odd-Numbered Review Questions

29. Visual Basic for Applications (VBA).

31. ActiveDocument.PageSetup.TopMargin = InchesToPoints(1.5)

33. Code Example:
    ```
    Dim Excel As Object, wbook As Object, wsheet As Object
    Set Excel = CreateObject("Excel.Application")
    Set wbook = Excel.Workbooks.Add
    Set wsheet = Excel.ActiveWorkbook.ActiveSheet
    ```

35. In the lstApplicants_Click event handler, the id number is retrieved from the ItemData array. This id is used with the Seek method to look up the record.

37. The user can double-click on a response topic, and the topic paragraph will appear.

39. The Check_Selections procedure verifies that an applicant was selected and at least one response topic was selected.

Chapter 10

1. Low-level tasks: hardware device drivers, high-speed video graphics, serial communications programming. High-level tasks: application programs, pop-up menus, printing reports, using SQL to build recordsets.

3. To handle time-critical tasks; to perform Windows programming tasks that are not directly supported by Visual Basic.

5. *Dynamic linking* allows compiled procedures to be stored in a separate file from the calling program. The procedures are loaded into memory only when called by another program.

7. Less memory is used, and the programs can pass data to each other via the DLL.

9. The C language is the traditional language for writing DLLs, and most DLLs assume that C data types will be used as arguments.

11. Some ActiveX components are DLLs, others are stand-along executable programs, and others are custom controls.

13. Sometimes, the name of a DLL procedure is the same as a Visual Basic keyword, or the name contains characters that would not be allowed in a Visual Basic identifier. Also, the names of Win32 API functions are slightly different frm the 16-bit API, so alias names can provide a way for the programmer to use the same names all the time.

15. Call the Windows API Sleep function.

17. A window handle is a long integer that is assigned a unique value when the window is created in memory. All Windows API functions acting on the window must refer to the window's handle.

19. It should be assigned to an array of characters.

21. It should be passed by value, unless the DLL procedure specifically asks for a pointer to an integer (notated as: int *, or long *).

23. Some of the function names are listed in Table 4 in this chapter.

25. The SendMessage function does this, with the LB_SETTABSTOPS argument.

Chapter 11

1. *Component software development* is the assembling of programs from tested, standardized components.

3. ActiveX provides the mechanism so that objects can work together, whether the objects are created from classes in a single program or the objects are created by external, out-of-process servers.

5. Before ActiveX was created, OLE servers were able to expose objects, methods, and properties. ActiveX is an extension of the same process.

7. ActiveX Controls, ActiveX Documents, and Code Components.

9. An ActiveX control.

11. No, they are compiled into DLL library files.

13. Unlike a class module which has no visual part, and ActiveX control can be visual, and can raise events.

15. Code Example:
    ```
    RaiseEvent FileError
    ```

17. The StudentIdText control does not contain code that will respond to a Resize event. However, that code could easily be added.

19. The Caption and BackColor properties.

21. Just provide a Property Get procedure, and either omit the Property Let or make it Private.

23. A BadDateFormat event is raised by the ActiveX control.

25. The UserControl_ReadProperties event.

27. It helps to reduce the size of the client program's form, because only values that are different from the default property values will be saved in the form file.

29. The four events are listed below:
    ```
    Public Event BadDateFormat(dt As String)
    Public Event BadTimeFormat(tm As String)
    Public Event MissingField(fieldName As String)
    Public Event CloseWindow(save As Boolean)
    ```

31. An *in-process component*, or *ActiveX DLL component*, shares the same address space with its client program. The component and its client are often part of the same application. An *out-of-process component*, or *ActiveX EXE component*, runs in its own address space, separate from the client program.

33. An ActiveX DLL is an in-process component.

35. Private, PublicNotcreatable, Multiuse, and GlobalMultiuse.

37. It opens the doctor appointments database. The Class_Initialize event handler.

39. The error is thrown backward to procedure X, where it can be handled by an On Error statement.

41. Yes, it can be run as a stand-alone executable program.

Index

Access (Microsoft), 172
    creating SQL queries, 284
    creating table relationships, 299
    creating validation rules, 296
ActiveX components, 439
    ActiveX control, 440
    ActiveX DLL, creating, 458
    code component, 440
    component object model, 439
    component software development, 439
    constituent controls, 448
    DoctorSchedule DLL, 458
    design mode properties, 447
    Instancing property, 461
    out-of-process component, 467
    property procedures, 453
    raising events in ActiveX controls, 445, 451
    run time properties, 447
    saving and restoring properties, 450
    Student ID number text box, 442
API, Windows (see *DLL procedures*)
App (application object, 517
    properties, 18, 42
application development cycle, 2
application INI file, 57
application testing, 5
arrays, 482
calculations
    invoice example, 43
    using arrays, 48
chapter exercises
    AddAppointment Control, 471
    Buttons Control Array, 106
    Changing Form Colors, 29
    Classical Music CD Catalog, 109-110
    Cleaning Equipment Rental Wizard, 112
    clsIniFile Class, Expanding, 434
    clsSchedule Class, 471
    Computer Mail-Order, 210, 367
    Concert Hall Ticketing, 267-269
    Customer Accounts, 116
    Depreciation Schedule, 67, 410
    Doctors Office Scheduling, 155, 157, 265-266
    E-Mail Address Book, 158, 208
    Express Travel Agency, 30
    Family Photo Album, 411
    Freight Forwarding Service, 29
    GetURLs ActiveX Control, 472
    Glossary Program, 106
    Hardbodies Health Club, 66-67, 410
    Indexed Random-Access File, 107
    IndexedFile Class, 157
    INI Files, Getting a List of, 438
    Kyoshi Karate School, 211-219, 367-368
    MixUp Game, 108
    Mozart Music Sales, 65-66, 108-109, 158, 209, 409
    Multiple-Choice Test, 30-31
    Personal Contact Manager, 263-264
    Personal Stock Portfolio, 413
    Record-Locking Program, 263
    Resizing Controls on a Form, 106
    Sorted Collection, 107
    Stellar Car Rental, 324-325, 471
    Student Collection, 156
    StudentIdText Control, 471
    Tab Stops in a List Box, Setting, 435
    Time Clock Program, 68, 158
    Yachting Regatta, 113-115, 325-327
class, 118
    creating class modules, 120
    creating instances, 122, 126
    Initialize event, 125
    methods, 126
    properties, 123
    Terminate event, 125
    using Public and Private, 124
coding guidelines
    code optimization, 25
    declaring, naming variables and constants, 13
    display optimization, 26
    incremental development, 236
    improving execution speed, 25
    indenting code, 17
    general procedures, 510
    line continuation symbol, 18
    naming controls, 509
    perceived speed optimization, 26
    predefined VB constants, 17
    prefixes for data types, 14
    prefixes for controls, 15-16
    procedure names, 16
    reducing code size, 24
    scope prefixes, 15

collections, 82
    Add method, 84
    built-in VB collections, 82
    DuplicateKeyError, 89
    Count property, 84
    Glossary program, 88
    introduction to, 483
    Item method, 85
    keys, 84
    programmer-defined, 83
    Remove method, 85-86
College Admissions program, 398
colors, changing on a form, 29
combo box
    loading from a file, 38-39
    removing items, 50
    using the ListIndex property, 49
common dialog control, 52
    properties, 53
    ShowColor, 55
    ShowFont, 56
    ShowOpen, ShowSave, 52
competency review test, 476
Concert Ticket Reports program, 345
constants, declaring, 13, 43
controls, standard Visual Basic, 503
    Check Box, 505
    Command Button, 504
    Default properties, 509
    Frame, 505
    Image, 506
    Label, 503
    Line, 506
    List Boxes and Combo Boxes, 507
    Option Button, 504
    Text, 503
    Timer, 506
    Scroll Barrs, 506
Crystal Reports, 330
    Concert Ticket Reports program, 345
    columnar report, 330
    cross-tab report, 340
    custom control, 343
    grouping records, 335
    group selection criteria, 338
    record selection criteria, 337
current directory, setting, 38
custom controls
    SSTab, 10-11
    StatusBar control, 351
Customer Accounts Program, 94
data-bound controls, 170
    combo, 186, 198
    controls that cannot be bound, 171
    DataSource, DataField, 170
    grid, 188
    list, 184
data control, 169
    DatabaseName, 169
    data-bound controls, 170
    properties, 169
    RecordSource, 169, 202
Data Form Designer utility program, 543
Data Manager utility program, 536
data types, variables, and constants, 478
database, 165
    BeginTrans, CommitTrans, Rollback, 258
    DBEngine.Idle method, 257
    creating databases using Access, 172
    creating indexes, 174
    creating SQL queries in Access, 284
    Data Access Objects (DAO), 221
    defining tables, 166
    designing a database, 273
    entering data, 175
    field types, 168
    filter, 272
    index, 272
    LockEdits parameter, 223
    multiuser database processing, 253
    OpenDatabase method, 222
    OpenRecordset method, 222
    primary key, 174
    query, 272
    record locking, 254
    Recordset object (see *Recordset object*)
    searching for records, 199
    table relationships, 297
    TableDefs property, 223
    Transaction processing, 258
    Workspace collection, object, 222
    validation, 272
    validation rules, 295
    view, 272
design
    goals, 4-5
    object-oriented, 4
    procedural, 3
designing programs, 3
DLL procedures, 416
    API Viewer utility program, 418
    clsIniFile class example, 429
    declaring and calling, 417
    flashing a window caption (program), 419
    GetWindowsDirectory procedure
    hWnd property, 420
    numeric parameters, 423
    parameters in DLL procedures, 421
    reading and writing INI files, 426
    string parameters, 422

Index

user-defined type parameters, 424
Doctors Office Scheduling program, 136, 241
Do-Unitil statement, 488
Do-While statement, 487
Excel
    OLE automation with, 394
    OLE objects, 372, 377, 383
    Statistical Score Analysis program, 395
Exit Sub, Exit Function, and Exit Property, 21
error handling, 20-24
    automatic backward chaining, 22
    causes of errors, 20
    error handler, 20
    Err object, 23
    On Error GoTo, 20-21
    Resume, 21
IF statements, 484
feasibility review, 2
file
    input (Mozart), 9
Format$ function, 511
    date and time, 512
    numeric, 48, 512
forms, 497
    events, 502
    methods, 499
    properties, 497
    Form-Loading program example, 500
For-Next statement, 487
Glossary Program, 88
icons
    loading at runtime, 79
    shuffling, 80
InputBox function, 515
Invoice Application, 33
Jumping Button program, 72
Linking, static and dynamic, 416
LoadPicture function, 79
loops, 486
keyboard
    predefined constants, 12
    input, 12
    KeyPress event, 12
    KeyDown, KeyUp events, 12
Mail-Order Computer Sales program, 193
MDI applications, 98
MDI Bitmap Viewer program, 99
menu design, 8, 41, 517
method (procedure),
    definition, 4, 118
MixUp Game (*Concentration*), 76
MouseMove event, 73
Mozart Music Sales program
    Version 1, 6
    Version 2, 40

Version 3, 46
Version 4, 190
MsgBox
    function, 39, 513
    procedure, 512
multiple-document interface (MDI), 98
object
    arrays, 73
    control arrays, 74
    creating controls at runtime, 75
    declaring and assigning, 71
    variables, 71
object linking and embedding (OLE), 369
    applications, 370
    College Admissions program, 398
    Close method, 383
    CreateLink method, 382
    embedded object, 371
    Excel 8.0 objects, 372, 377, 383
    history of, 370
    insertable objects, 371
    linked object, 371
    NegotiateMenus, 376
    NegotiatePosition, 376
    NegotiateToolbars, 376
    OLE automation server, 370, 388
    OLE container control, 373
    OLE objects, 370
    Update method, 383
    Word objects, 373, 384
object-oriented design, 4, 118
    attributes and operations, 119
    interface and implementation, 120
object-oriented programming, 117
    Doctors Office Scheduling program, 136
    Vehicle Reservation program, 303
OLE (see *object linking and embedding*)
online help, creating, 350
    StatusBar control, 351
    user assistance model, 350
    VB/HelpWriter Lite, 355
optimization
    code, 25
    display, 26
    perceived speed, 26
option buttons
    with IF statements, 43
Option Explicit statement, 13
Personal Contact Manager program, 225, 236
plug-in component, 5
Print method, 511
Printer object, 516
procedural design, 3
procedures, 489
    declaring, 489

function procedure, 491
optional parameters, 494
parameter arrays, 495
parameters, 490
passing by reference (ByRef), 492
passing by value (ByVal), 493
Private and Public, 494
property, 4
definition of, 118
tabstop, 11
prototyping, 3
query, 272
Query program (SQL), 203
random-access files, 92
Customer Accounts Program, 94, 116
Recordset
BOF, EOF properties, 181
changing the record order, 179
Index property, 179
optimistic and pessimistic locking, 254
moving the recordset pointer, 181
types of, 167
updatable, 189
Recordset methods
AddNew method, 178
Delete method, 179
FindFirst, FindNext, 205
FindLast, FindPrevious, 205
MoveFirst, MoveLast, 181
MoveNext, MovePrevious, 181
Seek, 200
SQL search, 202
Update method, 178
resizing controls on a form, 86
relational database management system (RDMS), 272
Rnd function, 72, 80
SalesStaff Table program, 182, 199, 205
Screen object, 516
Select Case statement, 485
sequential files (see *text files*)
settings, saving and retrieving, 57
example program, 61
GetAllSettings, 62
GetSetting, 60
SaveSetting, 60
splash screen, 7
SQL
action queries, 285
aggregate functions, 275
calculated columns, 278
clauses, 275
comparison operators, 278
creating indexes, 288
creating queries in Access, 284

creating tables, 288
data manipulation, 275
date formats, 278
DELETE statement, 286
DROP statement, 289
explanation, 274
JOIN clause, 281
inner join, 282
INSERT INTO statement, 287
left join, 283
logical operators (AND, OR, NOT), 279
Query program, 203
redundant queries, 280
removing tables and indexes, 289
right join, 283
sample database, 275
searching a recordset, 202
SELECT statement, 276
selecting from multiple tables, 280
structure, 274
UPDATE statement, 285
WHERE clause, 277
StatusBar control, 351
Stellar Car Rental program, 290, 355
string handling, 495
Student Class Example, 127
Student Collection Class, 130
system registry, 57
TableDef object, 223
Fields property, 223
table relationships, 297
creating, in Access, 299
one-to-many, 298
one-to-one, 298
testing an application, 5-6
text files
basic syntax, 521
FreeFile function, 38
reading from, 38, 522, 524
saving data to, 44
selecting and opening, 53
timer control
maninpulating in code, 81
Timer function, 69
Transaction processing, 258
user-defined types, 483
user interface design, 10-13
crowding forms, 10
form size, 11
setting the tab order, 11
standard menus, 13
validating user input, 151
validation rules (database)
creating in Access, 296
field-level, 296

Index

record-level, 296
Vehicle Reservations program, 303, 355
Viewing the SalesStaff Table (program), 175
VisData utility program, 529
visual design, 3
Word Document creating program, 389

While-Wend statement, 488
Windows API procedures (see *DLL procedures*)
Word
    classes, properties, and methods, 390